The History of Central Section Wrestling

(and more)

1952-2007

Compiled and Edited
By Mike Stricker

The History of California
Central Section Wrestling (and More)
1952-2007

Copyright © 2007 reprint 2021

by Mike Stricker

ALL RIGHTS RESERVED.
No part of this publication may be reproduced, stored in a retrieval system, or transmitted in any form or by any means whatsoever, whether electronic, mechanical, magnetic recording, or photocopying, without the prior written approval of the Copyright holder or Publisher, excepting brief quotations for inclusion in book reviews.

Compiled and Edited by: Mike Stricker

Reprinted by:

Janaway Publishing, Inc.
732 Kelsey Ct.
Santa Maria, California 93454
(805) 925-1952
www.JanawayGenealogy.com

2021

In many older books, foxing (or discoloration) occurs and, in some instances, print lightens with wear and age. Reprinted books, such as this, often duplicate these flaws, notwithstanding efforts to reduce or eliminate them. Corrections submitted with this reprint have been made, where possible, on the pages for easy reference.

ISBN: 978-1-59641-460-0

Made in the United States of America

The History of Central Section Wrestling (and more) 1952-2007

Compiled and Edited by Mike Stricker
First Edition © 2007 Mike Stricker

Credits:
- The Bakersfield Californian
- The Fresno Bee
- Visalia Times Delta
- Clovis Independent
- Amateur Wrestling News
- USA Wrestler
- Wrestling International News Magazine
- Cal-Hi Sports
- The California Wrestler
- Themat.com
- Sinai Enterprises

Special thanks to the numerous people in the Valley who took time to look in high school yearbooks for first names of wrestlers and coaches.

Funding for the printing of this book generously provided by:

- Harry and Ethel West Foundation
  Bakersfield, California
- Coyote Club Amateur Wrestling
  P.O. Box 9865
  Bakersfield, CA 93389

Please send corrections and/or additions:
Mike Stricker c/o The Coyote Club
P.O. Box 9865, Bakersfield, CA 99389
or **e-mail:** mikestricker@valleywrestling07.com
Visit the website: www.valleywrestling07.com

Disclaimer: The accuracy of the information here is limited to the accuracy of the sources and to the recording of the sources.

Design & Production
Bill Ramsey
Ramsey Design: www.wgramsey.com

Printed by Blueprint Service Co.
Bakersfield, California USA 2007

About the author

Mike Stricker has made numerous contributions to the sport of wrestling throughout his life. As founding executive board member and current CEO of the Coyote Club, an amateur wrestling support group established in 1986, Stricker has led the organization in raising almost $1.8 million during the last 20 years in support of "the world's oldest sport." In addition, he serves on various committees and associations, including the committee responsible for naming his hometown of Bakersfield the home of the state wrestling championships. Stricker was also a founding board member and officer of the Kern County Wrestling Association from 1974 to 1984. He is an inductee and executive committee member of the California Wrestling Hall of Fame and is the recipient of its prestigious 2006 Lifetime Service Award.

Stricker has been a wrestling competitor as a youth in high school and college, a referee and college coach, and continues to support the sport as a fan, booster and fundraiser. In 2000, Stricker was honored with the Irv Oliner Award by the California Wrestling Coaches Association at the state wrestling championships in Stockton. His 30-year coaching career began at Chico State under coaching legend Dick Trimmer. Stricker went on to coach with some of the finest coaches in the history of the Central Section, including Joe Seay, Art Chavez, Bob Lathrop and Gene Walker. He currently coaches alongside his son, Ty, at North Bakersfield High. Stricker wrestled at South Bakersfield High and Bakersfield College under coaching greats Bruce Pfutzenreuter and Harry Kane.

Stricker resides in Bakersfield with his wife, Lynn, and is very proud of his two sons, Ty (who is head wrestling coach at North Bakersfield High) and Tad (head wrestling coach at Loara High in Anahiem).

On the cover: 1965 CIF Finals
Roy Heath of South Bakersfield and Renaldo Contreras of Kingsburg. Heath won 2-1.

Introduction/Dedication

Over the years, I've spent countless hours researching the history of the San Joaquin Valley Wrestling Championships. In this book I have compiled the results of both Central Section qualifiers, beginning with the Yosemite Championships in 1952 and the Sierra-Sequoia Championships in 1966. In addition, this book documents the results of the South Yosemite League and the South Sequoia League Championships.

My research of the Central Section, or "Valley," has allowed me to share the rich wrestling history and bring forth the proud tradition of this area in the sport of wrestling. The Central Section is noted for its wrestling prowess through the state of California and across the nation. The Central Section has produced four NCAA wrestling champions and numerous wrestlers who have competed and captured victories at the highest level of competition

This book is dedicated to these four outstanding educators and coaches who 50 years ago jump-started high school wrestling in the Bakersfield and Kern County area.

Mike Stricker
Bakersfield, California
Spring 2007

Leon Tedder
Math Teacher/Coach
East Bakersfield High School

Win "Boot" Bootman
History Teacher/Coach
North Bakersfield High School

Bruce Pfutzenreuter
History Teacher/Coach
South Bakersfield High School

Olan Polite
Physical Educator/Coach
Arvin High School
Bakersfield High School

Contents

Section 1: Central Section — 1
South Yosemite League 1957-1994	2
South East Yosemite League 1995-2006	57
South West Yosemite League 1995-2006	73
South East & South West Yosemite League Area Tournament 1995-1998	89
South Sequoia League 1966-2006	99
Yosemite Divisional 1967-2006	143
Sierra-Sequoia Divisional 1966-2006	231
Central Section – Valley 1952-2000	277
Central Section – Masters 2001-2006	365
California State Championships 1973-2006	379
Southern Regional 1983	393
Northern California Invitational 1952-1960	395

Section 2: High School — 399
High School Championships 1990-2006	400
Dapper Dan Wrestling Classic	401
Amateur Wrestling News All-Americas	402
Wrestling USA Magazine All-American Team	403-404
Young Wrestler High School All-Americans	405
ASICS Tiger High School All-Americans	406
Junior USA National Wrestling Championships	407-408
Cadet USA National Championships	409-410
USWF Junior Nationals	411
National AAU Championships	411
Junior National AAU Championships	411
FILA Junior Nationals	412
FILA Cadet Nationals	412
Junior World Tournament	413
FILA Junior World Tournament	413
Cadet World Championships	413

Section 3: Collegiate — 415
NCAA Division I	416
NCAA Division II	417
National Association of Intercollegiate Athletics	418
Midlands Wrestling Championships	419
National Wrestling Coaches All-Star Classic	420

Section 4: National & International — 421
USA Wrestling Senior National Championships	422-423
Amateur Athletic Union National Championships	424-425
U.S. Wrestling Foundation Championships	426-427
World Championships	428
FILA World University Games	428
Pan-American Games	429
Olympic Games	430
USA Wrestling National Championships	431
University World	432
World Cup	433
Goodwill Games	434
U.S. Olympic Festival	435
ESPOIR USA Wrestling National Championships	436
ESPOIR FILA Juniors	436
Tbilisi, U.S.S.R.	437
National YMCA Championships	438

Section 5: Staff/Profiles/For The Record — 439
Kern County Coaching Staffs	440-458
Coach/Wrestler Profiles	459-464
For The Record	464

Section 6: 2007 Tournaments — 467
South East Yosemite League	468-469
South West Yosemite League	470
South Sequoia League	471
Sierra-Sequoia Division	472-473
Yosemite Division	474-475
Central Section Masters	476-477
State Championships	478
Notes/Corrections/Additions	479
Autographs	480
Career Wrestling Records Erratum and Additions	481

Abbreviations

SCHOOL	ABBREVIATION
Arvin	ARV
Bakersfield	BAK
Bakersfield Christian	BC
Buchanan	BUC
Bullard	BULL
Caruthers	CAR
Cesar Chavez	CC
Centennial	CEN
Central	CENT
Chowchilla	CHOW
Clovis	CLO
Clovis East	CE
Clovis West	CW
Coalinga	COAL
Corcoran	CORC
Delano	DEL
Dinuba	DIN
Dos Palos	DP
East Bakersfield	EB
Edison	ED
El Diamante	ELD
Exeter	EX
Farmersville	FARM
Firebaugh	FIRE
Foothill	FOOT
Fowler	FOW
Fresno	FRE
Frontier	FR
Golden Valley	GV
Golden West	GW
Granite Hills	GH
Hanford	HAN
Hanford West	HW
Highland	HIGH
Hoover	HOOV
Kerman	KER
Kingsburg	KING
Laton	LA

SCHOOL	ABBREVIATION
Lemoore	LEM
Liberty-Bakersfield	LIB-BAK
Liberty-Madera	LIB-MAD
Lindsay	LI
Madera	MAD
Madera South	MAD-S
McFarland	MCF
McLane	MCL
Mendota	MEN
Monache	MON
Mt. Whitney	MT.W.
North Bakersfield	NB
Orosi	O
Parlier	PAR
Porterville	PORT
Redwood	RED
Reedley	REED
Roosevelt	ROOS
Sanger	SANG
San Joaquin Memorial	SJM
Selma	SEL
Shafter	SHAFT
Sierra	SIE
South Bakersfield	SB
Stockdale	STOCK
Strathmore	STR
Sunnyside	SUNY
Taft	TAFT
Tehachapi	TEHA
Tranquility	TRAN
Tulare	TUL
Tulare Western	TW
Wasco	WASCO
Washington Union	WU
West Bakersfield	WB
Woodlake	WOOD
Yosemite	YOSE

Note: Some abbreviations may have changed during editing.

Section 1
South Yosemite League
1957-1994

South Yosemite League

Date	Location	Dual Champion		SYL Meet	Champion	Coach
1/30/57	BHS	BHS	5-1	East	BHS	Paul Briggs
2/8/58	North	BHS	6-0	East	BHS	Paul Briggs
2/13/59	East	BHS	8-1-1	East	BHS	Paul Briggs
2/13/60	Arvin	S	7-0-1	South	South	Bruce Pfutzenreuter
2/11/61	North	E	8-0	East	East	Leon Tedder
2/10/62	South	E	7-0	BHS	East	Leon Tedder
2/9/63	East	E	10-0	BHS	East	Leon Tedder
2/15/64	BHS	S	9-0-1	BHS	South	Bruce Pfutzenreuter
2/20/65	Foothill	S	9-0-1	South	South	Joe Seay
2/19/66	N	S	7-1	South	South	Joe Seay
2/11/67	BHS	S	6-2	South	South	Joe Seay
2/10/68	East	S	8-1-1	BHS	South	Joe Seay
2/15/69	BHS	S	10-0	South	South	Joe Seay
2/14/70	Foothill	BHS	10-0	BHS	BHS	Olan Polite
2/12/71	West	BHS	8-2	BHS	BHS	Olan Polite
2/19/72	BHS	BHS	11-1	BHS	BHS	Olan Polite
2/10/73	South	BHS	11-1	BHS	BHS	Olan Polite
2/9/74	Highland	W	6-0	Highland	Highland	Joe Barton
2/15/75	Foothill	HW	10-2	Highland	Highland	Joe Barton
2/14/76	Foothill	H	5-1	Highland	Highland	Joe Barton
2/11/77	Foothill	BHS	6-0	BHS	BHS	Steve Varner
2/15/78	Foothil	N	6-0	BHS	BHS	Steve Varner
2/10/79	Foothill	B N S	5-1 (All)	South	South	Gene Walker
2/16/80	Foothill	BHS	7-0	BHS	BHS	Steve Varner
2/12/81	Foothill	S	7-0	South	South	Gene Walker
2/12/82	Foothill	BHS	7-0	South	BHS South	S Varner G Walker
2/11/83	Foothill	F	7-0	Foothill	Foothill	Seymour Nerove
2/11/84	Foothill	A	7-0	Foothill	Foothill	Seymour Nerove
2/9/85	Foothill	F	7-0	Foothill	Foothill	Seymour Nerove
2/15/86	Foothill	S	7-0	South	South	Gene Walker
2/14/87	Foothill	S	7-0	South	South	Gene Walker
2/12/88	Foothill	A	7-0	Arvin	Arvin	Ruben Ramirez
2/11/89	Foothill	BHS	7-0	BHS	BHS	David East
2/10/90	Foothill	BHS	7-0	BHS	BHS	David East
2/9/91	Foothill	BHS	7-0	BHS	BHS	David East
2/8/92	East	N	6-0	BHS	North/BHS	R McKinney D. East
2/13/93	East	BHS	7-0	BHS	BHS	David East
2/12/94	East	BHS	7-0	BHS	BHS	David East

Notes
The point system was started in 1974 to determine the overall champion. Two points were awarded per dual victory, plus points for team place in the tournament, i.e., 12 first, 10 second, 8 third.

Outstanding Wrestlers SYL – Coaches Vote

Starting in 1985, the Coyote Club sponsored the
Most Outstanding Wrestler Awards – Lower and Upper Division

Year	Wrestler	School
1971	Gary Mayberry	Foothill
1972	Ed Valdes	South
1973		
1974	Ray Garza	East
1975	Paul Felez	South
1976		
1977		
1978		
1979		
1980	Joe Bisig	South
1980	Flint Pulskamp	Highland
1981	Richie Sinnott	Highland
1981	Dan Mayberry	Foothill
1982		
1982		
1983		
1983		
1984		
1984		
1985	Mike Dallas	Foothill
1985	Ben Lizama	Foothill
1986		
1987	Troy Beavers	Highland
1987	Chris Olinger	South
1988		
1989	Parris Whitley	South
1989	Jassen Froehlich	BHS
1990	Parris Whitley	South
1990	Tad Stricker	South
1991	Jeff Heberle	North
1991	Paul Carrillo	South
1992	Mario Gonzales	South
1992	Romel Green	Highland
1993	Chad Hobbs	North
1993	Willie Herron	Highland
1994	Kelly Miller	Bakersfield
1994	Jeremy Karle	Highland

SYL Tournament – BHS
January 30, 1957

103
Monji	Gary	N	Fall
Hess George	George	E	

112
Martinez	Tommy	E	Fall
Farrow	Vic	B	

120
Martwez		B	
Escalante	Luis	E	

127
Harlan	Earl	E	Fall
Burton		N	

133
Jeffrey	Dwight	E	
Bailey	Norman	N	

138
Noble	Lee	B	
Koontz	Dennis	E	

145
Escalante	Frank	E	
Montgomery	Keith	N	

154
Robbin	Marion	N	
Bookout	Ralph	E	

165
Albee	John	B	4-3
Kimbell	Carl	N	

175
Dooley	Clark	B	
Bowers	Ted	E	

191
Cardiel	Augie	E	
Edmonson	Dave	B	

HWT
Newcombe	Chuck	B	Fall
Tomlin	Harold	E	

Dual League
BHS	5-1
East	4-2
North	

SYL Tournament
East	48
BHS	39
North	26

Kneeling, left to right: Norman Bailey, Marion Drewry, Howard Wilson, Harry Hodges, Joe Greagrey, Gary Mongi, Riley Keester, Bob Orrick. Standing: Coach Dick Westbay, James Borgman, Jim Moneymaker, Roger Ellquist, Roger Bridgford, Zane Sherrill, Marion Robbins, Keith Montgomery, Blaine Rogers.

1957 North Bakersfield High School Wrestling Team

SYL Tournament – North
February 8, 1958

95
Bispo	Gene	S	9-0
Bridgeford	Charles	N	
Blankenship	C	A	10-6
Lo		B	

106
Wise	George	B	7-2
Jeffers	Ralph	S	
Hess	George	E	

112
Smith	Sammy	E	6-0
Bloomberg	Al	S	
Johnson	L	A	Fall/2
Keester	Riley	N	

123
Haddad	Angelo	E	8-1
Owens	Erby	S	
Hendricks		B	4-0
Miller		N	

130
Harland	Earl	E	8-4
Fulce	Tom	B	
Davis	Jim	S	6-0
Royal	Carlos	A	

136
Moreland	Danny	E	4-0
Bedford	Willard	S	
Bailey	Norman	N	
Walker	D	A	

141
Noble	Lee	B	6-0
Forrest	Clyde	A	
Haggard	Dennis	E	13-9
Young			

148
Koontz	Dennis	E	9-8
Morris	Bill	B	
Gutierrez	Steve	S	Fall/1
Shawn	Bob	N	

157
Bookout	Ralph	E	3-2
Nelson		B	
Tuculet	Jeff	N	5-0
Hernandez	Charles	S	

168
Sherrill	Zane	N	6-0
Albee	John	B	
Weese	Lloyd	E	Fall/3
Corley	Earl	S	

178
Hunt	Bill	B	8-1
Rivera	Don	E	
Smart	Gene	N	7-2
Sheppard	George	S	

194
Bridgeford	Roger	N	5-2
Bushfield	J	A	
Edmondson	Dave	B	Fall/1
Smith	Doug	S	

HWY
Newcombe	Chuck	B	Fall/1
Marshall	Roger	E	
Johnson			Fall/2
Farrell			

Dual League
BHS		8-0
East		
South		4-2-1
North		3-3
Arvin		

SYL Tournament
East	1
BHS	2
South	3
North	
Arvin	

SYL Tournament – East

February 13, 1959

95
Lewis	Jerry	D	5-4
Alvarez	David	S	

103
Bispo	Gene	S	6-1
Bridgeford	Charles	N	

112
Whitson	Larry	A	1:59
Keester	Riley	N	

120
Hodges	Harry	N	7-5
Stout	Royal	E	

127
Bedford	Willard	S	5-4
Haddad	Angelo	E	
Brisco	Jerry	N	

133
Moreland	Danny	E	7-6
Royal	Carlos	A	

138
Wells	Terry	S	4-1
Alvarez	Danny	E	

145
Schrader	Carl	B	5:16
Ethridge	Bob	A	

154
Carpenter	Larry	E	7-4
Kliewer	Jim	B	

165
Montgomery	Keith	N	1-0
Dewar	George	B	

175
Corley	Earl	S	5-0
Henry	Les	B	

191
Garrett	Joe	E	11-2
Adams	Alan	S	

HWT
Reade	Lynn	A	6-2
Brown	Charles	E	

East Unofficial Champion of SYL Tournament

Dual League		Season	
BHS	8-1-1		
South	7-2-1	11-2	
East	6-2		
North	3-5	4-6	
Arvin	1-6		
Delano	0-7		

1958 East Bakersfield High School Wrestling Team

SYL Tournament – Arvin
February 13, 1960

95
Bispo	Virgil	S	4-2*	
Pletcher	Delmar	E		
Sogo	Glen	B		4:45
Yeagar		N		

103
Martinez	Joe	E	9-7*	
Alvarez	David	S		
Bonds	David	A	13-8	
McKenzie	Stuart	B		

112
Villarreal	Manual	S	6-3	
Parmelee	Bob	B		
Belveal	Dan	N	9-4	
Gamboa	Danny	E		

120
Whitson	Larry	A		:40
Heckman	Jim	S		
Hooper	Frank	E		
Ford	Jerry	B		

127
Hallum	Bob	A		2:46
Metcalf	Ronnie	E		
Bloomburg	Alvin	S		

133
Washington	Drue	S	12-11*	
Royal	Carlos	A		
Baker	Larry	E	2-0	
Reyes	Joe	N		

145
Bridger	Jim	S	1-0	
Young	Barry	A		
Gold	David	B	1-0	
Alvarez	Danny	E		

154
Schrader	Carl	B	7-1	
Wells	Ken	A		
Gutierrez	Steve	S	9-6	
Haggard	Dennis	E		

165
Carpenter	Larry	E	DBL/OT	8-3
Dewar	George	B		
Stewart	Jim	S	4-0	
Meadows	Dave	N		

175
Salcido	John	E	2-1
Barrett	Marcel	B	
Diebel	Bob	S	6-0
Hill	Stan	N	

191
Corley	Earl	S	5-0
Beard	John	B	
Ford	Jack	A	5-0
Clark	Larry	N	

HWT
Garrett	Joe	E	6-0	
McGill	Danny	B		
Adams	Alan	S		4:57
Sanders		N		

*Undefeated in SYL

South Unofficial Champion of SYL Meet Season

Dual League		Season
South	7-0-1	11-0-1
East	4-3-1	
BHS	~~4x4~~ 5-3	7-3
Arvin	3-5	6-4
North	0-8	

1957 South Bakersfield High School Wrestling Team

SYL Tournament – North
February 11, 1961

95
Maynor	Don	E	10-5
Morris	Rufus	B	
Villarreal	Richard	S	

103
Pletcher	Delmar	E	8-3
Castro	Lupe	B	
Eyraud	Joe	S	

112
Martinez	Joe	E	7-2
Carr	Dave	B	
Stricker	Mike	S	Fall/1
Reese	Joe	N	

120
Whitson	Larry	A	4-0
Villarreal	Manual	S	
Norsworthy	Jim	E	4-1
Parmelee	Bob	B	

127
Alvarez	David	S	8-4
Johnson	Solomon	B	
Moreland	Terry	E	5-2
Churchwell	David	N	

133
King	Leon	B	7-1
Delis	Pete	E	
Hallum	Larry	A	3-1
DeWitt	Steve	S	

138
Fenton	Chuck	B	4-3
Moshier**	Jim	E	
Thompson	Jerry	S	4-1
Starr	Mike	N	

145
Cruz	Carl	E	3-2 OT
Bridger	Jim	S	
Roberson	Mike	B	Fall/2
Boyd	Eugene	N	

154
Meadows	Dave	N	Fall/3
Bigby	John	S	
Bradford	Claude	E	4-2
Gold	David	B	

165
Salcido	John	E	8-3
Van Worth	Ken	S	
Wells	Ken	A	4-2
Annis	Dale	B	

175
Dewar	George	B	2-1
Drew	Joe	S	
Dumble	Howard	E	Fall/1
Payton	David	N	

191
Adams	Alan	S	Fall/2
Beard	John	B	
Clark	Larry	N	3-0
Hammett	Lee	E	

HWT
Garrett	Joe	E	2-0
Statler	John	A	
Wilson	Lane	B	3-0
Brogdin	Mike	N	

Dual and SYL Meet Placings
East	8-0		1	
BHS	6-2	9x5*	2	11-4 *
South	4-4	9-4*	3	
Arvin	2-6		4	
North	0-8	0-13	5	

* Season records

** MIA (Missing In Action)
Jim Moshier, USMC
June 11, 1967
South Vietnam
You are not forgotten

SYL Tournament – South
February 10, 1962

95
Morgan	Quinnie	E	Fall
Stiles	Chuck	A	
Wiggins	Larry	B	Fall/3
Wilson	John	N	

103
Lindley	Jim	E	4-1
Hallum	Francis	A	
Harthorn	Dean	B	
Ramage	David	N	

112
Martinez	Joe	E	5-3
Morris	Rufus	B	14-5
Boado	Frank	A	Fall
Litterell	Ralph	N	

120
Belveal	Dan	N	7-0
Bispo	Virgil	S	
Fletcher	Delmar	E	3-1
Blake	Alex	B	

127
~~Strikex~~ Stricker	Mike	S	5-2
~~kkxxpex~~ Hopper	Frank	E	
Coy	John	B	
Robinson	Leon	A	

133
Norsworthy	Jim	E	5-1
Bridger	Bill	S	
Daniels	Glen	B	4-0
Shaden	Larry	A	

138
Moreland	Terry	E	Inj/Def
Fenton	Chuck	B	
Andrews	William	S	6-2
Boyd	Eugene	N	

145
King	Leon	B	4-0
Thompson	Jerry	S	
Delis	Peter	E	4-1
Findley	Ron	N	

154
Roberson	Mike	B	3-1
Nerove	Seymour	S	
Kinnett	Bill	N	6-2
Simmons	Richard	E	

165
Gold	Dave	B	5-3
Meadows	Dave	N	
Bradford	Claude	E	10-5
Montez	John	A	

175
Van Worth	Ken	S	7-3
Annis	Dale	B	
Sellers	Ben	E	4-2
Smith	Carl	N	

191
Beard	John	B	4-0
Statler	John	A	
Dumble	Howard	E	3-2 OT
Campbell	Pat	N	

HWT
Carter	John	S	2-1 OT
Brogdin	Mike	N	
McGill	Dan	B	Fall
Kinsman	Gary	E	

Dual League
East	7-0
BHS	5-2
South	4-3
North	2-6
Arvin	0-7

Season
	12-2
	9-3
	4-9

SYL Tournament
BHS	98
East	97
South	76
North	47
Arvin	37

SYL Tournament – East

February 9, 1963

95
Morgan	Quinn	E	5-0
Bracamonte	David	S	
Bingham	Jay	B	2:45
Roberts	Ron	N	

103
Heath	Roy	S	7-1
Harthron	Dean	B	
Kileen	John	E	Forfeit
Stiles	Chuck	F	

112
Boada	Frank	A	4-0
Herring	Jerry	B	
Hensley	Frank	E	4-1
Thompson	Clyde	S	

120
Lindley	Jim	E	5:58
Villarreal	Richard	S	
Metcalf	Ron	F	
Bachman	Milt	B	5:55

127
Bradford	Curtis	E	5-0
Errea	Larry	S	
Coy	John	B	3-2
Brown	Mike	~~A~~ B	

133
Norsworthy	Jim	E	6-2
Thornsberry	Tom	N	
Zawila	Charles	S	3-0
Brown	Mike	A	

138
Gamboa	Danny	E	5-3
Henson	Chuck	F	
Blake	Alex	B	4-1
Peeler	Dan	S	

145
Schnee	Al	E	4-3
Starr	Mike	N	
Creekbaum	Ray	S	5-3
Surbeck	Steve	B	

154
Kinnett	Bill	N	2-0
Sellers	Joe	E	
Christenson	Dean	B	3:45
Martin	John	S	

165
Greer	Jerry	S	2-0
Martini	Bob	E	
Findley	Ron	N	8-3
Munoz	Mike	B	

175
Van Worth	Ken	S	4-3
Harralson	Bill	B	
Smith	Carl	N	4:50
Sherrill		A	

191
Campbell	Pat	N	
Hammlett	Lee	E	
Askew	Gary	F	8-7
Rasley	Rocky	S	

HWT
Jackson	Garry	S	3-1
McGill	Dan	B	15-3 season rec
Bateman	Ray	E	4-2
Isaia	Joe	N	

Dual League
		Season
East	10-0	
South	7-3	13-3
BHS	6-4	10-5
North	3-7	4-9
Arvin		

SYL Tournament
East	114
South	101
BHS	59
North	53
Foothill	30
Arvin	18

SYL Tournament – Bakersfield High School
February 15, 1964

95
Nall	Barry	B	16-3	
Junkemeir	Mike	S		
Henson	Gene	F	4-2	
Howard	Jim	N		

103
Health	Roy	S	1-0	OT
Morgan	Quinn	E		
Bingham	Jay	B	11-0	
Roberts	Roy	N		

112
Stiles	Chuck	F	4-0	OT
Olgin	C	A		
Herring	Jerry	B	3-1	
Garcia	Tom	S		

120
Chavez	Art	S	3-2
Flores	Jess	E	
Roberts	Ron	N	4-2
Picardo	J	A	

127
Bradford	Curtis	E	3-1	
Brown	Mike	B		
Litterall	Ralph	N		5:20
Metcalf	Dan	F		

133
Lindley	Jim	E	9-2
Villarreal	Richard	S	
Sweetser	John	N	2-0
Popejoy	Joe	A	

138
Blake	Alex	B	3-0
Collier	Mike	S	
Coughran	Larry	F	2-0
Gonzaga	Robert	A	

145
Henson	Chuck	F	4-2
Welch	Ben	B	
Zisman	Terry	E	4-0
Bigby	Dennis	S	

154
Christensen	Dean	B	7-4
Wallace	Shayne	F	
Findley	Ron	N	4-2
Martin	John	S	

165
Munoz	Mike	B	5-2
Smith	Carl	N	
Williams	Jim	A	3-2
Brewer	Larry	S	

175
Cotton	Tim	S	6-0
Shore	Bob	N	
Subriar	Don	F	3-1
Valos	Tom	E	

191
Billington	Greg	B	6-2
Askew	Gary	F	
Barton	Joe	S	3-2
Aubrey	Richard	E	

HWT
Culliton	Lee	S		3:25
Sakai	Rob	B		
Defoor	Mike	F	Forfeit	
McWhorter	Lee	N		

Dual League
		Season
South	9-0-1	16-0-1
BHS	7-3	11-4
North	6-4	12-4
East	5-4-1	8-4-1
Foothill	2-8	6-9
Arvin		

SYL Tournament
BHS	95
South	92
Foothill	63
East	51
North	46
Arvin	23

SYL Tournament – Foothill

February 20, 1965

95
Serros	Jack	B	7-0
Cosme	Herb	N	
Junkemeir	Mike	S	8-1
Sanchez	Paul	F	

103
Henson	Gene	F	5:59
Howard	Jim	N	
Warren	Keith	E	8-0
Paregin	Bobby	S	

112
Herrera	Emmett	B	3-3 OT Refd
Health	Roy	S	
Gibson	Bob	E	Default
Scism	Robert	F	

120
Chavez	Art	S	6-1
Sanchez	Richard	F	
Lindley	Richard	E	1-0
Valdez	Albert	B	

127
Carolina	Mandell	B	6-3
Litterall	Ralph	N	
Pichardo	J	A	4-0
Pool	Jim	E	

133
Sousa	Frank	S	8-4
Sweetser	John	N	
Molano	Calvin	B	12-1
Pennell		F	

138
Collier	Mike	S	13-1
Kitchens	Gary	B	
Popejoy	Joe	A	4-0
Carlton		F	

145
Cosme	Alan	N	2-0
Bigby	Dennis	S	
Gollmyer	Sam	B	3-1
Simmons	Jerry	F	

154
Martin	John	S	2-0
Welch	Ben	B	
Townsend	Randy	N	3-2
Nash	Darrell	E	

165
Simmons	Richard	S	3-2
Christensen	Dean	B	
Litterell	Ron	N	4-3
Moss	Craig	E	

175
Barton	Joe	S	2-0
Munoz	Mike	B	
Haddad	Bob	E	6-3
Sherrill	Larry	A	

191
Rasley	Rocky	S	4-0
Shore	Bob	N	
Hultgren	Mark	F	5:35
Loving	Harry	E	

HWT
Culliton	Lee	S	4-1
Jeppi	Frank	B	
Aubrey	Richard	E	1:53
Davis	Clovis	A	

Dual League
South	9-0-1
BHS	8-1-1
North	6-4
Foothill	2-8
East	4-6
Arvin	0-10

Season
	15-0-1
	12-1-1
	10-4
	8-8
	8-8

SYL Tournament
South	113
BHS	97
North	67
Foothill	41
East	39
Arvin	16

SYL Tournament – North
February 19, 1966

95
Cosme	Herb	N	7-6	RT
Morgan	Larry	E		
Herrera	Don	B	4-1	
Williams	Tom	S		

103
Serros	Jack	B	6-2
Sanchez	Paul	F	
Seabourn	Bill	S	9-0
Varner	Roger	N	

112
Heath	Roy	S	4-0
Henson	Gene	F	
Roberts	Alan	N	4-3
Bares	Keith	B	

120
Sanchez	Richard	F	6-1
Varner	Vernon	S	
Gibson	Bob	E	7-0
Herrera	Bill	B	

127
Shearer	Ron	E	7-3
Stonebraker	Art	N	
Walker	Gene	S	7-4
Martinez	Mario	B	

133
Valdez	Albert	B	Default
Pool	Jim	E	
Burnett	Bruce	N	6-1
Nicholas	Gilbert	F	

138
Varner	Steve	B	8-7
Garcia	Ken	E	
Ivey	Cliff	S	3:35
Cady	Webb	N	

145
Goss	Jack	N	4-3
Horace	Brooks	E	
Gollmyer	Sam	B	1-0
Bispo	Jack	S	

154
Stock	Cliff	S	5-4
Brockman	Joe	E	
Blalock	Bob	N	3-1
Ochoa	Sam	B	

165
Martin	John	S	Default
Miller	John	N	
Shepard	Walt	B	2-0
Arriola	Andy	F	

175
Simmons	Richard	S	5:04
Litterell	Ron	N	
Rodman	Alan	E	4-2
Brand	Richard	B	

191
Hultgren	Mark	F	4-1
Estrada	Tom	S	
Valos	Tom	E	11-7
Robesky	Jim	B	

HWT
Culliton	Lee	S	6-1
Aubrey	Richard	E	
Brent	Chuck	F	1:51
Smith	Mark	B	

Dual League
South	7-1
East	4-4
BHS	5-3
North	2-6
Foothill	2-6

Season
11-1
10-3
8-6
2-6-1

SYL Tournament
South	98
East	77
North	66
BHS	64
Foothill	

SYL Tournament – Bakersfield High School
February 11, 1967

95
Williams	Tom	S	4-2	
Morgan	Larry	E		
Herrera	Bill	B	12-4	25-7
Higby	Russ	F		

103
Sanchez	Paul	F	5-3	
Lawrence	Mark	B		
Cosme	Herb	N	6-1	
Little	Larry	S		

112
Lindley	Dave	E		
Seabourn	Bill	S		
Watkins	Richard	B	5-1	
Amstutz	Doug	F		

120
Lindley	Richard	E	6-0	
Roberts	Allen	N		
Sloss	Jack	S	6-5	
Herrera	Karl	B		

127
Walker	Gene	S	6-2	
Crowder	Cecil	F		
Clifford	Jim	E	2-0	
Peterson	Chuck	B		

133
Burnett	Bruce	N	3-2	
Shearer	Ron	E		
Finch	John	S	11-5	
Manny	Bruce	B		

138
Jones	David	N	8-1	
King	Jack	S		
Garcia	Ken	E	8-3	
Miller	Ronnie	F		

145
Ivey	Cliff	S		5:35
Meaders	Chuck	E		
Meaders	Mike	F	5-1	
Sanborn	Dan	B		

154
Goss	Jack	N	5-1	
Alvarez	Richard	B		
Skaggs	Jack	E		
Smalley	Steve	S		

165
Shepard	Walt	B	9-1	30-7
Blalock	Bob	N		
Osborne	Pat	F		
Beasley	Lanny	E		

175
Miller	John	N	9-1	
Estrada	Tom	S		
Rodman	Alan	E	3-1	
Cook	Dick	B		

191
Robesky	Jim	B	16-0	Disq.
Padilla	Mark	S		
Kirk	Weldon	F		5:35
Brodsky	Tom	E		

HWT
Rucker	Sam	E		5:35
Williams	Wallace	S		
Fidler	Bob	N	6-4	
Thomas	Mark	B		

Dual League
South	6-2	
North	6-2	
BHS	4-4	
East	4-4	
Foothill	XX	

Season
South	7-3
North	9-2
BHS	11-4
East	4-5
Foothill	7-3

SYL Tournament
South	93
East	88
North	72
BHS	70
Foothill	41

SYL Tournament – East
February 10, 1968

95
Serros	Tony	B	10-2
Finch	Gary	S	
Adamson	Reed	N	4-2
Cortez	Eric	F	

106
Herrera	Billy	B	4-2
Gonzales	Rudy	E	
Rollins	Deight	S	3-2
Cargill	Mike	N	

115
Morgan	Larry	E	5-1
Little	Larry	S	
Watkins	Melvin	B	5-1
Amstute	Doug	F	

123
Lawrence	Mark	B	7-3
Morgan	Jon	E	
Galvez	Amaddor	S	4-0
Parker	Tom	W	

130
Seabourn	Bill	S	6-4
Manny	Bruce	B	
Blackhurst	Davis	E	3-0
Giggy	Dave	W	

136
Peterson	Chuck	B	3-0
Drennan	Bill	N	
Dickson	Chuck	W	Default
Finch	John	S	

141
Burnett	Bruce	N	15-7
Arechiga	Andy	E	
King	Jack	S	4-3
Rude	Alan	B	

148
Crowder Crower	Cecil	F	4-0
Saunders	Dean	B	
Tedder	Gary	E	4:45
Johnson	Don	N	

157
Garcia	Ken	E	5-3
Meadors	Mike	F	
Perry	Tom	S	9-2
Gollmyer	Bruce	W	

168
Alvarez	Richard	B	4-0
Rains	Brian	F	
Cagle	Wayne	N	2-0
Copenhaver	Dan	S	

178
Shapard	Walt	B	4-0
Blalock	Bob	N	
Lowe	Nick	E	5-2
Cotton	John	S	

194
Thomas	Mark	B	6-4
Rodman	Alan	E	
Fisher	Jack	S	1:35
Deboer	Noel	W	

HWT
Rucker	Sam	E	10-0
Williams	Wallace	S	
Lindsey	Joe	W	
Agness	Neil	F	

Dual League
		Season
South	8-1-1	12-1-1
BHS	8-2	11-2
East	7-2-1	
Foothill	3-7	
North	3-7	5-7
West	0-10	

SYL Tournament
BHS	117
East	93
South	79
North	46
Foothill	35
West	26

SYL Tournament – Bakersfield High School
February 15, 1969

95
Molina	Dick	S	11-2	
Cortez	Ernie	F		
Sanchez	Joe	E	Fall	
Valdez	Eddie	W		

103
Serros	Tony	B	18-0
Travers	Spencer	W	
Ave	John	S	
Hunter	Ted	N	

112
Herrera	Billy	B	9-6 OT
Vega	Joe	S	
Pon	Tom	F	10-1
Gonzalez	Tom	E	

120
Morgan	Larry	E	8-0	32-0*
Galvez	Amador	S		
Maldonado	Robert	B	6-0	
Kinoshita	Danny	W		

127
Little	Larry	S	10-2
Delis	Dean	E	
Espinoza	Ignacio	B	4-3
Kirby	Chris	F	

133
Giggy	Dave	W	2-1
Baker	Jeff	F	
Craig	Ray	B	3-2 OT
Ross	Eldon	N	

138
Peterson	Chuck	B	6-1
Roberson	Robert	E	
Finch	John	S	10-0
Harrer	Tom	F	

145
King	Jack	S	2:23
Verde	Frank	E	
Dickson	Chuck	W	7-5
Rhoades		F	

154
Crowder	Cecil	F	4-1
Harvick	Rick	N	
Domino	Ken	B	2-0
Oliveras	Abe	E	

165
Alvarez	Richard	B	6-1
Meadaers	Mike	F	
Cagle	Wayne	N	1-0
Perry	Tom	S	

175
Copenhaver	Dan	S	5-0
Lowe	Nick	E	
Alvarez	Danny	B	Fall
Osborn	Pat	F	

191
Blalock	Bob	N	7-0
Batsch	Dave	B	
Brodsky	Tom	E	2-1
Peeler	Dave	S	

HWT
Van Worth	Bill	S	2:57
Campbell	John	E	
Arvizu	Victor	F	3-1
Williams	Duane	N	

Dual League
South	10-0	
BHS	8-2	
East	5-5	
Foothill	5-5	
North	1-9	
West	1-9	

Season
South	15-0
BHS	13-2
East	8-7
North	5-9

SYL Tournament
South	99
BHS	81
East	72
Foothill	58
North	34
West	31

*Record

SYL Tournament - Foothill

February 14, 1970

95
Molina	Dick	S		:24
Gonzales	Johnny	E		
Gridiron	Harold	B	Fall	
Little	Mark	W		

103
Travers	Spencer	W		3:07
Burnett	Dennis	N		
Aguirre	Fernando	B	12-5	
Hill	Allan	F		

112
Serros	Tony	B	6-0
Lovelace	Paul	W	
Welte	Al	S	8-3
Cordova	Art	F	

120
Sanchez	Roy	E	10-2
Cortez	Ernie	F	
Shankle	Jerry	W	6-0
Lane	Kenny	B	

127
Higby	Russ	F	6-0
East	David	B	
Gonzales	Sal	E	5-4
McMasters	Dan	S	

133
Craig	Ray	B	14-2	(29-3)*
Moore	Mike	S		
Anderson	Sonny	N	7-2	
Buck	Mark	F		

138
Ross	Eldon	N	4-2	
Mitchell	Rodney	B		(23-7)
Powers	Randy	S	9-0	
Lundin	Mark	F		

145
Roland	Wilson	B	3:48
Clanahan	Ken	W	
Daniels	Leonard	B	6-0
Mayberry	Gary	F	

154
Domino	Ken	B	3-1
Oliveras	Abe	E	
Watts	Steve	S	8-2
Crenshaw	Don	F	

165
Davenport	Ed	E	4-3
Alvarez	Tony	B	
Montgomery	Dan	N	5-1
Robinson	Dan	W	

175
Alvarez	Danny	B	10-1
Campbell	John	E	
Hailey	Greg	F	5-3
Moe	David	S	

191
Battistoni	Mike	B	10-3
Jerri	Dave	F	
Durbin	Ken	S	4-3
Hunter	Pat	N	

HWT
Van Worth	Bill	S	:37
Smith	Weldon	E	
Brown	Jim	N	15-2
Raney	Tom	B	

Dual League
BHS	10-0
South	8-2
East	8-2
North	3-7
Foothill	1-9
West	

Season
12-0
20-3
18-4

SYL Tournament
BHS	114
East	65
South	62
Foothill	52
North	38
West	37

SYL Tournament – West

February 12, 1971

98
Ibarra	Joe	B	4-2
Hall	Rod	S	
Valdez	John	E	6-4
Smart	Marvin	N	
Porter	Rich	W	8-6
Rushing	Dennis	F	

106
Aguirre	Fernando	B	5-4
Sanchez	Pete	E	
Hunt	Bruce	F	5-1
Brewton	Briant	N	
Ochoa	Jerry	S	4-1
Lovelace	Charles	W	

115
Molina	Dick	S	5-1
Itokazu	Brad	E	
Riley	Larry	W	8-3
Stafford	Keith	N	
Maldonado		F	

123
Lovelace	Paul	W	2-1
Portillo	Vic	B	
Sanchez	Roy	E	3-1
Cordova	Art	F	
Valdez	Ed	S	6-1
Dugan	Mark	N	

130
Burnett	Dennis	N	13-4
Lane	Ken	B	(26-4)
McAtee	Fred	S	14-6
Shankle	Jerry	W	
Crenshaw	Matt	F	

136
East	David	B	18-4
O'Donnell	Rocky	N	
Cossey	Lester	S	:41
Arriaga	Tom	E	
Miller	Gary	W	4:59
Knight		F	

141
McMasters	Dan	S	5-1
Hunter	Ted	N	
Light	Mark	B	OT Ref Dec
Buck	Mark	F	
Lundin	Mark	E	14-2
Porter	Fred	W	

148
Mayberry	Gary	F	
Powers	Randy	S	
Mitchell	Rodney	B	3-0
Alexander	Ron	E	
Canaday	George	W	

157
Oliveras	Abe	E	3-1
Dickson	Russ	W	
Campbell	Guy	S	3-0
Brown	Gary	N	
Reed		B	2:59
De Orio		F	

168
Alvarez	Tony	B	14-8
Daniels	Lenord	E	
Cook	Rick	W	16-5
Moreno	Julio	S	
Porter	S	N	

178
Bull	Mike	S	6-0
Govea	John	B	
Owens	Jackie	F	3-2
Meadows	Dennis	N	
Newsome	Rufus	E	

194
Campbell	John	E	1:31
Mitchell	Roger	B	
Moe	David	S	:32
Young	Dick	N	
Powell	Steve	W	3:32
Akin		F	

(Continued on next page)

SYL Tournament – West
February 12, 1971

HWT
Bell	Bruce	E	Forfeit
Razo	George	F	
Van Worth	Bill	S	:26
Williams	Duane	N	

Dual League
BHS	8-2
East	8-2
South	8-2
North	4-6
West	2-8
Foothill	0-10

Season
	9-2
	15-2
	8-6

SYL Tournament
BHS	95
South	88
East	80
North	52
Foothill	36
West	33

Olan Polite: Arvin Coach 1958

1959 Arvin High wrestlers
Lynn Reade (left) – CIF Champion
Larry Whitson – 2nd in the CIF

Back row, left to right: Coach Polite, D. Walker, C. Forrest, R. Skaggs, R. Brown, D. Williams, O. Sherrill, J. Bushfield.
Front row, left to right: L. Hallum, C. Blankenship, B. Hallum, L. Johnson, L. Baker, C. Royal.

1958 Arvin High School Wrestling Team

SYL Tournament – Bakersfield High School
February 19, 1972

98
Gonzalez	Pete	H	5-0
Marshall	Mike	S	
Kinsinger	Tim	F	3-2
Peterson	Goe	B	

106
Valdez	John	E	Default
Hall	Rod	S	
Porter	Rich	W	5-4
Rushing	Dennis	F	

115
Parrin	Doug	H	2-1
Sanchez	Pete	E	
Carrillo	Eddie	B	4-3
Brewton	Ed	N	

123
Valdez	Ed	S	4-3
Pon	Art	H	
Beauford	Mark	E	Default
Coash	Tom	W	

130
Garza	Ray	E	Default
Chaffin	Doug	W	
Perez	Ray	B	Default
Long	Bob	S	

136
Lane	Kenny	B	3-1
Itokazu	Brad	E	
Blackhurst	Paul	H	9-3
Riley	Larry	W	

141
Light	Mark	B	2-1
Duckworth	Tony	H	
Jackson	Nick	N	5-0
Bigby	David	S	

148
East	David	B	3:15
Hambaroff	Pete	H	
Smrekar	Terry	S	18-3
Smart	Kevin	N	

157
Mitchell	Rodney	B	7-4
Brown	Gary	N	
Anderson	Mike	F	6-3
Torres	Jesse	S	

168
Alvarez	Tony	B	5-3
Campbell	Guy	S	
McNabb	Bryan	E	8-4
Carroll	Roy	F	

178
Rocha	Flo	B	8-5
Garcia	Reno	S	
Rasmussen	Eric	N	6-1
Mitchell	Jay	H	

194
Bull	Mike	S	15-4
Sheehan	Marvin	F	
Govea	John	B	2:05
Gomez	Tom	E	

HWT
Williams	Duane	N	13-4
McClintock	Brian	H	
Fowler	Bob	E	
Babb	Rich	W	

Dual League
BHS	11-1
South	10-2
East	8-4
Highland	7-5
Foothill	5-11
North	3-9
West	1-11

Season
	12-1
Foothill	5-15
North	3-10

SYL Tournament
BHS	94.5
South	77
East	66.5
Highland	66
North	41
Foothill	28
West	25

SYL Tournament – South

February 10, 1973

95
Peterson	Geo	B	4-1	29-6
Gonazlez	John	H		
Travers	Mickey	S	6-4	
Aleman	Juan	E		

103
Marshall	Mike	S	11-2
Parrin	Mike	H	
Canaday	Larry	W	12-0
Puente	Nick	E	

112
Sanchez	Pete	E	4-0
Rogers	J.B.	S	
Tobin	Mike	B	3-1
Gaitan	Jess	H	

120
Carrillo	Eddie	B	3-2
Dow	David	H	
Valdez	John	E	10-0
Kinsinger	Tim	F	

127
Garza	Ray	E	11-4
Coash	Tom	W	
York	Gary	B	3-2
Reynolds	Larry	S	

133
Perez	Ray	B	3-3 OT	(26-5)
Beauford	Mark	E		
Itokasu	Todd	H	2-1	
Hanline	Bob	W		

138
Blackhurst	Paul	H	7-2
Ward	Darrell	F	
Arriaga	Tom	E	6-5
Aubin	Tom	B	

145
Duckworth	Tony	H	
Stone	Jeff	W	
Smrekar	Terry	S	7-0
Tobin	Craig	B	

154
Anderson	Mike	F	5-2
Torres	Jess	S	
Sztorc	Ed	W	5-0 OT
Koons	Rocky	N	

165
Rocha	Flo	B	14-1
McKeehan	Dave	W	
Keese	Bill	F	6-5
Torres	James	S	

175
Garcia	Reno	S	8-6
Rivas	Tony	B	
Sheffel	Bill	H	4-1
Rassmussen	Eric	N	

191
Bull	Mike	S	12-0
Gomez	Tom	E	
Griffin	Randy	N	8-0
Ponce	Jess	B	

HWT
Williams	Duane	N	3:07
Fowler	Bob	E	
Jones	Bill	F	7-5
Cotton	Vince	S	

Dual League
BHS	11-1
South	10-2
Highland	9-3
East	6-6
Foothill	3-9
West	2-10
North	1-11

Season
Foothill	9-11
North	6-14

SYL Tournament
BHS	83.5
South	78.5
East	72.5
Highland	71
West	46
Foothill	41.5
North	31

SYL Tournament – Highland
February 9, 1974

95
Gonzalez	Pete	H	8-3	
Travers	Mickey	S		
Leyva	Anthony	B	2-0	
Davids	Brian	F		
Morrentine	Leonard	E		

103
Peterson	Geo	B	4-2	
Aleman	Juan	E		
Hull	Jeff	H	8-2	
Perez	Mike	S		
Sullivan	John	W		

112
Marshall	Mike	S	7-1	(112-8)*
Parrin	Mike	H		
Canaday	Larry	W	15-2	
Nickell	Steve	E		
Farmer	Vern	N		

120
Garza	Ray	E	8-1	(44-1)
Gaitan	Jess	H		
Tobin	Mike	B	12-0	
Ibarra	Francisco	W		
Feliz	Paul	S		

127
York	Gary	W	8-2	
Dow	Don	H		
Carroll	Chris	F	7-1	
Justice	Russ	S		
Torres	Primo	B		

133
Chambers	Scott	F	4-2	
May	Bill			
Champion	Dennis	S	4-3	
Machado	Barry	W		
Soles	Chandler	B		

138
Itokazu	Todd	H	8-0	
Hanline	Bob	W		
Alvarez	Jess	F	7-1	
Lozano	Jamie	B		
Russell	David	N		

*As of 2/9/74

145
Torres	Jess	S	7-0	
Martin	Ben	B		
Hill	Chester	F	10-6	
Thompson	Brad	H		
Allison	Scott	W		

154
Tobin	Craig	B		3:12
Conger	Kevin	F		
Torres	James	S		1:32
Ussery	Frank	N		
Bridgewater	Russell	E		

165
Sztorc	Ed	W	8-4	
Keese	Bill	F		
Delgado	Joe	H	3-2	
Eng	Stan	B		
Ackerman	Rick	N		

175
Ponce	Jess	B	4-3	
Sheffel	Bill	H		
Cummings	Alam	F	13-1	
McKeehan	Dave	W		
Farrelas	David	N		

191
Cotton	Vinson	S	6-2	
Greemore	Jim	B		
Marquex	Lorenzo	E	9-6	
Andrews	Joel	W		
Coons	Joe	N		

HWT
Clark	John	F		5:08
Van Worth	Lee	N		
Van Arkle	Tom	B	10-5	
Clift	Steve	W		
McNabb	Phil	E		

Dual League		Season	SYL Tournament	
West	6-0		Highland	85
Highland	4-2		BHS	80
BHS	4-2		Foothill	72.5
South	3-3		South	69
Foothill	3-3		East	32
North	1-5	7-12	North	15
East	0-6 7			

SYL Tournament – Foothill

February 15, 1975

95
Richard	Percey	E	10-9
Gonzales	Elfredo	B	
Burt	John	W	1:18
Duckworth	Aaron	H	
Wong	Wes	S	

103
Gonzalez	Pete	H	8-0 (26-2)*
Davids	Brian	F	
Gallegos	Ron	S	9-2
Stiener	Tim	B	
Acosta	Tim	E	

112
Leyva	Anthony	B	6-5
Hull	Jeff	H	
McCullouch	Glen	F	8-0
Nickell	Steve	E	
Perez	Mike	S	

120
Felez	Paul	S	6-3 (27-0)*
Torres	Primo	B	
Perrin	Mike	H	4-0 OT
Gonzales	William	F	
Canaday	Larry	W	

127
Gaitan	Jess	H	8-5
Reyes	Eddie	B	
Rollins	Steve	W	3-0
Clark	Tom	E	
Scott	Ronnie	F	

133
Dow	Don	H	3-2 OT
Chambers	Scott	F	
Machado	Barry	W	5-2
Peterson	Joe	B	
Flores	James	S	

138
Reynolds	Larry	S	8-6
Hanline	Bob	W	
May	Bill	H	9-0
Soto	Ray	B	
Gafford	Mike	N	

145
Hernandez	Paul	W	4-2
Chase	Bob	W	
Lozano	Jaime	B	5-2
Baker	Randy	F	
Parrish	Dennis	N	

154
Jones	Rick	S	6-5
Hill	Chesgter	F	
Dickson	Chet	W	2:01
Ussery	Frank	N	
Foy	Jeff	B	

165
Torres	James	S	7-3 (26-1)*
Farelas	Dave	E	
Osthimer	Mike	H	5-4
Cox	Mike	W	
Greek	David	F	

175
Herder	Jerry	W	4-0
Jennings	Everett	H	
Sugart	Ron	F	6-2
Knapp	Wes	N	
Finley	Gary	S	

191
Marquez	Lorenzo	E	13-5
Jelaca	Bob	W	
Greek	John	F	16-7
Blea	John	H	
Brown	Bruce	B	

HWT
Clanton	Brian	S	7-6
Clark	Dan	F	
Van Arkel	Tom	B	13-1
Leal	Pete	E	
Van Worth	Lee	N	

* Record

Dual League		Season	SYL Tournament	
West	10-2		Highland	92
Highland	10-2	12-2	West	79
BHS	7-5	9-5	South	69
South	6-6		Foothill	65
Foothill	6-6		BHS	61.5
North	7-10	3-13	East	47
East	0-12		North	14

SYL Tournament – Foothill
February 14, 1976

98
Richard	Percy	E	1-0
Gonzalez	Fred	H	
Reyes	Jessie	B	12-4
Blackford		F	
Hernandez	Larry	W	10-2
Burton	B	N	

106
Gonzalez	Pete	H	7-0 (26-1-1)*
Poteete	Jim	S	
Gonzales	Alfredo	B	7-1
Lewis		N	
Kinsinger		F	Forfeit
Soliz	Elias	E	

115
Burt	John	W	11-6 (25-5)*
Nickell	Steve	E	(23-2-2)*
Not Given			
Not Given			
Hargis	Darren	N	9-4
Morales	Eddie	B	

123
Gonzales	William	F	5-2
Johns	Deron	N	
Perez	Mike	S	6-0
Aleman	Juan	E	
Williams	Mike	H	9-2
Stiener	Tim	B	

130
Felez	Paul	S	11-0
Fahy	Jeff	W	
Higgins		F	9-4
Ballard	Jeff	H	
Dupuy	P	N	Default
Torres		B	

136
Reyes	Eddie	B	6-4
Best	Craig	H	
Churchman	Colby	N	4-0
McCullough	Glen	F	
Rollins	Steve	W	3-1
Schultz	Jon	S	

141
Chambers	Scott	F	1-1 OT Rf.d
Dow	Don	H	
Flores	James	S	2-1
Puente	Raul	E	
Cox	Ric	W	5-4
Johnson	R	N	

148
Chase	Bob	H	7-4 (23-0)*
Nipper	Waymon	S	
Choate	Steve	N	2-1
Najera	Mike	E	
Zimmerman	Brent	B	
No Sixth			

157
Johnson	Dave	H	5-3
Gause	Brian	N	
Cain	Tim	F	2-1
Walsh	Scott	W	
Salazar	Keith	S	
No Sixth			

168
Torres	James	S	16-2 (22-3)*
McNabb	Lewis	N	
McAbee	Larry	B	Forfeit
Stevens	C	N	
Vanderhook			
No Sixth			

178
Osthimer	Mike	H	2-0
Knapp	W	N	
Sogart	Ron	F	13-4
Harris	David	W	
Pierce	Bill	S	7-2
Lujan	Juan	B	

194
Brown	Bruce	B	6-2
Ackerman	Rick	N	
Greek	John	F	7-4
Jelica	Bob	W	
Purl	David	S	
No Sixth			

(Continued on next page)

SYL Tournament – Foothill
February 14, 1976

HWT

Hance	Alan	F	4-1 OT
Van Worth	Lee	N	
Whitmore		B	Default
Vanderhorst	Ed	S	
Long		N	
No Sixth			

Pete Gonzalez Four-Time SYL Champion

Dual League **Season**

Highland	5-1	
BHS	4-2	9-6
Foothill	4-2	
North	4-2	13-8
South	2-4	
West	2-4	
East	0-6	

SYL Tournament

Highland	118.5
Foothill	92
South	89.5
North	89
BHS	59
West	58.5
East	53.5

*Record

1961 Japanese National High School Champions

Bottom second from left Takatoshi Ikeda, Yojior Uetake, Katsuji Uchiyoma. Top second from left Tatsuo Sasaki, Shina Nakayama, Yukjharu AKiyama and Nobuyuki Motoyama. The Japan team wrestled McLane – Fresno and South Bakersfield. Yojiro Uetake would later win three NCAA championships at Oklahoma State and two Olympic gold medals for Japan.

SYL Tournament – Foothill
February 11, 1977

95
Gonzalez	Mike	H	5-2
Dallas	Willie	F	
Brisco	Mark	N	1-0
Neal	Tyrone	E	

103
Richard	Percy	E	7-2
Gonzalez	Fred	H	
Wong	Wes	S	4-0
Carrillo		F	

112
Poteete	Jim	S	4-0
Gonzales	Alfredo	B	
Martinez	Frank	F	2-1
Calvillo	Joe	H	

120
Nickell	Steve	E	4-3
Dow	Dale	H	
Morales	Eddie	B	14-7
Gann	Marty	F	

127
Duckworth	Aaron	H	2-1
McCullough	Glen	F	
Steiner	Tim	B	15-6
Miller	Bill	N	

133
Higgins	Dennis	F	3-2
Fahy	Jeff	W	
Pulskamp	Flint	H	5-1
Daniels	Eddie	B	

138
Mooney	Mike	B	6-5
Flores	James	S	
Kinsinger	Tony	F	15-3
Cobb	Ted	N	

145
Zimmerman	Brent	B	2-0
Roark	Gary	F	
Najera	Mike	E	5-3
Kincaid		N	

154
Castandeda	Danny	B	3-3 OT Rfd
Romine	Bob	H	
Lovell	Tim	W	6-1 OT
Choate	Steve	N	

165
McAbee	Larry	B	2-1
Ussery	Frank	N	
Cain	Tim	F	10-6
Stansbury	Tom	W	

175
McNabb	Lewis	N	3-2
Osthimer	Mike	H	
Jelica	Bob	W	9-3
Fabricius	Don	B	

191
Lujan	Juan	B	9-3
Harris	Dave	W	
Pierce	Bill	S	15-4
Leal		E	

HWT
Hall	Brian	N	4:21
Coronado	Junior	E	
Worley		F	3:30
Long	Dick	W	

Dual League
BHS	6-0
Highland	4-2
Foothill	4-2
North	3-3
West	3-3
South	0-5-1
East	0-5-1

Season
8-2

6-7-1

SYL Tournament
BHS	135.5
Highland	127
Foothill	118.5
North	89
East	71
West	59
South	51.5

SYL Tournament - Foothill
February 15, 1978

95
Gonazlez	Mike	H	11-6
Neal	Tyrone	E	
Wicks	Doug	S	4-0
Sztorc	Paul	W	
Carter	J	N	

103
Monsibies	Donny	H	4-2
Hidalgo	Larry	B	
Jones	Vernon	F	6-5
Luttrell	Darin	W	

112
Richards	Percey	E	5-2
Gonzalez	Fred	H	
Ibarra	Victor	B	5-1 OT
Bisig	Joe	S	
Dallas	Willie	F	

120
Reyes	Jessie	B	12-5
Calvillo	Joe	H	
Weaver	D	N	7-2
Villareal	Manuel	F	

127
Dow	Dale	H	12-5
Burt	John	W	
Hargis	Darrin	N	2-0
Morales	Eddie	B	

133
Kinsinger	Tony	F	Default
Nickell	Steve	E	
Govea	John	B	5-2
Hopkins	John	H	
Borrego		N	

138
Churchman	Colby	N	6-3
Mooney	Mike	B	
Montellano	Phillip	F	9-1
Tate	Tommy	W	

145
Pulskamp	Flint	H	2-0
Zimmerman	Brent	B	
Marquez	Phillip	F	2:11
Feliz		E	

154
Castaneda	Danny	B	5-3 OT
Choate	Steve	N	
Wicks	Bob	S	4-2
Campas	Joe	E	
Kincaid		H	

165
Romine	Bob	H	9-0
Torres	Fred	S	
Baker	Kevin	F	2-0
Eastwood	Brad	B	

175
McNabb	Lewis	N	(25-1)*
Fabricius	Don	B	
Saenz	Fernando	F	6-4
Simental	Leonard	E	
Herring	Tom	S	

191
Mayberry	Dan	F	9-7
Pierce	Bill	S	
Lujan	Juan	B	10-6
Duncan	D	N	

HWT
Saso	Dan	N	7-0
Marchant	Kyle	F	
Long	Dick	B	7-3
Ramirez	Cary	E	

Percey Richard (E) 4 SYL Titles
* Record

Dual League
North	6-0
BHS	5-1
Highland	4-2
South	2-4
Foothill	2-4
West	1-5
East	1-5

Season
14-1

5-8-1

SYL Tournament
BHS	138
Highland	132
North	98
Foothill	97.5
East	66.5
South	54
West	20

SYL Tournament - Foothill
February 10, 1979

95
Ray	Wynn	W	4-2	
Harris	Greg	S		
Diffenbaugh	Andrew	B	4:00	
Burns	Todd	N		

106
East	Mel	B	4-3	
Gonzalez	Mike	H		
Hood	Robby	W	6-0	
Carter	Jeff	N		

115
Slade	Steve	W	3-1	
Neal	Tyrone	E		21-4*
Villarreal	Marc	S	7-4	
Sinnott	Richie	H		

123
Poteete	Jim	S	9-0	26-1*
Dallas	Willie	F		
Ibarra	Victor	B	4-1	
Flowers	Charles	W		

130
Reyes	Jessie	B	7-3	28-0*
Hargis	Darin	N		
Calvillo	Joe	H	1-0	
Bisig	Joe	S		
Mays	Lamorris	F		

136
Cox	Greg	S	5-1 OT
Duran	Art	B	
Shaffer	Robbie	W	7-5
Gonzales	Henry	H	

141
Kinsinger	Tony	F		3:25
Fleischer	Matt	W		
Allison	Craig	N	13-8	
Mays	Mark	H		

148
Churchman	Colby	N	8-0
Annis	Jeff	S	
Eastwood	Brad	B	5-1
Devitt	Aaron	W	

157
Pulskamp	Flint	H	4-1	26-0*
Wicks	Bob	S		21-5*
Payne	Mike	W	7-3	
Atchley	Kyle	E		

168
McCullah	Lance	N	11-4
Suitor	Scott	W	
Zimmerman	Blair	B	9-3
Torres	Fred	S	

178
Baker	Kevin	F		3:12
Kennedy	Frank	W		
Choate	Steve	N	9-1	
Nielsen	Reed	S		

194
Pierce	Bill	S	15-2	25-0*
Kelsey	Forrest	N		
Campas	Jesse	E	Fall	
San Miguel	Rick	F		
Legg	Kevin	B		

HWT
James	Don	H	
Herring	Tom	S	
Worley	Donald	F	Fall
Ward	Kevin	N	

* Record

Dual League
South	5-1
BHS	5-1
North	5-1
West	3-3
Highland	2-4
East	1-5
Foothill	0-6

Season
South	14-1
North	9-3
West	4-4
Foothill	1-11

SYL Tournament
South	152
North	106
BHS	104.5
West	128
Highland	81.5
Foothill	36
East	33.5

SYL Tournament – Foothill
February 16, 1980

98
Ray	Wynn	W	14-2	23-3*
Oviveira	Dante	N		
Clevenland	Jeff	B	8-5	
Kimbrough	Brian	S		
Valdez		A		
No Sixth				

106
Gonzalez	Mike	H	5-0	
Sanchez	David	A		
Hudson	Darron	B	7-3	
Patrick	Rob	W		
Arriaga	Noe	E	OT Rfd	
Burns	Todd	N		

115
East	Mel	B	2:53
Geronimo	Ernie	A	
Seay	Mike	H	15-4
Gonzales	Art	S	
Blanton	Tim	W	
No Sixth			

123
Torres	Frank	B	3-1 OT	
Villarreal	Marc	S		
Luttrell	Darrin	W		4:25
Carter	Jeff	N		
Copeland		F		
No Sixth				

130
Bisig	Joe	S	6-5
Ibarra	Victor	B	
Shraland	Dirk	W	
Gonzales	Henry	H	
Bedford	Steve	N	9-8
Castillo		A	

136
Sanchez	Angel	A	4-1 OT
McCray	David	W	
Austin		N	
Hackney	Brad	H	
No Fifth			
No Sixth			

141
Sanchez	Art	A	1-0
Annis	Jeff	S	
Willey	Gary	B	9-4
Lovell	Dan	W	
No Fifth			
No Sixth			

148
Hendrix	Ramon	S	9-3
Devitt	Aaron	N	
Duran	Art	B	6-1
Flores		A	
Trowbridge	Dan	F	
No Sixth			

157
Froelich	John	B	8-6
Torres	Fred	S	
Smith	John	N	
Lathrop	Steve	W	
Van Wagoner	Jeff	F	
No Sixth			

168
Pulskamp	Flint	H	4:50	23-1*
Kelly	Tom	S		
Zimmerman	Blair	B	5-3	
Kennedy	Don	W		
Mendoza		A		2:55
Maldonado	Felix	F		

178
Neilson	Reed	S	5-1	
Greemore	Jason	B		
Orton	Jeff	W		2:48
Little	Greg	F		
Ludeke	Kevin	H	9-7	
Ansolabehere	Brian	N		

194
Park	Mark	N	6-4
Gause	Dennis	W	
Schallock	Mike	S	
Manriquez		A	
Legg	Kevin	B	
No Sixth			

(Continued on next page)

SYL Tournament – Foothill
February 16, 1980

HWT

James	Don	H		:08
Reyneveld	Willie	A		
Mudryk	Mark	F	2-0	
Cervantes	Victor	E		
McMenamy	John	S		
No Sixth				
* Record				

Dual League

		Season	
BHS	7-0		
West	6-1		
South	6-1	10-3	
Arvin			
North	2-5	4-9	
Highland			
Foothill		1-13	

SYL Tournament

BHS	157
South	152.5
West	150
Arvin	101.5
Highland	95
North	69
Foothill	22.5
East	17

1962 South Yosemite Champions

Bottom, left to right: Quinn Morgan, Jim Lindley, Joe Martinez, Mike Stricker and Jim Norsworthy.
Top, left to right: Terry Moreland, Leon King, Mike Roberson, Dave Gold, Ken Van Worth, John Beard, John Carter and (not picutred) Dan Belveal.

SYL Tournament – Foothill
February 12, 1981

101
Nerove	Darrell	F	Fall
Cleveland	Jeff	B	
Rodriguez	David	S	3:26
Lomas	Fred	E	

108
Ray	Wyn	W	1:21
Kimbrough	Brian	S	
Garcia	Hugo	A	1:40
Hinesley	Bruce	H	

115
East	Mel	B	10-3
Seay	Mike	H	
Ramirez	Anthony	A	4-1
Alvarado	Al	N	

122
Geronimo	Ernie	A	6-5
Torres	Frank	B	
Merritt	Joey	H	5-1
Jeffers	Nick	F	

129
Harris	Greg	S	7-5
Jeffry	Rick	W	
Gonzalez	Henry	H	7-3
Austin	Mark	N	

135
Sinnott	Richie	H	5-3 OT
Bisig	Joe	S	
DeVecchio	Matt	W	6-4
Flores	Joe	A	

141
McCray	David	W	11-2
Willey	Gary	B	
Castillo	Jose	A	8-3
Lathrop	Mike	S	

148
Hodges	Keith	B	1:59
Mills	Cary	S	
Larsen	DJ	N	Fall
Kurfess	Leland	W	

158
Annis	Jeff	S	16-6
Bellue	Chris	B	
Brown	Marlon	E	8-3
Sims	Rick	A	

170
Kelly	Tom	S	11-0 (21-1-1)*
Mass	David	W	
Ward	Kevin	N	2-0
Critchlow	Todd	H	

188
Mayberry	Dan	F	12-3
Orton	Jeff	W	
Greemore	Jason	B	3-2
Klugow	Scott	S	

203
Mudryk	Mark	F	6-0
Newcomb	Mike	W	
Toland	Al	N	5:22
Garza		A	

HWT
Cervantes	Victor	E	Fall
Duke	Russell	F	
Traffanstedd	Jim	B	4-2
Wilson	Dan	W	

* Record

Dual League
		Season	
South	7-0	12-6	
BHS	6-1		
Arvin	4-3	10-4	
West	3-2		
North	3-4	3-10	
Highland	2-5		
Foothill	1-6	3-13	
East	0-7		

SYL Tournament
South	134
West	132.5
BHS	125.5
Foothill	86.5
Highland	72
Arvin	70.5
North	54
East	49

SYL Tournament – Foothill
February 12, 1982

101
Nerove	Darrell	F	Fall
Ramirez	Pete	A	
Nickell	Jeff	E	
Williams	Joe	H	
Jarrard	Mike	B	
Glover	Logan	S	

108
Ray	Wynn	W	11-6
Cleveland	Jeff	B	
Valdez	Beto	A	4-2
Dallas	Mike	F	
Lui	Chang	E	10-2
Lewis	Kurt	N	

115
Kimbrough	Brian	S	6-5
Petrone	Tom	W	
Marin	Juan	A	
Lomas	Greg	E	
Jones	Mike	F	
No Sixth			

122
East	Mel	B	13-8
Hinesley	Bruce	H	
Blanton	Tim	W	
Carroll	Chip	S	
Puente	Bobby	F	
Garay	Manuel	A	

129
Prather	Brett	W	9-4
Merritt	Joey	H	
Harvey	Nick	B	6-2
Garcia	Hugo	A	
Brand	Chuck	S	11-5
Giggy	Mike	N	

135
Harris	Gregg	S	7-6
Morales	Tony	E	
Smith	Mark	W	
Pfutzreneuter	Dean	F	
Chamagni	Brad	H	Forfeit
Camareno	Tony	A	

141
Graham	Randy	B	5-4
Lathrop	Mike	S	
Marchant	Kris	F	4-1
Churchman	Rocky	N	
Zimmerman	Kevin	A	5-3
Cisneros	Gilbert	E	

148
Klugow	Scott	S	12-9
Hodges	Keith	B	
Slagle	Eric	F	14-12
Fussell	Trent	W	
Perez	Martin	E	Forfeit
Baeza	Ruben	A	

158
Mills	Cary	S	18-6
Creech	Jim	B	
Spiers	Jim	E	
William	Robert	W	
Hinesley	Jim	F	16-4
Smith	Ken	N	

170
Froehlich	John	B	2-0
Garnand	Blake	S	
Ward	Kevin	N	Fall
Critchlow	Todd	H	
Green	Richard	F	7-2
Wilson	Don	W	

188
Greenmore	Jason	B	Fall
Garcia	Andy	S	
Davidson	Linsey	W	
Gordillo	Martin	A	
Gonzales	Mac	E	
No Sixth			

203
Allen	Chris	S	10-5
Forrey	Matt	F	
Moore	Lenny	B	Fall
Hernandez	Carlos	W	
No Fifth			
No Sixth			

(Continued on next page)

SYL Tournament – Foothill
February 12, 1982

HWT

Lazama	Pete	F	Fall
Strong	Kurt	S	
Toland	Al	N	3-0
Madonza	Mike	A	
Traffenstedt	Jim	B	
Mendivel	Doc	E	

Mel East (B) 4 Time SYL Champion
Wynn Ray (W) 4 Time SYL Champion

Dual League		Season
BHS	7-0	
South	6-1	11-8
West	5-2	
Arvin	4-3	
Foothill	4-3	8-3
North	2-5	
East	1-6	
Highland	1-7	

SYL Tournament

South	161
BHS	154
West	110
Foothill	104.5
Arvin	67
Highland	49.5
East	39.5
North	31

East Bakersfield High School Coach Leon Tedder, left, presents captain Johnny Salcido with a team trophy.

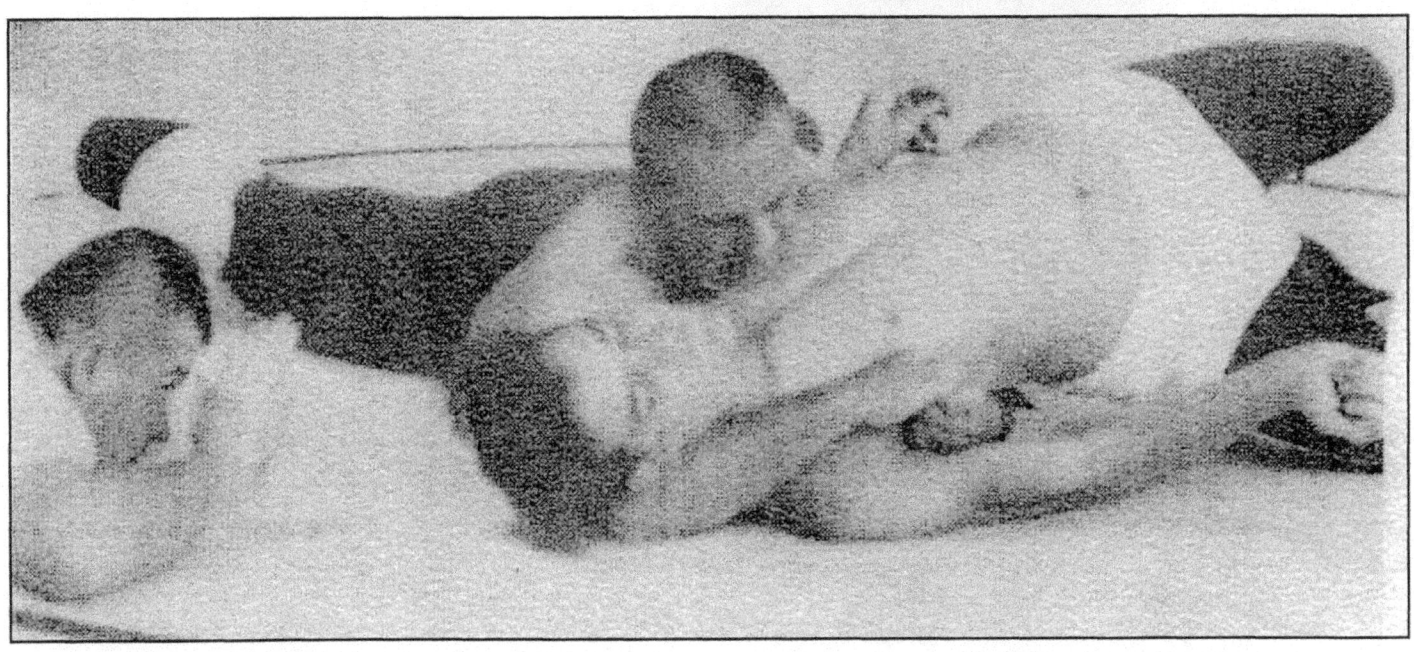

East Bakersfield's John Salcido – Two-time CIF Champion (1959/1960); 1961 2nd CIF
East Bakersfield High School varsity wrestler and team captain Johnny Salcido prepares to pin his opponent.

SYL Tournament – Foothill
February 11, 1983

101
Ramirez	Pete	A	9-5	
East	Brad	W		
Luevano	Mike	F	11-0	
Chavez	Tony	B		

108
Martinez	Joe	F	13-3	
Williams	Joe	H		
Glover	Logan	S	5-0 OT	
Camargo	Tim	B		

115
Dallas	Mike	F	8-1	(32-2)*
Nickell	Jeff	E		
Williams	Jim	A	Fall	
Carlson	Greg	B		

122
Nerove	Darrell	F	6-0	(34-0)*
Ramirez	Tony	A		
Petrone	Tom	W	Fall	
Leach	Brian	S		

129
Morales	Tony	E	7-4	
Garay	Manuel	A		
Hinsley	Bruce	H	2-1	
Puente	Bobby	F		

135
Perez	Noe	S	6-4	
Vasquez	Juan	A		
Orozco	Rick	F	4-0	
Champagne	Brad	H		

141
Merritt	Joey	H	9-5	(24-1)*
Marchant	Kris	F		
Chaves	Martin	B	8-6	
Blanton	Tim	W		

148
Graham	Randy	B	8-3	(28-5)*
Williams	Robert	W		
Slagle	Eric	F	11-5	
Zimmerman	Kevin	A		

158
Fussell	Trent	W	2-1	(30-7)*
Guerrro	Art	A		(20-9-1)*
Hinesley	Jim	F	10-7	
Clarksean	Mike	H		

170
Garnand	Blake	S	5-4	(35-3-1)*
Green	Richard	F		
Creech	Jim	B	Fall	
Towery	Scott	A		

188
Forry	Matt	F		(23-6-1)* 5:40
Gordillo	Martin	A		
Moore	Lenny	B	17-1	
Sanford	Guy	W		
Holland	Scott	S	Forfeit	
Gonzales	Mac	E		

203
Allen	Chris	S		(31-2)* 3:59
Lizama	Ben	F		
Mitchell	David	H	Fall	
Riemer	Don	W		

HWT
Duke	Russell	F	3-3 OT Crit.	
Mendivel	Doc	E		
Nordonza	Mike	A	6-2	
Kleiwer	Steve	H		
Reed	John	S		

No Sixth
* Record

Dual League		Season	SYL Tournament	
Foothill	7-0		Foothill	201
West	6-1		Arvin	144.5
Arvin	5-2		West	93.5
South	4-3	8-11-1	South	91.5
BHS	3-4		BHS	85
Highland	2-5		Highland	79
East	1-6		East	58
North	0-7		North	1.5

SYL Tournament – Foothill
February 11, 1984

101
Rameriz	Pete	A	Fall	(27-1)*
Garside	Erin	N		
Chavez	Tony	B	9-2	
Levario	Tony	E		
May	Mike	H	5-3	
Stormo	Ted	S		

108
East	Brad	W	Fall	(24-3)*
Camargo	Tim	B		
Eudy	Shannon	F	10-2	
Walker	Steve	E		
Beasley	Shawn	H		
Vela	Vale	A		

115
Leuvano	Mike	F	17-7
Gause	Darin	N	
Martinez	Mike	A	10-4
Eggers	Dave	W	
Henderson	Brian	S	10-5
Lanier	Don	E	

122
Dallas	Mike	F	18-5
Chavez	Ruben	B	
Beavers	Troy	H	4:36
Nickell	Jeff	E	
Marin	Juan	A	7-4
Leach	Brian	S	

129
Garay	Manuel	A	11-3
Jarrard	Mike	B	
Ballard	Bill	F	
Lewis	Delbert	N	
Seay	James	H	:51
Gonzales	Eddie		

135
Nerove	Darrell	F	8-0	(28-1)*
Ashjian	Brook	W		
Hinesly	Bruce	H	Default	
Shockley	Brian	B		
Herndon	Scott	S	5-3 OT	
Marin	Jose	A		

141
Merritt	Joey	H	5-1	(26-2)*
Hembree	James	S		
Hinojosa	Luis	E	Fall	
Toland	Richard	N		
Rangel	Jeff	F		
Garay	Rudy	A		

147
Pfutzenreuter	Dean	F	5-2
Fowler	Dale	W	
Padilla	Ray	A	9-6
Lomas	Fred	E	
Pulskamp	Greg	H	
Brewton	Mike	N	

157
Graham	Randy	B	7-3	(30-0)*
Zimmerman	Kevin	A		(22-9)*
Clarksean	Mike	H	6-0	
Grisedale	Mike	N		
Aguilar	James	E	Fall	
Walker	Brandon	S		

168
Green	Richard	F	7-4 23-5
Creech	Jim	B	
Leonard	Mike	A	Fall
Olinger	Eric	N	
Olinger	Scott	S	10-0
Ballew	Ron	H	

178
Gretlein	Jim	B	Fall
Holland	Scott	S	
Hulsey	Scott	F	Fall
Johnston	Roger	A	
No Fifth			
No Sixth			

194
Lizama	Ben	F	Fall
Sanford	Guy	W	
Byerly	Kevin	N	
Davis	Pat	B	
Mendez	Steve	S	Fall
Garcia	Willie	E	

(Continued on next page)

SYL Tournament – Foothill
February 11, 1984

HWT

Mendivel	Doc	E	Fall
Nadpmza	Mike	A	
Pierce	Vic	S	6-2
Nieto	Steve	F	
Ashbury	Darrin	N	Fall
Vasquez	Mike	B	

Dual League

		Season
Arvin	7-0	
Foothill	6-1	
South	5-2	6-12
BHS	4-3	
Highland	2-5	
West	2-5	6-12
East	2-5	
North	0-7	2xkx 3-10

SYL Tournament

Foothill	173
BHS	129
Arvin	127
West	74.5
East	74.5
North	74
Highand	64.5
South	49

* Record

Wrestling coach Grover Rains discusses a forthcoming match with several of his best wrestlers. Left to right: Royal Stout, Larry Carpenter, Danny Moreland, Coach Grover Rains, Charles Brown, Angelo Haddad, Jerry Garland.

1959 East Bakersfield High Wrestling Team

1962 Bakersfield High School Wrestling Coaches
Olan Polite (left) and Paul Briggs

SYL Tournament – Foothill
February 9, 1985

101
Beavers	Ted	H	18-7
Levario	Tony	E	
Mormolejo	Albert	A	Fall
Mancillas	Ferni	B	
Wiggs	Mike	F	
Gomez	Angel	S	

108
East	Brad	B	2:30
Lewis	Robert	S	
Vela	Vale	A	11-4
Bergman	Greg	E	
Salters	Danny	F	11-0
Ferris	Jeff	W	

115
Eudy	Shannon	F	10-5
Leach	Brian	S	
Walker	Steve	E	Fall
Robinson	Jimmy	A	
No Fifth			
No Sixth			

122
Luevano	Mike	F	11-0 OT
Marin	Juan	A	
Henderson	Brian	S	9-0
Pitoni	Steve	B	
Chavez	Art	W	
No Sixth			

129
Dallas	Mike	F	3:20
Beavers	Troy	H	
Marin	Jose	A	9-2
Gause	Darin	N	
Stricker	Ty	S	21-7
Bustomonte	Paul	W	

135
Chavez	Ruben	B	7-2
Ramos	Efarin	A	
Ballard	Bill	F	4-0
Lewis	Kurt	N	
Jolly	Joe	S	Fall
Nava	Brian	E	

141
Rangel	Jeff	F	11-7
Martinez	Barney	B	
Tamayo	Jose	A	8-4
Hinojosa	Luis	E	
Eggers	David	W	Fall
Casey	Marty	S	

147
Padilla	Ray	A	5-2
Toland	Richard	N	
Gannon	Joe	H	8-2
Oliver	Craig	B	
Olinger	Chris	S	13-2
Gilmore	Mark	F	

157
Spence	Jeff	S	3-2
Cotton	Bill	F	
Aguire	James	E	Fall
Leonard	Matt	A	
Robbins	Chris	B	10-6
Putman	David	H	

168
Olinger	Scott	S	8-6
Pulskamp	Greg	H	
Rangel	Alvaro	A	9-8
Gretlin	Jim	N	
Walker	Brandon	W	
No Sixth			

178
Leonard	Mike	A	1:52
Thomas	Frank	F	
Neri	John	E	
Castro	Pete	B	
Auxier	Tim	W	
Rodriguez	Jose	H	

194
Davis	Pat	B	10-7
Kelly	Pat	S	
Nahama	David	F	
Romero	Alfredo	A	
Woltz	John	N	Default
Mitchell	David	W	

(Continued on next page)

SYL Tournament – Foothill
February 9, 1985

HWT

Lizama	Ben	F	3:00
Pierce	Vic	S	
Pasqua	Brian	E	
Garcia	Marcos	A	
No Fifth			
No Sixth			

SYL Tournament

Foothill	156.5
Arvin	151
South	116
BHS	96
East	77
Highland	66
North	34.5
West	2

Dual League   **Season**

Foothill	7-0	
Arvin	6-1	
South	5-2	11-6
BHS	4-3	
East	2-4	
North	2-4	7-4-1
Highland	1-6	
West	0-7	

Lee Culliton (top) – South Bakersfield High two-time CIF Champion (1964-65); 3rd 1966
Career: 81-3

SYL Tournament – Foothill
February 15, 1986

101
Levario	Tony	E	Fall
Perez	Roy	S	
Wiggs	Mike	F	6-1
Padgett	Jeff	H	
James	Scott	W	
Cogdale	Jason	N	

108
Marmoletjo	Albert	A	9-3
Perez	Art	S	
Hernandez	David	E	10-2
Wilson	David	N	
Eggers	Brant	W	
No Sixth			

115
East	Brad	B	16-1
Autrey	Paul	H	
Lewis	Robert	S	4:55
Formbona	Pedro	A	
Cemo	Joe	N	
Compton	Brandon	F	

123
Eudy	Shannon	F	4:55
Walker	Steve	E	
Gaon	Jason	S	11-2
Hernandez	Austin	N	
Lopez	Joey	A	
Ferris	Jeff	W	

129
Shockley	Brian	B	5-3
Marin	Juan	A	
Henderson	Brian	S	6-4
Nava	Brian	E	
Chavez	Art	W	
Padilla		F	

136
Ramos	Efrain	A	9-5
Prather	Hugh	S	
Beavers	Troy	H	12-5
Aguilar	Jeff	E	
Myers	Shem	S	
Hwang	Kuopin	F	

141
Rangel	Jeff	F	:56
Stricker	Ty	S	
Martinez	Barney	B	
Bartlett	Steve	N	
Bradshaw	David	H	
Whitaker	John	E	

148
Herndon	Scott	S	8-2
Oliver	Craig	B	
Hinojosa	Luis	E	
Elliott	Shawn	W	
Garcia	Martin	A	
Putman	David	H	

157
Gannon	Joe	H	
Leonard	Matt	A	
Strenn	Steve	W	
Thomas	Frank	F	
Bird	Chuck	S	
Reynolds	Dirk	E	

169
Leonard	Mike	A	8-5
Olinger	Chris	S	
Hevely	Stacy	H	3:50
Walker	Brandon	W	
Smith	Eric	F	
Sizemore	John	B	

178
Pulskamp	Greg	H	
Cotton	Bill	F	
Pfeifle	Bob	S	
Ragpala	Mike	A	
Castanda	Mike	B	
Queen	Chris	E	

194
Davis	Pat		
Nahama	David	F	
Vasquez	Rick	S	
Taylor	Mike	N	
Garcia	Joey	A	
No Sixth			

(Continued on next page)

SYL Tournament – Foothill
February 15, 1986

HWT
Pierce	Vic	S
Woltz	John	N
Maricich	Jim	F
Peacock	Wayne	H
Garcia		A
Conrad		E

Dual League
		Season
South	7-0	15-1
Highland	6-1	
Foothill	5-2	
Arvin	4-3	
East	3-4	
BHS	2-5	
West	1-6	
North	0-7	0-11

SYL Tournament
South	165
BHS	109
Foothill	107.5
Arvin	104.5
Highland	98.5
East	81.5
North	45.5
West	19

Bakersfield High and South Bakersfield High wrestlers
Left to right, Jack Serros (Bakersfield High), Joe Seay, Art Chavez and Roy Heath (South Bakersfield)

SYL Tournament – Foothill
February 14, 1987

101
Mancillas	Frnie	B	16-2	
Contras	Paul	F		
Padget	Jeff	H	10-5	
Rodrigez	Danny	A		
Whitley	Parris	S	7-2	
Ward	Steve	N		

108
Patton	Dereck	A	9-4	(31-4)*
Perez	Art	S		
Lavario	Tony	E	Fall	
Ramero	George	B		
Clark	Allan	F	5-2	
Scott	James	W		

115
Mesa	Saul	E	15-7
Fammbona	Pedro	A	
Lewis	Robert	S	9-5
Frohlich	Jassen	B	
Long	Steve	W	Fall
Franks	Mike	N	

122
Gaon	Jason	S	Default
Cemo	Joe	N	
Marmolejo	Albert	A	8-1
Neito	Carl	F	
Beavers	Ted	H	11-5
Macias		E	

129
Garside	Erin	N	9-2
Marin	Joes	A	
Myers	Shem	S	9-0
Nava	Brian	E	
Frohlich	Jim	B	Forfeit
Pulskamp	Victor	H	

135
Beavers	Troy	H	10-9
Henderson	Brian	S	
Gallardo	Bennito	A	Fall
Miller	Scott	F	
Hernandez	Austin	N	11-0
Wofford	Mike	B	

141
Prather	Hugh	B	(35-4)*	3:03
Stricker	Ty	S		
Burbank	Tyler	W		
Jamie	Jesse	F	Forfeit	
Bergman	Greg	E	13-2	
Rizo	Gill	A		

148
Herndon	Scott	S	(38-1)*	1:10
Fletcher	David	W		
Wright	Cary	B	8-3	
May	Mike	H		
Deathridge	Larry	N	8-5	
Alcala	Jorge	A		

157
Romero	Robert	E	5-3
Pfeifle	Bob	S	
Guzman	Garry	N	Fall
Leary	Marcus	A	
May	Jason	H	5-0
Camenisch	Doug	B	

168
Olinger	Chris	S	15-0	(36-1)*
Leonard	Matt	A		
Brunelle	Jeff	N	8-6	
Putman	David	H		
Dimario	Mike	F	Forfeit	
Sizemore	John	B		

178
Walker	Brandon	W	12-10
Wren	John	S	
Zavala	George	B	Fall
Ragpala	Mike	A	
Langley	Kevin	N	Fall
Smith	Scott	F	

194
Nahama	David	F	9-4
Neri	John	E	
Taylor	Mike	N	Fall
Romero	Alfredo	A	
Reade	Scott	W	6-0 OT
Fanucchi	Gary	S	

(Continued on next page)

SYL Tournament – Foothill
February 14, 1987

HWT

Pierce	Vic	S	6-4 32-6
Woltz	John	N	
Alexander	Jiim	W	Forfeit
Maricich	Jim	F	
Vasquez	Jose	E	6-3
Gamez	Rudy		

*Record

SYL Tournament

South	194.5
Arvin	131.5
North	86.5
BHS	86
East	80
Foothill	62.5
West	59.5
Highland	

Dual League
South   7-0

Season
20-3-1

1961 Bakersfield High Wrestling Team
Back row, left to right: John Beard, Mike Roberson and David Gold
Front row, kneeling, left to right: Warren Fenton and Leon King

SYL Tournament – Foothill
February 12, 1988

101
Wright	Kenny	B	8-7	(31-2)*
Whitley	Parris	S		
Rodriguez	Danny	A	Default	
Contreras	Paul	F		
Ward	Steve	N		
Gonzales	Tony	E		

108
Armijo	Ted	E	12-8
Aceves	Feliz	A	
Heberle	Jeff	N	16-5
Roland	Justin	F	
Hamlin	Josh	B	
Molina	Jade	S	

115
Pombona	Pedro	A	18-3	(22-6)*
Fernandez	David	E		
Rogers	Josh	H	8-2	
Long	Steve	W		
Williams	Terry	B		
Clark	Alan	F		

122
Patton	Dereck	A	1:57
Desmaris	Joel	W	
Morales	Richrad	E	4-2 OT
Enriquez	Jim	S	
Backer	Steve	B	
Shoemaker	David	F	

129
Granillo	Dan	E	4-3
Eggers	Brant	W	
Harper	Dorrel	B	Fall
Maguire	Jay	S	
Sanchez	Alvaro	A	
No Sixth			

135
Cemo	Joe	N	10-4	(36-2)*
Chavez	Art	W		
Menchaca	Ray	A	Fall	
Torres	Travis	F		
Springer	Mark	B		
Millazzo	Mike	H		

141
Stricker	Tad	S	6-5	(17-6)*
Caldwell	Brandon	W		
Bergman	Greg	E		
Puskamp	Victor	H		
Froelich	Jim	B	Fall	
Arvizu	Joe	F		

148
Stricker	Ty	S	8-3	(39-5)*
Froehlich	Jason	B		(31-7)*
Ebarra	Jesse	A		
Bartlett	Steve	N		
Odell	Danny	W		
Wren	Brandon	F		

156
Fletcher	David	W	6-5
Deatherage	Larry	N	
Weir	Matt	S	9-4
Wright	Cary	B	
Scattini	Todd	A	
Williamson	Josh	F	

168
Leonard	Matt	A	Fall
Gonzales	Art	E	
Rogers	Brandon	S	
Lizama	Tom	F	
No Fifth			
No Sixth			

178
Madison	Mike	W	4-3
Leary	Mracus	A	
Olson	Gary	B	7-0
Bailey	Mike	N	
Nixon	Steve	E	
Paradez	John	S	

194
Langley	Kevin	N	Fall
Ragpala	Mike	A	
Queen	Chris	E	
Garcia	Mike	H	
Jennings	Jason	B	
Moore	Jerod	W	

(Continued on next page)

SYL Tournament – Foothill

February 12, 1988

248

Maricich	Jim	F		3:00
Rasley	Wade	W		
Fallis	Troy	S	Fall	
Pelham	Roger	E		
Garcia	Joe	A		
Alston	Rob	N		

* Record

SYL Tournament

Arvin	160.5
BHS	135.5
West	135.5
East	99
South	99
North	83.5
Foothill	53.5
Highland	20

Dual League

		Season
Arvin	7-0	
BHS	6-1	
East	5-2	
West	4-3	
North	3-4	
South	2-5	9-13
Foothill	1-6	
Highland	0-7	

1988 South Yosemite Champions
Bottom, left to right: Joe Cemo, Dan Granillo, Dereck Patton, Pedro Fambona, Ted Armiso, Kenny Wright.
Top, left to right: Jim Maricich, Kevin Langley, Mike Madison, Matt Leonard, David Fletcher, Ty Stricker and Tad Stricker

SYL Tournament – Foothill
February 11, 1989

98
Ward	Steve	N	4-3	(37-4)*
Marsh	Bill	B		(30-6-1)*
Sanchez	Mark	A	6-1	
McCray		F		
Radman	Aaron	W		
No Sixth				

103
Keester	Mike	N	6-0	(30-8)*
Gonzales	Tony	E		
Kolthoff	Cliff	B		
Padgett	Jeff	H		
Escobal	Dan	W		
No Sixth				

112
Whitley	Parris	S	11-7
Wright	Kenny	B	
Heberle	Jeff	N	Fall
Pimienta	Tom	E	
Rogers	Josh	H	6-5
Aceves	Jose	A	

119
Hernandez	Ryan	W	4-3	
Morales	Rich	E		(23-7)*
Roland	Justin	F	19-3	
Ramos	Tino	A		
Johnson	Scott	N		
Cox	Mark	B		

126
Harper	Dorrell	B	9-2
Sanches	Alvaro	A	
Enriquez	Jim	S	6-5
Boyd	Mike	W	

132
Cemo	Joe	N	7-1
Anderson	Demetrius	B	
Armijo	Ted	E	Default
Herrera	Juan	A	
No Fifth			
No Sixth			

138
Plott	Robert	S	12-11 OT
Williams	Terry	B	
Willard	Dan	N	18-2
Duenas	Gilbert	A	
Holguin	Luis	E	
Ashjan	Keller	F	

145
Caldwell	Brandon	W	5-4
Garcia	Isaac	B	
Puskamp	Victor	H	4-2
Menchaca	Ray	A	
Hardy	Jason	N	Fall
Clem	David	S	

154
Stricker	Tad	S	7-2
Froehlich	Jim	B	
Bartlett	Steve	N	3-0 OT
Ruiz	Danny	E	
Ramos	John	W	
Wren	Brandon	F	

165
Froehlich	Jassen	B	6-3
Leary	Marcus	A	
Brunelle	Jeff	N	6-5
Rogers	Brandon	S	
Bergman	Jeff	E	
Blanco	Anthony	H	

175
Madison	Mike	W	3-0
Olson	Gary	B	
Lizama	Tom	F	
Arenas	Stan	E	
Cardoza	Hector	A	
Anglin	Ben	S	

191
Langley	Kevin	N	Fall
Simmons	David	B	
Thomas	Josh	F	
Lee	Joe	W	
Leyva	Javier	A	
No Sixth			

(Continued on next page)

SYL Tournament – Foothill
February 11, 1989

HWT

Campbell	Glen	B	8-6
Reade	Scott	W	
Dearmoore	Wes	H	3-1
Garcia	Joe	A	
Alston	Rob	N	
No Sixth			

* Record

SYL Tournament

BHS	192
North	129
West	90.5
Arvin	80
South	73
East	66.5
Foothill	38.5
Highland	30

Dual League

		Season
BHS	7-0	
North	6-1	
West	5-2	
Arvin	4-3	
South	3-4	8-14-1
East	2-5	
Foothill	1-6	
Highland	0-7	

Mark Lawrence
Bakersfield High 1968 CIF Champion

1965 Bakersfield High CIF Champions
Left to right: Mike Munoz, Jack Serros and Ben Welch

SYL Tournament – Foothill
February 10, 1990

98
Sanchez	Mark	A	4-1	(19-8)*
Radman	Aaron	W		
Wright	Coby	B	6-1	
Fox	Jason	N		
Hawkins	Myron	E		
Roberts	Roy	S		

105
Winn	Robert	B	Fall	(18-5)*
Miller	Justin	W		(19-15)*
Aceves	Mike	A		
Chavez	Joey	H		
Trone	Derek	F		
No Sixth				

112
Jackson	Matt	N	17-4
Sherley	Jake	W	
Botts	Anthony	B	15-6
Gutcher	Joe	H	
Rocha	Gabe	S	

119
Whitley	Parris	S	8-1
Morales	Richard	E	
Aceves	Jose	A	7-6
Rogers	Josh	H	
Watkins	Ronnie	B	
No Sixth			

126
Heberle	Jeff	N	Fall
Hrenandez	Ryan	W	
Felix	Robert	E	5-0
Kolthoff	Cliff	B	
Smith	Eli	S	11-5
Calvillo	Isaias	A	

132
Williams	Terry	B	10-5	(33-4)*
Roland	Justin	F		
Enriquez	Jim	S	Forfeit	
Boyd	Mike	W		
Alejo	Alex	A	5-3	
Johnson	Scott	N		

138
Plummer	Kyle	A	7-6	(23-5)*
Harthorn	Brian	B	16-6*	
Gonzales	Mario	S	12-5	
Fernandez	Manuel	E		
King	Eric	F	Forfeit	
McFadden	Chris	W		

145
Sanchez	Mark	B	4-2	(27-4)*
Ruiz	Chris	E		
Goodwin	Chuck	A	Fall	
Gates	Ryan	H		
Brower		N	6-4	
Day		F		

154
Garcia	Isaac	B	(36-5)*	4:54
Ruiz	Dan	E		
Ramos	John	W	13-8	
Morgan	Steve	H		
Macedo	Frank	A	Forfeit	
Gonzales	Mark	S		

165
Stricker	Tad	S	26-11	(33-2)*
Wright	Chad	B		
Jones	Chris	E	Fall	
Matson	Tom	N		
Rasmussan		F	Forfeit	
Martinez		A		

175
Froehlich	Jassen	B	Fall
Rogers	Brandon	S	
Bergman	Jeff	E	Forfeit
Barton	Joe	W	
Gates	Aaron	H	10-0
Polston		N	

191
Simmons	David	B	8-6 OT	(31-4)*
Roberts	Mark	W		(24-3)*
Lizama	Tom	F	Fall	
Helston	Brenden	H		
Dermond	Mike	N	6-2	
Stewart	Tyson	S		

(Continued on next page)

SYL Tournament – Foothill (Continued)
February 10, 1990

245

Dearmore	Wes	H	3-2
Carrillo	Paul	S	
Hanson	Brad	F	Fall
Kinnick	Victor	N	
Jimenez	Robert	A	
No Sixth			

* Record

SYL Tournament

BHS	192
South	102
East	98
West	89.5
North	84.5
Arvin	76.5
Highland	65.5
Foothill	37.5

Dual League   Season

BHS	7-0	
East	5-2	
West	5-2	
North	4-3	5-3
Highland	3-4	
South	3-4	11-12
Arvin	1-6	
Foothill	0-7	

Tad Stricker
South Bakersfield High – 2nd State CIF Champion (1990)

SYL Tournament – Foothill
February 9, 1991

103
Radman	Aaron	W	2:40	(36-3)*
Fuqua	Brad	N		(26-12)*
Wright	Coby	B		
Roberts	Roy	S		
Arzate	Jeses	F		
Bell	Gavin	E		

112
Winn	Robert	B	6-4	(23-7-1)*
Miller	Justin	N		
Gonzales	Marcus	E	6-4	
Reyna	Sam	W		
Wilson	Don	S		
Covey	Josh	H		

119
Felix	Robert	E	7-5	(35-4)*
Jackson	Matt	N		(33-6)*
Botts	Anthony	B	15-0	
Gonzales	Abe	H		
No Fifth				
No Sixth				

125
Kolthoff	Cliff	B	7-6	(28-7)*
Cardona	Frank	N		
Skinner	Brian	W	11-8	
Holden	Stewart	S		
Zaragoza	Martin	E		
No Sixth				

130
Johnson	Scott	N	(28-8)*	3:57
Sherley	Jake	B		
Aguilar	Chris	E	7-4	
Azparren	Jeremy	W		
Griffis	Daryl	S		
Deck	Lee	F		

135
Herberle	Jeff	N	20-9	(36-1)*
McGuinn	Josh	B		
Martinez	Carlos	W	15-0	
Rock	Pat	F		
No Fifth				
No Sixth				

140
Gonzales	Mario	S	OT 14-7	(30-7)*
Oliver	James	B		(25-5)*
Warnock	Brian	N	Fall	3:35
Stewart	Bill	H		
No Fifth				
No Sixth				

145
Plummer	Kyle	B	TF Fall 3:35	(32-5)*
Russell	Bill	S		
Fernandez	Manuel	E		
Wilson	Charlie	W	Fall	2:59
Larroque	Mike	H		
Falk	Brian	N		

152
Spears	Travis	B	TF Fall	4:55
Armijo	Ted	E		(28-3-2)*
Gates	Ryan	H	10-2	
Brower	Phil	N		
Schaub	Wes	S		
Daugherty	Joe	F		

160
Jones	Chris	E	12-4	(30-8-2)*
Herron	Willie	H		
Thpene	Jake	N	Fall	2:58
Demos	Bob	B		
Rogers	Josh	S		
Jones	Jayson	W		

171
Wright	Chad	B	TF 2:57	(35-8)*
Arenas	Stan	H		
Gonzales	Mark	S		
Mooneyham	Jeff	N		
Martinez	Joe	E		
Clayton	Kevin	W		

189
Bergman	Jeff	E	7-6	(34-4)*
Helston	Brendon	H		(23-7)*
Scroggins	Jason	B	14-9	
Flanningan	Chris	W		
Azua	Isaac	S		
No Sixth				

(Continued on next page)

SYL Tournament – Foothill
February 9, 1991

275

Carrillo	Paul	S	(19-3)*	:49
Hanson	Brad	F		(31-5-1)*
Bloom	Corey	W	7-3	
Wolstenholm	Mike	H		
Moring	Rob	N		
Manning	Chad	B		

* Record

SYL Tournament

BHS	194.5
North	146
East	94
South	88
West	84.5
Highland	78.5
Foothill	18

Dual League

BHS	6-0
North	5-1
East	4-2
West	3-3
South	2-4
Highland	1-5
Foothill	0-6

Season

5-10

Roy Heath
South Bakersfield High – Three-time CIF Champion

SYL Tournament – East
February 15, 1992

103
Wright	Coby	B	(35-2)*	1:42
Fuqua	Brad	N	(36-5)*	
Radman	Aaron	W		2:15
Whitten	Stan	S		
Levario	Milo	E		
Moreno		H		

112
Winn	Robert	B	10-4	(32-9)*
Sherrill	Bobby	N		(30-8)*
Reyna	Sammy	W	12-6	
Roberts	Roy	S		
Gonzales	Anthony	H		
Gonzales	Marcus	E		

119
Sherley	Jake	B	9-8	(33-8)*
Miller	Justin	N		(32-9)*
Armijo	Jason	E	16-4	
Lock	Ranna	H		
Wilson	Don	S		
Newlen	Kyle	F		

125
Botts	Anthony	B	10-3	(24-7)*
Fox	Jason	N		(29-13)*
Garza	Anthony	S	8-2	
Machado	Johnny	W		
Esparza	Anthony	F		
Wolden	Brian	E		

130
Hobbs	Chad	N	12-1	(31-8)*
Lupercio	Carl	B		
Holden	Stuart	S	10-7	
Billingley	Alan	H		
Brar	Parminde	E		
Karr	Mike	F		

135
Heer	Ricky	N	(36-7)*	3:00
Collier	Sean	B		
Russell	Bill	S	Default	
Skinner	Brad	W		
Gonzales	Abe	H		
Johnson	Kurt	E		

140
Gonzales	Mario	S	13-9	
McGinn	Josh	B		
Warnock	Brian	N	6-2	
Azparren	Jeremy	W		
Bozeman	Ryan	E		
Horn	Austin	H		

145
Green	Romel	H	14-5	
Oliver	James	B		
Ramond	Randy	W	4:45	
Rassmussen	Chad	F		
Griffis	Daryl	S	15-7	
Le Rolland	Don	N		

152
Plummer	Kyle	B	(25-1)*	1:11
Schaub	Wes	S		
Barker	Shay	N	7-4	
Borjoquez	David	E		
Daughtery	Joe	H		
Dulan	Jason	F		

160
Pasquale	Kai	N		3:29
Gates	Ryan	H		
Garcia	Gabe	B	4-0	
Hopkins	Rick	S		
Wilson	Charley	W		
Evans	Brandon	F		

171
Herron	Willie	H	17-2	
Mooneyham	Jeff	N		
Azua	Isaac	S	5-2	
Clark	Brett	B		
Smith	Josh	W		
Garcia	Vic	F		

189
Helston	Brendon	H	4-1	
Demos	Bob	B		
Thoene	Jake	N		4:30
Azua	Adam	S		
Todd	John	E		

(Continued on next page)

SYL Tournament – East
February 15, 1992

HWT

Carrillo	Paul	S	8-0
Hyanson	Brad	F	
Godinez	Gabe	B	7-5
Karle	Jeremy	H	
Bolen	Justen	E	
No Sixth			

* Record

Dual League

North	6-0
BHS	5-1
Highland	4-2
South	3-3
West	2-4
East	1-5
Foothill	0-6

SYL Tournament

BHS	226
North	199.5
South	163.5
Highland	137.5
West	80.5
East	60
Foothill	46

1966 Bakersfield High CIF Champions
Front: Don Herrera (3rd CIF), Jack Serros
Back: Steve Varner, Sam Gollmyer and Albert Valdez

SYL Tournament – East
February 13, 1993

103
Adame	Anthony	F	8-6 OT	
Levario	Milo	E		
Schallberger	Phillip	B	7-0	
Vasquez	Nathan	W		
Zangrila	Marc	H	15-1	
Phaypaseuth	Than	A		

112
Brar	Prminder	E	10-5	
McCauley	Rob	B		
Reyna	Sammy	W	8-5	
Lock	Ronna	H		
Martinez	Ismael	F	5-4	
Harris	Justin	A		

119
Varner	Andy	B	8-6 OT	
Sherrill	Bobby	N		
Lopez	Juan	H	13-7	
Newloean	Kyle	F		
Parales	Josh	E		2:41
Hernandez	Anthony	W		

125
Miller	Justin	N	6-2	
Armijo	Jason	E		
Arzate	Jesse	F		4:15
Peet	Luke	B		
Rivera	Anthony	A		2:22
McNutt	Josh	S		

130
Lupergid	Carl	B	9-3	
Harvick	Kevin	N		
Champion	Joe	H	4-2	
Garcia	Juan	A		
Garcia	Nilo	E		3:08
Ransom	Mike	W		

135
Hobbs	Chad	N		3:51
Calderon	Angel	F		
Martinez	Mike	E	11-7	
Azparren	Jeremy	W		
Gonzales	Abe	H		2:02
Bedford	Wayne	B		

140
Fendrick	Jim	B	15-2	
Gaze	Luke	W		
Arrellano	Genaro	A	8-4	
Smith	Jesse	S		
Lawrence	Brandon	N		:59
Johnston	Kurt	E		

145
Graham	Bobby	A	10-6	
Amavisca	Eddie	B		
Rasmussen	Chad	F		4:11
Pasquini	Jeff	W		
Duncan	Craig	N		1:36
Griffis	Darryl	S		

152
Bojorquez	David	E	7-3	
Sanchez	Noni	A		
Holden	Stewart	S		:51
Christie	Joel	W		
Macias	Phil	B	Forfeit	
Evans	Brandon	F		

160
Garcia	Gabe	B	7-0	
Wilson	Charlie	W		
Hight	Dustin	N	13-3	
Johnson	Brandon	E		
Dougherty	Joe	H	Forfeit	

171
Herron	Willie	H	(34-0)*	3:00
Sheets	Ryan	N	(35-11)*	
Smith	Josh	W		2:35
Ashley	Fredrick	B		
White	Keith	F	Forfeit	

189
Clark	Brett	B		2:55
Brakeman	Chris	H		
Todd	John	E		2:25
Bazadua	Leo	A		
Adams	Kirk	F	8-5	
Abernathy	Jason	W		

(Continued on next page)

SYL Tournament – East
February 13, 1993

HWT

Karle	Jeremy	H	8-1	(31-2)*
Moring	Robert	N		
Maese	Ray	B	2-1	
Novella	Brian	E		
Cox	Travis	F	Forfeit	

* Record

Dual League

BHS 7-0

SYL Tournament

BHS	191
East	138
North	128.5
Highland	118
West	102.5
Foothill	96
Arvin	79.5
South	25

Rocky Rasley – 2nd CIF South Bakersfield (1965)
Rasley also played in the NFL for seven seasons (1969-1976) with the Detroit Lions,
New Orleans Saints, Kansas City Chiefs and San Francisco 49ers

SYL Tournament – East
February 12, 1994

103
Adame	Anthony	F	13-3	
Vasquez	Nathan	W		
Sherley	Ben	B	4-1	
Resseguie	Chris	E		
Wilson	Chris	N	Forfeit	
Lara	Frank	S		

112
McCauley	Rob	B		1:53
Reyes	Cirilo	E		
Martinez	Chris	F		4:35
Resales	Roy	A		
Edwards	Set	N		:40
Armstrong	Ken	H		

119
Elisondo	Steve	W	12-3	
Palamino	Chris	B		
Garcia	Nilo	E		2:55
Aguirre	Tommy	N		
Campos	Carl	H		:56
Uguez	Jacob	A		

125
Varner	Andy	B	14-3	
Perales	Josh	E		
Gonzales	Anthony	H	9-5	
Manes	Jeremy	W		
Marroquin	Jeremy	A	7-2	
Hogeland	Kalob	H		

130
Miller	Kelly	B	4-3	(31-8)*
Armijo	Jason	E		
Lopez	Juan	H	16-0	
Mazza	Mark	N		
McNutt	Josh	S	10-2	
Harris	Justin	A		

135
Calderon	Angel	F	13-5
Collier	Sean	B	
Plott	Steve	S	17-6
Gonzales	Abe	H	
Peterson	Isaac	A	

140
Queenan	Sean	S	18-6	
Harvick	Kevin	N		
Bedford	Wayne	B	3-1	
Rosales	Angel	A		
Champion	Joe	H	Default	
Pasquini	Jeff	W		

145
Bonner	Mitch	B	7-2
Bozeman	Ryan	E	
Barker	Howard	W	5-1
Guerra	Pete	H	
Aleman	Jose	S	5-1
Jackson	Cecil	N	

152
Bridges	Jeremy	B		2:32
Rasmussen	Chad	F		
Barker	Todd	N		1:35
Gaze	Luke	W		
Hill	Matt	S	8-0	
Amaya	Joel	A		

160
Bojorquez	David	E	7-3
Hight	Dusty	N	
Jimenez	Heliodoro	S	5-3
Hubbard	Damon	H	
Diniz	Chris	A	6-4
DuQuett	John	W	

171
Sheets	Ryan	N		1:54
Gonzalez	Leo	H		
Ochoa	Troy	S		3:31
Tingle	Jeremy	W		
Graffe	Michael	A	Default	
Johnson	Chris	E		

189
Clark	Brett	B		3:39
Daniels	Aaron	H		
East	Rocky	E	12-3	
Castro	Cesar	A		
Abney	Jacob	S	Default	
Marquez	Rudy	E		

(Continued on next page)

SYL Tournament – East
February 12, 1994

HWT

Karle	Jeremy	H	1:36
Galvan	Favian	S	
Rivera	Jose	F	3-1
Maese	Ray	B	
Ibarra	Jose	A	6-2
Lindsey	Bryan	N	

* Record

Dual League

BHS	7-0
East	6-1
North	3-2-1
Highland	3-3-1
South	2-5
West	2-4-1
Foothill	1-5-1
Arvin	1-6

SYL Tournament

BHS	196
Highland	127
North	111
East	109.5
South	106
Foothill	89
West	81
Arvin	66.5

Earl Corley
South Bakersfield High
1959 CIF Champion; 1960 2nd CIF (golf)

South East Yosemite League
1995-2006

Southeast Yosemite League

Date	Location	Dual Champion	Tournament Champion	Overall Champion	Coach
2/4/95	Highland	Bakersfield 4-0	Bakersfield	Bakersfield	David East
2/3/96	Highland	Bakersfield 4-0	Bakersfield	Bakersfield	David East
2/8/97	East	Bakersfield 4-0	Foothill	Foothill/Bakersfield	Alan Paradise
					David East
2/13/98	East	Bakersfield 4-0	Foothill	Foothill/Bakersfield	Alan Paradise
					David East
2/13/99	East	Bakersfield 4-0	Bakersfield	Bakersfield	David East
2/12/2000	East	East 4-0	Bakersfield	East/Bakersfield	Joe Triggs
					David East
2/10/2001	East	Bakersfield 4-0	Bakersfield	Bakersfield	David East
2/9/2002	East	Bakersfield 4-0	Bakersfield	Bakersfield	David East
2/15/2003	East	Bakersfield 5-0	Bakersfield	Bakersfield	Andy Varner
2/14/2004	East	Bakersfield 5-0	Bakersfield	Bakersfield	Andy Varner
2/12/2005	East	Bakersfield 4-0	Bakersfield	Bakersfield	Andy Varner
2/11/2006	East	Foothill 4-0	Bakersfield	Bakersfield	Andy Varner

Most Outstanding Wrestlers Lower/Upper Weights

Awards sponsored by The Coyote Club

Year	Wrestler	School
1995	Juan Lopez	Highland
	Fred Ashley	Bakersfield
1996	Anthony Adame	Foothill
	Jose Galarza	East
1997	Chris Ressequie	East
	Ryan McWilliams	Foothill
1998	Chris Felix	East
	Kirk Moore	Foothill
1999	Andrew Spradlin	Bakersfield
	Sam Burk	Ridgeview
2000	Tony Franco	Foothill
	Britt Mooney	East
2001	Anthony Marquez	Foothill
	Carlos Gonzalez	East
2002	Bakersfield High Team	
2003	Mike Marquez	East
	Jake Varner	Bakersfield
2004	Nathan Morgan	Bakersfield
	Kev Koy	Highland
2005	Addison Hay	Foothill
	Jake Varner	Bakersfield
2006	David Chaidez	Foothill
	Matt Peralta	Foothill

SEYL – Highland
February 4, 1995

103
Odom	Dustin	F	17-4
Confield	Greg	B	
Diaz	Abe	A	Default

112
Felix	Chris	H	
Elisondo	Steve	B	3:52
Moore	Kirk	F	
Estrada		A	7-6
Moroyoqui	Raymond	H	
Morqui			
None			

119
Vasquez	Larry	B	9-1
Reyes	Cirilo	E	
Martinez		F	1:20
Rosales	Nick	A	
Gonzales	Paul	H	

125
Vasquez	Nathan	B	18-6
Campos	Carl	H	
Villagomez	Allan	E	8-6
Hogeland	Kaleb	F	
Rosales		A	

130
Lopez	Juan	H	(40-2, 20 Falls)* 1:54
Rosales	Angel	A	
Garcia	Nilo	E	Default
Blaire	Luke	B	
Diniz	Adrian	F	

135
Miller	Kelly	B	18-6
Manes	Jeremy	F	
Guerra	Pete	H	5-2
Marroquin	Jeremy	A	
Reyes	Harvey	E	

140
Varner	Andy	B	T.F. 18-3 4:57
Padgett	Tim	H	
Harris		A	19-7
Crosthwaite	Victor	H	
None			

145
Williams	Ryan	H	10-6
Martinez	Mike	E	
Bedford	Wayne	B	2-1
Coffia	Martin	F	
Castro		A	

152
Bridges	Jeremy	B	T.F 22-7 4:06
Smith	Junior	E	
Urias	Albert	F	Default
Goodbye	Una		
None			

160
Keller	Tony	B	T.F. 22-7 4:41
Galarza	Jose	E	
Diniz	Chris	A	T.F. 4:45
Gospich	Nick	F	
None			

171
Ashley	Fred	B	:37
Bangloy	Anthony	E	
Shankey	Brandon	F	4:28
Gutierrez		A	

191
Maese	Ray	B	12-7
Hillis	Brandon	F	
Hanash		E 2	1-9
Duncan	Erik	H	
Overturf		A	

HWT
Clark	Brett	B	:48
Daugherty	Tim	F	
Ibarra	Jose	E	4-2
Schneider	C	A	
Stychovich	Van	H	

Dual League		Season	SEYL Tournament	
BHS	4-0	15-1	BHS	222
East	3-1	11-4	Foothill	128
Foothill	2-2	13-4	East	104.5
Highland	1-3	19-8	Highland	82
Arvin	0-4	10-12	Arvin	66.5

SEYL – Highland
February 2, 1996

103
Felix	Chris	H	7-4
Madradiaga	Oscar	A	
Resseguie	Chris	E	
Scott	Bennett	B	
Odom	Max	F	

112
Canfield	Greg	B	5-4
Diaz	Abraham	A	
Martinez	Mike	F	
Chavez	David	E	
Hootman	Cory	H	

119
Elisondo	Steve	B	7-5	
Moore	Kirk	F		39-5
Rosales	Nick	A		
Lock	Voeum	H		

125
Adame	Anthony	F	5-3
Vasquez	Nathan	B	
Villagomez	Allan	E	
Rosales	Angel	A	
Moreyoqui	Raymond	H	

130
Reyes	Cirilo	E	5:30
Sherley	Ben	B	
Hogeland	Kaler	F	
Allen	Mike	H	

135
Muralla	Ernesto	B	7-6
Diniz	Adrian	F	
Martinez	Eddie	H	
Garcia	Alex	E	
Piniential	E	A	

140
Molano	Fred	B	14-7
Reyes	Harvey	E	
Manes	Jeremy	F	
Ramirez	Chris	H	

145
Miller	Kelly	B	12-6
Padgett	Tim	F	
Sanchez	John	E	
Gonzales	Paul	H	

152
Rosales	A	A	1:02
Schallberger	Phillip	B	
Ulloa	Daniel	H	
Gospich	Nick	F	
Anaya	J	E	

160
Galarza	Jose	E	7-6
Dunn	J	B	
Lawson	Shannon	H	

171
Lomeli	David	B	11-3
Smith	Junior	E	
Urias	Albert	F	
Stevens	Greg	H	
Guttierrez	M	A	

189
Brogdon	Charlie	A	1:55
Scott	David	E	
Caudel	Brandon	B	
Duncan	Erik	H	

215
Maese	Ray	B	17-10
Schnelder	C	A	
Finn	Shannon	E	
Rivera	Adam	F	

HWT
Daugherty	Tim	F	17-6
Gonzalez	Tony	H	
Tapia	David	B	
Rivas	A	E	

Dual League / Season / SEYL Tournament

Dual League		Season	SEYL Tournament	
BHS	4-0	14-1	Bakersfield	199
East	2-2	11-3	East	140
Foothill	3-1	16-1	Foothill	125
Arvin	1-3	6-5	Arvin	97
Highland	0-4	0-6	Highland	84

SEYL - East
February 8, 1997

103
Felix	Chris	E	11-6
Maradiaga	Oscar	A	
Marquez	Phillip	F	5-2
Cole	Adam	B	

112
Ressequie	Chris	E	6-3
Diaz	Abraham	A	
Martinez	Michael	F	4-0
Dickerson	John	B	

119
Odom	Max	F	Fall
Bustamante	J.J.	A	
Chavez	David	E	Fall
Bell	Steven	B	

125
Scott	Bennett	B	5-1
Rosales	Nick	A	
Moroyoqui	Ray	H	9-6
Mooney	Britt	E	

130
Arellano	Jose	A	7-2
Hillis	Dustin	F	
Schallberger	Patrick	B	5-4
Perez	Phillip	E	

135
Meloche	Ryan	F	Fall
Villagomez	Alan	E	
Spradlin	Matt	B	4-1
Rosales	N	A	

140
Moore	Kirk	F	16
Muralla	Ernesto	B	2
Martinez	Ernesto	E	
Fallkwen	Jimmy	H	

145
Miller	Kelly	B	5-3
Reyes	Cirilo	E	
Guillen	Daniel	F	
Gonzalez	Paul	H	

152
Diniz	Adrian	F	7-3
Rosales	Angel	A	
Reyes	Harvey	E	7-3
Garcia	Juan	B	

160
McWilliams	Ryan	F	Fall
Caudel	Brandon	B	
Pimental	John	A	4-3
Sanchez	John	E	

171
Smith	Junior	E	10-1
Dunn	John	B	
Bravo	Mario	F	Forfeit

189
Brogdan	Charlie	A	7-1
Tobin	Eric	B	
Hernandez	Mario	H	Forfeit

215
Lomeil	David	B	Fall
Karle	Cory	H	
Dorado	Julien	F	Forfiet

275
Torres	Greg	F	3-2
Ibarra	Jose	E	
Gonzales	Tony	H	1-0
Tapia	David	B	

Dual League
BHS	4-0
Foothill	3-1
East	2-2
Arvin	1-3
Highland	0-4

Season
14-0

SEYL Tournament
Foothill	156.5
BHS	145
East	136
Arvin	111
Highland	45

SEYL – East
February 13, 1998

103
Cole	Adam	B
Onsurez	Andrew	E
Horl	Justin	F
Sanchez	Ivan	A

112
Felix	Chris	E
Dickerson	John	B
Bustamante	Johnny	A
Marquez	Phillip	F

119
Gutierrez	Miguel	F
Chicco	Caleb	B
Montoya	Miguel	H
Patino	Hector	E

125
Ashley	Benny	B
Rosales	Nick	A
Perez	Phillip	E
Hernandez	Steve	F

130
Odom	Max	F
Schallberger	Patrick	B
Arellano	Jose	A

135
Garcia	Juan	B
Meloche	Ryan	F
Mooney	Britt	E
Lock	Vouen	H

140
Villagomez	Alan	E
Wiebe	Justin	F
Valdez	Genero	B
Gonazales	Tommy	H

145
Diniz	Adrian	A	14-3
Spradlin	Matt	B	
Watson	Rick	H	
Frank	Zack	E	

152
Moore	Kirk	F
Bonilla	Ryan	B
Vasquez	Salvador	A
Pinagua	Arturo	H

160
Reyes	Harvey	E
Bravo	Mario	F
Navejos	John	B
Eaton	Eddie	H

171
Shankle	Brandon	F
Cantu	Andy	A
Maize	Paul	B
Pintoja	Jose	E

189
McDermott	Jermaine	B
Pantoja	Emmanuel	A
Monarrez	Omar	F
Palinksy	Willie	H

215
Graham	Aaron	B
Karle	Cory	H
Gutierrez	Cosmo	E
Jacobson	Nathan	F

275
Torres	Greg	F
Reyes	Alfredo	H
Tobin	Eric	B
Cabrera	George	E

Dual League | Season
	Dual League	Season
BHS	4-0	13-1
Foothill	3-1	5-2
East		
Highland		
Ridgeview	1-3	5-9

SEYL Tournament
Foothill	163.5
BHS	160.5
East	95
Arvin	67
Highland	54

SEYL - East
February 13, 1999

103
Vasquez	Darrell	B	5-1	
Onsurez	Andrew	E		
Franco	Tony	F		2:38
Ybarra	Richard	R		
Carrillo	George	H		

112
Spradlin	Andrew	B	8-6	
Marquez	Phillip	F		
Onsurez	Anthony	E		1:35
Mullen	Steve	H		

119
East	Drew	B	15-5	
Martinez	Josh	E		
Marquez	Anthony	F		:40
Garcia	Vincente	R		
Gonzales	Isaiah	H		

125
Chicca	Caleb	B	16-12	
Frank	Matt	E		
Diaz	Adrian	F		3:16
Ramirez	William	R		
Mollere	Christian	H		

130
Gutierrez	Miguel	F	Fall	3:07
Sherley	Josh	B		
Romero	David	R		
Marsh	Brian	H		

135
Hernandez	Joe	B	8-7	
Harl	Justin	F		
Beltran	Frank	E	Def.	
Faulkner	Salem	H		
Gomez	Juan	R		

140
Schallberger	Patrick	B	Fall	5:47
Hernandez	Steve	F		
Hernandez	S	E	Def.	
Salas	James	R		

145
Odom	Max	F	Fall	4:21
Valdez	Genard	B		
Jung	Brad	R		4:39
Anaya	Jason	E		
Tabangcora	Mark	H		

152
Mooney	Britt	E	6-4	
Guevara	Todd	F		
Hernandez	Ramero	B		:16
Duncan	Mathew	R		

160
Bravo	Mario	F	Fall	:34
McCauley	Nathan	B		
Rojas	Manuel	E		3:59
Heinz	Kevin	R		
Stevenson	Bobby	H		

171
Burk	Sam	R	Fall	1:05
Campbell	Cory	F		
Torrez	R	B		4:53
Kooren	David	E		

189
Tobin	Anthony	B	11-0	
Gonzales	Carlos	E		
Olgin	J.R.	F	1-0	
Ornelas	Silo	R		

215
Graham	Aaron	B	Fall	1:11
Jacobson	Nathan	F		
Carrasco	Richard	H	10-6	
Hoxsie	Jason	E		
Alyea	Joshua	R		

HWT
Robin	Eric	B	19-9	
Reyes	Alfredo	H		
Bunting	Dave	E		4:36
Dorado	Julien	F		

Dual League		Season	SEYL Tournament	
BHS	4-0	5-2	BHS	262.5
Highland		2-8	Foothill	216
Foothill		3-1	East	157.5
			Ridgeview	95
			Highland	51

SEYL – East
February 12, 2000

103
Onsurez	Angel	E	
Corona	Joseph	F	
Carrillo	Francesco	H	Default
Bullman	Eric	B	
None			

112
Onsurez	Andrew	E	Default
Vasquez	Darrell	B	
Hernandez	Jamie	H	
Cortez	Ryan	F	
Nichols	Travis	R	

119
Franco	Tony	F	
Onsurez	Anthony	E	
Carrillo	Gabe	H	
Miglas	Aaron	R	
None			

125
Chicca	Caleb	B	
Martinez	Josh	E	
Diaz	Marcos	F	
Gonzalez	Isaiah	H	
None			

130
East	Drew	B	
Frank	Matt	E	
Marquez	Anthony	F	16-6
Martinez	Frank	H	
None			

135
Gutierrez	Miguel	F	
Spradlin	Andrew	B	
Marquez	Tommy	E	2:35
Granillo	David	H	
Ray	Casey	R	

140
Hernandez	Steve	F	
Sherley	Josh	B	
Austin	Mark	E	15-0
Blackhurst	Zach	H	
Duncan	Tom	R	

145
Harl	Justin	F	
Hernandez	Joe	B	
Beltran	Frank	E	1-0
Suender	Matt	H	
Davis	Adam	R	

152
Kalivas	Karras	B	
Campbell	Corey	F	
Marsh	Brian	H	6-5
Wilen	Tyler	R	
Cacopardo	Nick	E	

160
Hernandez	Ramiro	B	
Rojas	Manuel	E	
Guevarra	Todd	F	1:21
Noriega	Aaron	H	
None			

171
Mooney	Britt	E	
Chambers	Matt	B	
Medina	Carlos	F	2:51
Eaton	Eddie	H	
Coleman	Eric	R	

189
Tobin	Anthony	B	
Gonzalez	Carlos	E	
Ortega	Jesus	H	2:09
Ornelas	Silo	R	
Campbell	Brandon	F	

215
Jacobson	Nathan	F	
Validaros	Juaquin	B	
Cabrasco	Richard	H	8-2
Hoxsie	Jason	E	
Barron	Craig	R	

275
Reyes	Alfredo	H	Injury Forfeit
Valdovinos	Lorenzo	B	
Cabrera	Luis	E	
Davis	Jason	R	
None			

(Continued on next page)

SEYL – East
February 12, 2000

Dual League   **Season**
East   4-0   13-0
BHS   3-1   5-2
Foothill   2-2   5-2
Highland   1-3   4-6
Ridgeview   0-4

SEYL Tournament
BHS   245.5
East   232
Foothill   212
Highland   198
Ridgeview   62

North Bakersfield High
Bill Kinnett (left) – 3rd in the CIF (1962), 1st in 1963
Pat Campbell – 4th in the CIF (1963)

SEYL – East
February 10, 2001

103
Morgan	Nathan	B	T.F. 19-4 6:00
Monsabias	Donny	H	
Eby	Eleanor	F	Forfeit

112
Franco	Tony	B	6-5
Morales	Carlos	E	
Cortez	Ryan	F	7-4
Hernandez	Jaime	H	

119
Vasquez	Darrell	B	11-3
Marquez	Mike	E	
Bustamante	Gabe	F	17-10
Carrillo	Francesco	H	

125
Herrera	Alex	B	8-7
Onsurez	Anthony	E	
Diaz	Marcos	F	1:30
Cox	Calvin	R	

130
Marquez	Anthony	F	11-4
Weimer	D.J.	B	
Marquez	Mark	E	13-4
Mullen	Steve	H	

135
Spradlin	Andrew	B	14-3
Frank	Matt	E	
Points	Jason	F	15-9
Blackhurst	Zack	H	

140
East	Drew	B	:35
Viahos	Nick	H	
Tigert	T.J.	F	16-3
Marquez	Ed	E	

145
Gutierrez	Miguel	F	3:37
Hernandez	Joe	B	
Tabangcora	Mark	H	:17
Galvan	Adan	R	

152
Sherley	Josh	B	4-0
Harl	Justin	F	
Salas	James	R	4-3
Suender	Matt	H	

160
Hernandez	Ramiro	B	13-0
Marsh	Brian	H	
Sanchez	Ruben	F	16-5
Armer	Brandon	E	

171
Mooney	Britt	E	1:55
Smart	Matt	B	
Noriega	Aaron	H	:55
Gabria	Delroy	R	

189
Gonzalez	Carlos	E	2:44
Schellenbe	Travis	R	
Peralta	Miguel	F	3:23
Battistoni	Alex	B	

215
Valladares	Joaquin	B	11-1
Barron	Craig	R	
Loera	Arnold	H	6-2
Campbell	Brandon	F	

HWT
Cornwell	Adam	B	1:46
Ruiz	Louis	F	
Cabbera	Luis	E	

Dual League
		Season	
BHS	4-0	12-0	
Foothill			
East			
Highland	3-1	10-2	
Ridgeview			

SEYL Tournament
BHS	277
Foothill	184.5
East	169
Highland	141
Ridgeview	96

SEYL – East
February 9, 2002

103
Espinoza	Robert	B	:51
Beckman	Frank	F	
Corn	Kevin	E	1:29
Martinez	Oscar	H	
Owen	Scott	R	

112
Morgan	Nathan	B	25-10
Monsibais	Donny	H	
Enriquez	Fernando	R	Default

119
Franco	Tony	B	3:11
Eades	Jerrod	R	
Hernandez	Jaime	H	9-2
Montijo	Rickey	E	

125
Vasquez	Darrell	B	11-3
Bustamante	Gabriel	F	
Marquez	Mike	E	Default

130
Herrera	Alex	B	11-4
Cox	Calvin	R	
Rozell	Colby	E	6-5
Valverde	Michael	F	
Gonzales	Mark	H	

135
Hernandez	Joe	B	4:40
Marquez	Mark	E	
Carillo	Francesco	H	13-7
Ray	Casey	R	
Toone	Tony	F	

140
Varner	Jake	B	1:22
Tigert	T.J.	F	
Ortega	Miguel	H	2:43
Herrera	Juan	R	
Torres	Gerardo	E	

145
Spradlin	Andrew	B	13-4
Diaz	Marcos	F	
Marquez	Ricky	E	5-4
Mullen	Steve	H	

152
East	Drew	B	4:40
Wilen	Tyler	R	
Schaffer	Mark	F	
Viahos	Nick	H	
Rodriguez	Steven	E	

160
Sherley	Josh	B	3:59
Gabriel	Delroy	R	
Suender	Matt	H	3-2
Moronnote	Jason	F	
Chavez	Isaac	E	

171
Hernandez	Ramiro	B	1:56
Armer	Brandon	E	
Noriega	Aaron	H	25-14
Martinez	Nathan	F	

189
Marquez	Josh	B	1:23
Mord	Tony	R	
Nunez	Jose	E	Default

215
Cornwell	Adam	B	4:47
Loera	Arnold	H	
Campbell	Brandon	F	2:19
Elliott	Mark	E	
Pierson	Jacob	R	

HWT
Valdivinos	Lorenzo	B	9-4
Cabrera	Luis	E	
Nelson	Doug	F	1:49
Tucker	Chad	R	

Dual League
	Dual League	Season
BHS	4-0	5-0
East		
Foothill	0-4	1-6-1
Ridgeview	1-3	3-4
Highland		

SEYL Tournament
BHS	311.5
East	137
Foothill	136.5
Ridgeview	132
Highland	129.5

SEYL – East
February 15, 2003

103
Land	Brett	B	Fall
Gorman	Jerry	R	
Martinez	Oscar	H	

112
Nacita	Elijah	B	4-2
Hernandez	Antonio	L	
Miranda	Joe	R	

119
Morales	Carlos	E	6-2
Neuman	Grant	B	
Boothe	Keenan	L	
Ornelas	Ricky	R	
Rivas	Kevin	F	

125
Morgan	Nathan	B	Tech Fall
Williams	Josh	L	
Monsibais	Tim	H	
Brown	Derek	E	

130
Marquez	Mike	E	8-6 OT
Bustamante	Gabriel	F	
Carreon	Chris	L	
Flores	Benny	B	
Limonies	Felix	H	

135
Herrera	Alex	B	Tech Fall
Mendoza	Santos	E	
Cemo	A.J.	L	
Valverde	Mike	F	
Gonzalez	Mark	H	

140
Marquez	Mark	E	Major 9-1
Hernandez	Jeremy	B	
Christensen	Ricky	L	
Torrez	Jake	H	
Ramirez	Phillip	F	

145
Points	Jason	L	Major 13-4
Kincaid	Mario	B	
Marquez	Ricky	E	
Noriega	Aaron	H	
Gaitan	Chris	R	
Roach	Ryan	F	

152
Varner	Jake	B	Tech Fall
Alderetti	Josh	H	
Aguilera	Steven	L	
Mireles	Vince	F	

160
Moronnolte	Jason	F	Major 10-2
Koy	Kev	H	
Freeborn	Mike	L	
Mahill	Mark	B	
Simpson	Josh	R	

171
Solis	Junior	L	Major 18-6
Czechowski	Nick	H	
Martinez	Nate	F	
Grimes	Ryan	R	

189
Nunez	Jose	E	5-1
Moore	Jamin	L	
Renteria	Anthony	B	
Hermosillo	Phillip	R	

215
Marquez	Josh	B	Fall
Ruiz	Louie	F	
Elliott	Mark	E	
Franco	Joseph	H	
Mord	Tony	R	
Patrick	C.J.	L	

275
Davis	Roy	F	Fall
Tucker	Chad	R	
Mahan	Robert	L	
McCorvey	James	B	
Shawn	Richie	E	

Dual League		Season	SEYL Tournament	
BHS	5-0	5-1	BHS	244
Liberty			Liberty	192
East			East	165
Foothill	3-2	5-2	Foothill	136.5
Highland	1-4	3-4	Highland	130
Ridgeview	1-4	1-6	Ridgeview	113

SEYL - East
February 14, 2004

103
Cisneros	Joe	B	Fall	:46
Chaidez	David	F		
Arreola	Edgar	H	12-1	
Magno	Jon	R		

112
Land	Brett	B	Fall	1:05
Hay	Addison	F		
Christensen	Colton	L	6-3	
Gorman	Jerry	R		
Ramirez	Robert	E		

119
Nacita	Elijah	B	Fall	1:16
Martinez	O.J.	F		
Christopher	Kelton	H	18-3	
Rodriguez	EZ	E		

125
Neumann	Grant	B	20-5 T.F. (35-5)*	
Chaidez	Bernard	F		
McCoy	Patrick	L	5-3	
Orneles	Ricky	R		

130
Morgan	Nathan	B	28-11 Tech Fall	
West	Matthew	L		
Peralta	Matt	F	Forfeit	

135
Webber	Tony	B	18-3 Tech Fall	
Johnson	Jimmie	R		
Rivas	Thomas	F	Forfeit	

140
Christensen	Ricky	L	9-6	(32-9)*
Box	Anthony	B		
Copeland	Josh	R	10-3	
Ramirez	Edward	F		

145
Herrera	Alex	B	Fall	:35
Points	Andrew	L		
Gaitan	Chris	R	8-6	
Gopnzalez	Mark	H		

152
Koy	Kev	H	Fall	1:26
Aguilera	Steven	L		
Cavanaugh	Mike	B	5-2	
Marquez	Ricky	E		
Ramirez	Phillip	F		
Gutierrez	Roy	R		

160
Marsh	David	H	Fall	5:57
Evans	Donny	F		
Sheets	Shane	L	9-6	
Wingate	Ryan	B		

171
Varner	Jake	B	Fall	:43
Degeare	Justin	L		
Crow	Mitchell	F	Fall	1:53
Ortega	Miguel	H		

189
Renteria	Anthony	B	Fall	3:27
Watkins	Blake	L		
Czechowski	Nick	H	4-2	
Martinez	Nate	F		
Duke	Nick	R		

215
Marquez	Josh	B	Fall	3:43
Stramler	Andrew	L		
Pierson	Jacob	R	Forfeit	

275
Tucker	Chad	R	5-0	
White	Kalen	B		
Goldberg	Trevor	L		
Arredondo	Dario	F		

Dual League		Season	SEYL Tournament	
BHS	5-0		BHS	303
Liberty	3-2	5-2	Liberty	197
Foothill	4-1	7-1	Foothill	180
Ridgeview	2-3	3-4	Ridgeview	144
Highland	1-5	1-7	Highland	135.5
East			East	61

* Record

SEYL – East
February 12, 2005

103
Chaidez	David	F	19-7
Arrelo	Edgar	H	
Kincaid	Dion	B	5-1
Zielsdorf	Jimmy	L	

112
Hay	Addison	F	6-4 OT
Lomas	Frank	B	
Demison	Nektoe	E	
Tarkington	Richard	H	

119
Martinez	Christian	B	16-4
Chaidez	Bernard	F	
Rios	Robert	L	Fall 1:33
Florez	Miguel	E	

125
Cisneros	Joe	B	20-1 Tech Fall
Christensen	Colton	L	
Miller	Justin	E	16-0 Tech Fall
Litton	Andrew	F	

130
Nacita	Elijah	B	Fall 3:44
Martinez	O.J.	F	
Gordillo	Derrik	E	9-2
Franco	Steve	H	

135
Webber	Tonny	B	13-0 (38-5 Season)
Sanchez	David	F	
Gonzales	Freddy	E	15-11
Martin	Jerry	H	

140
Land	Brett	B	15-0 T-F
Roers	Kail	L	
Lopez	Martin	E	5-2
Sanchez	Daniel	F	

145
Box	Anthony	B	13-5
Peralta	Matt	F	
Christian	Ricky	L	

152
Points	Andrew	L	Fall 1:58
Rodriguez	Zack	B	
Rivas	Thomas	F	8-0
Martinez	Miguel	H	

160
Williams	Josh	B	Fall 1:27
Evans	Donny	F	
Marsh	David	H	11-7
Swan	Zack	L	

171
Cavanaugh	Mike	B	4-0
Marquez	Ricky	E	
Degeare	Justin	L	10-2
Maese	David	F	

189
Varner	Jake	B	33-0 Fall 3:38
Czechowski	Nick	H	
Watkins	Blake	L	Fall :17
De La Rosa	Eric	F	

215
Travis	David	F	10-0
Goldberg	Trevor	L	
Holt	Shaun	B	11-3
Gomez	Brady	E	

275
White	Kalen	B	Forfeit
Arredondo	Dario	F	
Anders	Tamir	L	Fall :39
Burnett	Nick	H	

Dual League		Season	SEYL Tournament	
BHS	4-0	4-0	BHS	287
Foothill	3-1	11-2	Foothill	223
Liberty	2-2	7-4	Liberty	161.5
East			East	125.5
Highland	1-3	2-4	Highland	115

SEYL – East
February 11, 2006

103
Chaidez	David	F	Dec.
Gonzalez	Pete	E	
Ortiz	Nick	L	

112
Lomas	Frank	B	Dec.
Demesion	Nemeto	E	
Mioni	Keith	L	Fall
Hawkins	Angel	F	

119
Sanchez	Javier	B	Dec.
Kapler	Greg	L	
Tarkington	Richard	H	Dec.
Spear	Kyle	F	
Collier	Marc	E	

125
Booth	Derek	L	Dec.
Cruz	Jonah	B	
Gonzalez	Fred	E	Fall
Ramirez	Ritchie	H	
Christian	Jeff	F	

130
Rasmussen	Travis	B	Dec.
Socia	Mike	F	
Ruis	Robert	L	

135
Nacita	Elijah	B	Fall
Christensen	Colton	L	
Miller	Justin	E	MD
Franco	Steve	H	
Litton	Andrew	F	

140
Box	Anthony	B	Fall
Sanchez	David	F	
Baker	Mitch	L	Dec.
Gordillo	Derek	E	

145
Webber	Tony	B	TF
Lopez	Martin	E	
Hutchens	Colby	L	Fall
Mejia	Nefi	F	

Aguirre	Joseph	H	

152
Peralta	Matt	F	Dec.
Rodriguez	Jamie	B	
Rogers	Kail	L	Tech Fall
Torres	Victor	H	

160
Arriaga	Ruben	B	MD
Sheets	Shane	L	
Loera	Bernardo	H	Fall
Sandoval	Marcos	F	

171
De La Rosa	Eric	F	Dec.
Degeare	Justin	L	
Dollar	Greg	B	

189
Travis	David	F	Fall
Bishop	Jacob	L	
Daniel	Ziggy	B	

215
Goldberg	Trevor	L	Tech. Fall
Padilla	Anthony	B	
Cummings	Eddie	E	Fall
Burnett	Nick	H	
Evans	Donny	F	

275
Quiroz	Ivan	F	Fall
Alvarez	Lamar	B	

Dual League   **Season**

	Dual League	Season
Foothill	4-0	7-0
BHS	3-1	3-2
Liberty	2-2	3-2
East		
Highland	0-5	1-9

SEYL Tournament

BHS	266
Liberty	217
Foothill	198
East	152.5
Highland	102

South West Yosemite League
1995-2006

Southwest Yosemite League

Date	Location	Dual Champion	Tournament Champion	Overall Champion	Coach
2/4/95	Stockdale	Stockdale 4-0	Stockdale	Stockdale	Craig Schoene
2/3/96	Stockdale	South 4-0	South	South	Brian Henderson
2/8/97	Centennial	South 4-0	Centennial	South	Brian Henderson
				Centennial	Paul Olejnik
2/13/98	Centennial	Centennial 4-0	Centennial	Centennial	Paul Olejnik
2/13/99	Centennial	Centennial 4-0	Centennial	Centennial	Paul Olejnik
2/12/2000	Centennial	Centennial 4-0	Centennial	Centennial	Paul Olejnik
2/10/2001	Centennial	Centennial	Centennial	Centennial	Paul Olejnik
2/9/2002	Centennial	Centennial 4-0	Centennial	Centennial	Paul Olejnik
2/15/2003	Centennial	Centennial 3-1	Stockdale	Centennial	Paul Olejnik
		South 3-1			
2/14/2004	Centennial	Centennial 3-1			
		South 3-1			
		Stockdale 3-1	Stockdale	Stockdale	Paul Garcia
2/12/2005	Centennial	South 4-1			
		Centennial 4-1	Centennial	Centennial	Mike Hicks
2/11/2006	Centennial	South 5-0	Centennial	South	Brian Henderson
				Centennial	Mike Hicks

Most Outstanding Wrestlers Lower/Upper Weights
Awards sponsored by The Coyote Club

Year	Wrestler	School
1995	Tom Aguirre	North
	Rocky East	North
1996	Frank Lara	South
	Peter Ghitty	South
1997	Brian Leonard	South
	Juan Jimenez	South
1998	Joel Goings	West
	Josh Naus	Centennial
1999	Sean Sheets	Centennial
	Marcos Rivera	South
2000		
2001	Jason Matthews	Stockdale
	Colin Shields	South
2002	Derrick Hunter	North
	Jeff Baker	Centennial
2002	Derrick Hunter	North
	Jeff Baker	Centennial
2003	Rolland Parli	West
	Jeff Baker	Centennial
2004	Joe Kuntz	North
	Rolland Parli	West
2005	Freddie Vigil	South
	Bryce Horton	Centennial
2006	Eric Matthews	Stockdale
	Bryce Horton	Centennial

SWYL – Stockdale

February 4, 1995

103
Wilson	Chris	N	3:50
Lopez	Junior	D	
Green	Mitch	ST	Fall
Meeks	Jeff	W	

112
Lara	Frank	S	T.F. 17-1 5:42
Garcia	Adolph	ST	
Campus	Carlos	D	12-6
Blanks	Adam	N	

119
Aguirre	Tom	N	8-4
Mistler	Jeff	ST	
Tablit	Ian	D	Fall
Menendez	Robert	W	

125
Sansoni	Alex	ST	5:06
Media	Gabe		
Leonard	Brian	S	
Cervantes	Mike	D	

130
Amaya	Howard	ST	1:03
Morgret	Tim		
Macias	Dan	D	13-7
Frankovic	Ed	S	

135
Damsteadt	Derrick	ST	10-3
Mazza	Marc	N	
Escobedo	Vincent	D	11-10
Porter	Sean	W	

140
Pasquale	Jessie	ST	10-5
Hernandez	Tom	N	
Millikin	Randy	D	Injury Default
Sanchez	David	S	

145
Ransom	Mike	W	2:29
Merkeley	Ben	ST	
Elcano	Chris	S	
Uncontested			

152
Flynn	Scott	ST	(32-6)* 5:57
Jimenez	Juan	S	
Howard	Chris	N	Fall
Fernandez	Fernando	D	

160
Tingle	Jeremy	W	13-4
Hill	Matt	S	
Gamon	Tony	ST	6-5
Marquez	Frank	D	

171
East	Rocky	N	12-7
Heisey	Tim	ST	
Roberts	Josh	S	Fall
Cardenas	Mike	D	

189
Ferguson	Jon	ST	:50
DuQuette	John	W	
Van Tassel	Brent	N	Fall
Espinoza	Alonzo	D	

HWT
Eaton	Ricardo	N	3:22
Escamillia	Richard	W	
Esparza	Nick	D	

* Record

Dual League   **Season**

Stockdale	4-0	21-9
North	3-1	15-9
West	2-2	N/A
South	1-3	N/A
Delano	0-4	N/A

SWYL Tournament

Stockdale	189
North	138
West	96
Delano	84
South	73.5

SWYL – Stockdale
February 3, 1996

103
Green	Mitch	ST	2:56
Holeway	Pat	N	
King	Dan	W	:57
Matienzo	Anthony	D	

112
Lara	Frank	S	5:45
Mitler	Jeff	ST	
Torres	Victor	D	2:53
Meeks	Jeff	W	
Jorgenson	John		

119
Saldana	Richard	ST	4:45
Gorospe	Gary	D	
Kaiser	Mike	N	:53
Goings	Joel	W	

125
Alvarado	Lorezeno	D	5-2
Hembree	Derek	S	
Alvarez	Jessie	W	2:52
Wagoner	Mike	N	

130
Aguirre	Tommy	N	16-1
Ballard	Ryan	ST	
Vidal	Juan	D	Forfeit

135
Tablit	Ian	D	5:17
Leonard	Brian	S	
Bailey	Martin	N	12-5
Shephard	Erick	ST	

140
Muecke	Chris	S	8-4
Cervantes	Mike	D	
Sanchez	Joe	ST	T.F. 4:23
Howard	Nick	N	
Medeiros	John	W	

145
Mesa	Jason	ST	11-10
Guerrero	Paul	N	
Duff	Garred	S	5:52
Gillette	Scott	W	
Chacon	Ricky	D	

152
Hernandez	Tommy	N	4-1
Elcano	Chris	S	
Porter	Sean	W	Forfeit

160
Howard	Chris	N	8-4
Porter	Scott	W	
Blandburg	Rashad	S	Forfeit

171
Hill	Matt	S	5-2
Jimenez	John	W	
Van Tassell	Brent	N	2:15
Beyer	J.J.	D	

189
Ghitty	Peter	S	2:40
DuQuette	John	W	
Johnson	Russel	ST	Forfeit

215
Eaton	Richard	N	4:55
Patricio	Nick	W	
Graham	Aaron	S	10-2
Villarreal	Lorenzo	D	

HWT
Patricio	Rico	W	2:28
Perez	Jose	S	
Bolender	Bryce	N	Default
Delhoy	Jeff	D	

Dual League
	League	Season
South	4-0	5-3
North	3-1	8-8
Stockdale	0-4	0-7
West	2-2	4-12
Delano	1-3	1-3

SWYL Tournament
South	147
North	139.5
Stockdale	110
West	105
Delano	97

SWYL – Centennial
February 8, 1997

103
Marchant	Travis	ST	15-6
Duggan	Scott	C	
Romero	Horatio	W	:51
Enriquez	Nick	S	

112
Wilson	Chris	N	19-8
Goings	Joel	W	
Charles	Cruz	ST	

119
Bascom	Dwight	C	13-8
Alvarez	Jesse	W	
Clendon	Lalo	ST	

125
Lara	Frank	S	1:46
Green	Mitch	ST	
Delcid	Josh	C	8-4
Rice	Carl	N	

130
Branch	B.J.	C	2:58
Ballard	Ryan	ST	
Jorgenson	John	N	7-5
Elisondo	Elijah	W	

135
Wiebe	Justin	C	5:59
Tamayo	Jose	S	
Birkhauser	Bryan	ST	2:45
Reynolds	Mike	N	

140
Leonard	Brian	S	4:13
McNew	Neil	C	
Howard	Nick	N	
Pace	Eric	ST	

145
Hembree	Derek	S	11-4
Pasquini	Anthony	C	
Toomjan	Joe	ST	1:57
Morrison	Mike	N	

152
Harrington	Clint	C	Injury Default
Bennett	Donny	ST	
Duff	Garrad	S	9-0
Lawson	Shannon	W	

160
Jimenez	Juan	S	3:33
Lindsay	Shawn	C	
Pole	Aaron	N	8-0
Rosario	Gilbert	W	

171
Navs	Josh	C	3:03
Elcano	Chris	5	
Saenz	Sal	ST	3:35
Webb	Josh		

189
Morgan	Tim	C	5:03
Woltz	Justin	N	
Reyes	T.J.	ST	6-4
Hockett	Jeremy	S	

215
Graham	Aaron	S	3:50
McCague	Jeff	C	
Johnson	Russell	ST	10-0
Wood	Jake	N	

275
Strain	Brian	C	2:38
Virden	Tommy	ST	
Terrell	Dustin	N	1:00
Langston	Seth	S	

Dual League **Season**
South   4-0   18-7
Centennial 3-1

SWYL Tournament
Centennial 143
South   99
Stockdale   84
North   50
West   43

SWYL – Centennial
February 13, 1998

103
Chapman	Daniel	C	(35-5)*
King	Danny	W	
Bonilla	Gabe	ST	
Enriquez	Nick	S	

112
Marchant	Travis	ST
Ramirez	Aaron	C

119
Goings	Joel	W
Martinez	Joey	ST
Settlemire	Chris	S
Prendez	Matt	C
Hall	Jacob	N

125
Sheets	Sean	C
Cruz	Charles	ST

130
Alvarez	Jesse	W
Martin	Derick	ST
Jorgenson	John	N
Perez	Fernando	S

135
Gutierrez	Fred	C
Wahl	Ryan	ST
Ancheta	Alex	W

140
Ballard	Ryan	ST
Kaiser	Mike	N
Franey	John	C

145
Hembree	Derek	S
Pasquini	Anthony	C
Tyler	Ken	W
Birkhauser	Brian	ST

152
Duff	Garred	S
Mauro	Nick	N
Alexander	Jason	ST
Grealish	Rick	C

160
Jimenez	Juan	S
Francies	Courtney	ST
Baldwin	Treavor	C
Black	Byan	N

171
Rivera	Marcos	S
Lawson	Shannon	W
Herrera	Jason	C
Martin	Chago	ST

189
Naus	Josh	C
Woltz	Justin	N
Perez	Jose	ST
Farmer	Robert	S
Cochran	Matt	W

215
Langston	Seth	S
Stewart	Robert	C
Vilalobos	Manuel	W
Wood		N

275
Strain	Brian	C
DeQuiletts	Ryan	W
Prestridge	Mike	S
Virden	Tommy	ST

Dual League / Season
	Dual League	Season
Centennial	4-0	5-4
Stockdale	3-1	6-10
South	2-2 1	12-7
North	1-3	5-10
West	0-4	4-12

SWYL Tournament
Centennial	142.5
Stockdale	128
South	87
West	73
North	54

SWYL – Centennial
February 13, 1999

103
Chapman	Daniel	C	20-9
Bonilla	Gabe	ST	
Gonzalez	Damien	S	

112
Ramirez	Aaron	C	7-4
King	Danny	W	
Hunter	Derrick	N	8-6
Tamondong	Brandon	ST	
Villa	Danny	S	

119
Martinez	Joey	ST	6-4
Saran	Jaspinder	S	
Rivera	James	N	Inj. Def.
Blackwood	Chuck	C	

124
Goings	Joel	W	15-3
Baltierra	Felix	C	
Enriquez	Nick	S	15-3
Owens	Joe	N	
Owens	Tory	ST	

130
Morrison	Mike	ST	Inj. Def.	
Contreras	Manuel	S		
Gutierrez	Rudy	W	Fall	2:43
Woodruff	Mike	N		

135
Baker	David	C	8-4	
Martin	Derick	ST		
Mattley	Josh	S	Fall	1:48
Reynolds	Tyler	N		

140
Sheets	Sean	C	Fall	:53
Smith	Caleb	N		
Falco	Matt	ST	Fall	1:39
Sanchez	David	S		

145
Alexander	Jason	ST	Fall	3:15
Perez	Fernando	S		
Franey	Jon	C	2-0	
Jorgenson	John	N		

152
Duff	Garred	S	Fall	1:47
Gutierrez	Fred	C		
Branson	Robert	N	8-5	
Martin	Santiago	ST		

160
Ponce	Sean	ST	Fall	1:34
Baldwin	Trevor	C		
Jackson	Roy	S		

171
Rivera	Marcos	S	Fall	1:37
Grealish	Ricky	C		
Rios	Rick	ST		

189
Naus	Josh	C	Fall	1:19
Freeman	Brandon	ST		
Ehret	John	N		

215
Woltz	Justin	N	9-4	
Stewart	Robert	C		
Virden	Tommy	ST	Fall	2:44
Hinzo	Justin	W		
Shields	Colin	S		

HWT
Strain	Bryan	C	Fall	4:36
Langston	Seth	S		
DeQulletts	Ryan	W	Fall	2:26
Bratien	Chris	ST		

Dual League **Season**
Centennial   4-0   7-4

SWYL Tournament
Centennial	196
Stockdale	150
South	128
North	80
West	61

SWYL - Centennial
February 12, 2000

103
Botts	Mike	C	7-1
Gonzalez	Damien	S	
Lalban	Billy	W	17-1
Downhour	Tyler	N	

112
Cemo	Andy	C	3:48
Matthews	Jason	ST	
Morrow	Brandon	N	

119
Chapman	Daniel	C	:51
Hunter	Derrick	N	
Saran	Haspinder	S	4:39
Brown	Evan	ST	
Shaibi	Michael	W	

125
Baltierra	Felix	C	18-4
Gutierrez	Adam	S	
Atchley	Dustin	N	1:40
Defachelle	Jason	ST	
Wolfekuehl	Chris	W	

130
Ramirez	Aaron	C	:48
Franco	Richard	S	
Reynolds	Tyler	N	3-0
Owens	Tory	ST	
Alvarez	Sergio	W	

135
Middleton	Brian	ST	6-2
Horton	Chad	C	
Allen	Charles	S	4-0
Herrera	James	W	
Weikel	Richard	N	

140
Baker	Jeff	C	8-5
Martin	Derrick	ST	
Mattly	Josh	S	

145
Marchant	Travis	ST	1:56
Mullins	Brandon	W	
McNew	Jerry	C	

152
Sheets	Sean	C	1:30
Perez	Fernando	S	
Alexander	Jason	ST	2:57
Calantas	Beredick	W	

160
Griffith	Anthony	C	11-3
Birkhouser	Brian	ST	
Ramirez	Jose	W	

171
O'Reare	Scott	C	1:58
Bowens	Bryan	S	
Rios	Rick	ST	2:45
Rivas	Alexa	W	

189
Smotherman	Chris	C	7-3
Enos	Paul	ST	
Cheatham	Freddie	W	4:43
Ehret	John	N	

215
Henderson	Nate	C	11-4
Shields	Colin	S	
Thompson	Jackson	N	2-1
Hinzo	Justin	W	
Carr	Devin	ST	

275
DeQuillet	Ryan	W	5-3
Strain	Bryan	C	
Terrell	Dustin	N	:25
Braaten	Chris	ST	

* Record

Dual League		Season
Centennial	4-0	8-2
South	3-1	14-7
Stockdale	2-2	11-4
West	1-3	2-5
North	0-4	5-10

SWYL Tournament
Centennial	246
Stockdale	129
South	113.5
North	77
West	73.5

SWYL – Centennial
February 10, 2001

103
Perez	Rudy	N	1:52
Mercado	Frank	S	
Nguyen	Mike	W	Forfeit

112
Botts	Mike	C	1:45
Caliban	Billy	W	
Dowhour	Tyler	N	Default
Gonzales	Damien	S	

119
Matthews	Jason	ST	3:16
Camacho	Jason	C	
Atchley	Dustin	N	8-7
Caracas	David	S	

125
Chapman	Daniel	C	(23-2)* 3:56
Hunter	Derrick	N	(33-4)*
Vasquez	Manuel	S	Forfeit

130
Ramirez	Aaron	C	14-2
Rivera	James	N	
Gutierrez	Adam	S	3:59
Chacon	Adrian	ST	
Cartwright	Chris	W	

135
Franco	Richard	S	3:36
Hernandez	Nick	C	
Valverde	Josh	W	Forfeit

140
Horton	Chad	C	TF 22-7
Alvarez	Sergio	W	

145
Souvannahkh	Kevin	C	5:05
Tilton	Nate	ST	
Allen	Charles	S	2:31
Surratt	Gary	N	

152
Sheets	Sean	C	(30-2, 21 Falls) 2:33
Tamondong	Matt	ST	

160
Griffith	Anthony	C	2:52
Thompson	Jack	N	
Strawser	Chad	ST	3:40
Johnson	Jeff	W	

171
Baker	Jeff	C	TF 21-6
Bowens	Bryan	S	
Scarbrough	Anthony	N	7-0
Denison	David	ST	

189
O'Rear	Scott	C	TF 15-0(50-7 Season)*
Cheatham	Teddie	W	
Fuentes	Joe	S	7-4
Davis	Sean	ST	

215
Shields	Colin	S	7-4
Henderson	Nate	C	
Solis	Miguel	ST	6-1
Ballard	Josh	N	
Lozano	Frank	W	

HWT
Braaten	Chris	ST	2:27
Strain	Jacob	C	
Saso	Josh	N	Forfeit

* Record

SWYL Tournament
Centennial	263.5
North	115
Stockdale	115
South	112.5
West	66

Notes
Chapman and Sheets 4 Times SWYL Champions

SWYL – Centennial
February 9, 2002

103
Domingos	Jordan	ST	:53
Sanchez	Christian	C	

112
Perez	Rudy	N	12-6
Talbit	Mark	C	
Calban	Billy	W	3-2
Long	Matt	ST	

119
Holguin	Albert	W	5-3
Larkin	J.J.	N	
Talbit	Joel	C	12-2
Parker	Dustin	ST	

125
Hunter	Derrick	N	16-4
Vasquez	Manuel	S	
Hickey	Jason	ST	10-7
Comacho	Jason	C	

130
Franco	Richard	S	11-2
Rivera	James	N	
Grimm	Ryan	C	4:54
Quinones	Joe	ST	
Upchurch	Darryll	W	

135
Matthews	Jason	ST	9-5
Garay	Ernesto	C	
Cartwright	Chris	W	5:39
Nash	Greg	N	

140
Ramirez	Joe	C	21-5
Cupelli	Ryan	N	
Chacon	Adrian	ST	5-0
Estudillo	Jose	W	
Arredondo	Oscar	S	

145
Horton	Chad	C	11-4
Parli	Rolland	W	
Allen	Charles	S	7-3
Chisholm	John	N	
Riffe	Tim	ST	

152
Souvannakham	Kevin	C	:24
Johnston	Clayton	S	
Pericy	Ryan	N	3-1
Valverde	Josh	W	
Harvey	Marshall	ST	

160
Subia	Kris	C	1:42
Domingos	Josh	ST	
Medrano	Tony	N	

171
Baker	Jeff	C	13-4
Bowens	Bryan	S	
Patterson	Chris	ST	

189
Subia	Ken	C	5-3
Thompson	Jack	N	
Denison	David	ST	5-0
Nunez	Maurice	W	
Fuentes	Joseph	S	

215
Espejo	Joe	ST	5-0
Saso	Tyler	N	
Rivero	Robert	S	

HWT
Braaten	Chris	ST	5-0
Saso	Josh	N	
Hickman	Jacob	C	

Dual League | Season
	Dual League	Season
Centennial	4-0	6-6
Stockdale	3-1	13-4-1
North	2-2	3-3
South	1-3	6-7
West	0-4	1-5

SWYL Tournament
Centennial	193.5
North	148
Stockdale	119
South	79
West	60

SWYL - Centennial
February 15, 2003

103
Torrez	Frank	N	16-1	4:00
McKenzie	Thomas	ST		
Sanchez	Christian	C		
Hoffman	Mark	W		

112
Romero	Eric	S	10-6	
Knutz	Joe	N		
Nguyen	Mike	W		
Ambrose	Sean	C		

119
Perez	Rudy	N	4-3	
Talbit	Mark	C		
Garcia	Josh	W		
Domingos	Jordan	ST		
Shields	Steven	S		

125
Horton	Bryce	C	Fall	5:30
Klemman	Bryson	N		
Matthews	Sean	ST		
Bixler	Cody	W		
Singh	Gulwinder	S		

130
Vasquez	Manuel	S	7-2	
Grimm	Ryan	C		
McGill	Phillip	ST		

135
Lara	Martin	S	7-3	
Collins	Brendan	ST		
Woosley	Wendel	N		
Carmona	Anthony	W		

140
Parli	Rolland	W	10-5	
Nash	Greg	N		
Hayslett	Paul	C		
Mattly	Justin	S		
Lugo	Eric	ST		

145
Gibson	Brady	ST	Fall	3:33
Davis	Tysen	C		
Johnson	Ryan	W		

152
Horton	Chad	C	Major 18-7	
Harvey	Marshall	ST		
Estudillo	Jose	W		
Alcala	Juan	S		

160
Baker	Jeff	C	Fall	:41
Domingos	Josh	ST		
Gonzales	Julian	S		
Coronado	Matt	W		

171
Hacobian	Jon	ST	Fall	2:52
Nuno	Marcos	S		
Longcrier	Daniel	C		

189
Denison	David	ST	Major 9-1	
Gangl	Alex	W		
Greenhaw	Joel	S		

215
Davis	Tim	ST	5-3	
Saso	Tyler	N		
Fuentes	Daniel	S		
Lynnborgen	Travis	W		

275
White	Jerry	N	Fall	3:23
Rivero	Robert	S		
Morgan	David	C		

Dual League / Season
	Dual League	Season
Centennial	3-0-1	4-0-1
South	3-0-1	4-0-1
Stockdale	2-2	4-2
West	1-3	3-2
North	0-4	0-5

Final Standing
Centennial	8.5
Stockdale	8
South	6.5
North	5
West	2

SWYL Tournament
Stockdale	165
Centennial	162
North	142.5
South	113
West	94

SWYL – Centennial
February 14, 2004

103
Vigil	Freddie	S	9-2
Stuck	Ryan	C	
Barton	Bryant	ST	8-1
Peterson	Eugene	W	

112
Torres	Frankie	N	Fall	3:34
Romero	Eric	S		
Hurtado	Aaron	C	Fall	1:15
Henderson	James	ST		

119
Ambrose	Sean	C	3-1
Abruscato	Chris	ST	
Askew	Joel	S	

125
Kunts	Joe	N	Fall	4:30
Tablit	Mark	C		
Shields	Steven	S	Fall	4:59
Farr	Jameson	ST		

130
McGill	Phillip	ST	8-3
Thompson	Ross	C	
Davenport	David	S	3-2
Bixler	Cody	W	

135
Horton	Bryce	C	10-0
Mendez	Tony	S	
Steed	Mike	N	11-7
Smith	Chris	W	

140
Alcala	Francisco	S	4-3	
Matthews	Sean	ST		
Deathrage	Jared	N	Fall	3:48
Carmona	Anthony	W		

145
Harvey	Marshall	ST	10-2
Hefferan	Zylo	S	
Hopfe	Bryson	N	12-3
Villalobos	Tino	C	

152
Parli	Roland	W	14-5
Collins	Brendon	ST	
Alcala	Juan	S	8-6
Tanner	Will	C	

160
Hacobian	Ty	ST	8-6
Coranado	Matt	C	
Gonzalez	Johnny	W	

171
Domingos	Josh	ST	Fall	1:58
Estudillo	Jose	W		
Nuno	Macos	S	10-7	
Mills	Mitchell	C		

189
Dorsey	Matt	ST	Fall	5:54
Hyatt	Chris	N		
Halton	Derrick	S	Fall	3:50
Kennedy	Andrew	C		

215
Davis	Tim	ST	Fall	5:33
White	Jerry	N		
Egan	Jearal	S	Fall	1:20
Flemming	Weston	C		

275
Morgan	David	ST	7-5
Rivero	Robert	S	
Whitlock	Dan	ST	

Dual League   **Season**

	Dual League	Season
Stockdale	3-1	4-2
South	3-1	8-5
Centennial	3-1	4-2
North	1-3	2-3
West	0-4	1-6

SWYL Tournament

Stockdale	179
South	145.5
Centennial	139.5
North	95
West	57

SWYL – Centennial
February 12, 2005

103
Vigil	Freddie	S	8-3	
Gamboa	Buddy	W		
Hernandez	Christian	N	Fall	4:49
Magno	Jon	R		
Staffedo	Adom	C		

112
Romero	Erick	S	9-0	
Barton	Bryant	ST		
Stuck	Ryan	C		

119
Askew	Joel	S	Fall	1:59
Sanchez	Christian	C		
Matthews	Eric	ST	11-0	
Peterson	Eugene	W		
Thompson	Seth	R		

125
Ambrose	Sean	C	5-0	
Beltran	Andrew	S		
Garza	Rene	R	Fall	2:58
Kleeman	Brock	N		

130
Tablit	Mark	C	Fall	3:42
Gonzales	Vincent	S		
Ornelas	Rickey	R	7-2	
Pena	Mike	N		

135
McAtee	Hunter	C	5-1	
Steed	Mike	N		
Davenport	David	S		

140
McAtee	Carson	C	8-1	
Copeland	Josh	R		
Mendez	Tony	S	12-5	
Martin	Josh	ST		
Morrell	Robert	N	Fall	
Baker	Murray	W		

145
Horton	Bryce	C	Fall	1:54
Matthews	Sean	ST		
Hernandez	Cruz	N	Fall	2:59
Johnson	Jimmie	R		
Garcia	Johnny	W	Fall	
Alcala	Francisco	S		

152
Wilkin	Danny	C	Fall	5:23
Holguin	Albert	W		
Alcala	Juan	S	Fall	2:25
Roberts	Kenny	N		
Torgerson	James	ST		

160
Parli	Rolland	W	10-3	
Villalobos	Tino	C		
Deathrage	Jered	N	6-2	
Torres	Chris	S		

171
Musquez	John	C	10-4	
Hefferan	Zylo	S		
Estudillo	Jose	W	13-5	
Thampi	Advaith	ST		
Blake	Matt	N		

189
Halton	Derick	S	Fall	2:36
Grady	Tyler	N		
Ryder	Glen	C	Fall	1:59
Frasher	David	ST		

215
Pierson	Jacob	R	Fall	3:05
Moore	Quinn	S		
Hernandez	Carlos	ST	Fall	3:19
Castillo	Mike	C		

275
Morgan	David	C	Fall	3:29
Ruiz	Chris	R		
Banks	Prentice	S		

Dual League / Season
	Dual League	Season
Centennial	4-1	20-1
South	4-1	12-4
Ridgeview	2-3	5-8
Stockdale	2-3	5-9
North	3-2	4-2
West	0-5	0-6

SWYL Tournament
Centennial	205
South	187
Ridgeview	75
Stockdale	67
North	65
West	64

SWYL - Centennial
February 11, 2006

103
Vigil	Freddie	S	10-0	(26-1)*
Hernandez	Christian	N		
Perry	Ryan	ST		

112
Magno	Jonathan	R	Fall	:55
Johnston	Greg	S		
Staffero	Adam	C	Fall	3:16
Meyer	Chris	ST		
Hernandez	Mike	N		

119
Beltran	Andrew	S	6-4	(23-9)*
Magno	Bryan	R		
Sabo	John	N	14-8	
Hurtado	Aaron	C		
Haidze	Josh	ST		

125
Hicks	Seth	C	Fall	4:54
Abruscado	Chris	ST		
Arguello	Miguel	R	3-0	
Beltran	Xavier	S		
Turney	Kyle	N		

130
Garza	Rene	R	Fall	3:05
Kleeman	Brock	N		
Romero	Dominick	S	Fall	5:22
Payne	Jordan	ST		
Ballard	Austin	C		

135
Matthews	Eric	ST	Fall	1:51
Cox	Ty	N		
Rosenberge	Tommy	S	4-2	
Endes	Dalton	C		
Cavazos	Kyle	R		

140
McAtee	Carson	C	8-2	(20-7)*
Davenport	David	S		
Jones	Alex	ST	12-4	
Harrison	Alex	N		
Peterson	Eugene	W	11-2	
Flores	Jacob	R		

* Record

145
Horton	Bryce	C	Fall	3:22
Gonzales	Vincent	S		
Pena	Mike	N	Fall	:59
Ryther	Nathan	ST		

152
Wilkin	Danny	C	6-2	
Hernandez	Cruz	N		
Copeland	Josh	R	Fall	3:53
Alcala	Francisco	S		
Smith	Chris	W		

160
Torres	Chris	S	Fall	5:42 (33-7)*
Villalobos	Valentino	C		
Torgerson	James	S	4-2	
Johnson	Jimmie	R		
Sotelo	Nick	W	Fall	1:48
Thomason	Joey	N		

171
Muquez	John	C	Fall	2:22 (20-10)*
Ramirez	Jeremy	ST		
Blake	Mat	N	Fall	1:50
Gutierrez	Hernan	S		

189
Grady	Tyler	N	Fall	4:50
Ryder	Glenn	C		
Hernandez	Carlos	ST	Fall	3:55
Capaldi	Richie	S		

215
Moore	Quinn	S	10-3	(33-7)*
Hernandez	Antonio	N		
Quintero	Pedro	C	Fall	1:52
Mitchell	Aaron	ST		

275
Morgan	David	C	Fall	3:50
Banales	William	S		
Knoy	Mitch	N	Fall	:32
Perez	Jesus	R		

Dual League		Season	SWYL Tournament	
South	5-0	10-4	Centennial	214.5
Centennial	4-1	11-1	South	201.5
North	3-2	3-3	North	172.5
Stockdale	2-3	2-5	Stockdale	139
Ridgeview	1-4	2-4	Ridgeview	115
West	0-5	0-6	West	18

Florencio Rocha (kneeling), 3rd in State, and Bakersfield High Coach Olan Polite in 1973.

South East and South West Yosemite League Area Tournament
1995-1998

SWYL-SWYL Area Tournament 1995-98

Date	Location	Champion	Coach
2/11/95	East	Bakersfield	David East
2/10/96	East	Bakersfield	David East
2/15/97	East	Foothill	Alan Paradise
2/14/98	East	Foothill	Alan Paradise

Most Outstanding Wrestlers Lower/Upper Weights

Awards sponsored by The Coyote Club

Year	Wrestler	School
1995		
1996	Abraham Diaz	Arvin
	Charlie Brogdan	Arvin
1997	Max Odom	Foothill
	Cirilo Reyes	East
1998		

Area – East
February 11, 1995

103
Odom	Dustin	F		3:39
Lanfield	Greg	B		
Diaz	Abe	A	Default	
Felix	Chris	H		
Green	Mitch	ST		

112
Elisondo	Steve	B		5:00
Moore	Kirk	F		
Lara	Frank	S	10-2	
Garcia	Adolph			
Estrada	Sam	A		

119
Vasquez	Larry	B		:22
Reyes	Cirilo	E		
Aguirre	Tom	N	5-1	
Martinez	Ishmael	F		
Mistler	Jeff	ST		

125
Vasquez	Nathan	B		2:49
Villagomez	Alan	E		
Hogeland	Kaleb	F	13-6	
Sansoni	Alex	ST		
Leonard	Brian	S		

130
Lopez	Juan	H		1:10
Garcia	Nilo	E		
Diniz	Adrian	F	9-2	
Amaya	Howard	ST		
Morgret	Tim	N		

135
Manes	Jeremy	F	12-11	
Miller	Kelly	B		(28-5)*
Reyes	Harvey	E	13-4	
Mazza	Mark	N		
Guerra	Peter	H		

140
Varner	Andy	B		4:14
Pasquale	Jesse	ST		
Hernandez	Tom	N	8-2	
Harris	Justin	A		
Padgett	Tim	F		

* Record

145
Williams	Ryan	H		4:12
Martinez	Mike	E		
Bedford	Wayne	B	5-2	
Coffia	Marlin	F		
Elcano	Chris	S		

152
Bridges	Jeremy	B		:58
Flynn	Scott	ST		
Smith	Junior	E		1:45
Uries	Albert	F		
Jimenez	Juan	S		

160
Keller	Tony	B	T.F.	4:11
Tingle	Jeremy	W		
Hill	Matt	S		:34
Gamon	Tony	ST		
Galarzia	Jose	E		

171
Ashley	Fred	B		
Bangloy	Anthony	E	13-8	
Heisey	Tim	ST		
Sharkey	Brandon	F		

191
Maese	Ray	B	5-2	
Hanash	Mike	E		
Ferguson	Jon	ST		2:08
DuQuette	John	W		
Duncan	Eric	H		

HWT
Clark	Brett	B		1:16
Daugherty	Tim	F		
Eaton	Richard	N	7-3	
Schneider	Chris	A		
Escamilla	Richard	W		

Area Tournament
Bakersfield	306.5
Foothill	160
East	144.5
Stockdale	138.5
North	94
Highland	80
South	67.5
West	60.5
Arvin	53
Delano	18

South Area – East
February 10, 1996

103
Odom	Max	F	12-3
Resseguie	Chris	E	
Felix	Chris	H	6-0
Scott	Bennett	B	
Maradiaga	Oscar	A	15-4
Holloway	Pat	N	

112
Diaz	Abraham	A	4-2 O.T.
Canfield	Greg	B	
Martinez	Mike	F	8-5
Lara	Frank	S	
Torres	Victor	D	16-2
Jorgenson	John	N	

119
Moore	Kirk	F	4-3
Elisondo	Steve	B	
Rosales	Nick	A	1:32
Saldana	Richard	ST	
Kaiser	Mike	N	Fall
Goings	Joel	W	

125
Vasquez	Nathan	B	5-1
Adame	Anthony	F	
Alvardo	Lorenzo	D	11-7
Hembree	Derrick	S	
Villagomez	Allan	E	4-0
Alvarez	Jesse	W	

130
Reyes	Cirilo	E	3:10
Aguirre	Tommy	N	
Hogeland	Kaler	F	8-4
Sherley	Ben	B	
Ballard	Ryan	ST	4-2 O.T.
Vidal	Juan	D	

135
Muralla	Ernesto	B	3-0
Diniz	Adrian	F	
Leonard	Brian	S	Fall
Tablit	Ian	D	
Garcia	Alex	E	15-3
Bailey	Martin	N	

140
Molano	Fred	B	13-0
Manes	Jeremy	F	
Reyes	Harvey	E	4:44
Muecke	Chris	S	
Sanchez	Joe	ST	14-2
Cervantes	Mike	D	

145
Miller	Kelly	B	18-9
Mesa	Jason	ST	
Padgett	Tim	F	5:55
Duff	Garred	S	
Sanchez	John	E	9-6
Chacon	John	D	

152
Rosales	Angel	A	19-6
Hernandez	Tommy	N	
Schallberger	Phillip	B	15-3
Gospich	Nick	F	
Elcano	Chris	S	Fall
Porter	Sean	W	

160
Dunn	John	B	8-4
Galarza	Jose	E	
Howard	Chris	N	12-3
Lawson	Shannon	H	
Porter	Scott	W	Fall
Blandburg	Rashad	S	

171
Hill	Matt	S	7-2
Lomeli	David	B	
Smith	Junior	E	14-5
Ujrias	Albert	F	
Jimenez	John	W	2-1
Van Tassel	Brent	N	

189
Brogdan	Charlie	A	4-1
Ghitty	Peter	S	
DuQuette	John	W	3:01
Caudel	Brandon	B	
Scott	David	E	Fall
Johnson	Russell	ST	

(Continued on next page)

South Area – East
February 10, 1996

215

Maese	Ray	B	T.F. 25-10 5:37
Schneider	Chris	A	
Graham	Aaron	S	3-1
Patricio	Nick	W	
Rivera	Adam	F	Fall
Finn	Shannon	East	

HWT

Daugherty	Tim	F	2:44
Gonzalez	Tony	H	
Bolender	Bryce	N	Fall
Patricio	Rigo	W	
Delehoy		D	Fall
Tapia	David	B	

Area Tournament

Bakersfield	255.5
Foothill	207
South	134
East	122
Arvin	115.5
North	103
West	70
Delano	61
Stockdale	53
Highland	41

John Miller
North Bakersfield – Two-time CIF Champion
California Wrestler of the Year 1968

Area - East
February 15, 1997

135
Felix	Chris	E	
Maradiaga	Oscar	A	
Marquez	Phillip	F	
Duggan	Scott	C	
Marchant	Travis	ST	

112
Ressiquie	Chris	E	
Diaz	Abraham	A	
Dickerson	John	B	
Goings	Joel	W	
Martinez	Michael	F	

119
Odom	Max	F	
Bascom	Dwight	C	
Alvarez	Jessie	W	
Bustamante	J.J.	A	
Chavez	David	E	

125
Lara	Frank	S	5-3
Scott	Bennett	B	
Rosales	Nick	A	
Mooney	Ray	F	
Moroyoqul	Ray	H	

130
Schallenberger	Patrick	B	
Branch	B.J.	C	
Perez	Phillip	E	
Ballard	Ryan	ST	
Arellano	Jose	A	

135
Meloche	Ryan	F	
Wiebe	Justin	C	
Villagomez	Alan	E	
Spradlin	Matt	B	
Morales	Augie	A	

140
Moore	Kirk	F	15-5
Moralla	Ernesto	B	
Leonard	Brian	S	
Martinez	Eddie	E	
Howard	Nick	N	

145
Reyes	Cirillo	E	6-5
Miller	Kelly	B	
Hembree	Derek	S	
Pasquini	Anthony	C	
Guillen	Daniel	F	

152
Diniz	Adrian	F	
Rosales	Angel	A	
Reyes	Harvey	E	
Harrington	Cliint	C	
Garcia	Juan	B	

160
Jimenez	Juan	S	
McWilliams	Ryan	F	
Caudel	Bryan	B	
Pimental	Juan	A	
Lindsay	Shawn	C	

171
Naus	Josh	C	12-3
Smith	Junior	E	
Elcano	Chris	S	
Bravo	Mario	F	
Dunn	John	B	

189
Brogdan	Charlie	A	:20
Morgan	Tim	C	
Woltz	Justin	N	
Hernandez	Mario	H	
Tobin	Eric	B	

215
Graham	Aaron	S	(Season 41-8)*
Lomeli	David	B	
Karle	Corey	H	
McCague	Jeff	C	
Dorado	Julian	F	

(Continued on next page)

Area - East
February 15, 1997

275
Ibarra	Jose	E	2-1
Gonzalez	Tony	H	
Torres	Greg	F	
Tapia	David	B	
Strain	Bryan	C	

* Record

Area Tournament
Foothill	194.5
BHS	182
East	173.5
Centennial	160.5
Arvin	130.5
South	122.5
Highland	56.5
North	28
Stockdale	26
West	25

Earl Corley (top)
South Bakersfield – 1959 CIF Wrestling Champion
1960 – 2nd in the CIF Golf Championships

Area – East
February 14, 1998

103
Chapman	Daniel	C	11-3	
Harl Justin	Adam	B		
Sanchez	Ivan	A	4-2	
Onsurez	Andy	E		4:07
Felix	Marcox	H		

112
Dickerson	John	B	13-3
Felix	Chris	E	
Bustamante	Johnny	A	3-1
Marchant	Travis	ST	
Marquez	Phillip	F	16-1
Rameriz	Aaron	C	

119
Goings	Joel	W	3-2 O.T. (2)
Gutierrez	Miguel	F	
Chicca	Caleb	B	6-4
Montoya	Manuel	A	
Martinez	Joel	ST	13-3
Settlemire	Chris	S	

125
Ashley	Benny	B	9-6	
Rosales	Nick	A		
Hernandez	Steve	F		1:20
Sheets	Sean	C		
Perez	Phillip	E	7-0	
Charles	Cruz	ST		

130
Odom	Max	F	11-3
Schallenberger	Patrick	B	
Alvarez	Jessie	W	7-4
Arellano	Jose	A	
Jorgenson	John	N	7-2
Martin	Derick	ST	

135
Meloche	Ryan	F	5-4 O.T. (2)
Garcia	Juan	B	
Mooney	Britt	E	8-2
Gutierrez	Fred	C	
Ancueta		W	10-6
Wahl	Ryan	ST	

140
Gonzalez	Tommy	H	2-1 O.T. (2)
Villagomez	Alan	E	
Wiebe	Justin	F	7-0
Kaiser	Mike	N	
Valdez	Genero	B	11-4
Franey	John	C	

145
Spradlin	Matt	B	3-1 O.T.
Diniz	Adrian	F	
Pasquini	Anthony	C	7-2
Watson	Rick	H	
Hembree	Derek	S	23-7
Tyler	Ken	W	

152
Moore	Kirk	F	(45-0)* 1:06	
Duff	Garred	S		
Mauro	Nick	N	4-2	
Alexander	Jason	ST		
Grealish	Rick	C		4:30
Bonilla	Ryan	B		

160
Reyes	Harvey	E		3:33
Jimenez	Juan	S		
Bravo	Mario	F		2:56
Baldwin	Treavor	C		
Francies	Courtney	ST	14-12	
Navejos	John	B		

171
Shankle	Brandon	F	8-2
Herrera	Jason	C	
Rivera	Marcos	S	8-3
Lawson	Shannon	W	
Cantu	Andy	A	6-3
Maize	Paul	S	

189
Naus	Josh	C	(39-0)* !:15
McDermott	Jermaine	B	
Woltz	Justin	N	3:45
Pantosa	Emmanuel	A	7-4
Monarrez	Omar	F	

(Continued on next page)

Area – East
February 14, 1998

215				
Graham	Aaron	B		2:22
Langston	Seth	S		
Karle	Corey	H	3-2	
Stewart	Robert	C		
Gutierrez	Cosmo	E	5-1	
Jacobson	Nathan	F		

275				
Torres	Greg	F		5:09
Tobin	Eric	B	7-4	
Prestidge	Mike	S		
DeQuillett	Ryan	W		4:20
Reyes	Alfredo	H		

Area Tournament	
Foothill	250.5
BHS	210
Centennial	166
East	103.5
South	100.5
Arvin	84
Weest	71
Stockdale	69
Highland	66
North	52

* Record

North Bakersfield High wrestlers
Herb Cosme (left) – Two-time CIF Champion (1966-67)
Jack Goss – 2nd in the CIF (1966); 3rd in the CIF (1967)

Richard Alvarez, three-time CIF Champion (1967, 1968 and 1969), of Bakersfield High.
Career record: 112-8-1

South Sequoia League
1966-2006

South Sequoia League

Date	Location	Dual Champion	SSL Meet Champion	Overall Champion	Coach
2/11/66	West	Arvin 8-1	Arvin	Arvin	John Burton
1/11/67	West	West 6-0	West	West	Ray Juhl
2/10/68	Shafter		Arvin		
2/15/69	Wasco	Wasco/Shafter	Arvin	Wasco	Ted Hammack
2/14/70	Shafter	Shafter 8-0	Shafter	Shafter	Darrell Fletcher
2/11/71	Taft		Highland		
2/19/72	Shafter	Arvin 6-0	Arvin	Arvin	Phil McIntyre
2/9/73	Wasco	Shafter 5-0-1	Shafter	Shafter	Darrell Fletcher
2/9/74	Coalinga	Wasco 8-0	Wasco	Wasco	Gerald Brandon
2/15/75	Shafter	Wasco 8-0	Wasco	Wasco	Gerald Brandon
2/14/76	Corcoran	Wasco 8-0	Wasco	Wasco	Gerald Brandon
2/12/77	McFarland	Shafter 8-0	Shafter	Shafter	Darrell Fletcher
2/15/78	Wasco	Shafter 6-0	Shafter	Shafter	Darrell Fletcher
2/10/79	Corcoran	Shafter/Wasco	Shafter	Shafter	Don Burns
2/15/80	Shafter	Shafter 6-0	Shafter	Shafter	Lisle Gates
2/11/81	Shafter	Shafter 6-0	Shafter	Shafter	Lisle Gates
2/11/82	Shafter		Shafter		
2/10/83	Coalinga	Shafter 2-0	Shafter	Shafter	Joe Lopez
2/11/84	Wasco	Woodlake	Woodlake	Woodlake	Ron Barkley
2/9/85	Woodlake		Caruthers		
2/13/86	McFarland	Undefeated/Wasco	Wasco	Wasco	Phil Sullivan
2/12/87	Coalinga	Shafter 4-0			
2/12/88	Shafter	McFarland 4-0	Shafter	McFarland	Ed Levenson
2/9/89	Wasco		Corcoran		
2/8/90	McFarland	Corcoran	McFarland	Corcoran	
2/8/91	Arvin	Wasco	Arvin	Arvin	Ruben Ramirez
2/14/92	Shafter		Wasco		
2/11/93	Wasco	Tehachapi 4-0	Tehachapi	Tehachapi	John Caminiti
2/11/94	Stockdale	Wasco 6-0	Wasco	Wasco	Brett Clark
2/10/95	Centennial	Wasco	Wasco	Wasco	Brett Clark
2/10/96	Centennial	Centennial 5-0	Centennial	Centennial	Paul Olejnik
2/15/97	Shafter	Tehachapi	Wasco	Wasco/Tehachapi	Brent Clark/John Caminiti
2/12/98	Tehachapi		Shafter		
2/12/99	Tehachapi	Shafter 5-0	Shafter	Shafter	Gary Pederson
2/12/2000			Tehachapi		
2/9/2001	Shafter	Shafter 5-0	Shafter	Shafter	Gary Pederson
2/9/2002	Wasco	Shafter 5-0	Liberty	Liberty/Shafter	Joe Vega/Gary Pederson
2/14/2003	McFarland	Shafter 4-0	Shafter	Shafter	Gary Pederson
2/13/2004	Tehachapi	Shafter 4-0	Shafter	Shafter	Gary Pederson
2/11/2005	Arvin	Arvin	Arvin	Arvin	Miguel Sanchez
2/10/2006	Shafter	Tehachapi 5-0	Tehachapi	Tehachapi	Tony Kellor

Most Outstanding SSL Wrestler

Awards sponsored by The Coyote Club since 1993

Year	Wrestler	School
1966	John Lowe	Wasco
1967	Mike Garcia	West
1968	Mike Terry	Wasco
1969	Manuel Machado	McFarland
1970	Frank Ramos	Arvin
1971	Mike Machado	McFarland
1973	Mike Johnson	Wasco
1993	Aaron Rodriguez	Wasco
	Tony Kellor	Tehachapi
1994	Jeremy Roper	Shafter
	Dennis Clark	Wasco
1995	Eric Serda	Wasco
	Kevin Cierley	Centennial
1996	Jeremy Roper	Shafer
	Eli Espercueta	Shafter
1997	Sam Jameson	Wasco
	Rodney Leisle	Ridgeview
1998	Tony Madrigal	Shafter
	Narcy Martinez	Wasco
1999	Nick Rosales	Arvin
	Narcy Martinez	Wasco
2001	Matt Maldonado	Shafter
	Patrick Acosta	Wasco
2002	Antonio Hernandez	Liberty
	Jarred Ghilarducci	Liberty
2003	Rudy Tabada	Arvin
	Jedd Ingram	Tehachapi
2004	Dustin Cruz	Shafter
	Orlando Landois	Wasco
2005	Vincent Navarro	Shafter
	Marvin Statler	Shafter
2006	Frankie Castillo	Arvin
	Zack Johnson	Wasco

SSL - West
February 11, 1966

95
Lowe	John	WA	8-3	
Nelson	Dave	W		

103
Dickson	Chuck	W	14-7	
Vibe	Jim	A		

112
Winters	Jess	W	Fall	1:31
Silva	Jerry	WA		

120
Patino	Victor	A	8-5	
Salazar	Joe	S		

127
Garcia	Mike	W	12-0	
Rubinol	Jessie	A		

133
Bailey	Roger	A	6-3	
Carroll	Dave	W		

138
Popejoy	Joe	A	Fall	4:57
Janzen	Jerry	S		

145
Ramirez	Ruben	A	5-4	
Gilly	Steve	WA		
Forney	Bruce	W		

154
Herndon	Bob	A	Fall	:52
Sisemore	Tom	WA		

165
Tarver	Bill	A	5-0	
Forney	Doug	W		

175
Torres	Art	A	Fall	2:13
Blythe	Dan	WA		

191
Parker	Bob	A	8-6	
Hoseman	Steve	WA		

UNL
Davis	Clovis	A	8-2	
Williams	Don	W		

Dual League
Arvin	8-1
West	

Season
	14-3

SSL Tournament
Arvin	128
West	91
Wasco	73
Shafter	48

Arvin High wrestling coach John Bunton, right. Far right, Arvin High 1966 South Sequoia Leauge Champions.

Top Row: Coach Bunton, D. Campbell, M. Smith, T. Phillips, H. Thornburgh, B. Tarver, C. Davis, D. Brown, C. Tarver, R. Parker. 2nd Row: S. Soriano, M. Solario, A. Torres, E. Barron, B. Herndon, J. Popejoy, R. Bailey, L. Tarver, R. Ramirez, P. Rodriguez, B. Parker. Bottom Row: L. Ramos, B. Nakata, J. Rubinol, V. Patino, E. Espinoza, D. Clark, G. Patino, G. Feliz, J. Wesson, J. Vibe, G. Parent.

SSL – West
February 11, 1967

95
Velasquez	Tony	A	O.T. 3-1	
Kinoshita	Larry	W		
Banks	Donn	S	Fall	3:41
Kane	Danny	WA		

103
Kinoshita	Danny	W	2-0	
Rodriguez				
Steen	Mike	S	Fall	3:38
Garner	Phil	W		

112
Giggy	Dave	W	4-0
Silva	Jerry	WA	
Viebe	J	A	12-0
Salazar	Manuel	S	

120
Montecino	Mike	WA	Fall	2:37
Dickson		W		
Salazar	Sal	S	8-0	
Mendoza	M	A		

127
Winters	Jess	W	15-7	
Rodriguez	Vince	S		
Brown		WA	Fall	4:12
Chan	Stanley	A		

133
Chernabuff	Mike	WA	5-3
Gollmyer	Bruce	W	
Black	Danny	S	2-1
Patino	Gabae	A	

138
Garcia	Mike	W	Fall	3:40
Santillan	George	WA	(25-1)*	
Felix	G	A	5-2	
Ohanneson	Joe	S		

145
Bridges	Rich	W	7-2
Janzen	Jerry	S	
Terry	Mike	WA	
Eden	Doyle	A	

154
Forney	Bruce	W	Fall	2:47
Tarver	Charlie	A		
Nadal	Frank	WA		
Wegis	Rick	S		

165
Tarver	Bill	A	5-0	
Forney	Doug	W		
Moore	Johnny	S	Fall	5:13
Sanborn		WA		

175
Tarver	Larry	A	4-0
Kern	Rich	W	
Brown	Jim	S	6-1
Knupper	Max	WA	

191
Torres	Art	A	4-0
Teutsch	Don	W	
Wittenberg	Ken	S	7-0
Hester		S	

UNL
Cooper	Craig	W	Fall	1:41
Davis	Clovis	A		
Thomas	Jim	S	4-0	
Velasco	Everado	WA		

* Record

Dual League   **Season**
West   6-0   11-3
Shafter   2-4   4-8

SSL Tournament
West   132
Arvin   86
Wasco   65
Shafter   56

SSL – Shafter
February 10, 1968

95
Vasquez	Tony	A	9-0	
Herrera	Leo	S		
Loe	Ernie	W	Fall	3:07
McFarland	Mike	M		

103
Banks	Don	S	18-1	
Alvarez				
Gardner	Phil	W	Default	

112
Rodriguez	Paul	A	10-2	
Sizemore	Harold	W		
Futrell	Alan	S	Fall	3:43
Munoz	Art	M		

120
Salazar	Manual	S	Fall	4:29
Ramos	L	A		
Kring	Terry	M	Fall	3:22
Lee		W		

127
Rodriguez	Vince	S	
Parker	Randy	A	
Loe	D	W	

133
Black	Danny	S	12-3	
Ramos	Tom	A		
Chernabaeff	Mike	W	Fall	3:17
Quintana	Ralph	M		

138
Patino	Gabe	A	6-0
Striff	Rod	W	

145
Eden	Doyle	A	7-1	
Nadal	Frank	W		
Precie	Nole	M	Fall	4:30
Ellis	Doug	S		

154
Terry	Mike	W	15-4	
Nakata	Bill	A		
Moore	John	S	Fall	:58
Ross	Lawrence	M		

165
Wegis	Rick	S	6-5	
Clement	Randy	W		
Nakata	G	A	6-1	
McFarland	Steve	M		

175
Tarver	Larry	A	Fall	3:30
Samarin	Andrew	W		
Gladden	Mickey	S	9-0	
Kolosky	Drew	M		

191
Tarver	Charlie	A	6-4	
Brown	Jim	S		
Knupper	Max	W	Fall	1:30
Walker	Harold	M		

HWT
Davis	Clovis	A	Fall	3:07
Moreland	Ron	M		
Velesco	Everado	W	Fall	1:17
Voth	Jon	S		

SSL Tournament
Arvin	129
Shafter	102
Wasco	76
McFarland	39

Left to Right: Standing G. Patino, D. Eaton, B. Nakata, L. Tarver, C. Tarver, C. Davis, Kneeling E. Horton, T. Velasquez, P. Rodriquez, E. Patino, R. Parker, E. Ortiz, T. Ramos.

1968 Arvin High Wrestling Team

SSL - Wasco
February 15, 1969

95
Forges	Wayne	S	Ref Dec.	
Loe	Ernie	W		
Machado	Mike	M	9-6	
Romas	Frank	A		

103
Velasquez	Tony	A	6-1	
Herrera	Leo	S		
DeLasanto		A	Fall	4:58
Wooseley	Greg	T		

112
Combs	Steve	W	6-1	
Rodriguez		A		
Schultz	Danny	M	O.T. 1-0	
Banks	Don	S		

120
Sisemore	Harold	W	1-0	
Ramos	L	A		
Ketchem	P	A	12-10	
Gonzales	David	M		

127
Patino	Ernie	A	Fall	5:10
Velez	Nelson	A		
Gonzales	Joe	W	Fall	2:43
Abair	Larry	S		

133
Chan	Stanley	A	Fall	3:22
Diaz	Ricky	A		
Protor	Gerald	W	Fall	1:32
McMahan		M		

138
Black	Dan	S	Fall	3:17
Ramos	Tom	A		
Velasquez	Louis	A		
Lowe	D	W		

145
Machado	Manuel	M	11-2	
Patino	Gabe	A		
Strieff	Rod	W	6-4	
Hibbard	Charles	T		

154
Terry	Mike	W	17-0 (30-4)*	
Moore	Johnny	S		
Ortiz		A	8-2	
Garza	Ray	M		

165
Clement	Randy	W	13-5	
Kadel	Dave	S		
Precie	Noel	M	Fall	2:40
Blythe	Stanley	W		

175
Wilhite	Bill	W	8-0	
McGhee	Mitch	T		
Swanson		A	Fall	1:51
Cantu	S	A		

191
Brown	Jim	S	Fall	3:28
Morales	James	W		
Voth	Jon	S	Fall	:35
Kelly	Mark	T		

HWT
Jeffers	George	W	Fall	1:24
Cossum	Fred	T		
Hardwick	John	S	Fall	1:14
Conklin	Hank	M		

* Record

SSL Co-Champions Duals Meets
Wasco/Shafter

SSL Tournament
Arvin	145
Wasco	134
Shafter	96
McFarland	54
Taft	41

Jim Brown of Shafter

SSL – Shafter
February 14, 1970

95
Ramos	Frank	A	5-2	
Forbs	Wayne	S		
Lowe	Earle	W	Fall	1:50
Hass	Ted	M		

103
Velasquez	Tony	A	Fall	1:59
Holman	Steve	M		
Cates	Alam	S	9-8	
Thompson	Aubry	W		

112
De Los Santos	Manuel	A	6-0	
Garvin	Marcel	W		
Stowell	Robert	S	9-7	
Machado	Mike	M		

120
Herrera	Leo	S	O.T. Ref. Dec. 2-2	
Gonzales	David	M		
Powe	Keith	T	Fall	4:00
Raya	Junior	A		

127
Schultz	Danny	M	3-1	
Maldonado	Cain	S		
Diaz	Ricky	A	Fall	4:40
McCarthy	Gerry	T		

133
Sizemore	Harold	W	Fall	1:54
Morris	Gary	T		
Robertson	Richard	S	14-6	
Ramos	Tom	A		

138
Ohanneson	Jeff	S	8-3	
Velasquez	Luis	A		
Procter	Gerald	W	Fall	5:00
Hollingsworth	Brian	T		

145
Macado	Manual	M	Fall	2:38
Hollingsworth	G	T		
Ramos	Tom	A	1-0	
Clement	Marty	W		

154
Esquibel	Angel	M	3-2	
Sagaser	Grant	T		
Schultz	David	S	Fall	4:58
Reimer		W		

165
Moore	Johnny	S	Fall	1:44
Blythe	Stanley	W		
Rodriguez	David	M	O.T. 7-6	
Price	Greg	T		

175
Kadel	David	S	Fall	:30
Gehlert	Chuck	A		
McFarland	Steve	M	Fall	1:39
Saylor	Dale	T		

191
Hill	Tom	S	Fall	1:50
Tarver	Melvin	A		
Gates	Mike	M	1-0	
Morales		W		

HWT
Jeffers	George	M	Fall	3:09
Fraley	Phil	S		
Cossum	Fred	T		
Valles	Ruben	A		

Dual League
Shafter 8-0
Wasco

Season
6-5

SSL Tournament
Shafter 106
Arvin 76
McFarland 69
Wasco 57
Taft 39

SSL – Taft
February 11, 1971

145
Gonzales	John	H	9-1
George	Randy	T	
Lopeteguy	Joey	S	2-1
Rugnao	Johnny	A	

103
Ramos	Frank	A	13-0
Affentranger	Franc	S	
Gilley	Phil	W	6-3
Stroud	David	T	

112
Machado	Mike	M	15-1
Perrin	Doug	H	
Rodriguez	Richard	A	6-4
Thompson	Aubry	W	

120
Herrera	Leo	S	8-6	
Garvin	Marcel	W		
Pon	Art	H	Fall	1:50
Willingham	Jeff	T		

127
Gonzales	David	M	5-0
Gonzalez	Estevan	H	
Salvador	Ray	A	9-0
Powe	Keith	T	

133
Blackhurst	Paul	H	5-2
Velasquez	Luis	A	
Maldonado	Cain	S	8-7

138
Morris	Gary	T	10-4
Hamaroff	Pete	H	
Rodriguez	David	M	10-2
Reyna	J.R.	S	

145
Morroquin		M	6-2
Hollingsworth	Brian	T	
Harrer	John	H	Decision
Bustamente	Johnny	A	

154
Clement	Marty	W	2-3
Mitchell	Jay	H	
Parrish	Darrell	M	4-0
Campbell	Robert	S	

165
Schultz	David	S	6-2
Esquibel	Steve	M	
Clement	Terry	W	7-5
Burns		A	

175
Kadel	David	S	Fall	1:55
Gehlert	Chuck	A		
Holding	Jeff	H	9-4	
Poulton	Dennis	M		

191
Hll	Tom	S	Fall	4:25
McClintock	Brian	H		
Lynch	Brian	W	10-4	
Trout	Rick	T		

HWT
Jeffers	George	W	Fall	1:01
Valles	Ruben	A		
Arp	Bill	T	3-0	
Turner		H		

Dual League
Wasco

Season
2-10

SSL Tournament
Highland	92	McFarland	60
Shafter	81	Wasco	58
Arvin	65	Taft	56

Franc Affentranger (top) of Shafter High

SSL – Shafter
February 19, 1972

95
Filmore	Wayne	T	Fall	2:30
Machado	Ed	A		
Dodd	Emmitt	W	6-3	
Cruz	Alex	S		

103
Lopetguy	Joey	S	Fall	1:55
Perez		W		
George	Randy	T	Fall	3:03
Rugnad	Johnny	A		

112
Ramos	Frank	A	7-3	
Affentranger	Frank	S		
Camargo	Eddie	W	Default	

120
Rosales	Lupe	A	Fall	:55
Gilley	Philip	W		
Packard	Mark	S	Fall	5:28
Beck	Pat	T		

127
Lopez	Joe	S	Fall :	26
Guerrero	C	A		
Willingham	Jeff	T	8-6	
Thompson	Aubrey	W		

133
Smithee	Mike	A	Fall	:11
Powe	Keith	T		
Brown	Phillip	S	7-3	
Frank	R	W		

138
Ramos	Alvie	A	11-4	
Affentranger	Anton	S		
Butcher	T	W	Forfeit	

145
Ward	Darrell	T	2-1	
Long	William	W		
Painter	Paul	S	7-0	
Mirales	Cipriano	A		

154
Cota	Bucky	A	8-2	
Gutierres	P	W		
Williams	Gilbert	S		

165
Clement	Marty	W	Fall	:45
Reedy	Ron	T		
Fuller	Steve	S	Default	

175
Clement	Terry	W	19-1	
Mora	Brad	A		
Akman	Terry	S		

191
Johnson	Mike	W	Fall	2:31
Gelhert	Chuck	A		
Uncontested				

HWT
Jones	Billy	W	8-1	
Torrigiani	Jeff	S		
Arp	Bill	T	Fall	1:21
Michales	D	A		

Dual League
Arvin	6-0
Wasco	5-1
Shafter	2-4
Taft	0-6

SSL Tournament
Arvin	188.5
Wasco	173.5
Shafter	164.5
Taft	43

Shafter coaches Darrell Fletcher, left, and Kalman Matis

SSL - Wasco
February 9, 1973

95
| Machado | Ed | A | 7-0 | |
| Brashear | Charles | T | | |

103
| George | Randy | T | 10-0 | |
| Sanchez | Ruben | A | | |

112
| Lopeteguy | Joey | | 2-0 | |
| Rugnao | John | A | | |

120
| Affentranger | Franc | | 10-2 | |
| Rodriguez | Richard | A | | |

127
| Lopez | Joe | S | Fall | 2:19 |
| Stroud | David | T | | |

133
| Catles | Alan | S | Fall | 2:29 |
| McDonnell | Kevin | T | | |

138
| Tataum | Jesse | W | Fall | :33 |
| Sage | Bob | S | | |

145
| Affentranger | Anton | S | Fall | 2:31 |
| Lewis | David | W | | |

154
| Painter | Paul | S | Fall | 2:34 |
| Crosby | Randy | W | | |

165
| Williams | Carey | W | Default | |
| Williams | Gilbert | S | | |

175
| Clement | Terry | W | Fall | 1:33 |
| Shaw | Fred | T | | |

191
| Johnson | Mike | W | 32-4 | |
| Akman | Terry | S | | |

HWT
| Freitas | Stan | T | 6-3 | |
| Williams | Myron | W | | |

Dual League   Season
| Shafer | 4-2 | 5-0-1* |
| Wasco | | 7-1-1 |

SSL Tournament
Shafer	104
Wasco	96
Taft	58.5
Arvin	40

* Shafer won the dual meet championship

1966 – First Shafter High Wrestling Team

SSL – Coalinga
February 9, 1974

95
Affentranger	Martin	S	8-6	
Dillingham	Jimmy	W		
Corten	Heriberto	COR	9-1	
Rodriguez	Rudy	COAL		

103
Hunt	Ron	W	5-2	
Watts	Dwight	S		
Ceballos	Raul	COR	1-0	
Bowman	Earl	M		

112
Guerrero	Eugene	COR	9-4	
Sanders	Bobby	S		
Terry	Doug	W	3-2	
Moore	Bruce	COAL		

120
Balderama	Benny	COR	3-0	
Carmargo	Eddie	W		
Arredondo	Lupe	COAL	Fall	3:32
Woodruff	Ken	M		

127
Affentranger	Franc	S	Fall	2:18
Marroquin	Rene	M		
Gutierrez	Jose	W	Fall	2:20
Cruz	Ralph	COR		

133
Lopez	Joe	S	4-0	(40-1)*
Loomis	Kevin	W		
Howard	Chuck	COAL	7-2	
Perezoa	Richard	COR		

138
Lopeteguy	Joey	S	Fall	2:42
Ramirez	Tommy	M		
Barza		COR		
No Match				

145
Lewis	David	W	Fall	1:00
Turpin	Ben	COR		
No Match				

154
Moz	Danny	COR	9-7	
Roque		W		
Green	Dave	COAL	Fall	5:10
Williams	Marcus	S		

165
Williams	Cary	W	Fall	3:00
Williams	Norman	S		
Garcia	Matt	COR	Default	
Previtt	Bob	COAL		

175
Moz	B	COR	5-1	
Rey	Arthur	W		
Farmer	Scott	S	Dec.	
Neal	Roger	COAL		

191
Clement	Terry	W	Fall	:36
Gilbert	Jim	COR		
Whorton	Randy	M	Fall	2:19
Calder	Paul	S		

HWT
Williams	Myron	W	6-0	
Akman	Terry	S		
Kavarian	Don	M	Fall	3:27
Hernandez		COR		

* Season record

SSL Tournament
Wasco	109 (14-0 Season)
Shafter	90
Corcoran	83
Coalinga	41
McFarland	11

SSL - Shafter
February 15, 1975

95
Padilla	Tony	W	Fall	1:32
Marroquin	Tony	M		
Bender	Scott	S		
Mundy	Curtis	COAL		

103
Lamas	Mike	S	Fall	1:50
Arjornia	Rick	M		
Camargo		W	9-0	
Watanabe	John	COAL		

112
Sanders	Bob	S	Fall	1:45
Dillingham	Jim	W		
Cortez	Herberto	COR	14-3	
Herrera		M		

120
Arredono		COAL	9-7	
McWhorter	Steve	S		
Hunt	R	W	8-4	
Lerma	Armando	COR		

127
Mirelez	John	S	9-0	
Marroquin	John	M		
Terry	Doug	W	6-2	
Torres		COR		

133
Lopez	Joe	S	Fall	3:24
Myrick	Steve	M		
Foots	Lester	W	Forfeit	

138
Lovenguth	Chuck	COAL	8-0	
Cruz	Lolo	COR		
Hammett	Tomo	W	13-1	
Espinoza	Jose	S		

145
Rodriguez	Domingo	W	13-7	
Mejia	Tony	COR		
Turpin	Don	COAL	6-2	
Griffith	Steve	S		

154
Green	Dave	COAL	3-1	
Spoisdoff	George	W		
Branch	John	S	Fall	3:23
Hurst	Brian	M		

165
Williams	Cary	W	Fall	3:06
Longorgia	Luis	M		
Hernandez		COR	9-4	
Martin	Dennis	S		

175
Williams	Norman	S	11-0	
Spoisdoff	Alex	W		
Burk	Allen	M	Fall	2:14
Weekley	Gus	COAL		

191
Gilbert	Grant	COR	3-0	
Lovenguth	Desi	COR		
Richardson		W	Fall	3:24
Lowery	Mike	M		

HWT
Williams	Myron	W	Fall	2:41
Kavarian	Don	M		
Calder	Paul	S	Fall	2:41
Quintinilla	Ruben	COR		

SSL Tournament
WASCO	165
Shafter	149
McFarland	111 (7-6 Dual Season)
Coalinga	98
Cocoran	5.5

Notes
- Wasco was the undefeated dual meet champion of the SSL.
- Joe Lopez was Four-Time SSL Champion and never lost a SSL Dual or Tournament Match

SSL - Corcoran
February 14, 1976

95
Bender	Scott	S	4-1
Moreno	Vince	W	
Villerreal	Luis	COR	
Forfeit			

103
Padilla	Tony	W	Fall	1:47
Marroquin	Author	M		
Gallegos	P	COR	Fall	4:10
Duran	Francisco	COAL		

112
Affentranger	Martin	S	Fall	2:19
Salinas	Santos	M		
Foots	Julest	W	Fall	2:50
Cruz	Lalo	COR		

120
Lamas	Mike	S	12-6	
Hunt	Ron	W		
Cortez	Herbert	COR	Fall	:58
Salas	Joey	COAL		

127
Dillingham	Jim	W	16-10
McWorther	Steve	S	
Garza	Francisco	M	23-4
Aguirre	Manuel	COR	

133
Miralez	John	S	10-3
Myrick	Steve	M	
Foots	Lester	W	6-3
Baggs	Larry	COAL	

138
Hammett	Tom	W	O.T.	1:57
Cruz	Lalo	COR		
Smith	Robert	S	6-2	
Maroquin	Johnny	M		

145
Summers	Terry	W	4-3	
Mejia	Tony	COR		
Branch	John	S	O.T.	3-1
Venezuela	Angel	COAL		

154
Moz	Ray	COR	O.T.	6-0
Moore	Ray	W		
Vasquez	Urbano	M	O.T.	1-0
Lambert	Scott	COAL		

165
Spoidoff	Alex	W	24-0
Sanchez	Ray	COAL	
Hurst	Brian	M	
Forfeit			

175
Weekley	Gus	COAL	6-0
Soto	Albert	W	
Williams	Danny	COR	
Forfeit			

191
Williams	Norman	S	Fall	1:22
Richardson	Luis	W		
Chrisp	Willie	COR		
Forfeit				

HWT
Wedel	Jay	W	16-2	
Mata	Amando	COR		
Lovenguth	Desi	COAL	Fall	2:55
Kavarian	Don	M		

Dual League
Wasco	8-0
Shafter	6-2

SSL Tournament
Wasco	146
Shafter	91
Corcoran	76.5
Coaling	44
McFarland	42

Notes
Wasco Won 28 SSL Dual Meets in A Row

SSL – McFarland
February 12, 1977

95
Osorna	Ray	M	10-2	
Ramero	George	W		
Elrich	Ted	S	16-3	
Duran	Dave	COAL		

103
Bender	Scott	S	11-2	
Gonzales	Steve	M		
Moreno	George	W	11-2	
Apodaca	Victor	COAL		

112
Affentranger	Martin	S	10-5	
Padilla	Tony	W		
Mendez	Luis	M	7-0	
Villareal	Lewis	COR		

120
Affentranger	Henry	S	21-3	
Pachco	Tony	COR		
Marroquin	Arthur	M	6-1	
Guevera	M	W		

127
Lopez	Julio	S	5-1	
Skeels	K	W		
Garza	Francisco	M	Fall	5:55
Aguirre	Manuel	COR		

133
Apodaca	Ernie	COAL	
Froehlich			
Forfeit			
Forfeit			

138
Morales	John	S	Fall	3:36
Marroquin	Johnny	M		
Sanchez	M	W	Fall	3:45
Atarr		M		

145
Hernstedt	Dan	W	Fall	5:13
Martinez	Israel	COR		
Prewitt	Greg	COAL	6-2	
Reimer	D	W		

154
Giovanetti	Roger	S	4-0	
Vasquez	Urbano	M		
Boydstun	D	W	Fall	1:57
Venten				

165
Moore	Ken	W	14-2 Maj. Dec.	
Bartheime	Mike	M		
Griffith	Steve	S	12-5	
Lopez				

175
Guiton	Miles	W	7-3	
Sanchez		COR		
Lynch	Gary	S	3-0	
Guevarra		M		

191
*Martin	Dennis	S	Fall	3:36
Stenson	Steve	COR		
Colbert				
Forefeit				

HWT
Mootry	Ken	S	5-1	
Mata	Armando	COR		
Montoya	Richard	M	4-3	
Wedel	Jay	W		

*Martin 23-0 (record)

Dual League
Shafter	8-0
Wasco	6-2
McFarland	4-4

SSL Tournament
Shafter	178.5
Wasco	139.5
McFarland	113.5
Coaling	63.5
Corcoran	63

SSL – Wasco
February 15, 1978

95
Rodriguez	Phillip	S	14-10	
Torres	Juan	COAL		

103
Bender	Scott	S	Fall	3:06
Duran	Dave	COAL		

112
Romero	George	W	7-4
Bonilla	Marty	COR	
Elrich	Ted	S	

120
Affentranger	Henry	S	20-5
Pacheco	Tony	COR	
Camargo	Eric	W	

127
Lopez	Julio	S	9-1
Torres	Jelthe	W	
Villareal	Lewis	COR	

133
Delgado	Jose	S	7-1
Gallegos	Armando	COR	
Salas	Joey	COAL	

138
Reyna	Juan	W	Fall	3:14
Cruz	Richard	COR		
Cloud	Tommy	S		

145
Prewitt	Greg	COAL	9-5
Reimer	David	W	
Martinez	Israel	COR	

154
Giovannetti	Roger	S	Fall	3:37
Martinez	Isaac	COR		
Cole	Toby			

165
Hernandez	Ramero	W	Fall	4:22
Criswell	David	S		
Wilson	Lonnie	COAL		

175
Moore	Ken	W	Fall	5:28
Htumbo	Tom	S		

191
Mootry	Ken	S	6-3
Stenson	Steve	COR	
Funk	Kendall	W	

HWT
Martin	Dennis	S	Fall	4:44
Wilson	Danny	W		
Price	Mark	COR		

Dual League   **Season**
Shafter   6-0   7-1

SSL Tournament
Shafter   161.5
Wasco   127
Corcoran   95
Coaling   65

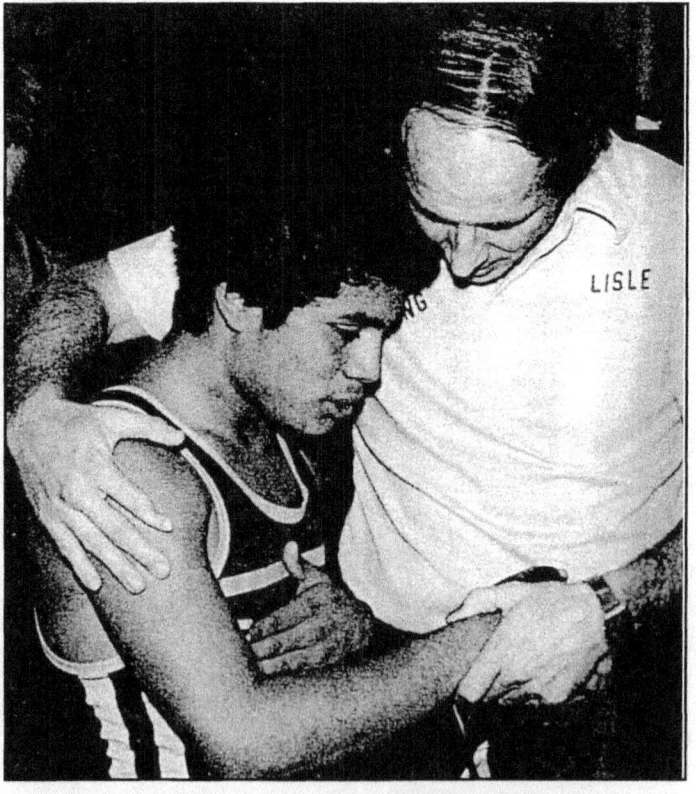

Coach Lisle Gates of Shafter High

SSL – Corcoran
February 10, 1979

95
| Harrison | Keith | W | |
| Torres | | COR | |

103
| Medina | Alex | COR | O.T. 4-0 |
| Case | Floyd | S | |

112
| Moreno | Vince | W | |
| Ulrich | Ted | S | |

120
NOT GIVEN

127
| Lopez | Julio | S | Fall | (21-2)* |
| Duran | Dave | COR | | |

133
| Salas | Ted | COAL | 12-6 |
| Camargo | Eric | W | |

138
| Martinez | Israel | COR | 9-3 |
| Mirelez | Tom | S | |

145
| Reyna | Juan | W | 13-0 |
| Duckett | Shane | S | |

154
| Valdez | Roy | S | 6-4 |
| Prewitt | Greg | COAL | |

165
| Giovannetti | Roger | S | 3-0 |
| Pierson | F | W | |

175
| Criswell | David | S | Fall |
| Jones | Kimmy | COR | |

191
| Stenson | Steve | COR | Fall |
| Ackman | Larry | S | |

HWT
| Valenzuela | Alex | COAL | |
| Wilson | Danny | W | |

* Record

SSL Tournament
Shafter	135.5
Wasco	129
Corcoran	100
Coalinga	91

Notes
Shafter and Wasco Tied for the SSL Dual Meet Championship 5-1

Back: Coach Gates, D. Vasquez, J. Plaza, E. Williams, M. Brown, H. Ricks, J. Jones. Front: A. Falcone, R. Gomez, D. Cruz, R. Delarosa, A. Belaza, R. Dooling, R. Brown, J. Flud.

1987 Shafter High Wrestling Team

SSL – Shafter
February 15, 1980

95
Cruz	Danny	S	Fall	2:25
Wood	N	W		
Reynolds		COR	Fall	
Swinney	Frank	COAL		

103
Gomez	Rene	S	Fall	1:59
Heady	Sam	COAL		
Blackwood		W		
Forfeit				

112
Borrego	Israel	S	12-10	
Smith		W		
Ambriz	Ernie	COR	Fall	5:16
Deathridge	Tim	COAL		

120
Sanchez		W	19-6	
Duran	David	COAL		
Dooling	Ronny	S	Fall	2:43
Martinez	Raul	COR		

127
Llanas	Ricardo	S	21-2
Hatassy		W	
Jones	Brian	COAL	9-0
Ambriz	Robert	COR	

133
Flud	Johnny	S	16-3
Comerer		COAL	
Edwards		W	7-5
Cruz	Gustavo	COR	

138
Bonilla	Henry	COR	Fall	2:04
Jones	Robert	COAL		
Duckett	Shane	S		
Forfeit				

145
Martinez	Israel	COR	2-0
Pearson	E	W	
Williams	Earl	S	13-4
Roberts	Mark	COAL	

154
Delgado	Jose	S		
Thierry	Leonard	COR		
Fowler	Charles	COAL		
Forfeit				

165
Ricks	Herbie	S	Fall	1:38
Millus	Clarence	COR		
Peters	Russell	W		
Forfeit				

175
Brown	Mike	S	Fall	2:05
West	Eddie	W		
Ramsey	Greg	COAL	Fall	4:27
Brown	Kevin	COR		

191
Torigani	Pat	S	14-2
Burganstarsser	Mark	W	
Reyna	Juan	COAL	
Forfeit			

HWT
Morley	Phillip	W	Fall	1:36
Preeds				
None				
None				

Dual League
Shafter 6-0

Season
8-1-1

SSL Tournament
Shafter 223.5
Wasco 140
Coalinga 109.5
Corcoran 90

Coalinga High's Brian Jones (top)

SSL – Shafter
February 11, 1981

95
Gomez	Rene	S	Fall	2:11
Pizana	Raul	COAL		
Adams	C	W	Fall	2:19
Freeman		O		

103
Cruz	Danny	S	Fall	1:58
Ward		W		
Simon	Jon	COAL		
Forfeit				

112
Presley	Joe	S	Fall	2:29
Pleceio		O		
Hinojosa	Cezar	W		
Forfeit				

120
Kurfess	Leland	S	Fall	2:11
Avila		O		
Heisley		W	12-7	
Deathridge	Tim	COAL		

127
Jones	Brian	COAL		
Garza	Ray	S		
Ambriz	Ernesto	COR	12-6	
Edwards		W		

133
Comerer	Leon	COAL	Fall	2:43
Edwards		W		
Dooling	Ronnie	S	Fall	5:38
Ramos	Ramon	COR		

138
Flud	Johnny	S	25-12	
Comerer	Greg	COAL		
Legis		W		
Morales	Bob	O		

145
Vasquez	Daniel	S	7-1	
Carmago	Eric	W		
Cruz	Gustavo	COR	Fall	4:36
Legos		W		

154
Williams	Earl	S	4-1	
Stamsbaugh	L	W		
Roberts	Mark	COAL		
Hernandez	Steve	COR		

167
West	Eddie	W	9-7	
Brown	Mike	S		
Fowler	Charles	COAL		
Forfeit				

180
Ricks	Herbie	S	Fall	1:19
Pacheco	Tommy	COR		
Skaggs	Robby	COAL	13-11	
Nelson		W		

200
Ramsey	Greg	COAL	10-6	
Burganstarsser	Mark	W		
Brown	Kevin	COR	Fall	2:00
Reyna	Daniel	O		

HWT
Morley	Phillip	W	Fall	4:26
Jones	James	S		
Anaya		COR	Fall	2:51
Rodriguez	Ramon	O		

SSL Tournament
Shafter	189	Corcoran	56.5
Wasco	146	Orosi	44
Coalinga	71.5	(Shafter 6-0 in SSLDuals)	

Coalinga High's Leon Comerer

SSL – Shafter
February 11, 1982

95
| Gonzales | Ricky | S | 10-2 |
| Nix | Bill | W | |

103
| Cruz | Danny | S | Fall 1:40 |
| Pizana | Raul | | |

112
| Gomez | Rene | S | Fall 2:06 |
| Wood | Norman | W | |

120
| Williams | Jeff | S | Fall 6-0 |
| Hinojosa | Cezar | W | |

127
| Presley | Joe | S | Fall 3:15 |
| Hallmark | Mike | W | |

133
| Cates | Roy | S | 11-5 |
| ElCarno | Cecino | W | |

138
| Jones | Brian | COAL | 8-4 |
| Cox | Greg | S | |

145
| Vasquez | Daniel | S | 11-4 |
| Comerer | Greg | COAL | |

154
| Brown | Rodney | S | 12-4 |
| Flower | Charles | COAL | |

167
| Brown | Mike | S | 14-2 |
| Skaggs | Robby | COAL | |

180
| Nelson | Melvin | W | 15-2 |
| Boger | Shane | COR | |

200
| Ramsey | Greg | COAL | Default |
| Jones | James | S | |

HWT
| Morley | Phillip | W | Fall 1:18 |
| Coffee | Pat | | |

SSL Tournament   **Dual League**
Shafter	212	6-0
Wasco	175	
Coalinga	45.5	
Corcoran	31.5	

Back: J. Lopez, G. Cox, R. Brown, M. Brown, J. Jones, B. Clark, P. Coffee, D. Vasquez, Coach Gates Front: R. Gonzales, D. Cruz, R. Gomez, R. Molina, J. Presley, R. Cates.

1982 SSL Champions Shafter High

SSL – Coalinga
February 10, 1983

100
| Lamas | Mark | S | Fall | 2:20 |
| Eastman | Jamie | COAL | | |

107
| Martinez | Manuel | S | 19-4 | |
| Reynaso | Jamie | W | | |

115
| Gomez | Rene | S | Fall 2nd Period | |
| Valenuela | Julian | COAL | | |

119
| Cruz | Dan | S | 9-0 | |
| Pizada | Raul | Coal | | |

126
| Molina | Robert | S | Fall | :35 |
| Hestar | Terriell | | | |

132
| Pressley | Joe | S | Fall 3rd Period | |
| Arridondo | Angel | COAL | | |

138
| Garza | Ray | S | 8-5 | |
| Lara | Jose | W | | |

145
| Cates | Roy | S | Fall | 1:49 |
| Kent | Dystary | W | | |

155
| Brown | Rodney | S | Fall | 3:50 |
| Jones | Robert | COAL | | |

167
| Clark | Brent | S | 19-8 | |
| Sanchez | Roger | | | |

180
| Pacheco | Tommy | COR | |
| Lee | Kenney | S | |

200
Not provided

245
| Pankey | Jeff | S | Fall 2nd Period |
| Ramey | Robert | COAL | |

SSL Tournament
Shafter
Wasco
Coalinga

Joe Presley (top) of Shafter High

SSL – Wasco
February 11, 1984

100
Not provided

105
| Maldonado | Louie | S | 1st |

112
| Lamas | Mark | S | 1st |

119
| Molina | Robert | S | 2nd |

126
| Williams | Jess | S | 1st |

132
Not provided

138
Not provided

145
| Presley | Joe | S | 2nd |

154
| Cates | Roy | S | 1st |

167
Not provided

180
Not provided

HWT
| Pankey | Jeff | S | 1st |

Dual Champion: Woodlake
Woodlake
Shafter
Caruthers
Wasco
Coalinga

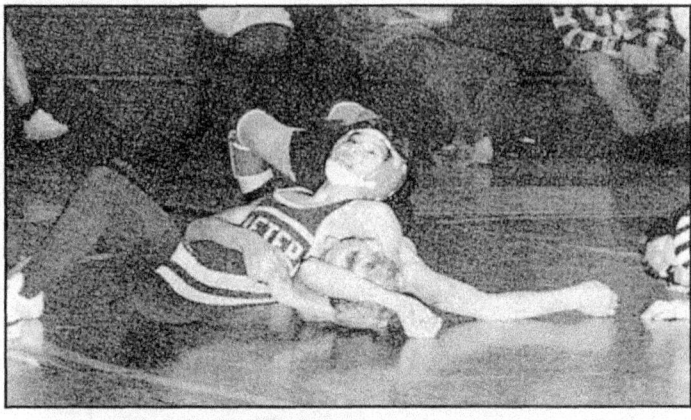

Louie Maldonado of Shafter High

Mark Lamas of Shafter High

SSL – Woodlake
February 9, 1985

100
Not provided

105
Maldonado Louie S 2nd

112
Not provided

119
Nickell Troy S 2nd

126
Not provided

132
Not provided

138
Hipolito Abel S 1st

145
Not provided

154
Not provided

167
Not provided

180
Not provided

HWT
Miller Tommy S 1st

SSL Tournament
Caruthers
Woodlake
Shafter

**Shafter High
Coach Steve Nickell**

Bottom Row left to right: R. George, D. Farris, D. Frashear, J. Willingham, H. Caneles, K. Powe, G. Morris. Top Row: Coach Garrett, D. Ward, B. Hollingsworth, G. Price, J. Watts, D. Saylor, M. Kelley.

1971 Taft High Wrestling Team

SSL – McFarland
February 13, 1986

100
Elisondo	Ben	S		2nd

105
Maldonado	Louie	S	9-2 (30-11)*1st	
Sullivan	Andrew	W		2nd

112
Not provided

119
Not provided

126
Perez	Sergio	S		3rd

132
Vaughn	Terry	S	Fall 1:35 (33-8)* 1st	
Gallardo	Juan	W		2nd

138
Lopez	Mondo	S		4th

145
Epperly	John	S		2nd

154
Gomez	Xavier	S		3rd

167
Hill	Jon	S		4th

180
Not provided

194
Thompson	Kelly	S		2nd

HWT

*Season Record

Unbeaten SSL Duals: Wasco
Shafter Season Record 1-9

SSL Tournament
Wasco	145
Shafter	109.5
McFarland	104.5
Coalinga	103
Avenal	77

Front row, l to r: M. Burleson, Mat Maid, B. Elisondo, P. Cloud, Mat Maid. Second row: J. Epperly, S. Valdez, L. Maldonado, X. Gomez. Third row: K. Thompson, R. Torigiani, Coach McKinney, T. Vaughn, P. Miller.

1986 Shafter High Wrestling Team

Shafter High Coach Rick McKinney

SSL – Coalinga
February 12, 1987

105
Arrelano   Danny   W   1st

112
Not provided

119
Not provided

125
Paul   Steve   W   2nd

130
Elholm   Garrett   W   3rd

135
Sanchez   Raul   W   3rd

140
Not provided

145
Not provided

152
Not provided

160
Not provided

171
Not provided

189
Gafner   Randy   W   2nd

215
Not provided

HWT
Ortiz   Johnny   W   5th

Dual League   **Season**
Shafter   4-0   7-9
Wasco   1-3

Shafter High's Ernie Hernandez (top)

Coalinga High's Jack Valenzuela (top)

SSL – Shafter
February 12, 1988

95
Serda	Mike	W	Fall	1:50
Salazar	Alan	S		
Garza	Jamie	M	Fall	3:13
Sirman	Leis			

103
Elisondo	Ben	S	Inj. Def.	
Tackett	Sal	W		
Barajas	Robert	COR	9-0	
Guerra	Jose	M		

112
Perez	Mario	S	15-2	
Huerta	Juan	M		
McGowen	Brent	COR	Fall	4:20
Rodriguez	Jose	W		

120
Bonilla	Gabe	COR	16-3	
Purcill	Sid	W		
Elisondo	Eli	S	Inj. Def.	
Escobar	Javier	COAL		

127
Soto	Fernando	M	8-2	
Ramirez	Andrew	COR		
Escondon	Robert	COAL	Fall	2:48
Tackett	Devin	W		

133
Paul	Brent	W	11-0	
Newby	James	Coal		
Perez	Sergio	S	7-6	
Perezchica	Sergio	M		

138
Paul	Steve	W	8-2	
Komin	Mike	S		
Thierry	Leland	COR	6-3	
Diaz	Ricardo	M		

145
Sullivan	Andrew	W	11-9	
Brice	Darrin	S		
Soliz	Mark	COR	Inj. Def.	
Salazar	Felincio	M		

154
Gomez	Fendencio	S	16-1	
Mellow	Brett	M		
Mereno	Javier	COAL	9-1	
Serda	Dan	W		

167
Deverick	Jason	COAL	Fall	:49
Soto	Alex	M		
Roper	Raymond	S	16-0	
Rollins	James	W		

174
Campos	Ed	COR	8-6	
McFarland	Jim	M		
Lopez	Mando	S	Fall	2:07
Acebedo	Ben	W		

191
Madrid	Ray	COR	19-14	
Martinez	Al	M		
Bloemhof	David	S	Fall	:30
Ince	Shawn	W		

HWT
Martinez	David	M	Fall	5:26
Aguillar	Thomas	COAL		
Martinez	Brian	S	16-22	
Giles	Brett	COR		

Dual League
McFarland	4-0
Shafter	3-1

Season
7-8

SSL Tournament
Shafter	160.5
McFarland	146.5
Wasco	140
Corcoran	119.5
Coalinga	75.5

SSL – Wasco
February 9, 1989

100
Serda	Mike	W	Fall	1:35
Bustos	E	COR		
Irigoyen	Julian	S		

105
Baraja	O	COR	15-5	
Salazar	Allen	S		

112
Elisando	Ben	S	11-8	
Huerta	Juan	M		

119
Perez	Roy	COR	Fall	5:10
Guerra				
Frey	Steve	S		

126
Donilla		COR	6-4	
Perez	Mario	S		

132
Perezchiza	Sergio	M	8-4	
Scott	Pat	W		
Jemenez	Frank	S		

138
Soto	Fernando	M	7-2	
Wise	Geordy	S		

145
Komin	Mike	S	6-2	
Thierry		COR		

154
Martinez	Nacho	W	5-2	
Moreno	Javier	COAL		
Bice	Darrin	S		

165
Soliz	Mark	COR	8-2	
Roper		S		

175
Deverick	Jason	COAL	Fall	:42
Gutierrez	Noe	S		

191
Mello	Brett	M	5-7	
Serda	Dan	W		
Velasco	Jimmy	S		

HWT
Aguillar	Jesus	COAL	Fall	5:20
Giles		COR		
Parish	Chris	S		

Dual League   **Season**
Shafter   3-1   9-6

SSL Tournament
Corcoran	136.5
Shafter	133
McFarland	108.5
Wasco	81
Coalinga	67

Shafter High's Mario Perez (top)

Shafter High's Darrin Bice

SSL - McFarland
February 8, 1990

95
| Serda | Mike | W | Fall | 2:00 |
| Pesina | Otillo | M | | |

103
| Alatorre | Salvador | M | Fall | 1:41 |
| Hobs | Chad | COAL | | |

112
| Salazar | Allen | S | Fall | 3:04 |
| Guzman | Freddy | | | |

120
| Rodriguez | Aaron | W | | |
| Default | | | | |

127
| Honea | Ryan | W | Fall | 4:20 |
| Barajas | Oscar | COR | | |

133
| Purcella | Sid | W | T.F. 21-4 |
| Gome | Joey | COR | |

138
| Guzman | Joseph | COR | 6-3 |
| Guerra | Jose | M | |

145

154
Brice	Darren	S	D.Q.
Martinez	Nacho	W	27-1
Connelly	John		

165
| Soto | Alex | M | 7-6 |
| Hair | Mike | S | |

175
| Claytoon | Terry | S | 5-4 |
| Rosas | Jesus | COR | |

191
| Mello | Brett | M | 4-2 |
| Soliz | Mike | COR | |

HWT
| Martinez | David | M | O.T. 3-2 |
| Ocampos | Fernando | W | |

Dual Season   Record
| Shafter | 3-1 | 6-2 |
| McFarland | 2-2 | |

*Corcoran was the Dual Meet champion plus SSL Champions

SSL Tournament
McFarland	147
Corcoran	127
Wasco	113.5
Shafter	112.5
Coalinga	76

Top Row: Mr. Cleveland, Mr. Peters, Josh Cleveland, Brian Hosman, Javier Moreno, Joesph Lopez, and J.J. Martinez. Middle Row: Lupe Espinoza, Jesus Rosas, Rigoberto Navarro, Mark Evans, Jesus Lopez, Leaf Sirman, and Lane Underwood. Bottom Row: Gerald Jones, Cole Gould, Justin Garcia, Chad Hobbs, and Mike Lopez.

1990 Coalinga Wrestling Team

SSL – Arvin
February 8, 1991

103
| Serda | Mike | W | Fall |
| Rubinol | Jesse | A | |

112
| Sanchez | Mark | A | Fall |
| Prendez | Jacob | S | |

119
| Aceves | Jose | A | 5-4 |
| Irogoyen | Julian | S | |

125
| Gonzales | Angel | A | Fall |
| Werdell | Jeremy | W | |

130
| Rodriguez | Aaron | W | Dec. |
| Calvillo | Isaias | A | |

135
| Alejo | Alex | A | Dec. |
| Salazar | Joe | S | |

140
| Wise | Geordy | S | Dec. |
| Sanchez | Miguel | A | |

145
| Goodwin | Chuck | A. | Dec. |
| Honea | Ryan | W | |

152
| Martinez | Nacho | W | Dec. |
| Duenas | Johnny | A | |

160
| Amaya | Julian | A | Dec. |
| Jones | Brian | S | |

171
| Serda | Daniel | W | Dec. |
| Clayton | Terry | S | |

189
| Gutierrez | Noe | S | Dec. |
| Bazaldua | Leo | A | |

HWT
| Godinez | Gabriel | A | Dec. |
| O'Campo | Fernando | W | |

Wasco: Dual Meet Champion
Arvin: Overall SSL Champion
Taft: No Varsity Team/First Year Back in Wrestling

Dual League		Season
Shafter	2-4	3-5

SSL Tournament
Arvin	200
Wasco	155
Shafter	135

Brian Jones (top) of Shafter High and Nacho Martinez of Wasco High

**Geordy Wise
Shafter High**

SSL – Shafter
February 14, 1992

103
Rubinal	Jesus	A	T.F. 15-0	
Coughenour	Chris	W		
Akerman	Matt	S		

112
Rivera	Anthony	A	(23-6)*	Fall 5:08
Prendez	Jacob	S		
Beltrain	Eric	W		

119
Aceves	Jose	A	4-1	(22-7)*
Delarosa	Johnny	S		(15-8)*
Zepeda	Carlos			

125
Negrete	Carlos	S	Maj. 16-5
De La Rosa	Ruben	W	(20-8)*
Galvan	Frank	A	

130
Garcia	Juan	A	Fall	5:00
Escalante	Juan	W		
Albiar	Fernando	S		

135
Rodriguez	Aaaron	W	Fall	2:16
Gomez	Raul	A		
Torres	Mario	S		

140
Sedillo	Alex	S	8-7
Graham	Bobby	A	
Wedel	Jeremy	W	

145
Colvert	Dusty	S	Fall	4:43

Siemens	Nate	W	
Sanchez	Nori	A	

152
Honea	Ryan	W	7-1
Goodwin	Chuck	A	
Brown	Mark	S	

160
Martinez	Nacho	W	Sup. Dec. 20-9
Amaya	Julian		
Sharp	Mark	S	

171
Smith	Jason	S	Fall	3:22
Bevan	Jascon	T		
Gallardo	Juan	W		

189
Bazaldua	Leo	A	5-4
Perez	Mario	S	
Chavez	Hector		

HWT
Gonzales	Jack	S	Fall	2:22
O'Campo	Eddie			
None				

* Record

Dual League
Shafter 3-2

Season
3-3

SSL Tournament
Wasco 167
Shafter 153
Arvin 151.5
Taft 22

Shafter High's Johnny DeLaRosa

**Fernando Albiar
Shafter High**

SSL – Wasco
February 11, 1993

103
Kingsbury	Ryan	TE	T.F. 18-3
Criner	Tony	W	
Gutierrez	Vincent	SH	
Josin	Joey	ST	

112
Misller	Jeff	ST	7-6
Dickerson	Joe	SH	
Serda	Eric	W	
Gropp	Barry	TE	

119
Beltran	Eric	W	O.T. 12-10
Dee	Matt	ST	
Rouse	Steve	TA	
Williams	David	TE	

125
Zendejas	Aaron	TE	Fall 3:09
Zepeda	Carlos	W	
Roper	Jeremy	SH	
Markely	Benny	ST	

130
De La Rosa	Johnny	SH	O.T. 11-9
Forshay	Ken	TE	
Foster	Damion	W	
Danstead	Derek	ST	

135
Rodriguez	Aaron	W	Fall 3:08
			(40-0 4xSSL Champion)
Davis	Jason	TE	
Mesa	Jason	ST	
Albair	Fernando	SH	

140
Flynn	Scott	ST	Fall 3:40
Escalante	Juan	W	
Castaneda	Ivan	TE	
Torres	Mario	SH	

145
Brommelsick	William	ST	6-4
Kingsbury	Tyson	TE	
Stockes	Rusty	SH	
Mudge	Tom	TA	

152
Sharp	Mike	ST	8-3
Siemans	Nate	W	
Bell	Brad	TE	
Hendricks	John	ST	

160
Kellor	Tony	TE	Fall 1:50
Lara	Loreto	SH	
Clark	Dennis	W	
No Fourth			

171
Beron	Jason	TA	Fall 2:21
Smith	Robert	SH	
Majonor	Steve	TE	
Gallardo	Alex	W	

189
Lockard	Mike	TE	5-2
Gallardo	Juan	W	
Yetter	Delbert	TA	
Montgomery	Brian	SH	

HWT
Gonzalez	Jack	SH	Fall :40
Cook	Shannon	ST	
Gutierrez	Larry	W	
Lockard	Ryan	TE	

Dual League
Tehachapi	4-0
Shafter	3-1
Wasco	2-2
Stockdale	1-3
Taft	0-4

SSL Tournament
Tehachapi	171
Shafter	153
Wasco	150
Stockdale	112
Taft	44

Season
8-5

SSL – Stockdale
February 11, 1994

103
Jamieson	Sam	W	Fall	1:10
Gutierrez	Art	SH		(23-2)*
Brooks	David	ST	10-3	
Bescom	Dewight	C		

112
Gutierrez	Vince	SH	O.T. 11-6	
Carrasco	Randy	T		
McGee	Aaron	ST	Fall	2:45
Kennedy	Steve	C		

119
Roper	Jeremy	SH	14-11	
Beltran	Eric	W		
Cervantez	Mike		6-4	
Odom	Dustin	T		

125
Zepeda	Carlos	W	11-2	
Prendez	Jacob	SH		
Machado	Matt	C	7-2	
Collins	Doyle	T		

130
Serda	Eric	W	11-5	
Mesa	Jason	ST		
Supertino	Victor	C	Fall	3:45
Albair	Fernando	SH		

135
Foster	Damion	W	9-1	
Uribe	Mark	St		
Espericueta	Eli	SH	7-6	
Gutierrez	Paul	C		

140
Flynn	Scott	ST	Fall	:47
Brown	Anthony	SH		
Cierley	Kevin	C	Maj. Dec. 13-0	
Caldwell	David	W		

145
Brommelsick	William	ST	9-4	
Linden	Joel	W		
Wilkins	Harvey	SH	Fall	:23
Moore	Jake	C		

152
Kingsbury	Tyson	T	Fall	
Gallardo	Alex	W		
Freeborn	Zak	SH	13-8	
Gentry	Sam	ST		

160
Arriaga	Ray	W	8-2	
Ferguson	Jon	ST		
Bender	Ted	C	Fall	2:28
Jimenez	Jose	SH		

171
Clark	Dennis	W	Fall	4:00
Colvard	Dusty	SH		
Kellor	Tony	T	Fall	2:37
Payne	Kevin	ST		

189
Gallardo	Juan	W	12-2	
Ray	Richey	ST		
Green	Mike	C	7-4	
Bermudez	Robert	SH		

HWT
Gutierrez	Larry	W	Fall	2:26
Espericueta	Frank	SH		
Cook	Shannon	ST	6-2	
Rocha	Jose	C		

* Record

Notes
■ Wasco 6-0 in Duals-SSL and 23-2 Season
■ Centennial was ineligible in team placing with 9th and 10th graders

SSL Tournament
Wasco	194.5
Shafter	153
Stockdale	138
Tehachapi	61

SSL – Centennial
February 10, 1995

103
Cortez	Danny	M	9-3
Bascon	Dwight	C	
Madrigal	Tony	S	7-5
Sanchez	Vincent	W	

112
Jameson	Sam	W	Fall 3:18 (32-7)*
Gutierrez	Art	S	
Wiebe	Justin	C	
No Entry			

119
Zepeda	Carlos	W	5-1
Cervantez	Mike	C	
Waldran	Jeremy	T	4-2
Gutierrez	Vince	S	

125
Serda	Eric	W	11-2
Roper	Jeremy	S	
Brooks	David	R	9-5
Spradlin	Matt	C	

130
Ramirez	Tommy	M	Fall 3:06
Criner	T.J.	W	
Cardova	Gabrial	S	Fall 1:47
Sandoval	Manny	T	

135
Espericueta	Eli	S	O.T. 10-8
Salinas	Elias	W	
Branch	B.J.	C	10-5
Salinas	Raul	T	

140
Landin	Jose	W	12-5
Hodges	Mark	S	
Lopez	Mike	M	4-3
Supertino	Vic	C	

145
Gallardo	Juan	W	Maj. Dec. 15-3
Kerste	Alman	T	
Gutierrez	Raul	C	Fall 3:57
Stone	Mark	S	

152
Cierley	Kevin	C	Maj. Dec. 15-3
Espericueta	Nate	S	
Ferrone	Robert	W	Fall 2:40
Carbajal	Daniel	T	

160
Freeborn	Zak	S	5-1
Gallardo	Alex	W	
Sandoval	Jose	C	11-5
Schneider	Luke	T	

171
Arriaga	Ray	W	Maj. Dec. 12-1
Bender	Ted	C	
Jimenez	Jose	S	Maj. Dec. 20-5
Ayon	Sid	M	

189
Martinez	Frank	W	Fall 5:41
Green	Mike	C	
Espericueta	Rocky	S	
No Entry			

HWT
Espericueta	Frank	S	4-2
Maldonado	Ruben	M	
Michael	Rooney	T	Fall 2:37
Angel	Mike	W	

* Record

SSL Tournament
Wasco	195.5
Shafter	157.5
Centennial	111
McFarland	71
Tehachapi	153
Ridgeview	21.5

SSL – Centennial
February 10, 1996

103
Cortez	Danny	M	9-5	
Baker	David	C		
Lopez	Juan	W	Fall	4:20
Cruz	Manual	S		

112
Bascom	Dwight	C	Tech. Fall. 17-2	
Sanchez	Anthony	S		
Long	Ken	W	7-5	
Jung	Brad	R		

119
Waldran	Jeremy	T	Fall	5:12
Weibe	Justin	C		
Armendaris	Alias	S		
Default				

125
Jameson	Sam	W	Fall	2:48
Gutierrez	Art	S		
Delcio	Josh	C		
Default				

130
Roper	Jeremy	S	8-4	
Branch	B.J.	C		
Burk	Sam	R		
Criner	T.J.	W		

135
Rushing	Eric	R	8-4	
Spradlin	Matt	C		
Farias	Rudy	S	10-2	
Landon	David	W		

140
Shearer	Ron	C	5-4	
Nickell	Jason	S		
Cox	Larry	R	Fall	1:38
Garza	Santos	M		

145
Gutierrez	Raul	C	Inj. Default	
Landin	Jose	W		
Renteria	Jesse	M		
Cardova	Gabriel	S		

152
Espericueta	Eli	S	5-3	
Reynolds	Steve	C		
Enriquez	Edger	M		
Default				

160
Harrington	Clint	C	Fall	5:13
Kerste	Alman	T		
Martinez	Narcy	W	T.F. 20-8	
Corbell	Scott	R		

171
Freeborn	Zak	S	10-5	
Schneider	Luke	T		
Herrera	Jason	C	Fall	2:05
Parton	Joe	W		

189
Martinez	Frank	W	Fall	5:19
Bender	Ted	C		
Nelson	Nick	T	Default	
Brown	Jeremy	S		

215
Sandoval	Jose	C	10-6	
Wedel	Nick	W		
Gonzales	John	M	Fall	4:25
Trotter	Jay	T		

275
Leisle	Rodney	R	Fall	3:52
Green	Mike	C		
Michael	Rodney	T	Fall	1:12
Marroquin	Gabe	W		

Dual League
		Season	
Centennial	5-0	16-5	
Shafter	4-1	5-3	
Wasco	2-2	3-3	
Tehachapi	2-3	2-3	
Ridgeview	1-4	1-4	
McFarland	0-4	0-4	

SSL Tournament
Centennial	203.5
Wasco	118
Shafter	113
Ridgeview	78.5
Tehachapi	67
McFarland	50.5

SSL – Shafter
February 15, 1997

103
Farrias	Matt	S	Fall	3:14
Macias	Eric	W		
Chin	Charles	R		
Forfeit				

112
Madrigal	Tony	S	Fall	3:52
Booker	Josh	T		
Barraza		W		
Forfeit				

119
Waldron	Jeremy	T	Fall	1:11
Jung	Brad	R		
Rodriguez		W	7-5	
Lucero		S		

125
Sanchez		W	Fall	4:28
Rueias				
Leyva	Nick	T		
Forfeit				

130
Landan		W	12-15	
Schneider	Josh	T		
Kroeker	Ryan	S		
Forfeit				

135
| Jameson | Sam | W | Fall | 3:11 |
| Schenider | Matt | T | | |

140
Wagner	Mike	R	Fall	3:51
Sandoval		S		
Collins	Doyle	T	Fall	2:35
Bell				

145
Brooks	David	R	8-0	
Juarez	Jose	S		
Marroquin	Gabe	W	Fall	3:20
Waldron	Jared	T		

152
Landin	David	W	Fall	1:20
Muller	Robert	R		
Noonan	Keith	T	8-4	
Morales		S		

160
Kerste	Alman	T	Fall	1:12
Froehlich		S		
Villalobos		W		
Forfeit				

171
Schneider	Josh	T	Fall	3:41
Corbell	Scott	R		
Garza		W		
Forfeit				

189
Martinez	Frank	W	11-7	
Tieyo	Jose	S		
Castella	Lon	T	6-5	
Corbeil	Scott	R		

215
Wedel	Nick	W	16-1	
Trofler	Jay	T		
Chicone		S		
Forfeit				

HWT
Leisle	Rodney	R	Fall	1:17
Michael	Rodney	T		
Nunez				
Forfeit				

Dual Meet Champion: Tehachapi
Co-Champions, SSL: Wasco and Tehachapi

SSL Tournament		Dual League	Season
Wasco			
Tehachapi			
Shafter	130	4-2	6-3
Ridgeview	107		

SSL – Tehachapi
February 12, 1998

105
| Macias | Eric | W | 1st |

112
| Madrigal | Tony | S | 1st |

119
| Farias | Matt | S | 1st |

125
| Waldrum | Jeremy | T | 1st |

130
| Jung | Brad | R | 1st |

135
| Sanchez | | W | 1st |

140
| Landin | David | W | 1st |

145
| Juarez | Jose | S | 1st |

152
| Sherry | Kris | T | 1st |

160
| Waldrum | Jared | T | 1st |

171
| Wagner | Mike | R | 1st |

189
| Wedel | | W | 1st |

215
| Martinez | Narcy | W | 1st |

275
| Michaels | Rodney | T | 1st |

Dual League   **Season**
Shafter   2-1   6-1
Ridgeview 2-2   3-2

SSL Tournament
Shafter   162
Ridgeview   145
Wasco   141
Tehachapi   139

1998 Shafter High Wrestling Team

SSL - Tehachapi
February 12, 1999

105
Stevens	Tim	S	Fall
Haddad	Tamara	T	

112
Sanchez	Ivan	A	Dec.
Madrigal	Freddy	S	
Clark	Justin	T	Dec.

119
Farias	Matt	S	Fall
Acosta	Pat	W	
Hernandez	Isaac	T	Dec.
Garcia		A	

125
Maldonado	Matt	S	Fall
Cox	Carvan	T	
Nunez		W	
Forfeit			

130
Angel	Jason	W	Dec.
Sampson	Mike	T	
Garcia	Jose	S	
Forfeit			

135
Rosales	Nick	A	Dec.
Preston	Josh	S	
Sawnson	Jeff	T	Dec.
Nunez		W	

140
White	Anthony	A	Dec.
Hooper	Jeremiah	S	
Lenichi		W	
Lynch	Sean	T	

145
Ruelas	Oscar	S	Fall
Greenan	Willie	T	
Clark		W	
Forfeit			

152
Jolly	Steven	S	Fall
Walz	Charlies	T	
Lopez		W	
Forfeit			

160
Landin	David	W	Dec.
Sherry	Kris	T	
Gullan		A	Dec.
Fraley	Matt	S	

171
Waldram	Jared	T	Dec.
Kroker	Ryan	S	

189
Pederson	Daniel	S	Fall
Nelson	Nathran	T	

215
Martinez	Narcy	W	Fall
Madrigal		A	
Bailey		S	Fall
Bray	Anthony	T	

HWT
Loyd	Greg	T	Fall
Sides	Daniel	S	

Dual League   **Season**
Shafter   5-0   7-1

SSL Tournament
Shafter   192
Tehachapi   148.5
Wasco   109
Arvin   82

SSL – Shafter
February 12, 2000

103
Carrasco	Jason	S
McCain		W
Whal	Danny	L
Renehau	Cari	T

112
Sanchez	Ivan	A
Alaniz	Luis	S
Leibman	David	T
Smith	Jason	L

119
Farias	Matt	S
Brook	Devin	A
Letourneau	Mike	L
Gonzales		W

125
Maldonado	Matt	S
Clark	Justin	T
Cemo	A.J.	L

130
Hernandez	Isaac	T
Angel		W
Stevens	Thomas	S
Phillips		L

135
Acosta	Patrick	W
Collins	Darren	T
Solis	Junior	L
Rodrigues		S

140
Hernandez	Joshua	T
Lopez	Juan	A
Lankford	Chris	L
Juarez		S

145
White	Anthony	A
Swanson	Jeff	T
Vega	Gilbert	L
Waldron	Lee	S

152
Jolley	Steven	S
Martinez		A
Baker		T
Lopez		W

160
Vasquez	Sal	A
Puch	Florian	S
Guilarducci	Jarred	L
Glass	Juston	T

171
Walz	Charlie	T
Rangel		W
Mireles	Vincente	A
Fraley	Matt	S

189
Pederson	Daniel	S
Nelson	Nathan	T
Garcia		W

215
Eilers	Justin	T
Myers	Grant	S
Vasquez		W
Singh	Mehtab	L

HWT
Loyd	Greg	T
Osuna	Marcos	A
Sides	Daniel	S
Amador		W

Dual League
		Season
Shafter	3-1	6-3

SSL Tournament
Tehachapi	178
Shafter	176
Arvin	109.5
Wasco	94.5
Liberty	

Note
League Rule: Liberty with F/S team couldn't score in SSL Tournament — League Record 3-1

Sal Vasquez
Arvin High

SSL – Shafter
February 9, 2001

103
Hernandez	Antonio	L	Fall	5:50
Parra	Joseph	S		
Rosales	Conrado	A	Fall	1:40
Gonzales		M		

112
Sanchez	Ivan	A	13-2	
Sanchez	Sal	W		
Alaniz	Luis	S	Fall	4:35
Wahl	Danny	L		

119
Carrasco	Jason	S	O.T. 6-4	
Landois	Orlando	W		
Aguirre	Daniel	A	11-5	
Williams	Jared	L		

125
Maldonado	Matt	S	Fall	1:27
Liebman	David	T		
Silva	Juan	W	7-3	
Salcido	Michael	A		

130
Madrigal	Freddie	S	10-8	
Cemo	A.J.	L		
Gonzalez	Dan	M	12-2	
Gonzales	Isaias	W		

135
Stevens	Tim	S	10-5	
Lorla	Rudy	M		
Lopez	Juan	A	Fall	:40
Brown	Collins	T		

140
Angel	Jason	W	13-9	
Lankford	Chris	L		
Lopez	David	S	6-3	
Eilers		T		

145
Acosta	Patrick	W	17-5	
Waldron	Lee	S		
Collins	Darren	T	12-3	
Glaser	Chad	L		

152
Jolley	Steven	S	13-8	
Swanson	Jeff	T		
Solis	Junior	L	5-2	
White	Anthony	A		

160
Rangel	Usbaldo	W	20-13	
Barker	Josh	T		
Guilarducci	Jarred	L	10-1	
Stevens	Thomas	S		

171
Aleman	Isaac	S	Fall :	34
Bishop	John	L		
Monge	Mario	A	9-5	
Wilson	Tim	T		

189
Garcia	Oscar	S	Fall	1:27
Garza	Nick	W		
Wilson	Ben	T	7-2	
Cervantes		L		

215
Eilers	Todd	T	Fall	1:23
Smith	Jason	L		
Ocampo	Raul	W	5-2	
Tomayo	Marco	A		

HWT
Sides	Dois	S	Fall	1:42
Gasco	Anthony	M		
Osuna	Marcos	A	Fall	3:55
Aguilera	Michael	W		

Dual League   Season
Shafter	5-0	6-1
Liberty	3-2	
Wasco	3-1-1	5-1-1
Tehachapi	2-2-1	
Arvin	2-3	
McFarland	0-5	

SSL Tournament
Shafter	227
Wasco	128
Liberty	125
Tehachapi	107
Arvin	104
McFarland	52

**Jason Carrasco
Shafter High**

SSL – Wasco
February 9, 2002

103
Hernandez	Antonio	L	9-2	
Parra	Joseph	S		
Gonzalez	Polo	M	2-1	
Hidalgo	Paul	A		

112
Cruz	Dustin	S	Fall	5:38
Herrera	Phillip	L		
Renehan	Cari	T	(Female) (10-14)*	

119
Anfonso	Chris	A	3-1	
Dawson	Beau	T		
Demers	Kyle	L	Fall	1:58
Plaza	M	S		

125
Tabada	Rudy	A	9-5	
Madrigan	Freddy	S		
Bullman		L	6-0	
Godschalk	Nelson	T		

130
Maldonado	Matt	S	14-3	
Cemo	A.J.	L		
Liedman	David	T	Fall	2:04
Cardoza	Chuck	M		

135
Carrasco	Jason	S	9-7	
Landois	Orlando	W		
Clark	Justin	T	5-2	
Christensen	Richard	L		

140
Points	Jason	L	15-4	
Hagar	Cody	T		
Tejeda	Alex	S	(15-1)	
Gaeta	Jose	A		

145
Collins	Darren	T	7-4	
Lankford	Chris	L		
Porter	J	S	Fall	2:59
Manriquez	David	A		

152
Hagar	Jared	T	Fall	1:49
Lopez	David	S		
Rodriguez	Matt	M	Bye	

160
Solis	Junior	L	13-2	
Clenard	Justin	T		
Mireles	Vincente	A	3-0	
Waters	Garret	S		

171
Bishop	John	L	10-3	
Statler	Marvin	S		
Wilson	Tim	T	5-4	
Harnandez	Humberto	W		

189
Guilarducci	Jarred	L	8-5	
Garcia	Marcos	S		
Ingraham	Jed	T	Fall	1:24
Marroquin	Jacob	M		

215
Sales	Marcelle	T	Fall	3:50
Espinoza	Adrian	M		
Picker	Cody	L	8-4	
Garza	Nick	W		

HWT
Williams	Jayson	S	5-3	
Osuna	Marcos	A		
Jensen	Jeremy	T	4-2	
Aguilera	Michael	W		

* Record

Dual League | Overall
Shafter	5-0	9-2
Liberty	4-1	5-2
Wasco	0-5	

SSL Tournament
(Co-Champs: Liberty, Shafter)

Liberty	201
Shafter	200
Tehachapi	197.5
Arvin	97
McFarland	54
Wasco	54

Matt Maldonado
Shafter High

SSL - McFarland Recreation Center
February 14, 2003

103
Gonzalez	Polo	M	5-3	
Parra	Joseph	S	(28-2)*	
Mesa	Rogelio	T	Fall	2:58
Kendig	Kayla	W		

112
Navarro	Vincent	S	Fall	1:22
Lazono	Eric	M		
Gonzalez	Rosa	W		

119
Cruz	Dustin	S	4-0	
Balasa	Joaquin	T		
Tamayo	Francisco	A	Fall	2:47
Sanchez	Earnie	W		
Navejar	Angel	M		

125
Tabada	Rudy	A	10-7	
Sanchez	Saul	W		
Block	Corey	S	12-8	
Avila	Osvaldo	M		

130
Espenicueta	Lucas	S	Forfeit	
Liebman	David	T		
Johnson	Zachery	W	Fall	3:10
Corona	Raul	A		

135
Tejeda	Alex	S	Fall	2:57
Clark	Jeremy	T		
Anaya	Robert	M		
Pineda	Carlos	A	Fall	2:20

140
Presley	Jason	S	Fall	5:54
Gaeta	Jose	A		
Cardoza	Chuck	M	4-0	
Poussan	Jeff	T		
Murritta	Isaac	W		

145
Landois	Orlando	W	Forfeit	
Waters	Garret	S		
Garcia	Jared	M	4-2	
Manriquez	David	A		
Liebengood	Thomas	T		

152
Carrasco	Jason	S	Fall	4:32
Paredes	Ricardo	A		
Tercy	Eric	T	Fall	5:55
Avila	Jacob	W		
Garcia	Manuel	M		

160
Clenard	Justin	T	12-5	
Mendez	Eddie	S		
Ramirez	Rudy	A	Forfeit	
Gonzalez	Ernie	M		

171
Wilson	Tim	T	10-6	
Garza	Nick	S		
Duran	Jason	A	6-3	
Marroquin	Jacob	M		

189
Ingram	Jedd	T	9-7	
Statler	Marvin	S		
Monge	Mario	A	7-3	
Flores	Jose	M		
Aguilera	Anthony	W		

215
Beltran	Francisco	S	6-2	
Balderas	Eric	A		
Sanchez	Carlos	W	Fall	5:45
Smith	Joe	T		

275
Williams	Jayson	S	Fall	3:31 (30-5)
Aguilera	Michael	W		
Alcala	Ricardo	A	Fall	2:30
Gonzalez	Sean	M		

Dual League   **Season**
Shafter   4-0   10-1

SSL Tournament
Shafter 257
Arvin 153
Tehachapi 150
Wasco 114.5
McFarland 111

Shafter's Coach Gary Pederson and Joseph Parra

SSL – Tehachapi
February 13, 2004

103
Solono	Phillip	W
Devera	Robert	
Navejar	Angel	M
Elliot	Jacob	T

112
Parra	Joseph	S
Castillo	Frankie	A
Mesa	Roger	T
Sandoval	Anthony	W

119
Moreno	A.J.	W
Franks	Ricky	S
Reyes	Josh	M

125
Tamayo	Francisco	A
Crosthwaite	Chris	M
Raya	Peter	W
Nelson	Tyler	T

130
Balassa	Joaquin	T
Snyder	Carlos	S
Sanchez	Ernie	W
Ramirez	Fernando	M

135
Cruz	Dustin	S
Sanchez	Sal	W
Dawson	Beau	T
Rosales	Julian	

140
Espericueta	Lucas	S
Enriquez	Jose	T
Aguilar	Uriel	M

145
Thompson	Zack	W
Tamayo	Jose	A
Stevens	Jason	S
Bolleau	Aaron	T

152
Landois	Orlando	W
Cardoza	Chuck	
Liebengood		T
Lopez	Jeremy	S

160
Clenard	Justin	T
Lookado	Ronald	S
Gallardo	Jose	A
Gonzales	Ernie	M

171
Duran	Jason	A
Garcia	Jared	M
Tercy	Eric	T
Sanchez	Carlos	W

191
Statler	Marvin	S
Smith	Joe	T
Coleman	Travon	W
Rodriguez	Matt	M

215
Garza	Ricky	S
Rocha	Gabe	T
Aguilera	Anthony	W
Gonzales	Sean	M

275
Alcala	Ricky	A
Perra	Trenton	T
Urrea	Larry	S
Gutierrez	Octaviano	M

Dual League
		Season
Shafter	4-0	11-3
Arvin	0-4	2-5

SSL Tournament
Shafter	195
Tehachapi	192.5
Wasco	175

Marvin Statler
Shafter High

SSL - Arvin
February 11, 2005

103
Diaz	Edgar	A	Fall	:51
Shehan	Ben	T		
Quintero	Robert	GV	14-2	
Ramiro	Beau	W		

112
Sanchez	Efrain	A	T.F. 15-0	
Mesa	Roger	T		
Najejar	Angel	M	Forfeit	
Alvarez	Jose	GV		

119
Castillo	Frankie	A	Fall	1:34
Reyes	Josh	M		
Franks	Ricky	S	Fall	:19
Reya	Peter	W		
Olmos	Guan	GV	6-2	
Martinez	Sergio	T		

125
Navarro	Vincent	S	12-0	
Ropsales	Julian	A		
Banducci	Mike	GV	9-7	
Chavez	Robert	M		
Mumby	Kyle	T		

130
Tamayo	Francisco	A	Fall	2:44
Ibarra	Mark	W		
Hernandez	Jesus	GV		5-2
Aleman	Jacob	S		
Nelson	Tyler	T		

135
Sullivan	Ryan	T	Fall	1:20
Varela	Abel	A		
Ramirez	Fernando	M	Fall	1:56
Lugo	Jose	GV		

140
Espericueta	Lucas	S	Fall	2:41
Montalvo	Raul	W		
Ramos	Esteban	M	Fall	1:58
Mundhenke	Matt	GV		
Rodriguez	Anthony	T		

145
Lopez	Jeremy	S	6-4	
Tamayo	Jose	A		
Gutierrez	Ivan	GV	15-5	
Ramirez	Jose	M		
Sanchez	Michael	W		

152
Johnson	Zack	W	1-0	
Post	Robert	T		
Duran	Jason	A	Fall	4:43
Casto	Mario	GV		
Jimenez	Martin	M		

160
Garcia	Jared	M	Fall	5:45
Coates	Marcys	T		
Solano	Michael	W	5-4	
Barron	Robert	S		

171
Coleman	Trevon	W	7-5	
Tercy	Eric	T		
Gallardo	Jose	A	Fall	1:00
Lucadoo	Ronald	S		
Castillo	Kendrick	GV		

189
Statler	Marvin	S	Fall	:17
Alcala	Alex	A		
Ortiez	Edgar	W	Fall	1:26
Gall	David	T		

215
Smith	Joe	T	6-0	
Coleman	Courtney	W		
Pantoja	Jesus	A		

275
Alcala	Ricky	A	Fall	1:42
Cisneros	Efrain	GV		
Cantu	Felipe	W		

Dual League
Arvin	4-1
Shafter	3-2
Wasco	2-3
McFarland	1-5
Golden Valley	1-4

Season
	10-5
	10-4
	5-3
	4-12
	1-5

SSL Tournament
Arvin	210
Tehachapi	146
Shafter	137
Wasco	127
McFarland	107
Golden Valley	102

SSL – Shafter
February 10, 2006

103
Diaz	Edgar	A	Fall	1:29
Steinbach	Jared	T		
Alvarez	Gilbran	GV		

112
Garcia	Raymond	M	6-5	
Martinez	Sergio	T		
Chavez	Leo	W	9-8	
Alcaraz	Jose	GV		

119
Sanchez	Efrain	A	19-10	
Alvares	Jose	GV		
Sheahan	Ben	T	Fall	:29
Garcia	Spencer	M		

125
Castillo	Frankie	A	Fall	2:22
Reyes	Josh	M		
Olmos	Juan	GV	Fall	3:41
Mumby	Kyle	T		

130
Navarro	Vincent	S	19-7	
Reyes	Reymundo	A		
Solorio	Phillip	W	15-5	
Banducci	Michael	GV		

135
Tamayo	Francisco	A	Fall	1:28
Marroquin	Daniel	M		
Hail	Jason	T	17-0	
Aleman	Jacob	S		

140
Varcia	Able	A	5-2	
Mundhanke	Aaron	GV		
Hack	Joey	T		

145
Espericueta	Lucas	S	Fall	1:35
Mundhanke	Matt	GV		
Rojo	Adolfo	A	10-6	
Ramos	Henry	W		

152
Johnson	Zack	W	4-0	
Post	Robert	T		
Molina	Guillermo	A	Fall	2:50
Gutierrez	Ivan	GV		

160
Hack	Tyler	T	8-4	
Mulligan	Mackenzie	S		
Vargas	Anthony	GV	Fall	1:34
Aguilera	Michael	W		

171
Garcia	Jared	M	Fall	;49
Wehust	Jerry	T		
Vileall	Angelo	GV		

189
Lookadoo	Ronald	S	3-0	
McBride	Evan	T		
Ricalde	Edwardo	A	Fall	1:34
Hansen	Robert	GV		

215
Smith	Joe	A	10-3	
Williams	Warren	S		
Rodriguez	David	GV		

275
Alcala	Ricky	A	Fall	1:09
Cisneros	Efren	GV		
Rodriguez	Arturo	M	Fall	1:09
Hood	Cameron	T		

Dual League
		Season	
Tehachapi	5-0		
Arvin	4-1	9-4	
Golden Valley	3-2	3-3	
Shafter	2-2-1	6-3-1	
McFarland	1-4	4-9	
Wasco	0-5	0-10	

SSL Tournament
Tehachapi	227.5
Golden Valley	226.5
Arvin	219.5
Shafter	126
McFarland	126
Wasco	88

Yosemite Divisional
1967-2006

Yosemite Divisional

Date	Champion	Coach	Location
2/18/67	McLane	Vern McCoy	Northern Division/Roosevelt Fresno
2/18/67			Central Division
2/18/67	South	Joe Seay	Southern Division/North Bakersfield
2/17/68	McLane	Vern McCoy	Northern Division/Dos Palos
2/17/68	Bakersfield	Olan Polite	Southern Division/South Bakersfield
2/21/69	Madera	Al Kiddy	McLane Fresno/Yosemite Division
2/21/70	Madera	Al Kiddy	Mt Whitney Visalia
2/20/71	South	Joe Seay	South Bakersfield
2/26/72	Bakersfield	Olan Polite	Bakersfield College
2/17/73	Clovis	Dennis Deliddo	Hanford
2/16/74	Clovis	Dennis Deliddo	Clovis
2/21/75	Clovis	Dennis Deliddo	Fresno High
2/21/76	Clovis	Dennis Deliddo	Hanford
2/19/77	Clovis	Dennis Deliddo	Hanford
2/18/78	Highland/Monache	Joe Barton/Drew Wiliams	Clovis
2/17/79	South	Gene Walker	Tulare Western
2/23/80	Clovis	Rodney Balch	Bakersfield College
2/21/81	Clovis	Rodney Balch	Clovis
2/20/82	Clovis West	Lewis Cowell	Hanford
2/19/83	Clovis West	Lennis Cowell	Tulare Western
2/18/84	Clovis West	Lewis Cowell	Arvin
2/16/85	Clovis	Rodney Balch	Tulare Western
2/22/86	Clovis	Rodney Balch	Bullard/Fresno
2/21/87	South	Gene Walker	Mt.Whitney/Visalia
2/20/88	Clovis West	Joe Faria	Arvin
2/18/89	Clovis West	Joe Faria	Hanford
2/17/90	Clovis	Rodney Balch	Clovis
2/16/91	Clovis	Rodney Balch	East Bakersfield
2/22/92	Clovis	Rodney Balch	Tulare Western
2/20/93	Madera	Corky Napier	Bullard/Fresno
2/19/94	Monache	Drew Williams	Arvin
2/18/95	Bakersfield	David East	Mt. Whitney/Visalia
2/17/96	Buchanan	Chris Hansen	Buchanan/Clovis
2/22/97	Clovis West	Brad Zimmer	East Bakersfield
2/21/98	Buchanan	Chris Hansen	Mt. Whitney/Visalia
2/20/99	Clovis	Steve Tirapelle	Clovis
2/18,19/2000	Buchanan	Dustin Riley	East Bakersfield
2/16,17/2001	Clovis	Steve Tirapelle	Clovis
2/15,16/2002	Bakersfield	David East	East Bakersfield
2/21,22/2003	Clovis	Steve Tirapelle	Lemoore
2/20,21/2004	Bakersfield	Andy Varner	Buchanan/Clovis
2/18,19/2005	Bakersfield	Andy Varner	East Bakersfield
2/17,18/06	Buchanan	Dustin Riley	Lemoore

Outstanding Yosemite Wrestlers
Starting in 1992 awards were sponsored by the Coyote Club

Year	Wrestler	School
1967	Joe Nigos	Delano
1968	Cecil Crowder	Foothill
1969		
1970		
1971	Dennis Burnett	North
1972		
1973		
1974		
1975		
1976		
1977		
1978		
1979		
1980		
1981		
1982		
1983		
1984		
1985		
1986		
1987		
1988		
1989		
1990		
1991		
1992	Mario Gonzales	South
1993		
1994		
1995		
1996	Jaime Garza	Selma
	or Adam Tirapelle	Buchanan
	Telly Sanders	Buchanan
	or Victor Leyva	Monache
1997	Jaime Garza	Selma
	Telly Sanders	Buchanan
	or Grant Harrington	Redwood
1998	Ben Martinez	Tulare Union
	Josh Naus	Centennial
1999	Ben Martinez	Tulare Union
	Max Odom	Foothill
2000	Darrell Vasquez	Bakersfield
	Chris Pendleton	Lemoore
2001	Gerard Contreras	Buchanan
	Miguel Gutierrez	Foothill
2002	Darrell Vasquez	Bakersfield
	Jacob Weaver	Sanger
2003	Chad Qkxxis Mendez	Hanford
	Jake Varner	Bakersfield
2004	Nathan Morgan	Bakersfield
	Josh Marquez	Bakersfield
2005	Mark Anderson	Lemoore
	Jake Varner	Bakersfield
2006	Alfonso Sanchez	McLane
	Tony Webber	Bakersfield

Northern Area Divisionals – Roosevelt/Fresno

February 18, 1967

95
Inouye	Bob	MCL
Smith	Clifton	ED
Castro	Pico	CEN
Grogg	Doug	HOOV
Marquez	Ruben	MAD
Gentile	Gary	BUL

103
Yoshida	David	CL
Ricardo	David	MCL
Ibarra,	George	CENT
McGough	Mike	ED
Arballo	Robert	MAD
Kabota	Russ	FRE

112
King	Sam	MAD	Fall
Jones	David	HOO	
Yamamoto	Tony	CL	
Martinez	Frank	FRE	
Moreno	David	ROOS	
Ramirez	Raymond	DP	

120
Moulton	Bill	MCL
Carr	Mike	ROOS
Whitehead	Steve	MAD
Harold	Mark	HOOV
Makries	Ralph	SIE
Howard	Frank	CL

127
Shimizu	Gene	CL
Waring	Dennis	ROOS
Vela	Tito	MCL
Hogan	Mel	MER
Harwell	Mel	BULL
Marin	Phil	ED

133
Ramirez	Bob	CL
Carbaal	John	CEN
Bracken	Tom	ROOS
Higgenbothem	Mark	MAD
Christy	Scott	SIE
Greco	Bob	MCL

138
Delbosque	Joe	DP
Montgomery	Dan	MCL
McCray	Mike	CL
Kerr	Bill	HOOV
Harman	David	BULL
Martinez	Dan	FRE

145
Ervin	Robert	ED
Ingraham	Bruce	MER
Sorenson	Steve	MCL
Atkins	Wayne	DP
Steggall	Chris	HOOV
Frutoz	Robert	CEN

154
Ball	Dennis	HOOV
Magdaleno	Vince	DP
Howe	George	CL
Bowser	Doug	CEN
Manooglan	John	BULL
White	Cecil	ED

165
Powell	Steve	MCL
McCorrey	Larry	ED
Smith	Carl	CEN
Napier	Corky	MAD
Thornburn	Kirk	CL
Fleming	Ken	

175
Watson	Don	MAD
Moreau	Woody	ED
Wagner	Tim	HOOV
Olivares	David	ROOS
Hoffman	Larry	MER
Barnett	John	DP

191
Vose	Doug	BULL
Echols	Larry	ED
Ede	Fred	MCL
Aquino	Albert	CHOW
Favila	Manuel	ROOS
Smith	David	FRE

(Continued on next page)

Northern Area Divisionals – Roosevelt/Fresno
February 18, 1967

UNL

Bedel	Jim	ROOS	Fall
Bigge	Roy	MCL	
Herrera	Art	FRE	
Morrell	Dan	CEN	
McGee	Pat	CL	
Love	Paul	DP	

Tournament

1. McLane — 99
2. Clovis — 70
3. Edison — 63
4. Roosevelt — 55
5. Madera — 55
6. Hoover — 48
7. Central — 44
8. Dos Palos — 40
9. Bullard — 26
10. Fresno — 19 Tied for 10th
10. Merced — 19 Tied for 10th
12. Sierra — 7 Tied for 12th
12. Chowchilla — 7 Tied for 12th

First Row: Stanley Moran, Ara Michaelion, Jim O'Neal, Art Parra, Hubert Donny, Bob Cherrie. Second Row: Louie Duran, Robert Donny, Dennis Isheim, Billy Young, Ken McCoy. Third Row: Tom Ryan, Armen Kiramidjian, Jerry Anderson, Eugene Sadoian, George Kezerian, Ara Der Garabedian, Charles Mann, Ray Ryals.

1952 Roosevelt High - Fresno Wrestling Team

Central Division
February 18, 1967

95
Lindholm	Carl	R
Kriuis	Steve	KING
Martinez	Ray	TW
Taylor	Dan	MT. W
Dames	Mark	PORT

103
Price	Terry	KING
Ensslin	Steve	PORT
Watson	Jerry	HAN
Claude	Rey	EX
Ashford	Terry	MT.W
Mulligan	Mike	TULARE

112
Nunez	Martin	
Kendig	Marty	MT.W
Coker	Gary	EX
Castillo	John	TULARE
Traving	M	KERMON

123
Contreras	Reynaldo	KING
Cardoza	Joe	HAN
Cook	Allyn	TULARE
Mendietta	Yno	SANGER
Martinez	Martin	PORT

127
Ramirez	Martin	KING
Santoga	Frank	SANGER
White	Rocky	MT. W
Molano	Fred	COR
Story	Wayne	PORT
Alvidrez	Pat	TULARE

133
Jones	Del	HAN
Wall	Jeff	PORT
Gomez	Pedro	COR
Ogawg	Eddie	
Gant	Glenn	W.U.

138
Anderson	Jeff	KING
Ketscher	David	REEDLEY
Pimintel	Bernard	HAN
Ogas	Tom	EX
Chavez	Jose	SANGER

145
Rabbon	Everett	PORT
Flores	Bob	REDWOOD
McManus	Dana	KING
Valverde	Ernesto	SANGER
Kofka	Neil	WOODLAKE
Grammer	R	TULARE

154
Williams	Wes	COR
Flores	Gabe	REDWOOD
Hines	Doug	HAN
Miguel	Chris	TW
Adams	Bruce	KING

165
Diaz	Rueben	REDWOOD
Maver	Ed	EX
Wall	Fred	PORT
Popp	Roger	TULARE
Naffgiger	Ken	MT. W

175
Nelms	Doyle	PORT
Burlson	Wayne	TW
Wortsmith	Dale	EX
Grist	Lyle	REDWOOD
Anderson	Tom	HAN
Waddell	Garry	WOODLAKE

191
Medrano	Paul	SANGER
Schnider	Gregg	REDWOOD
Pickrell	Alan	KING
Jackson	Dan	HAN
Gunning	Mike	TW

(Continued on next page)

Central Division
February 18, 1967

HWT
Borba	John	HAN
Benavides	Junior	WU
Rawls	Chris	EX
Medina	Mike	COR
Gonzales	David	REDWOOD

VARSITY WRESTLING--FRONT ROW: Rick Nitschke, Lee Torres, Richard Torres, Dennis Waring, Billy Carr, David Moreno, Ralph Makries, Steve Hardison. ROW 2: John Jastremsky, manager, David Olivares, John Figueroa, Jim Bedel, Gilbert Castenon, Bob Vaughn, Ken Duncan, Jack Clark, Bob Loney, Dudley Moordigian, manager, Coach Larry DeCarlo.

1966 Roosevelt High Wrestling Team

Southern Divisionals – North High/Bakersfield

February 18, 1967

95
Morgan	Larry	EB	8-0
Williams	Tom	SB	
Serna	Armando	DEL	O.T. 9-7
Higby	Russ	FOOT	

103
Sanchez	Paul	FOOT	10-3	
Lawrence	Mark	B		
Cosme	Herb	N	Fall	4:38
Little	Larry	SB		

112
Watkins	Richard	B	14-9
Seabourn	Bill	SB	
Lindley	David	EB	2-0
Armstutz	Doug	FOOT	

120
Herrera	Karl	B	Fofeit/Injury
Lindley	Richard	EB	
Roberts	Allen	NB	6-5
Sloss	Jack	SB	

127
Crowder	Cecil	FOOT	4-2
Walker	Gene	SB	
Winters	Jess	WB	3-2
Clifford	Jim	EB	

133
Shearer	Ron	EB	3-2	
Finch	John	SB		
Burnett	Bruce	NB	Fall	5:34
Gollmyer	Bruce	WB		

138
Jones	David	NB	Forfeit
Varner	Steve	B	
Garcia	Ken	EB	7-4
Garcia	Mike	WB	

145
Ivey	Cliff	SB	Fall	5:22
Bridges	Rich	WB		
Janzen	Jerry	SH	O.T. 4-0	
Meadors	Mike	FOOT		

154
Alvarez	Richard	B	5-0
Goss	Jack	NB	
Phillips		FOOT	8-0
Schallenbarger		DEL	

165
Nigos	Joe	DEL	Fall	3:18
Sheppard	Walt	B		
Beasley	Lanny	EB	8-7	
Osborn	Pat	FOOT		

175
Miller	John	NB	4-3	
Estrada	Tom	SB		
Rodman	Alan	EB	Fall	5:51
Cook	Dick	B		

191
Padilla	Mark	SB	Fall	2:18
Robesky	Jim	B		
Brewer		DEL	10-4	
Torres	Art	A		

UNL
Davis	Clovis	A	7-3	
Rucker	Sam	EB		
Williams	Wallace	SB	Fall	3:08
Lindsay	Joe	WB		

Tournament
1. South — 104
2. Bakersfield — 95
3. East — 85
4. North — 72
5. Foothill — 61
6. Delano — 46
7. West — 42
8. Arvin — 22
9. Shafter — 13
10. Wasco — 9

Northern Area Section Divisionals – Dos Palos
February 17, 1968

95
Gurule	Al	CENT	6-0
Inouye	Robert	MCL	
Grogg	Doug	HOOV	6-2
Garcia		ROOS	
Silverira			6-5
Lopez		FRE	

103
Clark	Lynn	HOOV	10-8
Valenzuela	Ruben	MCL	
Marquez	Ruben	MAD	2-1
Tatarakis		ROOS	
Castro	Pico	CENT	6-2
Rodriguez		ROOS	

112
Arballo	Robert	MAD	Default
Holman	Pete	MCL	
Jones	Dave	HOOV	
Howard		CL	
Ramirez		DP	7-3
Smith		ROOS	

120
Moulton	Bill	MCL	Default
Yamamoto	Tom	CL	
McGough	Mike	ED	3-2
Harold	Mark	HOOV	
Saenz		MER	Fall 1st Period
Tota		FRE	

127
Shimizu	Gene	CL	7-6
Vela	Tito	MCL	
Perez		DP	3-1
Carr		ROOS	
Collier		BULL	3-1
Moulton		MER	

133
Whitehead	Steve	MAD	8-1
Greco	Bob	MCL	
Christy	Scott	SIE	4-0
Costaies		DP	
Williams		FRE	8-6
Gaorian		MER	

138
Higgenbothem	Mark	MAD	Fall :47
Larabee	Dave	MER	
Maurer		HOOV	5-4
Bowser		CEN	
Hartwich		CHOW	Default
Larson		BULL	

145
Kerr	Bill	HOOV	8-3
Rogers		BULL	
Selwasser		CL	4-1
Arthur		MAD	
Martinez		ROOS	4-0
Heatrup		FRE	

154
Howe	George	CL	6-4
Mendia	Xavier	CEN	
Bell		HOOV	3-0
Chacon		FRE	
Cross		BULL	7-2
Koenig		MER	

165
Smith	Carl	CENT	5-3
Tribble	Larry	MAD	
Platten		ROO	5-2
Garabedian		MCL	
Hoffman	Larry	MER	6-3
Driggers	Dennis	ROO	

175
Smith	Al	CEN	6-2
Thornburn	Kirk	CL	
Hill		MAD	Fall 3rd period
Moreau	Woody	ED	
Otto		SIE	Fall 3rd period
Hanson		ROO	

191
Echols	Larry	ED	Fall 2nd period
Watson	Don	MAD	
McLaughlin		HOOV	4-2
Ede	Fred	MCL	
Rana		BULL	5-4

(Continued on next page)

Northern Area Section Divisionals – Dos Palos
February 17, 1968

UNL

Bigge	Roy	MCL	8-3
Delorio	Al	CL	
Aquino	Albert	CHOW	Fall 2nd period
Duncan	Mike	ROOS	
Cerreghino		MAD	Fall 3rd period
Ernsting		FRE	

Tournament

1. McLane	118	
2. Madera	109	
3. Hoover	85	
4. Central	78	
5. Clovis	74	
6. Roosevelt	37	
7. Edison	33	
8. Bullard	31	
9. Dos Palos	30	
10. Merced	24	Tied for 10th
10. Fresno	24	Tied for 10th
12. Chowchilla	17	
13. Sierra	11	

South Bakersfield 1958
Back, left to right, Gene Walker, Wallace Williams, Jack King
Front, left to right, Bill Seabourn, Larry Little

Madera's first wrestling team - 1952-53 Coach Mangini

Southern Divisional – South High/Bakersfield
February 17, 1968

95
Serros	Tony	B	8-0	
Velasquez	Tony	A		
Finch	Gary	SB	Fall	1:59
Herrera	Leo	SH		

103
Herrera	Bill	B	Double O.T. 6-5	
Gonzalez	Rudy	EB		
Cargill	Mike	NB	8-7	
Serna	Armando	DEL		

112
Morgan	Larry	EB	2-1	
Little	Larry	SB		
Watkins	Richard	B	Fall	2:58
Rodriguez	Paul	A		

120
Lawerance	Mark	B	4-0	
Morgan	Jon	EB		
Little	Ron	SB	1-0	
Baltazar		DEL		

127
Seabourn	Bill	SB	7-6	
Manny	Bruce	B		
Blackhurst	Dave	EB	6-5	
Giggy	Dave	WB		

133
Peterson	Chuck	B	7-0	
Dickson	Chuck	WB		
Black	Danny	SH	4-0	
Waterhouse		EB		

138
Burnett	Bruce	NB	4-1	
Arechiga	Andy	EB		
King	Jack	SB	3-1	
Rude	Alan	B		

145
Crowder	Cecil	FRE	Fall	3:46
Saunders	B	B		
Smart	Joe	NB	3-0	
Walker	Gene	SB		

154
Garcia	Ken	EB	5-3	
Meaders	Mike	F		
Parry	Tom	SB	Default	

165
Alvarez	Richard	B	6-0	
Rains	Brian	FRE		
Cagle	Wade	NB	4-2	
Wegins	Rick	SH		

175
Sheppard	Walt	B	3-2	
Blalock	Bob	NB		
Lowe	Nick	FOOT	6-5	
Fisher	Jack	SB		

191
Miller	John	NB	Fall	3:59
Rodman	Alan	EB		
Sheehan	Dennis	DEL	Fall	3:00
Thomas	Mark	B		

UNL
Rucker	Sam	EB	1-0	
Williams	Wallace	SB		
Brewer		DEL	Forfeit	

Tournament
1. Bakersfield 143
2. East 129
3. South 102
4. North 81
5. Foothill 54
6. Delano 46
7. West 36
8. Arvin 35
9. Shafter 27
10. Wasco 14
    McFarland 0

Bill Seaborn
South Bakersfield
1966 3rd CIF
1967 3rd CIF
1968 CIF Champion

Divisional – Fresno/McLane

February 21, 1969

95
Howard	Jim	CI	4-0	
Brock	Dennis	MAD		
Nebre	Pete	DEL	4-3	
Sanchez	Joe	EB		
Valdez	Eddie	WB	5-4	
Martinez	Zeke	PORT		

103
Serros	Tony	B	(Unbeaten) 2-0	
Ave	John	SB		
Travers	Spencer	WB	4-2	
Bloodworth	Bill	MAD		
Serna	Armando	DEL	8-3	
Morris	John	MT.W		

112
Marquez	Ruben	MAD	O.T. Ref. Dec.	
Grogg	Doug	HOOV		
Herrera	Billy	B	9-2	
Vega	Joe	SB		
Guerra	Ray	CL	9-3	
Gonzales	Tom	EB		

120
Morgan	Larry	EB	11-4	
Flemming	Henry	MAD		
Holeman	Pete	MCL	5-2	
Maldonado	Robert	B		
Harold	Mark	HOOV	3-0	
Smith	Clifton	ED		

127
Little	Larry	SB	10-5	(38-1)*
Arballo	Robert	MAD		(29-1)*
Espinoza	Ygnacio	B	14-2	
Martinez	Benito	DEL		
Delis	Dean	EB	10-5	
Kriby	Chris	FOOT		

133
McGough	Mike	ED	5-0	
King	Laddie	MAD		
Baker	Jeff	FOOT	1-0	
Ross	Eldon	NB		
Giggy	Dave	WB	8-0	
Sutherland	Bob	PORT		

138
Peterson	Chuck	B	5-1	(34-1)*
Roberson	Robert	EB		(38-1)*
Greco	Bob	MCL	3-2	
McIntyre	Ed	MAD		
Flores	Art	RED	10-1	
Hutchings	Steve	MT.W		

145
Cook	Allyn	TUL	8-0	
Rodgers	Roy	BULL		
Verde	Frank	EB	10-7	
Cesena	Ed	Mt.W		
McCowan	Greg	ED	14-3	
Benno	Al	DEL		

154
Crowder	Cecil	FOOT	12-4	(33-0)*
Wallace	Harlace	PORT		
Brock	Mike	MCL	2-0	
Domino	Kenny	B		
Harris	Tom	FRE	O.T. Ref. Dec.	
Flores	Robert	RED		

165
O'Conner	Steve	PORT	Fall	5:05
Hines	Doug	HAN		
Alvarez	Richard	B	5-0	
Mendes	Mike	HOOV		
King	Huston	MAD	10-0	
Driggers	Dennis	ROOS		

175
Tribble	Larry	MAD	5-3	
Copenhaver	Danny	SB		
Thornburn	Kirk	CL	7-3	
Alvarez	Danny	B		
Posey	Ken	DEL	Forfeit	
Wall	Fred	PORT		

191
Blalock	Bob	NB	Fall	1:10
Deltore	Tim	MAD		
Nelms	Doyle	PORT	9-3	
Forbes	Bob	MT.W		
Batach	Dave	B		
Duncan	Mike	ROOS		

(Continued on next page)

Divisional - Fresno/McLane
February 21, 1969

HWT

Shirley	Al	DEL	Fall	1:43
Watson	Don	MAD		(25-3)*
Hansen	Chris	REED	5-0	
Hernandez	Frank	RED		
Williams	Duane	NB	O.T. 2-0	
Arvizu	Victor	FOOT		

* Record

Tournament
1. Madera   115
2. Bakersfield   92
3. East   55
4. South   52
5. Porterville   49 Tied for 5th
5. Delano   49 Tied for 5th
7. McLane   48
8. Clovis   35
9. Foothill   31
10. North   27 Tied for 10th
10. Edison   27 Tied for 10th
12. Hoover   26
13. Mt. Whitney   23
14. West   19
15. Tulare Union   15 Tied for 15th
15. Redwood   15 Tied for 15th
15. Bullard   15 Tied for 15th
16. Hanford   14 Tled for 16th
16. Roosevelt   14 Tied for 16th
17. Fresno   5

LETTERMEN — FIRST ROW: Larry Nehring, Ed Davies, Dennis McCauley, Jerry Nelson, Leland Stephenson, Karl Smith. SECOND ROW: John Russell, Chuck Wright, Dennis Scott, Jack Reinold, Merle Inman, Ross Cariaga, Bob Aubery.

1958 Fresno High Wrestling Team

Yosemite Division – Mt. Whitney/Visalia
February 21, 1970

95
Gridiron	Harold	B	2-0	
Molina	Dick	SB		
Carter	Dennis	MT.W	6-3	
Dickenson	Dave	BULL		
Hall	Craig	MCL	6-0	
Gonzales	Mark	DEL		

103
Hughes	Gene	HOOV	4-3	
Howard	Jim	CL		
Tavers	Spencer	WB	4-0	
Burnett	Dennis	NB		
Klinchuch	Doug	DEL	O.T. Fall 6:22	
Lombardi	Joe	FRE		

112
Serros	Tony	B	5-0	(33-0)*
King	Pete	MAD		
Cafarelli	Danny	MCL	3-2	
Lovelace	Paul	WB		
Welte	Al	SB	7-2	
Cardova	Art	FOOT		

120
Reinhart	Gary	HOOV	2-0	
Byrd	Rick	CL		
Arrean	Art	MAD	7-4	
Symens	Terry	MCL		
Lane	Kenny	B	3-0	
Cortez	Ernie	FOOT		

127
Combs	Steve	HOOV	3-2	
McMasters	Dan	SB		
Higby	Russ	FOOT	5-2	
East	David	B		
Swindle	Marty	MON	13-3	
Gonzales				

133
Scroggs	Howard	MAD	7-2	
Peckler	David	HOOV		
Anderson	Sonny	NB	10-4	
Mulligan	Mike	TUL		
Salinas	Joe	PORT	Default	

138
Freeman	Charles	MAD	7-5	
McGough	Mike	ED		
Ross	Eldon	NB	4-1	
Houck	Jack	HOOV		
Powers	Randy	SB	3-1	
Gutierrez	Jerry	DEL		

145
Lopez	Bob	MAD	10-1	
Roland	Wilson	B		
Daniels	Leonard	EB	Fall	3:15
Powell	Randy	MCL		
Rodriguez	Mark	FRE	7-4	
Clanahan	Ken	WB		

154
Dasilva	Dan	MAD	3-1	
Tiner	Steve	ROOS		
Watts	Steve	SB	1-0	
Domino	Ken	B		
Oliveras	Abe	EB	6-0	
Howe	George	CL		

165
Davenport	Ed	EB	5-1	
Montgomery	Dan	NB		
Shaffer	Reed	TUL	3-0	
Taylor	Don	HOOV		
Alvarez	Tony	B	O.T. Fall 6:53	
Robison	Dan	WB		

175
Alvarez	Danny	B	4-3	
Crouch	Steve	HOOV		
Campbell	John	EB	10-5	
Rios	Steve	MAD		
Polotian	Don	MCL	2-0	
Sherman	Mike	MT.W		

191
Hatch	Brad	MAD	5-0	(27-0)*
Battistoni	Mike	B		
Westphal	Duane	RED	5-3	
Forbes	Bob	MT.W		
Tekado	George	FRE	3-0	
Durbin	Ken	SB		

(Continued on next page)

Yosemite Division – Mt. Whitney/Visalia
February 21, 1970

HWT

Van Worth	Bill	SB	Fall	1:30
Brown	Jim	NB		
Shirley	Al	DEL		
Murphy	Pat	HOOV		
Rodriguez	Robert	TUL	4-0	
Keck	Jeff	PORT		

Tournament

1. Madera — 107
2. Hoover — 86
3. Bakersfield — 84
4. South — 64
5. North — 51
6. East — 44
7. McLane — 29
8. Clovis — 26
9. West — 23
10. Tulare — 21 Tied for 10th
10. Mt.Whitney — 21 Tied for 10th
12. Delano — 19
13. Foothill — 17
14. Fresno — 14
15. Roosevelt — 13 Tied for 15th
15. Edison — 13 Tied for 15th
17. Redwood — 11
18. Porterville — 9
19. Bullard — 8
20. Monache — 5
Hanford — 0

Dick Molina
South Bakersfield
Two-time CIF Champion
1970 and 1971

Yosemite Division – South

February 20, 1971

95
Hill	Greg	MCL	O.T. Ref. Dec.
Woo	Lance	HOOV	
Morales	Julio	DEL	11-4
Sanches	Frank	FRE	
Valdez	John	EB	3-2
Silva	Ron	TUL	

103
Flores	Ernie	MAD	7-2
Mendoza	Lupe	TUL	
Aguirre	Fernando	B	17-4
Smith	Gregg	BULL	
Sanchez	Pete	EB	3-0
Klinchuch	Doug	DEL	

112
Molina	Dick	SB	Fall	1:01
Morris	John	MT.W		
Nebre	Pete	DEL	2-0	
Mendoza	Mario	TUL		
Salinas	Mario	RED	6-4	
Riley	Larry	WB		

120
Lovelace	Paul	WB	5-0
Brock	Dennis	MCL	
Sanchez	Roy	EB	5-2
Bloodworth	Dennis	MAD	
Portillo	Vic	B	6-0
Coronado	Eloy	ROOS	

127
Burnett	Dennis	N	6-5
Frost	Dale	DEL	
King	Pete	MAD	18-2
Symens	Terry	MCL	
Lane	Kenny	B	
Mendoza	Gabe	HAN	

133
Byrd	Rick	CL	12-9
East	David	B	
Cesena	Bob	MT.W	3-1
Kimbel	Neal	FRE	
Frances	Richard	HOOV	4-0
Macias	Ralph	HAN	

138
McMasters	Dan	SB	9-1
Devine	Stan	MT.W	
Yap	Frank	DEL	4-2
Lemos	Dennis	HAN	
Hunter	Ted	NB	Forfeit

145
Scruggs	Howard	MAD	20-2
Powers	Randy	SB	
Gutierrez	Jerry	DEL	6-1
Wong	Perry	MT.W	
Gleason	Cal	HOOV	4-1
Mayberry	Garry	FOOT	

154
Oliveras	Abe	EB	6-2
Dickson	Russ	WB	
Powell	Randy	MCL	9-2
Sanders	Bill	MAD	
Campbell	Guy	SB	4-3
Peffer	Tom	BULL	

165
Alvarez	Tony	B	10-0
Daniels	Leonard	EB	
Moreno	Julio	SB	6-2
Cemo	James	MON	
Mittlestead	Marc	DEL	4-2
Cook	Rick	WB	

175
Govea	John	B	5-4
Bull	Mike	SB	
Rios	Steve	BULL	4-2
Talbot	Tom	FRE	
Manuela	Ken	MT.W	6-0
Dillion	Bruce	HAN	

191
Hatch	Brad	MAD	9-0
Cardoza	Mike	HAN	
Davis	Jim	MCL	
Moe	David	SB	
Mitchell	Roger	B	11-3
Allen		CL	

(Continued on next page)

Yosemite Division – South
February 20, 1971

HWT

Van Worth	Bill	SB	Fall	1:49*
Bell	Bruce	EB		
Ford	Randy	RED	3-0	
Bough	Ron	MON		
Ryska	Tom	MCL	4-0	
Simmerman	Bob	FRE		

Tournament
1. South 99
2. Madera 82
3. Bakersfield 66
4. Delano 62
5. McLane 60
6. East 55
7. Mt. Whitney 47
8. West 33
9. Hanford 28
10. Fresno 25
11. Hoover 22
12. Tulare 21
13. North 20
14. Clovis 18
15. Redwood 17
16. Monache 16
17. Bullard 9
18. Roosevelt 7
19. Foothill 5
Porterville 0

*Bill Van Worth: 29 falls of 32 Matches 31-1

Bill VanWorth shows that weight has its advantages.

Bill Van Worth (right)
South Bakersfield
1970 CIF Champion
1971 CIF Champion

Neal Kimble (top)
Fresno High

Yosemite Division – Bakersfield College
February 26, 1972

95
Gonzalez	John	High	6-0	(26-3)*
Marshall	Mike	SB		
Kinsinger	Tim	FOOT	5-2	
Vanni	Vince	MON		
Lynn	Mike	TUL	3-0	
Peterson	George	B		

103
Morales	Julio	DEL	9-4	(2 yrs: 53-6)*
Martinez	Zeke	MON		
Ritter	Mike	BULL	8-7	
Silva	Ron	TUL		
Valdez	John	EB	Fall	4:45
Pereschica	Henry	SEL		

112
Perrin	Doug	High	2-0
Sanchez	Pete	EB	
Romero	Junior	REED	9-7
Hernandez	Chipy	SAN	
Flores	Gil	MAD	18-3
Howard	Ed	CL	

120
Mondoza	Lorenzo	TUL	Fall	3:58
Morren	Willard	CL		
Klinchuch	Doug	DEL	4-1	
Calabrese	Pat	FRE		
Beauford	Mark	EB	7-0	
Smart	Marvin	NB		

127
Montoya	Gabe	REED	8-3	
Red	Mike	HAN		
Balch	Rodney	CL	5-1	
Garza	Ray	EB		
Peevyhouse	Mike	DEL	Fall	4:56
Hoffman	Chris	ROOS		

133
Baxter	Randy	CL	Forfeit
Blackhurst	Paul	HIGH	
Coronado	Elroy	ROOS	3-1
Kimble	Neal	FRE	
Itokazu	Brad	EB	8-0
Jansen	Jim	SB	

138
Macias	Ralph	HAN	3-0	(36-0)*
Light	Mark	B		
Duckworth	Tony	HIGH	6-1	
Jackson	Nick	NB		
Bigby	David	SB	8-0	
Pandol	Jack	DEL		

145
East	David	B	7-4	(34-0-1)*
Guadaur	Chet	MCL		
Quintana	Mike	SEL	7-2	
Wilkinson	Ross	CL		
Lemos	Dennis	HAN	8-6	
Hambaroff	Pete	HIGH		

154
Mitchell	Rodney	B	Fall 5:40	(35-0-1)*
Anderson	Mike	FOOT		
McNeil	Randy	CL	6-2	
Torres	Jesse	SB		
Delarosa	Jerry	DEL	Fall	3:55
Monson	Gene	REED		

165
Alvarez	Tony	B	9-2	(33-1)*
Ramirez	Sam	HOO		
Campbell	Guy	SB	15-2	
Hunter	Roger	TW		
Sanders	Bill	MAD	6-4	
Posey	Don	MON		

175
Thompson	Sythel	SEL	6-1	(38-0)*
Cemo	Jim	MON		
Bodine	Mike	MAD	2-0	
Rocha	Flo	B		
Garcia	Reno	SB	6-1	
Lacey	Rich	HOOV		

191
Bull	Mike	SB	8-1	(36-1)*
Govea	John	B		
Gomez	Tom		13-3	
Ridge	Rick	MAD		
Richert	Tim	REED	6-2	
Bernard	Gary	TW		

(Continued on next page)

Yosemite Division – Bakersfield College
February 26, 1972

HWT

Gorras	Mike	MCL	4-3	
Gibson	Ray	REED		
Williams	Duane	NB	7-3	
Valov	Fred	DEL		
Simmerman	Bob	FRE	Fall	1:53
McClintock	Brian	High		

* Record

Tournament

1. Bakersfield 90.5
2. South 72
3. Highland 71.5
4. Clovis 71
5. East 55
6. Delano 54
7. Reedley 53.5
8. Hanford 43.5
9. Tulare 43
10. Monache 42.5
11. Madera 38.5
12. McLane 35.5
13. Selma 33.5
14. Foothill 31
15. Fresno 30.5
16. North 27
17. Tulare W. 24
18. Hoover 16.5
19. Roosevelt 16
20. Bullard 13
21. Sanger 11
22. Porterville 8 Tied for 22nd
22. Redwood 8 Tied for 22nd
24. West 2
Edison 0
Mt.Whitney 0

Joe Seay
South Bakersfield
Coached four
CIF Championship
Teams

Yosemite Division – Hanford
February 17, 1973

95
Borjas	Nick	CL	Default	
Peterson	Goe	BHS	2-1	29-6
Medina	Jose	DEL		
Iwamura	Gary	MT.W	3-0	
Quinonez	John	TW		

103
Huffman	Ray	MAD	6-0 (37-0)*
Marshall	Mike	SB	(29-3)*
Vanni	Vince	MON	3-0
Brenner	Rob	CL	
Pereachigia		SEL	Forfeit
Canaday	Larry	WB	

112
*Flores	Ernie	MAD	4-3
Romero	Junior	REED	
Sanchez	Pete	EB	5-2
Morales	Julio	DEL	
Steele	Bill	MCL	3-2
Markesano	Pat	SAN	

120
Carillo	Eddie	B	3-0
Garcia	Jim	TUL	
Moren	Willard	CL	13-3
Dow	David	HIGH	
Kiddy	Robert	MAD	Default
Ordiz			

127
Balch	Rodney	CL	8-6
Garza	Ray	EB	(36-1)*
Olson	Andy	MAD	Forfeit
Coash	Tom	WB	
Russell	Horace	RED	10-2
Randall	Kevin	HAN	

133
*Baxter	Randy	CL	6-3 (35-0)*
Peevyhouse	Mike	DEL	
Beauford	Mark	EB	5-1
Connell	Matt	HOOV	
Hanline	Bob	WB	7-1
Mollica	Mike	BULL	

138
Flores	Frank	CL	O.T. 4-0
Spotts	Lee	MAD	
Blackhurst	Paul	HIGH	13-5
Pimental	Mike	HAN	
Spickler	Kris	MCL	1-0
Ward	Darrell	FOOT	

145
Duckworth	Tony	HIGH	3-0
Smrekar	Terry	SB	
Combs	Roger	HOOV	3-0
Islas	Abundio	REED	
Bruer	Bob	MAD	Fall 5:10
Jurry	Jeff	CL	

154
Wilkerson	Ross	CL	12-0 (37-0)*
Cornell	Mike	HOOV	
Torres	Jesse	SB	3-0
Delarosa	Jerry	DEL	
Anderson	Mike	FOOT	4-3

165
Rocha	Florencio	B	9-5 (33-0)
Posey	Don	MON	
Rosenberger	Bob	DEL	16-4
McKeehan	David	W	
Johnson	Eddie	CL	Forfeit
Lovegren	Keith	SANG	

175
Bohna	Fred	CL	6-3
Richardson	Jeff	HAN	
Garcia	Reno	SB	3-2
Sheffel	Bill	HIGH	
Parrish	Mark	HOOV	Forfeit

191
*Bull	Mike	SB	Fall 1:20
Thomas	Jerrell	HAN	
Pratt	Richard	MT.W	10-5
Clark	Vic	TUL	
Ponce	Jess	B	3-2
Gomez	Tom	EB	

(Continued on next page)

Yosemite Division – Hanford
February 17, 1973

HWT
Robinson	Jeff	CL	Fall	1:20
Kelly	Keith	HOOV		
Williams	Duane	NB	3-0	
Valov	Fred	DEL		
Fowler	Bob	EB	Forfeit	
Lyons	Michael	MAD		

**Undefeated
* Record

Tournament
1. Clovis   143
2. Madera   79
3. South   71
4. Hoover   60
5. Delano   59.5
6. Bakersfield   58.5
7. East   52.5
8. Highland   50.5
9. West   39.5
10. North   13
11. Foothill   12

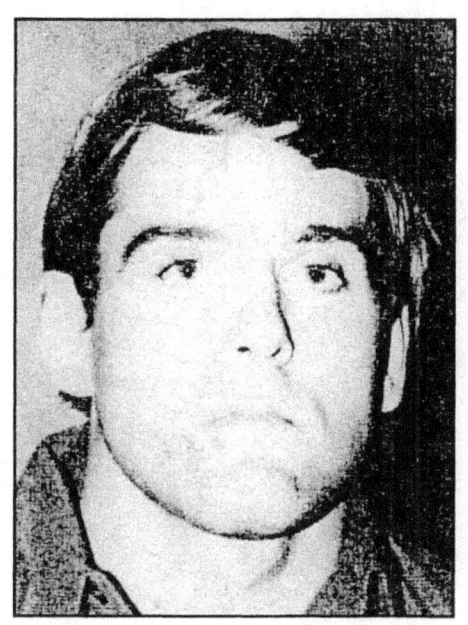

Fred Bohna
Clovis High
Two-time CIF Champion
State Champion
NCAA Champion

Coach Dennis DeLiddo
Clovis High
5 CIF and 3 State
Championship Teams

Yosemite Division – Clovis
February 16, 1974

95
Gonzalez	Pete	HIGH	4-0
Medina	Jose	DEL	
Travers	Mickey	SB	5-0
Balanos	Paul	CL	
Davids	Brian	FOOT	5-4
Bonilla	Charles	MAD	

103
Vanni	Vince	MON	7-2
Peterson	George	B	
Machado	Ed	A	4-2
Hasson	Scott	HOOV	
Hull	Jeff	HIGH	5-2
Aleman	Juan	EB	

112
Morales	Julio	DEL	13-7
Borjas	Nick	CL	
Canaday	Larry	WB	7-2
McConnaughy	Kevin	MT.W	
Murphy	Tim	HOOV	2-1
Perrin	Mike	HIGH	

120
Garza	Ray	EB	5-3
Gaitan	Jesse	HIGH	
Soltero	Chino	CL	Fall 2:27
Kachadururia	Allen	BULL	
Villarreal	Art	MAD	5-2
Markesano	Pat	SAN	

127
Gongora	Tom	CL	11-1
Russell	Horace	RED	
Sumida	Randy	LEM	17-6
Vejvada	Craig	TUL	
York	Gary	WB	11-1
Castaneda	Ismael	PORT	

133
Sanches	Luie	FRE	7-0
Davis	Eddie	HAN	
Jury	Jeff	CL	Ref. Dec.
May	Bill	HIGH	
Reimer	Greg	DEL	7-1
Bondietti	Bart	BULL	

138
Kiddy	Robert	MAD	3-1
Balch	Rodney	CL	
Oliveria	Frank	HAN	7-6
Itokazu	Todd	HIGH	
Hanline	Bob	WB	4-2
Guerrero	Vic	FRE	

145
Torres	Jesse	SB	3-1
Obar	Jim	CL	
Leroy	Loren	MAD	Forfeit
Combs	Roger	HOOV	
Islas	Abundi	REED	4-1
Roberts	Bob	FRE	

154
Tobin	Craig	B	3-1
Hutchings	Warren	MT.W	
Ramirez	Carlos	HOOV	4-2
Verduzco	Larry	ROOS	
Bridgewater	Russell	EB	6-2
Russell	Willy	RED	

165
Cookingham	Kevin	CL	5-2
Sztorc	Ed	WB	
Eng	Stanley	B	Forfeit
Lovgren	Keith	SANG	
Rosenberger	Bob	DEL	3-1
Grajada	Mark	HAN	

175
Ponce	Jesse	B	5-2
Sheffel	Bill	HIGH	
Henry	Titus	TW	4-3
Swanson	Rick	DEL	
Cummings	Alan	FOOT	4-3
Simpson	Michael	PORT	

191
Bohna	Fred	CL	7-2
Greemore	Jason	B	
Cotton	Vinson	SB	9-5
Diaz	John	MAD	
Duvall	Don	MT.W	3-1
Kawaiski	George	FRE	

(Continued on next page)

Yosemite Division - Clovis
February 16, 1974

HWT

Thomas	Jewell	HAN	4-0
Clark	John	FOOT	
Horn	Rod	HOOV	8-5
Van Arkle	Tom	B	
Arthur	Doug	CL	Fall 4:49
Bootz	Steve	TUL	

Tournament

1. Clovis — 133
2. Bakersfield — 84
3. Highland — 79
4. Delano — 57
5. Madera — 51
6. Hoover — 50
7. Hanford — 50
8. South — 46
9. West — 37
10. Mt. Whitney — 33
11. Fresno — 29
12. Foothill — 27
13. East — 26
14. Monache — 23
15. Redwood — 21
16. Tulare — 19
17. Tulare W. — 15
18. Arvin — 14
19. Bullard — 13 Tied for 19th
19. Lemoore — 13 Tied for 19th
19. Sanger — 13 Tied for 19th
22. Roosevelt — 11
23. Porterville — 10
24. Reedley — 8
25. McLane — 5
North — 0

ABOVE: VARSITY WRESTLING TEAM-BOTTOM ROW: Rick Oaxaca, Brad Montana, Larry Hymer, Biff Pietro, Greg Tsudama, Randy Morita. TOP ROW: Coach Gary Fascilla, Manager Robert Scott, Bob Bourbon, George Kowalski, Joe Coelho, Vince Mastro, Richard Guerrero, Luis Sanchez, Coach Rene Errotabere.

1974 Fresno High Wrestling Team

Yosemite Division – Fresno High
February 22, 1975

95
Bolanos	Paul	CL	6-0	
Burt	John	WB		
Gonzales	Alfredo	B	6-2	
Valasquez	Ray	RED		
Duckworth	Aaron	HIGH	3-1	
Markesano		SAN		

103
Gonzalez	Pete	HIGH	10-1	
Blanco	Tom	CL		
Dutra	Duane	HAN	5-1	
Ramirez	Michael	MAD		
Davids	Brian	FOOT	Ref. Dec.	
Flores	Ambrosio	RED		

112
Murphy	Tim	HOOV	Fall	1:16
Leyva	Anthony	B		
Jones	Bill	HAN	5-4	
Garcia	Onesimo	MAD		
Spencer	Bill	CL	Forfeit	
Machado	Ed	A		

120
Contreras	Rick	RED	6-4	(29-3)*
McConnaughey	Kevin	MT.W		(22-3-1)*
Felez	Paul	SB	5-1	
Villarreal	Art	MAD		
Perrin	Mike	HIGH	2-0	
Duffy	Mike	HOOV		

127
Borjas	Nick	CL	7-5	
Gaitan	Jess	HIGH		
Vejvada	Craig	TUL	Fall	2:55
Freeman	Neal	MAD		
Bell	Mike	MCL	O.T. 10-5	
Sanchez		A		

133
Dow	Don	HIGH	3-2	
Jury	Jeff	CL		
Pinera	Ernie	MAD	9-5	
Whitmore	Greg	FRE		
Flynn	Warren	BULL	Forfeit	
Juarez	Javaier	SANG		

138
Williams	Tom	CL	8-7	
Reynolds	Larry	SB		
Montana		FRE	8-3	
Coronado	Celzo	MAD		
Hanline	Bob	WB	Forfeit	
May	Bill	HIGH		

145
Kiddy	Robert	MAD	8-5	(34-0)*
Obar	Steve	CL		
Landeros	Mark	MON	2-1	
Chase	Bob	HIGH		
Hernandez	Paul	WB	5-4	
Parrish	Dennis	NB		

154
Roberts	Bob	FRE	2-0	
Leroy	Leren	MAD		
Hill	Chester	FOOT	9-6	
Cooksey	Phil	MON		
Thomas	Bill	HAN	10-6	
Wiedenhoffer	Curt	BULL		

165
Grimes	Bob	CL	4-3	
England	Rich	BULL		
Bradford	Walt	HOOV	7-4	
Torres	James	SB		
Sanders	Bill	MAD	3-2	
Negrette	John	RED		(30-3)*

175
Cookingham	Kevin	CL	6-2	(32-0-1)*
Torres	Lawrence	MAD		
Herder	Jerry	WB		
Buenafe	John	RED	9-0	
Suggart	Ron	FOOT	Forfeit	
Lemos	Frank	TW		

191
Johnson	Eddie	CL	9-6	
Diaz	John	MAD		
Smith	David	HAN	9-1	
Landeros	Mike	MON		
Duval	Don	MT.W		
Rodgers	Guy	DEL		

(Continued on next page)

Yosemite Division – Fresno High
February 22, 1975

HWT

Thomas	Jewrell	HAN	Fall	5:36
Authur	Doug	CL		
Van Arkle	Tom	B	Fall	2:05
Bootz	Steve	TUL		
Clark	Dan	FOOT	3-1	
Farris		SANG		

* Record

Tournament
1. Clovis — 155
2. Madera — 117.5
3. Highland — 69.5
4. Hanford — 60.5
5. Redwood — 45.5
6. West — 43
7. Foothill — 41
8. Fresno — 40
8. Monache — 40
10. Bakersfield — 39
11. South — 37.5
12. Hoover — 37.5
13. Tulare — 24
14. Bullard — 23.5
15. Mt. Whitney — 19.5
16. Arvin — 12
17. Sanger — 10.5
18. Tulare W. — 7
19. East — 6.5
20. McLane — 5 Tied for 20th
20. North — 5 Tied for 20th
22. Delano — 4.5
23. Lemoore — 1

Pete Gonzalez
Highland High
2nd in State 1974 and 1975
3rd in State 1976
Two-time CIF Champion
1974 and 1975
3rd Place 1973 and 1976

Undefeated Wrestlers
Jewrell Thomas
Robert Kiddy
Tim Murphy

One Loss
Paul Bolanos

Yosemite Division – Hanford
February 21, 1976

98
Richard	Percy	EB	Default	
Gonzalez	Fred	HIGH		
Blanco	Anthony	CL	9-3	
Bustamante	Johnny	A		
Morita	Gary	FRE	Forfeit	
Guerra	Rene	RED		

103
Bolanos	Paul	CL		
Gonzalez	Pete	HIGH		
Perez	Louie	FRE	5-0	
Gonazlez	Alfredo	B		
Poteete	Jiim	SB	21-3	
Sierra	Dave	PORT		

112
Blanco	Tom	CL	Fall	2:56
Gamboa	Joe	MAD		
Nickell	Steve	EB	2-0	
Martinez		FOOT		
Burt	John	WB	6-5	
Hargis	Darren	NB		

120
Gonzales	William	FOOT	6-3
Williams	Mike	HIGH	
Jones	Bill	HAN	4-3
Williams	Hakshick	BULL	
Garcia	Onesimo	MAD	7-3
Letts		ED	

127
Felez	Paul	SB	7-0	(25-0)*
McConnaghey	Kevin	MT.W		(29-2)*
Quiroz	Adam	CL	5-2	
Fahy	Jeff	W		
Freeman	Neal	MAD	14-1	
Aceves	Omero	A		

133
Contreras	Rick	RED	15-10	(27-2)*
Reyes	Eddie	B		
Rivera		BULL	8-0	
Salinas	Filomino	A		
Preez	Marco	FRE	3-1	
Best	Craig	HIGH		

138
Dow	Don	HIGH	Fall	5:28
Whitemore	Greg	FRE		
Flynn	Warren	BULL	1-0	
Inoyue	Craig	CL		
Pendergraft	Eric	RED	Forfeit	
Chambers	Scott	FOOT		

145
Williams	Tom	CL	8-4
Davis	Ed	HAN	
Chase	Bob	HIGH	9-5
Pinera	Ernie	MAD	
Nipper	Waymon	SB	9-0
Knopog		MON	

154
Johnson	Dave	HIGH	6-2	(17-0)*
Grimes	Bob	CL		
Duran	Albert	FRE		
Leroy	Lerron	MAD		
Gause	Brian	NB	Forfeit	
Garza		MON		

165
Cookingham	Kevin	CL	8-2
Torres	James	SB	
Thomas	Bill	HAN	9-3
Smith	Kreig	BULL	
Lett	Eric	ED	4-2
McNabb	Luis	NB	

175
Weidenhoft	Kurt	BULL	6-1
Landeros	Mike	MON	
Torosian	Ted	SANG	3-1
Winters	Randy	CL	
Nagrette	John	RED	
Thomas		HAN	Forfeit

191
Dias	John	MAD	8-1	(34-1)*
Maznanian	John	BULL		
Buenate	John	RED	4-3	
Molica	Lance	DEL		
Kline			Forfeit	
Dennis	Tim	MON		

(Continued on next page)

Yosemite Division – Hanford

February 21, 1976

HWT
Arthur	Doug	CL	7-2	(34-0)*
Hance	Alan	FOOT		
Smith	David	HAN	7-5	
Hill	Ed	MON		
Shamsloan		BULL	Fall	2:38
Van Worth	Lee	NB		

* Record

Tournament
1. Clovis — 162
2. Highland — 108.5
3. Madera — 94.5
4. Bullard — 92.5
5. Hanford — 85
5. Fresno — 85
7. Redwood — 66
8. South — 60
9. Foothill — 58
10. Monache — 49
11. East — 39.5
12. Bakersfield — 39
13. North — 34
14. Arvin — 28.5
15. Mt. Whitney — 26.5
16. West — 21
17. Delano — 15
18. Edison — 13
19. Sanger — 12
20. Porterville — 8.5
21. McLane — 5
21. Reedley — 5
23. Tulare — 4
24. Lemoore — 3.5
25. Roosevelt — 3

Paul Feliz (top) of South Bakersfield
1975 CIF Champion/1976 2nd in CIF/1976 3rd in State
Team captain of the U.S. Air Force Academy Wrestling Team

Waymon Nipper
South Bakersfield

Yosemite Division – Hanford

February 19, 1977

95
Blanco	Anthony	CL	18-3	
Gonzales	Mike	HIGH		
Vanni	Tim	MON	8-0	
Crane	Kris	MCL		
Dallas	Willie	FOOT	5-4	
Brown	Doug	HAN		

103
Gonzalez	Fred	HIGH	5-2	(28-3)*
Richard	Percey	EB		
Bustamante	Johnny	A	Forfeit	
Brieno	Mike	HAN		
Gutierrez	Alfred	RED	18-5	
Sandoval	Ventura	DEL		

112
Poteete	Jim	SB	3-2	(24-2)*
Marckesano	Jim	CL		
Estrada	Buff	FRE	5-4	
Gutierrez	Benji	RED		
Sierra	Frank	SANG	9-3	
Escobar	Simon	DEL		

120
Nickell	Steve	EB	6-2	(28-2)*
Rodriguez	Vince	TW		(29-1)*
Dow	Dale	HI	7-4	
Comacho	Hector	MAD		
Berry	Jeff	HOOV	6-1	
Franich	Ed	MT.W		

127
McCullough	Glen	FOOT	4-2	(24-5)*
Duckworth	Aaron	HIGH		(23-3)*
Couch	Fred	CL	8-4	
Cano	Alvarado	HAN		
Torres	Ralph	ROOS	Forfeit	
Weems	Monty	MT.W		

133
Fahy	Jeff	W	13-3	(26-2)*
Ribera	Mike	BULL		(25-2)*
Yoshida	Jay	RED	2-1	
Daniels	Eddie	B		
Higgins	Dennis	FOOT	Forfeit	
Salilnas	Filomeno	A		

138
Flores	James	SB	Fall	4:21
Mooney	Mike	B		
Inouye	Greg	CL	O.T. 12-10	
Duran	Albert	FRE		
Bejvada	Craig	TUL	6-0	
Aceves	Omero	A		

145
Roth	Mike	CL	Fall 1:55	(43-2)*
Zimmerman	Brent	B		
Juarez	Javier	SANG	5-0	
May	Alex	ROOS		
Avila	Robin	FRE	13-11	
Green	Clifford	ED		

154
Johnson	Chris	CL	6-2	
Ellis	Robert	BULL		
Castaneda	Danny	B	5-3	
Donnely	Russ	MCL		
Allen		HOOV		
Romine	Bob	HIGH	Forfeit	

165
Sanders	Tim	MAD	3-1	
Gouhart	Frank	RED		
Ussery	Frank	NB	6-5	
Buford	John	MCL		
McAbee	Larry	B	8-0	
Hill	Brian	MON		

175
Thomas	Bill	HAN	17-7	(34-0)*
McNabb	Lewis	NB		
Osthimer	Mike	HIGH	3-0	
Jelica	Bob	WB		
Juarez	Tony	FRE	7-2	
Lemos		TW		

191
Molica	Lance	DEL	13-7	(20-3)*
Landeros	Mike	MON		(25-2)*
Torosian	Ted	SANG	Fall	4:35
Harris	Dave	WB		
Henrick	Rodger	HAN	4-2	
Lujan	Juan	B		

(Continued on next page)

Yosemite Division – Hanford
February 19, 1977

HWT

Smith	Dave	HAN	11-3	(34-1)*
Parker	Barry	MT.W		
Bishop	Vernon	MAD	5-2	
Samshoian	Pete	BULL		
Lampp	Mike	CL	4-0	
Azzaro		ROOS		

* Record

Tournament
1. Clovis 139.5
2. Hanford 105
3. Highland 104.5
4. Bakersfield 86
5. Fresno 67
6. Redwood 60.5
7. Foothill 58
8. Monache 55 Tied for 8th
8. Mt. Whitney 55 Tied for 8th
10. West 54
11. Madera 52
12. Bullard 50
13. East 48
14. McLane 47
15. South 46
16. Delano 44
17. Sanger 43
18. North 40
19. Arvin 36
20. Tulare W. 28
21. Roosevelt 26
22. Hoover 24
23. Tulare 21
24. Porterville 7 Tied for 24th
24. Edison 7 Tied for 24th
26. Reedley 2
Lemoore 0

James Flores
South Bakersfield

Yosemite Division – Clovis

February 18, 1978

95
Vanni	Tim	MON	6-0	
Borjas	Rick	MCL		
Gonzales	Mike	HIGH	3-0	
Harautunian	Tom	HOOV		
Garcia	Jesse	CL	Fall	4:23
Gentry	Mike	MT.W		

103
Gutierrez	Alfred	RED	13-5	
Arredondo	Rene	MAD		
Vanni	Dan	MON	Fall	:35
Crouch		MCL		
Gorey	Ernesto	A	5-2	
Monsibais	Donny	HIGH		

112
Richard	Percey	EB	16-4	(30-3)*
Frausto	Jesse	MAD		
Gonzales	Fred	HIGH	Fall	:35
Silva	Dan	DEL		
Rodrigues	George	MON	Default	
Lynch	Pat	HOOV		

120
Estrada	Buff	FRE	6-2	(33-1)*
Reyes	Jesse	B		
Gutierrez	Benjie	RED		
Calvillo	Joe	HIGH		
Kapriellian	Larry	HOOV	8-3	
Sierra	Joel	PORT		

127
Dow	Dale	HIGH	16-5	
Hargis	Darin	NB		
Couch	Fred	CL	4-2	
Gonzalez	Adam	MON		
Franich	Ed	MT.W	1-0	
Morales	Eddie	B		

133
Nickell	Steve	EB	6-2	
Cano	Alvardo	HAN		
Blanos	George	CL	9-2	
Kinsinger	Tony	FOOT		
Hopkins	John	HIGH	5-0	
Morales	Jose	A		

138
Carley	Jeff	MT.W	13-8	
Churchman	Colby	NB		
Lett	Eric	ED	5-1	
Inouye	Scott	CL		
Hernandez	Ray	FRE	8-2	
Montellano	Phillip	FOOT		

145
May	Alex	ROOS	Fall	5:08
Ramsey	Cecil	MT.W		
Pulskamp	Flint	HIGH	9-1	
Avila	Mike	FRE		
Hines	Roy	HAN	Fall	:49
Ramos		TW		

154
Green	Robin	ED	4-2	
Ellis	Robert	BULL		
Buford	John	MCL	4-2	
Castaneda	Danny	B		
Wicks	Bob	SB	6-5	
Choate	Steve	NB		

165
Sischo	Richard	MAD	6-2	
Romine	Bob	HIGH		
Juarez	Tony	FRE	O.T. Crit	
Dunbar	Tim	HOOV		
Steelman	John	TUL	6-2	
Scott	Frank	ED		

175
Martinez	Rey	ROOS	17-3	
McNabb	Lewis	NB		
Drake	Jon	BULL	8-2	
Townsend	Dennis	MON		
Valov	Joel	DEL	7-6	
Fabricius	Don	B		

191
Haskins	Nonnie	ROOS	7-3	
Kropag	Bill	MAD		
Pierce	Bill	SB	16-5	
Lujan	Juan	B		
Mayberry	Dan	FOOT	Default	
Molica	Lee	DEL		

(Continued on next page)

Yosemite Division – Clovis
February 18, 1978

HWT
Molica	Lance	DEL	10-5	(15-1)*
Dennis	Tim	MON		
Lamp	Mike	CL	11-1	
Bishop	Vernon	MAD		
Castillo	Marvin	TUL	3-0	
Ezell	Craig	FRE		

* Record

Tournament
1. Monache — 130 Tied for 1st
1. Highland — 130 Tied for 1st
3. Roosevelt — 81
4. Bakersfield — 80.5
5. Clovis — 78.5
6. Fresno — 77
7. North — 76
8. Delano — 70
9. Mt. Whitney — 62.5
10. McLane — 61.5
11. Madera — 60.5
12. East — 52.5
13. Hoover — 50.5
14. Redwood — 49
15. Hanford — 45.5
16. Edison — 41
17. Foothill — 38
18. Bullard — 37
19. South — 34
20. Tulare — 34
21. Arvin — 20.5
22. Sanger — 14.5
23. Porterville — 7 Tied for 23rd
23. Reedley — 7 Tied for 23rd
23. Tulare W. — 7 Tied for 23rd
26. West — 3

RICHARD-NICKELL CHAMPS AGAIN!

Coach Rudy Gonzales has two fine seniors who capped their respective careers at East High in phenomenal fashion.

Percy Richard finished with a four year record of 130-18. He won four league titles, two valley, and a state title.

Steve Nickell finished 30-2 in '78. His four year record is 125-21. He also has league and valley titles to his credit.

As a team, the Varsity finished 1-5 in league and 5-8 overall. Other outstanding wrestlers were Tyrone Neal and Joe Campas.

Varsity Wrestling: Row 1 — Mike Gonzales, Donny Monsibais, Grant Itokazu, Freddie Gonzales and Joe Calvillo. Row 2 — Joe Barton, Bob Romine, Dave Kincaid, Flint Pulskamp, Dale Dow and Darrel Monsibais.

Highland High
1978 Co-Yosemite Division Champions

Yosemite Division – Tulare Western
February 17, 1979

95
Vanni	Tim	MON	6-3	
Sanchez	Dave	A		
Borges	Rick	MCL	7-0	
Long	Charlie	BULL		
Jimenez	Ricardo	MAD	13-2	
Caraveo	Jim	DEL		

103
Gutierrez	Alfred	RED	9-3	
Gonazlez	Mike	HIGH		
East	Mel	B	6-1	
Potter	Doug	MAD		
Saenz	Pablo	REED	6-2	
Geray	Nesto	A		

112
Slade	Steve	WB	11-2	
Neal	Tyrone	EB		
Villareal	Marc	SB	5-2	
Torres	Rene	ROOS		
Geronimo	Ernie	A		
Hasson	Jeff	HOOV		

120
Poteete	Jim	SB	14-1	(29-1)*
Ibarra	Victor	B		
Estrada	Buff	FRE	Forfeit	
Dallas	Willie	FOOT		
Jones	Del	TW	2-0	
Randall	Don	HAN		

127
Reyes	Jesse	B	7-2	(32-0)*
Hargis	Darin	NB		
Calvillo	Joe	HIGH	2-0	
Bisig	Joe	SB		
Gayer	Larry	RED	Forfeit	
Rodriguez	Joel	MAD		

133
Franich	Ed	MT.W	3-0	
Negrete	Ron	RED		
Evers	Rick	TUL	11-1	
Whitlock	Tim	MON		
Sanchez	Artie	A	3-0	
Cox	Greg	SB		

138
Kinsinger	Tony	FOOT	6-1	
Della	Mark	MON		
Thornton	Alvin	ED	5-3	
Boyles	Brian	HAN		
Christianson	Jim	SANG		
Fleischer	Matt	WB		

145
Hines	Roy	HAN	11-3	(32-2)*
Carrera	Kevin	HOOV		
Eastwood	Brad	B	5-0	
Juarez	Robert	SANG		
Nichols	Larry	FRE	7-2	
Ennis	John	MT.W.		

154
Pulskamp	Flint	HIGH xxxxxx	4-0	(28-0)*
Wicks	Bob	SB		(25-6)*
Goevara	Ezekiel	CL	7-5	
Ramsay	Cecil	MT.W		
Alvardo	Rich	HAN	5-2	
Besconeillo	Glen	DEL		

165
Scott	Malcomb	ED	4-1	
Suiter	Scott	WB		(25-3-2)*
Borchardt	Dave	BULL	3-2	
Steelman	John	TW		
Torres	Fred	SB	2-0	
McCullan	Lance	NB		

175
Emezian	Tom	ROOS	7-6	(27-1)
Townsend	Dennis	MON		
Baker	Kevin	FOOT	11-7	
Alva	Mark	FRE		
Adams	Allan	CL	20-6	
Ellis	Dino	Han		

191
Hansken	Nannie	ROOS	5-1	(28-0)*
Pierce	Bill	SB		(27-1-1)*
Dunbar	Tim	HOOV	8-3	
Dradga	Jeff	TUL		
Fann	Mike	HAN	Forfeit	
Diaz	Robert	BULL		

(Continued on next page)

Yosemite Division – Tulare Western
February 17, 1979

235

Jones	Scott	MT.W.	O.T. 1-0	
Walker	Calvin	SANG		
Castillo	Marvin	TUL	Fall	1:30
James	Don	HIGH		
Herring	Tom	SB	3-2	
Reyneveld	Willy	A		

* Record

Tournament
1. South — 125.5
2. Hanford — 91.5
3. Monache — 87
4. Bakersfield — 78.5
5. Mt. Whitney — 78
6. Highland — 74
7. Roosevelt — 72
8. Redwood — 65
9. West — 64
10. Fresno — 61.5
11. Foothill — 54
12. Hoover — 53
13. Bullard — 52.5
14. Clovis — 49
15. Tulare — 48
16. Sanger — 47 Tied for 16th
16. Arvin — 47 Tied for 16th
18. Edison — 41.5
19. Madera — 32.5
20. North — 31
21. Tulare W. — 27.5
22. East — 19
23. Delano — 18
24. McLane — 16
25. Reedley — 13
Porterville — 0
Lemoore — 0

Tim Vanni
Monache High
Two-time CIF Champion
Two-time Olympian

Jesse Reyes
Bakersfield High
3rd in CIF 1978
NCAA Champion

Yosemite Divison – Bakersfield College
February 23, 1980

95
Mendoza	Eddie	CL	7-4	
Ray	Wynn	WB		
Caraveo	Frank	DEL	Fall	3:51
Swan	Romeo	MON		
Gonzales	Gus	REED	6-4	
McNeill	Bobby	SANG		

103
Gonzalez	Mike	HIGH	2-0	
Crouch	Trent	FRE		
Saenz	Pablo	REED	3-2	
Potter	Doug	MAD		
Sanchez	David	A	Fall :	36
Hernandez	David	TW		

112
East	Mel	B	8-6	
Geronimo	Ernie	A		
Seay	Mike	HIGH	10-0	
Gonzales	Marty	EX		
Young	Robert	ED	12-5	
Chedester	Jeff	RED	(Career 84-18)	

120
Villareal	Willie	MON	5-2	
Jones	Del	TW		
Villareal	Marc	SB	7-2	
Luttrell	Darin	WB		
Severson	Jerry	EX	4-2	
Torres	Frank	B		

127
Ibarra	Victor	B	5-2	
Bisig	Joe	SB		
Hasson	Jeff	HOOV	1-0	
Dennis	Kenny	CL		
Trevino	Robert	FRE	6-5	
Ybarra	Ruben	ROOS		

133
Boyd	Sam	FRE	Fall	:43
McCray	David	WB		
Rodriguez	Joe	MAD	14-3	
Padilla	Mark	TUL		
Dieling	Dennis	CL	11-9	
Sanchez	Angel	A		

138
Negrette	Ron	RED	3-1	(22-0-1)*
Sanchez	Art	A		
Bilyeu	Scott	CL	Fall 2:13	
Townsend	Don	MON		
Navarro	Fred	EX	6-3	
Lovell	Dan	WB		

145
Carrera	Kevin	HOOV	10-0	(30-1)*
Salomonson	Robbie	PORT		
Inouye	Scott	CL	6-0	
Garza	Oscar	MON		
Coelho	Joe	TW	Fall	2:32
Gamble	Franie	HAN		

154
Juarez	Robert	SANG	6-2	
Aquafresca	Brian	EX		
Salazar	Emmet	DEL	Fall	4:15
Rogers	Leddis	ED		
Christiansen	Brian	CL	3-1	
Torres	Fred	SB		

165
Pulskamp	Flint	HIGH	7-4	(28-1)*
Scott	Malcolm	ED		
Kelly	Tom	SB	4-1	
Zimmerman	Blair	B		
Austin	Kevin	HAN	7-1	
Ferguson	Randy	RED		

175
Emerzian	Tom	ROOS	10-3	(32-1)*
Orton	Jeff	WB		
Snider	Kevin	HOOV	10-4	
Little	Greg	FOOT		
Neilson	Reed	SB	6-5	
Aguilar	Fabian	HAN		

191
Diaz	Robert	BULL	6-2	
Short	Jim	MON		
Jeffus	Craig	FRE	O.T. Ref. Dec.	
Sansinea	Joey	MAD		
Schallock	Mike	SB	Fall	3:40
Hamlin	Greg	PORT		

(Continued on next page)

Yosemite Divison – Bakersfield College
February 23, 1980

238

Jones	Scott	MT.W	Fall :38	(25-0)*
Long	Stan	TW		
Reyneveld	Willy	A	7-3	
Mudryk	Mark	FOOT		
Cervantes	Victor	EB	Fall	2:05
Millidrum	Carl	RED		

Tournament
1. Clovis   97.5
2. South   91.5
3. Monache   87
4. Arvin   82.5
5. Bakersfield   73
6. Highland   72
7. Fresno   69
8. Tulare W.   64.5
9. Exeter   63.5
10. West   60
11. Hoover   58.5
12. Redwood   52
13. Madera   45
14. Hanford   39.5
15. Sanger   37
16. Edison   33
17. Mt. Whitney   31 Tied for 17th
17. Roosevelt   31 Tied for 17th
19. Delano   28
20. Porterville   25.5
21. Reedley   25
22. Tulare   14

Clovis High
Dennis DeLiddo (top left)
Rodney Balch (bottom left)

Yosemite Division – Clovis
February 21, 1981

98
Mendoza	Eddie	CL	11-6
Patino	Bobby	EX	
Nerove	Darrell	FOOT	5-3
Mauricio	John	HAN	
Gonzales	Gus	REED	7-4
Suan	Romero	MON	

105
Quiroz	Joe	CL	10-4	
Garcia	Hugo	A		
Ray	Wynn	WB	Fall	:17
Hernandez	Carl	TW		
Rivera	Mark	MAD	4-2	
Martin	John	CW		

112
East	Mel	B	19-11
Seay	Mike	HIGH	
Caraveo	Jimmy	DEL	6-2
Hernandez	Dave	TW	
Jones	Randy	CW	6-5
Des Jardins	Shane	HAN	

119
Chedester	Jeff	RED	11-2	(33-2)*
Inouye	Darryl	CL		
Williams	Randy	MON	8-4	
Geronimo	Ernie	A		
Williams	S	BULL	Default	
Gonzales	Marty	EX		

126
Harris	Greg	SB	6-1
Jeffrey	Rick	WB	
Rodriguez	Alfonso	REED	2-1
Calderon	Abel	RED	
Gray	Edward	ED	Default
Severson	Jerry	EX	

133
Dennis	Kenny	CL	10-1	
Bisig	Joe	SB		
Sinnott	Richie	HIGH	Fall	4:20
Gamboa	Andrew	MAD		
Siebert	Shawn	Mt.W	5-4	
Briggs	Wayne	HAN		

138
Tice	Jeff	CW	O.T. 4-2	
Stout	Stephen	HAN		
Tillinghast	Mike	BULL	7-5	
Smith	Glen	Mt.W		
McGray	David	WB	Fall	2:59
Lathrop	Mike	SB		

145
Carrera	Kevin	HOOV	4-2
Bilyeu	Scott	CL	
Townsend	Don	MON	6-2
Zimmer	Brad	CW	
Mills	Cary	SB	8-6
Hernandez	Frank	EX	

154
Annis	Jeff	SB	9-5
Garza	Oscar	MON	
Christensen	Brian	CL	7-6
Lazalde	Ismael	FRE	
Stover	Rusty	EX	3-2
Campbell	Eric	CW	

167
Aquafresca	Brian	EX	15-4	(30-0)*
Kelly	Tom	SB		
Aguilar	Fabian	HAN	6-3	
Maas	David	WB		
Michell	Marty	TW	7-6	
Hill	Kirk	MON		

185
Mayberry	Dan	FOOT	4-3	
Peterson	George	CW		
Diaz	Robert	BULL	Fall	2:59
Austin	Kevin	HAN		
Stall	Dusty	MON	6-3	
Orton	Jeff	WB		

200
Sansinena	Joey	MAD	5-4	
Jeffus	Craig	FRE		
Madsen	Joey	Mon	Fall	:37
Hanneman	Cliff	CW		
Chadon	Joe	MT.W	Fall	3:45
Newcombe	Mike	WB		

(Continued on next page)

Yosemite Division – Clovis
February 21, 1981

245
Short	Jim	MON	5-4	(32-1)*
Wilson	Dan	WB		
Long	Stan	TW	Fall	2:30
Cervantes	Victor	EB		
Traffenstedt	Jim	B	Fall	5:30
Duke	Russel	FOOT		

* Record

Tournament
1. Clovis 140
2. Monache 136
3. West 113.5
4. South 110
5. Clovis West 106
6. Exeter 93
7. Hanford 85
8. Lemoore 70
9. Foothill 54
10. Madera 53
11. Tulare West 50
12. Highland 44
13. Bullard 43
14. Fresno 39
15. Bakersfield 38
16. Mt. Whitney 34
17. Arvin 31
18. Delano 29
19. Reedley 28
20. Hoover 26
21. Redwood 22
22. East 15
23. Edison 13 Tied for 23rd
23. Tulare 13 Tied for 23rd
25. McLane 3
26. Roosevelt 3
Sanger 0
Porterville 0
Golden West 0

Mel East
Bakersfield High
Three-time CIF Champion
1980 State Champion
1981 2nd in State
1982 4th in State

Yosemite Division – Hanford

February 20, 1982

98
Nerove	Darrell	FOOT	Fall	3:40
Mendoza	Ed	CL		
Patino	Bobby	EX		
Mauricio	John	HAN		
Kland	Kevin	HOOV		
Ramirez	Pete	A		

105
Ray	Wynn	WB	12-3	
Cleveland	Jeff	B		
Buccat	Chris	DEL		
Quiroz	Joe	CL		
Salgado	Larry	EX		
Santos	Willie	HOOV		

112
Rivera	Mark	MAD	4-3
Martin	John	CW	
Cottingham	Greg	EX	
Hernandez	David	TW	
Ybarra	Anthony	CL	
Austin	Brian	HAN	

119
East	Mel	B	Fall	4:46
Rangel	Pete	MAD		
Armstead	Mike	LEM		
Carrol	Chip	SB		
Enriquez	Ralph	TW		
Kong	Gary	DEL		

126
Des Jardins	Shane	HAN	10-1
Calderon	Abel	RED	
Williams	Randy	MON	
Prather	Brett	WB	
Johannas	Kirk	CL	
Media	Phil	PORT	

133
Harris	Greg	SB	4-3
Rosario	David	MAD	
Morales	Tony	EB	
Lewis	Brian	CW	
Munoz	Leroy	TUL	
Marquez	Jesse	GW	

138
Richburg	Allen	CW	6-0
Graham	Randy	B	
Lathrop	Mike	SB	
Marchant	Kris	FOOT	
Cantu	David	MAD	
Hollis	Jim	TW	

145
Tice	Jeff	CW	Fall	1:27
Hodges	Keith	B		
Klugow	Scott	SB		
Mays	Bill	SANG		
Gregory	John	MON		
Garcia	David	CL		

155
Townsend	Don	MON	13-3 (35-1)*
Christensen	Brian	CL	
Glass	Jon	HAN	
Mills	Cary	SB	
Zimmer	Brad	CW	
Creech	Jim	B	

167
Hill	Kirk	MON	O.T. 4-1
Campbell	Eric	CW	
Lazalde	Ismael	FRE	
Garnand	Blake	SB	
Frohlich	John	B	
Serr	Mike	MT.W	

185
Greemore	Jason	B	Fall	3:27
Davidson	Lindsey	WB		
Young	Todd	CW		
Torosian	Dan	MAD		
Tyler	Terry	RED		
Edmonds	Chris	REED		

200
Barnes	John	EX	6-5
Davis	Mark	TUL	
White	Donny	CW	
Keck	Ward	MON	
Forey	Matt	FOOT	
Ramirez	Juan	ROOS	

(Continued on next page)

Yosemite Division – Hanford
February 20, 1982

245
Estes	Barry	CW	11-5
Lizama	Pete	FOOT	
Garcia	Carlos	MAD	
Traffenstedt	Jim	B	
Bristol	Lloyd	HAN	
Toland	Al	NB	

* Record

Notes
Mel East was the first wrestler to win four Yosemite Division titles

Tournament
1. Clovis West   191.5
2. Bakersfield   164.5
3. Madera   107
4. South   105.5
5. Monache   98.5
6. Clovis   90
7. Hanford   86.5
8. Foothill   73
9. Exeter   69 Tied for 9th
9. West   69 Tied for 9th

Lennis Cowell
Clovis West
Coached three CIF and two State Championship teams

Yosemite Division – Tulare Western
February 19, 1983

98
Montoya	Greg	CL	11-9
Ramirez	Pete	AR	
Kland	Kevin	HOOV	10-9
Benavides	John	MT.W	
Henry	Casey	CW	7-0
Sullivan	Phillip	TW	

105
Patino	Bob	EX	13-0
Cardenas	Raul	MON	
Quiroz	Joe	CL	5-1
Martinez	Jiim	FOOT	
Hollender	Dan	CW	2-0
Williams	Joe	HIGH	

112
Dallas	Mke	Foot	11-3
Quintana	Diego	CL	
Salgado	Larry	EX	6-3
Bragg	Greg	RED	
Rodriguez	Abel	DEL	5-0
Carlson	Greg	B	

119
Nerove	Darrell	FOOT	Fall :35
Rangel	Pat	MAD	
Martin	John	CW	Fall 4:02 (34-4)*
Ramirez	Tony	A	
Moreno	Ed	ROOS	7-5
Ybarra	Anthony	CL	

126
Caladeron	Abel	RED	7-3
Morales	Tony	EB	
Gomez	Francisco	CL	10-3
Garay	Manuel	A	
Johanns	Kirk	CL	Forfeit
Able	Frank	TW	

133
Lewis	Brian	CW	7-4
Austin	Bryan	HAN	
Perez	Noe	SB	Fall 3:20
Sylvia	Darren	RED	
Cuevas	Tinee	EX	11-6
Collins	Kerry	GW	

138
Sapien	Kevin	Ex	11-9
Merritt	Joey	High	
Davis	Bret	Mon	7-4
Chavez	Martin	B	
Marchant	Kris	Foot	Forfeit
Barnes	Todd	CW	

145
Richburg	Allen	CW	7-2 (38-1)*
Graham	Randy	B	
Rosario	David	MAD	8-2
Williams	Robert	W	
Moody	Brian	GW	7-5
Klaasen	Randy	MT.W	

155
Zimmer	Brad	CW	13-3 (38-3)*
Glass	Jon	HAN	
Edmonds	Brett	REED	3-2
Hampton	Kelly	EX	
Hinsley	Jim	FOOT	6-4
Barboza	Lorenzo	CL	

167
Campbell	Eric	CW	31-2
Inouye	Les	CL	
Garnand	Blake	SB	17-4
Thompson	Matt	MON	
Lockwood	Rick	EX	3-2
Thompson	Terry	LEM	

185
Young	Todd	CW	7-1 (35-4)*
Forry	Matt	FOOT	
Moore	Lenny	B	Fall 4:09
Hill	Craig	MON	
Flowers	Randy	MCL	8-7
Stringer	John	CL	

200
Allen	Chris	SB	8-4
White	Don	CW	
Howe	Todd	CL	15-9
Imamura	Rod	FRE	
Lizama	Ben	FOOT	8-3
Elmore	Dan	TUL	

(Continued on next page)

Yosemite Division – Tulare Western
February 19, 1983

245

Estes	Barry	CW	Fall	5:47 (37-0)*
Sallas	Rick	MAD		
Duke	Russell	FOOT	Fall	1:27
Landseadel	Brad	RED		
Mendivel	Doc	EB	Fall	2:03
Machado	James	EX		

Tournament

1. Clovis West 240.5
2. Foothill 144
3. Clovis 137.5
4. Exeter 123
5. Monache 68
6. Arvin 67.5
7. Redwood 66
8. South 65
9. Madera 62.5
10. Bakersfield 60
11. Hanford 58
12. East 41
13. Highland 31.5
14. Fresno 25 Tied for 14th
14. Golden West 25 Tied for 14th
14. Mt. Whitney 25 Tied for 14th
17. Lemoore 24.5
18. Reedley 22 Tied for 18th
18. West 22 Tied for 18th
20. Tulare W. 20.5
21. Tulare Union 19
22. Hoover 15
23. Roosevelt 11 Tied for 23rd
23. McLane 11 Tied for 23rd
25. Delano 9.5
26. Sanger 7
27. Bullard 2
Porterville 0

Darrell Nerove of Foothill High
1984 State Champion scores a 2-point near fall

*Records as of 2-19-84

Yosemite Division – Arvin

February 18, 1984

98
Ramirez	Pete	A	Fall	(31-1)*
Martin	Sal	GW		(29-7)*
Benavides	John	MT.W		
Garcia	Sal	MAD		
Dutra	Darrin	HAN		
Brooks	Tim	SAN		

105
Henry	Casey	CW	3-2	(36-6)*
East	Brad	W		(27-4)*
Cantu	Roben	GW		
Rice	David	MON		
Lopez	Cruz	TW		
Quintero	Marty	CL		

112
Patino	Bobby	EX	14-2	(39-2)*
Bragg	Gregg	RED		(22-2)*
Ciprian	Peter	ROOS		
Ybarra	Anthony	CL		
Cardenas	Roy	MON		
Leuvano	Mike	FOOT		

119
Dallas	Mike	FOOT	15-3	(20-4-1)*
Chavez	Ruben	B		
Land	Robert	MON		
Calderon	Jerry	RED		
Hollender	Dan	CW		
Nickell	Jeff	EB		

126
Lewis	Brian	CW	O.T. Crit. Dec.
Garay	Manuel	A	
Rangel	Pat	MAD	
Erebia	Ruben	CL	
Armistead	Mike	LEM	
Jarrard	Mike	B	

133
Nerove	Darrel	FOOT	13-0	(32-1)*
Ashjian	Brook	WB		(28-5)*
Martin	John	CW		
Wooden	Bryan	TW		
Hinsley	Bruce	HIGH		
Cuevas	Tinee	EX		

138
Gomez	Francisco	CW	5-2	(38-2-1)*
Merritt	Joey	HIGH		(30-3)*
Hembree	James	SB		
Collings	Kerry	GW		
Austin	Brian	HAN		
Meneses	John	MON		

145
Rosario	David	MAD	12-14	(39-1)*
Thomas	Jerry	FRE		(21-7)*
Sandoval	Brent	CW		
Moody	Brian	GW		
Fowler	Dale	WB		
Padilla	Ray	A		

154
Graham	Randy	B	6-3	
Cowart	Lance	MON		
Cunningham	Randy	HOOV		
Martinez	Carmen	EX		
Barnes	Todd	CW		
Hammill	Chuck	GW		

165
Tice	Jeff	CW	6-3	(36-3)*
Creech	Jim	B		
Inouye	Les	CL		
Green	Richard	FOOT		
Green	Ron	TW		
Katuin	Kevin	SANG		

175
Hill	Craig	MON	10-1	(43-2-2)*
Telen	Dan	CL		
Cerda	David	CW		
Hadley	Anthony	FRE		
Gretlein	Jim	B		
Holland	Scott	SB		

191
Lizama	Ben	FOOT	10-5	(27-3)*
Flowers	Ron	FRE		
Flowers	Randy	MCL		
Christensen	Kevin	CL		
Velasco	John	MAD		
Kelley	Ron	GW		

(Continued on next page)

Yosemite Division - Arvin
February 18, 1984

245
Salas	Ricky	MAD	6-4	
Barnes	Trent	CW		(35-6)*
Mendival	Doc	EB		
Moore	Gailton	MT.W		
Machado	James	EX		
Pullin	Rich	MON		

* Record (as of 2-18-84)

Tournament
1. Clovis West 194
2. Monache 119.5
3. Clovis 102
4. Bakersfield 94
5. Madera 93.5
6. Foothill 87
7. Golden West 86.5
8. Exeter 75
9. Arvin 66.5
10. Fresno 59
11. West 55
12. Mt. Whitney 44
13. Tulare Union 36.5
14. Highland 35
15. Redwood 31
16. South 29.5
17. Hanford 29
18. East 25.5
19. McLane 25
20. Tulare W. 24.5
21. Sanger 22.5
22. Roosevelt 20
23. Hoover 18
24. Lemoore 10
25. Delano 6
26. Reedley 4
27. Porterville 4
28. Bullard 1
Edison 0
North 0

Varsity Wrestling. First row: Shannon Eudy, Luis Contreas, Mike Luevano, Jesse Pinon, Mike Dallas, Bill Ballard, Darrel Nerove, Frank Thomas. 2nd row: Coach Seymour Nerove, Dean Pfutzenreuter, Manuel Alderete, Jeff Rangel, Richard Green, Scott Hulcy, Ben Lizama, Steve Nieto, Coach Richie Sinnett.

1984 Foothill High South Yosemite League Champions

Craig Hill
6th in CIF 1983
3rd in CIF 1984
4th in State 1984

Lance Cowart
2nd in CIF 1984
2nd in State 1984
Monache High

Yosemite Division – Tulare Western

February 16, 1985

98
Snyder	Pete	MON	6-4	(39-5)*
Tamez	Anthony	CL		(32-6)*
Martinez	A	BULL	Inj. Default	
Dutra	Darrin	HAN		
Smithson	Chad	HOOV	4-3	
Garcia	Saliois	MAD		

105
East	Brad	B	Fall 2:40	(40-0)*
Cantu	Ruben	GW		(31-3)
Quintero	Marty	CL	Fall 4:36	
Hill	Charles	CW		
Sanchez	Eddie	MAD	6-3	
Burr	Bobby	PORT		

112
Henry	Casey	CW	13-4	(33-6-1)*
Eudy	Shannon	FOOT		(25-6)*
Lopez	Cruz	TUL	17-6	
Sweeney	Don	MAD		
Flores	Frank	HAN	15-8	
Barrios	Juan	MON		

119
Bragg	Greg	RED	11-0	(22-1)*
Richie	Jamie	CW		(15-6)*
Crosswhite	Shawn	CL	16-0	
Romero	Tony	TW		
Johansen	Keith	MAD	6-3	
Cuevas	Dan	EX		

126
Rangel	Pat	CL	Fall 5:08	
Morales	Perry	ROOS		(21-7)*
Dallas	Mike	FOOT	23-3	
Harlan	Robbie	CW		
Beavers	Troy	HIGH	7-2	
Marin	Jose	A		

133
Sordi	John	MAD	8-7	(22-5)*
Martinez	John	CL		(32-5-1)*
Valdez	Ric	SANG	9-5	
Chavez	Ruben	B		
Ballard	Bill	FOOT	2-0	
Pierro	Jon	CW		

138
Rangel	Jeff	FOOT	8-5	(38-7)*
Martinez	Joe	BULL		(25-4-1)*
Garcia	Frank	EX	10-4	
Olivas	Kelvin	CL		
Cano	Albert	HAN	13-2	
Martinez	Barney	B		

145
Flores	Luis	MAD	O.T. Crit. Dec.	
Sandoval	Brent	CW		(31-6-1)*
Cuevas	Miguel	EX	7-0	
Gannon	Joe	HIGH		
Ortega	Jesse	DEL	4-3	
Olinger	Chris	SB		

154
Cerda	Jerry	CW	Default	(31-6)*
McCauley	Phillip	HOOV		
Snyder	John	MON	6-5	
Cox	Steve	CL		
Cano	Chris	HAN	4-1	
Aguilar	James	EB		

165
Cunningham	Randy	HOOV	10-4	
Gretlein	Jim	NB		
Katuin	Kevin	SANG	5-2	
Pulskamp	Greg	HIGH		
Olinger	Scott	SB	18-11	
Howe	Ty	CL		

175
Hill	Craig	MON	19-6	(45-1)*
Hernandez	Robert	MT.W		
Leonard	Mike	A	4-3	
Williams	D	CW		
Flowers	Wes	ED	Forfeit	
Gatzka	Greg	ROOS		

191
Clark	David	MAD	6-2	
Telen	Dan	CL		
Fugman	Brett	CW	5-4	
Kelly	Ron	GW		(26.5)*
Davis	Pat	B	Fall 2:11	
Romera	Alfredo	A		

(Continued on next page)

Yosemite Division – Tulare Western
February 16, 1985

245
Lizama	Ben	FOOT	21-9	(35-3)*
Barnes	Trent	CW		(35-1)*
Fontes	Ken	CL	Default	
Pullen	Rich	MON		
Anderson	George	EX	13-2	
Slocum	Charles	ED		

* Record

Tournament
1. Clovis   190.5
Clovis West   182.5

Seated, from the left: Larry Clark, Jim Moneymaker, Jim Jones, Barry Young, Joe Reyes, Bob Shawn, Jim Pratt, Bill Downey, Stanley Hill, Ballard Barker. Kneeling: Jeff Tuculet, Glen Adams, Norman Bailey, Jerry Briscoe, Harry Hodges, Gary Monji, Riley Keester, Travis Smith, Charles Bridgford. Standing: Mr. Bootman, Coach; Jerry Collins, Jess Thoene, Clarence Elder, Roger Bridgford, Zane Sherrill, Keith Montgomery, Blaine Rogers, Marion Robbins, Marc Ratzlaff, Manager.

Kneeling, l. to r.: Monji, Hodges, Robbins, C. Bridgford. Standing: Bailey, Montgomery, R. Bridgford, Sherrill. Sherrill and Bridgford were the first North matmen to go to the state meet.

Mr. Bootman
Wrestling Coach

1958 North Bakersfield High Wrestling Team

Yosemite Division – Bullard
February 22, 1986

95
Garcia	Sal	MAD	2-1	
Zinkin	Harold	BULL		
Riley	Brandon	CL	8-2	
Hamaoka	Derek	CW		
Levanio	Tony	EB	Fall	4:45
Thulin	Billy	MON		

103
Tames	Anthony	CL	Fall	3:31
Tennison	Julius	ED		
Snyder	Pete	MON	10-3	
Blanco	Ray	CW		
Martinez	Alex	BULL	Fall	1:41
Melo	Vince	EX		

112
East	Brad	B	(34-2)*	
Dutra	Darren	HAN		
Salyer	Jimmy	TUL	Default	
Smithson	Chad	HOOV		
DeLuna	Osi	MAD	2-0	
Williams	Ken	EX		

120
Cavazos	Junior	MAD	6-5	
Gaon	Jason	SB		
Herron	Marc	EX	18-8	
Flores	Frank	HAN		
Eudy	Shannon	FOOT	Fall	1:35
Fierro	Henry	RED		

127
Crosswhite	Shawn	CL	10-2	
Shockley	Brian	B		
Cuevas	Dan	EX	O.T. 11-2	
Marin	Jose	A		
Johansen	Keith	FRE	10-5	
Duquette	James	MT.W		

133
Beavers	Troy	HIGH	4-2	(33-2)*
Islas	Andy	CL		
Prather	Hugh	B	Fall	3:13
Garcia	Joe	MAD		
Pierro	John	CW	6-0	
Ramos	Efrain	A		

138
Garcia	Frank	EX	9-5	
Rangel	Jeff	FOOT		
Olivas	Kelvin	CL	Fall	1:43
Stricker	Ty	SB		
Wright	Gary	LEM	8-4	
Nevez	Brian	HAN		

145
Herndon	Scott	SB	13-4	(21-1)*
Cerda	Jerry	ROOS		
Olivera	Craig	B	Fall	1:47
Threkeld	Wes	FRE		
Salgado	Fred	EX	6-3	
Starlin	Monty	CL		

154
Tripp	John	TUL	Fall 1:24	(28-1)*
Gannon	Joe	HIGH		
Romine	Joe	MAD	Default	
Leonard	Matt	A		
Brown	Wes	CW	5-0	
Percivel	Marc	RED		

165
Leonard	Mike	A	Default	
Olinger	Scott	SB		
Bruton	Terry	MT.W	5-2	
Warford	Scott	EX		
Howe	Ty	CL	TF 23-7	
Walker	Brandon	WB		

175
Pulskamp	Greg	HIGH	7-1	
Linsey	Cory	CW		
Gatzka	Greg	ROOS	4-2	
Flowers	Wes	ED		
Cox	Steve	CL	Fall	2:59
Pence	Keith	EX		

191
Tellen	Dan	CL	10-1	
Neal	Lorenzo	LEM		
Davis	Pat	B	Fall	4:52
Harris	Earl	TUL		
Blazevich	Scott	MCL	8-5	
Nahama	David	FOOT		

(Continued on next page)

Yosemite Division – Bullard

February 22, 1986

HWT

Barnes	Trent	CW	Fall	1:02
Pontes	Ken	CL		
Anderson	George	EX	Fall	4:14
Correa	Joseph	MAD		
Pullin	Richard	MON	3-0	
Waltz	John	NB		

Tournament

1. Clovis — 192
2. Exeter — 137
3. Madera — 112
4. Bakersfield — 107.5
5. Clovis West — 99.5
6. South — 88.5
7. Tulare — 79.5
8. Arvin — 76.5
9. Highland — 69.5
10. Hanford — 61

Foothill — 47.5
Monache — 41
East — 26
North — 12
West — 11

FIRST ROW, left to right: Jim Wise, Peter Delis, Frank Hopper, Royal Stout, Ronnie Betcalf, Angelo Haddad, Danny Moreland. SECOND ROW: Jerry Garland, Dennis Haggard, Lary Carpenter, Johnny Salcido, Mac Anderson, Charles Brown. THIRD ROW: Jerry Scott, Gene Trotter, Bob DiFrancisco, Lee Boyd, Bob Anglen, Al Gamboa, Carlos Garcia, Grover Rains, Coach. FOURTH ROW: Bob Aston, Coach; George Hess, Joe Meek, Claude Bradford, Mike Addy, Bill Sapp, Pete Wetzler, Jim May. FIFTH ROW: Don Lopez, William Huddleson, Jim Moshier, Joe Moss, Carl Cruz, Hollis Moss, Steve Magnus, Danny Avilez, Jack Chambers, Joe Garrett, Bob Piper, Ron Pratt.

1958 East Bakersfield Wrestling Team

Yosemite Division – Mt. Whitney/Visalia
February 21, 1987

98
Zinkin	Harold	BULL	3-2	
Hamoaka	Derrick	CW		
Sordi	Robbie	MAD	Fall	2:50
Mancillas	Fernie	B	(34-7)*	
Riley	Dustin	CL	5-2	
Rivera	Tom	MON		

105
Tamez	Anthony	CL	4-0
Zinkin	Dewayne	BULL	
Patton	Derrick	A	9-0
Perez	Art	SB	
Gobeli	David	HOOV	3-1
Tennyson	Julius	ED	

112
Salyer	Jimmy	TUL	8-5	(28-3)*
Flores	Frank	HAN		
Fambona	Pedro	A	4-2	
Riley	Brandon	CL		
Meza	Saul	EB	Maj. 17-8	
Costales	Ed	DEL		

119
Dutra	Darrin	HAN	7-5
Herron	Marc	EX	
Ortega	Mike	ROOS	TF 3:45
Gaon	Jason	SB	
Smithson	Chad	HOOV	8-4
Marmolejo	Albert	A	

125
Garcia	Joe	MAD	14-2
Myers	Shem	SB	
Garside	Erin	NB	6-3
Marin	Jose	A	
Johansen	Keith	FRE	8-3
Williams	Ken	EX	

132
Pierro	Jon	CW	8-2
Henderson	Brian	SB	
Beavers	Troy	HIGH	7-3
Harvey	Travis	MON	
Holland	Christian	TUL	O.T. 1-0
Slocum	Stacy	ED	

138
Sordi	John	MAD	7-2
Campos	Joe	FRE	
Prather	Hugh	B	6-2
Stricker	Ty	SB	
Richburg	Greg	CW	5-3
Gonzales	Frank	TW	

145
Hernadon	Scott	SB	Maj. 11-0	(42-1)*
Byrd	David	CW		
Neves	Brian	HAN	8-4	
Sever	Wes	HOOV		
Newton	Randy	LEM	Fall	2:52
Larrea	Mike	FRE		

154
Romine	Joe	MAD	9-2
Starlin	Monte	CW	
Treadwell	Otto	TUL	Sup. 14-2
Kessler	Tim	CW	
Threlkeld	Wes	FRE	7-2
Garcia	Adrian	EX	

165
Tripp	John	TUL	6-3	(33-0)*
Olinger	Chris	SB		
Alcorn	John	HAN	Maj. 11-0	
Leonard	Matt	A		
Percival	Marc	RED	Fall	2:50
Frantzich	Vince	CL		

175
Urzua	Jerry	FRE	Maj. 14-3	
Garcia	Mario	DEL		
Dominici	David	MAD	Maj. 12-2	
Nesbitt	Lee	MT.W		
Hailey	Lorenzo	TUL	Fall	1:35
Baserkanian	Art	BULL		

191
Neal	Lorenzo	LEM	9-2
Carlos	Rene	CL	
Blazevich	Scott	MCL	O.T.
Mayorene	Marcelino	FRE	
Scott	Greg	ED	9-2
Ramirez	Jimmy	HAN	

(Continued on next page)

Yosemite Division – Mt. Whitney/Visalia
February 21, 1987

HWT
Anderson	George	EX	6-3	(42-0)*
Fontes	Ken	CL		
Neal	Eddie	LEM	8-4	
Pierce	Vic	SB		
Woltz	John	NB	Fall	2:55
Sosa	Henry	RED		

Tournament
1. South 149.5
2. Clovis 129
3. Madera 104.5
4. Tulare 100
5. Hanford 99.5
6. Clovis West 99
7. Fresno 89.5
8. Arvin 75.5
9. Lemoore 64
10. Exeter 62
11. Bullard 58.5
12. North 37.5
12. Delano 37.5
14. Bakersfield 36.5
15. Hoover 36
16. Monache 34.5
17. Redwood 29.5
18. Edison 27.5
19. East 19.5
20. Mt. Whitney 19
21. McLane 17.5
22. Roosevelt 16.5
23. West 12
24. Tulare W. 11.5
25. Porterville 11.5
26. Foothill 4
27. Reedley 1

* Record

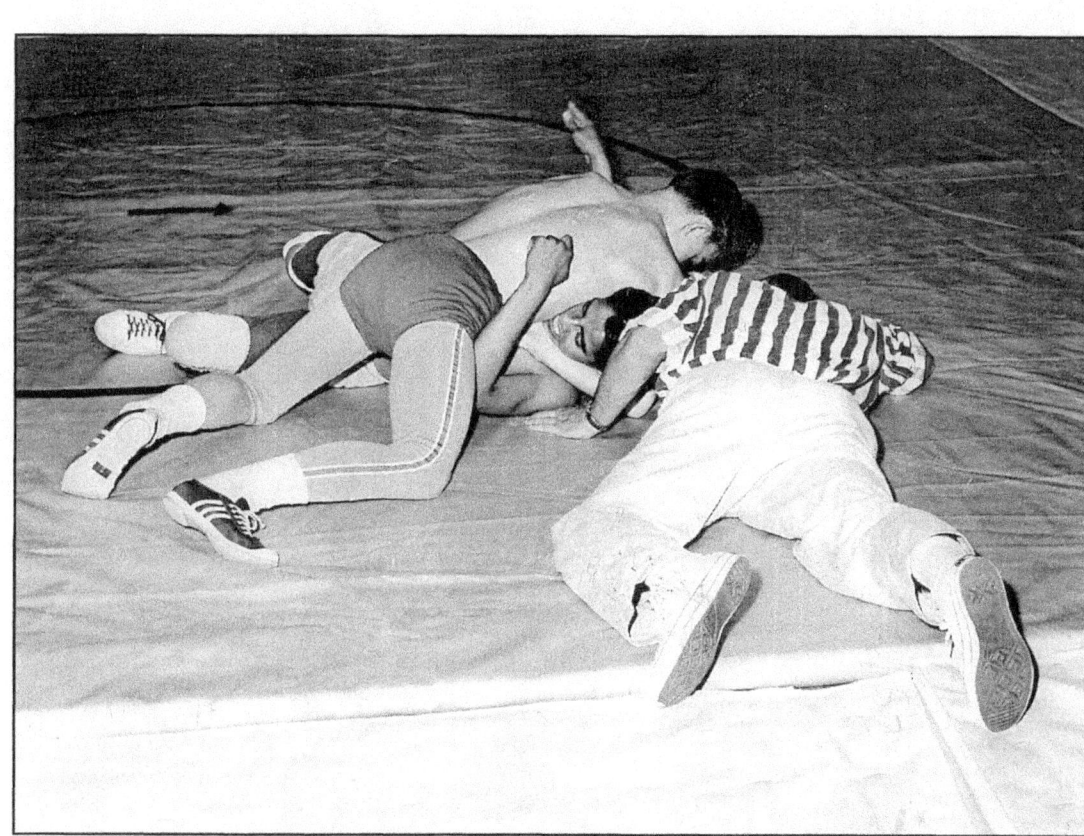
Jim Heckman (top) of South Bakersfield - 4th CIF 1960

Yosemite Division – Arvin
February 20, 1988

98
Sordi	Robbie	MAD	Maj. 10-1	
Crane	Shawn	CW		
Wright	Kenny	B	Fall	2:55
Villafona	Angel	RED		
Gant	Detran	ROOS	15-2	
Whitley	Parris	SB		

105
Valle	Levid	GW	6-5	
Hamaoka	Derrek	CW		(44-8)*
Rivera	Tom	MON	7-3	
Mendel	Henry	DEL		
Tamez	Mike	CL	8-7	
Heberle	Jeff	NB		

112
Zinkin	Dewayne	BULL	O.T. 2-0	
Gobeli	David	HOOV		
Solis	Robert	RED	9-4	
Fombona	Pedro	A		
Hood	Brett	MON		
Chester	Barry	HAN		

119
Salyer	Jim	TUL	9-7	
Patton	Derek	A		
Moreno	Jose	MAD	5-3	
Azcona	Robert	CL		
Desmarais	Joel	W	12-3	
Pegan	Del	GW		

126
Ortega	Mike	ROOS	16-1	(44-5)*
Soto	Steve	CW		
Melo	Vince	EX	6-2	
Olivas	Ralph	CL		
Flores	David	MAD		
Tripp	Ricky	RED		

132
Cemo	Joe	NB	Fall	3:40
Haupt	Heath	CL		
Gamulao	Danny	GW	9-6	
Chavez	Art	WB		
Williams	Ken	EX	Fall	1:59
McConnaughy	Rick	LEM		

138
Lopez	Narciso	ROOS	7-6	
Gonzales	Greg	TW		
Gomez	Gus	EX	Inj. Def.	
Stricker	Tad	SB		
Lawanson	Joseph	CW		
Caldwell	Brandon	W	3-1	

145
Stricker	Ty	SB	11-7	
Cuevas	Alfonso	MAD		
Hoyt	Brian	CL	O.T. 1-0	
Froehlich	Jassen	B		
Sandusky	Darren	CW	4-0	
Garcia	John			

154
Starling	Monty	CL	4-3	(32-12)*
DeGough	Scott	CW		
Camp	Scott	MON	13-9	
Deatherage	Larry	NB		
Fletcher	David	W	4-1	
Weier	Matt	SB		

165
Leonard	Matt	A	19-7	
Garcia	Adrian	EX		
Estrada	Richard	ROOS	7-0	
Smith	James	TUL		
Caldawell	Randy	CW	6-2	
Eckert	Danny	REED		

175
Urzua	Jerry	FRE	Fall	3:02
Madison	Mike	WB		
Cota	Ramon	HOOV	5-2	
Leary	Marcus	A		
Jones	Owen	DEL	Fall	4:51
Allen	Steve	REED		

191
Neal	Lorenzo	LEM	9-4	(32-0)*
Hailey	Lorenzo	TUL		
Langley	Kevin	NB	Fall	4:40
Jasso	Javier	RED		
Nesbitt	Lee	MT.W	6-0	
Williams	Gary	HOOV		

(Continued on next page)

Yosemite Division – Arvin
February 20, 1988

245
Carlos	Rene	CL	9-3	(34-5)*
Smith	Mark	CW		
Sosa	Henry	RED	Fall	2:48
Maricich	Jim	FOOT		
Barella	Mike	MON	Fall	:55
Fallis	Troy	SB		

*Record

Tournament
1. Clovis West 147.5
2. Clovis 139.5
3. Redwood 98.5
4. Arvin 87.5
5. Exeter 80.5
6. Roosevelt 79
7. West 77.5
8. Madera 72.5
9. North 68.5
10. South 67.5
11. Hoover 65
12. Tulare Union 62
13. Monache 61
14. Golden West 54.5
15. Bakersfield 43
16. Lemoore 39.5
17. Delano 29.5
18. Bullard 28
19. Fresno 26
20. Tulare W. 20
21. Foothill 14
21. Hanford 14
21. Mt. Whitney 14
24. East 11.5
25. Reedley 9.5
26. Sanger 5.5
27. Porterville 2
Highland 0
Edison 0
McLane 0

Left to right: Ty Stricker and Tad Stricker
South Bakersfield

Yosemite Division – Hanford
February 18, 1989

98
Alkire	Curtis	MON	2-0
Molano	David	GW	
Fuentes	Ed	SANG	3-2
Ward	Steve	NB	
Zinkin	Nick	BULL	11-9
Poor	Michael	MAD	

106
Aguirre	Jimmy	CL	7-6	
Sordi	Robi	MAD		
Gant	Detran	ROOS	Fall	5:30
Crain	Sean	CW		
Corona	Ralph	HAN	7-2	
Keester	Mike	NB		

112
Whitley	Parris	SB	O.T. 6-4
Heberle	Jeff	NB	
Wright	Kenny	B	5-2
Tamez	Mike	CL	
Villafano	Angel	RED	7-1
Ervin	Ben	MAD	

119
Honn	Troy	SANG	7-0
Arredeno	Rick	MAD	
Hood	Brett	MON	Default
Gobeli	David	HOOV	
Solis	Robert	RED	9-4
Hurtado	Steve	ROOS	

126
Zinkin	DeWayne	BULL	14-3
Hogue	Kelly	MAD	
Riley	Dustin	CL	15-2
Rodriguez	Jesse	REED	
Harper	Dorrell	B	2-1
Bennett	Mark	MT.W	

132
Mello	Vince	EX	6-5	
Cemo	Joe	NB		
Miller	David	CW	Fall	3:38
Anderson	Demetrius	B		
Kenner	Ricky	BULL	15-9	
Tripp	Ricky	RED		

138
Soto	Steve	CW	4-3
Williams	Ken	EX	(45-2-1)*
Olivas	Ralph	CL	6-1
Willard	Danny	NB	
Motl	Randy	LEM	6-0
Dominguez	Eddie	TW	

145
Lopez	Narciso	ROOS	6-5
Caldawell	Brandon	WB	
Cuevas	Alfonso	MAD	4-1
Campolongo	Jason	CW	
Garcia	Isaac	B	7-5
Pulskamp	Victor	HIGH	

154
Stricker	Tad	SB	7-1	
Lawanson	Joseph	CW		
Froelich	Jim	B	Fall	2:11
Bartlett	Steve	NB		
Gearhart	Henry	MCL	4-0	
Carranza	Francisco	PORT		

165
Sandusky	Darren	CW	5-4
Froelich	Jassen	B	
Chavez	Alberto	HOOV	6-4
Stringer	Don	CL	
Leary	Marcus	A	5-0
Cook	Greg	BULL	

175
Land	Ryan	MON	7-4
Martinez	Dan	TW	
Torres	Bryant	MAD	Default
Madison	Mike	WB	
Olsen	Gary	B	5-2
Lopez	Mark	ROOS	

191
Carlos	Rene	CL	7-4
Langley	Kevin	NB	
Bell	Brad	CW	4-2
Williams	Gary	HOOV	
Allen	Steve	RED	Default
Nesbitt	Lee	MT.W	

(Continued on next page)

Yosemite Division – Hanford
February 18, 1989

HWT

Neal	Lorenzo	LEM	6-3	
Smith	Mark	CW		
Jasso	Javier	RED	Fall	1:23
Campbell	Glen	B		
Reade	Scott	WB	13-7	
Klensch	Fred	FRE		

* Record

Tournament

1. Clovis West 163.5
2. Bakersfield 133.5
3. Madera 1 31
4. Clovis 114
5. North 112.5
6. Monache 85
7. Redwood 69
8. Bullard 64.5
9. Roosevelt 57
10. South 55
11. Hoover 52.5
12. Exeter 50.5
13. West 48
14. Sangaer 45
15. Tulare W. 44
16. Lemoore 40
17. Golden West 38.5
18. Mt. Whitney 22
19. Reedley 18
20. McLane 17
21. Arvin 15
22. Fresno 14.5
23. Hanford 11
24. East 9
25. Foothill 7
26. Tulare Union 6
27. Porterville 4
28. Highland 3
Delano 0

Joe Cemo (left)
North Bakersfield
1988 CIF Champion
1989 2nd CIF
1989 3rd in State

Steve Ward (left) of North Bakersfield

Yosemite Division – Clovis
February 17, 1990

98
Poore	Chad	MAD	8-0	
McGill	Mike	EX		
Amaya	Rick	Mon	3-0	
Radman	Aaron	WB		
Chandler	Travis	CL	Forfeit	
Sanchez	Mark	A		

105
Zinkin	Nick	CL	15-6	
Hamaoka	Tyson	CW		
Sanchez	George	PORT	8-1	
Winn	Robert	B		
Fuentes	Ed	SANG	6-2	
Watson	Ernie	GW		

112
Gant	Detran	ROOS	8-3	
Ervins	Ben	MAD		
Moland	Dvaid	GW	Fall	4:52
Hull	Brian	MON		
Mitchell	Matt	HAN	12-8	
Herrera	Chris	HOOV		

119
Aguirre	Jimmy	CL	Fall	1:13
Villafana	Angel	RED		
Gobeli	David	HOOV	Default	
Whitley	Parris	SB		
Washington	Yero	PORT	12-10	
Morales	Richard	EB		

126
Alkire	Curtis	MON	Fall	1:10
Hogue	Kelly	MAD		
Heberly	Jeff	NB	Forfeit	
Tamez	Mike	CL		
Hernandez	Ryan	WB	6-5	
Martinez	Marcelino	EX		

132
Riley	Dustin	CL	7-1	(37-1)*
Enriquez	Jimmy	SB		
Roach	Brian	CW	8-5	
Scalzo	Chad	MAD		
Rodriguez	Jesse	REED	4-1	
Williams	Terry	B		

138
Olivas	Ralph	CL	4-0	
Weber	Clayton	MAD		
Motl	Randy	LEM	10-7	
Zamarano	Carlos			
Alvarez	Michael	EX		
Harthorn	Brian	B		

145
Hall	Ken	MON	11-3	
Zeller	Jason	CW		
Chavez	Andres	HOOV	Default	
Sanchez	Mark	B		
Goodwin	Chuck	A	Fall	1:57
Gomez	Ruben	EX		

154
Cuevas	Alfonso	MAD	Fall	4:30
Parks	Gene	MON		
Garcia	Isaac	B	Fall	3:45
Ruiz	Dan	EB		
Ponce	Angel	ROOS	10-6	
Stalker	Rick	SANG		

165
Stricker	Tad	SB	18-7	(36-1)*
Covert	Wes	MON	(34-3)	
Silver	Scott	BULL	(31-3)	
Wright	Chad	B		
Smith	Doug	MT.W	8-5	
Castro	Mike	CL		

175
Froelich	Jassen	B	8-0	(43-0)*
Umada	David	MAD		(34-6-1)*
Parker	Jason	MON	Fall	3:00
Morales	Raul	CL		
Kachadorian	Ty	CW	6-4	
Rogers	Brandon	SB		

191
Bell	Brad	CW	14-2	(39-0-1)*
Moz	Lalo	HAN		
Atkins	Gene	CL	Fall	4:50
Roberts	Mark	WB		
Salinas	Noe	REED	Fall	2:10
Simmons	David	B		

(Continued on next page)

Yosemite Division – Clovis
February 17, 1990

HWT
Salven	Josh	CW	9-4	
Williams	Gary	HOOV		35-?
Dearmore	Wes	HIGH	Forfeit	
Carrillo	Paul	SB	Fall	4:55
Taylor	Chris	MON		

* Record (as of 02-17-90)

Tournament
1. Clovis   190.5
2. Monache   156
3. Madera   153.5
4. Bakersfield   126
5. Clovis West   121
6. South   84.5
7. Hoover   76
8. Exeter   67
9. Roosevelt   66
10. West   47.5
11. Hanford   44
12. Redwood   32
13. Reedley   28
14. Mt. Whitney   27
15. Highland   25

BOTTOM ROW, left to right: B. Nichols, L. Roberts, D. Roberts, R. Lazcano, E. Engebrits, M. Marquez, J. Welch, R. Oschner. TOP ROW: Mgr. H. Najarian, J. Green, B. McCrain, E. Newman, J. Elliot, A. Wise, S. Fuller, T. Operman, K. Oller, T. Holub.

1959 Fresno High Wrestling Team

Yosemite Division – East
February 16, 1991

103
Amaya	Rick	MON	4-1
McGill	Mike	EX	
Wright	Coby	B	Ing. Default
Radman	Aaron	WB	
Schuerman	Soowan	MAD	Ing. Default
Chandler	Trampis	CL	

112
Fuentez	Ed	SANG	6-2
Sanchez	Roger	ROOS	
Delacruz	Victor	EX	2-1
Rodriguez	Johnny	DEL	
Poor	Michael	MAD	Ing. Default
Watson	Ernie	GW	

119
Zinkin	Nick	CL	3-1
Juarez	Carlos	ROOS	
Jackson	Matt	NB	6-4
Corona	Ralph	HAN	
Enriquez	Zenaido	TUL	11-4
Aguierre	R	MAD	

125
Aguirre	Jimmy	CL	4-3
Gant	Detran	ROOS	
Fragosa	John	DEL	8-2
Gomez	Ricardo	EX	
Hull	Brian	MON	Fall 1:33
Sandoval	Gabriel	REED	

130
Ervin	Ben	MAD	9-1
Tamez	Mike	CL	
Villafana	Angel	RED	Ing. Default
Johnson	Ryan	BULL	
Martinez	Mike	EX	7-3
Gaitan	A	CW	

135
Alkire	Curtis	MON	3-1
Olivera	Jose	EX	
Pena	Chris	CL	5-3
Heberle	Jeff	NB	
Scalzo	Chad	MAD	17-10
McGinn	Josh	B	

140
Roach	Brian	CL	Maj. 17-4
Tucker	Alfonso	HOOV	
Williams	Ryan	MON	2-0
Percella	Sid	TW	
Romos	Eddie	PORT	13-8
Gonzales	Mario	SB	

145
Weber	Clayton	MAD	13-0
Ponce	Angel	ROOS	
Motl	Randy	LEM	7-0
Plummer	Kyle	B	
Wheeler	John	MON	8-3
Lentz	Steve	EX	

152
Spears	Travis	BHS	Fall 4:48 (31-4)*
Haupt	Brian	CL	
Rios	Alex	HAN	Fall 3:30
Workman	David	MAD	
Elhington	Robert	BULL	13-10
Graff	Daniel	RED	

160
Lopez	Narciso	ROOS	8-6
Arcure	Nick	MON	
Jones	Chris	EB	7-4
Herron	Willie	HIGH	
Napier	Jason	MAD	Fall 4:52
Gonzalez	Eric	HAN	

171
Silver	Scott	BULL	9-4
Castro	Mike	CL	
Umada	David	MAD	8-1
Salcido	Jose	MON	
Arenas	Stan	HIGH	13-5
Gonzales	Mark	SB	

189
Maz	Lalo	HAN	5-1
Bergman	Jeff	EB	
Scott	Raymond	ED	Fall :48
Atkins	Gene	CL	
Kachadorian	Ty	CW	3-2
Herrera	Paul	SB	5-3

(Continued on next page)

Yosemite Division – East
February 16, 1991

FRONT ROW left to right: Wiggins, L. Marino, R. Morris, A. Blake, W. Fenton, L. King, M. Brown, J. Coy, D. Mercald, B. Manley, Mgr. SECOND ROW: W. Beard, R. Sakai, H. Rue, M. Muniz, J. Hernandez, C. Hinson, D. Glen, D. Carr, B. Dorr, R. Tolson, P. Ramirez, THIRD ROW: J. Bingham, J. Beard, P. Tallman, R. Reese, S. Amundson, C. Havron, G. Kitchens, C. Hardison. FOURTH ROW: B. Harrelson, B. Rankin, Fl G. Jelletich, A. Silicz, M. DeFoor, G. Askew, D. Nunez, D. Annis, D. McGill, M. Roberson.

1962 Bakersfield High Wrestling Team

HWT

Carrillo	Paul	SB	5-3	
Falcon	Albert	SANG		
Jasso	Danny	RED	Fall	5:53
Bloom	Cory	WB		
Mast	Chad	CL	9-2	
Valov	Jerremy	DEL		

* Record

Tournament

1. Clovis	180
2. Madera	164
3. Monache	142.5
4. Roosevelt	120
5. Exeter	115
6. Hanford	88.5
7. Bakersfield	86.5
8. Bullard	82
9. Redwood	61
10. East	58
11. South	52
12. Clovis West	52
13. North	46
14. Delano	45
15. Sanger	43
16. West	39
Highland	22
Foothill	0

Yosemite Division – Tulare Western
February 22, 1992

103
Wright	Colby	B	4-3	(40-2)*
Radman	Aaron	WB		(35-3)*
Fuqua	Brad	NB	18-13	
Ruiz	Greg	MON		
Calandra	Steve	BULL	Maj. 16-0	
Sanchez	Angel	TUL		

112
Quintana	Nick	CL	5-3	
Enriquez	Zenido	TUL		
Delacruz	Victor	EX	10-0	
Asuncion	Ron	MON		
Ngo	Vinh	FRE	2-0	
Hogue	Chad	MAD		

119
Zinkin	Nick	CL	18-4	(37-0)*
Sherley	Jake	B		(36-9)*
Hull	Brad	MON	7-2	
Miller	Justin	NB		
Trujillo	Jose	GW	3-1	
Rodriguez	Johnny	DEL		

125
Hull	Brian	MON	Fall	:48
Summers	Curtis	CL		
Wilson	Jason	EX	6-5	
Ayers	Scott	LEM		
Maciel	Rafael	MAD	6-4	
Snyder	Jimmy	HAN		

130
Washington	Yero	PORT	Fall	5:36
Hammond	Patrick	ROOS		
Loyd	Johnny	CW	8-4	
Molano	David	GW		
Snapp	Chad	CL	9-3	
Covert	Greg	MON		

135
Meza	Fernando	MAD	O.T. 6-4	
Heer	Ricky	NB		(39-8)*
Frost	Kris	MON	Default	
Murphy	Ryan	TUL		
Swan	Kyle	CL	6-5	
Decastro	Luis	HAN		

140
Gonzales	Mario	SB	9-2	(40-5)*
Hill	Aaron	CW		
McGinn	Josh	B	Fall	2:00
Ramsey	Sam	BULL		
Ramos	Eddie	PORT	17-11	
Clays	Kenny	TUL		

145
Philp	Eric	MAD	Fall	:31
Munster	Bruce	CL		
Green	Romel	HIGH	5-4	
Ramos	Mario	ROOS		
Spike	Ben	SANG	9-3	
Alvarez	Mike	EX		

152
Tucker	Alfonso	HOOV	15-7	(40-1)*
Plummer	Kyle	B		(28-12)*
Crawford	Shane	CL	4-0	
Bushley	Dan	MCL		
Wood	Andy	RED	5-1	
Guzman	Lupe	LEM		

160
Haupt	Brian	CL	3-0	(32-5)*
Pasquale	Kai	NB		(42-5-1)*
Garcia	Milo	RED	7-3	
Graff	Daniel	REED		
Workman	David	MAD	Forfeit	
Garcia	Gabe	B		

171
Gonzalez	Eric	HAN	O.T. 4-2	
Herron	Willie	HIGH		(36-5)*
Napier	Jason	MAD	10-4	
Hine	Elliott	CL		
Paramo	Mark	LEM	6-5	
Tripp	Jeremy	TUL		

189
Moz	Lalo	HAN	Fall	3:21
Westbury	Kory	CL		
Helston	Brendon	HIGH	6-3	
Delacruz	Dan	MON		
Thoene	Jake	NB	TF 17-2	
Tejeda	Miguel	BULL		

(Continued on next page)

Yosemite Division – Tulare Western
February 22, 1992

HWT
Mast	Chad	CL	3-1
Carrillo	Paul	SB	
Falcon	Albert	SANG	5-1
Spradley	Sean	MT.W	
Chavira	Ramirel	MAD	7-2
Serjack	Chris	RED	

* Record

Tournament
1. Clovis 215.5
2. Madera 118.5
3. Monache 13.5
4. Bakersfield 109
5. North 93.5
6. Hanford 62
7. Tulare 60
8. Lemoore 59
9. Highland 56
10. South 48
11. Clovis West 45.5
11. Porterville 45.5
13. Exeter 44
14. Bullard 41
15. Roosevelt 38
16. Hoover 35
17. West 23
18. Mt. Whitney 21
19. Reedley 18
20. McLane 15
21. Delano 13
22. Fresno 9
23. Tulare W. 9
24. East 7
24. Foothill 7
Edison 0

Chuck Fenton (top)
Bakersfield High
Two-time CIF Champion
1961 and 1962

Yosemite Division – Bullard

February 20, 1993

103
Aguilar	Peter	PORT	7-6
Buckingham	Gary	TUL	
Taylor	Max	MAD	
Adams	Anthony	FOOT	
Ortiz	Jesus	CW	
Levario	Milo	EB	

112
Martinez	Miguel	MAD	12-0
Rubalcava	Oscar	CW	
Lake	Kenny	CL	
Petrig	Jason	LEM	
Sanchez	Angel	TUL	
Moreno	Manuel	RED	

119
Gutierrez	Gabe	EX	7-3
Esquivel	Benny	PORT	
Navarro	John	LEM	
Varner	Andy	B	
Rodriguez	Miguel	ROOS	
Lopez	Juan	HIGH	

125
Delacrauz	Victor	EX	5-4
Aguilar	Ron	MAD	
Hull	Brad	MON	
Miller	Justin	NB	
Ehn	Matt	CL	
Smithson	Russell	HOOV	

130
Snapp	Chad	CL	6-3
Jaimes	David	MAD	
Pantoja	Ben	CW	
Ellis	Jake	MON	
Harvick	Ken	NB	
Champion	J	HIGH	

135
Kuntz	Jesse	LEM	Fall	2:05
Smithson	James	HOOV		
Swan	Kyle	CL		
Gayton	Armando	CW		
Morrison	Darren	REED		
Hobbs	Chad	NB		

140
Ramos	Eddie	PORT	16-10
Hill	Aaron	CW	
Perez	Moises	MAD	
Moz	Tom	HAN	
Delao	Ronnie	CL	
Fendrick	Jim	B	

145
Crawford	Shane	CL	O.T. 15-13
Meza	Fernando	MAD	
Kagawa	Jason	CW	
Rasmussen	Chad	FOOT	
Messer	Toby	LEM	
Curry	Andy	HAN	

152
Philp	Eric	MAD	Fall	2:59
Wood	Andy	RED		
Miller	Doug	HAN		
Douthat	Fred	LEM		
Pectol	Erin	TUL		
Bejorquez	David	EB		

160
Munster	Bruce	CL	Fall	:55
Wheeler	John	MON		
Garcia	Gabe	B		
Houston	Antinon	LEM		
Zamarano	Elias	ROOS		
Llanes	Anthony	MAD		

171
Herron	Willie	HIGH	12-6
Cabral	Demes	HAN	
Salcido	Joe	MON	
Mills	Travis	CW	
Sheets	Ryan	NB	
Gloria	David	MT.W	

189
Mohammed	Jeremiah	ROOS	Fall	4:39
Avila	Ryan	MON		
Jasso	Jarold	RED		
Clark	Brett	B		
Gonzales	J.	CW		
Avila	Tim	PORT		

(Continued on next page)

Yosemite Division – Bullard
February 20, 1993

275
Mast	Chad	CL	10-3
Serjack	Chris	RED	
Karle	Jeremy	HIGH	
Smith	Jared	CW	
Holdren	Alex	LEM	
Rodriguez	Eric	MON	

Tournament
1. Madera 165.5
2. Clovis 161.5
3. Clovis West 139
4. Lemoore 122.5
5. Monache 105.5
6. Porterville 84.5
7. Redwood 79
8. Hanford 64.5
9. Highland 61
10. Bakersfield 57
11. Roosevelt 57
12. North 55
13. Tulare 50.5
14. Exeter 37.5
15. Foothill 33
16. Hoover 35

Brad Hull of Monache High
3rd in State 1992
3rd in CIF 1992
5th in State 1992
CIF Champion 1993
4th in State 1993

Yosemite Division – Arvin
February 19, 1994

103
Ortiz	Jesus	CW	13-3	(42-5)*
Garza	Albert	SANG		
Adame	Anthony	FRE	4-1	
Taylor	Max	MAD		
Smith	Ed	CL	8-0	
Vasquez	Nathan	WB		

112
Green	Stan	CL	12-0	(37-1)*
Phillips	Dallen	SANG		
McCauley	Rob	B	9-8	
Rublacava	Oscar	FRE		
Vanni	Chris	MON	6-5	
Ruiz	Parris	CW		

119
Lake	Kenny	CL	4-3 (2 O.T.)	(28-4)*
Esquivel	Benny	PORT		
Elisondo	Steve	WB	Fall	2:48
Ruiz	Frank	EX		
Thompson	Danny	RED	4-2	
Guerrero	Jon	TW		

125
Hull	Brad	MON	15-8	(42-4)*
Ehn	Matt	CL		
Varner	Andy	B	8-2	
Alamilla	Juan	PORT		
Davis	Jonte	ED	Fall	4:24
Carpenter	Rob	RED		

130
James	David	MAD	10-0	(25-7)*
Russell	David	HOOV		
Miller	Kelly	B	2-1	
Molano	Fred	GW		
Lopez	Juan	HIGH	10-8	
Maese	Jaime	MON		

135
Ellis	Jake	MON	3-1	(43-7)*
Demarre	Joe	LEM		
Duran	Ruben	GW	5-0	
Delao	Ronnie	CL		
Collier	Sean	B	9-8	
Demarco	Richards	ROOS		

140
Perez	Moises	MAD	9-0	(39-0)*
Smithson	Russell	HOOV		
Aldaco	Juan	MON	7-5	
Kraemer	Daron	HAN		
Queenan	Sean	SB	Fall	:56
Seals	Matt	RED		

145
Swan	Kyle	CL	T.F. 18-1	
Aldaco	Jose	MON		
Moz	Tom	HAN	10-3	
Arteaga	Jimmy	MCL		
Bozeman	Ryan	EB	6-3	
Kraft	Tim	HOOV		

152
Meza	Fernando	MAD	13-5	
Salcedo	Jose	EX		
Curry	Andy	HAN	Fall	4:11
Rasmussen	Chad	FRE		
Bridges	Jeremy	B	6-4	
Roach	Brandon	BULL		

160
Philp	Eric	MAD	Fall 1:53	(40-1)*
Cary	Ken	MON		
Bojorquez	David	EB	5-0	
Badillo	Julian	BULL		
Duarte	Mike	HOOV	T.F. 18-1	
Norman	Ramon	ED		

171
Sheets	Ryan	NB	9-5	
Strickland	Ben	CW		
Ashley	Fred	B	T.F. 15-0	
Gonazlez	Leo	HIGH		
Cabral	Demes	HAN	Fall	2:25
Ramirez	Steve	GW		

189
Muhammad	Jeremiah	ROOS	Fall	5:21
Ferguson	Vance	HAN		
Jasso	Jarold	RED	1:32	
Daniels	Aaron	HIGH		
Miller	Anthony	EX	6-4	
Salven	Ben	CW		

(Continued on next page)

Yosemite Division – Arvin

February 19, 1994

HWT

Rodriguez	Eric	MON	7-3	(43-5)*
Smith	Jered	CW		(36-4)*
Rodriguez	Efrain	MAD	Default	
Karle	Jeremy	HIGH		(43-2)*
Garcia	Chris	CL	3-1	
Beltran	Manuel	GW		

* Record

Tournament

1. Monache 152
2. Clovis 150
3. Madera 140.5
4. Hanford 97.5
5. Clovis West 90
6. Bakersfield 82.5
7. Hoover 73.5
8. Highland 63
9. Golden West 58
10. Exeter 52
11. Sanger 51
12. Redwood 47
13. East 40
14. Foothill 37
15. North 30
16. South 16
Arvin 0

Earl Corley
South Bakersfield
1959 CIF Champion

Above and right, 1959 Arvin High Wrestling Team

Yosemite Division – Mt. Whitney/Visalia
February 18, 1995

103
Garza	Albert	SANG	1:36	
Smith	Ed	CL		
Sar	Tee	MT.W	12-2	
Rosas	Tony	CW		
Diaz	Abe	A	Fall	4:00
Odom	Dustin	FOOT	(37-6)*	

112
Lake	K.L.	CL	14-6
Elisondo	Steve	B	
Ruiz	Parris	CW	10-0
Torres	Jerry	MON	
Telles	Robert	REED	Disqualified
Moore	Kirk	FOOT	

119
Vasquez	Larry	B	11-7
Rubalcava	Oscar	FRE	
Phillips	Dallen	SANG	9-8
Brown	William	HOOV	
Aguirre	Tom	NB	Default
Breceda	Sergio	BUC	

125
Davis	Jonte	ED	14-5
Lopez	Ralph	CW	
Ehn	Matt	CL	5-0
Barba	Esaul	HOOV	
Huizar	Antonio	LEM	6-4
Thompson	Danny	REED	

130
Russell	David	HOOV	6-0
Breceda	Victor	BUC	
Nichols	Kendall	PORT	6-1
Atchison	Scott	LEM	
Richards	Demasco	ROOS	8-3
Lopez	Juan	HIGH	

135
Pierro	Jerry	BUC	:41
Mazza	Marc	NB	
Miller	Kelly	B	6-5
Belvail	Kenny	LEM	
Manes	Jeremy	FOOT	6-1
Guerra	Pete	HIGH	

140
Varner	Andy	B	O.T. 6-4	
Molano	Fred	GW		
Rodriguez	Mike	BUC	Fall	4:50
Esajian	Paul	FRE		
Nelm	Ian	MT.W	9-0	
Duran	Darrich	ROOS		

145
Williams	Ryan	HIGH	Fall 3:15	(26th Fall)
Martinez	Mike	EB		
Duran	Ruben	GW	6-2	
Sanders	Telly	BUC		
Arteaga	Jimmy	MCL	6-2	
Taber	Jason	MON		

152
Bridges	Jeremy	B	Fall	3:59
Curry	Andy	HAN		
Milanesi	Vince	BUC	3:30	
Gutierrez	Tony	LEM		
Smithson	Russell	HOOV	6-1	
Burchett	Mike			

160
Wilson	Mike	MAD	8-4	
Hill	Matt	SB		
Keller	Tony	B	11-3	
Ray	Matt	LEM		
Aldaco	Jose	MON	Fall	2:30
Tingle	Jeremy	WB		

171
Askley	Fredrick	B	Fall	:56
East	Rocky	NB		
Cromer	A.J.	ED	Forfeit	
Costa	Mike	MON		
Armstrong	Chad	PORT	8-4	
Lunn	Tyler	BUC		

191
Maese	Ray	B	3-2	
Phillips	Damien	TUL		
Philp	Ryan	MAD	Fall	2:30
Serna	Emilio	BUC		
Merrill	Than	FRE	9-2	
Ferguson	Jon	STOCK		

(Continued on next page)

Yosemite Division – Mt. Whitney/Visalia

February 18, 1995

HWT

Clark	Brett	B	10-6
Rodriguez	Eric	MON	
Smith	Jarred	CW	1-0
Montoya	John	LEM	
Smith	Gary	ED	Fall 1:32
Daugherty	Tim	FOOT	

*Record

Tournament

1. Bakersfield 213
2. Buchanan 177
3. Lemoore 165.5
4. Monache 91.5
5. Edison 82.5
6. Clovis West 81.5
7. Hoover 72
8. Madera 62.5
9. Clovis 62
10. North 58.5

East 36.5
Foothill 35
Highland 33.5
South 28
Stockdale 22
Arvin 18
West 11

**Eric Rodriquez
Monache High
Two-time CIF Champion
1994 and 1995
5th in State 1995**

Yosemite Division – Buchanan/Clovis
February 17, 1996

103
Garza	Jaime	SANG	10-3
Guerrero	Brian	MAD	
Smith	Ed	CL	
Sar	Tee	MT.W	
Resseguie	Chris	EB	
Odom	Max	FOOT	

112
Garza	Alberto	SANG	Fall
Martinez	Ben	TUL	
Garcia	Abel	BUC	
Diaz	Abraham	A	
Roas	Tony	CW	
Cano	Eraldo	RED	

119
Ruiz	Parris	CW	3-2
Breceda	Sergio	BUC	
Sanchez	Jose	ED	
Valenzuela	Angel	ROOS	
Phillips	Dalen	SANG	Fall
Moore	Kirk	FOOT	

125
Lopez	Ralph	CW	11-10	(39-7)*
Vasquez	Nathan	B		(43-4)*
Adame	Anthony	FOOT		
Villareal	Guillermo	ROOS		
Banuelos	Antonio	TW		
Gutierrez	Chris	CL		

130
Rubalacava	Oscar	FRE	12-6
Brown	William	HOOV	
Reyes	Cirilo	EB	Fall
Araballo	Robert	MAD	
Hogeland	Caleb	FOOT	10-2
Hines	Tommy	HAN	

135
Ehn	Matt	CL	5-0
Huizar	Antonio	LEM	
Sherrick	Mike	CW	
Choske	Lonny	BUC	
Diniz	Adrian	FOOT	
Hoehn	Nathan	MON	

140
Tirapelle	Adam	BUC	5-1	
Molano	Fred	B		(40-2)*
Reyes	Harvey	EB	16-2	
Luna	Joaquin	GW		
Rodriguez	Felipe	PORT		
Work	Ryan	CL		

145
Duran	Derrick	ROOS	Default
Miller	Kelly	B	
Esajian	Paul	FRE	
Nelms	Ian	MT.W	
Lomelli	Daniel	CW	
Padgett	Tim	FOOT	

152
Sanders	Telly	BUC	12-9
Sheen	Charley	CL	
Burchett	Mike	MT.W	
Smithson	Russell	HOOV	
Garza	Damien	LEM	
Sheldon	Daniel	MON	

160
Sheen	Bill	CL	9-3
Aldaco	Jose	MON	
Lunn	Tyler	BUC	
Esqueda	Mike	CW	
Ainaya	Chris	MAD	
Reyna	Adolfo	HAN	

171
Stockton	Ryan	BUC	6-2
Badillo	Julian	BULL	
Hill	Matt	SB	
Ray	Matt	LEM	
Moran	Brandon	SANG	Fall
Smith	Junior	EB	

189
Philp	Ryan	MAD	9-7
Brogdon	Charlie	A	
Zieg	Elijah	BUC	
Winslow	Derek	BULL	
Costa	Chris	MCL	
Brughell	Matt	LEM	

(Continued on next page)

Yosemite Division – Buchanan/Clovis
February 17, 1996

215
Merrill	Than	FRE	Default
Serna	Emilio	BUC	
Rico	Ben	LEM	
Brewer	Otis	MAD	
Maese	Ray	B	8-4
Deleon	Carlos	CENT	

HWT
Leyva	Victor	MON	1:56
Smith	Gary	ED	
Harrington	Grant	RED	
Avila	Tim	PORT	
Garrett	Albert	MAD	
Stone	Jasen	BULL	

* Record

Tournament
1. Buchanan	189.5
2. Clovis West	115.5
3. Clovis	115.5
4. Madera	108.5
5. Bakersfield	93.5
6. Lemoore	79 Tied for 6th
6. Monache	79 Tied for 6th
8. Sanger	77
9. Foothill	76
10. Fresno	76
11. East	64
12. Edison	53 Tied for 12th
12. Mt. Whitney	53 Tied for 12th
12. Roosevelt	53 Tied for 12th
15. Bullard	51
16. Hoover	47
17. Arvin	45
18. South	34
19. Tulare	31 Tied for 19th
19. Redwood	31 Tied for 19th

Victor Leyva
Monache High
CIF Champion
5th in State 1996

Adam Tirapelle
Buchanan High
NCAA Champion
Also placed 2nd and 3rd
University of Illinois
Career records:
High school: 214-7
College: 127-21

Yosemite Division – East

February 22, 1997

103
Portillo	Angel	TUL	7-3	(43-4)*
Felix	Chris	E		
Morroquin	Jose	GW	1-0	
Nunez	Andres	ROOS		
Estrada	Juan	CEN	9-3	
Fuentes	Larry	FRE		

112
Garza	Jaime	SANG	16-1	
Nguyen	Tam	ED		
Resseguie	Chris	EB	10-4	
Mendez	Mondo	BUC		
Land	Eraldo	RED	Fall	2:18
Beck	Scott	TUL		

119
Banuelos	Antonio	CW	8-6
Guerrero	Brian	MAD	
Martinez	Ben	TUL	Inj. Def.
Garza	Albert	SANG	
Sanchez	Matt	FRE	6-5
Bascom	Dinity	CENT	

125
Sanchez	Jose	ED	Fall	:55
Rosas	Tim	CW		
Sanchez	Pablo	HOOV	7-5	
Rosales	Nick	A		
Scott	Bennett	B	4-1	
Arredondo	Jon	MAD		

130
Rosas	Tony	CW	3-1
Gutierrez	Chris	CL	
Hernandez	Josh	BULL	3-2
Cina	Edric	RED	
Sobaje	Justin	BUC	Inj. Def.
Prfitzer	Jeremy	TUL	

135
Lopez	Ralph	CW	14-5
Arballo	Robert	MAD	
Meloche	Ryan	FOOT	17-5
Spradlin	Matt	B	
Reyes	Gus	SANG	(won by disq.)

140
Moore	Kirk	FOOT	7-1
Muralla	Ernesto	B	
Hoehne	Nathan	MON	6-1
Jiminez	Paul	PORT	
Morales	Joseph	EX	7-3
Verduzco	Jerry	ED	

145
Miller	Kelly	B	9-4	
Duran	Darrio	ROOS		
Reyna	Adolfo	HAN	5-2	
Reyes	Cirilo	EB		
Brooks	Ryan	LEM	Fall	3:41
Albaniz	George	MON		

152
Pezzat	Yasser	EX	5-3
Botello	Isaac	TUL	
Perez	Noel	MAD	3-2
Lomelli	Daniel	CW	
Diniz	Adrian	FOOT	Inj. Def.
Harrington	Clint	CENT	

160
Sanders	Telly	BUC	Fall	:38
Gonzales	Todd	HOOV		
Nelms	Ian	MT.W	Fall	5:32
Cerda	Mauricio	ED		
Jimenez	Juan	SB	9-3	
Eck	Mike	HAN		

171
Lonn	Tyler	BUC	4-1
Nayen	Hussein	CW	
Naus	Josh	CENT	Inj. Def.
Moran	Brandon	SANG	
Smith	Junior	EB	Fall
Rojas	J.	MT.W	

189
Brogdon	Charlie	A	8-0
Fox	Ben	BUC	
Bowerman	Rodney	LEM	8-6
Shearer	Steven	MON	
Scott	Nad	CW	7-0
Morgan	Tim	CENT	

(Continued on next page)

Yosemite Division – East
February 22, 1997

215
Phillip	Ryan	MAD	1-0	
Matthews	Marcel	BULL		
Cash	Brandon	BUC	4-2	
Camacho	Baltazar	MON		
Perry	Ty	CW	Fall	2:33
Lomeli	David	B		

275
Harrington	Grant	RED	Fall	2:50
Simas	Pat	LEM		
Ibarra	Jose	EB	Ing. Def.	
Brewer	Otis	MAD		
Cabral	Dustin	HAN	6-3	
Gonzales	Tony	HIGH		

* Record (as of 2-22-97)

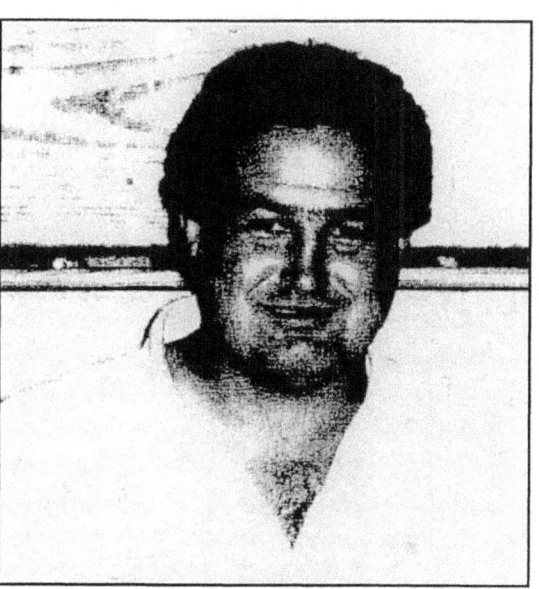

Rodney Balch
Clovis High
238-20-3

Tournament
1. Clovis West   154.5
2. Buchanan   123.5
3. Madera   110
4. East   99.5
5. Tulare   98
6. Bakersfield   81
7. Sanger   78.5
8. Edison   77.5
9. Foothill   74
10. Lemoore   66
11. Monache   62
12. Hoover   55
13. Centennial   54
14. Redwood   52
15. Exeter   47
16. Arvin   45
16. Clovis   45
16. Hanford   45
19. Bullard   43
20. Roosevelt   41.5
21. Mt. Whitney 35
22. Golden West 33
23. Fresno   25
24. South   24
25. Porterville 18.5
26. Central   13
27. Highland   10
28. Reedley   7.5
29. McLane   6
30. Delano   3

Yosemite Division – Mt. Whitney
February 21, 1998

103
Estrada	John	CEN	Fall	2:52
Castillo	Eddie	CL		
Onsurez	Andy	EB	4-1	
LaFrance	Devon	BUC		
Cole	Adam	B	10-1	
Harl	Justin	FOOT		

112
Dickerson	John	B	7-3	
Mendez	Mando	BUC		
Beck	Scott	TUL	7-3	
Gushiken	Brandon	CL		
Marquez	Phillip	FOOT	Fall	4:49
Leal	Ronnie	HAN		

119
Breceda	Sergio	BUC	6-5
Hernandez	Vince	LEM	
Gutierrez	Miguel	FOOT	8-0
Portillo	Angel	TUL	
Jones	Kevin	CW	10-1
Goings	Joel	WB	

125
Martinez	Ben	TUL	20-5
Calvert	James	LEM	
Ashley	Benny	B	11-5
Johnson	Gerald	ED	
Rosales	Nick	A	5-4
Alvarez	Frankie	CW	

130
Odom	Max	FOOT	2-1
Guiterrez	Chris	CL	
Calvert	Jason	LEM	3-1
Schallberger	Patrick	B	
Alvarez	Jesse	WB	7-4
Cano	Eraldo	RED	

135
Olson	Casey	CL	O.T. 5-3
Baca	Ben	BUC	
Meloche	Ryan	FOOT	3-0
Garcia	Juan	B	
Lopez	Juan	EX	11-3
Flores	Mike	TUL	

140
Lopez	Ralph	CW	Forfeit	
Prfitzer	Jeremy	TUL		
Villagomez	Alan	EB	3-1	
Reedy	John-Michael	BUC		
Lopez	Rudy	HAN	Fall	4:13
Gonzales	Tommy	HIGH		

145
Huizar	Juan	LEM	5-2	
Spradlin	Matt	B		
Diniz	Adrian	FOOT	Fall	1:41
Martinez	Miguel	MAD		
Owens	Jeremy	CL	15-0	
Escovedo	Nathan	MT.W		

152
Moore	Kirk	FOOT	10-3
Brooks	Ryan	LEM	
Gutierrez	Ryan	CL	7-1
Lomelli	Daniel	CW	
Buck	Richard	BUC	6-4
Botello	Isaac	TUL	36-7

160
Sanders	Telly	BUC	3-1
Sherrick	Mike	CW	
Reyes	Harvey	EB	Inj. Def.
Jimenez	Juan	SB	
Flores	Carlos	PORT	8-4
Bravo	Mario	FOOT	

171
Gonzales	Todd	HOOV	Inj. Def.
Perez	Noel	MAD	
Smith	Ryan	CW	Inj. Def.
Lunn	Tyler	BUC	
Shankle	Brandon	FOOT	3-0
Vasquez	Ed	LEM	

189
Naus	Josh	CENT	Fall	1:24
Cash	Brandon	BUC		
Roan	John	MAD	8-67	
Bowerman	Rodney	LEM		
Walbeck	Clint	CL	Fall	2:05
Waltz	Justin	NB		

(Continued on next page)

Yosemite Division – Mt. Whitney
February 21, 1998

215
Graham	Aaron	B	8-2	
Fox	Ben	BUC		
Camacho	Eduardo	REED	7-3	
Poo	Danny	EX		
Dix	Courtney	CL	6-3	
Donahue	Josh	LEM		

275
Sinas	Pat	LEM	Fall	5:58
Torres	Greg	FOOT		
Armendariz	Louie	MON	4-3	
Sanchez	Matt	BUC		
Gonzales	Robert	BULL	Fall	1:40
Austin	David	TUL		

Tournament
1. Buchanan 204
2. Foothill 175
3. Lemoore 165.5
4. Clovis 142.5
5. Bakersfield 133
6. Clovis West 116.5
7. Tulare Union 104.5
8. Madera 71
9. East 61
10. Centennial 47
11. Exeter 37.5
12. Monache 33.5
13. Hoover 33
14. Central 29
15. South 26.5
16. Hanford 24
17. Arvin 22
18. Mt. Whitney 20
19. West 16.5
20. Highland 16 Tied for 20th
20. North 16 Tied for 20th
20. Reedley 16 Tied for 20th
23. Edison 15 Tied for 20th
23. Bullard 15 Tied for 20th
25. Porterville 14
26. Redwood 13
27. Tulare W. 12.5
28. Stockdale 8
29. Roosevelt 6 Tied for 29th
29. Sanger 6 Tied for 29th
31. McLane 4 Tied for 31st
31. Fresno 4 Tied for 31st
33. Delano 1

Left to right, Jack Serros (Bakersfield), Joe Seay, Art Chavez, Roy Heath (South Bakersfield)

Yosemite Division – Clovis
February 20, 1999

103
Vasquez	Darrell	B	1-0
Onsurez	Andrew	EB	
Chapman	Daniel	CENT	10-3
Silva	Damen	LEM	
Reyes	Ray	HAN	Fall 1:00
Weber	Nick	MT.W	

112
Castillo	Eddie	CL	6-5
Marquez	Phillip	FOOT	
Spradlin	Andrew	B	6-4
Castillo	James	MAD	
Ramirez	Aaron	CEN	4-2
Berry	Adam	BULL	

119
East	Drew	B	7-3
Gusthiksen	Brandon	CL	
Leal	Ronnie	HAN	3-1
Castillo	Isaac	MON	
Facio	Paul	BUC	Fall 4:30
Marquez	Anthony	FOOT	

125
Tirapelle	Alex	CL	7-1
Beck	Scott	TUL	
Goings	Joel	WB	5-2
Esparza	Anthony	MT.W	
Chicca	Caleb	B	15-5
Siebert	Shane	MAD	

130
Martinez	Ben	TUL	8-3
Pendleton	Chris	LEM	
Jones	Kevin	CW	7-5
Gutierrez	Miguel	FOOT	
Spooner	Garrett	CL	17-8
Sanchez	Chilo	BUC	

135
Estrada	Robert	CEN	8-3
Bakaer	David	CENT	
Ramirez	Jessie	MT.W	3-2
Vasquez	Lino	HOOV	
Crane	Michael	BUC	
Portillo	Angel	TUL	1-0 (2) O.T.

140
Briggs	Charles	LEM	5-0
Bains	Jas	CL	
Schallberger	Patrick	B	7-0
Sheets	Sean	CEN	
Bernard	Evan	TUL	Fall 1:30
Reyes	Herman	CENT	

145
Odom	Max	FOOT	17-4
Diesslin	Justin	CL	
Rodgers	Brandon	MT.W	10-6
Valdez	Gendard	B	
Jacoby	Jon	CW	14-7
Herrera	Chuy	MON	

152
Yacoby	David	CW	7-6
Cross	Scott	MON	
Cotta	Nick	LEM	Inj. Def.
Escovido	Nathan	MT.W	
Mooney	Britt	EB	4-1
Guzman	Calos	FRE	

160
Brooks	Ryan	LEM	10-5
Tirado	Josue	MON	
Sanchez	Jesus	MAD	9-4
Mehr	Andonijah	ED	
Whitehead	Chris	CL	O.T. 4-2
Bravo	Mario	FOOT	

171
Gutierrez	Ryan	CL	Fall :56
Beechinor	Ted	MAD	
Weiner	Steffan	BUC	Inj. Def
Burke	Sam	RIDGE	
Bowman	Michah	TUL	Fall 1:55
Cortez	Jose	EX	

189
Silva	Ronnie	BUC	6-3
Hallmark	Jacob	CL	
Naus	Josh	CENT	Fall 2:15
Carrasco	Miguel	RED	
Tobin	Anthony	B	10-3
Nieto	Sonny	HOOV	

(Continued on next page)

Yosemite Division – Clovis
February 20, 1999

215
Graham	Aaron	B	4-3
Botehlo	Marcio	LEM	
Walbeck	Clint	CL	1-0
Pitino	Eddie	PORT	
Smoyer	Jason	BUC	Forfeit
Wotlz	Justin	NB	

275
Fox	Ben	BUC	3-1
Armendarez	Louie	MON	
Strain	Bryan	CEN	4-2
DeQuillett	Ryan	WB	
Reyes	Alfred	HIGH	15-4
Capella	Mike	MT.W	

Tournament
1. Clovis — 268.5
2. Bakersfield — 228
3. Lemoore — 199.5
4. Buchanan — 196
5. Centennial — 171.5
6. Foothill — 167.5
7. Tulare — 149.5
8. Monache — 135
9. Madera — 131
10. Mt. Whitney — 122
11. Hanford — 106.5
12. Clovis West — 95.5
13. Hoover — 76
14. East — 71.5
15. Exeter — 68
16. Roosevelt — 64.5
17. Stockdale — 55.5
18. Ridgeview — 54 Tied for 18th
18. Porterville — 54 Tied for 18th
20. West — 53
21. Golden West — 51
22. South — 49.5
23. Redwood — 46
24. Sanger — 43 Tied for 24th
24. Bullard — 43 Tied for 24th
26. Edison — 41
27. Central — 38.5
28. Highland — 37
29. Fresno — 34
30. North — 33
31. Delano — 26
32. Tulare W. — 18 Tied for 32nd
33. Reedley — 18 Tied for 32nd
32. McLane — 18 Tied for 32nd

East Bakersfield Wrestlers 1977
Left to right, State Champion Percy Richard, Steve Nickell, Jerry Balthis, Mike Najera, Junior Corando
Coach - Rudy Gonzalez

Yosemite Division – East
February 18-19, 2000

103
Ingram	Logan	BUC	2-0
Contreras	Gerrard	MAD	
Murillo	John	TW	Default
Mendes	Karl	HAN	
Sollis	Nick	RED	Fall :40
Ramirez	Isaac	MT.W	

112
Vasquez	Darrell	B	7-3	
Onsurez	Andrew	EB		38-2*
Reyes	Ray	HAN	8-2	
Martinez	Nick	TUL		
Goodpaster	Darrell	BUC	2-1	
Weber	Nick	MT.W		

119
Chapman	Daniel	CENT	Default
Castillo	Eddie	CL	
Facio	Paul	BUC	14-5
Silva	Damon	LEM	
Santos	Efrin	SANG	Default
Franco	Tony	FOOT	

125
Chicca	Caleb	B	5-3
Leal	Ronnie	HAN	
Stonehocke	Anthony	LEM	4-1
Morrison	Mike	CW	
Sanchez	Chris	BUC	3-2
Baltierra	Felix	CENT	

130
East	Drew	B	7-2
Sanchez	Chillo	BUC	
Spooner	Garrett	CL	14-3
Frank	Matt	EB	
Ramirez	Aaron	CENT	7-1
Ryder	Trevor	LEM	

135
Tirapelle	Alex	CL	5-2
Spradlin	Andrew	B	
Siebert	Shane	MAD	7-5
Gutierrez	Miguel	FOOT	
Serda	Craig	LEM	5-2
Marquez	Tommy	EB	

140
Hernandez	Steve	FOOT	8-6
Garcia	Pacifico	CL	
Weatherly	Steven	EX	8-7
Ramirez	Jesse	MT.W	
Sherley	Josh	B	19-6
Sarabia	Jose	BULL	

145
Pendleton	Chris	LEM	Fall :25
Harl	Justin	FOOT	
Estrada	Robert	BUC	18-0
Marchant	Travis	STOCK	
Hernandez	Joe	B	10-3
Joyner	Travis	REED	

152
Sheets	Sean	CENT	8-2
Kalivas	Karras	B	
Uriarte	Justin	MT.W	2-1
Baines	Jas	CL	
Medina	Ron	LEM	Fall 4:06
Campbell	Corey	FOOT	

160
Bardsley	Matt	HOOV	Fall 5:30
Sanchez	Jesus	MAD	
Madsen	Derek	HAN	Fall :51
Folmer	Daniel	BUC	
Griffith	Anthony	CENT	4-3
Hernandez	Ramiro	B	

171
Weimer	Steffan	BUC	5-2
Mooney	Britt	EB	
Sanchez	Mariano	REED	10-2
Stevens	Mike	LEM	
Whitehead	Chris	CL	3-1
Griffin	William	MAD	

189
Tobin	Anthony	B	15-9
Pickett	Robert	HOOV	
Silva	Ronnie	BUC	1-0
Gonzalez	Carlos	EB	
Costa	Jaime	CW	Default
Napier	Stephen	CL	

(Continued on next page)

Yosemite Division – East
February 18-19, 2000

215
Botello	Marcio	LEM	Default	
Muhammed	Omar	BULL		
Walbeck	Clint	CL	Default	
Scheesley	Brian	HAN		
Goodman	Will	BUC	Fall	2:32
Maffia	Broc	TW		

HWT
Patino	Ed	PORT	Fall	5:29
Smoyer	Jason	BUC		
Hallmark	Jacob	CL	3-2	
DeQuillett	Ryan	WB		
Murphy	Johnathan	HAN	Fall	4:57
Lovies	Brad	CW		

Chris Pendleton
Lemoore High
Two-time NCAA Champion
also placed 3rd
Oklahoma State University
Career records:
High school: 178-15
College: 115-11

Tournament
1. Buchanan   251
2. Bakersfield 226
3. Clovis   215
4. Lemoore   194.5
5. Centennial 164.5
6. Hanford   164
7. Madera   139
8. East   135
9. Foothill   133.5
10. Hoover   118.5
11. Clovis West 103.5
12. Mt.Whitney 98
13. Exeter   75.5
14. Bullard   69
15. Highland   67
16. Porterville 64.5
17. Stockdale 64
18. Tulare W. 62
19. Monache   60
20. Sanger   54
21. Reedley   52
22. Roosevelt 50
23. West   49.5
24. South   46.5
25. Delano   44
26. Tulare   39
27. Edison   38
28. Golden West 33
29. McLane   32
30. Redwood   29.5
31. North   25
32. Central   21
33. Fresno   17
34. Ridgeview 15

Yosemite Division – Clovis
February 16-17, 2001

103
Contereras	Gerard	BUC	5-2	
Morgan	Nathan	B		
Mendez	Chad	HAN	Fall	1:47
Carlson	Sean	HOOV		
Garza		CL	4-2	
Carillo	Gilbert	TUL		

112
Ingram	Logan	BUC	4-2	
Flores	Gabriel	MAD		
Franco	Tony	B	Fall	3:13
Williams	Jason	CL		
Ambriz	Alex	CE	14-6	
Gonzalez	Matt	EX		

119
Vasquez	Darrell	B	7-1
Tirapelle	Troy	CL	
Martinez	Nick	TUL	9-0
Settle	Isaac	CW	
Marquez	Mike	EB	3-0
Bustamante	Gabe	FRE	

125
Silva	Damon	LEM	Default	(42-4)*
Chapman	Daniel	CENT		(31-3)*
Santos	Efrain	SANG	Fall	1:49
Hunter	Derrick	NB		
Houck	Ryan	CW	Fall	5:53
Onsurez	Anthony	EB		

130
Ramirez	Aaron	CENT	13-11	
Juarez	Javier	CEN		(31-3)*
Marquez	Anthony	FRE	Default	
Perger	Cameron	CL		
Sanchez	Brandon	BUC	4-3	
Weimer	D.J.	B		

135
Spradlin	Andrew	B	4-3
Garcia	Pacifico	CL	
Salas	Jacob	MAD	7-0
Sierra	Lionel	REED	
Frank	Matt	EB	3-2
Mattox	David	BUC	

140
Tirapelle	Alex	CL	O.T. 5-0	
Seibert	Shane	MAD		
East	Drew	B	Fall	2:42
Sullivan	Daniel	GW		
Kesablyan	Vahe	HOOV	Fall	1:06
Bonita	Tim	DEL		

145
Gutierrez	Miguel	FOOT	3:31	
Breceda	Jesus	BUC		
Burnias	Matt	TUL	Fall	3:20
Ochoa	Josh	REED		
Rosa	Brian	MAD		7-6
Reyes	Richard	SANG		

152
Sheets	Sean	CENT	3-1
Shirley	Josh	B	
Cotta	Nick	LEM	5-4
Weatherly	Steven	EX	
Cooke	David	TUL	3-2
Harl	Justin	FOOT	

160
Hafenmeistger	Sven	LEM	7-3	(43-4)*
Bardsley	Matt	HOOV		
Griffith	Anthony	CENT	6-1	
Hernandez	Ramiro	B		
Garcia	Marcus	TUL	Fall	1:45
Napier	Mark	MAD		

171
Mooney	Britt	EB	13-5
Folmer	Daniel	BUC	
Botello	Edgar	EX	6-3
Griffin	William	MAD	
Roberts	Mitch	CL	17-3
Stewart	Brice	ED	

189
Sanchez	Mariano	REED	7-3	(34-3)*
Pickett	Robert	HOOV		
Stephens	Mike	LEM	6-3	
Negrete	Abel	CL		
Gonzales	Carlos	EB	13-0	
O'Rear	Scott	CENT		

(Continued on next page)

Yosemite Division – Clovis
February 16-17, 2001

215
Maffia	Broc	TW	13-7	(36-3)*
Cabrera	Bennie	LEM		
Goodman	Kyle	BUC	Fall	3:02
Torosian	Adam	CW		
Shields	Colin	SB	6-4	
Henderson	Nate	CENT		

HWT
Murphy	Jon	HAN	4-3	(39-6)*
Hallmark	Jacob	CL		
Wilson	Tyson	TW	3-1	
Braaten	Chris	STOCK		
Chretien	Jon	ED	2-1	
Rodriguez	Juan	MON		

* Record

Left to right, North Bakersfield Head Coach Ty Stricker, Derrick Hunter and Assistant Coach Parris Whitley

Tournament

1. Clovis 230.5
2. Bakersfield 225
3. Buchanan 203.5
4. Lemoore 172
5. Centennial 159.5
6. Madera 153
7. Tulare 135
8. Hoover 124
9. Foothill 116.5
10. East 111.5
11. Reedley 110.5
12. Hanford 104
13. Clovis West 88
14. Exeter 85
15. Tulare W. 82.5
16. Edison 68
17. Monache 67
18. Mt. Whitney 65
19. Bullard 62
20. Central 59.5
21. Sanger 55
22. North 54
23. Golden West 53.5
24. Stockdale 50
25. South 48.5
26. Highland 45.5
27. Redwood 42
28. Porterville 37
28. McLane 37
30. Ridgeview 31
31. Delano 30.5
32. Clovis East 25.5
33. Roosevelt 24
34. Fresno 23
35. Sunnywide 12
36. West 3

Bill Pierce (top) of South Bakersfield
1978 5th in CIF; 1979 2nd in CIF and 4th in State

Yosemite Division – East
February 15-16, 2002

103
Contreras	Gerrard	BUC	4-1
Perreira	Blake	TUL	
Juarez	Steven	HAN	11-9
Anderson	Mark	LEM	
Nelson	Jens	CW	4-1
Wilson	Rusty	CE	

112
Morgan	Nathan	B	5-2	
Mendes	Chad	HAN		
Ingram	Logan	BUC	Fall	1:37
Carlos	Sean	HOOV		
Carillo	Gilbert	TUL	8-1	
Harris	Travis	CL		

119
Flores	Gabe	CL	3-1	
Franco	Tony	B		
Martinez	Nick	TUL	Fall	3:00
Schneider	Justin	BUC		
Reyes	Eugene	HAN	Default	
Pena	Bobby	SANG		

125
Vasquez	Darrell	B	13-2
Holt	J.J.	TUL	
Bustamantae	Gabriel	FOOT	3-1
Williams	Jason	CL	
Marquez	Mike	EB	8-4
Hunter	Derrick	NB	

130
Tirapelle	Troy	CL	9-6
Goodpaster	Darrell	BUC	
Herrera	Alex	B	1-0
Anderson	Lucas	HAN	
Cox	Calvin	RIDGE	13-4
Setttle	Isaac	CW	

135
Roberts	David	CW	18-7
Hernandez	Joe	B	
Salas	Jacob	BUC	Default
Bonita	Tim	DEL	
Eck	Tony	HAN	11-0
Botello	Oscar	EX	

140
Varner	Jake	B	Fall	3:09
Sierra	Lionel	REED		
Mattox	David	BUC	3-1	
Hirata	Garin	CL		
Martinez	Chris	CW	3-2	
Daniels	Akili	ROOS		

145
Spradlin	Andrew	B	3:50
Nail	Norman	LEM	
Diaz	Marcos	FOOT	5-1
Thompson	Bryce	BUC	
Houck	Ryan	CW	5-1
Creason	Larry	TUL	

152
East	Drew	B	15-0
Breceda	Jesus	BUC	
Joyner	Travis	REED	2-0
Luna	Gabe	MON	
Thayn	Charlton	MT.W	13-6
Riojas	Adam	CW	

160
Sherley	Josh	B	9-4	
Hafaemeister	Sven	LEM		
Garcia	Marcus	TUL	Fall	4:41
Davis	Brian	MAD		
Cole	Jeff	CL	3-2	
Noak	Dustin	CW		

171
Weaver	Jacob	SANG	5-4	
Baker	Jeff	CENT		
Ferguson	Scott	CL	5-3	
Griffin	William	MAD		
Garcia	Jesse	GW	Fall	4:08
Hernandez	Ramiro	B		

189
Folmer	Daniel	BUC	Fall	4:24
Marquez	Josh	B		
Sanchez	Mariano	REED	5-1 (140 Wins)*	
Mercado	Eduardo	MAD		
Moore	Marcus	CL	4-2	
Mendonca	Frank	LEM		

(Continued on next page)

Yosemite Division – East
February 15-16, 2002

215
Goodman	Kyle	BUC	7-5
Maffia	Broc	TW	
Torosian	Adam	CW	3-1
Nadeau	Jeremiah	CL	
Chavez	Andy	REED	8-7
Cornwell	Adam	B	

HWT
Chretian	John	ED	Fall	5:10
Braaten	Chris	STOCK		
Parsons	Jared	CL	Default	
Camargo	Fernando	REED		
Landeros	Jake	MON	3-1 O.T.	
Valdovinos	Lorenzo	B		

* Career wins

John Martin
South Bakersfield
1966 CIF Champion
30-1

Tournament
1. Bakersfield 328
2. Buchanan 275
3. Clovis 234
4. Tulare 164.5
5. Clovis West 160.5
6. Reedley 144.5
7. Lemoore 133.5
8. Hanford 122.5
9. Madera 100.5
10. Centennial 92
11. Monache 80
12. Sangaer 79
13. Clovis East 76.5
14. Stockdale 68
15. Foothill 62
16. Edison 61.5
17. East 59.5
18. Ridgeview 59
19. Tulare W. 57
20. Exeter 55
21. Hoover 52
22. North 51
22. South 51
24. Porterville 50.5
25. Highland 50
26. Mt. Whitney 40
27. Bullard 37
28. Roosevelt 34.5
29. Redwood 34
30. Golden West 31.5
30. Delano 31.5
32. Central 29
33. Fresno 19
34. Sunnyside 18
35. McLane 17
36. West 12.5

Darrell Vasquez
Bakersfield High
Four-time State Champion
Career record: 191-7

Roy Heath
South Bakersfield
Three-time CIF Champion:
1964-66

Yosemite Division – Lemoore
February 21-22, 2003

103
Land	Brett	B	Fall	2:40 (37-8)
Vang	Chou	BULL		
Mercado	Edgar	MAD	7-2	
Winter	Brandon	BUC		
Ahumada	Fernando	PORT	Fall	:52
Uribe	Alex	HW		
Gibson	Keith	MT.W.	T.F.	
Simmons	Jordan	CW		

112
Parreira	Blake	TUL	4-0	
Orozco	Eric	MON		
Carlson	Sean	HOOV	Maj. 10-2	
Rocha	Dustin	LEM		
Rangell	Conrad	CEN	8-2	
Fisher	Reese	BUC		
Nacita	Elijah	B	6-2	(34-12)*
Hernandez	Antonio	LIB		

119
Mendez	Chad	HAN	T.F. 16-0	(56-2)*
Morales	Carlos	EB		
Carrillo	Gilbert	TUL	7-3	
Jaramillo	Tom	CW		
Neuman	Grant	B	Maj. 11-2	
Anderson	Mark	LEM		
Righi	Mike	RED	8-4	
Andaverde	Jose Gordy	MAD		

125
Morgan	Nathan	B	8-6	(33-1)*
Flores	Gabe	CL		
Waterston	Mike	BUC	6-4	
Reyes	Eugene	HAN		
Soto	Joe	PORT	Fall	3:32
Pierce	Tim	MAD		
Medina	Isaac	ROOS	3-1	
Horton	Bryce	CENT		

130
Tirapelle	Troy	CL	3:07	
Aguilar	Jacob	TUL		
Bustamonte	Gabe	FOOT	4-3	(37-6)
Schneider	Justin	BUC		
Ochoa	Joseph	REED	8-5	
Vasquez	Manuel	SB		
Klarcyk	Shawn	PORT		
Marquez	Mike	EAST		

135
Herrera	Alex	B	6-5	
Williams	Jason	Cl		
Moralez	Mark	Tul	5-4	
Anderson	Lucas	Han		
Caraveo	Jimmy	Del	9-4	
Jeffrey	Dwayne	Lem		
Gutierrez	Urbano	MAD	2-1	
Rojas	Alex	Reed		

140
Martinez	Chris	CW	17-11	
Dueck	Nick	SANG		
Perger	Cameron	CLO	2-4	
Marquez	Mark	E		
Hernandez	Jeremy	BHS	3-2	
Sanchez	Eric	MAD		
Pendleton	Willy	LEM	8-5	
Pari	Rolland	W		

145
Wender	K.B	CLO E	2-1	
Thompson	Bryce	CLO		
Points	Jason	LIB	11-4	
Guerrero	Joel	HAN		
Fielding	Coby	BUL	3-2	
Doherty	Randy	TUL		
Aguilar	Richard	HAN W	8-3	
Turkley	Chris	CW		

152
Varner	Jake	BHS	2:56	(32-2)*
Nail	Norman	LEM		
Houck	Ryan	CW	Major 11-2	
West	Doug	MON		
Thompson	Josh	MT.W	Default	
Mendez	James	HAN		
Packard	Kenneth	ROOS	6-3	
Aguilera	Steven	LIB		

160
Backer	Jeff	CENT	4-3	(43-3)*
Noack	Dustin	CW		
Lujand	Paul	BUL	1-0	
Perez	Nick	CL		
Wara	Garth	MAD	8-4	
Acevedo	Abel	MON		
Campos	Henry	LEM	15-2	
Moronnolte	Jason	FOOT		

(Continued on next page)

Yosemite Division – Lemoore
February 21-22, 2003

171
Griffin	William	Mad	4-2 O.T.
Ferguson	Scott	CLO	
Garcia	Marcus	Tul	6-2
Carey	Lammar	Hoov	
Mendonca	Frankie	Lem	8-5
Cooper	Casey	SANG	
Soils	Junior	LIB	Fall
Allen	Ben	Red	

189
Ceremello	Brandon	CLO	5:39
Mercado	Eduardo	MAD	
Clark	John	HAN	1:24
Medina	Daniel	ROOS	
Campos	Ray	LEM	6-0
Berry	Chad	HOOV	
Velasquez	Jesse	PORT	Fall
Lewis	Chris	CW	

215
Clutts	Tyler	CLO	5:09
Marquez	Josh	BHS	
Torosian	Adam	CW	10-3
Coleman	Chauncey	MAD	
Levay	Bryan	MAD	1:19
Garcia	Rudy	MON	
Davis	Tim	STOCK	
Curtis	Thomas	LEM	

275
Clark	James	MT.W	5:49
Thomas	Grant	BUL	
Camargo	Fernando	ED	
Rodriguez	Jordan	ED	
Preston	Wiley	CW	8-2
Garcia	Jesus	MON	
Engstrom	Jeremy	GW	10-2
White	Jerry	N	

* Record

Tournament
1. Clovis 275.5
2. Bakersfield 217
3. Clovis West 182.5
4. Madera 181
5. Buchanan 177
6. Lemoore 159
7. Tulare 153
8. Hanford 142.5
9. Monache 128
10. Clovis East 98
13. Liberty-B 84
14. East 81
15. Mt. Whitney 76
18. Centennial 65.5
20. Foothill 55
21. Stockdale 52
22. North 46
24. Redwood 44.5
26. Delano 42.5
29. South 38.5
30. West 34
33. Golden West 26
34. Highland 24
35. Ridgeview 23
36. Tulare W. 15

Note: Not all school records available.

Nathan Morgan
Bakersfield High
Four-time State Finalist
Three-time Champion
Career record: 166-6

Yosemite Division – Buchanan
February 20-21, 2004

103
Cisneros	Joe	B	Fall	1:35
Huizar	David	LEM		
Gomez	Lupe	MAD	11-9	
Contreras	Buck	BUC		
Mathews	Jordan	PORT		
Vigil	Freddie	SB	Fall	1:12
Williams	Galen	TW	Fall	3:40
Bocanegra	Daniel	HAN		

112
Land	Bret	B	7-2	
Parreire	Blake	TUL		
Mercado	Edgar	MAD	7-3	
Savala	Jimmy	CL		
Gibson	Keith	MT.W	Fall	3:59
Romin-Marin	Sean	LEM		
Wilson	Rusty	CE	Fall	1:37
Hay	Addison	FOOT		

119
Orozco	Eric	MON	5-3	
Nacita	Elijah	B		
Carrillo	Gilbert	TUL	7-1	
Masuta	Sabi	MAD		
Anderson	Mark	LEM	13-0	
Fisher	Reace	BUC		
Rangel	Conrad	CEN	Fall	3:48
Jordon	Vaughn	CW		

125
Soto	Joe	PORT	8-7	(35-5)*
Neuman	Grant	B		(37-7)*
Juarez	Steven	HAN		
Trevino	Rafael	BUC	Default	
Rocha	Dustin	LEM	6-1	
Andaverde	Gordy	MAD		
Galavis	Jerry	REED	17-10	
Tablit	Mark	CENT		

130
Morgan	Nathan	B	Fall	1:03
Williams	Jason	CL		
Ochoa	Joseph	REED	10-4	
Gibson	Coby	MT.W		
Quinones	Sergio	LEM		
Right	Daniel	RED	Fall	5:05
Rios	Johnny	MAD	9-8	
Strid	Sam	BUC		

135
Schneider	Justin	BUC	4-3	
Gutierrez	Urbano	MAD		
Moralez	Mark	TUL	12-3	
Webber	Tony	B		
Williams	Josh	CL	3-2	
Maldonado	Eric	GW		
Medina	Isaac	ROOS	4-1	
Dueck	Nick	SANG		

140
Tirapelle	Troy	CL	14-2	
Valenzuela	Don	BUC		
Pumarejo	Jay	CW	14-9	
Olivera	Mike	LEM		
Box	Anthony	B	Fall	3:56
Christensen	Ricky	LIB-B		
Martinez	Matt	TUL	4-2	
Gomez	Sam	REED		

145
Herrera	Alex	B	5-4	
Martinez	Chris	CW		
Pendleton	Willy	LEM	7-5	
Doherty	Randy	TUL		
Fielding	Coby	BUC		
Brooks	Wesley	MCL		
Metcalife	Josh	PORT	Fall	2:25
Gallegos	Jimmy	MAD		

152
Thompson	Bryce	CL	3-1	
Meredith	Chip	CEN		
Wender	K.B.	CE	3-0	
West	Doug	MON		
Sanchez	Eric	MAD	6-3	
Packard	Kenneth	ROOS		
Flores	Carlos	REED	Forfeit	
Koy	Kev	HIGH		

(Continued on next page)

*Cen = Central

Yosemite Division – Buchanan
February 20-21, 2004

160
Bernacchi	Tyler	CE	3-1
Noack	Dustin	CW	
Wara	Garth	MAD	5-4
Ceremello	Sean	CL	
Acevedo	Abel	MON	10-4
Amet	David	PORT	
Montez	Frank	MCL	5-4
Rincon	Mike	FRE	

171
Varner	Jake	B	Inj. Def.	
Griffin	Kyle	CE		
Garcia	Marcus	TUL	6-1	
Turley	Chris	CW		
Levay	Bryan	MAD	9-0	
Perez	Nick	CL		
Lujano	Paul	BUC	Fall	2:55
Madsen	Deke	HAN		

189
Ceremello	Brandon	CL	6-5	
Scheider	Will	CW		
Velasquez	Jesse	PORT		
Clark	John	HAN		
Flores	Ryan	BUC	8-2	
Vituccu	Anthony	CE		
Allen	Ben	RED	Fall	:52
Renteria	Anthony	B		

215
Marquez	Josh	B	Fall	:31
Garcia	Rudy	MON		
Lewis	Chris	CW	13-9	
Davis	Tim	STOCK		
Mercer	Daniel	CEN		
Moore	Marcus	CL		
Egan	Jearal	SB	Default	
Lanier	Will	MT.W		

HWT
Wiley	Preston	CW	2-1	
Leyva	Victor	FRE		
Torres	Carlos	MON	4-3	
Morgan	David	CENT		
Paulson	R.J.	FRE	Fall	2:36
Valov	Fred	DEL	(15-4)*	
Garza	Mike	BULL	Forfeit	
Salazar	Louie	SUNY		

Alex, Adam and Troy Tirapelle
10 CIF Championships
8 State Championships

Tournament
1. Bakersfield	293		33. Bullard	31
2. Clovis	229		34. Hoover	24.5
3. Clovis West	200		35. Hanford W.	18
4. Madera	195.5		36. Tulare W.	17
5. Buchanan	189.5		37. East	7
6. Clovis East	180		38. Granite Hills	3
7. Lemoore	172			
8. Tulare	163.5			
9. Monache	163			
10. Porterville	144.5			
11. Hanford	103			
12. Stockdale	75			
13. Redwood	69.5			
14. Centennial	67.5			
15. Mt.Whitney	66.5			
16. South	65			
17. Reedley	59.5			
18. Edison	54			
19. Foothill	53.5			
20. McLane	51			
21. Roosevelt	50.5			
22. Fresno	49			
23. Liberty-B	43.5			
23. North	43.5			
25. Central	40			
26. Sanger	35			
27. Sunnyside	33			
27. Golden West	33			
27. Delano	33			
30. Highland	32			
30. Ridgeview	32			
32. West	32			

Yosemite Division – East Bakersfield
February 18-19, 2005

103
Vigil	Freddie	SB	Fall 5:02	(38-5)*
Escandon	Pete	LEM		
Watts	Randall	ELD		
Weimer	Steve	CL		(36-16)*
Sanchez	Jesse	CE		
Cheidez	David	FOOT		(38-10)*
Arrelo	Edger	HIGH		
Gamboa	Buddy	WB		

112
Hay	Addison	FOOT	7-5	(44-9)*
Lomas	Frank	B		(38-14)*
Gibson	Keith	MT.W		
Watts	David	ELD		
Trevino	Ricky	FRE		
Conely	Matt	CE		(30-18)*
Perales	Anthony	MAD		
Contreras	Buck	BUC		

119
Savala	Jimmy	CL	10-6	
Chaidez	Bernard	FOOT	(41-10)	
Martinez	Christian	B	(36-12)	
Rodriguez	Alex	CL	(38-19)	
Huizar	David	LEM		
Padilla	Chris	CW		
Barbosa	Walt	BULL		
Gutierrez	Sid	BUC		

125
Anderson	Mark	LEM	Fall	3:13
Cisneros	Joe	B		
Jordan	Vaughn	CW		
Rangel	Conrad	CI		
Mercado	Edgar	MAD		
Trevino	Rafael	BUC		
Sanchez	Bengie	TW		
Saenz	Tyler	REED		

130
Nacita	Elijah	B	9-2	(44-5)*
Betancur	Josh	BUC		(49-9)*
Rocha	Dustin	LEM		
Rios	Johnny	MAD		
Christianson	Jessie	SANG		
Larson	Troy	CE		
Simmons	Jordan	CL		
Pavone	Chris	PORT		

135
Soto	Joe	PORT	7-2	(34-0)*
Gibson	Cody	MT.W		
Sanchez	Alfonso	MCL		
Velarde	Jovanny	BUC		(39-17)*
Ochoa	Joseph	REED		
Mendez	Michael	HAN		
Montelongo	Daniel	MAD		
Vukovic	Daniel	LEM		

140
Land	Brett	B	6-0	(46-8)*
Maldonado	Eric	GW		
Corona	Alex	MON		
Licon	Kenny	FRE		
Harris	Travis	CL		(27-10)*
Moralez	Mitch	TUL		
Cesena	Joseph	MAD		
Jeimini	Matt	CW		

145
Pendleton	Willy	LEM	14-2	
Rodriguez	Brian	CE		(32-12)*
Williams	John	CW		(31-10)*
Horton	Bryce	CENT		
Box	Anthony	B		
Martinez	Matt	TUL		
Peralta	Matt	FOOT		
Brooks	Wes	MCL		

152
Bardsley	Nick	CW	4-3	(42-13)*
Packard	Kenneth	ROOS		
Doherty	Randy	TUL		
Metcalf	Josh	PORT		
Olivera	Mike	LEM		
Gallegos	Jimmy	MAD		
Wilkin	Danny	CENT		
Mendez	Robert	MON		

(Continued on next page)

Yosemite Division – East Bakersfield
February 18-19, 2005

160
Williams	Josh	B	1-0	
Ceremellow	Shaun	CL		
Baughman	Scott	LEM		
Parli	Rolland	WB		(35-9)*
Rodriguez	Adrian	MON		
Tgaff	Tim	TUL		
Duran	Jordan	BULL		
Balch	Andrew	BUC		

171
Griffin	Christopher	MAD	6-1	
Cavanaugh	Mike	B		
Vitucci	Anthony	CE		
Rozario	Andrew	CL		
Degeare	Justin	LIB		
Marquez	Ricky	EB		
Rosebrock	Even	CW		
Ayers	Terrell	SUNY		

189
Varner	Jake	B	Fall 4:41	(39-0/35 Falls)
Timmerman	Nathan	MON		
Parrish	Zak	BUC		(34-14)*
Czechowski	Nick	HIGH		(32-10)*
Leyva	Raul	MCL		
Esparza	Kevin	CL		
De La Rosa	Eric	FOOT		
Wadkins	Blake	LIB		

215
Flores	Ryan	BUC	Default	(53-7)*
Clark	John	HAN		
Garcia	Rudy	MON		
Perez	Jose	PORT		
Guill	Westy	CE		
Pierson	Jacob	RIDGE		
Ferreria	Brennan	CL		
Valencia	Esteban	FRE		

275
Lewis	Chris	CW	4-0	(36-4)*
Morgan	David	CENT		
Valov	Fred	DEL		
Leyva	Luis	ROOS		
Dummar	Mike	GH		
Newman	Josh	GW		
Nichols	Tim	MAD		
Maxson	Jacob	RED		

Tournament
1. Bakersfield 235.5
2. Lemoore 196
3. Clovis 193
4. Buchanan 175.5
5. Madera 154.5
6. Clovis East 152.5
7. Clovis West 148.5
8. Monache 123.5
9. Foothill 120
10. Porterville 103
11. Centennial 88
12. South 81.5
13. Golden West 78.5
14. Tulare 73
15. McLane 72.5
16. Fresno 71.5
17. Bullard 69
18. Liberty 64
19. Hanford 62
20. Mt. Whitney 61
21. Sunnyside 50
22. Reedley 49.5 Tied for 22nd
22. Roosevelt 49.5 Tied for 22nd
24. Highland 49
25. El Diamante 47.5
26. Sanger 40 Tied for 26th
26. East 40 Tied for 26th
28. Redwood 38
29. Ridgeview 36
30. Granite Hills 32.5
31. Central 29.5
32. Edison 28.5 Tied for 32nd
32. West 28.5 Tied for 32nd
34. Delano 28
35. Tulare W. 25
36. Hanford W. 23
37. North 18
38. Stockdale 17
39. Cesar Chavez 12
40. Hoover 9.5

* Record

Art Chavez
South
Bakersfield
1964 3rd CIF
1965 CIF
Champion
Career record:
53-4

Yosemite Division – Lemoore
February 17-18, 2006

103
Vigil	Freddie	SB	9-0	
Gonzalez	Peter	EB		
Chaidez	David	FOOT	5-2	
Fitzgerald	Steven	CE		
Done	Chris	BUC	17-0	
Everwine	Chase	CW		
Rocha	Brandon	LEM	Fall	1:17
Hernandez	Christian	NB		

112
Arredondo	Justin	BUC	6-0	
Lomas	Frank	B		
Demison	Nektoe	EB	11-5	
Watts	Randall	ELD		
Weimer	Steve	CL	2-1	
Jaramillo	Al	LEM	8-3	
Mendoza	Sam	RED		

119
Conley	Matt	CE	10-7	
Watts	David	ELD		
Ramos	Chris	BULL	8-1	
Tucker	Warren	MAD		
Beltran	Andrew	SB	6-4	(34-12)*
Ortega	Paul	MCL		
Sabo	John	NB	Forfeit	
Chatman	Charles	ED		

125
Velarde	Jovanny	BUC	6-5	
Jordan	Vaughn	CW		
Rodriguez	Alex	CE	Fall	5:20
Roman-Marin	Sean	LEM		
Hicks	Seth	CENT	4-3	
Cruz	Jonah	B		
Sakaguchi	Scott	CL	Fall	1:16
Perez	Richard	HOOV		

130
Betancur	Josh	BUC	4-2	
Savala	Jimmy	CI		
Huizar	David	LEM	4-1	
Rios	Johnny	MAD		
Rasmussen	Travis	B	8-7	
Pavone	Ryan	PORT		
Parson	Tim	CE	Fall	4:41
Socia	Michael	FOOT		

135
Nacita	Edlijah	B	Fall	3:40
Pavone	Chris	PORT		
Larson	Troy	CE	8-5	
West	Stephen	BUC		
Christiansen	Colton	LIB-B		
Rubio	Vincent	LEM		
Christiansen	Jesse	SANG	8-0	
Esparza	Josh	CL		

140
Sanchez	Alfonso	MCL	Fall	3:58
Box	Anthony	B		
Morales	Mitch	TUL	5-3	
Cesena	Joseph	MAD		
West	Craig	BUC	4-3	
Licon	Kenny	FRE		
McAtee	Carson	CENT	9-6	
Aufderheld	Eric	CL		

145
Weber	Tony	B	3-2	
Horton	Bryce	CENT		
Rodriguez	Brian	CE	3-0	
Balch	Andrew	BUC		
Cox	Matt	CL	Fall	1:02
Lopez	Martin	EB		
Grayson	Jon	BULL	4-2	
Ireland	Lamont	SUNY		

152
Corona	Alex	MON	2-1	
Montez	Frank	MCL		
Pendleton	Willy	LEM	7-3	
Wilkin	Danny	CENT		
Tucker	Grant	MAD	1-0	
Smith	Eric	BUC		
Morales	Matt	TUL	7-2	(25-9)*
Peralta	Matt	FOOT		

(Continued on next page)

Yosemite Division – Lemoore
February 17-18, 2006

160
Boger	Matt	BUC	2-1
Bardsley	Nick	CW	
Righi	Daniel	RED	16-4
Bracamonte	Paul	CEN	
Torris	Chris	SB	Fall 3:11
Bays	Chris	CL	
Villalobos	Tino	CENT	6-4
Torgensen	James	STOCK	

171
Parrish	Zak	BUC	6-4
De La Rosa	Eric	FOOT	
Musquez	John	CENT	9-5
Ayers	Terrell	SUNY	
Vera	Jose	CEN	11-3
Allisoin	Dustin	MAD	
Sanchez	Brett	CL	7-3
Brandt	Phillip	BULL	

189
Timmerman	Nathan	MON	10-9
Boger	Josh	BUC	
Rozario	Andrew	CL	9-1
Blair	Tyler	MAD	
Travis	David	FOOT	Fall 5:23
Cabrera	Herman	LEM	
Jones	Donovan	RED	6-3
Bishop	Jacob	LIB-B	

215
Flores	Ryan	BUC	Fall 2:17
Perez	Jose	PORT	
Lopez	Vince	CL	4-2
Maxson	Jacob	RED	
Moore	Quinn	SB	Fall 1:18
Palmero	Matt	ELD	
Furstenburg	Shawn	MAD	Fall 3:42
Padilla	Anthony	B	

275
Lewis	Chris	CW	8-3
Morgan	David	CENT	
Newman	Josh	GW	6-4
Quiroz	Ivan	FOOT	
Zamora	Jonathan	CL	5-3
Hawkins	Ramon	FRE	
Rose	Ryan	MCL	6-4
Ayala	Javier	PORT	(22-12)*

Tournament
1. Buchanan 304.5
2. Clovis 187.0
3. Bakersfield 175
4. Lemoore 150.5
5. Clovis East 147
6. Centennial 146.5
7. Madera 133.5
8. Clovis West 129
9. Foothill 108
10. South 99
11. Porterville 96
12. Monache 95.5
13. Redwood 91
14. McLane 87.5
15. El Diamante 78.5
16. Bullard 77
17. Golden West 76
18. Fresno 69.5
19. East 66.5
20. Central 63
21. North 62.5
22. Sunnyside 56.0
23. Liberty-B 55
24. Tulare Union 51
25. Cesar Chavez 43
26. Hanford 37
27. Edison 35
27. Stockdale 35
29. Sanger 34
30. Reedley 31.5
31. Ridgeview 30.5
32. Hoover 25
33. Granite Hills 23
34. Hanford W. 21
34. Tulare W. 21
36. Highland 20
37. Delano 15
38. Mt. Whitney 12
39. Roosevelt 5
40. West 4

Alan Adam
South Bakersfield
2nd CIF 1961

Manuel Villarreal
2nd CIF 1960

Jim Bridger
South Bakersfield
4th CIF 1961

Jake Varner of Bakersfield High, the only four-time CIF Champion in the history of the Central Section.

Bakersfield High Coach Andy Varner hugs State Champion Joe Cisneros

Chris Martinez of Clovis West and Alex Herrera of Bakersfield High, three-time State finalist, wrestle at the 2004 State Finals.

Sierra-Sequoia Divisional
1966-2006

Sierra-Sequoia Division

Date	Champion	Coach	Location
2/19/66	Arvin	John Burton	Sequoia Divisional
			Corcoran-Southern Divisional
1967			
1968			
2/21/69	Tulare Western	Jerry Vinson	Small School Divisional: Selma
2/21/70	Selma	Dick Ravalin	Sequoia Divisional: Sanger
2/20/71	Washington Union	Bill Griffin	Sierra-Tollhouse
2/26/72	Washington Union	Bill Griffin	College of Sequoia-Visalia
2/17/73	Kingsburg	Sam Crandell	Arvin
2/16/74	Washington Union	Russ Simpson	Sierra-Tollhouse
2/22/75	Chowchilla	Eric Hansen	College of Sequoia-Visalia
2/21/76	Washington Union	Russ Simpson	Wasco
2/19/77	Kingsburg	Sam Crandell	Sierra-Tollhouse
2/18/78	Washington Union	Howard Zink	Sierra-Tollhouse
2/17/79	Shafter	Darrell Fletcher	Shafter
2/23/80	Washington Union	Howard Zink	Sierra-Tollhouse
2/21/81	Washington Union	Howard Zink	Central
2/20/82	Kingsburg	Sam Crandell	Wasco
2/19/83	Kingsburg	Sam Crandell	Firebaugh
2/18/84	Selma	Nick Quintana	Central
2/16/85	Washington Union	Howard Zink	Wasco
2/22/86	Selma	Nick Quintana	Dos Palos
2/21/87	Selma	Nick Quintana	Selma
2/20/88	Selma	Nick Quintana	Central
2/18/89	Selma	Nick Quintana	Central
*2/17/90	Selma	Nick Quintana	Shafter
	Tranquility	Joe Gomez	Shafter
2/16/91	Selma	Nick Quintana	Corcoran
2/22/92	Selma	Nick Quintana	Dos Palos
2/20/93	Dos Palos	Frank Lemos	Shafter
2/19/94	Firebaugh	Bill Mgnusson	Washington Union-Easton
2/18/95	Exeter	John Conley	Dos Palos
2/17/96	Firebaugh	Bill Magnusson	Shafter
2/22/97	Kingsburg	Ramiro Pereschica	Dos Palos
2/21/98	Dos Palos	Frank Lemos	Firebaugh
2/20/99	Dos Palos	Frank Lemos	Arvin
2/19/00	Dos Palos	Frank Lemos	Dos Palos
2/17/01	Dos Palos	Frank Lemos	Shafter
2/16/02	Firebaugh	Bill Magnusson	Hanford West
2/22/03	Shafter	Gary Pederson	Dos Palos
2/20-21/04	Washington Union	Howard Zink	Farmersville
2/18-19/05	Firebaugh	Bill Magnusson	Shafter
2/17-18/06	Dos Palos	Frank Lemos	Firebaugh

*The CIF ruled that Tranquility used two ineligible wrestlers, making Selma the champions in a decision on 3/17/90.

Outstanding Sierra-Sequoia Wrestlers

The Most Outstanding Wrestler Awards started in 1996 for lower and upper weights sponsored by the Coyote Club.

Year	Wrestler	School
1996	Charlie Uribe	Washington Union
	Clemente Moreno	Dinuba
1997	George Moreno	Firebaugh
	Dan Jackson	Kingsburg
1998	Keji Crane	Dos Palos
	Narcy Martinez	Wasco
1999	Jason Moreno	Firebaugh
	Narcy Martinez	Wasco
2000	Jorge Evangelis	Parlier
	Mike Van Worth	Dos Palos
2001	Jorge Evangelis	Parlier
	Riley Young	Sierra
2002	Matt Maldonado	Shafter
	Elvis Villegas	Mendota
2003	Matt Gonzales	Exeter
	Jason Carrasco	Shafter
2004	Pedro Olea	Farmersville
	Orlando Landois	Wasco
2005	Dan Weatherly	Exeter
	Marvin Statler	Shafter
2006	Frank Costillo	Arvin
	Lucas Espericueta	Shafter

Sierra-Sequoia Division – Corcoran
February 19, 1966

95
Hernandez	Alex	CORC	12-1
Lowe	John	WASC	
Rodriguez	Paul	A	

103
Guerrero		CORC	10-3
Nunez		REED	
Dickson	Chuck	W	

112
Rivera		REED	Fall
Espinoza	E	A	
Winters	Jess	W	

120
Santoya	Frank	SANG	1-0
Acord		REED	
Salazar	Joe	SHAFT	

127
Flores	Jess	TW	12-6
Garcia	Mike	W	
Patino	Vic	A	

133
Gonzales	Johnny	TW	2-1
Ogowa	Eddie	SANG	
Rubinol	Jesse	A	

138
Popejoy	Joe	A	Default
Renteria		REED	
Gollmyer	Bruce	W	

145
Ramirez	Ruben	A	7-4
Gilley	Steve	WASC	
Forney	Bruce	W	

154
Herndon	Bob	A	10-1
Forney	Doug	W	

165
Tarver	Bill	A	4-0
Ketcher	Mike	REED	

175
Lundgren	Don	SHAFT	Fall
Torres	Art	A	
Tutsch	Don	W	

191
Medrano	Paul	SANG	Fall
Parker	Bob	A	
Hosman	Steve	W	

UNL
Davis	Clovis	A	3-1
Ito		REED	
Engle	Jim	SHAFT	

Tournament
1. Arvin — 108
2. Reedley — 79
3. West — 55
4. Sanger — 45
5. Corcoran — 33 Tied for 5th
5. Wasco — 33 Tied for 5th
7. Tulare W. — 29
8. Shafter — 28

Don Lundgren
Shafter High

Small School Division – Selma
February 21, 1969

95
Hernandez	Alex	CORC	7-3
Hernandez	David	SANG	
Lowe	Ernie	W	6-4
Forbes	Wayne	SHAFT	

103
Tatarakis	Tom	DP	4-0
Inaba	Don	SANG	
Valesquez	Tony	A	4:32
Garcia		CORC	

112
Guerrero	Tony	CORC	10-1
Cantu	Gilbert	SANG	
Ramirez	Ramon	DP	4-1
Garcia	Fausto	WU	

120
Orosco	Sal	TW	6-2
Martinez	Mike	SANG	
Sisemore	Harold	W	6-0
Ketchum	P	A	

127
Price	Terry	KING	10-0
Wallace	Will	EX	
Gomez	Pedro	CORC	7-1
Miller	Dan	SIER	

133
Martin	Dean	TW	4-3
Pedroza	Humberto	DIN	
Silva	Leo	WOOD	6-2
Morales	Luis	WU	

138
Newman	Doug	TW	5-3
Black	Dan	SHAFT	
Ramos	Tom	A	
Sousa	Tony	SEL	

145
Machado	Manuel	MCF	4-3
Burris	Doug	KING	
Silva	Lionel	WOOD	8-3
Patrick	Stan	CORC	

154
Ernest	Mike	EX	3-2	
Martin	Tom	KING		
Terry	Mike	W	Fall	:55
Gill	Tony	REED		

155
Clement	Randy	W	Forfeit
Rawles	Eric	EX	
Kadel	Dave	SHAFT	8-4
Crandell	Oliver	KING	

175
Smith	Al	CENT	5-4
Wilhite	Bill	W	
Burleson	Dave	TW	9-5
Normi	Arvi	Reed	

191
Robinson	Wayne	SIER	Fall	3:22
Brown	Jim	SHAFT		
Scott		WOOD	8-0	
Niell	Randy	EX		

HWT
Mefford	Walt	TW	1-0	
Jeffers	George	SHAFT		
Duerkson	Don	REED	Fall	:43
Cossum	Fred	TAFT		

Tournament
1. Tulare Western	69		19. Kerman	1
2. Wasco	68		Coalinga	0
3. Corcoran	50		Laton	0
4. Exeter	43		Strathmore	0
5. Sanger	41	Tied for 5th		
5. Shafter	41	Tied for 5th		
7. Kingsbury	38			
8. Woodlake	31			
9. Dos Palos	26			
10. Arvin	23			
11. Sierra	20			
12. Reedley	19			
13. McFarland	15			
14. Washington U.	14			
15. Selma	12			
16. Dinuba	11			
17. Taft	5			
18. Tranquility	3			

Sierra-Sequoia Division – Sanger
February 21, 1970

95
Otomo	Tom	SEL	Fall	3:30
Ramos	Frank	A		
Forbs	Wayne	SHAFT	5-0	
Cavazos	Jess	DIN		

103
Hernandez	Alex	CORC	Fall 5:05 (40-0)*	
Hernandez	David	SANG		
Velasquez	Tony	A	7-2	
Flores	Michael	WU		

112
Caudle	Rex	EX	8-3
Garcia	Larry	WOOD	
Guerrero	Sebastian	CORC	6-5
Cantu	Gilbert	SHAFT	

120
Herrera	Leo	SHAFT	10-7	(26-5)*
Martinez	Mike	SANG		
Bowler	Jay	WOOD	11-6	
Hernandez	Victor	KING		

127
Wallis	Will	EX	11-4	(34-0-1)*
Munoz	Joe	SEL		
Gonzales	Armand	REED	Fall	3:23
Whitney		W		

133
Martin	Dean	TW	4-2
Quintana	Mike	SEL	
Silva	Jerry	WOOD	
Benevidez		EX	

138
Cruz	Dave	EX	8-1	(30-2)*
O'Hanneson	Jeff	SHAFT		
Davis	Darrell	CENT	2-0	
Allredge	Bruce	SIER		

145
Molano	Fred	CORC	Fall 1:15 (34-0)*	
Hollingworth	Gary	SHAFT		
Machado	Manuel	MCF	3-1	
Ramos	Tom	A		

154
Silva	Lionel	WOOD	Fall 3:45	
			(39-1/23 Falls)*	
Quintana	Nick	SEL		
Ketscher	William	SANG	5-2	
Andrews	Dani	LATON		

165
Moz	Lalo	CORC	4-1	(34-4)*
Thompson	Sythel	SEL		
Moore	Johnny	SHAFT		
Woods		CAR		

175
Candler Carl		WU	13-4
Watson Ken		TW	
Gonzales		SANG	3-1
Andrews	Dennis	EX	

191
Hill	Tom	SHAFT	10-6	
Cox	John	TW		
Gross	Pat	SEL	Fall	1:46
Mendoza	Mike	CENT		

HWT
Jefers	George	W	Fall 3:05 (17-0)*	
Johns	Earl	DP		
Lewis		SANG	3-0	
Aquino	Lupe	CHOW		

Tournament
1. Selma 69
2. Corcoran 63
3. Exeter 62
4. Shafter 58
5. Sanger 53
6. Woodlake 49
7. Tulare Western 46
8. Washington U. 42
9. Arvin 33
10. Wasco 19
11. Dos Palos 14
12. Central 13
13. Chowchilla 10 Tied for 13th
13. McFarland 10 Tied for 13th
13. Reedley 10 Tied for 13th
13. Taft 10 Tied for 13th
17. Tranquility 9 Tied for 17th
17. Sierra 9 Tied for 17th
19. Kingsburg 7 Tied for 19th
19. Caruthers 7 Tied for 19th
21. Laton 6
22. Dinuba 4
23 Kerman 3
24. Coalinga 2
24 OROSI 0

* Record

Sierra-Sequoia Division – Sierra High/Tollhouse
February 20, 1971

95
Gonzales	John	HIGH	12-8
Pardo	Gabe	REED	
Balderana	Bennie	CORC	3-0
Lopeteguy	Joey	SHAFT	

103
Otomo	Tom	SEL	6-5
Taterakis	Jim	DP	
Romero	Junior	REED	11-6
Cavazos	Jess	DIN	

112
Castillo	Armando	TW	9-6
Garecia	Robert	WU	
Leona	Richard	REED	Fall 4:40
Contreras	Rudy	OROSI	

120
Guerrero	Sebastian	CORC	8-1
Herrera	Leo	SHAFT	
Montoya	Gabe	REED	4-1
Garvin	Marcel	W	

127
Whitney	Mike	WOOD	Default
Miller	Steve	EX	
Carrasco	Tony	REED	Fall 3:34
Johnson	James	DP	

133
Castillo	Alberto	DP	14-7
Gonzales	Armand	REED	
Quintana	Mike	SEL	6-3
Pizarro	Larry	EX	

138
Correia	Larry	WU	6-2
Munoz		SEL	
Morris	Gary	TAFT	13-6
Turpin	Jimmy	COAL	

145
Gonzales	George	LATON	8-4
Kister	Mike	KER	
Merroquin	Rafael	MCF	6-3
Nichols	Clint	SIER	

154
Manning	Tony	WU	11-3
Torosian	Max	SANG	
Hendrix	Don	SIER	Fall 3:30
Lee		SEL	

165
Thompson	Sythel	SEL	Fall 3:55
McLennan	Tran		
Bentley	Leigh	EX	5-1
Delgado	Dan	SANG	

175
Moz	Lalo	CORC	10-5
Kadel	David	SHAFT	
Reichert	Tim	REED	Fall 2:25
Pitkin	Jim	EX	

191
Harmon	Charles	WU	5-1
Smith	Stan	CORC	
Andrews	Dennis	EX	6-4
Hill	Tom	SHAFT	

HWT
Jeffers	George	W	Fall 1:09
Gross	Pat	SEL	
Ramirez	Joe	WU	Ref. Dec.
Gonzales	Louis	CEN	

Tournament
1. Washington U.	70	
2. Selma	65	
3. Reedley	60	
4. Corcoran	53	
5. Exeter	46	
6. Shafter	39	
7. Dos Palos	31	
8. Wasco	22	
9. Sierra	20	Tied for 9th
9. Highland	20	Tied for 9th
11. Tulare Western	19	
12. Woodlake	18	Tied for 12th
12. Sanger	18	Tied for 12th
14. Kerman	14	Tied for 14th
14. Laton	14	Tied for 14th
16. Tranquility	13	
17. Orosi	12	Tied for 12th
17. Coalinga	12	Tied for 12th
19. Taft	11	
20. McFarland	9	
21. Central	7	
22. Dinuba	6	
23. Arvin	5	Tied for 23rd
23. Caruthers	5	Tied for 23rd
23. Kingsburg	5	Tied for 23rd
26. Chowchilla	3	
27. Lindsay	2	
Strathmore	0	

Sierra-Sequoia Div. – College of Sequoia/Visalia
February 26, 1972

95
Cavazos	Jesse	DIN	Fall 3:17
Contereras	Robert	KING	
Filmore	Wayne	TAFT	7-3
Alcantar	Mike	EX	

103
Guerrero	Eugene	CORC	5-2
Lopeteguy	Joey	SHAFT	
Rugnaid	John	A	2-0
Alfaro	Ron	EX	

112
Ramos	Frank	A	3-1
Affentranger	Franc	SHAFT	
Tataraki	James	DP	8-0
Balerama	Benny	CORC	

120
Moz	Roy	CORC	5-0
Silva	Augie	WOOD	
Castillo	Adolfo	DP	10-8
Balleza	Santon	MCF	

127
Maldonado	Frank	SHAFT	5-1
Bravo	Rick	EX	
Souza	Al	CENT	Fall 5:30
Cervantes	Pete	CORC	

133
Castillo	Alberto	DP	9-6
Smithee	Mike	A	
Rameros	Richard	KING	3-2
Martin	Rick	WU	

138
Ramos	Alvie	A	Fall 3:38
Pacheco	Ed	EX	
Baylon	Paul	DP	7-1
Gilmore	Steve	SIE	

145
Foglio	Ron	CENT	9-4
Correta	Larry	WU	
Almanza	Julian	EX	6-3
Ward	Darrell	TAFT	

154
Nichols	Clint	SIE	12-2
Parrish	Darrell	MCF	
Harris	Servain	WU	5-1
Mitchell	Ron	TRAN	

165
Manning	Tony	WU	20-1
Corbett	Bob	CORC	
Clement	Marty	W	Fall 1:49
Chambers	John	DP	

175
Bracamonte	Joe	CENT	9-6
Esquibel	Steve	MCF	
Clement	Terry	W	O.T. :55
Morra	Brad	A	

191
Harman	Charles	WU	3-1
Andrews	Dennis	EX	
Smith	Stan	CORC	Fall 1:46
Gehlert	Chuck	A	

HWT
Gonzalez	Luis	CENT	7-3
Vella	Emitto	KING	
Ramero	John	WU	Fall 2:10
Baughman	James	FOW	

Tournament
1. Washington U. 76.5
2. Arvin 65.5
3. Corcoran 55.5
4. Exeter 51
5. Dos Palos 51
6. Central 45
7. Kingsburg 37.5
8. Shafter 30
9. McFarland 27
10. Sierra 23.5
11. Woodlake 15.5
12. Wasco 15 Tied for 15th
12. Dinuba 15 Tied for 15th
14. Taft 12
15. Fowler 7
16. Kerman 6
17. Tranquility 5.5
18. Caruthers 5
19. Chowchilla 4
20. Coalinga 2

Ron Foglio
Central High

Sierra-Sequoia Division – Arvin
February 17, 1973

95
Contreras	Bob	KING	8-1
Machado	Ed	A	
Vasquez	Frank	DP	Ref. Dec.
Breshears	Charles	T	

103
Ruiz	Joe	KING	Fall 5:36
Orduna	Cosme	DP	
George	Randy	TAFT	5-0
Molina	Hector	EX	

112
Lopeteguy	Joey	SHAFT	3-1
Guerrero	Eugene	CORC	
Rugnao	John	A	12-3
Hurtado	Bob	KING	

120
Affentranger	Franc	SHAFT	5-0
Balverama	Ben	CORC	
Silva	Augie	WOOD	11-1
Esquivel	Roy	WU	

127
Garcia	Richard	EX	12-9
Lopez	Joe	SHAFT	
Souza	Al	CENT	6-4
Royal	Marlin	WU	

133
Ramirez	Richard	KING	14-0
Cates	Alan	SHAFT	
Royal	Eugene	WU	3-2
Bravo	Rick	EX	

138
Pacheco	Ken	EX	3-2
Wever	Randy	WU	
Swett	Ed	DP	7-1
Davis	Don	CAR	

145
Almanga	Julian	EX	9-7
Marroquin	Rafael	MCF	
Affentranger	Anton	SHAFT	3-0
Lopez	Randy	WU	

154
Watson	Geroge	EX	9-4
Scott	Amos	WU	
Painter	Paul	SHAFT	7-1
Wililams	Rick	CHOW	

165
Manning	Tony	WU	Fall 3:17
Kennedy	Burr	CHOW	
Flores	Fred	FOW	9-5
Williams	Gilbert	SHAFT	

175
Bracamante	Joe	CENT	6-1
Clement	Terry	W	
Johnson	Bruce	KING	6-1
Reynolds	Ted	KER	

191
Johnson	Mike	W	11-1
Gonzales	Luis	CENT	
Gomez	Manuel	KING	Fall 2:05
Handley	Don	CHOW	

HWT
Espinoza	Mike	TRAN	8-5
Nikitia	Dan	KER	
Kelarjain	Joe	WU	4-1
Freitas	Stan	TAFT	

Tournament
1. Kingsburg — 76.5
2. Washington U. — 75
3. Shafter — 69.5
4. Exeter — 67.5
5. Central — 38
6. Wasco — 31.5
7. Chowchilla — 28
8. Arvin — 27
9. Dos Palos — 24.5
10. Taft — 23.5
11. Woodlake — 22.5
12. Corcoran — 20.5 Tied for 12th
12. Kerman — 20.5 Tied for 12th
14. Fowler — 17
15. Tranquility — 15.5
16. McFarland — 13
17. Caruthers — 11.5
18. Lindsay — 4
19. Coalinga — 2
20. Laton — 1
Sierra — 0

**Luis Gonzales
Central High**

Sierra-Sequoia Division – Sierra High/Tollhouse

February 16, 1974

95
Stewart	Lyle	WU	7-6
Pereschica	Romero	SEL	
Badangeur	Dan	WOOD	6-2
Affentranger	Martin	SHAFT	

103
Hurtado	Bob	KING	Fall 2:58
Escavel	Gabe	DP	
Garcia	Javier	WU	6-3
Watts	Dwight	SHAFT	

112
Guerrero	Eugene	CORC	3-2
Pereschica	Henry	SEL	
Martinez	Juan	WOOD	6-0
Fontana	Bobby	CENT	

120
Carral	Victor	CENT	Fall 3:52
Carmago	Ed	W	
Esquivel	Roy	WU	O.T. 5-1
Gonzales	Charles	CAR	

127
Castillo	Adolfo	DP	11-6
Royal	Eugene	WU	
Nadeau	Brian	CENT	O.T. 4-2
Arvance	Brad	KER	

133
Lopez	Joe	SHAFT	6-5	(36-0)*
Royal	Marlin	WU		
Brower	Wayne	CAR	Fall 3:36	
Cunnings	Roger	SIER		

138
Lopeteguy	Joey	SHAFT	17-6
Swett	Ed	DP	
Peterson	Kip	WOOD	11-1
Ibarra	George	EX	

145
Lopez	Randy	WU	7-3
Bravo	Rick	EX	
Espinoza	Moe	DP	7-6
Garcia	Sal	WOOD	

154
Scott	Amos	WU	Fall 3:17
Campos	Manuel	WOOD	
Cruz	Ralph	CORC	O.T. 6-0
Flores	Fred	FOW	

165
Manning	Tony		Fall 3:32
			(37-0/35 Falls)*
Williams	Cary	W	
Kennedy	Burr	Chow	Fall 2:06
Williams	Norman	SHAFT	

175
Moz	Ben	CORC	6-0
Reynolds	Ted	CHOW	
Farmer	Scott	SHAFT	1-0
Rey	Arthur	W	

191
Gomez	Manual	KING	9-2
Clement	Terry	W	
Lawrence	Mark	LAT	Fall 1:56
Rogers	John	WU	

HWT
Hernandez	Carlos	EX	3-1
Akman	Terry	SHAFT	
Williams	Myron	W	9-0
Silva	Al	WOOD	

Tournament
1. Washington U. 96
2. Shafter 59.5
3. Wasco 49
4. Dos Palos 43
5. Woodlake 35.5
6. Corcoran 34
7. Kingsburg 32
8. Exeter 29
9. Central 27.5
10. Chowchilla 27
11. Selma 21.5
12. Caruthers 12.5
13. Laton 9
14. Fowler 6
15. Kerman 4 Tied for 15th
15. Sierra 4 Tied for 15th
17. Coalinga 3.5

* Record

**Sierra High
Coach Jerry Laird**

Sierra-Sequoia Div. – College of Sequoia/Visalia

February 22, 1975

*95
Parechica	Romero	SEL	Fall 3:02	
Cortez	Eddie	CORC		
Paramo	Noe	WOOD	2-1	
Carrejo		CHOW		

103
Hurtado	Bob	KING	10-1	(23-1)*
Bass	Leon	CHOW		
Cisneros	Gabe	EX	3-2	
Lamas	Mike	SHAFT		

112
Dillingham	Jim	W	2-1
Capata	Jesse	SEL	
Sanders	Bob	SHAFT	8-5
Hurado		KING	

120
Campos	Mike	KING	Fall :45
McWhorter	Steve	SHAFT	
Royal	Vernon	WU	4-3
Gonzales		CAR	

127
Corral	Vic	CENT	7-4
Gonzales	Tony	EX	
Arvance	Brad	KER	8-2
Pereschica	Henry	SEL	

133
Lopez	Joe	SHAFT	Fall 3:25	(26-0)*
Harris	Leon	CHOW		
Nadeau	Brian	CENT	4-0	
Wilcox	Dave	KER		

138
Brower	Wayne	CAR	
Ibarra	George	EX	
Williams	Tom	LAT	5-1
Villanueva	Felipe	TRAN	

145
Meza	Sal	LIND	10-4	(24-1)*
Lopez	David	CHOW		
Anderson		SEL	8-0	
Peterson	Kip	WOOD		

154
Spoisdoff	George	W	3-2
Idho	Steve	CENT	
McClellan	Tom	TRAN	Fall 3:55
Fagundes	Ralph	CHOW	

165
Scott	Amos	WU	Fall 3:45
Williams	Cary	SHAFT	
Groesbeck	Bruce	EX	3-2
Turner	Mike	CAR	

175
Williams	Norman	SHAFT	5-0
Kasparian	Sylex	SEL	
Reynolds	Ted	CHOW	4-0
Barcellos	Mark	CAR	

191
Curtis	Mark	WOOD	7-0	(23-2-1)*
Lovenguth	Desi	COAL		
Bedrosian	Brian	FOW	6-2	
Miller	Dirk	KER		

HWT
Hernandez	Carlos	EX	5-2	(31-3)*
Williams	Myron	W		
Handley	Don	CHOW	2-1	
Rodgers	John	WU		

Tournament

1. Chowchilla	67.5	18. Caruthers	1
2. Selma	51.5	Tied for 18th	
3. Wasco	49	18. Sierra	1
4. Shafter	47.5	Tied for 18th	
5. Exeter	44	Strathmore	0
6. Corcoran	42	Orosi	0
7. Central	41		
8. Kingsburg	39.5	* Record	
9. Washington U.	32		
10. Woodlake	27		
11. Kerman	17		
12. Tranquility	15		
13. Coalinga	13		
14. Lindsay	12		
15. Fowler	7		
16. Dos Palos	2 Tied for 16th		
16. McFarland	2 Tied for 16th		
18. Dinuba	1 Tied for 18th		

Sierra-Sequoia Division – Wasco
February 21, 1976

95
Pereschica	Romero	SEL	14-4
Carrillo	Ruben	TRAN	
Carrejo	Juan	CHOW	3-0
Bender	Scott	SHAFT	

103
Padilla	Tony	W	15-11
Tiller	Stan	WU	
Cortez	Don	CAR	11-2
Powell	Mike	EX	

112
Esquivel	Gabriel	DP	Fall 3:01
Sweet	Lyle	WU	
Bass	Leon	CHOW	
Dei	Chris	CENT	

120
Hurtado	Bob	KING	Fall 3:18
Cortez	Eddie	CORC	
Hunt	Ron	W	3-0
Harris	Jim	WU	

127
McWhorther	Steve	SHAFT	9-2
Dillingham	Jim	W	
Lopez	Ralf	SEL	5-4
Nava	Raul	DP	

133
Royal	Vernon	WU	13-4
Bowser	Jim	CENT	
Webb	Clint	KER	6-2
Miralez	John	SHAFT	

138
Klawitter	Daryl	CHOW	5-1
Padilla	David	WOOD	
Harvey	Ed	SIE	7-4
Hammett	Tom	W	

145
Fagundes	Ralph	CHOW	1-0
Herdia		KING	
Scott	Frank	WU	6-2
Mejia	Tony	CORC	

154
Peterson	Aaron	KING	5-3
Moz	Ray	CORC	
McClellan	Tully	TRAN	Fall 5:37
Bufford	John	WU	

165
Idhe	Steve	CENT	6-3
Larson	Scott	SIE	
Peterson	Tony	WOOD	O.T. 3-2
Ortiz	Victor	WU	

175
Kastarian	Alan	SEL	3-1
Bracmonte	Luis	CENT	
Shiene	Dick	TRAN	2-0
Conway	Rick	DIN	

191
Williams	Norman	SHAFT	Fall 3:11 (25-0)*
Hester	Vernon	CHOW	
Curtis	Mark	WOOD	Fall 3:24
Reckas	Tykee	SIE	

HWT
Hernandez	Carlos	EX	9-4	(29-1)*
Rodgers	John	WU		
Lovengut	Desi	COAL	5-4	
Wedel	Jay	W		

Tournament
1. Washington U. 110.5
2. Wasco 65
2. Kingsburg 65
4. Chowchilla 64
5. Tranquility 63.5
6. Selma 63
7. hafter 61.5
7. Central 61.5
9. Woodlake 54
10. Sierra 35.5
11. Corcoran 35
12. Exeter 29
13. Caruthers 16.5
14. Kerman 15.5
15. Coalinga 14.5
16. Dinuba 11
17. McFarland 9
18. Strathmore 7
19. Orosi 2

* Record

Ed Harvey
Sierra High

Sierra-Sequoia Division – Sierra High/Tollhouse
February 19, 1977

95
Paramo	Noe	WOOD	4-2
Martinez	Ken	CENT	
Romero	George	W	8-3
Orsorno	Ray	MCF	

103
Bender	Scott	SHAFT	3-2
Gonzales	Juan	STRA	
Carnejo	Juan	CHOW	5-4
Hurtado	Sal	KING	

112
Padilla	Tony	W	O.T. 2-0
Affentranger	Martin	SHAFT	
Kimbler	Ben	SIE	5-1
Pigg	Willie	DP	

120
Powell	Mike	EX	8-1	(23-2-1)*
Esquivel	Gabe	DP		
Ramirez	David	WOOD	6-0	
Crisp	Darryl	CAR		

127
Raya	Gabe	LIND	14-2
Betancour	Dan	WOOD	
Garcia	David	TRAN	Fall
Garza	Francisco	MCF	

133
Hurtado	Ramiro	KING	11-9
Ball	John	SIE	
Castillo	Junior	WOOD	Fall 2:15
Cornaggia	Chris	CHOW	

138
Miralez	Johnny	SHAFT	3-1
Marroquin	Johnny	MCF	
Escovedo	Anthony	KING	10-2
Lichti	Russel	WU	

145
Scott	Frank	WU	11-2
Hernstedt	Danny	W	
Pena	Aaron	KING	10-0
Yescas	Xavier	LAT	

154
Vigil	Mark	EX	5-4
Peterson	Aaron	KING	
Scott	Forrest	WU	6-1
Reese	Billy	SIE	

165
Larson	Scott	SIE	17-4
Moore	Kenny	W	
Barthelme	Mike	MCF	6-5
Rocker	Rick	KING	

175
Shienle	Duke	TRAN	5-4
Shannon	Rick	STRA	
Reya	Rich	WOOD	3-0
Guyton	Miles	W	

191
Martin	Dennis	SHAFT	Fall 2:55 (27-0)*
Stenson	Steve	CORC	
Lopez	Abe	KING	Fall :59
Goolsby	Wayne	KER	

235
*Hernandez	Carlos	EX	Fall 3:13 (20-0)*
Hester	Raymond	CHOW	(28-1)*
Fajardo	Carlos	CENT	1-0
Mootry	Ken	SHAFT	

*Carlos Hernandez 4-Time Sierra-Sequoia Champion 125-14 Career Record as of 2/19/77

Tournament
1. Kingsburg 111
2. Shafter 110.5
3. Wasco 94
4. McFarland 76
5. Woodlake 70.5 Tied for 5th
5. Sierra 70.5 Tied for 5th
7. Exeter 59
8. Tranquility 47
9. Chowchilla 45
10. Washington U. 43
11. Lindsay 42.5
12. Central 40
13. Dos Palos 29
14. Corcoran 26
15. Caruthers 21.5
16. Strathmore 19
17. Selma 12.5
18. Kerman 11.5
19. Coalinga 10
20. Orosi 6
Dinuba 0
Firebaugh 0

* Record

Sierra-Sequoia Division – Sierra High/Tollhouse
February 18, 1978

95
Martinez	Ken	CENT	15-3	
Rodriguez	Phil	SHAFT		
Rios	Mark	LIND	5-0	
Torres	Juan	COAL		

103
Taterakis	Chris	FIRE	5-4	
Bender	Scott	SHAFT		
Cortez	Don	CAR	3-0	
Quintana	Jesse	SEL		

112
Carillo	Ruben	TRAN	11-4	
Sims	Bill	CENT		
Cervantes	Albert	EX	3-1	
Barton	Bob	SIE		

120
Kimbler	Ben	SIE	Fall 1:42	
Albidrez	John	SEL		
Cardenas	Fred	EX	14-2	
Prieto	Eusesio	KER		

127
Powell	Mike	EX	5-3	(26-0)*
Lopez	Julio	SHAFT		
Wortley	Todd	SIE	4-3	
Valasquez	Pete	OROSI		

133
Pineda	John	WU	6-3	
Harshman	John	SIE		
Yescas	Jim	LAT		
Cervantes	Martin	EX		

138
Gomez	Raul	KING	7-2	
Reyna	Juan	W		
Willits	Larry	DP	Fall 3:01	
Cloud	Tom	SHAFT		

145
Garcia	Moses	LIND	18-4	(24-0)*
Aldredge	Gaylon	WU		
Gonzales	Joe	KING	4-1	
Prewitt	Greg	COAL		

154
Vigil	Mark	EX	7-3	(26-0)*
Giovannetti	Roger	SHAFT		
Flores	Ralph	FIRE	5-1	
Ramirez	Robert	WOOD		

165
Scott	Frank	WU	9-1	
Rocker	Rick	KING		
Pollard	Shawn	WOOD	7-2	
Vasquez	Ricardo	MCF		

175
Scott	Forest	WU	7-3	
Semainiego	Sam	KER		
Flagher	David	SEL	13-5	
Moore	Ken	W		

191
Verwey	John	TRAN	7-5	
Mootry	Ken	SHAFT		
Lopez	Abe	KING	11-5	
Goolsby	Wayne	KER		

HWT
Rossi	Eric	CENT	11-2	
Hernandez	George	TRAN		
Martin	Dennis	SHAFT	10-4	
Long	Darren	EX		

Tournament
1. Washington U. 126
2. Shafter 113
3. Exeter 96
4. Tranquility 74.5
5. Sierra 73
6. Central 69.5
7. Kingsburg 63.5
8. Wasco 56.5
9. Selma 47.5
10. Firebaugh 47
11. Lindsay 41
12. Kerman 39.5
13. Woodlake 38
14. Laton 31
15. Dos Palos 30
16. Caruthers 29
17. McFarland 28
18. Coalinga 27.5
19. Corcoran 13
20. Chowchilla 6
21. Clovis West 5.5
22. Dinuba 1.5
Fowler 0
Parlier 0
Strathmore 0

* Record

Sierra-Sequoia Division – Shafter
February 17, 1979

95
Gutierrez	Anacleto	WU
Corral	Armando	CENT
Torrez	Juan	COAL
Rangel	Lucky	PAR

103
Quintana	Jesse	SEL
Kimbler	Wade	SIE
Garcia	Danny	TRAN
Raney	Tom	DP

112
Cortez	Don	CAR
Elrich	Ted	SHAFT
Moreno	Vince	W
Gongora		CW

119
Barton	Bob	SIE
Sims	Bill	CENT
Cervantes	Albert	EX
Ramirez	Tony	WOOD

127
Lopez	Julio	SHAFT
Albidrez	John	SEL
Kimbler	Ben	SIE
Cardanes	Fred	EX

133
Pigg	William	DP
Vera	Armando	CAR
Hashman	John	SIE
Lopez	Abe	KING

138
Gonzales	Jose	KING
Loftis	Mike	CAR
Willis	Larry	DP
Flores		FIRE

145
Gomez	Raul	KING
Haro	Frank	WOOD
Peterson	George	CW
Escalante	Ruben	DP

154
Valdez	Roy	SHAFT
Marichal	John	OROSI
Fry	David	KING
Van Fosson	Chris	WOOD

165
Snell	Mike	WU
Giovannetti	Roger	SHAFT
Ramirez	Robert	WOOD
Gonzales	Paul	TRAN

191
Lopez	Abe	KING
Smith	Jeff	CW
Stensin	Steve	CORC
Sanchez		COAL

235
Blacksill	John	WU
Walker	Calvin	SANG
Hernandez	George	TRAN
Wilson	Dan	W

* Record

Tournament
1. Shafter   104
2. Kingsburg   103.5
3. Washington U.   80.5
4. Woodlake   75
5. Dos Palos   72
6. Sierra   66.
7. Central   62
8. Caruthers   60
9. Clovis West   46
10. Selma   40.5
11. Tranquility   29
12. Kerman   27.5
13. Coalinga   27 Tie d for 13th
13. Wasco   27 Tied for 13th
15. Exeter   20 Tied for 15th
15. Orosi   20 Tied for 15th
17. Parlier   15
18. Firebaugh   14
19. Chowchilla   11
20. Corcoran   8
21. Laton   6
22. Lindsay   4
23. McFarland   3
24. Strathmore   2

Sierra-Sequoia Division – Sierra High/Tollhouse

February 23, 1980

95
Piccolo	David	KING	9-5
Corral	Mando	CENT	
Scherer	Larry	MCF	Fall 1:25
Alcorn	Brett	KER	

103
Soto	Sal	KING	7-2
Quintana	Diego	SEL	
Sharp	Gilbert	SIE	Fall 3:25
Ratcliff	Clifford	CAR	

112
Esquivel	Jose	WU	5-1
Nakagawa	Randy	CENT	
Salazar	Robert	SEL	5-2
Erebia	Danny	KING	

120
Gomes	Roy	FIRE	Fall 2:40
Miles	Skyler	WU	
Ramirez	Tony	WOOD	8-2
Duran	Dave	COAL	

127
Garcia	Rudy	SEL	Fall 1:40
Marroquim	Bobby	MCF	
De La Cruz	David	KING	5-2
Prieto	Raul	PAR	

133
Barton	Bob	SIE	Default
Ortiz	Frankie	WU	
Vera	Armando	CAR	10-3
Ward	Jim	SEL	

138
Lopez	Manuel	KING	Fall 5:30
Bonilla	Henry	CORC	
Rodriguez	Jose	FIRE	17-9
Joens	Brian	COAL	

145
Loftis	Mike	CAR	Default
Gomez	Raul	KING	
Martinez	Israel	CORC	Default
Pearson	F	W	

154
Fry	David	KING	5-0
Delgado	Jose	SHAFT	
Hoegh	Buddy	SEL	5-8
Flores	Miguel	FIRE	

165
Bowlden	Mike	CENT	Fall 4:25
Escalante	Ruben	DP	
Herrera	Cessario	WU	7-5
Harris	Brian	LAT	

175
Snell	Mike	WU	13-3
Zambrano	Mario	PAR	
Castillo	Sal	WOOD	6-5
McDaniel	Robert	SEL	

191
Ochoa	Eddie	WU	9-0
Fry	Gary	KING	
Torigiani	Pat	SHAFT	9-6
Rodriguez	Ruben	WOOD	

235
Avila	Joe	STRA	11-3
Pickens	Carl	WU	
Gomes	Victor	TRAN	4-3
Morley	Phillip	W	

Tournament

1. Washington U.	161.5		18. Kerman	22
2. Kingsburg	158		Tied for 18th	
3. Selma	93		20. Lindsey	16
4. Central	81		Chowchilla	0
5. Firebaugh	68.5		Dinuba	0
6. Woodlake	59.5			
7. Caruthers	56.5			
8. McFarland	55.5			
9. Sierra	50			
10. Shafter	45			
11. Corcoran	34			
12. Parlier	28.5			
13. Laton	28			
14. Dos Palos	27			
15. Strathmore	26.5			
16. Wasco	25			
17. Tranquility	23			
18. Coalinga	22	Tied for 18th		

Sierra-Sequoia Division – Central
February 21, 1981

98
Gomez	Rene	SHAFT	6-2
Aguilar	George	WU	
Woods	Jon	KING	7-2
Madrid		CENT	

105
Quintana	Diego	SEL	2-0
Erebia	Ruben	KING	
Aguilar	Martin	WU	8-6
Corral	Mando	CENT	

112
Erebia	Danny	KING	8-6
Salazar	Robert	SEL	
Valez	Fred	CAR	14-3
Nakagawa	Randy	CENT	

122
Gomez		FIRE	9-4
Piccolo	David	KING	
Rangel	Lucky	PARL	6-5
Lopez		DP	

126
Kellerhals	Bud	WU	7-1
Aulakh	Jagbir	KER	
Flores	Luis	WOOD	21-4
Marroquin	Bobby	MCF	

132
Anderson	Steve	SIE	12-10
Castillo	Eddie	WOOD	
Abeyta	Tim	KING	6-4
Comerer	Leon	COAL	

138
Ortiz	Frankie	WU	Fall 3:34
Gonzales	Sal	KING	
Watts	Dave	CAR	17-6
Comerer	Greg	COAL	

145
Vasquez	Daniel	SHAFT	
Camargo	Eric	W	
Stockton	Ronnie	LAT	O.T.
Lara	Emilio	WOOD	

154
Williams	Earl	SHAFT	4-3
Lombardo	Mark	CENT	
Lafleur	Jeff	WOOD	17-6
Flores	Miguel	FIRE	

167
Brown	Mike	SHAFT	9-6
Watley	Randy	CHOW	
Sisney	Steve	KING	112-3
Fowler	Charles	COAL	

185
Zambrano	Mark	PAR	Fall 1:03
Ochoa	Eddie	WU	
Ricks	Herbie	SHAFT	12-8
Garza	Junior	CAR	

200
Thornton	Alvin	WU	Fall 1:58
Gomes	V.	TRAN	
Garcia	Mario	PAR	10-9
Turett		CENT	

245
Pickens	Carl	WU	Fall 5:24
Morley	Phillips	W	
Corrnet	Rebel	WOOD	5-0
Jones	James	SHAFT	

Tournament
1. Washington U. 159
2. Kingsburg 131.5
3. Shafter 129
4. Woodlake 80.5
5. Central 70.5
6. Parlier 61.5
7. Caruthers 53
8. Wasco 44
9. Coalinga 43.5 Tied for 9th
9. Selma 43.5 Tied for 9th
11. Dos Palos 41.5
12. Firebaugh 39.5
13. Tranquility 34
14. Sierra 31.5
15. Kerman 28
16. Chowchilla 26.5
17. McFarland 20
18. Laton 19
19. Yosemite 1

**Roger Giovannetti
Shafter High**

Sierra-Sequoia Division – Wasco

February 20, 1982

98
Barron	Rick	WU	6-0
Lewis	Tony	KING	
Sanchez	Gil	TRAN	9-7
Nashkawa	Randy	CENT	

105
Aguilar	Martin	WU	7-2
Woods	Jon	KING	
Carrillo	Augustine	KER	6-3
Gomez	Ed	CAR	

112
Quintana	Diego	SEL	
Aguilar	George	WU	
Gomez	Rene	SHAFT	5-2
Varner	Todd	KING	

119
Salazar	Robert	SEL	
Erebia	Danny	KING	
Gomez	Ray	CAR	16-3
Gomez	Martin	TRAN	

126
Abeyta	Tim	KING	4-2
Gomez	Fred	DP	
Aulakh	Jagbir	KER	13-4
Presley	Joe	SHAFT	

132
Palomar	Vince	KING	4-1
Flores	Louie	WOOD	
Nishikawa	Clark	CAR	Fall :51
Cates	Roy	SHAFT	

138
Palomar	Ernie	KING	6-4
Jimenez	Pablo	DP	
Mitchell	John	CAR	5-1
Alvardo	Ernie	WU	

145
Vasquez	Daniel	SHAFT	Default
Watts	David	CAR	
Comerer	Greg	COAL	1-0
Camacho	Danny	MCF	

154
Lafleur	Jeff	WOOD	Fall 3:39
Quianjo	Alex	PAR	
Brown	Rodney	SHAFT	11-1
Quiros	Serjio	CAR	

167
Brown	Mike	SHAFT	3-0
Clifton	Jim	PAR	
Sanchez	Gabe	CENT	Fall 4:54
Gonzales	Rick	KER	

185
Garcia	Mario	PAR	16-8
Uhlir	Bob	WU	
Scott	James	KING	13-4
Clark	Brent	SHAFT	

200
Cornet	Rebel	WOOD	1-0
Garza	Oscar	KING	
Reitz	Dennis	CENT	5-2
Ramsey	Greg	COAL	

HWT
Pickens	Carl	WU	Fall 3:29
Morley	Phillip	W	
Grijalva	Eddie	MCF	Fall 1:22
Roberts	Joe	KING	

Tournament
1. Kingsburg 176
2. Washington U. 136
3. Shafter 119.5
4. Caruthers 84
5. Parlier 70 Tied for 5th
5. Kerman 70 Tied for 5th
7. Woodlake 60
8. Dos Palos 50.5
9. Selma 43.5
10. Central Union 43
11. Coalinga 41
12. Wasco 32
13. Tranquility 31.5
14. McFarland 27
15. Yosemite 9
16. Sierra 6
17. Dinuba 3
18. Firebaugh 2.5
19. Orosi 2 Tied for 19th
19. Chowchilla 2 Tied for 19th
Corcoran 0
Laton 0

Sierra-Sequoia Division – Firebaugh

February 19, 1983

98
Gomez	Eddie	CAR	
Lewis	Tony	KING	
Lomas	Mark	SHAFT	(29-8)*
Sanchez	Giblert	TRAN	

105
Barron	Rick	WU	6-1	
Martinez	Manuel	SHAFT		(17-7)*
Gomez	George	CAR		
Serna	Isial	MCF		

112
Gomez	Rene	SHAFT	3-2	(37-7)*
Aguilar	George	WU		
Woods	Jon	KING		
Pimental	Guillermo			

119
Erebia	Danny	KING	
Santellano	Vinny	WU	
Cruz	Danny	SHAFT	Fall (27-7)*
Fanning	Rob	CHOW	

126
Sahagun	Xavier	WOOD
Ortiz	Tony	WU
Soltero	Jesse	CENT
Lopez	Jesus	DP

132
Poindexter	Jim	PAR	7-2
Pressley	Joe	SHAFT	(31-8/23Falls)*
Palomar	Vince		
Morales	Averiel	MCF	

138
Gomez	Joe	TRAN
Erebia	Ruben	KING
Carlson	Brian	WOOD
Willis	Rodney	DP

145
Watts	David	CAR	
Castro	Ruben	TRAN	
Cates	Roy	SHAFT	(26-8)*
Bowser	Morgan	CENT	

154
Souza	Shane	LAT
Quijano	Alejandro	PAR
Brown	Rod	SHAFT
Fierra	Mark	TRAN

167
Henson	Scott	SEL
Cornett	Rebel	WOOD
Camacho	Dan	MCF
Munoz	Tony	WU

185
Scott	James	KING
Selvin	Danny	DP
Clifton	Jim	PAR
Estes	John	AVE

200
Reitz	Dennis	CENT
Gomez	David	TRAN
Haves	Ernest	WU
Roberts	Joe	KING

245
Tierce	Kevin	CAR
Baptista	Eddie	KER
Lopez	Paul	KING
Pankey	Jeff	SHAFT

Tournament
1. Kingsburg 148
2. Shafter 136
3. Washington U. 119
4. Caruthers 102
5. Tranquility 101
6. Parlier 65
7. Dos Palos 63.5
8. Woodlake 59
9. Central 57.5
10. Selma 42.5

* Record

Sierra-Sequoia Division – Central High/Fresno
February 18, 1984

98
Gomez	Eddie	CAR	13-1	(37-1)*
Rangel	Raymond	PAR		
Lara	Armando	SEL	13-1	
Skinner	Don	YOSE		

103
Barron	Rick	WU	14-7	(37-5)*
Salazar	Nick	SEL		
Serna	Ismael	MCF	Fall 2:19	
Maldonado	Luis	SHAFT		

112
Lamas	Mark	SHAFT	5-2
Gonzales	Mario	MCF	
Garza	Ray	CHOW	5-2
Escamilla	Steve	PAR	

119
Gonzales	Arnold	WU	7-1
Mendoza	Victor	SEL	
Nakagowa	Randy	CENT	16-2
Casanova	Joey	TRAN	

126
Santellano	Vinnie	WU	6-2
Soltero	Jesse	CENT	
Zarate	Elias	SEL	Fall 1:43
Marruto	Ramone	DP	

132
Sahaoun	Xavier	WOOD	O.T. 1-0	(24-0)*
Nunez	Jesus	DP		
Sandoval	Esoie	TRAN	3-0	
Zarate	Ocile	SEL		

138
Lopez	Victor	CENT	12-2	(25-3)*
Pickens	Kenny	WU		
Quiroz	Seroio	CAR	19-8	
Morales	Lorenzo	SEL		

145
Pressley	Joe	SHAFT	Fall 5:30	(20-5)*
Carlson	Brian	WOOD		
Gomez	Joe	TRAN	10-1	
Dean	William	CHOW		

154
Hayes	Ernest	WU	Fall 5:41	(25-5)*
Jimenez	Pablo	DP		
Henson	Robert	SEL	6-0	
Cates	Roy	SHAFT		

165
Aulakh	Abe	KER	5-3
Ravalin	Rick	SEL	
Gonzales	Vince	TRAN	Fall 4:59
Howard	Fred	WU	

175
Henson	Scott	SEL	6-2	(35-1)*
Jackson	Rick	KING		
Clifton	Jim	PAR	5-3	
Reitz	Darrin	CENT		

191
Reitz	Dennis	CENT	10-4	(33-2)*
Mitchell	Russ	SEL		
Slevin	Don	DP	Fall :47	
Landsteadel	Vince	KING		

145
Alarcon	Eloy	DP	
Torosian	Alan	SEL	
Pankey	Jeff	SHAFT	Fall 2:52
Stackhouse	Harry	WU	

*Record

Tournament
1. Selma   187.5
2. Washington U. 143.5
3. Dos Palos   117.5
4. Central   100
5. Shafter   98.5
6. Woodlake   74.5
7. Tranquility   69
8. Caruthers   62
9. Kingsburg   61
10. McFarland   57
11. Parlier   49.5
12. Chowchilla   34.5
13. Kerman   34.5
14. Yosemite   25
15. Laton   12
16. Coalinga   4 Tied for 16th
16. Firebaugh   4 Tied for 16th
18. Avenal   3
19. Sierra   2

Sierra-Sequoia Division – Wasco
February 16, 1985

98
Gomez	Eddie	CAR	Fall 2:42
Reyes	Lee	WU	
Skinner	Don	YOSE	
Ramirez	Pedro	FIRE	

105
Rangel	Raymond	PAR	Fall 1:23
Ramirez	Richard	KING	
Lara	Armando	CAR	
Pimentel	Armando	DP	

112
Chavez	Richard	CENT	4-3
Morales	Manuel	SEL	
Serna	Ismael	MCF	
Zepeda	Francisco	KER	

119
Nishikawa	Randy	CENT	6-5
Hurtado	Alex	KING	
Aguilar	Carlos	WU	
Avalos	Jose Manuel	WOOD	

127
Gonzalez	Arnold	WU	7-1
Zarate	Elias	SEL	
Briseno	Aaron	KER	
Avalos	Jose Luis	WOOD	

133
Santellano	Vinnie	WU	Inj. Default
Zarete	Ocile	SEL	
Ornelas	Stevie	TRAN	
Sahagun	Richard	WOOD	

138
Morales	Lorenzo	SEL	9-8
Nunez	Jesus	DP	
Sharp	Patrick	SIER	
Jurado	Santiago	PAR	

145
Pickens	Kenny	WU	5-0
Davila	David	CAR	
Cintora	Bradley	DP	
Ramos	Mago	PAR	

154
Rosario	David	FIRE	Inj. Default
Hansen	Robert	SEL	
Mendoza	Jose	KING	
Faubel	Terry	WOOD	

165
Thornberg	Tim	SEL	7-2
Howard	Fred	WU	
Quinonez	Javier	TRAN	
Lincoln	Kent	YOSE	

175
Jackson	Rick	KING	7-3
Lincoln	Bob	YOSE	
Granados	Tony	WU	
Bonilla	DJ	SEL	

191
Ravalin	Rick	SEL	3-2
Slevin	Don	DP	
Boucieques	Luis	WU	
Reyes	Javier	TRAN	

245
Jackson	Bill	KING	Fall 5:40
Torosian	Alan	SEL	
Stackhouse	Harry	WU	
Aguilar	Marcello	COAL	

Tournament
1. Washington U. 171.5
2. Selma 169.5
3. Kingsburg 125.5
5. 4. Dos Palos 82.5
6. Caruthers 65.5
7. Woodlake 61.5
8. Tranquility 57
9. Parlier 54
10. Firebaugh 49.5
11. Central 47

Sierra-Sequoia Division – Dos Palos
February 22, 1986

98
Munoz	Rito	WU	19-14
Madgallanes	Magdaleno	FIRE	
Arellano	Danny	W	
Deltoro	Tony	CAR	

105
Maldonado	Luie	SHAFT	11-6
Sullivan	Andrew	W	
Moreno	Mauricio	DP	
Rodriguez	Thomas	SEL	

112
Perez	Eddie	FIRE	Fall :22
Pollard	Tim	KING	
Morales	Manuel	SEL	
Pimentel	Armando		

119
Rangel	Ray	PAR	9-1
Avalos	Manuel	WOOD	
Sanchez	Eddie	FIRE	
Macias	Manuel	WU	

127
Morales	John	SEL	9-6
Woods	Matt	KING	
Aguilar	Carlos	WU	
Lopes	Joe	SIER	

133
Gonzales	Arnold	WU	7-4
Zarate	Ociel	SEL	
Vaughn	Terry	SHAFT	
Pickerel	Ted	YOSE	

138
Ramirez	Jesus	FIRE	7-1
Wright	Scott	KING	
Zarate	Elias	SEL	
Vandenack	Rick	CHOW	

145
Davila	David	CAR	4-2
Klaprath	Bert	YOSE	
Zapata	Robert	SEL	
Holland	Mike	FIRE	

154
Bonilla	B.J.	SEL	15-8
Murphy	Robbie	FIRE	
Mendoza	Jose	KING	
Reyes	Adrian	TRAN	

165
Grenada	Tony	WU	Fall
Gonzales	Lupe	WOOD	
Lincoln	Kent	YOSE	
Vera	Roy	CAR	

175
Ravalin	Rick	SEL	8-3
Boucieques	Louis	WU	
Vest	Cletus	MCF	
Boggs	Keith	COAL	

191
Briner	Skip	YOSE	10-9
Powell	Darin	WOOD	
Torosian	Alan	SEL	
Gonzales	Javier	MCF	

245
Jackson	Bill	KING	Fall 5:19
Cuellar	Ricardo	PAR	
Brewster	Willie	DP	
Mesz	Phillip	WOOD	

Tournament
1. Selma 171
2. Washington U. 141
3. Firebaugh 115
4. Kingsburg 95.5
5. Woodlake 79.5
6. Yosemite 79
7. Dos Palos 63
8. Shafter 57.5
9. Parlier 53
10. Caruthers 51.5

Sierra-Sequoia Division – Selma
February 21, 1987

98
Munoz	Rito	WU	4-1
Legarreta	Eric	SEL	
Ramirez	Bryan	KING	
Cintora	Theo	DP	

105
Magallenes	Magdalgno	FIRE	15-3	
Behill	Raymond	CAR		
Contreras	Michael	DIN		
Campos	Raul	DP		

112
Reyes	Lee	WU	7-4
Rodriguez	Thomas	SEL	
Misquez	Mario	WOOD	
De La Cruz	Richard	FIRE	

119
Macias	Manuel	WU	5-1
Lucatero	Valdo	WOOD	
Hesser	Scott	KING	
Ramirez	Louie	SEL	

126
Rangel	Raymond	PAR	7-6	(24-1)*
Watts	Terry	CAR		
Quintana	Ismael	SEL		
Pollard	Tim	KING		

132
Briseno	Aaron	KER	3-1
Oliva	Navor	TRAN	
Ramirez	Richard	KING	
Morales	Johnny	SEL	

138
Woods	Matt	KING	8-5
Aguilar	Carlos	WU	
Medrano	Jesus	TRAN	
Klaproth	M	YOSE	

145
Kalproth	Bert	YOSE	12-6
Pilgrim	Randy	LAT	
Davilla	David	CAR	
Enyart	Gerald	WU	

154
Morin	Mike	SEL	5-2
Reyes	Adrian	Tran	
Roope	Caleb	Yose	
Zarasua	Marty	Cent	

165
Zapata	Robert	SEL	15-0	(41-2)*
Herrera	Richard	KER		
Sahagun	Richard	WOOD		
Sanchez	S	SIE		

175
Bonilla	B.J.	SEL	16-0	(42-2)*
Sessions	Bill	WU		
Gonzales	Lupe	WOOD		
Westfall	T	YOSE		

191
Lincoln	Kent	YOSE	4-0
Tsang	Alan	CAR	
Jones	Glen	SEL	
Estrada	Herman	LAT	

245
Jackson	Bill	KING	Forfeit
Raney	Brian	DP	
Henderson	Jimmy	KER	
Gamez	Jesus	TRAN	

Tournament
1. Selma 171.5
2. Washington U. 121.5
3. Kingsburg 109
4. Tranquility 88.5
5. Yosemite 88
6. Caruthers 86
7. Woodlake 83
8. Kerman 67
9. Dos Palos 60
10. Firebaugh 45.5
11. Parlier 44
12. Laton 33.5
13. Shafter 21.5
14. Central 18
15. Dinuba 16
16. Sierra 14
17. Corcoran 12
18. Coalinga 7.5
19. Wasco 7.5
20. Lindsay 6
21. Chowchilla 4 Tied for 21st
21. McFarland 4 Tied for 21st

* Record

Randy Pilgram
Laton High

Sierra-Sequoia Division – Central High
February 20, 1988

98
Ramirez	Brian	KING	4-0
Marez	Joseph	SEL	
Garcia	Robert	WU	Fall 2:38
Cintora	Theo	DP	

103
Legarreta	Eric	SEL	
Munoz	Rito	WU	
Sanders		TRAN	Fall 2:15
Alvarez	Mike	KING	

112
Medrano	Daniel	WU	12-6
Del Toro	Tony	CAR	
Compos	Raul	DP	3-1
Martinez	Richard	CENT	

119
Lucatero	Valdo	WOOD	12-2
Hurtado	Nacho	KING	
Solano	David	DP	8-4
Medina	Jose	SEL	

126
Ramirez	Louie	SEL	12-5
Alonzo	Ronaldo	CENT	
Archuleta	Jason	WU	Fall 3:58
Novikoff	Billy	KER	

132
Quintana	Ismael	SEL	6-1	(42-4)*
Paul	Brent	W		
Ruelas	Miguel	DIN	11-6	
Alvarez	Louie	PAR		

138
Watts	Terry	CAR	Fall	(39-1)*
Morales	Johnny	SEL		
Paul	Steve	W	2-1	
Cortez	Roman	WOOD		

145
Salazar	Felicio	MCF	12-9
Grijalva	K	CENT	
Sullivan	Andrew	W	7-2
Medano		TRAN	

154
Roop	Caleb	YOSE	14-3
Jenkins	Brandy	FIRE	
Enyart	Gerald	WU	T.F. 3:36
Cintaura			

165
Morin	Mike	SEL	14-5
Herrera	Richard	KER	
Lopez	Jorge	WU	9-3
Soto	Alex	MCF	

175
Zapata	Robert	SEL	10-3	(44-3)*
Sahagun	Richard	WOOD		(30-2)*
Lowery	Casey	YOSE	Fall 1:56	
Reyes	Lazaro	TRAN		

191
Lincoln	Kent	YOSE	Fall
Ordaz	Tony	CENT	
Mesa	Chuck	WOOD	7-2
Martinez	Al	MCF	

HWT
Williams	Rodney	WU	8-4
Gomez	Jesus	TRAN	
Gomez		FIRE	Fall :57
Martinez	Brian	SHAFT	

Tournament
1. Selma 193.5
2. Washington U. 120
3. Woodlake 108
4. Central 85
5. Kingsburg 77.5
6. Tranquility 76.5
7. Dos Palos 75
8. Yosemite 74.5
9. McFarland 63
10. Caruthers 58
11. Firebaugh 57.5
12. Wasco 56.5
13. Kerman 48.5
14. Shafter 32.5
15. Sierra 23.5
16. Dinuba 16
17. Parlier 15.5
18. Coalinga 15
19. Chowchilla 10.5
20. Corcoran 7
21. Laton 5.5
22. Avenal 5
23. San Joaquin Memorial 3

* Record

Sierra-Sequoia Division – Central
February 18, 1989

98
Pumarejo	Isaac	KING	Inj. Forf. 4:46
Quintana	Nick	SEL	
Serda	Mike	W	6-5
Munoz	Andy	WU	

105
Mares	Joseph	SEL	17-5
Garcia	Robert	WU	
Magallanes	Magdaleno	FIRE	15-0
Bustamante	Pedro	A	

112
Quintana	Gary	SEL	1-0
Ramirez	Bryan	KING	
Encizo	Rafael	WU	9-6
Cintora	Theo	DP	

119
Legarretta	Eric	SEL	5-2
Perez	Roy	CORC	
Solano	Alex	DP	3-0
Martinez	Luis	TRAN	

125
Rodriguez	Thomas	SEL	Fall 1:46
Perez	Mario	SHAFT	
Bonilla	Gabriel	CORC	
Vargas	Frank	FIRE	

132
Ramirez	Louie	SEL	15-6
Gomez	Johnny	TRAN	
Patton	David	DP	
Scott	Patrick	W	

138
Medrano	Berto	TRAN	4-5
Alvarez	Louie	PAR	
Rodriguez	Eric	WU	6-4
Takeuchi	Travis	CENT	

145
Watts	Terry	CAR	8-0
Quintana	Ismael	SEL	
Ruiz	Abe	PAR	13-6
Komin	Mike	SHAFT	

154
Roope	Caleb	YOSE	8-0
Martinez	Nacho	W	
Soto	Alex	MCF	8-5
Bruce	Brian	KING	

165
Lopez	Jorge	WU	3-2
Jenkins	Brady	FIRE	
Soliz	Mark	CORC	4-3
Valdiva	Eric	KER	

175
Morin	Mike	SEL	14-6
Corchado	Manuel	DP	
Reyes	Lozano	TRAN	Fall 2:45
Longoria	Danny	KING	

191
Mendiola	Tom	TRAN	16-4
Lowery	Casey	YOSE	
Nelson	Scott	CHOW	6-1
Casillas	Martin	DP	

HWT
Aguilar	Jesus	COAL	11-1
Gomez	Jaime	FIRE	
Williams	Rodney	WU	14-4
Castro	Joe	TRAN	

Tournament
1. Selma 202.5
2. Tranquility 142.5
3. Washington U. 132
4. Firebaugh 112
5. Dos Palos 94.5
6. Kingsburg 89.5
7. Corcoran 85.5
8. Caruthers 54.5
9. Yosemite 53
10. Wasco 49.5

Sierra-Sequoia Division – Shafter
February 17, 1990

98
Munoz	Andy	WU	3-1	(31-0)*
Ruiz	Joe	KING		
Serda	Mike	W		

105
Quintana	Nick	SEL	Fall :55
Lango	Kevin	SIE	
Flores	Tony	CENT	

112
Montalvo	Leo	TRAN	3-1
Lee	Brian	SIE	
Alvarez	Mike	KING	

119
Garcia	Robert	WU	12-7
Sanchez	Frank	TRAN	
Solano	Alex	DP	

126
Quintana	Gary	SEL	12-3	(34-1-1)*
Martinez	Luis	TRAN		(31-6)*
Cintora	Theo	DP		
Zambrando	Steve	FIRE		

132
Purcella	Sid	W	11-6
Mull	Craig	SEL	
Benavides	Ray	CAR	

138
Ramirez	Louie	SEL	9-6	(42-3)*
Gamez	John	TRAN		(36-3)*
Gonzales	Alfred	FIRE		

145
Medrano	Beta	TRAN	12-1
Hesser	Scott	KING	
Cleveland	Josh	COAL	

154
Martinez	Nacho	W	4-3
Bice	Darin	SHAFT	
Rodriguez	Eric	WU	

165
Norred	Roger	FIRE	5-1	(33-2)*
Bruce	Brian	KING		
Soto	Alex	MCF		

175
Perry	Jim	CAR	6-1
Clayton	Terry	SHAFT	
Magdaleno	Mike	DP	

191
Mello	Brett	MCF	8-5
Dias	John	LAT	
Montgomery	Norman	CENT	

245
William	Rodney	WU	8-1
Gomez	Jaime	FIRE	
Barron	Vic	DP	

Tournament

1. Tranquility	149.5		7. Wasco	82
2. Selma	119.5		8. Shafter	74
3. Washington U.	116.5		9. McFarland	67
4. Dos Palos	113.5		10. Corcoran	49
5. Kingsburg	100.5		11. Caruthers	43
6. Firebaugh	90.		12. Kerman	41
			13. Sierra	38

* Record

Former Fresno High wrestling coach Rene Errotabere presents the 1990 Most Oustanding Lower Weight Award to Gary Quintana of Selma at the Clovis High Tournament

Sierra-Sequoia Division – Corcoran
February 16, 1991

103
Serda	Mike	W	18-3	
Pimental	Junior			
Ruiz	Joey	KING	Fall 4:30	
Gonzales	Chris	TRAN		

112
Quintana	Nick	SEL	6-3 (34-2)*	
Pumarejo	Isaac	KING		
Sanchez	Mark	A	Fall 4:12	
Brown	Jeremy	KER		

119
Mares	Eric	SEL	10-2
Mantalvo	Leo	TRAN	
Irogoyen	J	SHAFT	4-0
Veliz	Gabriel	FIRE	

125
Zambrano	Steven	FIRE	Fall 2:54
Zermino	Beto	TRAN	
Cortez	Carlos	MCF	6-2
De La Rosa	Eddie	PAR	

130
Quintana	Gary	SEL	Fall 1:23 (30-1)*
Gonzalez	Alfredo	FIRE	
Rodriguez	Aaron	W	Fall 2:45
Cavillo	Isaias	A	

135
Encizo	Rafael	WU	9-6
Lopez	Tony	PAR	Fall :35
Friend	Mike	SEL	

140
Mull	Craig	SEL	19-4	(29-7)*
Gamez	Johnny	TRAN		(32-2)*
Wise	Geordy	SHAFT	Fall 4:58	
Fernandez	Johnny	WOOD		

145
Husein	Naser	SEL	12-3
Honea	Ryan	W	
Gasca	Jay	KING	8-3
Guzman	Joseph	CORC	

152
Martinez	Nacho	W	8-4	(32-1)*
Smith	Matt	SEL		
Vallez	Johnny	KER	Dec.	
Cleveland	Josh	COAL		

160
Moreno	Javier	COAL	9-6
Nunez	Juan	DP	
Hernandez	Javier	CORC	Fall 1:02
Capell	Vince	SJM	

171
Rosas	Jesus	COAL	2-0
Turman	Arlie	DP	
Clayton	Terry	SHAFT	5-2
Serda	Daniel	W	

189
Banda	Marlo	SEL	O.T.
Barron	Vic	DP	
Garcia	A	KING	12-4
Gutierres	Noe	SHAFT	

275
O'Campo	R	W	8-3
Godinez	Gabriel	A	
Lewis	Jon	KER	Fall 3:20
Gonzales	Jack	SHAFT	

Tournament
1. Selma 203.5
2. Wasco 122
3. Dos Palos 107
4. Kingsburg 92
5. Tranquility 86.5
6. Arvin 79
7. Shafter 78.5
8. Firebaugh 77.5
9. Coalinga 72
10. Washington U. 66.5
(24 Teams Entered)

* Record

Sierra-Sequoia Division – Dos Palos
February 22, 1992

103
Pimentel	Junior	DP	9-2
Mestaz	Matt	WOOD	
Rubinol	Jesus	A	7-3
Perez	Jessie	SEL	

112
Pumarrejo	Isaac	KING	Fall
Veliz	Gabriel	FIRE	
Ruiz	Tony	DP	22-6
Gutierrez	Dan	CORC	

119
Ruiz	Joey	KING	7-6
Montalvo	Leo	TRAN	
Lujan	Jesse	SEL	16-2
Brown	Jeremy	KER	

125
Mares	Eric	SEL	5-0
Lopez	Mike	COAL	
Rivera	Moi	DP	2-1
Cerillo	Mike	WU	

130
Medrano	Jaime	TRAN	5-3
Morsin	Cesar	SEL	
Mora	Jose	FIRE	Fall
Gonzalez	Javier	WU	

135
Rodriguez	Aaron	W	6-4
Benavides	Ray	CAR	
Buckley	Damoni	CENT	5-0
Gomez	Paul	A	

140
Lopez	Tony	PAR	Inj. Def.
Mull	Craig	SEL	
Willis	Brian	SIE	9-5
Gomez	Jody	CORC	

145
Hussein	Naser	SEL	10-5
Tomasini	Dominic	SJM	
Gasca	Jay	KING	5-2
Suarez	Tony	DP	

152
Honea	Ryan	W	8-7
Cleveland	Josh	COAL	
Goodwin	Chuck	A	4-2
Negrete	Nosh	FIRE	

160
Martinez	Nacho	W	Fall
Suarez	Yurin	DP	
Rico	Daniel	WU	5-2
Schneider	Clayton	KER	

171
Rosas	Jesus	COAL	8-4
Connelly	John	McF	
Criado	Joseph	TRAN	10-5
Moreno	Aaron	PAR	

189
De Santiago	Juan	WOOD	Fall
Reyes	Jose	WU	
Moreno	Miguel	DIN	7-2
Casteneda	Emilio	PAR	

HWT
Gonzales	Jack	SHAFT	Fall
Briseno	Lewis	WU	
Anguiano	Richard	MCF	Fall
Chavez	Manuel	PAR	

Tournament
1. Selma 125
2. Dos Palos 124
3. Washington U. 115.5
4. Tranquility 94.5
5. Kingsburg 92
6. Wasco 82
7. Parlier 80
8. Firebaugh 73
9. Arvin 66.5
10. Coalinga 60

Sierra-Sequoia Division – Shafter
February 20, 1993

98
Borocio	Francisco	DP	O.T. 5-0
Hernandez	Adrian	CORC	
Sobaje	Jason	BUC	3-0
Garcia	Selso	WOOD	

112
Ruiz	Tony	DP	Fall 3:15
Perez	Jesse	SEL	
Mestaz	Matthew	WOOD	Fall 2:20
Montalvo	Raul	KER	

119
Pierro	Jeremy	BUC	9-4
Cones	Greg	DP	
Barbeau	Trevor	DIN	6-4
Campos	Felipe	FIRE	

125
Lopez	Mike	COAL	6-0
Rodriguez	Mike	SEL	
Rios	Steven	CENT	14-11
Galvan	Marcus	WU	

130
Jimenez	Manuel	KING	9-3
Castro	Jaime	PAR	
Cerrillo	Michael	WU	9-2
Valencia	Jesus	DP	

136
Rodriguez	Aaron	W	3-1
Mora	Jose	FIRE	
Valencia	Jose	DP	7-4
Duarte	Josue	CORC	

140
Buckley	Damani	CENT	Fall 3:05
Plaza	Eric	WU	
Williams	Mike	FIRE	Fall 3:37
Breceda	Victor	BUC	

145
Negrete	Nacho	FIRE	Maj. 14-4
Mello	Ben	MCF	
Rodriguez	Javier	DIN	3-1
Kingsbury	Tyson	TEHA	

152
Ontiveros	Ruben	TRAN	4-1
Rodriguez	Tony	WU	
Williams	Shawn	CAR	8-6
Quintana	Esdras	MCF	

160
Maldonado	Adam	FIRE	9-8
Wareham	Willie	DP	
St. Martin	Cliff	Wood	Fall 4:04
Rivera	Anthony	DIN	

171
Pascual	Maurilio	WU	9-4
Criado	Joe	TRAN	
Montoya	Jaime	KER	1-0
Ramirez	Raul	DP	

189
Herrera	George	FIRE	10-8
De Santiago	Juan	WOOD	
Lockard	Mike	TEHA	Fall 1:41
Gallardo	Juan	W	

275
Flores	Joe	WOOD	3-0
Briseno	Luis	WU	
Gonzales	Jack	SHAFT	Fall :52
Garcia	Rigo	FIRE	

Tournament
1. Dos Palos 152.5
2. Firebaugh 145.5
3. Washington U. 116
4. Woodlake 95
5. Parlier 63.5
6. Dinuba 62
7. Tranquility 61
8. Central 58.5
9. Selma 57 Tied for 9th
9. Buchanan 57 Tied for 9th
11. Corcoran 56
12. Wasco 52
13. Tehachapi 50
14. McFarland 48.5
15. Kingsburg 33
16. Shafter 29 Tied for 16th
16. Coaling 29 Tied for 16th
18. Kerman 28.5
19. Caruthers 27
20. Stockdale 14
21. Chowchilla 5
22. Yosemite 2
23. Taft 1
Avenal 0
San Joaquin Memorial 0
Sierra 0

Sierra-Sequoia Division – Washington Union
February 19, 1994

103
Sobate	Jason	BUCH	10-4
Garcia	Santos	WOOD	
Jameson	Sam	W	11-9
Mosaqueda	Ricardo	DP	

112
Mestaz	Matt	WOOD	8-4
Barocio	Francisco	DP	
Ortiz	Alex	CORC	Fall 3:29
Perez	Jesse	SEL	

119
Noain	Joey	CHOW	4-3
Cones	Billy	DP	
Garcia	Carlos	WOOD	4-1
Ropier	Jeremy	SHAFT	

125
Duarte	Josue	CORC	Fall 3:11
Barba	Saul	TRAN	
Cones	Greg	DP	11-4
Zepada	Carlos	W	

130
Pierro	Jeremy	BUCH	T F 4:00
Serda	Eric	W	
Jiminez	Manuel	KING	8-2
Lopez	Onismo	SEL	

135
Mora	Jose	FIRE	3-1
Breceda	Victor	BUCH	
Valencia	Jesus	DP	7-2
Mann	Cory	SIE	

140
Wiliams	Mike	FIRE	11-2
Pena	Mike	CORC	
Urena	Joel	KER	7-3
Cerrillo	Mike	SU	

145
Negrete	Nosh	FIRE	5-4
Rossetti	Jason	SEL	
Ortiz	Albert	CORC	7-3
Plaza	Eric	WU	

152
Pereschica	Sonny	KING	8-4
Ontiberos	Ruben	MKEN	
Navarro	Erik	FIRE	9-5
Moreno	Clemente	DIN	

160
Maldonado	Adam	FIRE	12-3
Thompson	Mike	BUCH	
Castro	Rene	PAR	Fall 3:11
Moran	Fernando	SEL	

171
Jackson	Daniel	KING	6-2
Criado	Joe	TRAN	
Waremham	Willy	DP	Fall 4:05
Clark	Dennis	W	

189
Herrera	George	FIRE	8-3
Moreno	Quillermo	DIN	
Gallardo	Juan	W	7-1
Bracamonte	Louie	CEN	

HWT
Urena	Ralph	WOOD	Fall 2:23
Ortiz	Evan	SEL	
Espericueta	Frank	SHAFT	Fall 4:30
Catania	Joseph	FIRE	

Tournament
1. Firebaugh 168
2. Dos Palos 121.5
3. Buchanan 116
4. Wasco 88
5. Corcoran 87.5
6. Woodlake 87 Tied for 6th
6. Selma 87 Tied for 6th
8. Kingsburg 77.5
9. Tranquility 62
10. Parlier 44
11. Washington U. 36
12. Dinuba 31
12. Shafter 31
14. Central 27
15. Mendota 23
16. Tehachapi 21
17. Chowchilla 20
18. McFarland 18 Tied for 18th
18. Caruthers 18 Tied for 18th
20. Kerman 17
21. Coalinga 16
22. Sierra 13
23. Stockdale 12
24. Yosemite 7
Centennial 0
San Joaquin Memorial 0

Sierra-Sequoia Division – Dos Palos
February 18, 1995

*103
Eastman	Dustin	EX	6-1	
Mendez	M	SEL		
Bazan	Jose	COAL		
Padilla	Tim	YOSE		

112
Garcia	Selso	WOOD	6-4	(36-0)*
Mosqueda	Richard	DP		
Perez	Jesse	SEL	2-0	
Arias	Cesar	FIRE		

119
Moreno	George	FIRE	4-3	
Jiminez	Victor	KING		
Garcia	Santos	WOOD	8-5	(35-3)*
Barocio	Francisco	DP		

125
Ruiz	Frank	EX	6-4
Serda	Eric	W	
Cantu	Herberto	TRAN	5-3
Campos	Felipe	FIRE	

130
Jimenez	Manuel	KING	4-1
Garcia	Arturo	SEL	
Morales	Joseph	EX	4-1
Castro	Jaime	PAR	

136
Pena	Mike	CORC	O.T. 7-5
Morales	Jason	EX	
Valencia	Jesus	DP	3-1
Hernandez	Edgar	TRAN	

140
Salcido	Felipe	EX	Fall
Harris	William	WOOD	
Arias	Francisco	FIRE	5-4
Landin		W	

145
Ensign	Warren	EX	5-2
Gallardo	Juan	W	
Gastelum	Rudy	CAR	7-6
Lupian	Jose	DP	

152
Salcido	Jose	EX	Fall 1:40
Pereschica	Sonny	KING	
Cierley	Kevin	CENT	11-2
Becerra	Isaac	CORC	

160
Rossotti	Jason	SEL	7-4
Moreno	Clemente	DIN	
Freeborn	Zak	SHAFT	
Rosas	Norberto	COAL	

171
Jackson	Daniel	KING	6-4
St. Martin	Cliff	WOOD	
Pezzat	Art	EX	4-1
Arraga		W	

189
Criado	Joe	TRAN	6-1
Jones	Arturo	DP	
Miller	Anthony	EX	6-2
Martinez	Frank	W	

HWT
Espericueta	Frank	SHAFT	3-0
Van Worth	Bryan	DP	
Maldonado	Ruben	MCF	3-1
Cantania	Joseph	FIRE	

Tournament

1. Exeter — 195
2. Dos Palos — 125
3. Kingsburg — 98.5
4. Firebaugh — 90
5. Selma — 88
6. Woodlake — 83
7. Wasco — 81
8. Shafter — 68.5
9. Corcoran — 62.5
10. Tranquility — 60
11. Kerman — 43
12. Centennial — 42.5 Tied for 12th
12. Coalinga — 42.5 Tied for 12th
14. Dinuba — 39
15. Sierra — 32
16. McFarland — 28 Tied for 16th
16. Parlier — 28 Tied for 16th
16. Caruthers — 28 Tied for 16th
18. Washington U. — 24
19. Yosemite — 16.5
20. Chowchilla — 16
21. Tehachapi — 13
22. Mendota — 5
23. Ridgeview — 2

* Record

Sierra-Sequoia Division – Shafter
February 17, 1996

103
Johnson	Cleo	FIRE	12-3
Valdovinos	Abel	PAR	
Montez	Julio	DIN	8-3
Sepulveda	Robert	SEL	

112
Mendez	Mondo	SEL	7-6
Crane	Kenji	DP	
Bascom	Dwight	CENT	Default
Orosco	Armando	FIRE	

119
Arias	Cesar	FIRE	5-4
Mosqueda	Ricardo	DP	
Waldrom	Jeremy	TEHA	10-3
Arredondo	Dominick	COAL	

125
Moreno	George	FIRE	7-2
Jameson	Sam	W	
Jimenez	Victor	KING	3-1
Cones	Bill	DP	

130
Ortiz	Alex	CORC	5-3
Cantu	Herbert	FIRE	
Roper	Jeremy	SHAFT	6-2
Sandoval	Juanny	TRAN	

135
Plaza	Aldo	W	10-7
Lopez	Cassidy	COAL	
Avila	Alfred	FIRE	5-1
Gutierrez	Jim	CORC	

140
Uribe	Charlie	WU	6-4
Garcia	Arturo	SEL	
Campos	Federico	CORC	7-4
Molina	Juan	FIRE	

145
Salcido	Felipe	EX	8-4
Lupian	Jose	DP	
Gutierrez	Paul	CENT	6-0
Rios	Gabe	DIN	

152
Espericueta	Eli	SHAFT	17-6
Rivera	Phillip	DIN	
Gennoe	Nick	WOOD	13-8
Bouhaben	Michael	KER	

160
Moreno	Clemente	DIN	13-11
Salcido	Jose	EX	
Pereschica	Sonny	KING	Fall 1:23
Cisneros	Jose	DP	

171
Gonzales	Mike	CAR	3-1
Freeborn	Zak	SHAFT	
Becerra	Isaac	CORC	7-1
Murphy	Joe	FOW	

189
Miller	Anthony	EX	Fall 1:33
Martinez	Frank	W	
Bluadau	Ryan	SIE	Fall 1:40
Reed	William	DP	

215
Alvardo	Chris	FIRE	Fall 3:11
Ramirez	Mario	CORC	
Miligan	Conner	CAR	2-1
Wilson	Albert	W	

HWT
Van Worth	Bryan	DP	5-3
Smith	Ryan		
Leslie	Rodney	RIDGE	Fall 1:56
Michael	Rod	TEHA	

Tournament:
Sequoia Division
1. Dos Palos 150.5
2. Corcoran 117.5
3. Dinuba 102.5
4. Exeter 98.5
5. Washington U. 97
6. Selma 82.5
7. Shafter 71

Tournament:
Sierra Division
1. Firebaugh 164
2. Caruthers 48
3. Parlier 39

Sierra-Sequoia Division – Dos Palos

February 22, 1997

103
Johnson	Cleo	FIRE	TF 5:55 (53-0)*
Sepulveda	Robert	SEL	
Rodriguez	Jose	CHOW	4-2
Garcia	Fidel	PAR	

112
Moreno	Jason	Fire	11-5
Ramos	Jesus	DIN	
Madriga	Tony	SHAFT	Inj. Default
Codero	George	SEL	

119
Waldrum	Jerremy	TEHA	8-5
Crane	Kenji	DP	
Sanchez	Francisco	KER	8-3
Orosco	Armando	FIRE	

125
Valenzuela	Ricky	WU	7-4
Estrada	Steve	PAR	
Arredondo	Mariano	Chow	5-1
Solis		CORC	

130
Moreno	George	FIRE	Fall 3:53
Pereschica	Danny	King	
Pacheco	Nestor	WU	Fall 2:45
Snyder	Keith	DP	

135
Jameson	Sam	W	1-0
Jimenez	Victor	KING	
Negrete	Carlos	FIRE	7-4
Ramsey	Dustin	COAL	

140
Garcia	Arturo	SEL	9-3
Gutierrez	Jimmy	CORC	
Cazares	Juvenal	PAR	10-0
Amaro	Omar	WU	

145
Rios	Gabriel	DIN	5-4
Molina	Juan	FIRE	
Brooks	Ryan	RIDGE	8-3
Matson	Max	YOSE	

152
Landin	Jose	W	5-3
Lupian	Jose	DP	
Gennoe	Nick	WOOD	8-3
Hansen	Bryan	YOSE	

160
Kerste	Alman	TEHA	11-5
Arreola	Ramon	CORC	
Van Worth	Mike	DP	5-0
Martinez	Manny	WOOD	

171
Pereschica	Sonny	KING	Tech. Fall 5:48
Chaddock	Nick	COAL	
Schneider	Luke	TEHA	Fall 4:38
Reed	William	DP	

189
Jackson	Dan	KING	T. Fall 5:01 (33-0)*
Bludau	Ryan	SIE	
Martinez	Narcy	W	6-3
Tredjo	Jose	SHAFT	

215
Milligan	Conor	CAR	3-0
Rodriguez	David	WU	
Gai	Joe	KING	2-1
Molina	Chris	DP	

HWT
Leslie	Rodney	RIDGE	Fall :37
Michael	Rodney	TEHA	
Brady	Aaron	KING	7-4
Davila	Hector	CAR	

* Record

Tournament

1. Kingsburg	150.5		12. Kerman	57
2. Firebaugh	150		13. Coalinga	52
3. Dos Palos	124		14. Ridgeview	51
4. Washington U.	90.5		15. Yosemite	41 Tied
5. Wasco	89.5		15. Sierra	41 Tied
6. Tehachapi	88		17. Woodlake	40
7. Selma	72		18. Mendota	34
8. Dinuba	71.5		19. Shafter	32
9. Corcoran	70.5		20. Chowchilla	31
10 Caruthers	60		21. McFarland	26
11. Parlier	59		22. Tranquility	25
			23. Fowler	

Sierra-Sequoia Division – Firebaugh
February 21, 1998

103
Moreno	Jason	FIRE	Fall 2:22
Cuevas	Clemetne	MEN	
Serrano	Eddie	KER	Fall 1:05
Macias	Eric	W	

112
Sanchez	Francisco	KER	8-3
Madrigal	Tony	SHAFT	
Sandoval	Miguel	TRAN	5-1
Devora	Rene	DIN	

119
Sepulveda	Robert	SEL	Fall 3:31
Maldonado	Fernando	FIRE	
Rivera	Eleuto	DP	7-3
Argueta	Miguel	MEN	

125
Waldram	Jeremy	TEHA	5-0
Venegas	Cookie	WU	
Evangelist	Jorge	PAR	4-0
Molina	Rudy	FIRE	

130
Crane	Kenji	DP	Fall 3:26
Pereschica	Danny	KING	
Ramirez	Jessie	WOOD	6-1
Areyano	Joe	SEL	

135
Negrete	Carlos	FIRE	3-1
Valenzuela	Ricky	W	
Cornaggia	Luke	CHOW	9-1
Rivera	Pedro	DIN	

140
Landin	David	W	10-8
Cummins	Jimmy	CAR	
Evangelist	Billy	PAR	5-3
Diaz	David	MEN	

145
Garcia	Roger	KER	5-3
De La Rosa	Ricardo	DP	
Chavarria	Jose	MEN	15-7
Huerta	Sam	DIN	

152
Daniell	Beau	CHOW	6-1
Cantu	Wilfred	FIRE	
Marroquin	Gabe	W	5-1
Sherry	Kris	TEHA	

160
Prudeck	Jack	CAR	8-7
Rodriguez	Jo Jo	WU	
Burke	Sam	RIDGE	Fall 4:15
Valenzuela	Robert	KER	

171
Gennoe	Nick	WOOD	Fall 2:40
Hemman	Rodney	CAR	
Vasquez	Joe	SEL	Dec.
Willis	Baron	DP	

189
Van Worth	Mike	DP	6-4
Gross	Paxton	CORC	
Dennis	Brad	CAR	9-4
Ochoa	Carlos	MEN	

215
Martinez	Narcy	W	10-6
Kragie	Ken	CHOW	
Casillas	Johnny	KER	7-6
Estrada	Gabriel	FOW	

275
Michael	Rodney	TEHA	Fall :35
Ramos	Mike	CORC	
Calvert	Josh	DP	3-1
Cruz	Richard	FOW	

Tournament
1. Dos Palos — 156.5
2. Firebaugh — 143.5
3. Kerman — 127 Tied for 3rd
3. Mendota — 127 Tied for 3rd
5. Caruthers — 101
6. Tehachapi — 85
7. Wasco — 84
8. Chowchilla — 79
9. Selma — 75
10. Washington U. — 70
11. Dinuba — 63
12. Shafter — 60.5
13. Corcoran — 56.5
14. Ridgeview — 56
15. Woodlake — 52.5
16. Parlier — 37.5
17. Sierra — 32
18. Kingsburg — 30
19. Fowler — 29
20. Tranquility — 22
21. Yosemite — 20
22. Farmersville — 11
23. McFarland — 10
24. Coalinga — 3 Tied
24. Lindsey — 3 Tied

Sierra-Sequoia Division – Arvin
February 20, 1999

103
Hernandez	Victor	WU	9-5	
Augilera	Antonio	TRAN		
Argutes	Ulies	MEN	17-11	
Jenkins	Ricky	YOSE		

112
Moreno	Jason	FIRE	21-7	(52-1)*
Cuevas	Clemente	MEN		
Campos	Ignacio	DP	4-3	
Sanchez	Ivan	A		

119
Rodriguez	Robert	DP	6-5
Farias	Matt	SHAFT	
Acosta	Pat	W	12-10
Harris	Terrence	CHOW	

125
Sepulveda	Robert	SEL	T.F.
Arguata	Miguel	MEN	
Downs	Eric	DP	
Ramos	Jesus	DIN	

130
Venegas	Cookie	WU	2-1
Evangelista	Jorge	PAR	
Rivera	Gabriel	DP	8-3
Oceguera	Luis	CHOW	

135
Rosales	Nick	A	Fall 2:22	(36-2)*
Preston	Joseh	SHAFT		(31-6)*
Jimenez	Victor	KING	7-5	
Rivera		WU		

140
Coinagga	Luke	CHOW	10-3
Pena	Albert	WOOD	
Smith	Greg	DP	8-2
Garcia			

145
Diaz	David	MEN	7-3
Garcia	Carlos	WOOD	
Perez	Armando	FARM	12-9
Moreno	Anthony	PAR	

152
De La Rosa	Ricardo	DP	7-2
Chavarria	Jose	MEN	
Reedy	John Michael	YOSE	6-2
Yegar		SANG	

160
Landin	David	W	9-8
Corrasco	Ernie	SEL	
Hemen	Rodney	CAR	16-10
William	Dan	YOSE	

171
Nystem	Eric	CAR	Dec Fall 1:54
Waldrum	Jared	TEHA	
Clark	Granson	DP	5-4
DeLoura	Luis	MEN	

189
Van Worth	Mike	DP	Fall
Cantu	Leo	KER	
Ochoa	Carlos	MEN	6-2
Moisa	Giblert	YOSE	

215
Martinez	Narcy	W	15-10	(39-1)*
Kargle	Ken	CHOW		(36-3)*
Vasquez	Joe	SEL	Fall	
Mosqueda	Santiago	DP		

275
Ramirez	Johnny	DIN	4-1
Harris	Walter	CHOW	
Calvert	Josh	DP	2-0
Frowsing	Nathan	SIE	

Tournament
1. Dos Palos	195
7. Shafter	76
8. Wasco	67
11. Tehachapi	52.5
15. Arvin	48.5
21. McFarland	19.5

*Record

Sierra-Sequoia Division – Dos Palos
February 19, 2000

103
Argueta	Ulysses	MEN	
Cortez	Greg	PAR	
Soldano	Andy	CORC	
Vega	Alfredo	SEL	

112
Sanchez	Ivan	A	
Clevas	Clemente	MEN	
Silva	George	MCF	
Arias	Eric	FIRE	

119
Farias	Matt	SHAFT	8-7
Campos	Vincent	DP	
Guerrero	Modesto	CAR	
Brook	Devin	A	

125
Maldonado	Matt	SHAFT	
Taftos	Javier	SEL	
Rojas	Elias	DIN	
Barragan	Richard	HW	

130
Evangelista	Jorge	PAR	
Venegas	Cookie	WU	
Berrera	Isaac	TEHA	
Cortina	Rene	SEL	

135
Rivera	Eleuto	DP	
Ocegurea	Luis	CHOW	
Acosta	Patrick	W	
Bebout	Jeremy	YOSE	

140
Necnerte	Carlos	FIRE	
Glenn	Douglas	DP	
Hallmyer	Daniel	WOOD	
Orosco	Ignacio	CAR	

145
Garcia	Carlos	WOOD	
Silvia	Tony	KER	
Gorman	Robert	YOSE	
Zavala	Hugo	DP	

152
Erddey	John	YOSE	
Corall	Carlos	CORC	
Soltero	Anthony	KER	
Arroyo	Silerio	FOW	

160
Cantu	Wilfredo	FIRE	
Moreno	Michael	PAR	
Chavarria	Jose	MEN	
Rojas	Andy	SEL	

171
Clark	Granson	DP	
Yager	Jacob	SEL	
Walz	Charlie	TEHA	
Martinez	Freddie	LIN	

189
Van Worth	Mike	DP	10-2
Pederson	Daniel	SHAFT	
Nelson	Nate	TEHA	
Rocha	Michael	KER	

215
Kragie	Ken	CHOW	
Young	Riley	SIE	
Banuelos	Andres	DP	
Gonzalez	Luis	WOOD	

275
Jackson	Immanuel	HW	
McCoy	Shawn	YOSE	
Harris	Walter	CHOW	
Medina	Rudy	CORC	

Tournament
1. Dos Palos	177.5		14. Caruthers	47
2. Mendota	108.5		15. Arvin	45.5
3. Firebaugh	105		16. Farmersville	42.5
4. Yosemite	95		17. Sierra	40
5. Shafter	91.5		18. Kingsburg	39
6. Woodlake	84.5		19. Fowler	26 Tied
7. Tehachapi	84.5		19. McFarland	26 Tied
8. Selma	84		21. Washington U.	24.5
9. Chowchilla	74.5		22. Dinuba	20
10. Parlier	67.5		23. Clovis East	14 Tied
11. Corcoran	61		23. Wasco	14 Tied
12. Kerman	54.5		25. Lindsey	13
13. Hanford West	49		26. Coalinga	8
			27. Sunnyside	7

Sierra-Sequoia Division – Shafter
February 17, 2001

103
Lee	Kou	WU	3-2
Kinbler	Jay	SIE	
Garcia	Sonny	KING	5-0
Hernandez	Antonio	LIB	

112
Sanchez	Ivan	A	9-0
Arguella	Ulysses	MEN	
Cortez	Greg	PAR	10-2
Cortina	Willie	SEL	

119
Loredo	Francisco	COAL	7-2
Fierro	Paul	KING	
Landois	Orlando	WASCO	7-3
Saldana	Andy	CORC	

125
Maldonado	Matt	SHAFT	Fall 1:40
Campos	Javier	SEL	
Arias	Eric	FIRE	Fall 4:40
Gomez	Jose	W	

130
Evangelist	Jorge	PAR	Fall 2:31
Madrigal	Freddy	SHAFT	
Sanchez	Marcus	HW	9-7
Cortina	Rene	SEL	

135
Oceguara	Luis	CHOW	12-7
Mendoza	Adam	FIRE	
Alvarez	Derek	YOSE	5-2
Rubio	Sam	MEN	

140
Rivera	Gabriel	WU	Fall 5:00
Douglas	Glen	DP	
Rodriguez	Emilio	MEN	13-7
Gaumnitz	Cole	CHOW	

145
Garcia	Carlos	WOOD	10-1
Acosta	Pat	W	
Bebout	Jeremy	YOSE	5-0
Castro	Roberto	FIRE	

152
Arroyo	Silverio	FOW	4:28
Applewhite	Wesley	HW	
Zavala	Hugo	DP	10-4
Gorman	Robert	YOSE	

160
Valdez	Sergio	MEN	Fall 4:55
Mora	Lupe	FIRE	
Soltero	Anthony	KER	4-0
Gulium	Michael	FOW	

171
Moreno	Anthony	PAR	13-2
Luna	Moises	MEN	
Toone	Jonathan	CORC	17-4
Rodriguez	Abraham	WOOD	

189
Clark	Gronson	DP	9-5
Villegas	Elvis	MEN	
Mejia	Gabe	FOW	10-6
Jackson	Justin	KING	

215
Young	Riley	SIE	Fall 5:59
Gonzalez	Luis	WOOD	
Powers	Cole	DP	2:54
Montgomery	Greg	YOSE	

HWT
Jackson	Emanuel	HW	1-0
Medina	Rudy	CORC	
Rodriguez	Juan	DP	5-4
Lopez	Gabe	COAL	

Tournament
1. Dos Palos 135
2. Mendota 123
3. Firebaugh 98
4. Shafter 89
5. Woodlake 89
6. Parlier 80.5

Sierra-Sequoia Division – Hanford West
February 16, 2002

103
Garcia	Sonny	KING	9-2
Ruiz	Paul	FIRE	
Hernandez	Antonio	LIB	4-3
Olea	Angel	FARM	(29-12)*

112
Flores	Matt	KING	6-4
Saldana	Andy	CORC	
Jenkins	Ricky	YOSE	9-6
Acevedo	Luis	FARM	(31-6)*

119
Kimbler	Jay	SIE	7-0
Rangel	Francisco	FIRE	
Husein	Ali	SEL	17-6
Downs	Sergio	DP	

125
Loredo	Francisco	COAL	5:25
Hernandez	Luis	WU	
Siegers	Andrew	YOSE	7-5
Solis	Miguel	WU	

130
Maldonado	Matt	SHAFT	Fall 5:33 (36-0)*
Martinez	Lorenzo	PAR	
Silva	Thomas	KER	6-3
Perez	Adam	FIRE	

135
Carrasco	Jason	SHAFT	13-4
Arias	Eric	FIRE	
Landois	Orlando	W	8-2
Orosco	Gabe	CORC	

140
Rivera	Gabriel	WU	3-1
Points	Jason	LIB	
Hagar	Cody	TEHA	6-3
Nevarro	George	CORC	

145
Garcia	J.R.	FARM	Fall 1:46
Ferrer	Andy	CAR	
Aguilar	Richard	HW	Fall 1:19
Collings	Darren	TEHA	

152
Haidey	Santiago	CAR	5-4
Mendoza	Adam	FIRE	
Dias	Chad	CORC	5-2
Pezzat	Sinai	FARM	

160
Gulian	Michael	FOW	2-1
Castro	Roberto	FIRE	
Pacheco	Alex	WU	5-3
Rivera	Mario	COAL	

171
Rodriguez	Abraham	WOOD	9-4
Gorman	Robert	YOSE	
Becerra	Jonathan	FARM	Fall 1:30
Torres	Bernadino	CAR	

189
Villegas	Elvis	MEN	5-0
Howard	Brent	COAL	
Gaona	Alex	WU	Fall 4:38
Hernandez	Alfredo	FARM	

215
Powers	Cole	DP	O.T. 2-1
Vincent	Chad	HW	
Trejo	Juan	SEL	6-1
Picker	Cody	LIB	

HWT
Jackson	Emanual	HW	Forfeit
Wililam	Jason	SHAFT	
Lopez	Gabe	COAL	3-1
Rivas	Modesto	FARM	(20-9 Season)*

* Record

Tournament
1. Firebaugh 147
2. Shafter 117.5
3. Hanford West 114
4. Farmersville 110
5. Coalinga 105.5
6. Washington U. 101
7. Corcoran 78
8. Woodlake 77.5
9. Liberty 75.5
10. Caruthers 59.5
11. Tehachapi 57 Tied
11. Dos Palos 57 Tied
13. Selma 52.5
14. Yosemite 47
15. Kingsburg 45
16. Mendota 36
17. Sierra 34
18. Fowler 31.5
19. Kerman 28.5
20. Parlier 28
21. Dinuba 20
22. Wasco 16
23. Arvin 13
24. Granite Hills 9
25. Lindsay 8
26. Chowchilla 7
27. McFarland 6
28. Orosi 3

Sierra-Sequoia Division – Dos Palos
February 22, 2003

103
Ruiz	Paul	FIRE	Maj. 12-4
Olea	Angel	FARM	(Season 45-11)*
Para	Joseph	SHAFT	5-3
Gonzales	Polo	MCF	
Naranjo	Francisco	PAR	2-1
Morales	Que	DP	

112
Mestaz	Mike	WOOD	O.T. 5-3
Cruz	Gus	CORC	
Coronado	Albert	FIRE	Maj. 13-0
Navarro	Vincent	SHAFT	
Subia	Isaac	COAL	Maj. 12-4
Partida	Alex	DP	

119
Husein	Ali	SEL	10-4
Weatherly	Daniel	EX	
Flores	Matt	King	7-0
Hamilton	Josh	DP	
Santana	Rene	DIN	15-9
Cruz	Dustin	SHAFT	

125
Sanchez	Sal	W	15-7
Gaxiola	David	KER	
Siegers	Andrew	YOSE	7-5
Torres	Anthony	EX	
Martinez	Ramon	FIRE	Fall
Arriola	Scott	SEL	

130
Espericueta	Lucas	SHAFT	4:43 (35-6)*
Martinez	Lorenzo	PAR	
Smith	Will	WOOD	Default
Goff	Kayne	COAL	
Liebman	David	TEHA	Fall
Silvaker	Tomas		

135
Gonzalez	Matt	EX	1:02
Loredo	Francisco	COAL	
Flores	Santos	PAR	Tech. Fall 15-0
Rodriguez	Steven	WOOD	
Maldonado	Anthony	FIRE	5-2
Hamilton	Jacob	DP	

140
Coronado	John	FIRE	9-7
Pezzat	Sinai	FARM	
Gomez	Rene	WU	Fall
Gillihan	Chris	SIE	
Presley	Jason	SHAFT	Fall
Vargas	Samnuel	PAR	

145
Landois	Orlando	W	T. Fall. 15-0 2:26
Torres	Manuel	FIRE	
Manriquez	David	A	4-2
Serna	Miguel	DP	
Bustamante	Nick	SIE	Fall
Farmer	Matt	COAL	

152
Carrasco	Jason	SHAFT	3:31 (30-4)
Watson	James	COAL	
Urena	Rafa	WOOD	11-6
Cuevas	Jose	DIN	
Lopez	Guillermo	WU	Fall
Guerrero	Armando	FIRE	

160
Boger	Matt	COAL	13-10
Castillo	Cain	WOOD	
Soltero	Andrew	KER	T.F. 15-0
Mendez	Eddie	SHAFT	
Saucedo	Israel	FIRE	5-3
Delgadillo	Martin		

171
Becerra	Jonathan	FARM	2-1
Pacheco	Alex	WU	
Hall	Chris	DIN	Default
Torres	Bernardino	DIN	
Nunez	Francisco	DP	Default
Vasquez	Erik	SEL	

189
Merrell	Jacob	DP	11-9 O.T.
Gaona	Alex	WU	
Statler	Marvin	SHAFT	Major 19-9 (34-9)
Rodriguez	Abraham	WOOD	
Iriye	Bryan	LIN	5-2
Ingram	Jedd	TEH	

(Continued on next page)

Sierra-Sequoia Division – Dos Palos
February 22, 2003

215
Trejo	Juan	SEL	Major 14-2
Puga	Homar	CAR	
Cervantes	Alex	FIRE	Major 14-4
Beltran	Francisco	SHAFT	
LeLendias	Mark	DP	Fall
Resenediz	Johnny	PAR	

275
Williams	Jason	SHAFT	1:57	(30-5)*
Sconiers	Decovan	WU		
McGuire	Joe	SIE	5-2	
Vargas	Jamie	SEL		
Serrano	Nabor	FIRE	Fall	
Padilla	Sergio	DP		

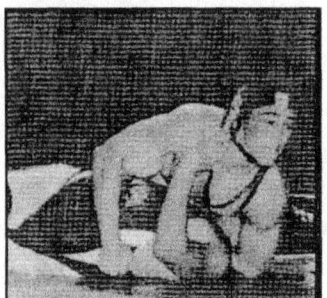

Matt Farmer
Coalinga High

Tournament
1. Shafter 206
2. Firebaugh 188.5
3. Dos Palos 139
4. Coalinga 119.5 Tied for 4th
4. Woodlake 119.5 Tied for 4th
6 Washington U. 106
7. Selma 94.5
8. Parlier 93
9. Exeter 85
10. Dinuba 78.5
11. Farmersville 77
12. Sierra 68
13. Wasco 67.5
14. Kerman 56
15. Caruthers 36
16. Arvin 32
17. Tehachapi 30.5
18. Corcoran 29.5
19. Yosemite 28
20. McFarland 24.5
21. Kingsburg 24
22. Lindsay 17
23. Fowler 15
24. Mendota 10
25. Madera Lib. 7
26. Orosi 3
27. Chowchilla 2
28. Tranquility 1

* Record

2002 McFarland High Wrestling Team

2003 Shafter High Wrestling Team

Sierra-Sequoia Division – Farmersville
February 20-21, 2004

103
Olea	Pedro	FARM	MDec.14-0(41-9)*
Rivera	David		
Dominguez	Christian	CORC	Maj. Dec. 8-0
Naranjo	Francisco	PAR	
Martinez	Rolando	DIN	Maj. Dec. 14-6
Gallegos	Robert	WU	

112
Olea	Angel	FARM	Def. (36-5)*
Cruz	Gus	CORC	
Para	Joseph	SHAFT	10-2
Larson	Dan	YOSE	
Castillo	Frankie	A	Dec.
Powell	Michael	EX	

119
Coronado	Albert	FIRE	Default
Contreras	Nick	SEL	
Santana	Rene	DIN	4-3
Subia	Isaac	COAL	
Nelson	Robbie	KING	Maj. Dec. 13-2
Loretz	Martin		

125
Husein	Ali	SEL	10-9
Torres	Anthony	EX	
Martinez	Fernando	FIRE	Fall 1:59
Tamayo	Francisco	A	
Cole	Galvin	COAL	10-3
Crosthwaite	Chris	COAL	

130
Weatherly	Daniel	EX	10-7
Balassa	Joaquin	TEHA	
Argueta	Eddie	MEN	6-1
Campos	Adam	KING	
Arriola	Scott	SEL	112-5
Workman	Junior	WU	

135
Sanchez	Sal	W	12-6
Cruz	Dustin	SHAFT	
Gonzales	Matt	EX	4-2
Mora	Jaime	FIRE	
Barron	Mark	WU	Maj. Dec. 21-9
Gaxiola	David	KER	

140
Espercueta	Lucas	SHAFT	13-7
Pezzat	Sinai	FARM	
Ramos	Anthony	WOOD	10-6
Torres	Manual	FIRE	
Hamilton	Jacob	DP	Maj. Dec. 11-3
Timblin	Jason		

145
Botello	Oscar	EX	10-5
Coronado	Johnny	FIRE	
Johnson	Zack	W	Forfeit
Chavez	Richard	FARM	
Stevens	Jason	SHAFT	Forfeit
Serna	Miguel	DP	

152
Landios	Orlando	W	Fall 3:31
Urena	Rafa	WOOD	
Rodriguez	Steven	WU	Fall 1:15
Downs	Sergio	DP	
Ray	Kenny	CAR	Fall 3:41
Liebengood	Thomas	THS	

160
Boger	Matt	COAL	Maj. Dec. (20-10)*
Castillo	Cain	WOOD	
Clenard	Justin	TEHA	4-1
Huff	Drake	DP	
Williams	Cody	SIE	Maj. Dec. 13-4
Lopez	Guillermo	WU	

171
Acosta	Jesse	COAL	6-2
Pacheco	Alex	WU	
Delgadillo	Martin	DIN	Fall 2:33
Guzman	Ricardo	PAR	
Duran	Jason	A	Fall 1:43
Ward	Ray	SIE	

189
Statler	Marvin	SHAFT	Fall 3:51
Rodriguez	Abraham	WOOD	
Gaona	Alex	WU	
Merrell	Jacob	DP	
Guzman	Jose	PAR	Fall 1:44
Valencia	Alvaro	DIN	

(Continued on next page)

Sierra-Sequoia Division – Farmersville
February 20-21, 2004

215
Trejo	Juan	SEL	Fall 1:36
Garza	Nick	SHAFT	
Cervanstes	Alex	FIRE	Fall 3:34
Caywood	Ryan	YOSE	
Lucas	Terry	DIN	Fall 5:54
Garcia	Adam	FOW	

275
McGuire	Joe	SIE	Fall 5:44 (29-2/23 falls)
Sconiers	Decovan	WU	(27-9/26 falls)
Gomez	Daniel	FOW	1-0
Bonila	Chris	CORC	Default
Magallon	Sal	EX	
Padilla	Sergio		

Tournament
1. Washington U. 141.5
2. Exeter 137
3. Shafter 135
4. Firebaugh 131.5
5. Selma 126
6. Dos Palos 100
7. Dinuba 97
8. Woodlake 95 Tied for 8th
8. Wasco 95 Tied for 8th
10. Farmersville 87.5 Tied for 10th
10. Sierra 87.5 Tied for 10th
12. Coalinga 86
13. Tehachapi 62
14. Yosemite 61
15. Arvin 57
16. Corcoran 56.5
17. Parlier 54.5
18. Fowler 35
19. Kingsburg 31
20. Caruthers 28
21. McFarland 26.5
22. Mendota 23
23. Kerman 16
24. Lib-Madera 9.5
25. Chowchilla 9
26. Orosi 6
27. Tranquility 3

VARSITY--First Row: T. Guerrero, A. Garcia, A. Hernandez, S. Guerrero. Second Row: P. Gomez, A. Terronez, S. Patrick, H. Terronez. Third Row: S. Smith, L. Moz, A. Diaz, M. Porras, T. Medina. Fourth Row: Coach Robert Stevens.

1969 Corcoran High Wrestling Team

Top Row: Coach White, Coach Sanchez, Oscar Martinez, Sal Vasquez, Marcos Osuna, Anthony White, Vincente Mireles, Mario Monge, Coach Serros. Bottom Row: Jarred White, Ivan Sanchez, Devin Brook, Ernesto Garay, Juan Lopez.

2000 Arvin High Wrestling Team

Sierra-Sequoia Division II – Shafter
February 18-19, 2005

103
Garcia	John	FIRE	6-3	(46-6)*
Martinez	Rolando	DIN		
Alverado	Nick	FOW	14-10	
Gutierrez	Emanuel	DP		
Gallegos	Robert	WU	7-1	
Avila	Fernando	EX		

112
Olea	Angel	FARM	14-5	(33-0/143-28)*
Sanchez	Efrain	A		
Mesa	Roger	TEHA	8-4	
Randrup	Tyler	YOSE		
Dominguez	Christian	CORC	Tech. Fall. 15-0	
Nevejar	Angel	MCF		

119
Ruiz	Paul	FIRE	15-4	(50-2/149-9)*
Ramirez	Ernesto	EX		
Castillo	Frankie	A	Forfeit	(28-10)*
Morales	Que	DP		
Franks	Ricky	SHAFT	17-10	
Cruz	Gus	CORC		

125
Husein	Ali	SEL	8-5	
Subia	Isaac	COAL		
Navarro	Vincent	SHAFT	9-1	(26-8)*
Coronado	Albert	FIRE		
Campos	Adam	KING	8-5	
Powell	Mike	EX		

130
Martinez	Fernando	FIRE	T.F. 15-0	(27-9)*
Gillihan	Jacob	SIE		
Tamayo	Francisco	A	Fall 2:59	
Tovar	Archie	SEL		
McEver	Jacob	DP	Fall 5:18	
Rodriguez	Miguel	WOOD		

135
Perez	Matt	FIRE	Fall 5:37	(36-13)*
Arriola	Scott	SEL		
Silva	David	KER	5-4	
Varela	Abel	A		
Hamilton	Josh	DP	Fall :30	
Garcia	Angel	FARM		

140
Weatherly	Dan	EX	5-2	
Espericueta	Lucas	SHAFT		(44-5)*
Gallegos	Manuel	YOSE	5-1	
Martinez	Ricky	FIRE		
Vasquez	Eleazar	SEL	9-2	
Gonzales	Josh	DP		

145
Chavez	Richard	FARM	5-3
Serna	Miguel	DP	
Garcia	Pedro	FIRE	5-4
Smith	Steve	LIB-MAD	
Vereide	C.JU.	SIE	Fall 1:22
Ortiz	Jacob	YOSE	

152
Johnson	Zach	WAS	5-0	(33-10)*
Post	Robert	TEHA		
Flores	Santos	PAR	11-7	
Serna	Ray	COAL		
Duran	Jason	A	Fall 2:43	
Terrones	Zeke	WU		

160
Garrison	Chris	FOW	12-7
Garcia	Jared	MCF	
Vonallman	Kurt	DP	Fall :28
Vanderpool	Shane	LIB-MAD	
Coates	Marcus	TEHA	Forfeit
Bautista	Alejandro	COAL	

171
Boger	Matt	COAL	12-2
Merrell	Jacob	DP	
Coleman	Trevon	WAS	9-5
Guillien	Raul	FOW	
Grffis	Brandon	CAR	4-2
Cervantes	John	FIRE	

189
Statler	Marvin	SHAFT	17-4	(31-7)*
Boger	Josh	COAL		
Noriega	Gino	TRAN	Fall 5:35	
LeLandais	Marc	DP		
Alcala	Alex	A	Fall 5:40	
Alfaro	Erik	FIRE		

(Continued on next page)

Sierra-Sequoia Division II – Shafter
February 18-19, 2005

215
Cervantes	Alex	FIRE	Fall :38
Smith	Joe	TEHA	
Lopez	Vince	COAL	9-4
Mendoza	Francisco	DP	
Tovar	Juan	FOW	Fall 3:03
Polston	Zack	FIRE	

275
Gomez	Daniel	FOW	10-6
Alcala	Ricky	A	
Jimenez	Leobardo	DP	4-1
Cisneros	Efren	GV	
Caywood	Ryan	YOSE	Fall :11
Aguilar	Andrew	COAL	

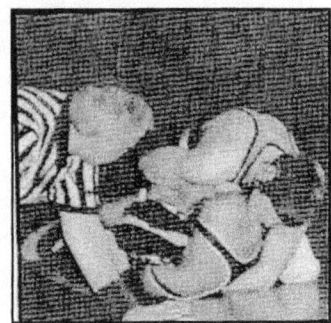

Matt Boger
Coalinga High

Tournament
1. Firebaugh 213.5
2. Dos Palos 197
3. Arvin 137.5
4. Coalinga 132.5
5. Fowler 108.5
6. Selma 103.5
7. Shafter 82
8. Tehachapi 86.5
9. Yosemite 79
10. Exeter 77.5
11. Farmersville 68
12. Wasco 55
13. Sierra 52
14. Washingotn U. 49
Liberty-Madera
15. Ranchos 43
16. Caruthers 42.5
17. McFarland 42
18. Corcoran 37.5
19. Tranquility 30
20. Golden Valley 28
21. Parlier 28
22. Kerman 26
23. Dinuba 24
24. Woodlake 20
25. Kingsburg 13
26. Mendota 11
27. Chowchilla 4

* Record and career record

Back Row: Coach Eddie Zuniga, Coach Darryl Cleveland, Jose Contreras, Jesus Perez, George Sanchez, Jame Quesada, Coach Joe Lopez. Middle Row: Tim Meltabarger, Dominic Arredondo, Horacio Moreno, Mike Adams Nick Chaddock, Brandon Holland, Cassidy Lopez. Bottom Row: Alex Garcia, Amado Gonzales, Dustin Ramsey Joe Bazan.

1994 Coalinga High Wrestling Team

Sierra-Sequoia Division – Firebaugh
February 17-18, 2006

103
Camacho	Gilbert	WU	Fall
Diaz	Edgar	A	
Gonzales	Juan	KER	Fall
Avila	Fernando	EX	
Steinbach	Jared	TEHA	Fall
Alvaro	Armando	MEN	

112
Olea	Pedro	FARM	Dec.
Quintana	Diego	SEL	
Alvardo	Nick	FOW	Fall
Arroyo	Jay	DP	
Garcia	Raymond	MCF	Dec.
Rojas	Kevin	KER	

119
Cole	Calvin	COAL	Dec.
Vanni	Garrett	LIB-MAD	
Mendoza	Jose	SEL	Forfeit
Sanchez	Efrain	A	
Patino	Robert	EX	Fall
Alvares	Jose	GV	

125
Castillo	Frankie	A	Dec.
Ramirez	Ernesto	EX	
Reyes	Josh	MCF	Dec.
Arreola	Alberto	WU	
Ferrer	Ruben	CAR	Fall
Langford	Michael	DP	

130
Contreras	Nick	SEL	Dec.
Nelson	Robby	KING	
Navarro	Vincent	SHAFT	Fall
Lorentez	Martin	SIE	
Perez	Fabian	CORC	Default
Quiroz	Isaac	DP	

135
Ballesteros	Adam	DP	Dec.
Tovar	Archie	SEL	
Arreola	Diego	WU	Fall
Doss	Noland	LIB-MAD	
Tamayo	Francisco	A	Fall
Rocha	Mario	MEN	

140
Cisneros	Joe	SEL	Fall
Martinez	Ricky	FIRE	
Varcia	Abel	A	Fall
Merrell	Cody	DP	
Terronies	Ezequiel	WU	Dec.
Mundhanke	Aaron	GV	

145
Espericueta	Lucas	SHAFT	Fall
Merrell	Caleb	DP	
Barajas	Eddie	MEN	Fall
Hicks	Chris	KER	
Sotelo	Erik	YOSE	Fall
Rojo	Adolfo	A	

152
Johnson	Zach	WASCO	Dec.
Post	Robert	TEHA	
Eskew	Brian	KING	Dec.
Cuen	Memo	FIRE	
Jaime	Jeff	CORC	Fall
Gutierrez	Ivan	GV	

160
Bautista	Alejandro	COAL	Dec.
Van Allman	Kurt	DP	
Hack	Tyler	TEHA	Dec.
Smith	David	LIB-MAD	
Mulligan	MacKenzie	SHAFT	Fall
Saran	Simon	WU	

171
Garcia	Jared	MCF	Fall
Valencia	Pedro	DP	
Ruiz	Abel	SEL	Dec.
Cervantes	Johnny	FIRE	
Wehurst	Jerry	TEHA	Default
Walker	Justin	SIE	

189
Noriega	Gino	TRAN	Fall
Lopez	Orlando	COAL	
Rodriguez	Abraham	WU	Fall
Lokadoo	Ronald	SHAFT	
Allarez	Jesus	DP	Forfeit
Vasquez	Chris	SEL	

(Continued on next page)

Sierra-Sequoia Division – Firebaugh
February 17-18, 2006

215
Mendoza	Francisco	DP	Dec.
Smith	Joe	TEHA	
Realteria	Michael	WU	Dec.
Lopez	Andrew	PAR	
Williams	Warren	SHAFT	Dec.
Furnish	Theodore	KER	

275
Alcala	Ricky	A	Fall
Bonilla	Chris	CORC	
Jimenez	Leobardo	DP	Fall
Celedon	Jacdob	SEL	
Aguilar	Andrew	COAL	Fall
Anderzon	Zach	LIB-MAD	

Tournament
1. Dos Palos 235
2. Selma 174.5
3. Arvin 146
4. Washington U. 134.5
5. Coalinga 113
6. Tehachapi 106.5
7. Shafter 89.5
8. Exeter 89
9. Liberty 87
10. Firebaugh 78
11. Caruthers 73
12. Kerman 63
13. McFarland 62
14. Golden Valley 57
15. Fowler 45 Tied for 15th
15. Mendota 45 Tied for 15th
17. Kingsburg 37
18. Corcoran 35
19. Wasco 30
20. Farmersville 29.5 Tied for 20th
20. Tranquility 29.5 Tied for 20th
22. Sierra 28
23. Parlier 27
24. Yosemite 16
25. Chowchilla 15
26. Dinuba 6

1977 Arvin High Wrestling Team

2002 Arvin High Wrestling Team

Central Section – Valley
1952-2000

Central Section

Date	Champion	Coach	Location
1/26/52	Roosevelt	Vico Bondietti	Oakdale
1/31/53	Roosevelt	Vico Bondietti	Fresno High
2/6/54	Roosevelt	Vico Bondietti	Tulare Union
2/12/55	Roosevelt	Vico Bondietti	Roosevelt/Fresno
2/11/56	Madera	Vern Brooks	Fresno High
1957	No Finals	N/A	N/A
2/15/58	Fresno	Dick Francis	Roosevelt/Fresno
2/21/59	Madera	Vern Brooks	Tulare Union
2/20/60	Madera	Vern Brooks	Bakersfield High
2/18/61	Madera	Vern Brooks	McLane/Fresno
2/17/62	East Bakersfield	Leon Tedder	Mt. Whitney/Visalia
2/16/63	East Bakersfield	Leon Tedder	Bakersfield College
2/22/64	Madera	Vern Brooks	McLane/Fresno
2/27/65	South Bakersfield	Joe Seay	Tulare Western
2/26/66	South Bakersfield	Joe Seay	South Bakersfield
2/25/67	South Bakresfield	Joe Seay	McLane/Fresno
2/24/68	Bakesfield High	Olan Polite	Reedley College
3/01/69	Madera	Al Kiddy	Bakersfield College
2/28/70	Madera	Al Kiddy	McLane/Fresno
2/27/71	South Bakersfield	Joe Seay	Monache/Porterville
3/04/72	Bakersfield High	Olan Polite	McLane/Fresno
2/24/73	Clovis	Dennis DeLiddo	Highland/Bakersfield
2/23/74	Clovis	Dennis DeLiddo	Mt. Whitney/Visalia
3/02/75	Clovis	Dennis DeLiddo	Tulare Western
2/2876	Clovis	Dennis DeLiddo	Fresno City College
2/26/77	Highland	Joe Barton	West Bakersfield
2/25/78	Monache	Drew Williams	Hanford
2/24/79	South Bakersfield	Gene Walker	Clovis
3/01/80	Highland	Jim Seay	Bakersfield College
2/28/81	Clovis	Dennis DeLiddo	Monache/Porterville
2/27/82	Clovis West	Lennis Cowell	Clovis West
2/26/83	Clovis West	Lennis Cowell	Bakersfield High
2/25/84	Clovis West	Lennis Cowell	Hanford
2/23/85	Clovis	Rodney Balch	Clovis West
3/01/86	Clovis	Rodney Balch	Bakersfield High
2/28/87	South Bakersfield	Gene Walker	Monache/Porterville
2/27/88	Clovis	Rodney Balch	Bullard/Fresno
2/25/89	Selma	Nick Quintana	Arvin
2/24/90	Madera	Corky Napier	Hanford
2/23/91	Clovis	Rodney Balch	Clovis
2/29/92	Clovis	Rodney Balch	Bakersfield College
2/27/93	Clovis	Rodney Blach	Mt. Whitney/Visalia
2/26/94	Clovis	Rodney Balch	Clovis
2/25/95	Bakersfield	David East	Arvin
2/24/96	Buchanan	Chris Hansen	Monache/Porterville
3/01/97	Buchanan	Chris Hansen	Clovis
2/28/98	Buchanan	Chris Hansen	Shafter
2/27/99	Clovis	Steve Tirapelle	Mt. Whitney/Visalia
2/26/2000	Clovis	Steve Tirapelle	Buchanan/Clovis

Central Section Most Outstanding Wrestlers

Starting in 1992 the Coyote Club sponsored the Lower/Upper Weights
Most Outstanding Wrestler Award

Year	Wrestler	School
1952	George Kezarian	Roosevelt
1953	Don Taylor	Hughson
1954	Don Westerling	Tulare
1955	Marvin Parnell	Roosevelt
1956	Bob Carr	Roosevelt
1959	Larry Carpenter	East Bakersfield
1966	Richard Simmons	South Bakersfield
1992	Coby Wright	Bakersfield
1992	Lalo Moz	Hanford
1993	Aaron Rodrigues	Wasco
1993	Ryan Silva	Monache
1994	Moises Perez	Madera
1994	Demes Cabral	Hanford
1995	Albert Garza	Sanger
1995	Dan Jackson	Kingsburg
1996	Alex Ortiz	Corcoran
1996	Sonny Pereschica	Kingsburg
1997	Jamie Garza	Sanger
1997	Tyler Lunn	Buchanan
1998	Ralph Lopez	Clovis West
1998	Tyler Lunn	Buchanan
1999	Jason Moreno	Firebaugh
1999	Josh Naus	Centennial
2000	Daniel Chapman	Centennial
2000	Chris Pendleton	Lemoore

Central Section – Oakdale High School
January 26, 1952

103
Asaki	Tom	HAN	Dec.
O'Neal	Jim	ROOS	

112
Rarber	Herb	FRE	Dec.
Venhaus	Jim	OAK	

120
Desouza	Dennis	OAK	
Hines	Ted	HUGH	

127
Parra	Art	ROOS	Dec.
Strautmanie	Augie	HUGH	

133
Hitchcock	Joe	TUL	Dec.
Rena	Mat	CORC	

138
Reynoso	Bill	HAN	Fall
McCleeny	Reese	FRE	

145
Sherman	Grant	HAN	Dec.
Myers	Vern	OAK	

154
Martinho	Tony	CORC	Fall
Gomes	Bob	HUGH	

166
Kezarian	George	ROOS	Fall
Roberts	Ed	FRE	

175
Knecht	Vern	OAK	Dec.
Der Garabedian	Ara	ROOS	

191
Dee	Vince	HUGH	Dec.
Short	Phil	HUGH	

HWT
Kelly	Gordon	FRE	Dec.
Anderson	Jerry	ROOS	

Tournament
1. Roosevelt   20
2. Fresno   17
2. Hughson   17
4. Oakdale   16
4. Hanford   16
6. Corcoran   9
7. Tulare   5

*94 wrestlers participated

Coaches Stan Pavko and Chuck Coker of Modesto Junior College selected the Most Outstanding Wrestler: Goerge Kezarian

First Row: Stanley Moran, Ara Michaelian, Jim O'Neal, Art Parra, Hubert Donny, Bob Cherrie. Second Row: Louie Duran, Robert Donny, Dennis Isheim, Billy Young, Ken McCoy. Third Row: Tom Ryan, Armen Kiramidjian, Jerry Anderson, Eugene Sadoian, George Kezerian, Ara Der Garabedian, Charles Mann, Ray Ryals.

1952 Roosevelt High Wrestling Team – CIF Champions

Central Section – Fresno High
January 31, 1953

103
Zakar	Bob	ROOS	Ref. Dec.
Jones	Gary	HUGH	

112
Jones	David	HUGH	2-0
Asaki	Jack	HUGH	

120
Padilla	Manuel	TUL	1-0
Escobar	Herb	HAN	

127
Gomes	Norman	HAN	Ref. Dec.
Jones	Alan	FRE	

133
Ishiam	Dennis	ROOS	Ref. Dec.
Harris	Ted	HUGH	

138
Hitchcock	Kenneth	TUL	Ref. Dec.
Moran	Stan	ROOS	

145
Harrison	Stanley	HUGH
Loring	Jesse	TUL

154
Taylor	Don	HUGH	Fall
Amey	Wilbert	MAD*	

165
Latoueau	Eddie	OAK	2-0
Stragio	Bob	HAN	

175
Duran	Louie	ROOS	Fall
Leimbach	Chuck	ROOS	

191
Fox	Calvin	ROOS	Ref. Dec.
Kloppenburg	Don	ROOS	

HWT
Ryan	Tom	ROOS	1-0
Nickell	Otto		

Tournament
1. Roosevelt 40
2. Hughson 29
3. Hanford 13
4. Tulare 10
5. Oakdale 8
6. Madera 6
7. Fresno 3

*Only Loss All Season

Officials
Hans Widenhoefer
Doug Bray
Bob Schoendube

Central Section – Tulare Union
February 6, 1954

Tournament
1. Roosevelt 34
2. Hanford 26
3. Tulare 22
4. Madera 15
5. Oakdale 7
6. Fresno 5
7. Hughson 0

103
Parnell	Marvin	ROOS	Dec.	
Trilloo	Al	MAD		

112
Zaker	Bob	ROOS	Fall	5:53
Hernandez	Fernando	HAN		

120
Asaki	Jack	HAN	Dec.
Friske	Merle	OAK	

127
Carr	Bob	ROOS	Dec.
Padilla	Manuel	Tul	

133
Marquez	Marvin	MAD	Fall	5:56
Reynoso	Ralph	HAN		

138
Isheim	Dennis	ROOS	Dec.
Hagadorn	Larry	HAN	

145
Richmond	Charles	HAN	Dec.
Hubert	Donny	ROOS	

154
Jordan	Eddie		Dec.
McCoy	Kenneth	ROOS	

165
Allen	John	TUL	Dec.
Liddle	Ted	OAK	

175
Bockenoogen	Ken	MAD	Dec.
Krouse	Ray	TUL	

191
Westerling	Don	TUL	Dec.
Fox	Calvin	ROOS	

HWT
Moses	Jiim	HAN	Dec.
Carvalho	Richard	TUL	

Central Section – Roosevelt/Fresno
February 12, 1955

103
Jaramillo	Louie	TUL	Dec
Rodriguez	Frank	MAD	

112
Nelson	Jim	FRE	Dec.
Turk	Jan	TUL	

120
Parnell	Marvin	ROOS	Fall
Martinez	Dale	CORC	

127
Padillo	Manuel	TUL	Dec.
O'Neal	Jim	ROOS	

133
Jones	Robert	MAD	Fall
Taylor	Don	HAN	

138
Carr	Bob	ROOS	Dec.
Castro	Merle	TUL	

145
Richmond	Charles	HAN	Dec.
Hubert	Donny	ROOS	

154
Hadadoen	Laqwrence	HAN	Dec.
Baker	Lee	FRE	

165
Rose	Don	ROOS	Dec.
Musick	Bill	MAD	

175
Bockenoogen	Ken	MAD	Dec.
Marino	Eddie	ROOS	

191
Westerling	Don	TUL	Fall
Rauta	Karl	HAN	

HWT
Palacios	Eddie	ROOS	Fall
Wilson	Don	MAD	

Tournament
Roosevelt	34
Tulare	26
Madera	22
Hanford	17
Fresno	8
Corcoran	3

*72 Wrestlers Participated

Officials
Hans Widenhoefer
Doug Bray

Central Section – Fresno High
February 11, 1956

Tournament
1. Madera   32
2. Tulare   27
3. Roosevelt 26
4. Corcoran   13
5. Fresno   3
6. Hanford   0

103
| Rodriguez | Frank | MAD | Fall |
| Castro | Richard | TUL | |

112
| Parnell | Marvin | ROOS | Dec. |
| Martinez | Dale | CORC | |

120
| Bilvado | Manuel | TUL | Dec. |
| Zakar | Bob | ROOS | |

127
| Seagraves | Art | MAD | Dec. |
| Hernandez | | ROOS | |

133
| Marquez | Ismael | MAD | Dec. |
| Villanueva | Phil | ROOS | |

138
| Carr | Bob | ROOS | Dec. |
| Owens | Gerald | TUL | |

145
| Terronez | Gabe | CORC | Dec. |
| Gallegos | Ernie | MAD | |

154
| Saenz | Jim | TUL | Dec. |
| Lilles | John | MAD | |

165
| Allen | John | TUL | Fall |
| Martin | | MAD | |

175
| Lasher | Roland | MAD | Dec. |
| Laird | Jerry | TUL | |

191
| Sanders | Louis | ROOS | Dec. |
| Ortega | Jose | CORC | |

HWT
| Streshley | Bill | CORC | Fall |
| Mogenan | Paul | FRE | |

Central Section

1957: No Central Section Championship Meet

North San Joaquin Valley – Roosevelt/Fresno
February 16, 1957

103
Rodriguez	Ace	MAD
Nehring	Larry	FRE
Garcia	Fay	ROOS
William	Earl	CHOW

112
Rodriguez	Frank	MAD
Quinonez	Jerry	ROOS
Stevenson	Leland	FFRE
Vanderveen	Norman	CHOW

120
Davies	Ed	FRE
Faulkner	Brent	ROOS
Amey	Bob	CHOW
Diaz	Ed	MAD

127
Villanueva	Phil	ROOS
Mariscal	Albert	CHOW
McCracken	Richard	
McCauley	Dennis	

133
Marquez	Ismael	MAD
Nelson	Jim	FRE
Beza	Martin	ROOS
No Fourth		

138
Kohl	Norman	FRE
Oliver	Roy	MAD
Cochran	Stan	ROOS
Boyer	Don	CHOW

145
Ortega	Joe	FRE
Lloyd	Eli	CHOW
Hammer	Jack	ROOS
Brown	Travis	MAD

154
*Tony	Larry	FRE
Hance	Burton	ROOS
Flanigan	Terry	CHOW
McGaughey	Kelvyn	MAD

165
Lilles	John	MAD
Carmichael	Jim	ROOS
Wamhof	Don	FRE
Rhoades	Leonard	CHOW

175
Lasher	Roland	MAD
Morris	John	ROOS
Aquino	Joe	CHOW
Bridges	Beau	FRE

191
Sanders	Louis	ROOS
Rankin	Frank	FRE
Vancil	Ken	MAD
Aquino	Manuel	CHOW

HWT
Rodarte	Narcy	ROOS
Hollbroom	Bill	FRE
Maneer	Ken	MAD
No Fourth		

Tournament
1. Fresno 44
2. Roosevelt 38
3. Madera 38
4. Chowchilla 8

Top two in each weight qualified for Northern California Championships

Outstanding Wrestler
Larry Tone

Coach Bruce Pfutzenreuter South Bakersfield

Central Section – Roosevelt/Fresno
February 15, 1958

103
Nehring	Larry	FRE
Garcia	Ray	ROOS

112
Rodriguez	Ausencio	MAD
Smith	Karl	FRE

120
Rodriguez	Frank	MAD
Crouch	Gary	ROOS

127
Bilvado	Manuel	TUL
Beza	Martin	ROOS

133
Marquez	Ismael	MAD
Reyes	Ted	ROOS

138
Grooms	Bill	CORC
Ortega	Joe	FRE
Noble	Lee	B

145
Brammer	Jack	ROOS
Holquin	Adrian	TUL
Morris	Bill	B

154
Bookout	Ralph	EB
Bridgeford	Roger	NB

165
Cariaga	Ross	FRE
Sherrill	Zane	NB

175
Hunt	Bill	B
Aquino	Joe	CHOW
Rivera	Don	EB

191
Vorhees	Bob	MAD
Putnam	Dave	MT.W
Edmondson	Dave	B

HWT
Newcomb	Chuck	B
Turner	Ron	ROOS
Marshall	Roger	EB

Tournament
1. Fresno 84
2. Madera 78
3. Roosevelt 68
4. Bakersfield 56
5. Hanford 34
6. Tulare 33
7. E. Bakersfield 32
8. Corcoran 26
9. N. Bakersfield 25
10. Mt. Whitney 21
11. Chowchilla 19
12. Porterville 12
13. Redwood 6
14. Arvin 6
15. S Bakersfield 1

Total Teams: 16

Roger Bridgeford and Zane Sherrill
Both 2nd in the CIF - 1958
North Bakersfield

Alan Adams
South Bakersfield
2nd CIF 1960

Central Section – Tulare
February 21, 1959

103
Fimbrez	Louie	MAD	
Rodriguez	Frank	ROOS	
Bispo	Gene	SB	(21-3)*
Bridgeford	Charles	NB	

112
Rodriguez	Ausencio	MAD	
Whitson	Larry	A	(15-3)*
Bloomberg	Al	SB	

120
Marquez	Sam	MAD	
Whittemore	Clem		
Hodges	Harry	NB	

127
Bush	Ron	ROOS	
Bedford	Willard	SB	(32-11)*
Haddad	Angelo	EB	

133
Reyes	Ted	ROOS	
Moreland	Danny	EB	

138
Nelson	Jerry	FFRE	
Wells	Terry	SB	
Allen	Richard		
Varner	Bob	B	

145
Johnson	Errol	MAD	
Ortega	Joe	FRE	
Ethridge	Bob	A	(14-5)*

154
Carpenter	Larry	EB
Brown	Travis	MAD

165
Salcido	John	EB
Bressler	Richard	HAN

175
Corley	Earl	SB	(22 Falls/38-7)* (22-1)*
Ford	Jack	A	

191
Aquino	Joe	CHOW
Edmondson	Dave	B

HWT
Reade	Lynn	A	(15-4-1)*
Brown	Charles	EB	
Solis	Joe	CORC	

Tournament
1. Madera 66
2. E. Bakersfield 47
3. Fresno 42
4. Roosevelt 42
5. S. Bakersfield 41

Top three in each weight to the Northern California in Turlock

* Career records

**Earl Corley
South Bakersfield
1959 CIF Champion
Wrestling
1960 2nd CIF Golf**

Central Section – Bakersfield
February 20, 1960

103
Rodriguez	Frank	ROOS	Dec.
Martinez	Joe	EB	
Figg	Joe	BULL	Dec.
Montez	John	DEL	

112
Stuckey	Roy	MAD	Dec.
Villarreal	Manuel	SB	
Jones	James	HAN	
Alcarez	Marshall	FRE	

120
Whittlemoore	Clem	FRE	Dec.
Whitson	Larry	A	
King	John	MAD	
Heckman	Jim	SB	

127
Marquez	Sam	MAD	
Aguilar	Steve	HAN	
Raasch	Lol	PORT	Dec.
McCamey	Dennis	ROOS	

133
Patterson	Andy	HAN	Dec.
Wagoner	Ron	FRE	
Gillock	Chuck	ROOS	Dec.
Son	Larry	MT.W	

138
Washington	Drue	SB		(20-3)*
Barker	Roger	MAD		
Stephenson	Ron	FRE	Fall	
Royal	Carlos	A		

145
Vasquez	Ben	ROOS	Dec.
Allen	Richard	MAD	
Lucio	Dave	TUL	Dec.
Flores	Manuel	RED	

154
Thetford	Dan	ROOS	Dec.	
Schrader	Carl	B		(11-3)*
Wells	Ken	A	Dec.	
Main	Ron	MT.W		

165
Kirby	Larry	PORT	Dec.
Bressler	Richard	HAN	
Shipley	Bill	FRE	Dec.
Enrique	Armando	MAD	

175
*Salcido	John	EB	Dec.
Crook	Ron	MAD	
Gallegos	Frank	HAN	Dec.
Clark	Jack	TUL	

191
McGrew	John	TUL	Dec.
Gillis	Paul	MCL	
Dewhirst		REED	Dec.
Moss	Bill	MT.W	

HWT
Garrett	Joe	EB	
Adams	Alan	SB	
Watkins	Charlies	MT.W	Dec.
Anderson	Robert	TUL	

Tournament
1. Madera 72
2. Roosevelt 55
3. Hanford 47
4. S. Bakersfield 39
5. Fresno 39
6. Tulare Union 39
7. E. Bakersfield 35
8. Mt. Whitney 23
9. Porterville 21
10. Arvin 16
11. Bakersfield 14
12. McLane 13
13. Bullard 8
14. Reedley 8
15. Redwood 4
16. Delano 4
17. Sanger 3
18. Kingsburg 1
Caruthers 0
Chowchilla 0
Corcoran 0
Dinuba 0
N. Bakersfield 0
Exeter 0

* Reedley is Small Schools Champion

* Undefeated

( ) Record

Manuel Villarreal
South Bakersfield
2nd CIF

Central Section – McLane/Fresno
February 18, 1961

103
Johanson	Steve	MAD	4-0
Bowman	Dan	RED	
Pletcher	Delmer	EB	
Flores	Robert	MT.W	

112
Rodriguez	Frank	ROOS	4-3
Marquez	Dave	MAD	
Cooper	Al	MCL	
Martinez	Joe	EB	

120
Whitson	Larry	A	4-3
Jones	James	HAN	

127
Mendoza	Jim	MAD	7-3
Gearhart	Dave	MCL	
Moreland	Terry	EB	

133
Aguilar	Steve	HAN	Fall	3rd
Jacobson	Bob	ROOS		
**King	Leon	B		
Clifton	Jim	MAD		

138
Fenton	Chuck	B	3-2
Daily	John	KING	

145
Sullivan	Phil	TW	Fall	2nd
Zinkin	Harold	FRE		
Vizcarra	Milo	MAD		
Bridger	Jim	SB		

154
Lung	Bob	FRE	3-0
Andrews	Fred	MCL	

165
Wells	Ken	A	3-1	
Salcido	John	EB		(20-1-1)

175
Gibson	Jewett	SANG	2-0	
Dewar	George	B	13-1-1	(21-4-1)*

191
*Burroughs	Bob	DEL	14-6
Adam	Alan	SB	

HWT
Garrett	Joe	EB	Fall	1st
Pye	Ernie	DEL		

Tournament
1. Madera 76
2. E. Bakersfield 46
3. McLane 39
4. Bakersfield 30
5. Hanford 29
6. Fresno 28
7. Roosevelt 28
8. Arvin 26
9. Delano 24
10. Kingsburg 19

Total Schools: 31

*Unbeaten
**One loss
( ) Record

**Drue Washington of South Bakersfield
CIF Champion**

Central Section – Mt. Whitney/Visalia
February 17, 1962

103
*Lindley	Jim	EB	
Hernandez	Robert	TUL	
Horton		SANG	
Elander	Robert	KING	

112
Johanson	Steve	MAD	
Garcia	John	TUL	
Nunez	Joe	REED	
Carter		RED	

120
Marquez	David	MAD	
Gonzales	Jack	TUL	
Belveal	Dan	NB	
Pletcher	Delmer	EB	

127
Cox	Ed	SANG	
Wing	Chet	ROOS	
Simpson	Russ	MCL	
Stricker	Mike	SB	

133
Figg	Joe	BULL	
Mendoza	Jim	MAD	
Machado	Ron	TW	
Gonzales	Fernando	Tul	

138
Fenton	Chuck	B	18-1
Moreland	Terry	EB	
Clifton	Jim	MAD	
Doucette	Carl	MT.W	

145
Jacobson	Bobby	HAN	
King	Leon	B	
Delis	Pete	EB	
Knapp	Jim	BULL	

154
Reed	Harold	HAN	
Robertson	Mike	B	15-3
Kennett	Bill	NB	
Parks	Bill	BULL	

165
Sullivan	Phil	TW	
Bradford	Claude	EB	
Kirby	Frank	MCL	
Gold	David	B	12-3

175
Van Worth	Ken	SB	47-7
Tullis	Don	DIN	
Haskins	Arthur	HAN	
Stiers	Bill	FRE	

191
Dimble	Howard	EB O.T. Ref. Dec.	
**Beard	John	B	19-1 29-8-4
Aquina	Tony	CHOW	
Gillis	David	TUL	

HWT
Gartung	Mark	PORT
Ruby	George	MCL
Brogdin	Mike	NB
Carter	John	SB

Tournament
1. E. Bakersfield 58
2. Bakersfield 55
3. Madera 42
4. Tulare 34
5. McLane 29
6. S. Bakersfield 26
7. Sangaer 26
8. Roosevelt 24
9. Hanford 24
10. Tulare W. 22
11. Bullard 21
12. N. Bakersfield 21
13. Porterville 15
14. Chowchilla 10
14. Dinuba 10
16. Mt. Whitney 9
17. Reedley 6
18. Kingsburg 5
19. Redwood 5
20. Delano 4
21. Fresno 2
22. Arvin 1
22. Clovis 1
22. Corcoran 1

Merced-El Capitan 0
Merced 0
Exeter 0
Dos Palos 0

*Unbeaten
**One Loss

Central Section – Bakersfield College
February 16, 1963

95
Morgan	Charles	MCL	Fall	1:11
Bingham	Jay	B		(17-5)*
Morgan	Quinn	EB	2-0	
Amasalian	Charles	ROOS		

103
Marquez	Ron	FRE	3-0	
Sordi	Doug	MAD		
Guerrero	Fred	CORC	10-2	
Davenport	Bob	Ex		

112
Hernandez	Robert	TUL	1-0	
Boado	Frank	A		
Richards	Craig	MCL	Fall	3:22
Engebits	Ernie	FRE		

120
Lindley	Jim	EB	9-5
Nino	Nick	EX	
April	Ray	MAD	2-0
Martinez	Leroy	REED	

127
Simpson	Russ	ROOS	4-2
Rocha	Dave	FRE	
Turek	Dennis	HAN	4-2
Bradford	Curtis	EB	

133
Scales	Jim	BULL	Fall	6:22 O.T.
Wing	Chet	ROOS		
Manfredi	Stell	MAD	1-0	
Leach	Brad	TUL		

138
Mendoza	Jim	ROOS	4-1	
Kataiun	Al	MCL		
Machado	Ron	TW	Fall	4:25
Jones	Del	CORC		

145
Jacobo	Armando	ROOS	4-1
Starr	Mike	NB	
Schnee	Al	EB	7-3
Bonilla	Steve	CORC	

154
Kinnett	Bill	NB	2-0
Sellers	Joe	EB	
Mancini	Ken	PORT	4-2
Lott	Ron	MCL	

165
Greer	Jerry	SB	6-2	(21-0)*
Woods	John	RED		
Marcy	Richard	MAD	2-0	
Massey	Clydell	TW		

175
Kirby	Frank	MCL	2-1	
Van Worth	Ken	SB	(42-7)	
Harralson	Bill	B	Forfeit	(16-5)*
Mackey	Allen	MAD		

191
Haskins	Art	HAN	5-1
Hammlett	Lee	EB	
Aquino	Tony	CHOW	4-3
Campbell	Pat	NB	

HWT
Smith	Van	PORT	3-2
Bateman	Ray	EB	
Newman	Jim	MT.W	
Masaoka	Calvin	SANG	

Tournament

1. E. Bakersfield	68	
2. McLane	60	
3. Roosevelt	44	
4. Madera	39	
5. N. Bakersfield	30	
6. Fresno	28	
7. S. Bakersfield	27	
8. Porterfield	25	
9. Bakersfield	23	
10. Hanford	19	
10. Tulare	19	
12. Corcoran	17	
13. Bullard	16	
14. Exeter	15	
15. Tulare W.	13	
16. Redwood	11	
17. Sanger	10	
18. Arvin	9	
18. Mt. Whitney	9	
20. Reedley	6	
20. Chowchilla	6	
22. Clovis	2	
22. Delano	2	
22. Dos Palso	2	
22. Kingsburg	2	
26. Foothill	1	
Merced	0	

Jim Lindley Undefeated
Frank Kirby won 22 consecutive matches
Ken Van Worth's 42-7 record was a career record

* Record

Central Section – McLane
February 22, 1964

95
Harris	Larry	MER	
Sanborn	Ray	MCL	
Nall	Barry	B	(16-5)*
Abunois	Frank	MAD	

103
Heath	Roy	SB	5-1	(26-1)*
Bingham	Jay	B		
Sordi	Doug	MAD		
Madrigal	Richard	MCL		

112
Rios	Pedro	MAD	
Stiles	Chuck	FOOT	
Alvedriz		TUL	
Richer	Eddie	DEL	

120
Flores	Jesse	EB	
Johansen	Bob	MAD	
Chavez	Art	SB	
Jones	Roy	HAN	

127
King	Tim	MAD	
Bradford	Curtis	EB	
Dove	Gary	PORT	
Brown	Mike	B	(17-2-1)*

133
Lindley	Jim	EB	
Turek	Dennis	HAN	
Oller	Kim	FRE	
Archuleta	Joe	CENT	

138
Green	Steve	HAN	
Collier	Mike	SB	
Morrison		REED	
Blake	Alex	B	

145
Machado	Ron	TW	
Hinson	Chuck	FOOT	
Edwards	Marshall	DEL	
Baker	Willie	MAD	

154
Possum	Neil	TUL	
Manuels	Gary	MT.W	
Christiansen	Dean	B	
Findley	Ron	NB	

165
Woods	John	RED	(68-8)*
Munos	Mike	B	
Smith	Carl	NB	
Noland		HAN	

175
Cotton	Tim	SB	(20-0)*
Mackey	Allen	MAD	
Droullard	Mike	MCL	
McClaughry	Roger	CHOW	

191
Tate	Bill	MAD	
Graves	Jody	MT.W	
Polzin	Bill	ROOS	
Barton	Joe	SB	

HWT
Culliton	Lee	SB	(21-2)*
Smith	Van	PORT	
Brase	Ben	MCL	
Gilson	Bob	REED	

Tournment
1. Madera 79
2. S. Bakersfield 56
3. Bakersfield 48
4. E. Bakersfield 41
5. McLane 37
6. Hanford 34
7. Tulare 23
8. Mt. Whitney 22
9. Foothill 21
10. Porterville 18

Total Schools: 32

* Record

John Woods
Redwood High
Record 68-8
2nd NCAA
Cal Poly

Tim Cotton
1964 CIF Champion
South Bakersfield

Central Section - Tulare Western
February 27, 1965

95
Serros	Jack	B	6-2	(27-1)*
Abundis	Frank	MAD		
Cosme	Herb	NB	Fall	

103
Moraga	John	ROOS	Fall	1:46
King	Sam	MAD		

112
Heath	Roy	SB	2-1	
Contreras	Renaldo	KING		(28-1)*
Herrera	Emmett	B		(22-4)*

120
Chavez	Art	SB	4-0 (27-0)
Sanchez	Richard	FOOT	

127
Roberts	Luis	FRE	
Litterell	Ron	NB	

133
Folmer	Jerry	ROOS	4-2	
Vasquez	Mike	MT.W		
Sweetser	John	NB		
Moland	Calvin	B		(22-6-1)*

138
Collier	Mike	SB	4-2	(25-0)*
Morrison		REED		

145
Green	Steve	HAN	2-0
Nichols	Bob	FRE	

154
Welch	Ben	B	9-1 (24-4)*(35-10)**
Vaughn		SANG	

165
Simmons	Richard	SB	8-4	
Christenson	Dean	B		(24-4)*

175
Munoz	Mike	B	O.T. Inj. Def.	***
Barton	Joe	SB		(24-5)*

191
Tate	Bill	MAD	8-2	
Rasley	Rocky	SB		(23-1-1)*
Graves	Jody	MT.W		

HWT
Cullition	Lee	SB	10-3	(26-0/21 Falls)*
Jeppi	Frank	B		(21-9)*
Castaneda	Roger	PORT		

Tournament
1. S. Bakersfield 98
2. Bakersfield 84
3. Madera 60
4. Roosevelt 42
5. N. Bakersfield 32
6. Porterville 28
7. Mt. Whitney 25
7. Fresno 25
9. Hanford 24
9. Hoover 24
11. Reedley 21

Career Records
Art Chavez 53-4-1
Mike Collier (40-4)
Joe Barton (48-9)

* Record
**Career

Lee Cullton
South Bakersfield
Two-time CIF Champion
One-time 3rd CIF
81-3 career wins with 54 falls

***Munoz, Mike 24-5* 48-23**

Central Section – South Bakersfield
February 26, 1966

95
Cosme	Herb	NB	8-3	
Banvelos	Rudy	HAN		
Herrera	Don	B	4-3	
Ensslin	Steve	PORT		

103
Serros	Jack	B	6-0	(29-1)*
Molina	Hilario	RED		
Seabourn	Bill	SB	5-4	
Sanchez	Paul	FOOT		

112
Heath	Roy	SB	3-0	(34-1)*
King	Sam	MAD		
Rivera	Joe	REED	4-3	
Henson	Gene	FOOT		

120
Contreras	Renaldo	KING	7:35 O.T.	
Bolgara	Ray	FRE		
Yamamoto	Gordon	CL	2-0	
Sanchez	Richard	FOOT		

127
Jones	Roger	HAN	5-0	**
Mason	Louie	WI		
Walker	Gene	SB	9-6	
Patino	Vic	A		

133
Valdez	Albert	B	1-0	(28-1)*
Diaz	Charles	FRE		
Burnett	Bruce	NB	2-1	
Turner	Sam	TUL		

138
Varner	Steve	B	7-6 O.T.	(24-5)*
Bauers	Wayne	FRE		
Montgomery	Danny	MCL	15-4	
Rabbon	Everett	PORT		

145
Gollmyer	Sam	B	Fall 5:43	(28-1)*
Goss	Jack	NB		
Pacini	Mike	FRE	8-2	
Holcomb	Billy	MAD		

154
Herndon	Bob	A	15-5	**
Duncan	Ken	ROOS		
Hudson	Gary	HOOV		
Mayberry	George	PORT		

165
Martin	John	SB	9-1	(30-1)*
Hull	Brad	MCL		
Roche	Dan	EX	6-0	
Ketscher	Mike	REED		

175
Simmons	Richard	SB	1:25	(35-0/31 Falls)*
Ballinger	Rick	DP		
Medaris	John	FRE	6-0	
Riser	Bruce	MCL		

191
Hultgren	Mark	FOOT	2-0	
Valos	Tom	EB		
Ortiz	Ed	HOOV	6-0	
Medrano	Paul	SANG		

HWT
Castaneda	Roger	PORT	2-1	
Graves	Jody	MT.W		
Culliton	Lee	SB	Fall 3:18	(34-1)
Hulana	Al	MERC		

Tournament
1. S. Bakersfield 71
2. Bakersfield 66
3. Fresno 48
4. N. Bakersfield 33
5. Porterville 31
6. McLane 30
7. Foothill 28
8. Hanford 25
9. E. Bakersfield 22
10. Madera 20

Career
Richard Simmons (54-1/40 Falls)
Roy Heath (106-6-1)
Lee Culliton (81-3/xxxxxxx) (57 Falls)
Jack Serros (xxxx)(59-2)
Sam Gollmyer (48-8-1)
Sam King (91-11)

* Record
** Undefeated

Richard Simmons
South Bakersfield
California Wrestler of the Year 1966
Two-time CIF Champion

Central Section – McLane
February 25, 1967

95
Williams	Tom	SB	4-2	(34-4-1)*
Morgan	Larry	EB		
Inouye	Bob	MCL	4-3	
Serros	Tony	B		
Krivis	Steve	KING	5-0	
Smith	Clifton	ED		

103
Cosme	Herb	NB	8-5	
Yoshida	David	CL		
Lawrence	Mark	B	4-0	(33-8)*(83-13)
Little	Larry	SB		
Price	Terry	KING	3-0	
Ensslin	Steve	PORT		

112
King	Sam	MAD	5-0	
Jones	David	HOOV		
Seabourn	Bill	SB	7-3	(30-9)*
Amstutz	Doug	FOOT		
Yamamoto	Tony	CL	3-0	
Lindley	David	EB		

120
Contreras	Renaldo	KING	10-2	(29-0)*
Roberts	Alan	NB		
Herrera	Karl	B	4-1	(33-6)*
Moulton	Bill	MCL		
Carr	Mike	ROOS	Fall	2:47
Harold	Mark	HOOV		

127
Walker	Gene	SB	5-0	(37-4)*
Crowder	Cecil	FOOT		
Vela	Tito	MCL	7-5	
Shimuzu	Gene	CL		
Story	Dwayne	PORT	5-0	
Smart	Joe	NB		

133
Shearer	Ron	EB	3-2	
Burnett	Bruce	NB		
Jones	Del	HAN	4-1	
Gomez	Pedro	CORC		
Wall	Jeff	PORT	4-2	
Finch	John	SB		

138
Delbosque	Joe	DP	7-0	(41-0)*
Garcia	Mike	WB		
Jones	David	NB	5-2	
Garcia	Ken	EB		
Anderson	Jeff	KING	Def.	
Ketscher	David	REED		

145
Ivery	Cliff	SB	12-5	(39-1)*
Rabbon	Everett	PORT		
Ingraham	Bruce	MERC	6-1	
Ervin	Robert	ED		
Flores	Bob	RED	2-1	
Sorenson	Steve	MCL		

154
Alvarez	Richard	B	Fall 4:36	(34-4-1)*
Williams	Wes	CORC		
Goss	Jack	NB	Fall	3:04
Hines	Doug	HAN		
Phillips	Tom	FOOT	6-0	
Magoaleno	Vincent	DP		

165
Nigos	Joe	DEL	Fall	1:49
Powell	Steve	MCL		
Smith	Carl	CENT	7-1	
Napier	Corky	MAD		
Beasley	Lanny	EB	4-0	
Diaz	Ruben	RED		

175
Miller	John	NB	7-1	(44-0)*
Rodman	Alan	EB		
Nelms	Doyal	PORT	5-4	
Wurtsmith	Dale	EEX		
Estrada	Tom	SB	12-1	(31-9-2)
Sheehan	Dennis	DEL		

191
Robeskey	Jim	B	5-0	(36-3)*
Padilla	Mark	SB		
Pickrell	Alan	KING	D/F	
Vose	Doug	BULL		
Medrano	Paul	SANG	5-4	
Schnider	Greg	RED		

(Continued on next page)

Central Section – McLane
February 25, 1967

HWT
Bedel	Jim	ROOS	11-6
Herrera	Art	FRE	
Rucker	Sam	EB	Default
Borba	John	HAN	
Williams	Wallace	SB	4-0
Thomas	Mark	B	

Tournament
1. S. Bakersfield 78
2. N. Bakersfield 76
3. Bakersfield 60
4. E. Bakersfield 57
5. McLane 40
6. Kingsburg 33
7. Porterville 31
8. Madera 27
9. Clovis 25
10. Roosevelt 22
10. Foothill 22

Total Teams: 42

* Record

Career
Sam King 65-2 2 years – Career 91-11
Joe Nigos Unbeaten 2 ties
Renaldo Contreras 96-4
Herb Cosme – 79-7
Ron Shearer – 50-6

John Martin of South Bakersfield
CIF Champion

1966 CIF Champions
South Bakersfield
Back (l-r) Lee Culliton, Mark Padilla, Richard Simmons, John Martin, Cliff Stock, Ed Henderson, Vernon Peeling
Front (l-r) Eugene Walker, Vernon Varner, Jack Sloss, Roy Heath, Bill Seaborn, Tom Williams

Central Section – Reedley College
February 24, 1968

95
Serros	Tony	B	9-1	(43-0)*
Hernandez	Alex	CORC		
Inouye	Robert	MCL	2-0	
Garcia	Joe	ROOS		
Grogg	Doug	HOOV	20-0	
Enos	Dennis	TW		

103
Herrera	Billy	B	7-0 O.T.	(38-8)*
Gonzalez	Rudy	EB		
Marquex	Ruben	MAD	3-0	
Tetarakis	Tony	DP		
Cantu	Gilbert	SANG		
Clark	Lynn	HOOV		

112
Little	Larry	SB	8-6
Jones	David	HOOV	
Morgan	Larry	EB	7-0
Guerrero	Tony	CORC	
Watkins	Richard	B	10-4
Holman	Pete	MCL	

120
Lawrence	Mark	B	6-0 (83-13 career)
Morgan	Jon	EB	
Moulton	Bill	MCL	Fall 1:30
Yamamoto	Tom	CL	
Kendig	Marty	MT.W	5-4 O.T.
Price	Terry	KING	

127
Seabourn	Bill	SB	Fall 3:41
Manny	Bruce	B	
Shimizo	Geno	CL	5-4
Vela	Tito	MCL	
Moland	Fred	CORC	4-0
Perez	Gilbert	DP	

133
Whithead	Steve	MAD	4-3	
Peterson	Chuck	B	(36-2-2)*	(73-24-3)
Greco	Bob	MCL	5-1	
Black	Danny	SHAFT		
Costales	Edward	DP	3-1	
Christy		SIE		

138
Burnett	Bruce	NB	7-0	(42-2)
Arechiga	Andy	EB		
Cook	Allyn	TUL	1-0	
Rude	Allan	B		
Morrison	Bob	DEL	10-4	
Larabee	Dave	MERC		

145
Crowder	Cecil	FOOT	3-1
Saunders	Dean	B	
Walker	Gene	SB	5-1
Smart	Joe	NB	
Karr	Bill	HOOV	2-0
Salwasser	George	CENT	

154
Rabbon	Everett	PORT	12-0
Lindholm	Ray	RED	
McManus	Dana	KING	6-1 O.T.
Mendia	Xavier	CENT	
Ball	Dennis	HOOV	7-0
Howe	Goerge	CL	

165
Alvarez	Richard	B	6-5	(39-1)*
Tribble	Larry	MAD		
Smith	Carl	CENT	6-1	
Platten	Mike	HOOV		
Garabedian	Wayne	MCL		
Rains	Brian	FOOT		

175
Shepard	Walt	B	9-4	(42-1)*
Blalock	Bob	NB		
Wurtsmith	Dale	EX	4-1	
Wall	Fred	PORT		
Smith	Al	CENT	5-1 O.T.	
Diaz	John	RED		

191
Miller	John	NB	5-1	
Rodman	Alan	EB		
Watson	Don	MAD	7-2	
Cox	Ron	MT.W		
Grist		RED	Fall	3:22
McLaughlin	Dennis	HOOV		

Correction – Serros, Tony 44-0 Career 122-9-2

(Continued on next page)

Central Section – Reedley College
February 24, 1968

HWT

Bigge	Roy	MCL	4-0	
Aquino	Albert	CHOW		
Rucker	Sam	EB	Fall	3:03
Dalerio	Al	CL		
Cereighino	Dan	MAD	6-5 O.T.	
Rawls	Chris	EX		

Tournament

1. Bakersfield	131
2. E. Bakersfield	77
3. McLane	67
4. N. Bakersfield	57
5. Madera	53
6. Hoover	46
7. S. Bakersfield	44
8. Porterville	29
9. Clovis	28
10. Central	27
10. Corcoran	27
12. Redwood	26
13. Foothill	21
14. Chowchilla	18
15. Dos Palos	17
16. Kingsburg	16
17. Mt. Whitney	15
18. Tulare	12
18. Exeter	12
20. Sanger	10
20. Shafter	10
22. Roosevelt	7
22. Delano	7
24. Reedley	4
24. Tulare Western	4
26. Hanford	2
26. Merced	2
26. Bullard	2
26. Washington U.	2
26. Sierra	2
31. Woodlake	1
31. Edison	1
31. Arvin	1
Dinuba	0
Fresno	0
Laton	0
Selma	0

* Record

Bob Miller
McFarland High
First wrestling coach

Bob Blalock
North Bakersfield
1969 2nd CIF

John Miller career 112-6-1
John Miller 40-1 1 loss over two years
Sam Rucker 1 loss all year
Bill Seabourn 82-30-1 career
Gene Walker 98-23-1 career
Walt Shpard 72-8 career

Mike Munoz (left) CIF Champion
Dean Christenson – 2nd CIF
Bakersfield High 1965

Emmett Herrera (left) 3rd CIF
Ben Welch – CIF Champion
1965 Bakersfield High

Central Section – Bakersfield College
March 1, 1969

95
Hernandez	Alex	CORC	17-6	
Howard	Jim	CL		
Hernandez	David	SANG	3-0 O.T.	
Nebre	Pete	DEL		
Brock	Dennis	MCL	10-5	
Sanchez	Joe	EAST		

103
Tatarakis	Tom	DP	10-2	
Velasquez	Tony	A		
Serros	Tony	B	5-3	(38-3-1)*
Ave	John	SB		
Travers	Spencer	WB	3-2	
Inaba	Don	SANG		

112
Guerrero	Tony	CORC	3-1	
Marquez	Ruben	MAD		
Gross	Doug	HOOV	7-6	
Ramirez	Ramon	DP		
Herrera	Billy	B	6-1	
Vega	Joe	SB		

120
Morgan	Larry	EB	9-1	(41-0)*
Holeman	Pete	MCL		
Fleming	Henry	MAD	6-0	
Maldonado	Robert	B		
Martinez	Mike	SANG	6-4	
Orosco	Sal	TW		

127
Little	Larry	SB	9-4	(41-1)*
Arballo	Robert	MAD		(31-2)*
Espinoza	Ygnacio	B	4-2	
Willis	Will	EX		
Gomez	Pedro	CORC	4-2	
Price	Terry	KING		

133
King	Laddie	MAD	6-0	
McGough	Mike	ED		
Giggy	Dave	WB	14-5	
Silva	Leo	WOOD		
Pedroza	Humberto	DIN	4-2	
Ross	Eldon	NB		

138
Greco	Bob	MCL	4-1	
Peterson	Chuck	B		
McIntyre	Ed	MAD	2-1 O.T.	
Roberson	Robert	EB		
Black	Danny	SHAFT	7-0	
Newman	Doug	TW		

145
Cooke	Allyn	TUL	5-0	
Machdo	Manuel	MCF		
Burris	Doug	KING	6-3	
Verde	Frank	EB		
Rodgers	Roy	BULL	10-2	
Silva	Lionel	WOOD		

154
Wallace	Harlace	PORT	13-5	
Domino	Kenny	B		
Terry	Mike	W	4-1 O.T.	
Brock	Mike	MCL		
Crowder	Cecil	FOOT	5-2	(37-2)**
Ernst	Mike	EX		

165
Alvarez	Richard	B	7-2	(39-3)*
O'Connor	Steve	PORT		
King	Huston	MAD	1-0	
Mendes	Mike	HOOV		
Hines	Doug	HAN	6-1	
Rawls	Eric	EX		

175
Tribble	Larry	MAD	4-3	
Copenhaver	Dan	SB		
Thorburn	Kirk	CL	Fall 2:35	
Alvarez	Danny	B		
Smith	Al	CENT	4-1	
Wilhite	Bill	W		

191
Deltoro	Tim	MAD	3-1	
Blalock	Bob	MT.W		
Nelms	Doyle	PORT		
Forbes	Bob	MT.W		
Batch	Dave	B	6-0	
Brown	Jim	SHAFT		

(Continued on next page)

Central Section - Bakersfield College
March 1, 1969

HWT

Watson	Don	MAD	2-1
Shirley	Al	DEL	
Jeffers	George	W	Fall 3:45
Hansen	Chris	ROOS	
Williams	Duane	NB	4-2
Hernandez	Frank	RED	

Tournament

1. Madera	106
2. Bakersfield	73
3. South	36
4. McLane	36
5. Porterville	36
6. East	33
6. Corcoran	33
8. Dos Palos	21
9. Clovis	20
10. Delano	19
10. North	19
12. Wasco	17
13. Hoover	16
14. West	14
14. Tulare	14
14. Sanger	14
17. Edison	12
17. Exeter	12
17. McFarland	12

Total Schools: 36

Larry Morgan only undefeated wrestler in CIF. Two-year record: 82-2. Estimated career record: 156-12
Allyn Cooke one loss all season
Richard Alvarez career ~~12x8x1~~ 115-12-1
Career record for Larry Little: 101-25 – 82-5 Jr./Sr. years

** Record

Alex Hernandez
Corcoran High
1968 2ne CIF
Two-time CIF Champion
1969 and 1970

Larry Morgan
East Bakersfield
CIF Champion
1969
3rd place 1968
2nd place 1967

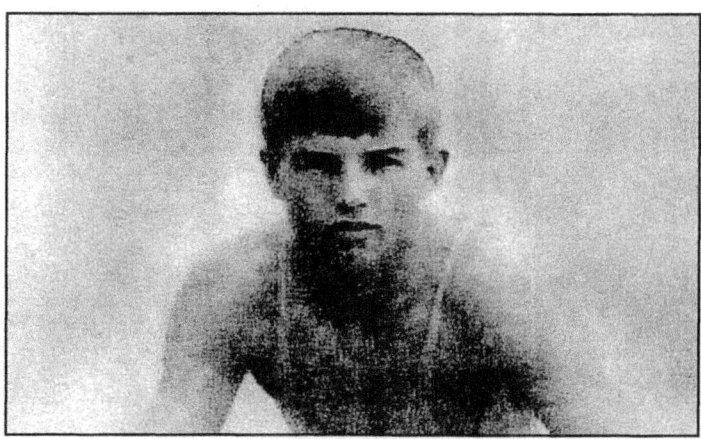

Larry Little of South Bakersfield
Two-time CIF Champion
1968 and 1969
1967 4th in CIF

Corcoran High
(Left to right) Sebastian Guerrero, Fred Maland, Lalo Moz, Alex Hernandez

Central Section – McLane/Fresno
February 28, 1970

95
Molina	Dick	SB	8-0	
Gridiron	Harold	B		(26-6-2)*
Dickenson	Dave	BULL	4-2	
Carter	Dennis	MT.W		
Otomo	Tony	SEL	10-7	
Ramos	Frank	A		

103
*Hernandez	Alex	CORC	7-4	
Hernandez	David	SANG		
Hughes	Gene	HOOV	3-0	
Howard	Jim	CL		
Travers	Spencer	WB	Fall 3:40	
Burnett	Dennis	NB		

112
**King	Pete	MAD	1-0	
**Serros	Tony	B		(36-0-1)*
Caudle	Rex	EX	9-0	
Welte	Al	SB		
Lovelace	Paul	WB	9-4	
Garcia	Larry	WOOD		

120
Reinhart	Gary	HOOV	7-1	(34-1-1)*
Arrean	Art	MAD		
Martinez	Mike	SANG	6-5	
Bowler	Jay	WOOD		
Lane	Kenny	B	2-0	
Byrd	Rick	CL		

127
Combs	Steve	HOOV	8-4	
Higby	Russ	FOOT		
Wallis	Will	EX	1-0	
McMasters	Danny	SB		
Munoz	Joe	SEL	7-5	
East	David	B		(24-12-1)*

133
Martin	Dean	TW	2-0	
Quintana	Mike	SEL	2	
Mulligan	Mike	TUL	O.T. Ref. Dec.	
Anderson	Sonny	NB		
Silva	Jerry	WOOD		
Salinas	Joe	PORT		

138
Freeman	Charles	MAD	3-2	
McGough	Mike	ED		
Ross	Eldon	NB	5-4	
Cruz	Dave	EX		
Hauck	Jack	HOOV	Fall 4:32	
Davis	Darrell	CENT		

145
***Machado	Manuel	MCF	3-1	
Roland	Wilson	B		(32-7)*
Lopez	Bob	MAD	6-0	
Powell	Randy	MCL		
Moland	Fred	CORC	11-0	
Rodriguez	Mark	FRE		

154
Dasilva	Dan	MAD	3-0 O.T.	
Watts	Steve	SB		
Silva	Lionel	WOOD	4-1	
Oliveras	Abe	EB		
Domino	Kenny	B	8-4	(32-5-1)*
Quintana	Nick	SEL		

165
Moz	Lalo	CORC	Fall 5:02	
Davenport	Ed	EB		
Thompson	Sythel	SEL	5-1	
Moore	Johnny	SHAFT		
Alvarez	Tony	B	6-4	
Shaffer	Reed	TUL		

175
Alvarez	Danny	B	11-2	(36-1-1)*
Crouch	Steve	HOOV		
Candler	Carl	WU	5-1	
Campbell	John	EB		
Watson	Ken	TW	3-1	
Rios	Steve	MAD		

191
Hatch	Brad	MAD	7-0	(30-0)*
Westphal	Duane	RED		
Battistoni	Mike	B	5-4	
Forbes	Bob	MT.W		
Hill	Tom	SHAFT	12-0	
Cox	John	TW		

(Continued on next page)

Central Section – McLane/Fresno
February 28, 1970

HWT
Shirley	Al	DEL	1-0
Van Worth	Bill	SB	
Brown	Jim	NB	Fall 2:30
Jeffers	George	W	
Johns	Earl	DP	Fall
Murphy	Pat	HOOV	

Tournament
1. Madera 79
2. Bakersfield 71
3. Hoover 58
4. S. Bakersfield 54
5. Corcoran 34
6. Selma 31
7. N. Bakersfield 30
8. Exeter 26
9. E. Bakersfield 25
10. Woodlake 22
10. Tulare W. 22
12. Sanger 20
13. Delano 15
13. Mt. Whitney 15
15. McFarland 14
16. Foothill 11
16. Shafter 11
16. Edison 11
16. Redwood 11
20. Bullard 10
20. West 10
22. Washington U. 9
23. Wasco 8
24. McLane 7
25. Dos Palos 6
26. Arvin 2
26. Porterville 2
26. Central 2
26. Fresno 2

Alex Hernandez 44-0/35 Falls
Protest Co-Champs
One loss all year
Tony Serros career 122-9-2

* Record

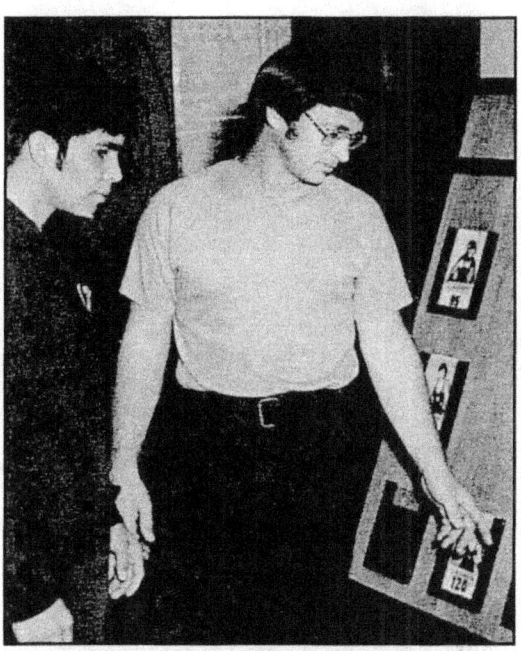

Shafter wrestler Joe Lopez, left, and Coach Darrell Fletcher

Central Section – Monache/Porterville

February 27, 1971

95
Hall	Greg	MCL	L 8-2	
Sanchez	Frank	FRE		
Valdez	John	EB	8-2	
Pardo	Gabe	REED		
Gonzalez	John	HI	4-0	
Woo	Lance H	HOOV		

103
Flores	Ernie	MAD	10-2	(56-6 Jr/Sr)
Mendoza	Lupe	TUL		
Aguirre	Fernando	B	5-2	(27-6-1)**
Tatarakis	Jim	DP		
Otomo	Tom	SEL	2-0	
Sanchez	Pete	EB		

112
Molina	Dick	SB	9-2	(34-2)**
Nebre	Pete	DEL		
Morris	Johnny	MT.W	7-5	
Garcia	Robert	WU		
Mendoza	Mario	TUL	12-5	
Castillo	Armando	TW		

120
Lovelace	Paul	WB	5-2	(34-1-1)**
Sanchez	Roy	EB		
Guerrero	Sebastian	CORC	4-3	
Brock	Dennis	MCL		
Bloodworth	Dennis	MAD	11-5	
Herera	Leo	SHAFT		

127
King	Pete	MAD	12-0	
Burnett	Dennis	NB		
Frost	Dale	DEL	O.T. Ref. Dec.	
Symens	Terry	MCL		
Miller	Steve	EX	2-0	
Lane	Kenny	B		

133
Byrd	Rick	CL	7-2 O.T.	
East	David	B		(24-7)**
Quintana	Mike	SEL	8-5	
Kimble	Neal	FRE		
Castillo	Alberto	DP	6-2	
Cesena	Bob	MT.W		

138
McMasters	Dan	SB	11-1	(34-1)**
Devine	Stan	MT.W		(36-3)**
Correia	Larry	WU	12-0	
Lemos	Dennis	HAN		
Munoz		SEL	12-2	
Yap	Frank	DEL		

145
Powers	Randy	SB	8-4	(29-4-1)**
Scruggs	Howard	MAD		
Gutierez	Jerry	DEL	11-0	
Gonzales	George	LAT		
Kister	Mike	KER	6-0	
Merroquin	Rafael	MCF		

154
Oliveras	Abe	EB	12-2	
Manning	Tony	WU		
Dickson	Russ	W	7-5	
Sandaers	Bill	MAD		
Torosian	Max	SANG	O.T. Ref. Dec.	
Campbell	Guy	SB		

165
Thompson	Sythel	SEL	2-0	(37-3)**
Alvarez	Tony	B		(33-2)*
Daniels	Lenord	EB	5-2	
Cemo	James	MON		
Moreno	Julio	SB	13-0	
McClennan		TRAN		

175
Moz	Lalo	CORC	15-5	
Kadel	David	SHAFT		(28-4)**
Bull	Mike	SB	6-1	(24-9-1)**
Rios	Steve	MAD		
Govera	John	B	8-1	(27-7)**
Reichert	Tim	REED		

191
Hatch	Brad	MAD	2:50	(37-1)**
Mitchell	Roger	B		(21-11)**
Harmon	Charles	WU	7-0	
Moe	David	SB		
Andrews	Dennis	EX	7-0	
Cardoza	Mike	HAN		

(Continued on next page)

Central Section – Monache/Porterville

February 27, 1971

HWT

Van Worth	Bill	SB	2:50 (34-0/30 falls)**
Ford	Randy	MT.W	
Ryska	Tom	MCL	7-2
Gross	Pat	SEL	Forfeit
Bell	Bruce	EB	

Tournament

1. S. Bakersfield — 84
2. Madera — 72
3. E. Bakersfield — 52
4. Bakersfield — 47
5. Selma — 41
6. Washington U. — 38
7. McLane — 37
8. Delano — 35
9. Mt. Whitney — 24
9. Corcoran — 24
11. W. Bakersfield — 23
12. Fresno — 18
13. Dos Palos — 16
13. Tulare — 16
15. Clovis — 14
16. Shafter — 12
17. Monache — 11
17. North — 11
17. Redwood — 11
20. Hanford — 9
20. Exeter — 9
20. Reedley — 9
23. Laton — 7
24. Highland — 5
25. Hoover — 3
25. Sanger — 3
27. Kerman — 2
McFarland — 0
Sierra — 0
Taft — 0
Wasco — 0
Woodlake — 0

Joe Seay
South Bakersfield
Coached 4 CIF
Championship teams
Record: 117-13-2

Lalo Moz
Two-time CIF Champion
1970 and 1971
Corcoran High

Dick Molina career 91-18/42 Falls
Lao Moz 1 loss in two years
Bill Van Worth career 89-7/74 Falls
Hatch, Brad career 76-1
** Record

Central Section – McLane/Fresno
March 4, 1972

95
Gonzalez	John	HI	11-0	
Cavazos	Jesse	DIN		
Marshall	Mike	SB		(32-8)*
Kinsinger	Tim	FOOT		
Vanni	Vince	MON		
Contreras	Robert	KING		

103
Lopeteguy	Joe	SHAFT	6-2
Valdez	John	EB	
Morales	Julio	DEL	5-0
Rugnao	John	A	
Guerrero	Eugene	CORC	
Ritter	Mike	BULL	

112
Perrin	Doug	HI	5-3
Romera	Junior	REED	
Ramos	Frank	A	11-2
Tatarakis	James	DP	
Flores	Gil	MAD	
Affentranger	Franc	SHAFT	

120
Klinchuch	Doug	DEL	15-12
Mendoza	Lorenzo	TUL	
Beauford	Mark	EB	3-2
Moz	Roy	CORC	
Calarese	Pat	FRE	
Silva	Augie	Wood	

127
Garza	Ray	EB	5-4
Peevyhouse	Mike	DEL	
Maldonado	Frank	SHAFT	9-2
Montoya	Gabe	REED	
Red	Mike	HAN	
Rand		EX	

133
Baxter	Randy	CL	4-1 O.T.
Coronado	Elroy	ROOS	
Castillo	Alberto	DP	
Kimble	Neal	FRE	
Smithee	Mike	A	F/F
Blackhurst	Paul	HI	

138
Macias	Ralph	HAN	5-4	(39-0)*
Duckworth	Tony	HI		
Light	Mark	B	3-0	
Bigby	David	SB		
Jackson	Nick	NB		

145
East	David	B	7-3	(37-0-1)*
Quintana	Mike	SEL		
Gaudaur	Chet	MCL		
Foglio	Ron	CENT	2-1	
Correia	Larry	WU		
Wilkinson	Ross	CL		

154
Mitchell	Rodney	B	11-6	(38-0)*
McNeil	Randy	CL		
Delarosa	Jerry	DEL		
Anderson	Mike	FOOT	9-2	
Torres	Jesse	SB		
Parrish	Darrell	MCF		

165
Alvarez	Tony	B	9-7	(36-1)*28 Falls
Manning	Tony	WU		
Campbell	Guy	SB		(34-6)*
Ramirez	Sam	HOOV	2-1	
Hunt	Roger	TW		
Clement	Marty	W		

175
Thompson	Sythel	SEL	8-4	(41-0)*
Bodine	Mike	MAD		
Rocha	Florencio	B		(34-5)*
Cemo	Jim	MON		
Garcia	Reno	SB		
Clement	Terry	W		

191
Harmon	Charles	WU 3-2		(26-0)*
Andrews	Dennis	EX		
Bull	Mike	SB 9-1		(36-3/21 Falls)*
Govea	John	B		(32-7)*(59-14-29 Falls)
Richert	Tim	REED		
Smith	Stan	CORC		

(Continued on next page)

Central Section – McLane/Fresno
March 4, 1972

HWT

Williams	Duane	NB	8-2	(126-39)
Velov	Fred	DEL		
Gorras	Mike	MCL	5-0	
Vella	Emitto	KING		
Simmerman	Bob	FRE	F/F	
Gilson	Ray	REED		

Tournament

1. Bakersfield	72.5
2. Delano	56
3. S. Bakersfield	48
4. Highland	43.5
5. Washington U.	36
6. E. Bakersfield	34.5
7. Clovis	28
8. Reedley	25.5
9. Selma	25
10. Arvin	21
11. McLane	19
11. Hanford	19
11. N. Bakersfield	19
14. Foothill	18
14. Shafter	18
Taft	12.5
Wasco	4.5
McFarland	2

Total Teams: 32

Sythell Thompson unbeaten two years
Tony Alvarez and Tony Manning one loss each all season to each other
David East career: ~~86x19x1~~ 85-19-2 (42-0-1 season correction)
Tony Alvarez career: ~~94x15x3~~ 95-15-5
Mitchell, Rodney career 70-20-1
* Record

Olan Polite, left, and Paul Briggs
Bakersfield High
Briggs was the first Driller wrestling coach

Olan Polite
Head coach at Arvin High

Central Section – Highland/Bakersfield

February 24, 1973

95
Contreras	Bob	KING	1-0	
Machado	Ed	A		
Gonzalez	Pete	HI	10-0	
Inwanura	Gary	MT.W		
Vasquez	Frank	DP	4-2	
Quinonez	John	TW		

103
Huffman	Ray	MAD	7-5	(34-2)*
Marshall	Mike	SB		(38-2)*
Vanni	Vince	MON	7-0	
Orduna	Cosmo	DP		
Pereschina	Henry	SEL	11-4	
George	Randy	TAFT		

112
Flores	Ernie	MAD	2-1	
Romero	Junior	REED		
Guerrero	Eugene	CORC	3-2	
Morales	Julio	DEL		
Sanchez	Pete	EB	4-2	
Lopeteguy	Joey	SHAFT		

120
Moren	Willard	CL	9-0	
Kiddy	Robert	MAD		
Affentranger	Franc	SHAFT	3-0	
Dow	David	HI		
Carrillo	Eddie	B	1-0	(32-7-1)*
Silva	Augie	WOOD		

127
Balch	Rodney	CL	4-3	
Russell	Horace	RED		
Garza	Ray	EB	5-1	
Garcia	Richard	EX		
Lopez	Joe	SHAFT	5-1	
Coash	Tom	WB		

133
Baxter	Randy	CL	6-4	(40-0)*
Peevyhouse	Mike	DEL		
Cates	Allan	SHAFT	14-0	
Connell	Matt	HOOV		
Beauford	Mark	EB	Default	
Ramirez	Richard	KING		

138
Blackhurst	Paul	HI	7-2	(33-1)*
Spickler	Kris	MCL		
Spotts	Lee	MAD	4-1	
Flores	Frank	CL		
Swett	Ed	DP	9-4	
Pachelo	Ken	EX		

145
Duckworth	Tony	HI	4-3	(37-1)*
Almanza	Julian	EX		
Combs	Roger	HOOV	7-4	
Bruer	Bob	MAD		
Marroquin	Rafael	MCF	19-11	
Islas	Abundio	REED		

154
Wilkinson	Ross	CL	3-1	(41-0)*
Anderson	Mike	FOOT		
Torres	Jess	SB	2:04	
Delarosa	Jerry	DEL		
Scott	Amos	WU	F/F	
Watson	George	EX		

165
Manning	Tony	WU	8-6	(35-1)*
Rocha	Florencio	B		(42-2)
Posey	Don	MON	2:48	
Johnson	Eddie	CL		
Kennedy	Burr	CHOW	7-5	
Flores	Fred	FOW		

175
Bracamonte	Joe	CENT	9-7
Bohna	Fred	CL	
Clement	Terry	W	4:23
Johnson	Bruce	KING	
Garcia	Reno	SB	3-2
Richardson	Jeff	HAN	

191
Bull	Mike	SB	12-0	(47-0)*
Ponce	Jess	B		
Gonzales	Luis	CENT	2-1	
Johnson	Mike	W		
Pratt	Richard	MT.W		
Gomez	Manuel	KING		

(Continued on next page)

Central Section – Highland/Bakersfield
February 24, 1973

HWT
*Williams	Duane	NB	4-0	(44-6)*
Robenson	Jeff	CL		
Kelly	Keith	HOOV	4-2	
Fowler	Bob	EB		
Valov	Fred	DEL	2-0	
Kelarjian	Joe	WU	3-0	

Tournament
1. Clovis — 87
2. Madera — 57.5
3. Highland — 48
4. S. Bakersfield — 42
5. Delano — 30.5
6. Shafter — 27
7. Bakersfield — 26.5
8. E. Bakersfield — 26
8. Hoover — 26
10. Exeter — 25.5
11. Central — 25
12. Washington U. — 23
13. Kingsburg — 20
14. Monache — 20
15. Wasco — 17
16. N. Bakersfield — 16
17.. Reedley — 14
18. Mt. Whitney — 13
19. Arvin — 11
19. Redwood — 11
19. McLane — 11
22. Foothill — 10
22. Dos Palos — 10
24. Corcoran — 9
25. McFarland — 5
25. Chowchillla — 5
27. Selma — 4
28. Hanford — 3
29. W. Bakersfield — 2
29. Fowler — 2
29. Tulare Western — 2
29. Woodlake — 2

Dennis DeLiddo
Clovis High
Record: 147-7-1
Coached 3 State
Championship teams

Williams 126-39 Career

* Record

Central Section – Mt. Whitney/Visalia

February 23, 1974

95
Gonzalez	Pete	HI	10-2	(31-2)*
Travers	Mickey	SB		
Medina	Jose	DEL	DF	(33-2)*
Bolanos	Paul	CL		
Stewart	Lyle	W	:57	
Pereschica	Romero	SEL		

103
Hurtado	Bob	KING	2-0	(36-0)*
Vannie	Vince	MON		
Peterson	Geroge	B	2-0 O.T.	
Hull	Jeff	HI		
Hasson	Scott	HOOV	1:22	
Esquivel	Gabriel	DP		

112
Canaday	Larry	WB	7-1	
Guerrero	Eugene	CORC		
Morales	Julio	DEL	3-1	(34-1)*
Pereschica	Henry	SEL	4-0	
McConnaughy	Kevin	MT.W		

120
Garza	Ray	EB	13-1	(44-1)*
Villareal	Art	MAD		
Carmago	Ed	W	7-6	
Esquivel	Roy	WU		
Soltero	Chino	CL	5-1	
Carral	Victor	CENT		

127
Russell	Horace	RED	3-1	
Gongora	Tom	CL		
Royal	Marlin	WU	4:00	
Vejvada	Craig	TUL		
Sumida	Randy	LEM	4-3	
Nadeau	Brian	CENT		

133
Lopez	Joe	SHAFT	9-7	(35-0)*
Royal	Eugene	WU		
Sanchez	Luie	FRE	8-4	
Brower	Wayne	CORC		
Reimer	Greg	DEL	3-2	
Jury	Jeff	CL		

138
Balch	Rod	CL	3-2	
Kiddy	Robert	MAD		
Lopetecuy	Joey	SHAFT	12-5	
Itokazu	Todd	HI		
Oliveria	Frank	HAN	8-2	
Swett	Ed	DP		

145
Torres	Jesse	SB	8-4	(42-3)*
Islas	Abundi	REED		
Combs	Roger	HOOV	2-1	
Lopez	Randy	WU		
Leroy	Loren	MAD	15-8	
Edspinoza	Moe	DP		

154
Hutchings	Warren	MT.W	6-2	
Tobin	Craig	B		(39-4)
Ramirez	Carlos	HOOV	3-1	
Scott	Amos	WU		
Verdusco	Larry	ROOS	5-0	
Cruz	Ralph	CORC		

165
Cookingham	Kevin	CL	5-4	(30-3)*
Manning	Tony	WU	(39-1/37 falls)*	
Rosenberger	Bob	DEL	Default	
Kennedy	Burr	CHOW		
Sztorc	Ed	WB	5-2	
Williams	Cary	W		

175
Ponce	Jess	B	7-3	(35-5)*
Sheffel	Bill	HI		
Henry	Titus	TW	6-5	
Moz	Ben	CORC		
Reynolds	Ted	CHOW	3:25	
Swanson	Rick	DEL		

191
Bohna	Fred	CL	11-6	(31-1)*
Gomez	Manuel	KING		
Clement	Terry	W	12-4	
Diaz	John	MAD		
Cotton	Vinson	SB	Default	
Duvall	Don	MT.W		

(Continued on next page)

Central Section – Mt. Whitney/Visalia
February 23, 1974

HWT
Thomas	Jeweal	HAN	Default
Horn	Rod	HOOV	
Clark	John	FOOT	8-4
Hernandez	Carlos	EX	
Akman	Terry	SHAF	6-3
Van Arkle	Tom	B	

Tournament
1. Clovis — 70
2. Washington U. — 65
3. Hoover — 45
4. Highland — 43
5. Delano — 40
6. Bakersfield — 38.5
7. Madera — 35.5
8. S. Bakersfield — 33
9. Shafter — 30
10. Kingsburg — 26

* Record

Corrections

103 Peterson, George (24-7-1)* career 67-29-1

Fred Bohna
Clovis High
NCAA Champion
UCLA

Central Section – Tulare Western

March 1, 1975

95
Bolanos	Paul	CL	3-0	(35-1-1)*
Gonzales	Alfredo	B	2	
Burt	John	WB	11-5	
Pereschica	Romero	SEL		
Cortez	Eddie	CORC	4:23	
Paramo	Noe	WOOD		

103
Gonzalez	Pete	HI	6-3	
Dutra	Duane	HAN		(33-2-1)*
Blanco	Tom	CL	6-3	
Bass	Leon	CHOW		
Davids	Brian	FOOT	5-0	
Cisneros	Gabe	EX		

112
Murphy	Tim	HOOV	4-2	(31-0)
Leyva	Anthony	B		
Garcia	Onesimo	MAD	8-3	
Sanders	Bobby	SHAFT		
Spencer	Bill	CL	7-0	
Dillingham	Jim	W		

120
Felez	Paul	SB	6-0	(33-1)*
Contreras	Nick	RED		
McConnaughy	Kevin	MT.W	9-4	
Parrin	Mike	HI		
Villareal	Art	MAD	F/F	
Royal	Vernon	WU		

127
Corral	Vic	CENT	8-4	
Arvance	Brad	KER		
Borjas	Nick	CL	3-2	
Vejvada	Craig	TUL		
Freeman	Neal	MAD	2-1	
Gaitan	Jess	HI		

133
Lopez	Joe	SHAF	3-1	
Nadeau	Brian	CENT		
Whittmore	Greg	FRE	9-4	
Flynn		BULL		
Jury	Jeff	CL	7-3	
Harris	Leon	CHOW		

138
Brower	Wayne	CAR	4:46	
Wililams	Tom	CL		
Coronado	Celzo	MAD	9-2	
Ybarra	George	EX		
Montana		FRE	4-0	
Hanline	Bob	WB		

145
Kiddy	Robert	MAD	3-2	(37-0)*
O'Bar	Steve			
Chase	Bob	HI	1-0	
Landeros	Mark	MON		
Hernandez	Paul	WB	7-0	
Parrish	Dennis	NB		

154
Roberts	Bob	FRE	3-2	
Leroy	Loren	MAD		
Cooksley	Phil	MON	6-2	
McClellan	Tom	TRAN		
Spoisdoff	George	WASCO	F/F	
Thomas	Bill	HAN		

165
Scott	Amos	WU	4-1	(35-1)*
Torres	James	SB		
England	Rich	BULL	5-3	
Grimes	Bob	CL		
Bradford	Walt	HOOV	6-3	
Groesbeck	Bruce	EX		

175
Cookingham	Kevin	CL	7-3	(33-0-1)*
Williams	Norman	SHAFT		
Torres	Lawrence	MAD	3-0	
Kasperian	Sylex	SEL		
Reynolds	Ted	CHOW	5-4	
Herder	Jerry	WB		

191
Johnson	Eddie	CL	10-4	
Diaz	John	MAD		
Smith	David	HAN	5-1	
Landeros	Mike	MON		
Curtis	Mark	WOOD	8-6	
Bedrosian	Brian	FOW		

(Continued on next page)

Central Section – Tulare Western
March 1, 1975

HWT

Thomas	Jeweal	HAN 7-4	(34-0)*
Author	Doug	CL	
Hernandez	Carlos	EX 8-3	
Van Arkel	Tom	B	
Handley	Don	CHOW 2:00	
Williams	Myron	WASCO	

Tournament

1. Clovis — 111
2. Madera — 80
3. Hanfaord — 39
4. Highland — 34
5. Shafter — 33.5
6. Bakersfield — 31
7. Fresno — 30
8. S. Bakersfield — 28
9. Monache — 25.5
10. Central — 25
11. Caruthers — 22
12. Exeter — 21
12. Chowchilla — 21
14. Hoover — 19.5
15. W. Bakersfield — 19
16. Washington U. — 18
17. Bullard — 17
18. Selma — 15.5
19. Kerman — 12
20. Redwood — 11
21. Mt. Whitney — 10
22. Wasco — 8
23. Tulare — 7.5
24. Tranquility — 7
25. Foothill — 5
26. N. Bakersfield — 3
27. Fowler — 2

Joe Lopez
Shafter High
1975 2nd State
1974 3rd State

Central Section – Fresno City College
February 28, 1976

95
Richard	Percy	EB	6-2	(32-1)*
Gonzalez	Fred	HI		
Pereschica	Romero	SEL	6-5	
Blanco	Anthony	CL		
Carrejo	Juan	CHOW	9-8	
Bustamonte	Johnny	A		

103
Bolanos	Paul	CL	6-0	(41-2)*
Perez	Louie	FRE		
Gonzalez	Pete	HI	3-0	
Poteete	Jim	SB		
Gonzales	Alfredo	B	9-4	
Tiller	Stan	WU		

112
Blanco	Tom	CL	13-1
Gamboa	Joe	MAD	
Esquivel	Gabriel	DP	4:58
Nickell	Steve	EB	
Bass	Leon	CHOW	3-2
Stewart	Lyle	WU	

120
Jones	Bill	HAN	6-2	(40-1)*
Gonzales	William	FOOT		(38-2)*
Williams	Mike	HI	3-1	
Garcia	Onesimo	MAD		
Hunt	Ron	W	2-0	
Williams	Hakshik	BULL		

127
McConnaughey	Kevin	MT.W	6-5	
Felez	Paul	SB		(30-1)*
Fahy	Jeff	WB	4-2	
McWhorter	Steve	SHAFT		
Freeman	Neal	MAD	7-2	
Dillingham	Jim	W		

133
Contreras	Rick	RED	7-2	
Reyes	Eddie	B		(35-3)*
Bowser	Jim	CENT	5-3	
Salinas	Filomino	A		
Royal	Vernon	WU	14-5	
Rivera		BULL		

138
Dow	Don	HI	4-3	(29-5)*
Whitemore	Greg	FRE		
Flynn	Warren	BULL	12-0	
Inouye	Craig	CL		
Harvey	Ed	SIE	5-1	
Kiawitter	Daryl	CHOW		

145
Pineida	Ernie	MAD	4-3	
Chase	Bob	HI		(26-2)*
Williams	Tom	CL	17-3	
Davis	Ed	HAN		
Scott	Frank	WU	8-4	
Nipper	Waymon	SB		

154
Grimes	Bob	CL	4-3	
Johnson	Dave	HI		(20-1)*
Leroy	Lerron	MAD	14-2	
McClellan		TRAN		
Peterson	Ray	KING	5-3	
Duran	Albert	FRE		

165
Cookingham	Kevin	CL	3-1	(36-1)*
Torres	James	SB		
Thomas	Bill	HAN	10-0	
Smith	Kreig	BULL		
Lett	Eric	Ed	F/F	
Peterson	Tony	WOOD		

175
Kasperian	Alan	SEL	F/F
Weidenhoft	Kurt	BULL	
Negrete	John	RED	7-6
Landeros	Mike	MON	
Winter	Randy	CL	3-2
Bustamonte	Luis	CENT	

191
Diaz	John	MAD	18-4	(36-1)*
Buenafe	John	RED		
Curtis	Mark	WOOD	3:43	
Molica	Lance	DEL		
Williams	Norman	SHAFT	12-3	
Masmanian	John	BULL		

(Continued on next page)

Central Section – Fresno City College
February 28, 1976

HWT

Author	Doug	CL	6-2	(38-0)*
Hernandez	Carlos	EX		
Smith	David	HAN	3-2	
Rogers	John	WU		
Hill	Ed	MON	F/F	
Van Worth	Lee	NB		

Tournament

1. Clovis — 120
2. Highland — 78
2. Madera — 78
4. Hanford — 50
5. Bullard — 44
6. S. Bakersfield — 39
6. Redwood — 39
8. Washington U. — 33
9. Fresno — 30
10. Selma — 27
11. E. Bakersfield — 26
12. Bakersfield — 20
13. Monache — 17

* Record

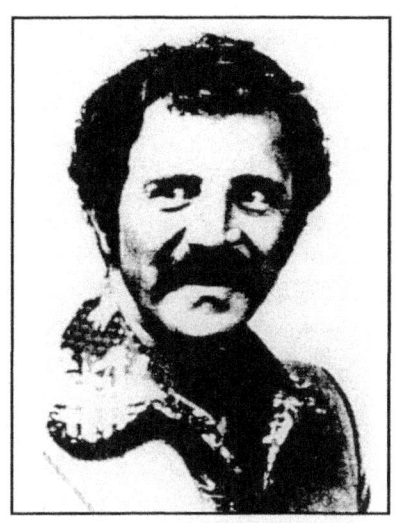

Coach Ruben Ramirez
Arvin High

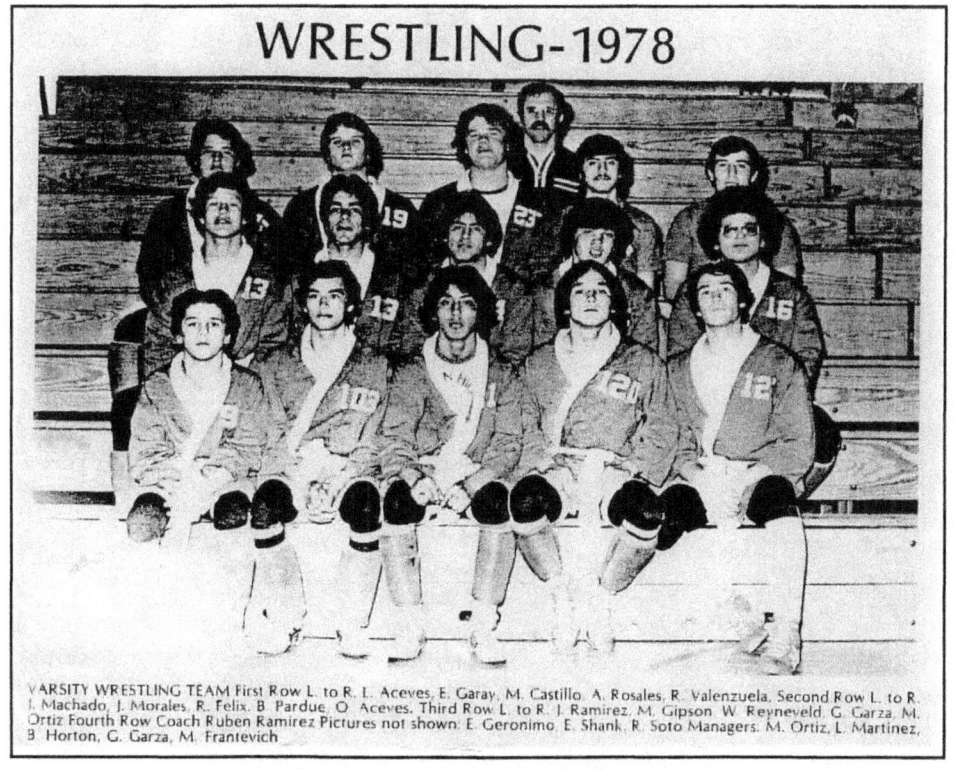

1978 Arvin High Wrestling Team

Central Section – West Bakersfield
February 26, 1977

95
Blanco	Anthony	CL	3:49	(48-3)*
Gonzalez	Mike	HI		
Vanni	Tim	MON	6-2	
Dallas	Willie	FOOT		
Martinez	Ken	CENT	2-1 O.T.	
Crane	Kris	MCL		

103
Richard	Percy	EB	9-0	(38-4)*
Gonzalez	Fred	HI		
Bustamonte	Johnny	A	7-2	
Gutierrez	Al	RED		
Carnejo	Juan	CHOW	Default	
Brieno	Mike	HAN		

112
Poteete	Jimi	SB	7-1	(27-4)*
Estrada	Buff	FRE		
Padilla	Tony	WASCO		
Sierra	Frank	SANG		
Gutierrez	Alfred	RED	Default	
Affentranger	Martin	SHAFT		

120
Nickell	Steve	EB	2-1	(33-4)*
Dow	Dale	HI		
Rodriguez	Vince	TW	2-1 O.T.	
Powell	Mike	EX		
Ramirez	David	WOOD	Default	
Esquivel	Gabriel	DP		

127
McCullough	Glen	FOOT	4-3
Duckworth	Aaron	HI	
Torres	Ralph	ROOS	7-4
Raya	Gabe	LIN	
Cano	Slavardo	HAN	15-3
Betencourt	Dan	WOOD	

133
Fahy	Jeff	WB	4-0	(41-2)*
Yoshida	Tay	RED		
Ball	John	SIE	5-1	
Riberia	Mike	BULL		
Hurtado	Romero	KING	4:43	
Daniels	Eddie	B		

138
Inouye	Greg	CL	12-5
Mooney	Mike	B	
Vejvoda	Mike	TUL	3-1
Duran	Albert	FRE	
Marroquin	Johnny	MCF	Default
Mirelez	Johnny	SHAFT	

145
Roth	Mike	CL	9-3	(36-1)*
Juarez	Javier	SANG		
Rena	Aaron	KING	3-2	
May	Alex	ROOS		
Scott	Frank	WU	1:54	
Zimmerman	Brent	B		

154
Elis	Robert	BULL	2-1
Donnelly	Russ	MCL	
Castaneda	Danny	B	5-2
Pederson	Aaron	KING	
Virgil	Mark	EX	8-2
Scott	Forrest	WU	

165
Sanders	Tim	MAD	2-1
Ussery	Frank	NB	
Bufford	John	MCL	7-2
Gouhart	Frank	RED	
Bartholine	Mike	MCL	2:30
Larson	Scott	SIE	

175
Thomas	Bill	HAN	6-2	(36-0)*
Osthimer	Mike	HI		
McNabb	Lewis	NB	1:30	
Shannon	Rick	STRM		
Juarez	Tony	FRE	6-4	
Jelaca	Bob	WB		

191
Landeros	Mike	MON	6-3
Molica	Lance	DEL	
Torosian		SANG	5-0
Harris	Dave	WB	
Lopez	Abe	KING	12-6
Hedrick	Rodger	HAN	

(Continued on next page)

Central Section – West Bakersfield
February 26, 1977

HWT
Hernandez	Carlos	EX	3-1
Smith	Dave	HAN	
Hester	Raymond	CHOW	:59
Fajardo	Jose	CENT	
Parker	Barry	MT.W	O.T. Ref. Dec.
Mootry	Ken	SHAFT	

Tournament
1. Highland 81.5
2. Clovis 68
3. Hanford 60
4. Redwood 43.5
5. E. Bakersfield 43
6. Sanger 40.5
7. W. Bakersfield 39
8. Bakersfield 38.5
9. Fresno 38
10. Monache 37
11. Kingsburg 36
12. McLane 32
13. Bullard 30.5
14. Foothill 30
15. N. Bakersfield 28
16. Exeter 27
17. Chowchilla 26.5
18. Bakersfield 22
18. Roosevelt 22
18. Delano 22
21. Madera 20
22. Sierra 18
23. Shafter 17
23. McFarland 17
25. Central 16
26. Wasco 15
27. Washington U. 14
28. Tulare 13
28. Woodlake 13
30. Arvin 12.5
30. Tulare Western 12.5
32. Strathmore 11
33. Lindsay 10
34. Dos Palos 7
35. Mt. Whitney 6

1958 Arvin High Wrestling Team

* Record
Carlos Hernandez was 24-0 with four divisional titles in the
CIF — Placed in the CIF 4,3,2,1
Bill Thomas had 141 career wins

Central Section – Hanford
February 25, 1978

95
Vanni	Tim	MON	5-3	(32-0)*
Garcia	Jesse	CL		
Gonalez	Mike	HI	4-0	
Borjas	Rick	MCL		
Harautunian	Tom	HOOV	10-0	
Rodriguez	Phil	SHAFT		

103
Gutierrez	Alfred	RED	2:37	(30-1)*
Vannie	Dan	MON		(29-3)*
Cortez	Dan	CCAR	4-2	
Tatarakis	Chris	FIRE		
Bender	Scott	SHAFT	3-2	
Arrendendo	Rene	MAD		

112
Gonzalez	Fred	HI	6-3	(31-6)*
Richard	Percy	EB	(33-4)	(130-18)*
Frausto	Jessie	MAD	8-1	
Carrillo	Ruben	TRAN		
Sims	Bill	CENT	1:46	
Silva	Dan	DEL	30.5	

120
Estrada	Buff	FRE	11-2	(36-1)*
Kaprielian	Larry	HOOV		
Reyes	Jessie	B	8-1	
Kimbler	Ben	SIE		
Calvillo	Joe	HI	5-0	
Cardenas	Fred	EX		

127
Dow	Dale	HI	7-2	(32-2)*
Powell	Mike	EX		
Franich	Ed	MT.W	5-3	
Lopez	Julio	SHAFT		
Hargis	Darin	NB	7-0	
Worthey	Todd	SIE		

133
Nickell	Steve	EB	5-3 (35-2)	(125-21)*
Balanos	George	CL		
Kinsinger	Tony	FOOT	2-0	
Cano	Alvardo	HAN		
Harshman	John	SIE	4:29	
Pineda	John	WU		

138
Carley	Jeff	MT.W	13-0	(32-1)*
Hernandez	Ray	FRE		
Churchman	Colby	NB	10-2	
Gomez	Raul	KING		
Willits	Larry	DP	6-3	
Reyna	Juan	W		

145
May	Alex	ROOS	5-4	(24-1)*
Hines	Roy	HAN		
Ramsey	Cecil	MT.W	3:00	
Avila	Mike	FRE		
Aldredge	Gaylon	WU	Default	
Garcia	Moses	LIND		

154
Virgil	Mark	EX	6-3	(28-0)*
Green	Robin	ED		
Ellis	Robert	BULL	O.T. Ref. Dec.	
Castaneda	Danny	B		
Bufford	John	MCL	5-3	
Giovanetti	Roger	SHAFT		

165
Scott	Frank	WU	10-7	(34-2)*
Sischo	Richard	MCL		
Romine	Bob	HI	4-3	
Juares	Tony	FRE		
Rocker	Rick	KING	2-0	
Dunbar	Tim	HOOV		

175
Martinez	Rey	ROOS	17-3	(28-0/24 Falls)*
McNabb	Lewis	NB		(30-3)*
Scott	Forest	WU	3-1	
Semainiego	Sam	KER		
Townsend	Dennis	MON		
Valov	Joel	DEL	30.5	

191
Kropog	Bill	MON	5-4	(29-2)*
Haskins	Nonnie	ROOS		
Mootry	Ken	SHAFT	6-5	
Lopez	Abe	KING		
Pierce	Bill	SB	Defafult	(37-7-1)*
Mayberry	Dan	FOOT		

(Continued on next page)

Central Section – Hanford
February 25, 1978

HWT

Molica	Lance	DEL	4-1	(25-2)*
Dennis	Tim	MON		(24-7)*
Bishop	Vernon	MAD	8-3 O.T.	
Martin	Dennis	SHAFT		
Lamb	Mike	CL	3-2	
Castillo	Marvin	TUL		

Tournament

1. Monache	79	18. Bakersfield South	22	
2. Highland	77	19. Redwood	22.5	
3. Roosevelt	62	20. Sierra	20	
4. Fresno	59.5	21. Edison	18	
5. Shafter	50	22. Foothill	12	
6. Washington U.	48	22. Kerman	12	
7. Mt. Whitney	46	22. Bullard	12	
8. Exeter	44.5	25. Caruthers	11	
9. E. Bakersfield	39	26. Tranquility	9.5	
9. Clovis	39	27. South	9	
11. North	35.5	27. Firebaugh	9	
11. Madera	35.5	29. Dos Palos	8.5	
13. Hoover	32.5	30. Central	8	
14. McLane	31	31. Lindsey	5	
15. Delano	29	31. Wasco	5	
16. Hanford	28.5	33. Tulare	4.5	
16. Kingsburg	28.5			

* Record

Monache Ends With 10-0 Log

Coach Drew Williams of Monache High
Coaching record: 368-71-4

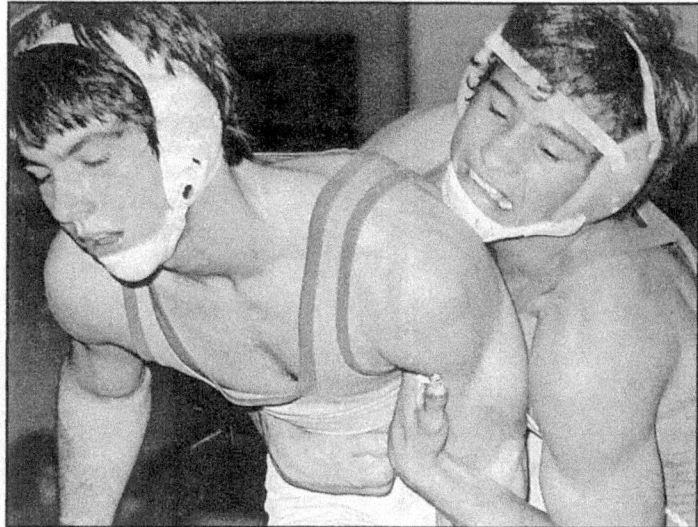

Greg Harris of South Bakersfield (left)
Jessie Reyes of Bakersfield High
NCAA Champion at CSUB
College career record: 151-22-1

Bill Kropog (top) of Monache High
CIF Champion

Tim Vanni (left) of
Monache High
Two-time CIF Champion
Career record: 98-12
Two-time Olympian

Central Section – Clovis
February 24, 1979

98
Vanni	Tim	MON	13-0	(34-1)*
Borges	Rick	MCL		
Gutierrez	Anacleto	WU	8-7	
Sanchez	David	A		
Corral	Armondo	CENT	4-3	
Long	Charlie	BULL		

106
Gutierrez	Al	RED	11-9
East	Mel	B	
Saenz	Pablo	REED	4-3
Garay	Ernesto	A	
Gonales	Mike	HI	2-1
Potter	Doug	MAD	

115
Torres	Rene	ROOS	8-3	(28-3)*
Slade	Steve	WB		
Moreno	Vince	W	10-6	
Hasson	Jeff	HOOV		
Geronimo	Ernie	A	O.T. Ref. Dec.	
Villareal	Marc	SB		

123
Poteete	Jim	SB	7-3	(36-1)*
Estrada	Buff	FRE		(35-3)*
Dallas	Willie	FOOT	9-6	
Sims	Bill	CENT		
Barton	Bob	SIE	10-4 O.T.	
Jones	Del	TW		

130
Kimbler	Ben	SIE	7-4	(28-3)*
Calvillo	Joe	HI		
Hargis	Darrin	NB	3:41	
Albidrez	John	SEL		
Lopez	Julio	SHAFT	1-0	
Bisig	Joe	SB		

136
Francish	Eddie	MT.W	2-1	(35-3)*
Negrete	Ron	RED		
Harshman	John	SIE	11-0	
Pigg	William	DP		
Vera	Armondo	CAR	8-5	
Evers	Rick	BULL		

141
Gonzales	Jose	KING	9-2
Willis	Larry	DP	
Della	Mark	MON	3-1
Thornton	Alvin	ED	
Loftis	Mike	CAR	11-6
Boyles	Brian	HAN	

148
Hines	Roy	HAN	3:25	(35-2)*
Gomes	Paul	KING		
Carrera	Kevin	HOOV	1:48	
Nichols	Larry	FRE		
Juarez	Robert	SANG	9-1	
Haro	Frank	WOOD		

157
Guevara	Ezekiel	CL	Forfeit Default
Pulskamp	Flint	HI	
Ramsey	Cecil	MT.W	7-5
Wicks	Bob	SB	
Alvarado	Rick	HAN	13-2
Fry	David	KING	

168
Scott	Malcolm	ED	9-2	(31-2)*
Borchardt	Dave	BULL		
Suitor	Scott	WB	5-2	
Snell	Mike	WU		
Giovannetti	Roger	SHAFT	1-0	
Steelman	John	TUL		

178
Alva	Mark	FRE	5-0
Sameniego	Sam	KER	
Emerzinn	Tom	ROOS	7-1
Townsend	Dennis	MON	
Harris	Bruce	LAT	
Forfeit			

194
Hanskens	Nonnie	ROOS	5:11 (31-0/29 Falls)*	
Pierce	Bill	SB		(32-4-1)*
Lopez	Abe	KING	3-2	
Dunbar	Tim	HOOV		
Smith	Jeff	CLW	9-0 O.T.	
Fann	Mike	HAN		

(Continued on next page)

Central Section – Clovis
February 24, 1979

238
Castillo	Marvin	TUL	O.T. Ref. Dec.
Jones	Scott	MT.W	
Walker	Calvin	SANG	5-2
Blacksill	John	WU	
Fajardo	Jose	CENT	6-5
James	Donnie	HI	

Tournament
1. S. Bakersfield	61.5		22. Kerman	18
2. Roosevelt	60.5		23. Bakersfield	16
3. Kingsburg	55		23. Caruthers	16
4. Mt. Whitney	53		23. McLane	16
5. Monache	52		26. North	13.5
6. Fresno	49.5		27. Selma	13
7. Highland	47.5		28. Shafter	12
8. Hanford	39		29. Foothill	11.5
9. Sierra	38		30. Reedley	11
10. Redwood	36		30. Wasco	11
11. Edison	34		32. Laton	10
12. Hoover	33		33. Clovis West	9.5
13. Washington U.	31		34. Madera	7
14. Bullard	28.5		35. Tulare Western	5
15. Dos Palos	28		36. Woodlake	4
16. W. Bakersfield	28		Tranquility	0
17. Tulare Union	25		Orosi	0
18. Arvin	24		Exeter	0
19. Clovis	22		Corcoran	0
19. Central	22			
21. Sanger	21.5		* Record	

Ben Kimbler 125-35 career

Jim Poteet of South Bakersfield
1979 State Champion
Two-time CIF Champion
1977 and 1979
4th place in 1976

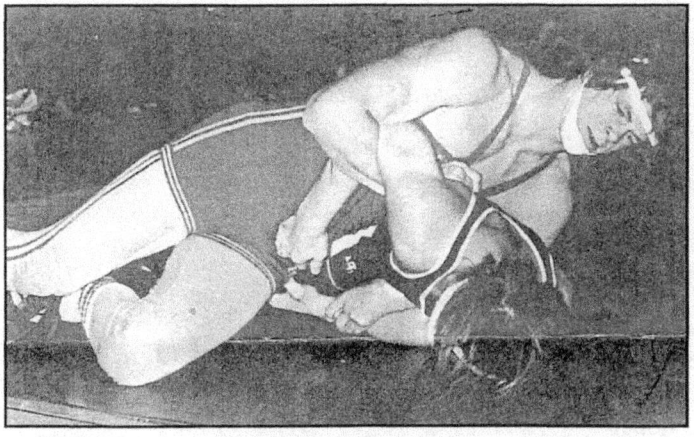

Nonnie Haskens (top) of Roosevelt High
CIF Champion

1979 State Meet: Back (l-r) Mike Stricker and
Gene Walker. Front (l-r) Bill Pierce (4th) and
Jim Poteete (State Champion)
South Bakersfield

Central Section – Bakersfield College
March 1, 1980

95
Ray	Wynn	WB	5:04	(24-9)*
Suan	Romero	MON		(28-5)*
Corral	Jeff	CENT	7-4	
Piccolo	David	KING		
Mendoza	Ed	CL	F/F	
Caraveo	Frank	DEL		

103
Gonzales	Mike	HI	5-2	(29-3)*
Saenz	Pablo	REED		
Crouch	Trent	FRE	3-2	
Potter	Doug	MAD		
Sanchez	David	A		
Quintana	Diego	SEL		

112
East	Mel	B	9-5	(33-1)*
Seay	Mike	HI		(30-7)*
Gonzales	Marty	EX	5-1	
Geronimo	Ernie	A		
Esquivel	Jose	WU	7-3	
Salazar	Robert	SEL		

120
Jones	Del	TW	2-1	
Villareal	Willie	MON		
Ramirez	Tony	WOOD	6-2	
Severson	Jerry	EX		
Luttrell	Darrin	WB		
Gomes	Roy	FRE		

127
Ibarra	Victor	B	6-4	
Trevino	Robert	FRE		
Bisig	Joe	SB	3-0 O.T.	
Hansson	Jeff	HOOV		
Dennis	Kenny	CL	11-8	
De La Cruz	David	KING		

133
Rodriguez	Joel	MAD	8-2	
Vera	Rob	CAR		
Dieling	Dennis	CL	10-3	
McCray	David	WB		
Boyd	Sam	FRE	1-0	
Ortiz	Frank	WU		

138
Sanchez	Art	A	2-0 O.T.	
Negrette	Ron	RED		
Bilyeu	Scott	CL	12-0	
Townsend	Don	MON		
Lopez	Manuel	KING	13-6	
Bonilla	Henry	CORC		

145
Carrera	Kevin	HOOV	3-2	(33-1)*
Inouye	Scott	CL		(33-6)*
Salmonson	Robbie	PORT	5-2	
Gomez	Raul	KING		
Loftis	Mike	CAR	7-1	
Martinez	Israel	CORC		

154
Aquafresca	Brian	EX	3-2	
Delgado	Jose	SHA		
Juarez	Robert	SANG	10-1	
Hoegh	Buddy	SEL		
Fry	David	KING	6-5	
Christiansen	Brian	CL		

165
Pulskamp	Flint	HI	6-2	(31-1/21 Falls)*
Scott	Malcolm	ED		
Bowlden	Mike	CENT	9-3	
Austin	Kevin	HAN		
Kelly	Tom	SB	Default	
Herrera	Cessario	WU		

175
Snell	Mike	WU	7-1	(31-2)*
Emerzian	Tom	ROOS		(34-2)*
Orton	Jeff	WB	7-2	
Little	Greg	FOOT		
Snider	Kevin	HOOV	12-2	
Zambrano	Mario	PAR		

191
Sansinena	Joe	MAD	8-2	
Short	Jim	MON		
Diaz	Robert	BULL	5-3	
Jeffus	Craig	FRE		
Ochoa	Eddie	WU	13-4	
Torigiani	Jeff	SHAFT		

(Continued on next page)

Central Section – Bakersfield College
March 1, 1980

235

Jones	Scott	MT.W	5-4	(27-0)*
Reynevel	Willy	A		
Long	Stan	TW	6-2	
Avila	Joe	STA		
Mudryk	Mark	FOOT	:59	
Pickens	Carl	WU		

Tournament
1. Highland — 66.5
2. Clovis — 61
3. Monache — 61
4. W. Bakersfield — 59
5. Arvin — 57.5
6. Madera — 52
7. Fresno — 48
8. Washington U. — 46.5
9. Exeter — 45
10. Bakersfield — 42.5
11. Hoover — 37
12. Tulare Western — 33
13. Kingsburg — 32
14. Central — 26
15. Mt. Whitney — 24
16. Caruthers — 21
16. Foothill — 21
18. Shafter — 20
19. Selma — 19
20. Redwood — 18
21. Roosevelt — 18
21. S. Bakersfield — 18
23. Edison — 16.5
24. Reedley — 16
25. Bullard — 13
26. Sangaer — 12.5
27. Woodlake — 11
28. Hanford — 10
28. Porterville — 10
30. Strathmore — 8
31. Delano — 5
31. Firebaugh — 5
33. Corcoran — 4
33. Parlier — 4

Willy Reyneveld
Arvin High
2nd in CIF
1980

Jessie Reyes of Bakersfield High
Head wrestling coach
Purdue University

* Record

Correction

Jones, Scott (31-0)*

Central Section – Porterville/Monache

February 28, 1981

101
Mendoza	Ed	CL	6-3	(43-4)*
Gomez	Rene	SHAFT		(34-3)*
Nerove	Darrell	FOOT	1:20	
Gonzales	Gus	REED		
Mauricio	John	HAN	5-0	
Woods	Jon	KING		

108
Quiros	Joe	CL	3-3 O.T.	(35-3)*
Quintana	Diego	SEL		
Rivera	Mark	MAD	5-1	
Erebia	Ruben	KING		
Ray	Wynn	WB	12-10	
Aguilar	Martin	WU		

115
East	Mel	B	14-5	(20-0)*
Caraveo	Jimmy	DEL		
Seay	Mike	HI	4-3	
Jones	Randy	CLW		
Hernandez	Dave	TW	8-6	
Salazar	Robert	SEL		

122
Chedester	Jeff	RED	2-0
Inouye	Darryl	CL	
Williams	Randy	MON	11-0
Gomes	Roy	FIRE	
Geronimo	Ernie	A	10-5
Rangel	Lucky	PAR	

129
Kellerhals	Bud	WU	7-3
Flores	Louis	WOOD	
Jeffery	Rick	WB	4-0
Aulakh	Jagbir	KER	
Rodriguez	Alfonso	REED	6-5
Harris	Greg	SB	

135
Dennis	Kenny	CL	1-1 O.T.	(46-6)*
Bisig	Joe	SB	Criteria	(22-2)*
Sinnott	Richie	HI	:49	
Gamboa	Andrew	MAD		
Abeyta	Tim	KING	6-3	
Anderson	Steve	SIE		

141
Ortiz	Frankie	WU	1:02
Smith	Glen	MT.W	
McCray	Dave	WB	6-2 O.T.
Tice	Jeff	CLW	
Tillinghast	Mike	BULL	9-4
Watts	Dave	CAR	

148
Carrera	Kevin	HOOV	8-0	(30-2)*
Bilyeu	Scott	CL		(46-5)*
Townsend	Don	MON	11-5	
Zimmer	Brad	CLW		
Camargo	Eric	W	2:59	
Vasquez	Danny	SHAFT		

158
Garza	Oscar	MON	3-1	
Lazalde	Ismael	FRE		
Christenson	Brian	CL	5-0	
Stover	Rusty	EX		
Annis	Jeff	SB	Default	(35-3-1)*
Lafleur	Jeff	WOOD		

170
Aquafresca	Brian	EX	11-10 (37-0)
Kelly	Tom	SB	
Aguilar	Fabian	HAN	12-1
Mass	Dave	WB	
Brown	Mike	SHAFT	2-0
Sisney	Steve	KING	

188
Peterson	George	CLW	6-3	(42-4)*
Mayberry	Dan	FOOT		(29-3-1)*
Diaz	Robert	FULL	10-3	
Stall	Dusty	MON		
Austin	Kevin	HAN	Default	
Ochoa	Eddie	WU		

203
Sansinena	Joe	MAD	9-4	(27-0)*
Jeffus	Craig	FRE		(30-9-1)*
Thornton	Alvin	WU	4:40	
Madsen	Joey	MON		
Hanneman	Cliff	CLW	6-1	
Gomes	Victor	TRAN		

(Continued on next page)

Central Section – Porterville/Monache

February 28, 1981

248
Long	Stan	TW	Default
Cervantes	Victor	EB	
Short	Jim	MON	9-3
Wilson	Dan	WB	
Pickens	Carl	WU	1:49
Morley	Phil	W	

Tournament
1. Clovis	111.5
2. Monache	88
3. Washington U.	79
4. Clovis West	62
5. W. Bakersfield	54.5
6. S. Bakersfield	49.5
7. Madera	48
8. Fresno	36
9. Exeter	31.5
10. Foothill	31
10. Tulare Western	31
12. Hanford	30.5
13. Highland	28
14. Shafter	26.5
14. Kingsburg	26.5
16. Bakersfield	23
17. Woodlake	20
17. Redwood	20
17. Bullard	20
17. Selma	20
17. E. Bakersfield	20
22. Reedley	16.5
23. Delano	16
23. Mt. Whitney	16
25. Wasco	14.5
26. Firebaugh	12
27. Kerman	10
28. Arvin	7.5
29. Caruthers	4
29. Parlier	4
29. Sierra	4
Central	0
Chowchilla	0
Edison	0
Laton	0
Hoover	?

* Record

Bruce Burnett of North Bakersfield
Head wrestling coach, United States Naval Academy

Central Section – Clovis West

February 27, 1982

101
Mendoza	Ed	CL	14-10
Nerove	Darrell	FOOT	
Mauricio	John	HAN	5-3
Patino	Bobby	EX	
Lewis	Tony	KING	3-1
Kland	Kevin	HOOV	

108
Ray	Wynn	WB	7-6
Aguilar	Martin	WU	
Buccat	Chris	DEL	11-0
Carrillo	Augustine	KER	
Quiroz	Joe	CL	4-1
Salgado	Larry	EX	

115
Rivera	Mark	MAD	3-0
Cottingham	Greg	EX	
Martin	John	CLW	18-11
Aguilar	George	WU	
Quintaqna	Diego	SEL	5-2
Hernandez	David	TW	

122
East	Mel	B	3-2	(31-0)*
Rangel	Pat	MAD		
Salazar	Robert	SEL	12-6	
Armstead	Mike	LEM		
Gomez	Ray	CAR		
Erebia	Danny	KING		

129
Williams	Randy	MON	10-9
Des Jardins	Shane	HAN	
Abeyta	Tim	KING	5-3
Aulakh	Jagbir	KER	
Prather	Brett	WB	:51
Calderon	Abel	RED	

135
Rosario	David	MAD	4-3
Harris	Greg	SB	
Lewis	Brian	CLW	7-4
Polomar	Vince	KING	
Flores	Louie	WOOD	7-5
Marquez	Jessi	GOLD	

141
Richburg	Allen	CLW	4-0
Graham	Randy	B	
Lathrop	Mike	SB	3-2
Marchant	Kris	FOOT	
Mitchell	John	CAR	2:53
Cantu	David	MAD	

148
Hayes	Bill	SANG	5-3
Vasquez	Daniel	SHAFT	
Watts	David	CAR	7-4
Klugow	Scott	SB	
Gregory	John	MON	Default
Tice	Jeff	CLW	

158
Townsend	Don	MON	9-2	(48-2)*
Christiansen	Brian	CL		
Mills	Cary	SB	7-4	
Brown	Rodney	SHAF		
Zimmer	Brad	CLW	2:52	
Glass	Jon	HAN		

170
Hill	Kirk	MON	7-2
Campbell	Eric	CLW	
Lazalde	Ismael	FRE	1:53
Garnand	Blake	SB	
Clifton	Jim	PAR	10-6
Brown	Mike	SHAFT	

188
Greemore	Jason	B	O.T. Ref. Dec.
Young	Todd	CLW	
Torosian	Dan	MAD	6-4
Tyler	Terry	RED	
Garcia	Mario	PAR	
Uhlier	Bob	WU	

203
Corniet	Rebel	WOOD	11-7
Garza	Oscar	KING	
Barnes	John	EX	1:30
Reitz	Dennis	CER	

(Continued on next page)

Central Section – Mt. Whitney/Visalia
February 17, 1982

248
Estes	Barry	CLW	8-3
Lazama	Pete	FOOT	
Garcia	Carlos	MAD	3-2
Traffanstedd	Jim	B	

Tournament
1. Clovis West — 126
2. Madera — 95.5
3. Bakersfield — 77
4. Monache — 74
5. S. Bakersfield — 67
6. Kingsburg — 52.5
7. Exeter — 51.5
8. Foothill — 50
9. Clovis — 45
10. Hanford — 38.5
11. Washington U. — 37
12. W. Bakersfield — 31
13. Shafter — 30
14. Caruthers — 27
14. Woodlake — 27
16. Sanger — 20
17. Selma — 18
17. Kerman — 18
19. Redwood — 16
20. Fresno — 12
20. Delano — 12
22. Parlier — 11
22. Wasco — 11
22. Central — 11
25. Lemoore — 5
25. Tulare — 5
27. Hoover — 4
27. Golden West — 4
27. Tulare Western — 4
Dos Palos — 0
E. Bakersfield — 0
McFarland — 0
Tranquility — 0

Lennis Cowell
Clovis West
Coached two State
Championship teams
Record: 97-5

* Record

Central Section – Bakersfield High

February 26, 1983

101
Ramirez	Pete	A	8-0
Montoya	Greg	CL	
Gomez	Eddie	CAR	11-2
Benavides	John	MT.W	
Kland	Devin	HOOV	4-3
Lewis	Tony	KING	

108
Quiroz	Joe	CL	8-7
Patino	Bob	EX	
Barron	Rick	WU	3-0
Cardenas	Roy	MON	
Hollender	Dan	CLW	2-1
Gomez	George	CAR	

115
Aguilar	George	WU	5-3
Gomez	Rene	SHAFT	
Dallas	Mike	FOOT	:42
Quintana	Diego	SEL	
Woods	John	KING	4-2
Rodriguez	Abe	DEL	

122
Nerove	Darrell	FOOT	11-0	(50-0)*
Rangel	Pat	MAD		
Martin	John	CLW	6-2	
Erebia	Danny	KING		
Ramirez	Tony	A	6-1	
Cruz	Danny	SHAFT		

129
Gomez	Francisco	CLW	8-0
Calderon	Abel	RED	
Morales	Tony	EB	3-1
Garay	Manuel	A	
Ortiz	Tony	WU	2:10
Johanns	Kirk	CL	

135
Pressley	Joe	SHAFT	1:19
Poindexter	Jim	PAR	
Lewis	Brian	CLW	6-4
Palomar	Vince	KING	
Austin	Brian	HAN	15-6
Cuevas	Tinee	EX	

141
Davis	Bret	MON	5-4
Sapien	Kevin	EX	
Merritt	Joey	HI	2-1
Marchant	Kris	FOOT	F/F
Erebia	Ruben	KING	
Chavez	Martin	B	

148
Richburg	Allen	CLW	19-1
Rosario	David	MAD	
Graham	Randy	B	1-0
Watts	David	CAR	
Cates	Roy	SHAFT	6-3
Williams	Robert	WB	

158
Glass	Jon	HAN	Default
Hampton	Kelly	EX	
Zimmer	Brad	CLW	Default
Edmonds	Brett	REED	
Hinsley	Jim	FOOT	6-4
Quijano	Alejandro	PAR	

170
Campbell	Eric	CLW	4-2
Inouye	Les	CL	
Cornett	Rebel	WOOD	9-7
Camacho	Dan	MCF	
Henson	Scott	SEL	9-7
Lockwood	Rick	EX	

188
Young	Todd	CLW	9-5
Moore	Lenny	B	
Forry	Matt	FOOT	4:45
Scott	James	KING	
Clifton	Jim	PAR	5-1
Hill	Craig	MON	

203
Allen	Chris	SB	7-1	(38-4)*
Reitz	Dennis	CENT		(30-1)*
White	Don	CW	6-5	
Howe	Todd	CL		
Imanura	Rod	FRE	9-3	
Gomez	David	TRAN		

(Continued on next page)

Central Section – Bakersfield High
February 26, 1983

248
Salas	Rick	MAD	7-2
Estes	Barry	CLW	
Landseadel	Brad	RED	11-6
Duke	Russell	FOOT	
Mendivel	Doc	EB	3:20
Baptista	Eddie	KER	

Tournament
1. Clovis West 172
2. Foothill 82
3. Clovis 77.5
4. Exeter 60
5. Madera 54
6. Shafter 52
7. Monache 46.5
8. Kingsburg 44.5
9. Washington U. 42
10. Arvin 34.5
11. Bakersfield 32
12. Hanford 31.5
13. Redwood 30
14. Caruthers 28
15. Parlier 27
16. S. Bakersfield 22
17. E. Bakersfield 21.5
18. Central 18
19. Mt. Whitney 13
20. Highland 12
20. Woodlake 12
22. Reedley 10
23. Fresno 9
23. McFarland 9
23. Selma 9
26. Hoover 6
27. W. Bakersfield 5.5
28. Delano 4
28. Kerman 4
28. Tranquility 4

* Record

David Watts of Caruthers
Winner over Ruben Castro
Tranquility
Sierra/Sequoia Finals

Central Section – Hanford
February 25, 1984

101
Gomez	Eddie	CAR	4-2	
Ramirez	Pete	A		
Benavides	John	MT.W		
Martin	Sal	GW		
Rangel	Ray	PAR		
Garcia	Sal	MAD		

108
Baron	Rick	WU	
Henry	Casey	CLW	
East	Brad	B	
Lopez	Cruz	TUL	
Rice	David	MON	
Serna	Ismael	MCF	

115
Patino	Bobby	EX	
Cardenas	Roy	MON	
Bragg	Gregg	RED	
Ciprian	Peter	ROOS	
Ibarra	Anthony	CL	
Garza	Ray	CHOW	

122
Dallas	Mike	FOOT	12-1	(31-4-1)*
Gonzales	Arnold	WU		
Land	Robert	MON		
Nishikawa	Randy	CENT		
Hollender	Dan	CLW		
Calderon	Jerry	RED		

129
Lewis	Brian	CLW	(40-0-1)*
Armistead	Mike	LEM	
Rangel	Pat	MAD	
Santellano	V.	WU	
Erebia	Ruben	CL	
Soltero	Jesse	CENT	

135
Martin	John	CLW	(36-3)*
Nerove	Darrell	FOOT	(34-2)*
Ashjian	Brook	WB	
Wooden	Bryan	TUL	
Nunez	Jesus	DP	
Sahacun	Xavier	WOOD	

141
Gomez	Francisco	CLW	10-4	(43-1)*
Hembree	James	SB		
Collins	Kerry	GW		
Quiroz	Serrio	CAR		
Austin	Brian	HAN		
Merritt	Joey	HI		

148
Rosario	David	MAD	(45-1)*
Thomas	Jerry	FRE	
Moody	Brian	GW	
Gomez	Joe	TRAN	
Dandoval	Brent	CLW	
Pressley	Joe	SHAFT	

157
Graham	Randy	B	6-3	(41-0)*
Cowart	Lance	MON		
Barnes	Todd	CLW		
Hansen	Robert	SEL		
Martinez	Carmen	EX		
Cunningham	Randy	HOOV		

168
Inouye	Les	CL
Tice	Jeff	CLW
Green	Richard	FOOT
Creech	Jim	B
Gonzales	Vince	TRAN
Aulakh	Abel	KER

178
Cerda	David	CLW	
Jackson	Rick	KING	
Hill	Craig	MON	
Clifton	Jim	PAR	(35-5)*
Telen	Dan	CLW	
Gretlein	Jim	B	

194
Flowers	Randy	MCL
Christensen	Kevin	CL
Flowers	Ron	FRE
Lizama	Ben	FOOT
Slevin	Don	DP
Velasco	John	MAD

(Continued on next page)

Central Section – Hanford
February 25, 1984

245

Mendivel	Doc	EB	4-3	
Salas	Ricky	MAD		(45-2)*
Barnes	Trent	CLW		
Moore	Gailton	MT.W		
Alarcon	Eloy	DP		
Torosian	Alan	SEL		

Tournament

1. Clovis West — 151.5
2. Monache — 67
3. Clovis — 64.5
4. Foothill — 64
5. Madera — 60
6. Washington U. — 48
7. Golden West — 41.5
8. Bakersfield — 39
9. Exeter — 31
10. Caruthers — 29
11. Fresno — 27
11. W. Bakersfield — 27
13. Dos Palos — 26
14. Mt. Whitney — 25.5
15. E. Bakersfield — 22
16. Arvin — 20
16. McLane — 20
18. Kingsburg — 18
18. Tranquility — 18
20. Redwood — 16.5
21. Lemoore — 16
21. S. Bakersfield — 16
23. Darlier — 15
23. Selma — 15
25. Central — 14
26. Roosevelt — 12
26. Tulare Western — 12
28. Hanford — 11
29. Tulare — 10
30. Chowchilla — 6
31. Hoover — 5
31. Shafter — 5
33. Highland — 4
33. Kerman — 4
33. McFarland — 4
33. Woodlake — 4

* Record

1986 South High Wrestling Team
SYL Wrestling Champions
League record: 7-0
Overall record: 15-1

Central Section – Clovis West
February 23, 1985

98
Gomes	Eddie	CAR	5-1	(141-12)*
Snyder	Pete	MON		
Dutra	Darrin	HAN	5-0	
Smithson	Chad	HOOV		
Tames	Anthony	CL	2:40	
Reyes	Lee	WU		

105
East	Brad	B	15-4	(43-0)*
Quintero	Marty	CL		
Cantu	Ruben	GW	2:09	
Rangel	Raymond	PAR		
Hill	Charles	CLW	Default	
Lara	Armando	CAR		

112
Lopez	Cruz	TUL	2-1
Henry	Casey	CLW	
Eudy	Shannon	FOOT	7-6
Morales	Manuel	SEL	
Chavez	Richard	CENT	11-4
Serna	Ismael	MCF	

119
Crosswhite	Shawn	CL	
Bragg	Greg	RED	
Richey	Jamie	CLW	7-4
Nishikawa	Randy	CENT	
Hurtado	Alex	KING	9-4
Ramero	Tony	TW	

126
Rangel	Pat	CL	8-4	
Dallas	Mike	FOOT		(37-3)*
Zarate	Elias	SEL	2:41	
Beavers	Troy	HI		
Gonzales	Arnold	WU	5-0	
Briseno	Aaron	KER		

132
Chavez	Ruben	B	15-2 (38-4-1)
Martinez	John	CL	
Sordi	John	MAD	4-0
Ornelas	Stevie	TRAN	
Valdez	Ric	SANG	7-1
Santellano	Vinnie	WU	

138
Martinez	Joe	BULL	10-6
Olivas	Kelvin	CL	
Rangel	Jeff	FOOT	7-3
Nunez	Jesus	DP	
Garcia	Frank	EX	11-2
Morales	Lorenzo	SEL	

145
Sandoval	Brent	CLW	8-0
Flores	Luis	MAD	
Cuevas	Miguel	EX	6-2
Pickens	Kenny	WU	
Davila.	David	CAR	6-5
Cintora	Bradley	DP	

154
Rosario	David	FIRE	Default
Hansen	Robert	SEL	
Cerda	Jerry	CLW	2-1
Snyder	John	MON	
Mendoza	Jose	KING	4:06
Cano	Chris	HAN	

165
Cunningham	Randy	HOOV	9-5
Thornberg	Tim	SEL	
Howard	Fred	WU	3-1
Pulskamp	Greeg	HI	
Katuin	Kevin	SANG	Default
Olinger	Scott	SB	

175
Hill	Craig	MON	8-2
Jackson	Rick	KING	
Leonard	Mike	A	7-4
Hernandez	Robert	MT.W	
Lincoln	Bob	YOSE	9-5
Granadoz	Tony	WU	

191
Clark	David	MAD	
Telen	Dan	CL	
Slevin	Don	DP	14-5
Kelly	Ron	GW	
Fugman	Brett	CLW	F/F
Ravalin	Rick	SEL	

(Continued on next page)

Central Section – Clovis West
February 23, 1985

245
Barnes	Trent	CLW	12-10 (37-1/34 Falls)*
Lizama	Ben	FOOT	(36-4)*
Fontes	Ken	CL	2:28
Jackson	Bill	KING	
Slocum	Charles	ED	5-4
Torosian	Alan	SEL	

Tournament
1. Clovis 134
2. Clovis West 106
3. Selma 77
4. Foothill 62
5. Madera 53
6. Monache 50
7. Bakesfield 45
8. Kingsburg 44
9. Washington U. 40
10. Hoover 33
11. Caruthers 32
12. Golden West 26
12. Firebaugh 26
14. Dos Palos 25
15. Highland 21
16. Tulare 20
16. Bullard 20
18. Exeter 19
19. Hanford 17
19. Redwood 17
21. Sanger 16
22. Darlier 15
22. Central 15
24. Arvin 13
25. Mt. Whitney 11
25. Tranquility 11
27. Yosemite 9
28. Edison 8
29. Kerman 6
30. S. Bakersfield 5
31. Tulare Western 4
31. McFarland 4

* Record

Gomes career 141-12
Junior/Senior years 80-2

Top Row (L. to R.): T. Dennis, B. Kropog, D. Townsend, D. Williams; Middle Row (L. to R.): T. Whitlock, M. Della, R. Whitlock, J. Loflin; Bottom Row (L. to R.): A. Gonzales, W. McNutt, G. Rodriguez, D. Vanni, T. Vanni

1978 Monach High Wrestling Team
CIF Champions

Drew Williams
Heach Coach
Monache High

Central Section – Bakersfield High
March 1, 1986

102
Garcia	Sal	MAD	10-2
Zinkin	Harold	BULL	
Riley	Brandon	CL	10-3
Munoz	Rito	WU	
Hamaoka	Derrick	CLW	2:40
Madgallanes	M	FIRE	

109
Tamez	Anthony	CL	4-2 O.T.
Snyder	Pete	MON	
Tennison	Julius	ED	3-2 O.T.
Martinez	Alex	BULL	
Blanco	Ray	CLW	8-3
Sullivan	Andrew	W	

116
East	Brad	B	7-2
Dutra	Darren	HAN	
Smithson	Chad	HOOV	4-2
Perez	Eddie	FIRE	
Morales	Manuel	SEL	10-2
Deluna	Osi	MAD	

123
Cavazos	Junior	MAD	7-6
Rangel	Ray	PAR	
Herron	Marc	EX	1:15
Sanchez	Eddie	FIRE	
Avalos	Manuel	WOOD	10-6
Eudy	Shannon	FOOT	

130
Crosswhite	Shawn	CL	8-3
Cuevas	Dan	EX	
Shockley	Brian	B	8-1
Marin	Jose	A	
Duquette	James	MT.W 1	2-4
Aguilar	Carlos	WU	

136
Beavers	Troy	HI	12-4
Gonzales	Arnold	WU	
Zarate	Ociel	SEL	6-2
Pierro	John	CLW	
Garcia	Joe	MAD	2-0 O.T.
Islas	Andy	CL	

142
Olivas	Kelvin	CL	12-3
Zarate	Elias	SEL	
Rangel	Jeff	FOOT	2:12
Stricker	Ty	SB	
Wright	Scott	KING	Default Inj.
Wright	Gary	LEM	

149
Herndon	Scott	SB	5-2 (44-1)
Davila	David	CAR	
Oliver	Craig	B	:45
Cerda	Jerry	ROOS	
Klaprath	Bert	YOSE	7-5
Threlkeld	Wes	FRE	

158
Tripp	John	TUL	1:54
Romine	Joe	MAD	
Gannon	Joe	HI	6-5
Brown	Scott	CLW	
Mendoza	Jose	KING	2:41
Murphy	Robbie	FIRE	

167
Leonard	Mike	A	3:59
Bruton	Terry	MT.W	
Howe	Ty	CL	16-5
Gonzales	Lupe	WOOD	
Warford	Scott	EX	
Olinger	Chris	SB	Default Inj.

179
Ravalin	Rick	SEL	6-5	(34-3)*
Pulskamp	Greg	HI		(36-2)*
Flowers	Wes	ED	12-4	
Gatzka	Greg	ROOS		
Lindsey	Cory	CLW	7-5	
Boucieques	Louis	WU		

195
Telen	Dan	CL	12-2
Neal	Lorenzo	LEM	
Harris	Earl	TUL	15-4
Powell	Darin	WOOD	
Davis	Pat	B	10-4
Briner	Skip	YOSE	

(Continued on next page)

Central Section – Bakersfield High
March 1, 1986

249

Barnes	Trent	CLW	:28 (124-12/84 Falls)*
Anderson	George	EX	
Pullin	Richard	MON	7-3
Correa	Joseph	MAD	
Fontes	Ken	CL	2:48
Cullar	Ricardo	PAR	

Tournament

1. Clovis — 122
2. Madera — 78
3. Clovis West — 69
4. Selma — 58.5
5. Exeter — 56
6. Highland — 51.5
7. Bakersfield — 44
8. Tulare — 38.5
9. Washington U. — 38
10. Bullard — 36.5
11. S. Bakersfield — 36
12. Arvin — 36
13. Firebaugh — 32.5
14. Monache — 29.5
15. Woodlake — 27.5
16. Parlier — 27
17. Edison — 24.5
18. Roosevelt — 23
19. Mt. Whitney — 22.5
20. Lemoore — 20
21. Foothill — 19
22. Hanford — 18.5
23. Caruthers — 18
24. Kingsburg — 16
25. Hoover — 12.5
26. Yosemite — 11
27. Wasco — 4
28. Fresno — 3
E. Bakersfield — 0
Dos Palos — 0
Shafter — 0
McFarland — 0
McLane — 0

* Record

Trent Barnes career

Coby Wright of Bakersfield High.
CIF Champion, State Champion,
two-time NCAA All-American CSUB

Randy Graham of Bakersfield High
1984 State Champion

Central Section – Monache/Porterville
February 28, 1987

98
Zinkin	Harold	BULL	10-2	
Hamaoka	Derek	CLW		
Sordi	Robbie	MAD	6-0	(44-11)*
Munoz	Rito	WU		
Ramirez	Bryan	KING	1-0	
Legarreta	Eric	SEL		

105
Tamez	Anthony	CL	8-7	
Zinkin	Dewayne	BULL		
Patton	Derek	A	5-2	(37-8)*
Perez	Art	SB		
Gobeli	David	HOOV	2-1	
Behill	Raymond	CAR		

112
Salyer	Jimmy	TUL	11-7	
Flores	Frank	HAN		
Riley	Brandon	CL	11-0	
Fambona	Pedro	A		(34-14)*
Rodriguez	Thomas	SEL	1:10	
Meza	Soul	EB		

119
Dutra	Darren	HAN	9-1	
Herron	Marc	EX		
Ortega	Mike	ROOS	3:30	
Gaon	Jason	SB		(31-11)*
Macias	Manuel	WU	2-1	
Lucatero	Valdo	WOOD		

126
Rangel	Ray	PAR	4-2
Watts	Terry	CAR	
Garcia	Joe	MAD	2-1
Johanson	Keith	FRE	
Quintana	Ismael	SEL	19-3
Garside	Darrin	NB	

132
Beavers	Troy	HI	16-13	(143-39)*
Pierro	John	CLW		
Briseno	Aaron	KER	8-4	
Harvey	Travis	MON		
Henderson	Brian	SB	1:10	
Ramirez	Richard	KING		

138
Sordi	John	MAD	15-8	
Prather	Hugh	B		(38-6)*
Campos	Joe	FRE	7-6	
Stricker	Ty	SB		
Richburg	Greg	CLW	4-2	
Medrano	Jesus	TRAN		

145
Herndon	Scott	SB	7-3	(48-4)*
Byrd	David	CLW		
Davila	David	CAR	4-3	
Neves	Brian	HAN		
Kaproth	Bert	YOSE	1:30	
Pilgrim	Randy	LAT		

154
Romine	Joe	MAD	15-8
Threlkeld	Wes	FRE	
Treadwell	Otto	TUL	6-0
Kessler	Tim	CLW	
Starlin	Monty	CL	9-4
Reyes	Adrian	TRAN	

165
Tripp	John	TUL	2:53	
Olinger	Chris	SB		(45-6)*
Zapata	Robert	SEL	7-4	
Sahagun	Richard	WOOD		
Leonard	Matt	A	8-7	
Alcorn	John	HAN		

175
Urzua	Jerry	FRE	14-8
Hailey	Lorenzo	TUL	
Bonilla	B.J.	SEL	113-4
Sessions	Billy	WU	
Dominici	David	MAD	
Gonzales	Lupe	WOOD	

191
Neal	Lorenzo	LEM	6-2
Carlos	Rene	CL	
Lincoln	Kent	YOSE	6-5
Blazevich	Scott	MCL	
Tsang	Alan	CAR	5-0
Maytorena	Marcelino	FRE	

(Continued on next page)

Central Section – Monache/Porterville
February 28, 1987

245
Anderson	George	EX	7-3
Neal	Eddie	LEM	
Fontes	Ken	CL	Default
Jackson	Billy	KING	
Raney	Brian	DP	10-1
Henderson	Jimmy	KER	

Tournament
1. S. Bakersfield — 82
2. Tulare — 79
3. Clovis — 75
4. Clovis West — 70.5
5. Madera — 70.5
6. Fresno — 61
7. Hanford — 58.5
8. Selma — 44.5
9. Caruthers — 41.5
10. Exeter — 40.5
10. Lemoore — 40
12. Bullard — 33.5
12. Arvin — 33.5
14. Washington U. — 29.5
15. Yosemite — 23
16. Highland — 20.5
17. Kingsburg — 20
17. Parlier — 20
19. Kerman — 19.5
20. Woodlake — 19
21. Bakersfield — 16.5
22. Roosevelt — 16
23. Monache — 11.5
24. McLane — 11
25. N. Bakersfield — 8
25. Tranquility — 8
27. Dos Palos — 7.5
28. Hoover — 6
29. Laton — 5
30. E. Bakersfield — 4
Delano — 0
Dinubia — 0
Edison — 0
Firebaugh — 0
Sierra — 0
Redwood — 0
Mt. Whitney — 0

* Record

1987 South Bakersfield Wrestling Team – CIF Champions

Parris Whitley, left, 3rd in State for South Bakersfield 1990

Lorenzo Neal, Lemoore, Three-time CIF Champion Placed 4, 2 and State Champion NCAA All-American Fresno State All Pro – NFL

Central Section – Bullard/Fresno

February 27, 1988

98
Sordi	Robbie	MAD	7-1	(49-3)*
Ramirez	Bryan	KING		
Mares	Joseph	SEL	2:59	
Garcia	Robert	WU		
Wright	Kenny	B	4-1	
Crane	Shawn	CLW		

105
Munoz	Rito	WU	7-5
Hamaoka	Derek	CLW	
Rivera	Tom	MON	9-8
Legarreta	Erc	SEL	
Valle	Levid	GW	2-0
Mendez	Henry	DEL	

112
Zinkin	DeWayne	BULL	11-4
Gobeli	David	HOOV	
Fambona	Pedro	A	7-2
Solis	Robert	RED	
Deltoro	Tony	CAR	3-1
Hood	Brett	MON	

119
Patton	Derek	A	1-02
Salyer	Jimmy	TUL	
Lucatero	Valdo	WU	8-2
Arcona	Robert	CL	
Hurtado	Nacho	KING	4:20
Moreno	Jose	MAD	

126
Melo	Vince	EX	4-1
Olivas	Ralph	CL	
Ortega	Mike	ROOS	1:48
Soto	Steve	CLW	
Archveleta	Jason	WU	5-2
Flores	David	MAD	

132
Cemo	Joe	NB	4-2
Williams	Ken	EX	
Quintana	Ismael	SEL	1:55
Haupt	Heath	CL	
Chavez	Art	WB	4-1
Paul	Brent	W	

138
Watts	Terry	CAR	2:53
Morales	Johnny	SEL	
Gomez	Gus	EX	4:58 TF
Stricker	Tad	SB	
Lawanson	Joseph	CLW	1-0
Lopez	Narcisco	ROOS	

145
Hoyt	Brian	CL	6-3	
Stricker	Ty	SB	(47-6)	(110-48)*
Sandusky	Darrin	CLW	6-4	
Cuevas	Alfonso	MAD		
Froehlich	Jassen	B	F/F	
Grijalva	K.	CENT		

154
Starling	Monte	CL	11-9
Fletcher	David	WB	
Roop	Caleb	YOSE	2:15
Deatherage	Larry	NB	
Enyart	Gerald	WU	17-4
Degough	Scott	CLW	

165
Leonard	Matt	A	4-3	(89-18)*
Morin	Mike	SEL		
Estrada	Richard	ROOS	1:43	
Garcia	Adrian	EX		
Lopez	Jorgie	WU	6-3	
Smith	James	TUL		

175
Zapata	Robert	SEL	8-0
Urzua	Jerry	FRE	
Sahagun	Richard	WOOD	18-5
Madison	Mike	WB	
Jones	Owen	DEL	11-10
Lowery	Casey	YOSE	

191
Neal	Lorenzo	LEM	9-5
Hailey	Lorenzo	TUL	
Lincoln	Kent	YOS	6-5
Jasso	Javier	RED	
Nesbit	Lee	MT.W	2-1
Mesa	Chuck	WOOD	

(Continued on next page)

Central Section - Bullard/Fresno
February 27, 1988

245

Carlos	Rene	CL	10-1
Smith	Mark	CLW	
Marucuch	Jim	FOOT	11-1
Barella	Mike	MON	
Sosa	Henry	RED	
Gamez	Jesus	TRAN	

Tournament
1. Clovis — 106.5
2. Selma — 99.5
3. Clovis Wsest — 75
4. Exeter — 65
5. Arvin — 55
6. Washington U. — 51.5
7. Madera — 42
8. Tulare — 41
9. Roosevelt — 35.5
10. W. Bakersfield — 35
11. Redwood — 34
12. Yosemite — 33
13. N. Bakersfield — 31.5
14. Caruthers — 30.5
15. Woodlake — 30
16. S. Bakersfield — 27.5
17. Kingsburg — 26.5
18. Monache — 26
19. Lemoore — 22.5
20. Bullard — 21
21. Fresno — 18
21. Hoover — 18
23. Bakersfield — 17
24. Delano — 15
25. Foothill — 13.5
26. Golden West — 6.5
27. Wasco — 4
28. Tranquility — 2
McFarland — 0

* Record

Ty Stricker career
Matt Leonard career

Left to right, Ty and Tad Stricker
South Bakersfield
CIF placing:
Ty: 4, 4, 2   Tad: 4, 2, 1

Terry Watts (top) of Caruthers
Darren Dutra (bottom) of Hanford

Central Section – Arvin
February 25, 1989

98
Zinkin	Nick	CL	4-2	
Alkire	Curtis	MON		(39-8)*
Serda	Mike	W	5-2	(35-3)*
Fuentes	Ed	SANG		
Pumarejo	Isaac	KING	Default	
Quintana	Nick	SEL		

132
Aguirre	Jim	CL	3-2	
Sordi	Robbi	MAD		(48-4)*
Gant	Detran	Roos	11-9	
Crain	Sean	CLW		
Mares	Joseph	SEL	9-0	
Garcia	Robert	WU		

112
Quintana	Gary	SEL	Fall	
Ramirez	Brian	KING		
Whitley	Parris	SB	2-1	
Heberle	Jeff	NB		(51-10)*
Wright	Kenny	B	2-0	
Tamez	Mike	CL		

119
Legarreta	Eric	SEL	5-4
Gobeli	David	HOOV	
Solano	Alex	DP	7-5
Perez	Roy	CORC	
Arredondo	Rick	MAD	8-5
Solis	Robert	RED	

126
Zinkin	Dewayne	BULL	9-1
Riley	Dustin	CL	
Rodriguez	Jesse	REED	15-4
Rodriguez	Thomas	SEL	
Perez	Mario	Sha	7-0
Harper	Darrell	B	

132
Melo	Vince	EX	1-0	
Cemo	Joe	NB		(51-5)*
Ramirez	Louie	SEL	10-6	
Kenner	Ricky	BULL		
Patton	David	DP	Default	
Gomez	Johnny	TRAN		

138
Soto	Steve	CLW	3-2
Williams	Ken	EX	
Olivas	Ralph	CL	4-0
Motl	Randy	LEM	
Alvarez	Louie	PAR	10-2
Rodriguez	Eric	WU	

145
Watts	Terry	CAR	13-2 (47-1/32 Falls)*	
Lopez	Narcisco	ROOS		
Garcia	Isaac	B	15-8	(39-9-1)*
Quintana	Ismael	SEL		
Cuevas	Alfonso	MAD	16-0	
Compolongo	Jason	CLW		

154
Roop	Caleb	YOSE	8-5	(42-2)*
Stricker	Tad	SB		(34-7)*
Bartlett	Steve	NB	10-4	
Martinez	Nacho	W		
Lawanson	Joseph	CLW	9-3	
Froehlich	Jim	B		

165
Sandusky	Darren	CLW	:53
Leary	Marcus	A	
Froehlich	Jassen	B	1:59
Stringer	Don	CL	
Jenkins	Brady	FIRE	:34
Lopez	Jorge	WU	

175
Morin	Mike	SEL	4-1
Land	Ryan	MON	
Madison	Mike	WB	4-3
Reyes	Lozano	TRAN	
Torres	Bryant	MAD	4:35
Olsen	Gary	B	

191
Carlos	Rene	CL	5-2	(36-3)*
Langley	Kevin	NB		(50-6-1)*
Lowry	Casey	YOSE	13-7	
			(100-35 Career)	
Bell	Brad	CLW		
Williams	Gary	HOOV	F/F	
Mendiola	Tom	TRAN		

(Continued on next page)

Central Section – Arvin
February 25, 1989

245

Neal	Lorenzo	LEM	6-0	(43-0)*	
				(147-8-1 Career)*	
Smith	Mark	CLW		(38-4)*	
Jasso	Javier	RED	5-1		
Gomez	Jamie	FIRE			
Campbell	Glen	B	F/F	(30-10)*	
Reade	Scott	WB			

Tournament
1. Selma — 112
2. Clovis West — 99.5
3. Clovis — 88.5
4. Bullard — 62
5. Bakersfield — 59
6. N. Bakersfield — 58
7. Madera — 45
8. Exeter — 40
9. Lemoore — 35
10. Yosemite — 34.5
11. S. Bakersfield — 29.5
12. Roosevelt — 29
13. Kingsburg — 27
13. Redwood — 27
15. Caruthers — 24
16. Tranquility — 22
16. Firebaugh — 22
18. Wasco — 21
19. Dos Palos — 20
20. W. Bakersfield — 17.5
21. Arvin — 16
22. Washington U. — 15
23. Corcoran — 9
24. Parlier — 8
24. Sanger — 8
26. Shafter — 7
27. Reedley — 5
Highland — 0
McFarland — 0

Terry Watts (top) of Caruthers High
Two-time CIF Champion
State Champion
All-American at Fresno State
Photo: J. Shinkawa

12 other schools scored no points

* Record
Terry Watts: career 177-13/108 falls

Central Section – Hanford
February 24, 1990

98
Munoz	Andy	WU	5-3	(35-0)*
Poore	Mike	MAD		(35-7)*
Serda	Mike	W	4:42	
Radman	Aaron	WB		
Amaya	Rick	MON	4-1	
Chandler	Trampis	CL		

105
Quintana	Nick	SEL	6-2	(41-5-1)*
Zinkin	Nick	CL		(42-2-2)*
Fuentes	Ed	SANG	4:12	
Lango	Kevin	SIE		
Sanchez	Roger	ROOS	5:00	
Winn	Robert			

112
Gant	Detran	ROOS	25-8 T.F.	
Molano	David	GW		(30-6)*
Ervin	Ben	MAD	4-2	
Michell	Matt	HAN		
Hull	Brian	MON		
Alvarez	Mike	KING		

119
Aguirre	Jim	CL	8-4	(47-2)*
Gobeli	David	HOOV		(38-7)*
Whitley	Parris	SB	8-7	(44-3)*
Solano	Alex	DP		(49-4)*
Garcia	Robert	WU	1:40	
Washington	Yero	PORT		

126
Alkire	Curtis	MON	Default	(27-1)*
Hogue	Kelly	MAD		(28-9)*
Quintana	Gary	SEL	11-5	
Heberle	Jeff	NB		
Tamez	Mike	CL	11-5	
Cintora	Theo	DP		

132
Roach	Brian	CLW	3-2	
Riley	Dustin	CL		
Scalzo	Chad	MAD	9-4	(39-2)*
Rodriguez	Jesse	REED		
Benavides	Ray	CAR		
Purcella	Sid	WASCO		

138
Ramirez	Louie	SEL	4-3	(15-2-1)*
Olivas	Ralph	CL		(31-3-2)*
Weber	Clayton	MAD	9-1	
Motl	Randy	LEM		
Gomez	John	TRAN	8-6	
Zamorano	Carlos	ROOS		

145
Medrano	Beto	TRAN	5-3	(40-2)*
Hall	Ken	MON		
Chavez	Andrez	HOOV	5-1	
Cleveland	Josh	COAL		
Zeller	Jason	CLW	9-4	
Hesser	Scott	KING		

154
Cuevas	Alfonso	MAD	11-7	(39-2)*
Garcia	Isaac	B		(43-7)*
Bice	Darin	SHAFT	2:42	
Ruiz	Danny	EB		
Parks	Gene	MON	11-10	
Ponce	Angel	ROOS		

165
Stricker	Tad	SB	Fall 2:57	(45-3)*
Silver	Scott	BULL		(34-4)*
Covert	Wes	MON	Fall 4:30	
Soto	Alex	MCF		
Wright	Chad	B	3-2	
Smith	Doug	MTW		

175
Froehlich	Jassen	B	Fall	(46-0)*
Umada	David	MAD		(39-8-1)*
Parker	Jason	MON	2-0	
Morales	Paul	CL		
Perry	Jim	CAR	Default	
Clayton	Terry	SHAFT		

191
Bell	Brad	CLW	10-1	(41-0-1)*
Atkins	Gene	CL		(32-13)*
Moz	Lalo	HAN	13-1	
Salinas	Noe	REED		
Dias	John	LAT	3:55	
Robert	Mark	WB		

(Continued on next page)

Central Section – Hanford
February 24, 1990

245

Williams	Gary	HOOV	Fall	(34-3)*
Salven	Josh	CLW		(39-4)*
				(Career 84-23)*
Gutierrez	David	MTW	2-0	
Williams	Rod	WU		
Gomez	Jamie	FIRE	2:50	
Carrillo	Paul	SB		

Tournament

1. Madera	118	21. Dos Palos	15
2. Clovis	117	21. W. Bakersfield	15
3. Monache	90.5	23. E. Bakersfield	11
4. Clovis West	74	24. Firebaugh	10
5. Bakersfield	57	24. Kingsburg	10
6. Selma	53	24. Sierra	10
6. Hoover	53	27. Coalinga	9
8. Roosevelt	45	27. Laton	9
9. S. Bakersfield	41.5	27. Lemoore	9
10. Washington U.	39	27. McFarland	9
11. Tranquility	28	27. N. Bakersfield	9
12. Hanford	25	32. Porterville	5
13. Mt. Whitney	21	Arvin	0
14. Reedley	20	Central	0
15. Caruthers	19	Exeter	0
16. Golden West	18	Highland	0
16. Shafter	18	Redwood	0
16. Wasco	18	San Joaquin	0
19. Bullard	17	Memorial	0
19. Sanger	17		

* Record

Tad Stricker and Coach Gene Walker
South Bakersfield

Left to right, Tad Stricker (2nd State), Paul Carrillo (4th and 5th State) and Parris Whitley (3rd State)
South Bakersfield

Ralph Olivas
Clovis High
State Champion 1990
6th in State 1988

Corky Napier (right) of Madera High
Coaching record: 314-48
1990 CIF Championship Team

Central Section – Clovis
February 23, 1991

103
Serda	Mike	W	11-4	(37-0)*
Amaya	Rick	MON		(40-7)*
Radman	Aaron	WB	2-0	
Scheverman	Sowan	MAD		
Wright	Coby	B	9-2	
Ruiz	Joey	KING		

112
Quintana	Nick	SEL	4-2
Pumarejo	Isaac	KING	
Fuentes	Ed	SANG	5-0
Rodriguez	Johnny	DEL	
Poore	Mike	MAD	5-4
Sanchez	Roger	ROOS	

119
Zinkin	Nick	CL	6-4
Mares	Erik	SEL	
Montalvo	Leo	TRAN	20-14
Jackson	Matt	NB	
Corona	Ralph	HAN	9-6
Enriquez	Zenaido	TUL	

125
Gant	Detran	ROOS	8-3 O.T.	(54-3)*
Aguire	Jim	CL	(167-21-99 Falls)**	
Hull	Brian	MON	6-4	
Zambrano	Steven	FIRE		
Gomez	Ricardo	EX	F/F	
Cortez	Carlos	MCF		

130
Quintana	Gary	SEL	16-12	(44-1)*
Ervin	Ben	MAD		
Tamez	Mike	CL	14-2	
Martinez	Mike	EX		
Johnson	Ryan	BULL	3-2	
Gonzales	Alfredo	FIRE		

135
Alkire	Curtis	MON		
Scalzo	Chad	MAD		
Heberle	Jeff	NB	6-4	153-40-1**
Pena	Chris	CL		
Olivera	Jose	EX	11-6	
Lopez	Tony	PAR		

140
Roach	Brian	CLW	Fall
Tucker	Alfonzo	HOOV	
Gamez	Johnny	TRAN	F/F
Purcella	Sid	TW	
Ramos	Efrain	PORT	7-3 O.T.
Williams	Ryan	MON	

145
Motl	Randy	LEM	6-3
Weber	Clayton	MAD	
Ponce	Angel	ROOS	14-3
Plummer	Kyle	B	
Wheeler	John	MON	2:40
Gasca	Jay	KING	

152
Martinez	Nacho	W	9-3	(36-1)*
Spears	Travis	B		(35-5)*
Rios	Alex	HAN	4:45	
Haupt	Brian	CL		
Workman	David	MAD	F/F	
Smith	Matt	SEL		

160
Lopez	Narcisco	ROOS	7-3
Napier	Jason	MAD	
Arcure	Nick	MON	3:37
Herron	Willie	HI	
Nunez	Juan	DP	14-1
Moreno	Javier	COAL	

171
Silver	Scott	BULL	11-3	(111-24/60 Falls)*
Castro	Mike	CL		
Umada	David	MAD	:40	
Turmkan	Arlie	DP		
Clayton	Terry	SHAFT	9-5	
Rosas	Jesus	COAL		

189
Moz	Lalo	HAN	16-6
Scott	Raymond	ED	
Bergman	Jeff	EB	10-4
Katchadorian	Ty	CLW	
Atkins	Gene	CL	6-2
Barron	Vic	DP	

(Continued on next page)

Central Section – Clovis
February 23, 1991

275
Carrillo	Paul	SB	10-2	(32-5)*	(114-26)**
Falcon	Albert	SANG		(28-5-1)*	
Lewis	Jon	KER	1:45		
Mast	Chad	CL			
Bloom	Cory	WB	1:52		
Jasso	Danny	RED			

Tournament
1. Clovis — 116
2. Madera — 110
3. Monache — 74
4. Roosevelt — 67
5. Selma — 64
6. Hanford — 48
7. Wasco — 41
8. Bakersfield — 37
9. Clovis West — 35
10. Sanger — 32
11. Bullard — 30
12. Kingsburg — 26.5
13. Exeter — 26
14. Tranquility — 24
15. West — 23
15 Dos Paslos — 23
15. South — 23
18. North — 21
18. Lemoore — 21

* Record
** Career

Addition

130 Quintana, Gary 123-7-47 Falls**

Jimmy Aguirre (right) of Clovis High
Three-time State Champion: 1989, 1990 and 1991
Two-time CIF Champion: 1989 and 1990
2nd place 1991

Detren Gant
Roosevelt High
State Champion
1990
2nd in State
1989 and 1991
CIF Champion
1990 and 1991
3rd place 1989

Central Section – Bakersfield College
February 29, 1992

103
Wright	Coby	B	3:56	(46-2)*
Radman	Aaron	W		
Calandra	Steve	BULL	6-5	
Fuqua	Brad	NB		
Ruiz	Greg	MON	13-0	
Rubinol	Jesus	A		

112
Enriquez	Zenaido	TUL	12-7	
Delacruz	Victor	EX		
Pumarejo	Isaac	KING	5-2	
Asuncion	Ron	MON		
Veliz	Gabrial	FIRE	5-4	
Ngo	Vinh	FRE		

119
Zinkin	Nick	CL	15-4	(46-1)*
Trujillo	Jose	GW		
Hull	Brad	MON	6-3	
Ruiz	Joey	KING		
Lujan	Jesse	SEL	:30	
Montalvo	Leo	TRAN		

125
Hull	Brian	MON	8-7
Mares	Eric	SEL	
Summers	Curtis	CL	5-0
Wilson	Jason	EX	
Ayers	Scott	LEM	5-3
Lopez	Mike	COAL	

130
Washington	Yero	PORT	13-4
Hammond	Patrick	ROOS	
Molano	David	GW	T.F. 5:00
Lloyd	Johnny	CLW	
Snapp	Chad	CL	7-2
Morfin	Cesar	SEL	

135
Rodriguez	Aaron	W	4-2	(37-2)*
Frost	Kris	MON		(39-9)*
Swan	Kyle	CL	2-0 O.T.	
Meza	Fernando	MAD		
Buckey	Damani	CENT	11-2	
Heer	Ricky	N		

140
Ramos	Eddie	PORT	16-9
Lopez	Tony	PAR	
McGinn	Josh	B	4:18
Ramsey	Sam	BULL	
Hill	Aaron	CLW	T.F. 4:56
Gomez	Jody	CORC	

145
Munster	Bruce	CL	5:36
Philips	Eric	MAD	
Spike	Brian	SANG	9-7
Hussein	Naser	SEL	
Green	Romel	HI	8-4
Gasca	Jay	KING	

152
Tucker	Alfonso	HOOV	9-2	(42-1)*
Plummer	Kyle	B		
Cleveland	Josh	COAL	11-4	
Crawford	Shane	CL		
Goodwin	Chuck	A	9-5	
Honea	Ryan	W		

160
Martinez	Nacho	W	10-4	(36-0)*
Haupt	Brian	CL		
Pasquale	Kai	N	9-5	
Graff	Daniel	REED		
Workman	David	MAD	2:40	
Suarez	Yurin	DP		

171
Napier	Jason	MAD	5:05
Hine	Elliot	CL	
Rosas	Jesus	COAL	4-2
Herron	Willie	HI	
Criado	Joseph	TRAN	4-1
Gonzales	Eric	HAN	

189
Moz	Lalo	HAN	1:50	
				(43-0/33 Falls)*
Helston	Brendon	HI		
De Santiago	Juan	WOOD	7-6	
Westbury	Kory	CL		
Reyes	Jose	WU	5-2	
Delacruz	Dan	MON		

(Continued on next page)

Central Section – Bakersfield College
February 29, 1992

HWT
Mast	Chad	CL	7-1	(49-3)*
Carrillo	Paul	SB		(46-3)*
Falcon	Albert	SANG	6-2	
Gonzales	Jack	SHAFT		
Spradley	Sean	MT.W	7-1	
Briseno	Lewis	WU		

Tournament
1. Clovis	155.5		23. Roosevelt	16.0
2. Monache	75.5		24. Reedley	14.0
3. Bakersfield	58.5		25. Tranquility	13.0
4. Madera	56.0		26. Washington U.	12.0
5. Wasco	48.0		27. Woodlake	11.0
6. Porterville	45.5		28. Arvin	10.0
7. Selma	40.0		28. Shafter	10.0
8. Highland	37.0		30. Lemoore	8.0
9. North	32.0		31. Central	7.0
10. Golden West	30.5		31. Firebaugh	7.0
10. Coalinga	30.0		33. Mt. Whitney	5.0
10. Kingsburg	30.0		34. Corcoran	4.0
13. Hanford	29.0		34. Dos Palos	4.0
14. Exeter	28.0		Caruthers	0
15. Sanger	25.0		Delano	0
16. South	23.0		Dinuba	0
17. Hoover	22.0		Kerman	0
18. Clovis West	21.5		McFarland	0
19. Bullard	20.0		McLane	0
19. Tulare Union	20.0		Redwood	0
21. West	18.0		San Joaquin	0
22. Parlier	16.0		Memorial	0
			Sierra	0

* Record

Rodney Balch
Clovis High
Record: 238-20-3
Coached 7 CIF Championship teams

Nick Zinking of Clovis High
CIF Champion 1989-1991, 1992
2nd in 1990

Left to right, Yero Washington, Eddie Ramos and Benny Esquivel – CIF Champions, Porterville High

Central Section – Mt. Whitney/Visalia

February 27, 1993

103
Taylor	Max	MAD	3-2	(29-2)*
Adame	Anthony	FOOT		(33-8)*
Aguilar	Peter	PORT	8-4	
Ortiz	Jesus	CLW		
Sobaje	Jason	BULL	4-2	
Buckingham	Gary	TUL		

112
Lake	Kenny	CL	8-3	
Petrig	Jason	LEM		(38-12)*
Ruiz	Tony	DP	4-3	
Sanchez	Angel	TUL		
Martinez	Miguel	MAD	2-1	
Mestaz	Matahew	WOOD		

119
Navarro	John	LEM	4-2 O.T.	(49-5)*
Gutierrez	Gabe	EX		(42-4)*
Rodriguez	Miguel	ROOS	2-1	
Esquivel	Benny	PORT		
Varner	Andy	B	8-6	
Cones	Greg	DP		

125
Aguilar	Ronnie	MAD	5-0	(42-6)*
De La Cruz	Victor	EX		(32-7)*
Hull	Brad	MON	3-1	
Lopez	Mike	COAL		
Miller	Justin	N	:45	(39-10)*
Rodriguez	Mike	SEL		

130
Snapp	Chad	CL	10-2	(42-4)*
Jimenez	Manuel	KING		(36-5)*
Pantoja	Ben	CLW	6-4	
James	David	MAD		
Castro	Jaime	PAR	4-3	
Cerrillo	Michael	WU		

135
Rodriguez	Aaron	W	3-1	(46-0)*
Kuntz	Jesse	LEM		(40-12)*
Swan	Kyle	CL	2-0	
Gaytan	Armando	CLW		
Mora	Jose	FIRE	2-0	
Morrison	Darren	REED		

140
Perez	Moises	MAD	11-10 O.T.	(35-3)*
Ramos	Eddie	PORT		(34-4)*
Hill	Aaron	CLW	6-2	
Buckley	Damani	CENT		
Wiliams	Mike	FIRE	5-1	
Moz	Tom	HAN		

145
Crawford	Shane	CL	6-3	(38-3)*
Meza	Fernando	MAD		(37-8)*
Negrete	Nacho	FIRE	6-1	
Mello	Ben	MCF		
Kagawa	Jason	CLW	8-7	
Rodriguez	Javier	DIN		

152
Phillip	Eric	MAD	4-2 O.T.	(29-4)*
Miller	Doug	HAN		(46-11)*
Pectol	Erin	TUL	6-5	
Douthaf	Fred	LEM		
Wood	Andy	RED	Default	
Rodriguez	Tony	WU		

160
Munster	Bruce	CL	11-10	(32-1)*
Wheeler	John	MON		(43-11)*
Zamorano	Elias	ROOS	8-7	
Garcia	Gabe	B		
Huston	Antwon	LEM	2-0	
Wareham	Willy	DP		

171
Herron	Willie	HI	8-7	(42-2)*
Cabral	Dexxxxb Dems	HAN		
Salcido	Joe	MON	11-3	(43-8)*
Pascual	Maurillo	WU		
Mills	Travis	CLW	7-2	
Montoya	Jaime	KER		

189
Avila	Ryan	MON	6-3	(50-5)*
Mohammad	Jeremiah	ROOS		(33-9)*
Herrera	George	FIRE	9-7	
Jasso	Jarold	RED		
De Santiago	Juan	WOOD	:22	
Clark	Brett	B		

(Continued on next page)

Central Section – Mt. Whitney/Visalia
February 27, 1993

HWT
Mast	Chad	CL	4-0	(43-0)
Karle	Jeremy	HI		(38-4)
Smith	Jared	CLW	8-2	
Serjak	Chris	RED		
Flores	Joe	WOOD	7-3	
Gonzales	Jack	SHAFT		

Tournament
1. Clovis 119
2. Madera 116
3. Lemoore 73
4. Monache 64
5. Clovis West 63
6. Hanford 39
7. Highland 39
8. Portrerville 38.5
9. Exeter 37.5
10. Firebaugh 37
10 Roosevelt 37
12. Redwood 32
13. Tulare 30
14. Dos Palos 28
15. Bakersfield 24
16. Woodlake 20
16. Wasco 20
18. Washington 18
18. Foothill 18
20. Kingsburg 16

* Record

Coach Rick McKinney
North Bakersfield

Central Section – Clovis
February 26, 1994

103
Sobaje	Jason	BULL	1:18 O.T.	(41-1)*
Ortiz	Jesus	CLW		
Garza	Albert	SANG	4:43	
Taylor	Max	MAD		
Smith	Edward	CL	1:33	
Jameson	Sam	W		

112
Green	Stan	CL	3:39	(45-1)*
Mestaz	Matt	WOOD		
Rubalcava	Oscar	FRE	10-8	
Philips	Dallen	SANG		
McCauly	Rob	B	13-9	
Ortiz	Alex	CORC		

119
Lake	K.L.	CL	4-1	(31-4)*
Esquivel	Benny	PORT		
Ruiz	Frank	EX	4-2 O.T.	
Elisondo	Steve	W		
Thompson	Danny	RED	2:45	
Cones	Billy	DP		

125
Hull	Brad	MON	8-1	(45-4)*
Varner	Andy	B		(39-7)*
Alamilla	Juan	PORT	5-3 O.T.	
Davis	Jonte	ED		
Ehn	Matt	CL	9-0	
Cones	Greg	DB		

130
Pierro	Jeremy	BULL	3-0	(41-4)*
Jimenez	Manuel	KING		
Miller	Kelly	B	6-0	
Russell	David	HOOV		
Moland	Fred	GW	13-0	
Serda	Eric	W		

135
Ellis	Jake	MON	4-3	(45-7)*
Mora	Jose	FIRE		
Breceda	Victor	BULL	8-4	
Duran	Ruben	GW		
Demarro	Joe	LEM	5-3	
Delad	Ronnie	CL		

140
Perez	Moises	MAD	10-3	(47-1)*
Williams	Mike	FIRE		
Urena	Joel	KER	10-3	
Kraemer	Daron	HAN		
Queenan	Sean	SB	11-3	
Smithson	Russell	HOOV		

145
Swan	Kyle	CL	7-0	(42-5)*
Moz	Tom	HAN		
Negrete	Josh	FIRE	4-3	
Ortiz	Albert	CORC		
Arteaga	Jimmy	MCL	1-0	
Bozeman	Ryan	ED		

152
Meza	Fernando	MAD	6-2	(40-3)*
Curry	Andy	HAN		
Navarro	Erick	FIRE	15-1	
Bridges	Jerremy	B		
Salcedo	Jose	EX	11-7	
Ontiberos	Ruben	MEN		

160
Philp	Eric	MAD	4-0	(47-1)*
Maldonado	Adam	FIRE		
Duarte	Mike	Hoov	5-3	
Bojorquez	David	E		
Thompson	Mike	BUC	8-6 O.T.	
Badillo	Julian	BULL		

171
Cabral	Demes	HAN	10-1	(29-4)*
Sheets	Ryan	NB		(44-5)*
Jackson	Daniel	KING	5-3	
Stricklnad	Ben	CL		
Wareham	Willy	DP	13-3	
Criado	Joe	TRAN		

189
Mohammed	Jeremiah	ROOS	12-6	(41-1)*
Jasso	Jarold	RED		
Ferguson	Vance	HAN	12-3	
Moreno	Guillermo	DIN		
Daniels	Aaron	HI	9-2	
Herrera	George	FIRE		

(Continued on next page)

Central Section – Clovis
February 26, 1994

HWT

Rodriguez	Eric	MON	3:55	(49-5)*
Urena	Ralph	WOOD		
Kale	Jeremy	HI	7-2	
Smith	Jared	CLW		
Ortiz	Evan	SEL	5-2	
Garcia	Chris	CL		

Tournament

1. Clovis 91.5
2. Hanford 82
3. Firebaugh 81
4. Madera 76
5. Monache 65
6. Buchanan 62.5
7. Bakersfield 42
8. Clovis West 39.5
9. Woodlake 33
10. Kingsburg 30
11. Porterville 28
12. Hoover 27
13. Sanger 26
14. Redwood 24
15. Roosevelt 23
16. Highland 17
17. North 16
17. East 16
19. West 12
19. Dos Palos 12
19. Kerman 12
22. Wasco 10
22. Dinuba 10
24. Lemoore 8
24. Selma 8
24. South 8
27. Memdota 7
27. McLane 7
29. Bullard 5
29. Tranquility 5

* Record

Eric Philp (left) and Moises Peres
Madera High
Both two-time CIF Champions

Central Section – Arvin
February 25, 1995

103
Garza	Albert	SEL	2:16	(51-1)*
Smith	Ed	CL		
Eastman	Dustin	ED	Fall	
Rojas	Tony	CLW		
Sar	Tee	MT.W	14-5	
Bazan	Jose	COAL		

112
Lake	K.L.	CL	9-5	
Elisondo	Steve	B		(32-9)*
Garcia	Selco	WOOD	6-4 O.T.	
Ruiz	Parris	CLV		
Telles	Robert	REED	4:50	
Perez	Jesse	SEL		

119
Vasquez	Larry	B	5-4	(42-5)*
Rubalcava	Oscar	FRE		
Moreno	Geroge	FIRE	8-3	
Phillips	Dallen	SANG		
Brown	William	HOOV	8-2	
Garcia	Santos	WOOD		

125
Lopez	Ralph	CLW	5-4
Davis	Jonte	ED	
Cantu	Herbert	TRAN	1-0
Serda	Eric	W	
Ehn	Matt	CL	6-2
Ruiz	Frank	EX	

130
Russell	David	HOOV	5-4
Jimenez	Manuel	KING	
Morales	Joseph	EX	4-1
Garcia	Arturo	SEL	
Richards	Demasco	ROOS	13-6
Breceda	Victor	BUC	

135
Pierro	Jeremy	BUC	7-1
Miller	Kelly	B	
Belvail	Kenny	LEM	17-8
Valencia	Jesus	DP	
Mazza	Mark	NB	7-3
Manes	Jeremy	FOOT	

140
Varner	Andy	B	3:15
Molano	Fred	GW	
Rodriguez	Mike	BUC	4:43
Esajian	Paul	FRE	
Arias	Francisco	FIRE	7-2
Nelms	Ian	MT.W	

145
Williams	Ryan	HI	12-0	
			(47-1/28 Falls)*	
Arteaga	Jimmy	MCL		
Gallardo	Juan	W	3-0	
Duran	Ruben	GW		
Ensign	Warren	EX	7-5 O.T.	
Sanders	Telly	BULL		

152
Bridges	Jeremy	B	6-4 O.T.
Smithson	Russell	HOOV	
Curry	Andy	HAN	12-4
Milanesi	Vince	BUC	
Peres	Sonny	KING	7-5
Cierley	Kevin	CENT	

160
Wilson	Mike	MAD	3-2	
Keller	Tony	B		(41-9)*
Rossotti	Jason	SEL	14-6	
Aldaco	Jose	MON		
Freeborn	Zak	SHAFT	19-4	
Ray	Matt	LEM		

171
Jackson	Dan	KING	10-3
Ashley	Fredrick	B	
Pezzat	Art	EX	8-7
St. Martin	Cliff	WOOD	
Cromer	A.J.	ED	:22
East	Rocky	NB	

191
Miller	Anthony	EX	14-2
Phillips	Damien	Tul	
Phillips	Ryan	MAD	10-2
Criado	Joe	TRAN	
Jones	Arturo	DP	6-3
Maese	Ray	B	

(Continued on next page)

Central Section - Arvin
February 25, 1995

HWT

Rodriguez	Eric	MON	7-4
Clark	Brett	B	(37-3)*
Smith	Jarred	CLW	8-4
Espericueta	Frank	SHAFT	
Montoya	John	LEM	T.F. 15-0
Van Worth	Bryan	DP	

Tournament

1. Bakesfield 161.5
2. Exeter 73
3. Clovis Weset 62
4. Buchanan 58
5. Clovis 50.5
6. Hoover 47
7. Kingsburg 44
8. Madera 35
9. Sanger 33.5
10. Monache 32
11. Lemoore 30.5
12. Selma 28.5
13. Fresno 27.5
14. Edison 27
15. Golden West 25
15. Dos Palos 25
17. Woodlake 24
18. Highland 23
18. Tranquility 23
20. Wasco 22
21. Shafter 20.5
22. Firebaugh 20
23. Tulare 16
23. McLane 16
25. Hanford 14
26. North 12
27. Reedley 9
28. Roosevelt 6
28. Foothill 6
30. Coalinga 5
31. Mt. Whitney 4
31. Centennial 4

* Record (as of 02-25-95)

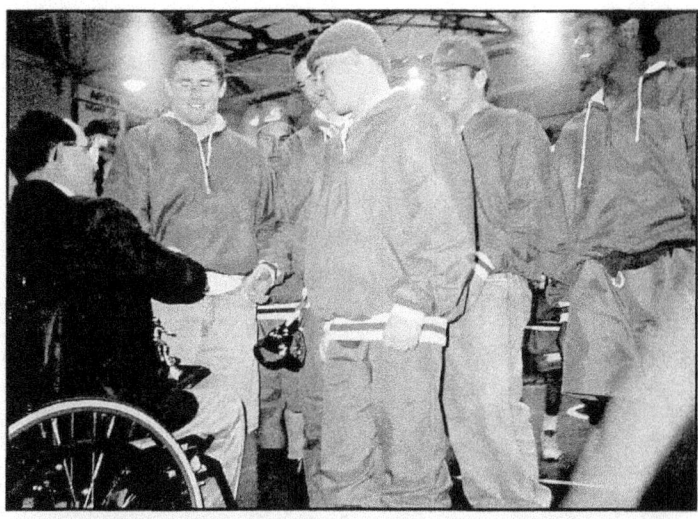

Arvin Coach Ruben Ramierz presenting the CIF Championship Award to Bakersfield High

Brett Clark of Bakersfield High - 2nd CIF

Central Section – Monache/Porterville

February 24, 1996

103
Garza	Jaime	SANG	10-1
Johnson	Cleo	FIRE	
Ressesguie	Chris	EB	6-1
Sar	Tee	MT.W	
Smith	Ed	CL	1:55
Sepulveda	Robert	SEL	

112
Garza	Alberto	SANG	1:57
Martinez	Ben	TUL	
Rosas	Tony	CLW	Default
Garcia	Abel	BUC	
Diaz	Abraham	A	8-2
Crane	Kent	DP	

119
Ruiz	Parris	CLW	6-5
Breceda	Sergio	BUC	
Valenzuela	Angel	ROOS	12-5
Mosqueda	Ricardo	DP	
Phillips	Dalen	SANG	11-2
Areas	Cesar	FIRE	

125
Vasquez	Nathan	B	Default (46-4)*
Lopez	Ralph	CLW*	
Moreno	George	FIRE	6-5
Adame	Anthony	FOOT	
Gutierrez	Chris	CL	8-3
Jamison	Sam	W	

130
Ortiz	Alex	CORC	11-4
Rubalcava	Oscar	FRE	
Brown	Willim	HOOV	2:30
Arballo	Robert	MAD	
Hogeland	Kaleb	FOOT	1-0
Cantu	Herbert	FIRE	

135
Ehn	Matt	CL	5-2
Sherrick	Mike	CLW	
Huizar	Antonio	LEM	7-4
Diniz	Adrian	FOOT	
Lopez	Cassidy	COAL	11-8
Choske	Lonny	BUC	

140
Tirapelle	Adam	BUC	11-4	(42-1)*
Molano	Fred	B		(43-3)*
Garcia	Arturo	SEL	8-3	
Reyes	Harvey	EB		
Uribe	Charlie	WU	6-4 O.T.	
Campos	Frederico	CORC		

145
Nelms	Ian	MT.W	3-2 O.T.
Miller	Kelly	B	
Duran	Derrick	ROOS	8-5
Lupian	Jose	DP	
Lomeli	Daniel	CLW	Default
Esajian	Paul	FRE	

152
Smithson	Russell	HOOV	10-5
Espericueta	Ely	SHAFT	
Sanders	Telly	BUC	3-1
Sheen	Charlie	CI	
Burchett	Mike	MT.W	9-4
Gennor	Nick	WOOD	

160
Pereschica	Sonny	KING	:53
Aldaco	Jose	MON	
Moreno	Clemente	DIN	3-2
Salcedo	Jose	EX	
Sheen	Bill	CL	7-5 O.T.
Lunn	Tyler	BUC	

171
Hill	Matt	SB	4-3
Ray	Matt	LEM	
Moran	Brandon	SANG	10-8
Gonzalez	Mike	CAR	
Stockton	Ryan	BUC	
Becerra	Isaac	CORC	

189
Miller	Anthony	EX	9-7
Philp	Ryan	MAD	
Martinez	Frank	W	Default
Winslow	Derek	BULL	
Brogdon	Charlie	A	8-6
Zieg	Elijah	BUC	

(Continued on next page)

Central Section – Monache/Porterville
February 24, 1996

215
Maese	Ray	B	15-7
Merrill	Than	FRE	
Alvardo	Chris	FIRE	8-3
Serna	Emilio	BUC	
Rico	Ben	LEM	4-2 O.T.
Ramirez	Mario	CORC	

HWT
Leyva	Victor	MON	3:57
Harrington	Grant	RED	
Garrett	Albert	MAD	2-1
Avila	Tim	PORT	
Smith	Garry	ED	Defeat
Leslie	Rodney	RIDGE	

Adam Tirapelle
Buchanan High
Career record: 214-7
NCAA Champion
Placed 2nd and 3rd
University of Illinois
Career record: 127-21

Tournament
1. Buchanan 99
2. Bakersfield 79
3. Clovis West 75
4. Sanger 71.5
5. Firebaugh 53
5. Clovis 53
7. Madera 42.5
7. Fresno 42.5
9. Monache 40.5
10. Mt. Whitney 40
11. Hoover 36.5
12. Lemoore 35
12. Corcoran 35
14. Exeter 30
15. Foothill 25
16. Roosevelt 24.5
16. East Bakerfield 24.5
18. Kingsburg 24
19. Dos Palos 23
20. Wasco 20
20. South 20

Ralph Lopez leading 14-8 with 18 second left injury default elbow dislocation

* Record

Central Section – Clovis
March 1, 1997

103
Johnson	Cleo	FIRE	21-9	(53-0)*
Portillo	Angel	TUL		
Felix	Chris	EB	5-3	(27-6)*
Sepulveda	Robert	SEL		
Nunez	Andreas	ROOS	10-2	
Estrada	John	CEN		

112
Garza	Jaime	SANG	12-3	(45-0)*
Resseguie	Chris	EB		(45-5)*
Mendez	Mando	BUC	3-0	
Cano	Eraldo	RED		
Nguyen	Tam	Ed	Fall 2:05	
Madrigal	Tony	SHAFT		

119
Banuelos	Antonio	CLW	4-3	(62-?)*
Martinez	Ben	TUL		
Guerrero	Brian	MAD	4-1	
Crane	Kenji	DP		
Garza	Albert	SANG	10-9	
Sanchez	Matt	FRE		

125
Sanchez	Jose	ED	7-4	
Roas	Tim	CLW		(39-7)*
Sanchez	Pablo	HOOV	T.F. 4:20	
Rosales	Nick	A		(39-7)*
Scott	Bennett	B	4-1	(28-8)*
Arredondo	Mariano	CHOW		

130
Moreno	George	FIRE	13-6
Rosas	Tony	CLW	
Hernandez	Josh	BULL	4-0
Sobaje	Justin	BUC	
Pereschica	Danny	KING	T.F. 3:00
China	Eric	RED	

135
Lopez	Ralph	CLW	9-3	(62-0)*
Jameson	Sam	W		(44-4)*
Arballo	Robert	MAD	Fall 2:47	
Jiminez	Victor	KING		
Spradlin	Matt	B	6-1	(26-11)*
Reyes	Gus	SANG		

140
Moore	Kirk	FOOT	11-3	(49-4/29 Falls)*
Garcia	Arturo	SEL		
Hoehn	Nathan	MON	Forfeit	
Morales	Joseph	EX		
Gutierrez	Jimmy	CORC		
Jiminez	Paul	PORT		

145
Miller	Kelly	B	5-2	(45-5)*
Duran	Darrick	ROOS		
Reyes	Cirillo	EB	Fall 3:10	(34-5)*
Reyna	Adolfo	HAN		
Brooks	Ryan	LEM	9-3	
Molina	Juan	FIRE		

152
Pezzat	Yasser	EX	8-7	
Landin	Jose	W		(26-4)*
Diniz	Adrian	FOOT	4-3	
Lupian	Jose	DP		
Gennoe	Nick	WOOD	5-3	
Botello	Isaac	TUL		

160
Sanders	Telly	BUC	6-2	
Nelms	Ian	MT.W		(48-3)*
Kerste	Alman	TEHA	6-4	(23-4)*
Jimenez	Juan	SB		(47-9)*
Arreola	Ramon	CORC	12-2	
Van Worth	Mike	DP		

171
Lunn	Tyler	BUC	8-2	
Perschica	Sonny	KING		
Smith	Junior	EB	6-1	(47-8)*
Moran	Brandon	SANG		
Schneider	Luke	TEHA	8-2	(20-3)*
Naus	Josh	CENT		

189
Jackson	Dan	KING	5-4	(36-0)*
Brogdon	Charlie	A		(40-5)*
Blodau	Ryan	SIE	14-0	
Scott	Nad	GW		
Martinez	Narcy	W	4-1	
Fox	Ben	BUC		

(Continued on next page)

Central Section – Clovis
March 1, 1997

215
Philp	Ryan	MAD	8-5
Matthews	Marcel	BULL	
Camacho	Baltazar	MON	6-2
Cash	Brandon	BUC	
Rodriguez	David	WU	Fall 2:59
Milligan	Conor		

275
Harrington	Grant	RED	O.T. 3-1
Leisle	Rodney	RIDGE	(30-4)*
Simas	Pat	LEM	8-4
Brewer	Otis	MAD	
Brady	Aaron	KING	6-5
Cabral	Dustin	HAN	

Steve Tirapelle
Clovis High

Tournament
1. Buchanan 86
2. Clovis Wesst 76.5
3. Kingsburg 67.5
4. Madera 63.5
5. E. Bakersfield 61
6. Sanger 47
7. Firebaugh 45
8. Wasco 40
9. Tulare 37
10. Foothill 36
10. Redwood 36
12. Edison 32
12. Bakersfield 32
14. Monache 31
15. Exeter 30
16. Arviin 29
17. Bullard 28
18. Dos Palos 27
19. Selma 26
19. Roosevelt 26
21. Lemoore 20
22. Ridgeview 18
22. Tehachapi 18
24. Hanford 16
24. Mt. Whitney 16
24. Corcoran 16
27. Sierra 15
28. Hoover 13.5
29. S. Bakersfield 10
30. Golden West 9

Alex, Adam and Troy Tirapelle

* Record

Central Section – Shafter
February 28, 1998

103
Moreno	Jason	FIRE	15-4	
LaFrance	Devon	BUC		
Castillo	Eddie	CL	4-3	
Estrada	John	CENT		
Serrano	Eddie	KER	4-2 O.T.	
Onsurez	Andy	EB		

112
Dickerson	John	B	8-6 O.T.	
Beck	Scott	TUL		(53-4)*
Mendez	Mendo	BUC	6-2	
Madrigal	Tony	SHAFT		(48-8)*
Gushiken	Brandon	CL	13-2	
Marquez	Phillip	FOOT		

119
Gutierrez	Miguel	FOOT	2:22	(54-11)*
Braceda	Sergio	BUC		
Jones	Kevin	CLW	5:15	
Sepulveda	Robert	SEL		
Portello	Angel	TUL	:43	(47-7)*
Rivera	Eleuto	DP		

125
Martines	Ben	TUL	1:48	(55-0)*
Ashley	Benny	B		(46-7)*
Rosales	Nick	A	6-5	(47-6)*
Calvert	James	LEM		
Venegas	Cookie	WU.	6-3	
Evangelist	Jorge	PAR		

130
Odom	Max	FOOT	5:01 (48-3/22 Falls)*
Gutierrez	Chris	CL	
Schallberger	Patrick	B	4:37 (38-9)*
Crane	Kenji	DP	
Calvert	Jason	LEM	4:45
Preschica	Danny	KING	

135
Olson	Casey	CL	5-3 O.T.	
Meloche	Ryan	FOOT		(47-7)*
Lopez	Juan	EX	4-3	
Baca	Ben	BUC		
Garcia	Juan	B	Default	(39-9)*
Valenzuela	Ricky	WU		

140
Lopez	Ralph	CLW	14-2	(61-1/232-16)*
Lopez	Rudy	HAN		
Villagomez	Allen	EB	6-4	(44-10)*
Pfitzer	Jeremy	TUL		(49-5)*
Cummings	Jimmy	CORC	4-2	
Evangelist	Billy	PAR		

145
Spradlin	Matt	B	5-2	(41-8)*
Huizar	Juan	LEM		
Diniz	Adrian	FOOT	8-4	(52-9)*
Owens	Jeremy	CL		
Delarosa	Richard	DP	12-?	
Martinez	Miguel	MAD		(57-0/27 Falls)*

152
Moore	Kirk	FOOT	10-1 (57-0/27 Falls)*
Brooks	Ryan	LEM	
Lomelli	Daniel	CLW	Default
Gutierrez	Ryan	CL	
Danieli	Beau	CHOW	7-4
Cantu	Wilfred	FIRE	

160
Sanders	Telly	BUC	7-6	
Sherrick	Mike	CLW		
Jimenez	Juan	SB	4:25	(35-6)*
Reyes	Harvy	EB		(26-12)*
Burke	Sam	RIDGE	7-5	
Flores	Carlos	PORT		

171
Lunn	Tyler	BUC	4-1
Perez	Noel	MAD	
Smith	Ryan	CLW	1:37
Gonzales	Todd	HOOV	
Gennoe	Nick	WOOD	12-1
Hemman	Rodney	CAR	

189
Naus	Josh	CENT	9-4	(51-0)*
Cash	Brandon	BUC		
Van Worth	Mike	DP	10-0	
Roan	John	MAD		
Bowerman	Rodney	Lem	6-2	
Gross	Paxton	LEM		

(Continued on next page)

Central Section – Shafter
February 28, 1998

215
Graham	Aaron	B	2-0	(22-1)*
Fox	Ben	BUC		
Martinez	Narcy	W	4:12	
Poo	Danny	EX		
Kragle	Ken	CHOW	8-2	
Dix	Courtney	CL		

275
Simas	Pat	LEM	5:57
Torres	Greg	FOOT	
Michael	Rodney	TEHA	:59
Armendarez	Louie	MON	
Sanchez	Matt	BUC	2-1
Calvert	Josh	DP	

Tournament
1. Buchanan	144.5
2. Foothill	129
3. Bakersfield	105.5
4. Clovis West	91
5. Clovis	83
6. Lemoore	82.5
7. Tulare	61.5
8. Dos Palos	43
9. Madera	34.5
10. E. Bakersfield	28
11. Firebaugh	26
12. Centennial	24
13. Exeter	21
14. Hanford	16
15. S. Bakersfield	15.5
16. Wasco	15
16. Tehachapi	15
18. Monache	14
18. Hoover	14
18. Chowchilla	14
18. Arvin	14
22. Selma	12
23. Washington U.	11
23. Caruthers	11
25. Shafter	10
25. Central	10
27. Woodlake	9
28. Ridgeview	8
28. Parlier	8
30. Kerman	6
31. Porterville	4
31. Kingsburg	4
31. Corcoran	4

* Record

Max Odom of Foothill High
CIF Champion
State Champion
National Champion
173-17 with 93 falls

One win away at NCAA's for Harvard his sophomore year to be an All-American. After two shoulder surgeries, his wrestling career was cut short. Odom now has a degree from Harvard.

Nancy Schultz presents Max Odom with the Dave Schultz High School Wrestling Excellence Award Western Region 1999 Other Central Section winners: 2002 Darrell Vasquez 2001 Alex Tirapelle

Central Section – Mt. Whitney/Visalia
February 27, 1999

103
Chapman	Daniel	CENT	4-3	(48-6)*
Darrell	Vasquez	B		(43-4)*
Onsurez	Andrew	EB	3-0	(41-9)*
Silva	Damen	LEM		(48-9)*
Reyes	Ray	HAN	7-0	
Aguilera	Antonio	TRAN		

112
Moreno	Jason	FIRE	11-4	(50-0)*
Castillo	Eddie	CL		
Marquez	Phillip	FOOT	9-4	(45-15)*
Castillo	Jaime	MAD		
Spradlin	Andrew	B	Fall 4:59	(27-16)*
Cuevas	Clemente	MEN		

119
East	Drew	B	5-2	(32-6)*
Gushiken	Brandon	CL		(35-14)*
Leal	Ronnie	HAN	13-4	
Farias	Matt	SHAFT	(32-8-21 Falls)*	
Castillo	Isaac	MON	3-2	
Rodriguez	Robert	DP		

125
Tirapelle	Alex	CL	3-0	(47-2)*
Goings	Joel	WB		(41-6)*
Beck	Scott	TUL	4-0	(40-6)*
Esparza	Anthony	MT.W		
Chicca	Caleb	B	Fall 4:39	(43-16)*
Downs	Eric	DP		

130
Martinez	Ben	TUL	7-5	(53-0)*
Pendleton	Chris	LEM		
Vasquez	Cookie	WU	7-5	
Gutierrez	Miguel	FOOT		(48-9)*
Jones	Kevin	CLW	3-2	
Evangelista	Jorge	PAR		

135
Estrada	Robert	CEN	7-3	(32-4)*
Rosales	Nick	A		(43-5)*
Bakers	David	CENT	2-1	(19-6)*
Crane	Michael	BUC		
Vasquez	Lino	HOOV	8-6	
Preston	Josh	SHAFT		

140
Schallberger	Patrick	B	11-9 O.T.	(30-5)*
Briggs	Charles	LEM		
Sheets	Sean	CENT	12-7	(28-10)*
Bains	Jas	CL		
Bernard	Evan	TUL		
Reyes	Herman	CENT		

145
Odom	Max	FOOT	Fall 3:45	(52-0/30 Falls)*
Diesslin	Justin	CI		
Perez	Armando	FARM	4-3	
Yacoby	Jon	CLW		
Garcia	Carlos	WOOD	2-0	
Rodgers	Brandon	MT.W		

152
Yacoby	David	CLW	7-6	
Delarosa		DP		
Cruess	Scott	MON	4-0	
Cotta	Nick	LEM		
Chavarria	Jose	MEND	8-5	
Mooney	Britt	EB		

160
Brooks	Ryan	LEM	9-4	(35-2)*
Whitehead	Chris	CL		
Tirado	Josue	MON	2-1	
Landin	David	W		(11-4)*
Mehr	Andonijah	ED	9-3	
Carrasco	Ernie	SEL		

171
Burke	Sam	RIDGE	Default	(37-4)*
Weiner	Steffan	BUC		
Beechiner	Ted	MAD	Inj. Def.	
Nystrem	Eric	CAR		
Clark	Granson	DP	Inj. Def.	
Gutierrez	Ryan	CL		

189
Naus	Josh	CENT	Fall 1:38	(51-1/41 Falls)*
Silva	Ronnie	BUC		
Van Worth	Mike	DP	Fall	
Carrasco	Miguel	RED		
Cantu	Leo	KER	11-5	
Tobin	Anthony	B		

(Continued on next page)

Central Section – Mt. Whitney/Visalia

February 27, 1999

215
Botelho	Marcio	LEM	6-3	
Krague	Ken	CHOW		
Walbeck	Chris	CL	Inj. Def.	
Graham	Aaron	B		(19-5)*
Smoyer	Jason	BUC	7-6	
Vasquez	Joe	SEL		

HWT
Fox	Ben	BUC	5-2	(44-4/20 Falls)*
Armendarez	Louie	MON		
Ramirez	Johnny	DIN	3-2	(28-14)*
Straw	Ryan	CENT		(28-14)*
Harris	Walter	CHOW	13-8	
DeQuillett	Ryan	WB		

Ben Martinez 2-year record 105-0

Tournament
1. Clovis	122	20. Mt. Whitney	17	
2. Lemoore	99	21. Shaftaer	15	
3. Bakersfield	95	22. Dinuba	14	
4. Centennial	80.5	23. Tranquility	12.5	
5. Buchanan	74	24. Washington U.	12	
6. Monache	50	25. Caruthers	11	
7. Foothill	49	25. Redwood	11	
8. Dos Palos	48	25. Woodlake	11	
9. Tulare	42.5	25. Farmersville	11	
10. Clovis West	35	25. Mendota	11	
11. Central	27	30. Wasco	10	
12. Madera	26	31. Yosemite	9	
12. Ridgeview	26	31. Kerman	9	
14. Chowchilla	23	33. Selma	8	
15. East	21.5	34. Hoover	7	
16. W. Bakersfield	21	34. Edison	7	
16. Firebaugh	21	36. Parlier	4	
18. Hanford	19	South	No entry	
19. Arvin	17.5			

* Record

Addition
145 Odom, Max career 167-17

Coach Paul Olejnik (left) and Josh Naus
Centennial High
CIF Champion
State Champion

Left to right, Daniel Chapman, Coach Paul Olejnik and Sean Sheets of Centennial High

Lemoore High Wrestling Team

Central Section – Buchanan/Clovis
February 26, 2000

103
Ingram	Logan	BUC	4-4	
Contreras	Gerrard	MAD		
Cortez	Greg	PAR	Forfeit	
Solis	Nick	RED		
Murrillo	John	TW	7-6	
Mendez	Karl	HAN		

112
Vasquez	Darrell	B	3-2	(54-1)*
Onsurez	Andrew	EB		(44-4)*
Martinez	Nick	TUL	1:42	
Cuevas	Clemente	MEN		
Reyes	Ray	HAN	3-1	
Goodpaster	Darrell	BUC		

119
Chapman	Daniel	CENT	3-2	(34-3)*
Castillo	Eddie	CL		
Silva	Damen	LEM	6-2	
Farias	Matt	SHA		
Facio	Paul	BUC	7-6	
Guerrero	Modesto	CAR		

125
Chicca	Caleb	B	12-9
Leal	Ronnie	HAN	
Morrison	Mike	CLW	4-3
Sanchez	Chris	BUC	
Campos	Javier	SEL	4-3
Stonehocker	Anthony	LEM	

130
Spooner	Garett	CL	4-3 (35 Falls)
Venegas	Cookie	WU	
Evangelista	Jorge	PAR	1:35
Sanchez	Chilo	BUC	
Becerra	Isaac	TEHA	7-0
Frank	Matt	EB	

135
Tirapelle	Alex	CL	9-2	
Sierbert	Shane	MAD		
Gutierrez	Miguel	FOOT	8-1	(49-7)*
Serpa	Craig	LEM		
Spradlin	Andrew	B	12-5	
Oceguero	Lui	CHOW		

140
Hernandez	Steve	FOOT	5-2	(47-4)*
Negrete	Carlos	FIRE		
Ramirez	Jesse	MT.W	4-3	
Garcia	Pacifico	CL		
Sherley	Josh	B	14-7	
Glenn	Douglas	DP		

145
Pendleton	Chris	LEM	3:03	(62-0/51 Falls)
Estrada	Robert	BUC		
Garcia	Carlos	WOOD	7-2	
Hernandez	Joe	B		
Marchant	Travis	STOCK	20-4	(38-11)*
Silva	Tony	KER		

152
Kalivas	Karris	B	5-4	
Sheets	Sean	CENT		(44-6)*
Uriarte	Justin	MT.W	7-3	
Bains	Jaskarin	CL		
Soltero	Anthony	KER	13-5	
Medina	Ron	LEM		

160
~~Bradley~~ Bardsley	Matt	HOOV	9-4	
Madsen	Derek	HAN		
Folmer	Daniel	BULL	5-2	
Chavarria	Jose	MEND		
Griffith	Anthony	CENT	4-2	(25-13)*
Sanchez	Jesus	MAD		

171
Weiner	Steffan	BUC	5-3	
Mooney	Britt	EB		(42-5)*
Clark	Granson	DP	5-2	
Whitehead	Chris	CI		
Yeager	Jacob	SEL	1:22	
Waiz	Charlie	TEHA		

189
Tobin	Anthony	B	3-2	(45-3)*
Van Worth	Mike	DP		
Silva	Ronnie	BUC	3-2	
Pickett	Robert	HOOV		
Gonzalez	Carlos	EB	12-4	
Pederson	Daniel	SHAFT		

(Continued on next page)

Central Section – Buchanan/Clovis
February 25, 2000

215
Botehlo	Marcio	LEM	3-1	(62-1)*
Walbeck	Clint	CL		
Goodman	Will	BC	14	
Kraggie	Ken	CHOW		
Scheesley	Brian	HAN	7-4	
Young	Riley	SIER		

HWT
Hallmark	Jacob	CL	4-2
Patino	Eddie	PORT	
Harris	Walter	CHOW	:50
Jackson	Emmanuel	HAN W	
Murphy	Johnathan	HAN	2-1 O.T.
DeQuilletts	Ryan	WB	

Tournament
1. Clovis — 138.5
2. Buchanan — 128
3. Bakersfield — 114
4. Lemoore — 81
5. Hanford — 66
6. East — 51
7. Centennial — 44
8. Madera — 43
9. Dos Palos — 39
10. Hoover — 37
11. Foothill — 36

21. Shafter — 16

26. Stockdale — 10.5

27. Tehachapi

31. West — 5

*Record

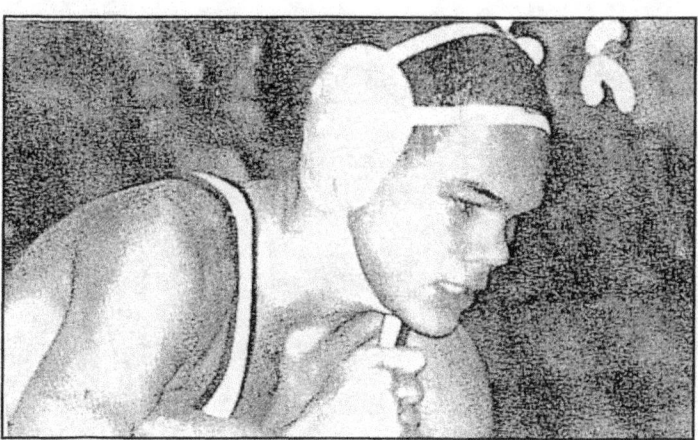

Chris Pendleton of Lemoore High
Two-time NCAA Champion
Also placed 3rd
Oklahoma State University record: 115-11
Lemoore High record: 178-15

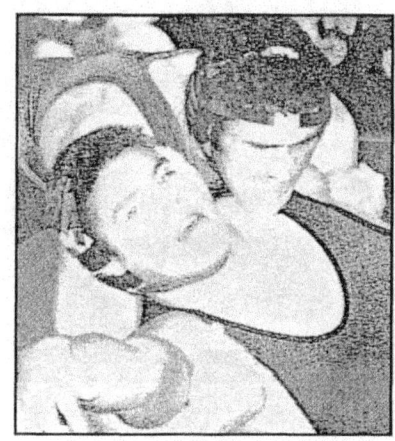

Marcio Botelho (top)
Lemoore High
CIF Champion
State Champion
All-American at
Fresno State

Alex Triapelle of Clovis High
Three-time CIF Champion
Three-time State Champion
University of Illinois
Two-time All-American
College career record: 128-18

Karris Kalivas of Bakersfield High – CIF Champion
Wrestled for his father, Bill, at Bakersfield College and Portland State

Left to right, Coach Gary Chapman, Daniel Chapman, Coach Paul Olenjnik, Coach Derek Scott, Sean Sheets and Josh Naus of Centennial High

Central Section – Masters
2 0 0 1 - 2 0 0 6

Central Section Masters

Date	Champion	Coach	Location
2/24/2001	Bakersfield	David East	East Bakersfield
2/23/2002	Bakersfield	David East	Clovis
3/1/2003	Clovis	Steve Tirapelle	East Bakersfield
2/28/2004	Bakersfield	Andy Varner	Lemoore
2/26/2005	Bakersfield	Andy Varner	Buchanan
2/25/2006	Buchanan	Dustin Riley	East Bakersfield

Outstanding Wrestlers
Lower and Upper Weights

Year	Wrestler	School
2001	Gerrard Contreras	Buchanan
	Miguel Gutierrez	Foothill
2002		
	Darrell Vasquez	Bakersfield
	Drew East	Bakersfield
2003		
	Troy Tirapelle	Clovis
	William Griffin	Madera
2004		
	Nathan Morgan	Bakersfield
	Chip Meredith	Central
2005		
	Paul Ruiz	Firebaugh
	Jake Varner	Bakersfield
2006		
	David Chaidez	Foothill
	Ryan Flores	Buchanan

Awards sponsored by The Coyote Club

Central Section Masters Championships – East
February 14, 2001

103
Contereras	Gerrard	BUC	7-1	(32-3)*
Morgan	Nathan	B		(46-4)*
Mendez	Chad	HAN	4:32	
Lee	Kou	WU		
Garcia	Sonny	KING	3:23	
Kimbler	Jay	SIE		

112
Ingram	Logan	BUC	8-4	
Franco	Tony	B	(43-5/25 Falls)*	
Flores	Gabe	MAD	5-4	
Sanchez	Ivan	A		(24-4)*
Williams	Jason	CL	10-5	
Arguela	Ulises	MEN		

119
Vasquez	Darrell	B	8-4	(49-1)*
Tirapelle	Troy	CL		
Martinez	Nick	TUL	1:44	
Fierro	Paul	KING		
Settle	Isaac	CW	7-2	
Loredo	Francisco	COAL		

125
Silva	Damon	LEM	7-2	
Santos	Efrain	SANG		
Maldonado	Matt	SHAFT	8-4	(43-4)*
Campos	Javier	SEL		
Houck	Ryan	CW	7-6	
Osurez	Anthony	ED		

130
Ramirez	Aaron	CENT	7-4	(27-5)*
Weimer	D.J.	B		(22-6)*
Evangelista	Jorge	PAR	9-6	
Sanchez	Brandon	BUC		
Juarez	Javier	CENT	15-4	
Madrigal	Freddy	SHAFT		

135
Spradlin	Andrew	B	21-5	(47-2)*
Salas	Jacob	MAD		
Garcia	Pacifico	CL	5-0	
Frank	Matt	EB		
Sierra	Lionel	REED	2-0	
Mendoza	Adam	FIRE		

140
Tirapelle	Alex	CL	7-0	(51-1)*
East	Drew	B		(46-4)*
Seibert	Shane	MAD	4-0	
Sullivan	Daniel	GW		
Rivera	Gabriel	WU	10-9	
Rodriguez	Emilio	MEN		

145
Gutierrez	Miguel	FOOT	4:24	(50-3)*
Garcia	Carlos	WOOD		
Acosta	Pat	WASCO	8-5	(31-9)*
Burnias	Matt	TUL		
Ochoa	Josh	REED	O.T. 8-6	
Breceda	Jesus	BUC		

152
Sherley	Josh	B	4-1	(41-9)*
Sheets	Sean	CENT	(32 Falls/41-3)*	
Cotta	Nick	LEM	5-2	
Arroyo	Silverio	FOW		
Weatherly	Steven	EX	2:42	
Zavala	Hugo	DP		

160
Hafemeister	Sven	LEM	8-4	
Bardsley	Matt	HOOV		
Soltero	Anthony	KER	17-14	
Valdez	Sergio	MEN		
Griffith	Anthony	CEN	9-8	(29-10)*
Hernandez	Ramiro	B		

171
Mooney	Britt	EB	8-6	(25-4)*
Folmer	Daniel	BUC		
Moreno	Anthony	PAR	11-3	
Botello	Edgar	EX		
Luna	Moises	MEN	4-1	
Griffin	William	MAD		

189
Sanchez	Mariano	REED	7-1	
Gonzalez	Carlos	EB		(31-12)*
Clark	Granson	DP	9-6	
Stephens	Mike	LEM		
Negrete	Abel	CL	7-1	
Villegas	Elvis	MEN		

(Continued on next page)

Central Section Masters Championships – East
February 14, 2001

215
Goodman	Kyle	BUC	6-3	
Maffia	Broc	TW		
Cabrera	Bennie	LEM	14-5	
Torosian	Adam	CW		
Shields	Colin	SB	4:33	(35-14)*
Gonzalez	Luis	WOOD		

275
Hallmark	Jacob	CL	3:01	(24-3)*
Murphy	Jon	HAN		(43-8)*
Wilson	Tyrone	TW	1:15	
Rodriguez	Juan	DP		
Braaten	Chris	STOCK	D.Q.	(38-13)*
Jackson	Emanuel	HW		

Tournament
1. Bakersfield — 141.5
2. Buchanan — 100
3. Clovis — 93
4. Lemoore — 86.5
5. East — 54
6. Madera — 50
6. Centennial — 50
8. Hanford — 34
8. Reedley — 34
10. Mendota — 31.5
11. Tulare Western — 31
12. Parlier — 30
13. Dos Palos — 29
14. Tulare — 28
15. Clovis West — 26
15. Foothill — 26
17. Woodlake — 24
18. Exeter — 21
18. Hoover — 21
20. Washington U. — 19
20. Shafter — 19
22. Kingsburg — 16
23. Sanger — 14
23. Wasco — 14
23. Kerman — 14
26. Golden West — 12
27. Arvin — 10
27. Selma — 10
29. Fowler — 9
29. Stockdale — 9
31. South — 8
32. Central — 7
33. Sierra — 5
33. Firebaugh — 5
35. Coalinga — 4

* Record

Darrell Vasquez
Four-time State Champion
Three-time CIF Champion
Two-time Most Outstanding Wrestler in the State Championships
Bakersfield High

Central Section Masters – Clovis High
February 23, 2002

103
Contreras	Gerrard	BUC	4-1	(45-1)*
Parreira	Blake	TUL		
Garcia	Sonny	KING	Fall 1:04	
Anderson	Mark	LEM		
Hernandez	Antonio	LIB-BAK		(33-11)*
Nelson	Jens	CW		

112
Morgan	Nathan	B	3-1	(39-1)*
Mendes	Chad	HAN		(34-6)*
Carillo	Gilbert	TUL	Inj. Def.	
Ingram	Logan	BUC		(27-7)*
Carlson	Sean	HOOV		
Saldana	Andy	COR		

119
Flores	Gabe	CL	13-7	(46-1)*
Franco	Tony	B		(42-7)*
Martinez	Nick	TUL	7-1	**(40-8)***
Schneider	Justin	BUC		
Reyes	Eugene	HAN		
Husein	Ali	SEL		

125
Vasquez	Darrell	B	13-4	(48-1)*
Holt	J.J.	TUL		(37-14)*
Williams	Jason	CL	3-1	(33-4)*
Bustamante	Gabriel	FOOT		(37-10)*
Martinez	Mike	EB		(44-12)*
Siegers	Andrew	YOSE		

130
Tirapelle	Troy	CL	3-1	(46-3)*
Herrera	Alex	B		(36-7)*
Goodpaster	Darrel	BUC	Inj. Def.	
Maldonado	Matt	SHAFT		(39-5)*
Anderson	Lucas	HAN		
Silva	Thomas	KER		

135
Roberts	David	CW	22-5	(55-6)*
Hernandez	Joe	B		(32-14)*
Salas	Jacob	BUC	15-1	
Carrasco	Jason	SHAFT		(25-7)*
Bonita	Tim	DEL		(41-5)*
Landois	Orlando	W		(25-10)*

140
Varner	Jake	B	3-2	(37-7)*
Martinez	Chris	CW		(18-14)*
Hirata	Garin	CI		
Piontes	Jason	LIB		
Mattox	David	BUC		
Rivera	Gabriel	WU		

145
Spradlin	Andrew	B	2:31	(38-2)*
Nail	Norman	LEM		
Diaz	Marcos	FOOT	Fall 5:37	(44-10)*
Thompson	Bryce	BUC		
Garcia	J.R.	FARM		
Ferrer	Andy	CAR		

152
East	Drew	B	3:26	(40-2)*
Breceda	Jesus	BUC		
Luna	Gabe	MON	O.T. 1-1	
Joyner	Travis	REED		
Thayn	Charlton	MT.W		
Mendoza	Adam	FIRE		

160
Sherley	Josh	B	7-4	(38-1)*
Hafemeister	Swen	LEM		(49-6)*
Garcia	Marcus	TUL	9-3	
David	Brian	MAD		
Pacheco	Alex	WU		
Cole	Jeff	CL		

171
Ferguson	Scott	CL	6-3	
Griffin	Wiliam	MAD		
Baker	Jeff	CENT	10-5	(35-6)*
Weaver	Jake	SANG		
Becerra	Jonathan	FARM		(46-9/23 Falls)*
Garcia	Jesse	GW		

189
Sanchez	Mariano	REED	Forfeit	
Folmer	Daniel	BUC		(42-4)*
Mercado	Eduardo	MAD	5:09	
Grona	Alex	WU		
Villegas	Elvis	MEN		
Marquez	Josh	B	Inj. Def.	(29-12)*

(Continued on next page)

Central Section Masters – Clovis High
February 23, 2002

215

Goodman	Kyle	BUC	11-5	(20-2)*
Maffia	Broc	TW		
Nadeau	Jeremiah	CL	7-2	
Torosian	Adam	CW		
Trego	Juan	SEL		
Powers	Cole	DP		

HWT

Chretien	Jon	ED Fall 3:02	(49-2/35 Falls)*
Braaten	Chris	STOCK	(48-6)*
Jackson	Emmanuel	HW 5-3	
Parsons	Jared	CL	
Landeros	Jake	MON	
Lopez	Gabriel	COAL	

Tournmanet

1. Bakersfield 198
2. Buchanan 148
3. Clovis 127
4. Tulare 75
5. Clovis West 55.5
6. Lemoore 46
7. Madera 40
8. Hanford 39.5
9. Reedley 38
10. Foothill 37
11. Edison 24
12. Shafter 21
13. Washington U. 19
14. Monache 19
15. Stockdale 17
16. Liberty 17
17. Tulare Western 15
18. Kingsburg 14
18. Hanford West 14

* Record

Correction

103 Contreras, Gerrard (43-1)*

Drew East of Bakersfield High
State Champion 2002
3rd in State 2001

Josh Shirley of Bakersfield High
State Champion 2002
2nd in State 2001

CIF Central Section Masters – East Bakersfield
March 11, 2003

103
Land	Brett	B	WB Inj. Def.	(37-8)*
Ruiz	Paul	FIRE		(50-8)*
Olea	Angel	FARM	5-0	(45-11)*
Gonzalez	Polo	MCF		(26-11)*
Mercado	Edgar	MAD	112-0	
Vang	Chou	BULL		

112
Carlson	Sean	HOOV	2-0	(55-7)*
Parreira	Blake	TUL		
Rangell	Conrad	CE	5-2	
Orozco	Eric	MON		
Rocha	Dustin	LEM	14-4	
Fisher	Reace	BUC		

119
Mendes	Chad	HAN	16-8	(56-2)*
Carillo	Gilbert	TUL		
Neuman	Grant	B	4-3	(33-14)*
Morales	Carlos	EB		(42-9)*
Andersen	Mark	LEM	10-2	
Weatherly	Daniel	EX		

125
Morgan	Nathan	B	5-3	(42-1)*
Flores	Gabe	CL		
Reyes	Eugene	HAN	Fall :40	
Pierce	Tim	MAD		
Soto	Joe	PORT	3-0	
Sanchez	Sal	W		(29-9)*

130
Tirapelle	Troy	CLO	Fall 2:45	
Aguilar	Jacob	TUL		
Bustamante	Gabe	FOOT	12-5	(37-6)*
Espericueta	Lucas	SHAFT		(39-10)*
Schneider	Justin	BUC	FF	
Ochoa	Joseph	REED		

135
Herrera	Alex	B	7-4	(39-3)*
Williams	Jason	CL		
Anderson	Lucas	HAN	Inj. Def.	
Caraveo	Jimmy	DEL		(15-11)*
Moralez	Mark	TUL	3-0	
Loredo	Francisco	COAL		

140
Martinez	Chris	CW	Inj. Def.	
Perger	Cameron	CL		
Marquez	Mark	EB	16-5	(44-11)*
Pendleton	Willie	LEM		
Sanchez	Eric	MAD	5-4	
Dueck	Nick	SANG		

145
Thompson	Bryce	CL	5-2	
Guerrero	Joel	HAN		
Wender	K.B.	CE	3-2	
Points	Jason	LIB-BAK		(36-10)*
Fielding	Coby	BUC	3-2	
Doherty	Randy	TUL		

152
Varner	Jake	B	O.T. 7-5	(39-3/31 Falls)*
Carrasco	Jason	SHAFT		(44-4/26 Falls/123-26 Career)*
Nail	Norman	LEM	D O.T. 2-2	
Houck	Ryan	CW		
West	Doug	MON	7-0	
Watson	James	COAL		

160
Baker	Jeff	CENT	8-2	(49-4)*
xxxxxxNoak	Dustin	CW		(42-9)*
Lujano	Paul	Buc	3-0	
Wara	Garth	MAD		
Castillo	Cain	WOOD	WB FF	
Boger	Matt	COAL		

171
Griffin	William	MAD	4-0	
Ferguson	Scott	CL		
Garcia	Marcus	TUL	10-8	
Becerra	Jonathan	FARM		(41-10/20 Falls)*
Carey	Lammar	HOOV	9-8	
Pacheco	Alex	WU		

189
Ceremello	Brandon	CL	7-4	
Mercado	Eduardo	MAD		
Campos	Ray	LEM	12-9	
Rodriguez	Abraham	WOOD		
Medina	Daniel	ROOS	9-2	
Merrell	Jacob	DP		

(Continued on next page)

CIF Central Section Masters – East Bakersfield
March 11, 2003

215
Clutts	Tyler	CL	8-0	
Marquez	Josh	B		(37-9)*
Coleman	Chauncey	MCL	14-1	
Levay	Bryan	MAD		
Torosian	Adam	CW	FF	
Trejo	Juan	SEL		

275
Thomas	Grant	BUC	O.T. 3-1	
Clark	James	MT.W		
Wiley	Preston	CW	5-1	
Rodriguez	Jordan	ED		
Camargo	Fernando	REED	FF	
Williams	Jayson	SHAFT		(30-5)*

Alex Herrera
State Champion
Two-time State runner-up
Bakersfield High

Tournament
1. Clovis	175.5		23. Edison	14
2. Bakersfield	140.5		24. McFarland	13
3. Madera	104		25. Foothill	11
4. Clovis West	91		25. Roosevelt	11
5. Tulare	85		27. Porterville	10
6. Hanford	79		27. Liberty	10
7. Lemoore	69.5		27. Exeter	10
8. Buchanan	62		30. Wasco	9
9. Shafter	47		31. Sanger	8
10. Woodlake	34		31. Selma	8
11. Hoover	33		33. Bullard	7
12. Clovis East	27.5		34. Washington U.	6
13. Monache	27		35. Dos Palos	5
13. Farmersville	27		35. Dinuba	5
15. Firebaugh	26.5		37. Parlier	4
16. Centennial	25		38. Kingsburg	3
17. East	24.5		38. Sierra	3
18. Mount Whitney	20		40. Hanford West	2
19. Reedley	19		40. Kerman	2
19. Coalinga	19		42. South	1
21. Delano	15		42. Arvin	1
21. McLane	15			

* Record

Addition
103 Olea, Angel career 143-54

Nathan Morgan
Three-time State Champion
State runner-up
Bakersfield High

Central Section Masters – Lemoore
February 28, 2004

103
Cisneros	Joe	B	O.T. 4-2	(45-4)*
Matthews	Jordan	PORT		
Gomez	Lupe	MAD	6-5	
Olea	Pedro	FARM		(41-9)*
Contreras	Buck	BUC	12-3	
Vigil	Freddie	SB		(36-11)*
Dominguez	Christian	COR	7-5	
Huizar	David	LEM		

112
Land	Brett	B	5-0	(46-4)*
Parreira	Blake	TUL		
Savala	Jimmy	CL	3-2	(42-15)*
Olea	Angel	FARM		(36-5)*
Mercado	Edgar	MAD	9-5	
Roman-Marin	Sean	LEM		
Gibson	Keith	MT.W		
Larson	Don	YOSE		

119
Carillo	Gilbdert	TUL	Fall 1:42	(39-2)*
Masuta	Sabi	MAD		(38-9)*
Nacita	Elijah	B	Fall 5:34	(40-4)*
Subia	Isaac	COAL		(39-12)*
Orozco	Eric	MON	Default	
Coronado	Albert	FIRE		(33-21)*
				(Career 95-55)*
Fisher	Rease	BUC	2-0	
Andersen	Mark	LEM		

125
Soto	Joe	PORT	3-2	(39-3)
Juarez	Steven	HAN	(40-5/93-10 Career)*	
Rocha	Dustin	LEM	Inj. Default	(45-11)*
Husein	Ali	SEL		
Torres	Anthony	EX	Default	
Trevino	Rafael	BUC		
Martinez	Fernando	FIRE	7-5	
Andaverde	Grody	MAD		

130
Morgan	Nathan	B	Inj. Def.	
			(39-0/Career 167-6)*	
Williams	Jason	CL		(23-3)*
Weatherly	Daniel	EX	Default	
Ochoa	Joseph	REED		
Balasse	Joaquin	TEHA	Default	(35-5)*
Gibson	Cody	MT.W		
Quinones	Sergio	LEM	10-2	
Righi	Daniel	RED		

135
Moralez	Mike	TUL	9-0	(45-2)*
Webber	Tony	B		(41-13)*
Schneider	Justin	BUC	1-0	(41-13)*
Maldanado	Eric	GW		
Gutierrez	Urbano	MAD	3-1	(39-6)*
Sanchez	Sal	W		(39-8)*
Mora	Jaime	FIRE	9-6	
Williams	Josh	CL		

140
Tirapelle	Troy	CL	11-2	
			(47-2/27 Falls)*	
Valenzuela	Don	BUC	(34-12/Career 89-43)*	
Espericueta	Lucas	SHAFT	Fall 3:29	(47-5)*
Oliveira	Mike	LEM		
Pezzat	Sinai	FAR	12-5	(34-12)*
Box	Anthony	B		(35-12)*
Pumarejo	Jay	CW	9-2	
Ramos	Anthony	WOOD		

145
Martinez	Chris	CW	O.T. 3-3	(49-4)*
Herrera	Alex	B		(45-4)*
Felding	Coby	BUC	8-4	
			(34-15/106-55 Career)*	
Pendleton	Willie	LEM		
Doherty	Randy	TUL	Default	
Coronado	Johnny	FIRE		
Botello	Oscar	EX	Fall 1:59	
Brooks	Wesley	MCL		

152
Meredith	Chip	CENT	8-5	(35-1)*
Thompson	Bryce	CL		(38-13)*
Landois	Orlando	W	Fall 5:32	(40-7)*
Wender	K.B.	CE	(40-7/153-37 Career)*	
Packard	Kenneth	ROOS	Default	
West	Doug	MON		
Sanchez	Eric	MAD	Fall 3:23	
Urena	Rafe	WOOD		

160
Bernacchi	Tyler	CE		(51-4)*
Noack	Dustin	CW		(39-6)*
Castillo	Cain	WOOD		
Boger	Matt	COAL		
Ceremello	Sean	CL	7-2	
Wara	Garth	MAD		
Acevedo	Abel	MON	Fall 1:49	
Clenard	Justin	TEHA		

(Continued on next page)

Central Section Masters – Lemoore
February 28, 2004

171
Varner	Jake	B	5-0	
			(41-0/34 Falls)*	
Griffin	Kyle	CE	(42-8)*	
Garcia	Marcus	TUL	Default (43-4)*	
Levay	Bryan	MAD		
Turley	Chris	CW	7-5	
Pacheco	Alex	WU		
Acosta	Jesse	COAL	10-6	
Delgadillo	Martin	DIN		

189
Ceremello	Brandon	CL	4-2	
			(45-10/197-26 Career)*	
Schneider	Will	CW	(42-8)*	
Flores	Ryan	BUC	8-4	
Statler	Marvin	SHAFT	(42-7)*	
Merrill	Jacob	DP	Default	
Clark	John	HAN		
Velasquez	Jesse	PORT	8-3	
Vitucci	Anthony	CE		

215
Marquez	Josh	B	2-0	
Trejo	Juan	SEL		
Lewis	Chris	CW	6-2	
Garcia	Rudy	MON		
Davis	Tim	STOCK	Default (38-7)*	
Moore	Marcus	CL		
Mercer	Daniel	CE	Fall 4:17	
Garza	Nick	SHAFT		

HWT
Sconiers	Decovan	WU	4-2	
Torres	Carlos	MON	(32-7)*	
McGuire	Joe	SIE	2-1	
Wiley	Preston	CW		
Gomez	Daniel	FOW	Fall 2:32	
Leyva	Victor	ROOS		
Paulson	R.J.	FRE	1-0	
Morgan	David	CENT		

Tournament
1. Bakersfield	157
2. Clovis	107.5
3. Clovis West	80
4. Tulare	75
5. Madera	66
5. Buchanan	66
7. Clovis East	60
8. Lemoore	51
9. Porterville	40
10. Monache	36
11. Washington U.	27
12. Farmersville	26
13. Shafter	25
14. Selma	24
15. Exeter	20
15. Coalinga	20
15. Central	20
18. Hanford	17
19. Firebaugh	16
19. Woodlake	16
21. Wasco	15
22. Reedley	14
23. Golden West	12
23. Roosevelt	12
25. Sierra	10
26. Tehachapi	9
27. Mt. Whitney	7
27. Fowler	7
27. Dos Palos	7
30. Stockdale	5
30. S. Bakersfield	5
32. McLane	4
33. Corcoran	3
34. Dinuba	2
34. Fresno	2
34. Redwood	2
34. Yosemite	2

Josh Marquez
2003 - 4th in State
2004 - 5th in State
Bakersfield High

Jake Varner
Two-time State
Champion
State runner-up
4th in State
Bakersfield High

* Record

Addition

171 Griffin, Kyle career 125-25

Central Section Masters – Buchanan
February 26, 2005

103
Garcia	John	FIRE	5-0	
Weimer	Steve	CL		
Vigil	Freddy	SB	15-5	(38-5)*
Cheidez	David	FOOT		(38-10)*
Watts	Randall	ELD		
Escandon	Pete	LEM		
Martinez	Rolando	DIN	5-2	
Sanchez	Jesse	CE		

112
Olea	Angel	FARM	12-14	(33-0/143-28 Career)*
Hay	Addison	FOOT		(44-9)*
Gibson	Keith	MT.W	2-0	(45-14)*
Watts	David	ELD		(32-16)*
Lomas	Frank	B	8-7	(38-14)*
Coneay	Matt	CL		
Trevino	Ricky	FRE	9-3	
Sanchez	Efrain	A		

119
Ruiz	Paul	FIRE	Fall :45	
Castillo	Frankie	A		(28-10)*
Ramirez	Ernesto	EX	16-14	(36-10)*
Salvala	Jimmy	CL		
Martinez	Christian	B	Inj. Def.	(36-12)*
Chaidez	Bernard	FOOT		(41-10)*
Rodriguez	Alex	CE	7-1	
Huizar	David	LEM		

125
Anderson	Mark	LEM	Fall 1:28	(50-6)*
Rangel	Conrad	CE		
Subia	Isaac	COAL	8-0	
Vaughn	Jordan	CW		
Husein	Ali	SEL	Fall 1:42	
Navarro	Vincent	SHAFT		
Trevino	Rafael	BUC	5-1	
Mercado	Edgar	MAD		

130
Nacita	Elijah	B	13-3	(45-4)*
Betancur	Josh	BUC		
Rocha	Dustin	LEM	9-6	
Martinez	Fernando	FIRE		
Rios	Johnny	MAD	6-0	
Larsen	Troy	CE		
Tovar	Archie	SEL	9-4	
Gillhar	Jacob	SIE		

135
Soto	Joe	PORT	9-3	(42-0/103-38 Career)*
Gibson	Cody	MT.W		
Ochoa	Joseph	REED	5-1	
Sanchez	Alfonso	MCL		
Velarde	Jovany	BUC	5-3	
Montolongo	Daniel	MAD		
Perez	Matt	FIRE	Fall 4:02	
Aridia	Scott	SEL		

140
Land	Brett	B	Fall 3:55	(46-8)*
Weatherly	Dan	EX		
Maldonado	Eric	GW	5-0	(46-4)*
Espericueta	Lucas	SHAFT		(44-6)*
Corona	Alex	MON	7-4	
Licon	Kenny	FRE		
Moralez	Mitch	TUL	6-3	
Gallegos	Manuel	YOSE		

145
Pendleton	Willy	LEM	7-4	(43-9)*
Williams	John	CW		
Horton	Bryce	CENT	Fall 2:58	(47-10)*
Martinez	Matt	TUL		
Box	Anthony	B	Inj. Def.	
Rodriguez	Brian	CE		
Chavez	Richard	FARM	6-4	(32-9)*
Serna	Miguel	DP		

152
Packard	Kenneth	ROOS	4-1 (52-7/18 Falls)	(131-39 career)*
Metcalf	Josh	PORT		
Doherty Randy		TUL	2-1	(123-50 Career)*
Olivera	Mike	LEM		
Bardsley	Nick	CW	15-0	
Gallegos	Jimmy	MAD		
Johnson	Zack	W	9-4	(33-10)*
Serna	Ray	COAL		

160
Ceremellow	Shaun	CL	9-4	(47-6)*
Williams	Josh	B		(34-8)*
Baughman	Scott	LEM	9-0	
Garrison	Chris	FOW		
Graff	Tim	TUL	9-2	
Garcia	Jared	MCF		(26-11)*
Parli	Rolland	WEST	8-5	(35-9)*
Rodriguez	Adrian	MON		

(Continued on next page)

Central Section Masters – Buchanan
February 26, 2005

171
Boger	Matt	COAL	Fall 1:46	
Merrill	Jacob	DP		
Rozario	Andrfew	CL	Inj. Default	
Griffin	Christopher	MAD		
Cavanaugh	Mike	B	Fall 3:30	(42-12)*
Degeare	Justin	LIB		(30-14)*
Vitucci	Anthony	CE	Fall 4:23	
Coleman	Trevon	WASCO		

189
Varner	Jake	B	Fall 1:42 (47-0/43 Falls/ Career 157-10/132 Falls)*	
Timmerman	Nathan	MON		(47-6)*
Statler	Marvin	SHAFT	Fall 4:20	(31-7)*
Czechowski	Nick	HIGH		(32-10)*
Leyva	Raul	MCL	8-5	
Boger	Josh	COAL		
Esparza	Kevin	CL	6-2	
Parrish	Zak	BUC		

215
Flores	Ryan	BUC	Fall 2:34	
Garcia	Rudy	MON		
Pierson	Jacob	RIDGE	Fall 2:50	(34-12)*
Mendoza	Francisco	DP		
Guill	Westy	CE	Inj. Default	
Cervantes	Alex	FIRE		
Lopez	Vince	COAL	5-2	
Ferrera	Brandon	CL		

275
Lewis	Chris	CW	10-3	(35-4)*
Morgan	David	CENT		(37-8)*
Gomez	Daniel	FOW	3-1	
Alcala	Ricky	A		(30-11)*
Dummar	Mike	GH	2-1	
Leyva	Luis	ROOS		
Newman	Josh	GW	2-1	
Jiminez	Leobardo	DP		

* Record

Tournament
1.	Bakersfield	132
2.	Lemoore	102
3.	Clovis	71
4.	Firebaugh	64
5.	Buchanan	58
6.	Clovis West	57.5
7.	Clovis East	56
8.	Coalinga	54
9.	Monache	45
10.	Porterville	37
10.	Tulare Union	37
12.	Dos Palos	35
12.	Madera	35
14.	Foothill	34
15.	Centennial	33
16.	Shafter	32.5
17.	Arvin	32
18.	Exeter	31
19.	Mt. Whitney	30
20.	Roosevelt	27
21.	Fowler	26
21.	McLane	26
23.	Farmersville	24.5
24.	Golden West	17.5
25.	El Diamonte	17
26.	Ridgeview	16
27.	Reedley	15.5
28.	Selma	15
28.	South	15
30.	Highland	14
31.	Granite Hills	9
32.	Fresno	8
33.	Liberty	7
34.	Dinuba	5
34.	McFarland	5
34.	W. Bakersfield	5
37.	Sierra	4
37.	Yosemite	4
39.	Wasco	2
	Delano	0
	Tehachapi	0

Brett Land
Two-time CIF Champion
Bakersfield High

Central Section Masters – East Bakersfield
February 25, 2006

103
Chaidez	David	FOOT	11-1	(51-6)*
Done	Chris	BUC		
Vigil	Freddie	S	12-2	
			(42-4/Career 123-21)*	
Camacho	Gilbert	WU		(35-12)*
Gonzalez	Peter	EB	Fall 1:26	(39-11)*
Evenwine	Chase	CW		
Fitzgerald	Steven	CE	Fall 5:56	(41-15)*
Gonzales	Juan	KER		

112
Arredondo	Justin	BUC	8-6	(46-10)*
Weimer	Steven	CL		(39-21)*
Lomas	Frank	B	3-1	(45-12)*
Watts	Randall	ELD		(34-10)*
Demison	Neketo	EAST	Fall 5:12	(41-10)*
Quintana	Diego	SEL		
Olea	Pedro	FARM	10-5	
			(102-26 career)*	
Sanchez	Jesse	CE		

119
Watts	David	ELD	5-1	(35-6)*
Conley	Matt	CE		(36-12)*
Romas	Chris	BULL	5-0	
Cole	Calvin	COAL		
Tucker	Warren	MAD	4-2	
Mendoza	Jose	SEL		
Vanni	Garret	LIB-MAD	16-11	
Patino	Robert	EX		

125
Valarde	Jovanny	BUC Tech. Fall.		
		(40-7/Career 109-40)*		
Castillo	Frankie	A		
Jordan	Vaughn	CW	9-5	
Rodriguez	Alex	CE		
Roman-Marin	Sean	LEM	5-3	
Cruz	Jonah	B	(34-18)	
Ramirez	Ernesto	EX	14-2	
Hicks	Seth	CENT		

130
Betancur	Josh	BUC	9-4	(51-5)*
Savala	Jimmy	CL		(19-6)*
Rios	Johnny	MAD	12-1	
Nelson	Robby	KING		
Huizar	David	LEM	Fall 3:34	
Rasmussen	Travis	B		(39-13)*
Contreras	Nick	SEL	9-4	
Pavone	Ryan	PORT		(35-10)*

135
Nacita	Elijah	B	Fall 4:05	(35-0)*
Pavone	Chris	PORT		(31-8)*
Larson	Troy	CE	9-4	(26-19)*
Tovar	Archie	SEL		
West	Stephen	BUC	Fall 5:54	
Christensen	Colton	LIB-BAK		
Arreola	Diego	WU	13-7	
Ballesteros	Adam	DP		

140
Sanchez	Alfonso	MCL	7-6	(48-1)*
Cisneros	Joe	SEL		
Cesena	Joseph	MAD	8-3	
Morales	Mitch	TUL		(44-9)*
Box	Anthony	B	5-1	(31-8)*
Martinez	Ricky	FIRE		
Licon	Kenny	FRE	4-2	
West	Craig	BUC		

145
Webber	Tony	B	5-4	(51-5)*
Espericueta	Lucas	SHAFT		(44-4)*
Rodriguez	Brian	CE	4-2	(26-10)*
Horton	Bryce	CENT		(48-6)*
Balch	Andrew	BUC	Fall 1:50	
Merrell	Caleb	DP		
Cox	Matt	CL	6-0	
Barajas	Eddie	MEN		

152
Pendleton	Willy	LEM	14-5	(59-6)*
Wilkin	Danny	CENT		(33-11)*
Montez	Frank	MCL	5-2	
Johnson	Zach	W		(34-14)*
Corona	Alex	MON	Default	(46-6)*
Smith	Eric	BUC		
Tucker	Grant	MAD	10-2	
Post	Robert	TEHA		

(Continued on next page)

Central Section Masters – East Bakersfield
February 25, 2006

160
Boger	Matt	BUC	5-4	(47-6)*
Bardsley	Nick	CW		(40-12)*
Righi	Dan	RED	Tech Fall	(50-8)*
Bays	Chris	CL		
Bautista	Alejandro	COAL	2-1	
Bracamonte	Paul	CEN		
Torres	Chris	S	11-4	(40-10)*
Smith	David	LIB-MAD		

171
Parrish	Zak	BUC	14-7	(42-13)*
Garcia	Jared	MCF		(31-4)*
De La Rosa	Eric	FOOT	10-8	(39-11)*
Ayers	Terrell	SUNY		
Musquez	John	CENT	4-0	(31-14)*
Ruiz	Abel	SEL		
Vera	Jose	CEN	8-4	
Allison	Duston	MAD		

189
Timmerman	Nathan	MON	9-6	(42-0)*
Boger	Josh	BUC		(25-7)*
Rozario	Andrew	CL	Fall 2:20	(41-11)*
Blair	Tyler	MAD		
Travis	David	FOOT	5-4	(41-10)*
Lopez	Orlando	COAL		
Cabrerra	Herman	LEM	Fall 5:05	
Lookadoo	Ronald	SHAFT		

215
Flores	Ryan	BUC	14-0	(54-1/30 Falls)
Maxson	Jacob	RED		(45-19)*
Mendoza	Francisco	DP	4-1	
Perez	Jose	PORT		(35-12)*
Lopez	Vincent	CL	12-1	(29-9)*
Smith	Joe	TEHA		(40-12)*
Moore	Quinn	S	5-4	(43-11)*
Renteria	Michael	WU		

275
Lewis	Chris	CW	6-3	(48-4)*
Alcala	Ricky	A		(36-4)*
Morgan	David	CENT	1-0	(40-9)*
Zamora	Jonathan	CL		
Jimenez	Leobardo	DP	Default	
Newman	Josh	GW	(56-10)	
Hawkins	Roman	FRE	Default	
Quiroz	Ivan	FOOT		

Tournament

1. Buchanan	207.5
2. Clovis	83.5
3. Bakersfield	77
4. Clovis East	61.5
5. Clovis West	58
6. Centennial	55
7. Selma	54.5
8. Madera	52
9. Lemoore	49
10. Foothill	47
11. Arvin	35
12. Porterville	34
12. Dos Palos	34
12. McLane	34
15. Monache	33
16. El Diamante	32
17. Redwood	31.5
18. Coalinga	24
19. S. Bakersfield	22
20. Shafter	21
21. Washington U.	17
22. McFarland	16
22. East Bakersfield	16
24. Sunnyside	16
25. Bullard	14
26. Kingsburg	12
27. Tulare	11
27. Wasco	11
27. Central	11
30. Fresno	10
31. Golden West	7
31. Liberty-Bak	7
31. Liberty-Mad	7
31. Tehachapi	7
35. Exeter	6
36. Farmersville	5
36. Firebaugh	5
38. Mendota	2
38. Kerman	2
Hanford	0
Stockdale	0
Parlier	0
Fowler	0
Dinuba	0
Roosevelt	0
Reedley	0
Delano	0
Caruthers	0
Corcoran	0
Highland	0
Mt. Whitney	0
Sanger	0
Sierra	0
Tranquility	0
Tulare Western	0
Woodlake	0
Yosemite	0

* Record

Riley, Dustin coaching record 7 years - 81-13

Elijah Nacita
State Champion
State runner-up
7th in State 2004
Bakersfield High

California State Championships
1973-2006

Central Section State Meet Results Team Top 10

Year	School	Place	Points	Year	School	Place	Points
1973	Clovis	2	38	1996	Bakersfield	9	55.5
1974	Clovis	Champion	57	1997	ClovisWest	4	71.5
1975	Clovis	Champion	46	1997	Madera	8	49.5
1975	Madera	2	40	1998	Buchanan	2	102
1976	Clovis	Champion	65.5	1998	Foothill	3	93
1976	Hanford	5	40	1998	ClovisWest	7	81
1979	South	4	38	1999	Clovis	3	69
1979	Mt. Whitney	5	34.5	1999	Foothill	6	64
1980	Bakersfield	5	35	1999	Centennial	9	57.5
1981	Clovis	3	59.5	1999	Tulare	10	53
1982	ClovisWest	5	45	2000	Clovis	2	106.5
1983	ClovisWest	Champion	88.5	2000	Lemoore	4	66.5
1984	ClovisWest	Champion	117.5	2000	Buchanan	5	61.5
1984	Madera	2	69	2000	Bakersfield	6	53.5
1985	Clovis	6	41	2000	Hanford	10	41.5
1986	Clovis	4	51.5	2001	Bakersfield	2	129
1988	Selma	5	47	2001	Clovis	5	71.5
1988	Roosevelt	6	35	2001	Buchanan	7	60.5
1989	ClovisWest	Champion	57	2001	Lemoore	8	54
1989	Clovis	3	51.5	2001	Madera	9	48.5
1990	Clovis	Champion	78.5	2002	Bakersfield	Champion	226.5
1990	Selma	7	42	2002	Buchanan	2	101.5
1990	South	9		2002	Clovis	3	96
1991	Clovis	Champion	88.5	2003	Clovis	Champion	151.5
1991	Selma	4	64	2003	Bakersfield	4	106
1991	Madera	5	53.5	2003	ClovisWest	6	69.5
1991	Roosevelt	8	43.5	2003	Hanford	9	38.5
1992	Clovis	Champion	95	2004	Bakersfield	Champion	170.5
1992	Bakersfield	10	37	2004	Clovis	2	93.5
1993	Clovis	3	65	2004	ClovisWest	7	63
1993	Madera	6	52	2005	Bakersfield	2	111
1994	Madera	3	68	2005	Lemoore	8	62
1994	Clovis	4	63	2006	Buchanan	Champion	134
1995	Bakersfield	3	98.5	2006	Bakersfield	6	73
1995	ClovisWest	10	42	2006	Clovis	8 Tie	55
1996	Buchanan	5	65.5				

State Wrestler of the Year*

*Named by Cal-Hi Sports

Year	Wrestler	School	Weight
1958	Ausencio Rodriguez	Madera	112
1959	Ausencio Rodriguez	Madera	112
1966	Richard Simmons	South Bakersfield	175
1968	John Miller	North Bakersfield	191
1973	Mike Bull	South Bakersfield	191

Outstanding Wrestlers of the California State Championships

Year	Wrestler	School	Weight
1999	Ben Martinez	Tulare	130
2000	Chris Pendleton	Lemoore	145
2001	Darrell Vasquez	Bakersfield	119
2002	Darrell Vasquez	Bakersfield	125
2003	Nathan Morgan	Bakersfield	130
2004	Jake Varner	Bakersfield	189

Rey Martinez
Two-Time State Champion. 1977 Righetti Southern Section. 1978 Roosevelt Central Section

Terry Watts
Member of the 1986 State Champions Poway. As a freshman, he won the Divisoin I CIF at 126 and placed 2nd in the San Diego Masters. State Meet: By today's standards he would have wrestled for 7th-8th, one victory from the top 6. At Caruthers, Terry's top placings: 3, 2, 1.

Adam Tirapelle
Four-Time CIF Champion. Hiram Johnson SAC-Joaquin Section 1993, 1994, 1995. Buchanan Central Section 1996. Adam's state placings: 2, 1, 1

David Roberts
State Placings: Bear River-SAC-Joaquin Section 2000 6th, 2001 3rd
Clovis West-Central Section 2002 2nd

California State Wrestling Championships
Started 1973

Name	School	WT/Record	Place
1973			
Robert Contreras	KING	95	Champion
Ernie Flores	MAD	112	Champion
Eugene Guerrero	CORC	112	2
Randy Baxster	CLOVIS	133	2
Ross Wilkerson	CLOVIS	154	3
Mike Anderson	FOOT	154	4
Tony Manning	WU	165	2
Florencio Rocha	B	165	3
Joe Bracamonte	CEN	175	2
Mike Bull	SB	191	Champion
Jeff Robinson	CLOVIS	HWT	5
1974			
Pete Gonzalez	HIGH	95	2
Eugene Guerrero	CORC	112	5
Julio Morales	DEL	112	6
Ray Garza	EB	120	4
Tom Gongora	CLOVIS	127	Champion
Horace Russell	RED	127	6
Joe Lopez	SHAFT	133 (40-1)	2
Rodney Balch	CLOVIS	138	Champion
Jess Torres	SB	145	Champion
Tony Manning	WU	165	3
Kevin Cookingham	CLOVIS	165	4
Fred Bohna	CLOVIS	191	Champion
Jeweal Thomas	HAN	235	3
1975			
Paul Bolanos	CLOVIS	95	3
Pete Gonzalez	HIGH	103	2
Tommy Blanco	CLOVIS	103	3
Tim Murphy	HOOV	112	6
Rick Contreras	RED	120	6
Joe Lopez	SHAFT	133	2
Robert Kiddy	MAD	145 (137-13)*	2
Leron Leroy	MAD	154	2
Bob Roberts	FRE	154	5
Ed Johnson	CLOVIS	191	3
Mike Diaz	MAD	191	4
Jeweal Thomas	HAN	235	Champion
1976			
Percy Richard	EB	95	2
Ram Pereschica	SEL	95	4
Paul Bolanos	CLOVIS	103	2
Pete Gonzalez	HIGH	103	3
Bill Jones	HAN	120	2
Paul Felez	SB	127	3
Rich Contreras	RED	133	2
Eddie Reyes	SB	133	4
Don Dow	HIGH	138	5
Ernie Pinieda	MAD	145	5
Bob Grimes	CLOVIS	154	4
Loren Leroy	MAD	154	5
Kevin Cookingham	CLOVIS	165	2
Bill Thomas	HAN	165	3
John Negrete	RED	175	4
Doug Arthur	CLOVIS	235	2
1977			
Anthony Blanco	CLOVIS	95	2
Percy Richard	EB	103	Champion
Fred Gonzalez	HIGH	103	2
Buff Estrada	FRE	112	3
Tony Padilla	WASCO	112	5
Glen McCullough	FOOT	127	2
Jeff Fahy	WB	133	2
Greg Inouye	CLOVIS	138	3
Bill Thomas	HAN	175 (141-?)*	2
Mike Landeros	MON	191	2
Lance Molica	DEL	191	4
Carlos Hernandez	EX	235	4
1978			
Tim Vanni	MON	95	6
Alfred Gutierrez	RED	103	3
Fred Gonzalez	HIGH	112	2
Steve Nickell	EB	133	6
Mark Vigil	EX	154	5
Frank Scott	WU	165	4
Rey Martinez	ROOS	175	Champion
Lewis McNabb	NB	175	4
Forrest Scott	WU	175	6
Lance Molica	DEL	235	3

Additions

Rocha, Florencio (76-7-23 Falls)
Richard, Percy (130-18)
Nickell, Steve (125-21)

California State Wrestling Championships

Name	School	WT/Record	Place
1979			
Tim Vanni	MON	95 (98-12)*	2
Alfred Gutierrez	RED	103	Champion
Pablo Saenz	REED	103	6
Steve Slade	WB	112	4
Jim Poteete	SB	120	Champion
Buff Estrada	FRE	120	2
Eddy Franich	MT.W	133	3
Nonnie Haskins	ROOS	191	3
Bill Pierce	SB	191	4
Scott Jones	MT.W	235	4
Marvin Castillo	TUL	235	6
1980			
Mike Gonzalez	HIGH	103	3
Mel East	B	112	Champion
Joe Bisig	SB	127	5
Victor Ibarra	B	127	6
Flint Pulskamp	HIGH	165	5
Mike Snell	WU	175	5
Joe Sansinena	MAD	191	6
Scott Jones	MT.W	235	Champion
1981			
Ed Mendoza	CLOVIS	98	6
Mel East	B	112	2
Mike Seay	HIGH	112	4
Kenny Dennis	CLOVIS	132	3
Frankie Ortiz	WU	138	3
Scott Bilyeu	CLOVIS	145	2
Kevin Carrera	HOOV	145	3
Brian Aquafresca	EX	167	Champion
George Peterson	CLOVIS W	185	2
Robert Diaz	BULL	185	6
Joe Sansinena	MAD	200	2
1982			
Darrell Nerove	FOOT	98	2
Ed Mendoza	CLOVIS	98	3
Wynn Ray	WB	105	2
Mel East	B	119	4
Pete Rangel	MAD	119	5
Don Townsend	MON	155	2
Todd Young	CLOVIS W	185	3
Barry Estes	CLOVIS W	245	5
1983			
Greg Montoya	CLOVIS	102	2
George Aguilar	WU	116	5
Darrell Nerove	FOOT	123	Champion
John Martin	CLOVIS W	123	2
Brian Lewis	CLOVIS W	136	2
Bret Davis	MON	142	6
Allen Richburg	CLOVIS W	149	2
Brad Zimmer	CLOVIS W	155	5
Eric Campbell	CLOVIS W	171	5
Todd Young	CLOVIS W	189	3
Lenny Moore	B	189	5
Barry Estes	CLOVIS W	249	3
Ricky Salas	MAD	249	5
1984			
Eddie Gomez	CAR	98	2
Pete Ramirez	A	98	3
Rick Barron	WU	105	6
Brian Lewis	CLOVIS W	126	Champion
Pat Rangel	MAD	126	2
Mike Armstead	LEM	126	4
Darrell Nerove	FOOT	132 (78-1 Jr-Sr)*	3
John Martin	CLOVIS W	132	4
Francisco Gomez	CLOVIS W	138	3
Kerry Collings	GOLDEN W	138	4
David Rosario	MAD	145	Champion
Randy Graham	B	154	Champion
Lance Cowart	MON	154	2
Todd Barns	CLOVIS W	154	3
Les Inouye	CLOVIS	165	2
Jeff Tice	CLOVIS W	165	3
Craig Hill	MON	175	4
Randy Flowers	MCL	191	5
Ricky Salas	MAD	220	Champion
Doc Mendivel	EB	220	2
Trent Barnes	CLOVIS W	220	4
1985			
Eddie Gomez	CAR	98 (141-12)*	Champion
Pete Snyder	MON	98	2
Brad East	B	105	3
Mike Dallas	FOOT	126	3
Elias Zarate	SEL	126	4
Ruben Chavez	B	132	3
David Rosario	FIRE	154 (105-21)*	3
Robert Henson	SEL	154	6
Dan Telen	CLOVIS	191	2
Trent Barnes	CLOVIS W	HWT	Champion
Ben Lizama	FOOT	HWT	3

California State Wrestling Championships

Name	School	WT/Record	Place
1986			
Anthony Tamez	CLOVIS	105	3
Brad East	B	112	4
Darrin Dutra	HAN	112	6
Ray Rangel	PAR	119	3
Shawn Crosswhite	CLOVIS	126	3
Trent Barnes	CLOVIS W	(84 Falls/138-14)*	
		245	Champion
George Anderson	EX	245	4
1987			
Harold Zinkin	BULL	98 (75-8)*	4
Robbie Sordi	MAD	98	6
Darrin Dutra	HAN	119	4
Mike Ortega	ROOS	119	5
Terry Watts	CAR	126	3
John Pierce	CLOVIS W	132 (126-26)*	6
John Sordi	MAD	138	5
Scott Herndon	SB	145 (79-10)*	6
Joe Romine	MAD	154	5
John Tripp	TUL	165	3
Chris Olinger	SB	165 (111-35-1)*	6
Lorenzo Hailey	TUL	175	6
Kent Lincoln	YOS	191	6
Ken Fontes	CLOVIS	245	Champion
George Anderson	EX	245	3
1988			
Robbie Sordi	MAD	98	Champion
Derek Patton	A	119	2
Mike Ortega	ROOS	126	Champion
Ralph Olivas	CLOVIS	126	6
Terry Watts	CAR	138	2
Robert Zapata S	SEL	175	Champion
Jerry Urzua	FRE	175	5
Lorenzo Neal	LEM	191	2

Name	School	WT/Record	Place
1989			
Nick Zinkin	BULL	98	4
Curis Alkire	MON	98	6
Jim Aguirre	CLOVIS	105	Champion
Robbie Sordi	MAD	105 (144-18)*	2
Petran Gant	ROOS	105	3
Sean Crain	CLOVIS W	105	4
Gary Quintana	SEL	112	2
Roy Perez	CORC	119	5
Eric Legareta	SEL	119	6
Dewayne Zinkin	BULL	126 (120-13)*	6
Joe Cemo	NB	132 (155-35)*	3
Steve Soto	CLOVIS W	138	3
Terry Watts	CAR	145 (177-19/108 Falls)*	
			Champion
Narcisco Lopez	ROOS	145	5
Caleb Roope	YOSE	154	2
Jassen Froehlich	B	165	4
Darren Sandusky	CLOVIS W	165	5
Renee Carlos	CLOVIS	191	2
Lorenzo Neal	LEM	HWT (147-8-1)*	
			Champion
Javier Jasso	RED	HWT	5
1990			
Andy Munoz	WU	98	2
Mike Serda	WASCO	98	6
Nick Quintana	SEL	105	3
Nick Zinkin	CLOVIS	105 (198-15-3)*	5
Detran Gant	ROOS	112	Champion
Jiim Aguirre	CLOVIS	119	Champion
Parris Whitely	SB	119 (124-41-1)*	3
Al Solano	DP	119	5
Gary Quintana	SEL	126	4
Brian Roach	CLOVIS W	132	7
Ralph Olivas	CLOVIS	138	Champion
Tad Stricker	SB	165 (116-27)*	2
Jassen Froehlich	B	175 (125-16)*	2
Brad Bell	CLOVIS W	191	2
Gary Williams	HOOV	245	4
Rod Williams	WU	245	6

California State Wrestling Championships

Name	School	WT/Record	Place
1991			
Mike Serda	WASCO	103	3
Soowan Scheuermann	MAD	103	8
Nick Quintana	SEL	112	Champion
Eduardo Fuentes	SANG	112	2
Isaac Pumarejo	KING	112	5
Nick Zinkin	CLOVIS	119	4
Eric Mares	SEL	119	6
Jim Aguirre	CLOVIS	130 (167-21/99 Falls)*	Champion
Ben Ervin	MAD	130	4
Mike Tamez	CLOVIS	130	5
Curtis Alkire	MON	135	2
Chad Scalzo	MAD	1315	7
Brian Roach	CLOVIS W	140	3
Alfonso Tucker	HOOV	140	7
Clayton Webber	MAD	145	7
Angel Ponce	ROOS	145	8
Brian Haupt	CLOVIS	152	6
Nacho Martinez	WASCO	152	8
Narcisco Lopez	ROOS	160	5
Scott Silver	BULL	171 (111-24/60 Falls)*	Champion
David Umada	MAD	171	6
Lalo Moz	HAN	189	Champion
Paul Carrillo	SB	245	4
1992			
Coby Wright	B	103	Champion
Aaron Radman	WB	103	3
Isaac Pumarejo	KING	112	4
Nick Zinkin	CLOVIS	119 (198-15-3)*	3
Joey Ruiz	KING	119	6
Curtis Summers	CLOVIS	125	4
Eric Mares	SEL	125	7
Yero Washington	PORT	130	Champion
David Molano	Golden W	130	4
Tony Lopez	PAR	140	6
Bruce Munster	CLOVIS	145	3
Alfonso Tucker	HOOV	152 (101-20-1)*	7
Josh Cleveland	COAL	152	8
Elliott Hine	CLOVIS	171	5
Lalo Moz	HAN	189 (126-11 90 Falls)*	Champion
Kory Westbury	CLOVIS	189	6
Paul Carrillo	SB	HWT (114-26)*	5
Chad Mast	CLOVIS	HWT	6
1993			
John Navarro	LEM	119	7
Johnny Esquivel	PORT	119	8
Brad Hull	MON	125	5
Chad Snapp	CLOVIS	130	5
Manuel Jimenez	KING	130	8
Aaron Rodriguez	WASCO	135	3
Kyle Swan	CLOVIS	135	4
Eddie Ramos	PORT	140	Champion
Moises Perez	MAD	140	2
Eric Philp	MAD	152	3
Erin Pectol	TUL	152	6
Elias Zamorano	ROOS	160	6
Joe Salcido	MON	191	5
Chad Mast	CLOVIS	245	Champion
1994			
Stan Green	CLOVIS	112	3
K.L. Lake	CLOVIS	119	4
Brad Hull	MON	125	4
Andy Varner	B	125	6
Juan Alamilla	PORT	125	8
Jeremy Pierro	BUC	130	7
Moises Perez	MAD	140	3
Kyle Swan	CLOVIS	145	2
Tom Moz	HAN	145	4
Fernando Meza	MAD	152	2
Eric Philp	MAD	160	Champion
Jeremiah Muhammed	ROOS	189	3
Jared Smith	CLOVIS W	245	4
1995			
Albert Garza	SANG	103	4
Paris Ruiz	CLOVIS W	112	3
Larry Vasquez	B	119	3
Jonte Davis	ED	125	5
Eric Serda	WASCO	125	7
David Russell	HOOV	130	6
Kelly Miller	B	135	3
Ismael Cordova	CEN	135	5
Andy Varner	B	140	3
Fred Molano	GOLDEN W	140	6
Tony Keller	B	160	7
Dan Jackson	KING	171	5
Fred Ashley	B	171	7
Anthony Miller	EX	189	6
Brett Clark	B	245	4
Eric Rodriguez	MON	245	5
Jared Smith	CLOVIS W	245	7

California State Wrestling Championships

Name	School	WT/Record	Place
1996			
Ed Smith	CLOVIS	103	3
Jaime Garza	SANG	103	4
Tee Sar	MT.W	103	5
Albert Garza	SANG	112	5
Paris Ruiz	CLOVIS W	119 (112-19)*	2
Ricardo Mosqueda	DP	119	5
Sergio Breceda	BUC	119	7
Nathan Vasquez	B	125	3
Anthony Adame	FOOT	125	8
Oscar Rubalcava	FRE	130	3
William Brown	HOOV	130	6
Mat Ehn	CLOVIS	135	5
Mike Sherrick	CLOVIS W	135	7
Adam Tirapelle	BUC	140 (213-7 134 Falls)*	Champion
Fred Molano	B	140	3
Arturo Garcia	SEL	140	8
Darrick Duran	ROOS	145 (114-24)	6
Ian Nelms	MT.W	145	7
Telly Sanders	BUC	152	4
Russell Smithson	HOOV	152	7
Charlie Sheen	CLOVIS	152	8
Sonny Pereschica	KING	160	2
Anthony Miller	EX	189	8
Ray Maese	B	215	4
Than Merrill	FRE	215	7
Victor Leyva	MON	275	5
Grant Harrington	RED	275	8

Name	School	WT/Record	Place
1997			
Cleo Johnson	FIRE	103	Champion
Chris Felix	EB	103	4
Angel Portillo	TUL	103	8
Jaime Garza	SANG	112	2
Mondo Mendez	BUC	112	6
Chris Resseguie	EB	112	8
Antoni Banuelos	CLOVIS W	119	3
Albert Garza	SANG	119	5
Tim Rosas	CLOVIS W	125	2
Jose Sanchez	ED	125	4
George Moreno	FIRE	201-25 130	5
Tony Rosas	CLOVIS W	130	7
Ralph Lopez	CLOVIS W	135	Champion
Robert Arballo	MAD	135	4
Sam Jameson	WASCO	135	8
Kirk Moore	FOOT	140	2
Kelly Miller	B	145	3
Jose Landin	WASCO	152	5
Adrian Diniz	FOOT	152	8
Telly Sanders	BUC	160	2
Ian Nelms	MT.W	160	3
Sonny Pereschica	KING	171	6
Dan Jackson	KING	189 (137-12)*	Champion
Ryan Philp	MAD	215	Champion
Rodney Leisle	RIDGE	275	7

California State Wrestling Championships

Name	School	WT/Record	Place
1998			
Jason Moreno	FIRE	103	6
Mando Mendez	BUC	112	6
Scott Beck	TUL	112	7
Kevin Jones	CLOVIS W	119	8
Ben Martinez	TUL	125 (197-15)*	Champion
Benny Ashley	B	125	8
Max Odom	FOOT	130	Champion
Chris Gutierrez	CLOVIS	130	8
Ben Baca	BUC	135	5
Casey Olson	CLOVIS	135	6
Ralph Lopez	CLOVIS W	140 (192-14)*	Champion
Jeremy Pfitzer	TUL	140	5
Adrian Diniz	FOOT	140	2
Kirk Moore	FOOT	152 (173-19)*	Champion
Daniel Lomeli	CLOVIS W	152	5
Telly Sanders	BUC	160 (147-?/50 falls)*	Champion
Mike Sherrick	CLOVIS W	160	2
Tyler Lunn	BUC	(137-?43 Falls)* 171	3
Noel Perez	MAD	171	6
Josh Naus	CENT	189	4
Mike Van Worth	DP	189	6
Aaron Graham	B	215	4
Ben Fox	BUC	215 (118-25)*	5

Name	School	WT/Record	Place
1999			
Darrell Vasquez	B	105	Champion
Jason Moreno	FIRE	114	2
Phillip Marquez	FOOT	114	6
Alex Tirapelle	CLOVIS	127	Champion
Scott Beck	TUL	127	3
Joel Goings	W	127	4
Ben Martinez	TUL	132 (191-15)*	Champion
Miguel Gutierrez	FOOT	132	3
Chris Pendleton	LEM	132	4
Cookie Venegas	WU	132	5
Kevin Jones	CLOVIS W	132	7
Nick Rosales	A	137	7
Sean Sheets	CENT	142	7
Max Odom	FOOT	147 (167-17/86 Falls)*	Champion
Ricardo Pelarosa	DP	154	6
Ryan brooks	LEM	162	4
Josh Naus	CENT	191 (141-9/40 Falls)*	Champion
Mike Van Worth	DP	191	4
Miguel Carrasco	RED	191	8
Clint Wolbeck	CLOVIS	217	Champion
Ken Kragie	CHOW	217	6
Marcio Botehlo	LEM	217	7
Ben Fox	BUC	277 (118-25/67 Falls)*	2
Louie Armendarez	MON	277	5

Corrections

Ralph Lopez (232-16)
Ben Martinez (197-15)

California State Wrestling Championships

Name	School	WT/Record	Place
2000			
John Murillo	TW	103	8
Darrell Vasquez	B	112	Champion
Andrew Onsurez	E	112 (136-38)*	2
Ray Reyes	HAN	112	8
Eddie Castillo	CLOVIS	119	3
Daniel Chapman	CENT	119	5
Matt Farias	SHAFT	119	7
Garrett Spooner	CLOVIS	130 (81-46/49 Falls)*	Champion
Cookie Venegas	WU	130	5
Alex Tirapelle	CLOVIS	135	Champion
Miguel Gutierrez	FOOT	135	3
Craig Serpa	LEM	135	5
Shane Seibert	MAD	135	6
Andrew Spradlin	B	135	8
Jesse Ramirez	MT.W	140	2
Steve Hernandez	FOOT	140	3
Chris Pendleton	LEM	145 (170-25/106 Falls)*	Champion
Robert Estrada	BUC	145	4
Carlos Garcia	WOOD	145	6
Sean Sheets	CENT	152	2
Justin Uriarte	MT.W	152	5
Derek Madsen	HAN	160	6
Steffan Weiner	BUC	171	3
Mike Van Worth	DP	189 (189-32)	2
Anthony Tobin	B	189	4
Marcio Botelho	LEM	215 (136-15/90 Falls)*	Champion
Clint Walbeck	CLOVIS	215	2
Ken Kragie	CHOW	215	7
Brian Sheesley	HAN	215	8
Jacob Hallmark	CLOVIS	275	5
Ed Patino	PORT	275	7
2001			
Gerrard Contreras	BUC	105	Champion
Nathan Morgan	B	105	2
Chad Mendes	HAN	105	8
Logan Ingram	BUC	114	2
Gabriel Flores	MAD	114	3
Tony Franco	B	114	5
Ivan Sanchez	A	114	8
Darrell Vasquez	B	121	Champion
Damon Silva	LEM	127	3
Matt Maldonado	SHAFT	127	7
Jorge Evangelista	PAR	132	5
Javier Juarez	CEN	132	6
Pacifico Garcia	CLOVIS	137	2
Andrew Spradlin	B	137	3
Lionel Sierra	REED	137	5
Alex Tirapelle	CLOVIS	142 (190-23/99 Falls)*	Champion
Shane Seibert	MAD	142	2
Drew East	B	142	3
Miguel Gutierrez	FOOT	147 (203-30/131 Falls)*	Champion
Carlos Garcia	WOOD	147	8
Sean Sheets	CENT	154 (120-19)*	Champion
Josh Sherley	B	154	2
Nick Cotta	LEM	154	7
Sven Hafemeister	LEM	162	4
Matt Bardsley	HOOV	162	6
Brett Mooney	EB	173	3
Anthony Moreno	PAR	173	4
Jacob Hallmark	CLOVIS	277	5
Jon Murphy	HAN	277	6

California State Wrestling Championships

2002

Name	School	WT/Record	Place
Gerrard Contreras	BUC	103	2
Sonny Garcia	KING	103	7
Nathan Morgan	B	112	Champion
Logan Ignram	BUC	112 (165-24/88 Falls)*	3
Chad Mendes	HAN	112 (56-2)	5
Gabe Flores	CLOVIS	119	Champion
Tony Franco	B	119 (139-33/79 Falls)*	2
Darrell Vasquez	B	125 (191-7/47 Falls)*	Champion
Jason Williams	CLOVIS	125	2
J.J. Holt	TUL	125	3
Troy Tirapelle	CLOVIS	130	Champion
Alex Herrera	B	130	2
Darrell Goodpaster	BUC	130 (125 Wins)*	3
Matt Maldonado	SHAFT	130	6
Lucas Anderson	LEM	130	7
David Roberts	CLOVIS W	135 (183-27/98 Falls)*	2
Joe Hernandez	B	135	6
Jake Varner	B	140	4
Andrew Spradlin	B	145 (191-15/38 Falls)*	2
Marcos Diaz	FOOT	145	4
Drew East	B	152 (189-13/53 Falls)*	Champion
Josh Sherley	B	160 (186-29/53 Falls)*	Champion
Sven Hafaemeister	LEM	160 (105-12/61 Falls)*	2
Brian Davis	MAD	160	7
Mariano Sanchez	REED	189	3
Dan Folmer	BUC	189	4
Broc Maffia	TUL W	215	2
Kyle Goodman	BUC	215	7
Jon Chretien	ED	275	2

2003

Name	School	WT/Record	Place
Paul Ruiz	FIRE	103	7
Chad Mendes	HAN	119 (152-20)*	3
Grant Newman	B	119	7
Nathan Morgan	B	125	Champion
Gabe Flores	CLOVIS	125 (170-23)*	2
Joe Soto	PORT	125	7
Troy Tirappelle	CLOVIS	130	Champion
Alex Herrera	B	135	2
Lucas Anderson	LEM	135 (105-40)*	6
Jason Williams	CLOVIS	135	8
Chris Martinez	CLOVIS W	140	Champion
Mark Marquez	EB	140	6
K.B. Wender	CLOVIS E	145	6
Bryce Thompson	CLOVIS	145	8
Jake Varner	B	152	2
Ryan Houck	CLOVIS W	152	3
Jeff Baker	CENT	160	2
Dustin Noack	CLOVIS W	160	6
William Griffin	MAD	171 (256-40)*	2
Scott Ferguson	CLOVIS	171	3
Brandon Ceremello	CLOVIS	189 (197-26)*	4
Tyler Clutts	CLOVIS	215	Champion
Josh Marquez	B	215	4
Adam Torosian	CLOVIS W	215	7

Correction

Darrell Vasquez (197-7)

California State Wrestling Championships

Name	School	WT/Record	Place
2004			
Joe Cisneros	B	103	Champion
Brett Land	B	112	3
Jimmy Savala	CLOVIS	112	7
Sabi Masuta	MAD	119	4
Elijah Nacita	B	119	7
Steven Juarez	HAN	125	Champion
Dustin Rocha	LEM	125	6
Torres Anthony	EX	125 (159-6)*	8
Nathan Morgan	B	130 (166-6)*	Champion
Jason Williams	CLOVIS	130	2
Troy Tirapelle	CLOVIS	140 (198-16)*	Champion
Alex Herrera	B	145 (154-19)*	Champion
Chris Martinez	CLOVIS W	145 (113-25)*	2
Coby Fielding	BUC	145	5
Bryce Thompson	CLOVIS	152 (166-55)*	8
Tyler Bernacchi	CLOVIS E	160 (151-38)*	4
Dustin Noack	CLOVIS W	160 (112-41)*	6
Jake Varner	B	171	Champion
Marcus Garcia	TUL	171	3
Bryan Levay	MAD	171	7
Will Schneider	CLOVIS E	189	7
Josh Marquez	B	215	5

Name	School	WT/Record	Place
2005			
Keith Gibson	MT.W	112 (136-39)*	8
Paul Ruiz	FIRE	119	2
Alex Rodriguez	CLOVIS E	119	8
Mark Anderson	LEM	125 (165-53 58 Falls)*	Champion
Conrad Rangel	CLOVIS E	125	2
Ali Husein	SEL	125	8
Elijah Nacita	B	130	2
Josh Betancur	BUC	130	3
Dustin Rocha	LEM	130	4
Joe Soto	PORT	135 (148-30 43 Falls)*	Champion
Eric Maldonado	GOLDEN W	140	2
Brett Land	B	140	6
Lucas Espericueta	SHAFT	140	8
Brice Horton	CENT	145	7
Kenneth Packard	ROOS	152 (131-39)*	3
Shaun Ceremello	CLOVIS	160	Champion
Josh Williams	B	160	6
Jake Varner	B	189 (157-10 132 Falls)*	Champion
Nathan Timmerman	MON	189	7
Ryan Flores	BUC	215	5
Chris Lewis	CLOVIS W	275	2

California State Wrestling Championships

Name	School	WT/Record	Place	
2006				
David Chaidez	FOOT	103	4	
Justin Arredondo	BUC	112 (131-32)*	3	
Steven Weimer	CLOVIS	112	6	
Frank Lomas	B	112	7	
Josh Betancur	BUC	130 (142-32)*	3	
Jimmy Savala	CLOVIS	130	4	
Elijah Nacita	B	135	Champion	
		(165-25)* 65 Falls		
Alfonso Sanchez	MCL	140 (120-19)*		
Joe Cisneros	SEL	140	4	
Lucas Espericueta	SHAFT	145	3	
		(166-18/110 Falls)*		
Bryce Horton	CENT	145	5	
Tony Webber	B	145	6	
Willy Pendleton	LEM	152 (181-36)*	5	
Matt Boger	BUC	160 (~~183-22~~)*	3	(185-22)* correction
Nick Bardsley	CLOVIS W	160 (109-31)*	5	
Nathan Timmerman	MON	189	Champion	
Andrew Rozario	CLOVIS	189	7	
Ryan Flores	BUC	215	Champion	(54-1)*
Vincent Lopez	CLOVIS	215	8	
Ricky Alcala	A	275 (65-13)*	3	(76-15 Jr & Sr years)*
David Morgan	CENT	275	5	

* Career record

Kelly Miller of Bakersfield High
3rd in CIF 1994 • 2nd in CIF 1995 • 2nd in CIF 1996 • CIF Champion 1997

Southern Regional
1983

Mira Mesa High School - San Diego
March 4-5, 1983

Weight	Wrestler	School	Place	Record
102	Montoya, Greg	Clovis	3	
116	Aguilar, George	Washington Union	2	
123	Nerove, Darrell	Foothill	1	45-0
123	Martin, John	Clovis West	2	39-6
136	Lewis, Brian	Clovis West	3	
142	Davis, Bret	Monache	4	
149	Richburg, Allen	Clovis West	1	45-1
159	Zimmer, Brad	Clovis West	3	
171	Campbell, Eric	Clovis West	3	45-3
189	Young, Todd	Clovis West	1	41-4
189	Moore, Lenny	Bakersfield	2	
249	Estes, Barry	Clovis West	2	42-2
249	Salas, Ricky	Madera	4	

The finalist from the Central Section qualified for the first and last Southern Regional won by Clovis West. There were two regional tournaments that qualified wrestlers into the state meet.

Regional Team Results

1	Clovis West	108.5
5	Foothill	33
14	Clovis	24.5

Northern California Invitational
1952-1960

Northern California Invitational
Central Section Results (Team) 1952-1960

1952
Hayward High School
- 5th   Roosevelt
- 12th   Fresno
- 14th   Hanford

1953
Hughson High School
- 4th   Roosevelt
- 7th   Hanford
- 8th   Tulare
- 13th   Madera

1954
Santa Cruz High School
- 4th   Madera
- 4th   Roosevelt
- 10th   Tulare

1955
Tulare High School
- 1st   Tulare – Coach Oscar Edminister
- 4th   Fresno
- 7th   Roosevelt
- 14th   Madera

1956
San Jose (Camden)
- 1st   Roosevelt – Coach Vern McCoy
- 5th   Tulare
- 8th   Madera

1957
Hughson High School
- 1st   Madera – Coach Vern Brooks
- 5th   Tulare
- 6th   Roosevelt
- 13th   Fresno

1958
UC-Berkeley
- 1st   Madera – Coach Vern Brooks
- 2nd   Fresno
- 4th   Roosevelt
- 7th   Tulare
- 9th   Bakersfield

1959
Turlock High School
- 4th   Madera
- 5th   Roosevelt
- 7th   Fresno

1960
UC-Berkeley
- 2nd Hanford
- 5th Madera
- 7th Roosevelt

Northern California Invitational
Central Section Results (Individual) 1952-1960

1952
Hayward High School

175	1	Dergarabedian, Ara	Roosevelt

1953
Hughson High School

138	2	Hitchcock, Kenneth	Tulare
175	2	Duran, Louie	Roosevelt
191	1	Fox, Calvin	Roosevelt

1954
Santa Cruz High School

103	2	Trillo, Al	Madera
133	1	Marquezs, Marvin	Madera
138	1	Ishiam, Dennis	Roosevelt
175	2	Crouse, Ray	Tulare
191	2	Fox, Calvin	Roosevelt

1955
Tulare High School

103	1	Jarmillo, Louie	Tulare
120	1	Nelson, Jim	Fresno
*127	1	O'Neal, Jim	Roosevelt
133	2	Jones, Robert	Madera
165	2	Baker, Lee	Fresno
191	1	Westerling, Don	Tulare

1956
San Jose (Camden)

103	1	Rodriguez, Frank	Madera
103	2	Castro, Richard	Tulare
112	1	Parnell, Marvin	Roosevelt
112	2	Martinez, Dale	Corcoran
120	1	Zakar, Bob	Roosevelt
120	2	Bilvado, Manuel	Tulare
127	1	Hernandez	Roosevelt
133	4	Marquez, Ismael	Madera
138	4	Carr, Bob	Roosevelt
165	4	Allen, John	Tulare
191	3	Sanders, Louis	Roosevelt
HWT	3	Palacios, Eddie	Roosevelt

1957
Hughson High School

103	1	Rodriguez, Ausencio	Madera
112	1	Rodriguez, Frank	Madera
120	1	Bilvado, Manuel	Tulare
133	1	Marquez, Ismael	Madera
154	1	Hance, Tom	Roosevelt
154	2	Tone, Larry	Fresno
165	1	Lilles, John	Madera
165	3	Hoot	Hanford
175	1	Lasher, Roland	Madera
175	2	Allen, John	Tulare

1958
UC-Berkeley

103	1	Nehring, Larry	Fresno
103	2	Garcia, Ray	Roosevelt
103	3	Fimbrez, Louie	Madera
112	1	Rodriguez, Ausencio	Madera
112	2	Quintero	Tulare
120	1	Crouch, Gary	Roosevelt
120	3	Rodriguez, Frank	Madera
120	4	Davies	Fresno
127	1	Bilvado, Manuel	Tulare
127	2	Stevenson	Fresno
127	4	Solis	Corcoran
133	1	Marquez, Ismael	Madera
133	3	Reyes, Ted	Roosevelt
138	3	Ortega, Joe	Fresno
165	3	Edsell	Porterville
165	4	Cariaga, Ross	Fresno
175	1	Hunt, Bill	Bakersfield
191	4	Voorhees, Bob	Madera
HWT	2	Newcomb, Chuck	Bakersfield

Northern California Invitational
Central Section Results (Individual) 1952-1960

1959
Turlock High School

103	1	Fimbrez, Louie	Madera
103	2	Rodriguez, Frank	Roosevelt
103	4	Marquez	Fresno
*112	1	Rodriguez, Ausencio	Madera
120	2	Marquez, Sam	Madera
120	3	Whitmore, Clem	Fresno
127	3	Bush, Ron	Roosevelt
133	1	Reyes, Ted	Roosevelt
133	3	Patterson, Andy	Hanford
138	4	Wells, Terry	South Bakersfield
145	2	Ortega, Joe	Fresno
154	4	Mains	Mt. Whitney
165	3	Dow	Corcoran
191	3	Aquino, Joe	Chowchilla

1960
UC-Berkeley

103	1	Rodriguez, Frank	Roosevelt
103	2	Martinez, Joe	East Bakersfield
103	4	Figgs, Joe	Bullard
112	1	Jones, James	Hanford
120	3	Whitmore, Clem	Fresno
127	1	Marquez, Sam	Madera
127	3	Aguilar, Steve	Hanford
133	3	Patterson, Andy	Hanford
133	4	Wagoner, Ron	Fresno
145	2	Vasques, Ben	Roosevelt
145	3	Allen, Richard	Madera
165	4	Bressler, Richard	Hanford
191	2	McGrew, John	Tulare

*Outstanding Wrestler

Ausencio Rodriguez-Madera
Three-Time Champion 1956, 1957, 1958

From 1952 until 1960, the top three placers from the Central Section qualified to wrestle five other CIF Section placers: North, North Coast, Oakland, SAC-Joaquin, Central Coast and Central. This was the closest to a state championship until the 1973 state wrestling meet.

Section 2
National High School Wrestling Championships

High School Championships
1990-2006

1991
Jimmy Aguirre	119	1st	Clovis
Gary Quintana	130	1st	Selma *

1992
Lalo Moz	189	4th	Hanford
Coby Wright	103	7th	Bakersfield

1993
Chad Mast	275	3rd	Clovis
Eddie Ramos	135	6th	Porterville

1994
Moises Perez	140	5th	Madera
Eric Philp	160	7th	Madera

1996
Adam Tirapelle	135	1st	Buchanan
Paris Ruiz	112	6th	Clovis West

1997
Cleo Johnson	103	7th	Firebaugh
Dan Jackson	189	7th	Kingsburg
Albert Garza	112	7th	Sanger

1998
Chris Felix	103	3rd	East Bakersfield
Telly Sanders	160	4th	Buchanan
Kirk Moore	152	5th	Foothill

1999
Max Odom	140	1st	Foothill
Joshua Naus	189	2nd	Centennial
Ben Fox	275	2nd	Buchanan
Ben Martinez	119	7th	Tulare Union

2000
Chris Pendleton	145	4th	Lemoore
Andrew Onsuerez	112	8th	East Bakersfield

2001
Alex Tirapelle	135	1st	Clovis
Miguel Gutierrez	145	4th	Foothill

2002
Darrell Vasquez	125	2nd	Bakersfield
Josh Sherley	160	3rd	Bakersfield
Gerrard Contreras	103	4th	Buchanan
Sven Hafemeister	152	5th	Lemoore

2003
Chad Mendes	119	3rd	Hanford
Gabe Flores	125	3rd	Clovis

2004
Troy Tirapelle	135	3rd	Clovis

2005
Mark Anderson	125	3rd	Lemoore
Joe Soto	135	7th	Porterville
Jake Varner	189	2nd	Bakersfield

2006
David Chaides	103	3rd	Foothill
Josh Betancur	130	8th	Buchanan
Lucas Espericueta	145	5th	Shafter

*Outstanding Wrestler Award
All Placers Awarded All-American Status

Pittsburgh Post-Gazette
Dapper Dan Wrestling Classic

The most prestigious high school All-Star wrestling meet in the United States began in 1975 in Pittsburgh, Pennsylvania.

Year	Wrestler	School	Weight	Won/Lost
1986	Trent Barnes	Clovis West	HWT	Lost 11-5
2001	Alex Tirapelle	Clovis	140	Won 8-6 O.T.
2002	Darrell Vasquez	Bakersfield	125	Lost Fall 5:45
2004	Nathan Morgan	Bakersfield	130	Won 13-5

Darrell Vasquez
Bakersfield High
Record: 191-7
Four-time State
Champion

Nathan Morgan
Bakersfield High
Record: 166-6
Three-time State
Champion
Four-time finalist

Trent Barnes
Clovis West
Two-time State Champion
1985 and 1986
4th place 1984
Two-time CIF Champion
1985 and 1986
3rd place 1984

Amateur Wrestling News All-Americans
1986-2006

1986
Trent Barnes Clovis West First Team

1988
Mike Ortega Roosevelt *

1989
Terry Watts Caruthers 6
Lorenzo Neal Lemoore 4

1990
Jassen Froehlich Bakersfield *

1991
Jimmy Aguirre Clovis 2
Detran Gant Roosevelt 7
Gary Quintana Selma 3

1992
Nick Quintana Selma 8
Nick Zinkin Clovis 8
Lalo Maz Hanford 3

1993
Chad Mast Clovis 3

1994
Moises Perez Madera *

1996
Adam Tirapelle Buchanan 2

1997
Dan Jackson Kingsburg *

1998
Ralph Lopez Clovis West 3
Kirk Moore Foothill 6
Telly Sanders Buchanan *

1999
Ben Martinez Tulare Union 2
Max Odom Foothill First Team
Joshua Naus Centennial 3
Ben Fox Buchanan 9

2000
Chris Pendleton LeMoore 5
Marcio Botelho LeMoore 5
Garrett Spooner Clovis *
Mike Van Worth Dos Palos *
Clint Walbeck Clovis *

2001
Alex Tirapelle Clovis First Team
Miguel Gutierrez Foothill 8
Sean Sheets Centennial *

2002
Darrell Vasquez Bakersfield First Team
Josh Sherley Bakersfield 5
Logan Ingram Buchanan 9
Gerrard Contreras Buchanan 11
Tony Franco Bakersfield 9
David Roberts Clovis west 11
Shane Seibert Madera 11
Drew East Bakersfield 7

2003
Chad Mendes Hanford 4
Gabe Flores Clovis 3

2004
Nathan Morgan Bakersfield First Team
Troy Tirapelle Clovis First Team
Alex Herrera Bakersfield 9
Chris Martinez Clovis East 10

2005
Mark Anderson Lemoore 9
Jake Varner Bakersfield First Team

2006
Elijah Nacita Bakersfield 11

*Honorable Mention
(Number represents team number)

Wrestling USA Magazine All-American Team
1969-1999

1969
Richard Alvarez	Bakersfield
Larry Morgan	East Bakersfield

1970
Alex Hernandez	Corcoran
Charlie Freeman	Madera *
Tony Serros	Bakersfield *

1971
Pete King	Madera
Paul Lovelace	West *
Bill Van Worth	South *
Dan McMasters	South *

1972
Sythell Thompson	Selma
Tony Alvarez	Bakersfield *
Rodney Mitchell	Bakersfield *

1973
Mike Bull	South
Ernie Flores	Madera *
Randy Baxter	Clovis *

1974
Rodney Balch	Clovis *
Fred Bohna	Clovis *

1978
Reynaldo Martinez	Roosevelt
	Dream Team

1984
Randy Graham	Bakersfield
Brian Lewis	Clovis West *

1985
Eddie Gomez	Caruthers
	Dream Team

1986
Trent Barnes	Clovis West
	Dream Team

1989
Terry Watts	Caruthers

1991
Jimmy Aguirre	Clovis
	Dream Team
Gary Quintana	Selma

1992
Lalo Moz	Hanford

1996
Adam Tirapelle	Buchanan
	Dream Team

1999
Max Odom	Foothill
	Academic Team
Ben Martinez	Tulare Union
Josh Naus	Centennial
Ben Fox	Buchanan *

Wrestling USA Magazine All-American Team
2000-2006

2000
Garrett Spooner	Clovis
Chris Pendleton	Lemoore
Marcio Botehlo	Lemoore
Clint Walbeck	Clovis *

2001
Alex Tirapelle	Clovis Dream Team
Miguel Gutierrez	Foothill
Sean Sheets	Centennial *

2002
Darrell Vasquez	Bakersfield Academic Team
Drew East	Bakersfield
Josh Sherley	Bakersfield
Logan Ingram	Buchanan *
Tony Franco	Bakersfield *
David Roberts	Clovis West *
Andrew Spradlin	Bakersfield *
Sven Hafemeister	Lemoore *

2003
Gabriel Flores	Clovis
Chad Mendes	Hanford *

2004
Nathan Morgan	Bakersfield Dream Team
Troy Tirapelle	Clovis Dream Team
Chris Martinez	Clovis West
Alex Herrera	Bakersfield
Steve Juarez	Hanford *

2005
Mark Anderson	Lemoore
Joe Soto	Porterville
Jake Varner	Bakersfield

2006
Elijah Nacita	Bakersfield
Lucas Espericueta	Shafter *

*Honorable Mention

Buchanan High – 2006 State Champions

Young Wrestler High School All-Americans
1975-1978

Year	Wrestler	School	Team
1975	Robert Kiddy	Madera	Fourth Team
1975	Jewrel Thomas	Hanford	Sixth Team
1978	Rey Martinez	Roosevelt	First Team

ASICS Tiger High School All-Americans
1986-2006

1986
Trent Barnes	Clovis West	HWT First Team

1989
Lorenzo Neal	Lemoore	HWT Second Team
Terry Watts	Carruthers	145 Honorable Mention

1990
Jimmy Aguirre	Clovis	119 Honorable Mention

1991
Jimmy Aguirre	Clovis	125 Second Team
Detran Gant	Roosevelt	125 Honorable Mention
Gary Quintana	Selma	130 Third Team
Lalo Moz	Hanford	189 Second Team

1992
Lalo Moz	Hanford	189 Second Team

1993
Chad Mast		HWT Second Team

1995
Adam Tirapelle	Hiram Johnson	130 Honorable Mention

1996
Adam Tirapelle	Buchanan	Third Team

1998
Max Odom	Foothill	Honorable Mention
Ralph Lopez	Clovis West	Honorable Mention
Telly Sanders	Buchanan	Honorable Mention

1999
Max Odom	Foothill	Third Team
Josh Naus	Centennial	Third Team
Ben Martinez	Tulare Union	Honorable Mention

2000
Darrell Vasquez	Bakersfield	Third Team
Marcio Botelho	Lemoore	Honorable Mention

2001
Alex Tirapelle	Clovis	First Team
Darrell Vasquez	Bakersfield	Third Team
Miguel Gutierrez	Foothill	Honorable Mention

2002
Darrell Vasquez	Bakersfield	Second Team
Nathan Morgan	Bakersfield	Third Team
Josh Sherley	Bakersfield	Honorable Mention
Sven Hafemeister	Lemoore	Honorable Mention

2003
Nathan Morgan	Bakersfield	Second Team
Troy Tirapelle	Clovis	Second Team
Gabe Flores	Clovis	Honorable Mention

2004
Nathan Morgan	Bakersfield	First Team
Troy Tirapelle	Clovis	Second Team
Jake Varner	Bakersfield	Honorable Mention

2005
Jake Varner	Bakersfield	Second Team
Mark Anderson	Lemoore	Honorable Mention

2006
Ryan Flores	Buchanan	Second Team

Junior USA National Wrestling Championships

Year	Wrestler	Weight	Style	Place	School
1972	Bull, Mike	191.5	Greco	Champion	South
1974	Bohna, Fred	191.5	Freestyle	3	Clovis
1974	Gongora, Tom	143	Greco	2	Clovis
1975	Bolanos, Paul	105.5	Freestyle	3	Clovis
1976	Blanco, Tom	114.5	Freestyle	6	Clovis
1976	Arthur, Doug	HWT	Greco	2	Clovis
1976	Arthur, Doug	HWT	Freestyle	6	Clovis
1978	Martinez, Rey	191	Freestyle	Champion	Roosevelt
1981	Nerove, Darrell	98	Greco	3	Foothill
1985	Lizama, Ben	286	Greco	Champion	Foothill
1987	Tripp, John	165	Greco	6	Tulare
1987	Tripp, John	178	Freestyle	6	Tulare
1988	Zapata, Robert	178	Freestyle	3	Selma
1988	Neal, Lorenzo	220	Greco	3	Lemoore
1988	Neal, Lorenzo	220	Freestyle	3	Lemoore
1988	Smith, Mark	275	Freestyle	8	Clovis West
1989	Aguirre, Jim	105.5	Freestyle	3	Clovis
1990	Munoz, Andy	98	Freestyle	Champion	Washington Union
1990	Quintana, Gary	123	Freestyle	7	Selma
1990	Heberle, Jeff	132	Greco	7	North
1990	Moz, Lalo	191.5	Greco	6	Hanford
1990	Salven, Josh	275	Greco	4	Clovis West
1990	Salven, Josh	275	Freestyle	8	Clovis West
1991	Fuqua, Brad	98	Greco	7	North
1991	Zinkin, Nick	114.5	Freestyle	8	Clovis
1991	Quintana, Gary	132	Freestyle	5	Selma
1991	Heberle, Jeff	143	Greco	7	North
1991	Silver, Scott	178	Greco	8	Bullard
1991	Moz, Lalo	191.5	Greco	2	Hanford
1992	Fuqua, Brad	98	Greco	5	North
1992	Moz, Lalo	191.5	Greco	6	Hanford
1992	Moz, Lalo	220	Freestyle	7	Hanford
1992	Zinkin, Nick	123	Freestyle	8	Clovis
1992	Mast, Chad	275	Freestyle	2	Clovis
1993	Karle, Jeremy	275	Greco	8	Highland
1995	Tirapelle, Adam	143	Greco	5	Buchanan
1995	Ashley, Fred	178	Greco	4	Bakresfield
1995	Clark, Brett	275	Greco	2	Bakersfield
1995	Clark, Brett	275	Freestyle	5	Bakersfield
1996	Tirapelle, Adam	143	Freestyle	4	Buchanan
1998	Martinez, Ben	123	Greco	Champion	Tulare
1998	Naus, Joshua	191.5	Greco	7	Centennial
1999	Martinez, Ben	132	Greco	3	Tulare
1999	Martinez, Ben	132	Freestyle	4	Tulare
1999	Odom, Max	143	Freestyle	Champion	Foothill

Junior USA National Wrestling Championships

Year	Wrestler	Weight	Style	Place	School
1999	Botelho, Marcio	220	Freestyle	3	Lemoore
2000	Vasquez, Darrell	114.5	Freestyle	2	Bakersfield
2000	Hafemeister, Sven	165	Greco	3	Lemoore
2000	Botelho, Marcio	220	Freestyle	4	Lemoore
2000	Botelho, Marcio	220	Greco	5	Lemoore
2001	Vasquez, Darrell	123	Freestyle	4	Bakersfield
2001	Franco, Tony	123	Freestyle	6	Bakersfield
2002	Morgan, Nathan	119	Freestyle	2	Bakersfield
2002	Mendez, Chad	119	Freestyle	8	Hanford
2002	Holt, James	125	Greco	2	Tulare
2002	Holt, James	130	Freestyle	8	Tulare
2002	Franco, Tony	125	Freestyle	8	Bakersfield
2002	Vasquez, Darrell	130	Freestyle	2	Bakersfield
2003	Land, Brett	112	Greco	4	Bakersfield
2003	Land, Brett	112	Freestyle	4	Bakersfield
2003	Herrera, Alex	140	Freestyle	7	Bakersfield
2003	Bernacchi, Tyler	160	Greco	5	Clovis East
2003	Varner, Jake	160	Greco	6	Bakersfield
2004	Morgan, Nathan	130	Freestyle	4	Bakersfield
2004	Varner, Jake	189	Freestyle	3	Bakersfield
2006	Watts, Randall	125	Freestyle	6	El Diamante
2006	Nacita, Elijah	135	Freestyle	7	Bakersfield

All Placers Awarded All-American Status

Lorenzo Neal
Lemoore High
Two-time State Champion
1988 and 1989
4th place in 1987
Three-time CIF Champion
2nd in 1986

Max Odom
Foothill High
National Champion

Jimmy Aguirre
Clovis High
Three-time State Champion

Cadet USA National Championships

Year	Wrestler	Weight	Style	Place	School
1986	Stricker, Tad	121	Greco	4	South Bakersfield
1987	La Garetta, Eric	103.5	Greco	5	Selma
1989	Munoz, Andy	94.5	Freestyle	3	Washington Union
1989	Zinkin, Nick	103.5	Freestyle	3	Clovis
1989	Moz, Lalo	182.5	Freestyle	8	Hanford
1991	Green, Stan	83.5	Freestyle	2	Clovis
1992	Perez, Moises	154	Freestyle	6	Madera
1993	Tirapelle, Adam	121	Greco	2	Buchanan
1993	Tirapelle, Adam	121	Freestyle	6	Buchanan
1993	Clark, Brett	209	Greco	2	Bakersfield
1993	Smith, Jared	242	Greco	2	Clovis West
1993	Smith, Jared	242	Freesyle	2	Clovis West
1994	Johnson, Cleo	83.5	Freestyle	8	Firebaugh
1994	Guerrero, Brian	94.5	Freestyle	6	Madera
1994	Brecedo, Sergio	112	Freestyle	8	Buchanan
1994	Jackson, Dan	182.5	Freestyle	6	Kingsburg
1995	*Sanders, Telly	154	Greco	2	Buchanan
1996	Beck, Scott	94.5	Freestyle	7	Tulare
1996	Beck, Scott	94.5	Greco	5	Tulare
1996	Odom, Max	103.5	Freestyle	5	Foothill
1996	Martinez, Ben	112	Greco	2	Tulare
1997	Villa, Daniel	88	Freestyle	7	South Bakersfield
1997	Odom, Max	121	Freestyle	Champion	Foothill
1997	Martinez, Ben	121	Freestyle	4	Tulare
1997	Martinez, Ben	121	Greco	Champion	Tulare
1997	Naus, Josh	182.5	Greco	5	Centennial
1998	Holt, James	83.5	Freestyle	7	Tulare
1998	Holt, James	83.5	Greco	2	Tulare
1998	Moreno, Jason	103.5	Freestyle	Champion	Firebaugh
1998	Moreno, Jason	103.5	Greco	Champion	Firebaugh
1998	Portillo, Angel	121	Greco	4	Tulare
1998	Gutierrez, Miguel	132	Freestyle	8	Foothill
1998	Patino, Edward	209	Greco	8	Porterville
1999	Morgan, Nathan	88	Freestyle	Champion	Bakersfield
1999	Holt, James	94.5	Greco	4	Tulare
1999	Roberts, David	121	Freestyle	8	Clovis West
1999	Gutierrez, Miguel	143	Freestyle	8	Foothill
2000	Morgan, Nathan	103.5	Freestyle	5	Bakersfield
2000	Flores, Gabe	103.5	Greco	4	Clovis
2000	*Franco, Tony	121	Freestyle	2	Bakersfield
2001	Land, Brett	83.5	Greco	Champion	Bakersfield
2001	Land, Brett	83.5	Freestyle	2	Bakersfield
2001	Mendes, Chad	112	Greco	4	Hanford
2001	Herrera, Alex	121	Freestyle	4	Bakersfield

Cadet USA National Championships

Year	Wrestler	Weight	Style	Place	School
2001	Flores, Gabe	121	Freestyle	6	Clovis
2001	Bernacchi, Tyler	154	Greco	8	Clovis East
2002	Ruiz, Paul	98	Freestyle	3	Firebaugh
2002	Herrera, Alex	130	Freestyle	Champion	Bakersfield
2002	Sierra, Lionel	140	Greco	5	Reedley
2002	Landois, Orlando	145	Greco	7	Wasco
2002	Varner, Jake	152	Freestyle	4	Bakersfield
2002	Griffin, Kyle	160	Greco	2	Clovis East
2002	Griffin, Kyle	160	Freestyle	7	Clovis East
2003	Soto, Joe	135	Freestyle	5	Porterville
2004	Watts, Randall	98	Greco	8	El Diamante
2004	Boger, Matt	171	Freestyle	3	Coalinga
2004	Boger, Matt	171	Greco	7	Coalinga
2004	Flores, Ryan	215	Freestyle	3	Buchanan
2005	Timmerman, Nathan	189	Freestyle	7	Monache
2006	Zimmer, Zach	84	Freestyle	5	Clovis West
2006	Boger, Josh	215	Greco	3	Buchanan
2006	Boger, Josh	215	Freestyle	4	Buchanan

*Most Falls Award
All Placers Awarded All-American Status

Chuck Fenton of Bakersfield High
Two-time CIF Champion 1961 and 1962
40-3-1 career

USWF Junior Nationals

Year	Wrestler	Weight	Style	Place	School
1972	Campbell, Guy	165	Greco	2	South
1972	Bull, Mike	191.5	Greco	1	South

National AAU Championships
High School Division

Year	Wrestler	Weight	Style	Place	School
1971	Campbell, Guy	154	Greco	1	South

Junior National AAU Championships

Year	Wrestler	Weight	Style	Place	School
1979	Vanni, Tim	98	Freestyle	1	Monache
1979	Vanni, Tim	105	Greco	1	Monache

FILA Junior Nationals

Year	Wrestler	Weight	Style	Place	School
1999	Martinez, Ben	127.7	Greco	2	Tulare
1999	Martinez, Ben	127.7	Freestyle	1	Tulare
1999	Nelms, Ian	167.5	Greco	3	Mt. Whitney
1999	Nelms, Ian	167.5	Freestyle	7	Mt. Whitney
2003	Roberts, David	145.5	Freestyle	8	Clovis West
2005	Varner, Jake	185	Freestyle	4	Bakersfield

FILA Cadet Nationals

Year	Wrestler	Weight	Style	Place	School
2005	Lewis, Chris	220.25	Freestyle	1	Clovis West

1968 Bakersfield High Wrestling Team – CIF Champions
Front row, left to right: Tony Serros, Billy Herrera, Richard Watkins, Mark Lawrence, Bruce Manny, Chuck Peterson
Back row, left to right: Dave Batsch, Alan Rude, Dean Sanders, Dan Sanborn, Coach Olan Polite, Walt Shapard, Richard Alvarez, Richard Alvarez, Mark Thomas

Junior World Tournament

Year	Wrestler	Weight	Style	Place	School	Location
1967	Morgan, Larry	106	Freestyle		East	Canceled
1967	Shearer, Ron	132	Freestyle		East	Canceled
1967	Miller, John	178	Greco		North	Canceled
1969	Morgan, Larry	123	Freestyle	Champion	East	Colorado Springs, CO
1969	Little, Larry	132	Freestyle	2	South	Colorado Springs, CO
1971	Powers, Randy	143	Greco	6	South	Tokyo, Japan
1973	Bull, Mike	198	Greco	Injured	South	Miami Beach, FLA
1981	Vanni, Tim	105.5	Freestyle	D.N.P.	Monacue	Vancouver, BC

FILA Junior World Tournament

Year	Wrestler	Weight	Style	Place	School	Location
1990	Neal, Lorenzo	HWT	Freestyle		Lemoore	
1997	Tirapelle, Adam	143	Freestyle	5	Buchanan	Helsinki, Finland
1998	Vasquez, Nathan	154	Greco	D.N.P.	Bakersfield	
1999	Martinez, Ben	127.5	Freestyle	8	Tulare	
2005	Varner, Jake	185	Freestyle	Injured	Bakersfield	Budapest, Hungary

Cadet World Championships

Year	Wrestler	Weight	Style	Place	School	Location
1998	Moreno, Jason	105.5	Greco	D.N.P.	Firebaugh	Pretoria, S. Africa

Larry Morgan
1969 Junior World
Tournament

Lorenzo Neal (right)
Lemoore High

Larry Little
1969 Junior World
Tournament

Buchanan High
2006 California State Champions

Buchanan High
2006 League and State Champions

Ryan Flores of Buchanan, two-time state champion.

Josh Betancur of Buchanan

Section 3
Collegiate Wrestling

University Division 1

Before there were NCAA Divisions II and III, there was the NCAA College Division created in 1963 for smaller college programs. In 1975, the NCAA split the college division into Division II and Division III.

National Collegiate Athletic Association NCAA Division 1

Year	Wrestler	Weight	Place	College
1969	John Woods	167	2	Cal Poly
1969	Ben Welch	167	5	Navy
1971	Lee Torres	142	3	Cal Poly
1972	Larry Morgan	134	5	Cal Poly
1973	Allyn Cooke	158	4	Cal Poly
1976	Sythell Thompson	177	4	Cal Poly
1977	Franc Affentranger	134	3	CSUB
1978	Franc Affentranger	134	3	CSUB
1979	Fred Bohna	UNL	1	UCLA
1983	Al Gutierrez	118	8	Cal Poly
1984	Jesse Reyes	142	1	CSUB
1988	Darrel Nerove	142	7	Army
1992	Lorenzo Neal	275	7	Fresno
1993	Harold Zinkin	134	5	Fresno
1994	Terry Watts	150	5	Fresno
1995	DeWayne Zinkin	134	5	Fresno
1996	Coby Wright	126	4	CSUB
1996	Yero Washington	134	6	Fresno
1997	Coby Wright	126	5	CSUB
1997	Yero Washington	134	3	Fresno
1996	Alfonso Tucker	158	4	Fresno
1998	Stan Green	126	4	Fresno
1999	Stan Green	133	5	Fresno
1999	Adam Tirapelle	149	3	Illinois
2000	Adam Tirapelle	149	2	Illinois
2001	Adam Tirapelle	149	1	Illinois
2003	Alex Tirapelle	157	2	Illinois
2003	Chris Pendleton	174	3	Oklahoma State
2003	Marcio Botelho	197	8	Fresno
2004	Darrel Vasquez	133	4	Cal Poly
2004	Alex Tirapelle	157	4	Illinois
2004	Chris Pendleton	174	1	Oklahoma State
2005	Chris Pendleton	174	1	Oklahoma State
2006	Chad Mendes	125	6	Cal Poly
2006	Nathan Morgan	133	6	Oklahoma State

NCAA Division II

Year	Wrestler	Weight	Place	College
1964	Roy Stuckey	123	3	Fresno
1965	Steve Johansen	115	1	Fresno
1965	Phillip Sullivan	177	1	Cal Poly
1966	Steve Johansen	115	2	Fresno
1968	Sam King	123	3	Cal Poly
1968	John Woods	167	2	Cal Poly
1969	Art Chavez	123	5	San Francisco
1969	Jesse Flores	130	5	Cal Poly
1969	John Woods	167	1	Cal Poly
1970	Lee Torres	150	2	Cal Poly
1970	Richard Simmons	177	2	Cal Poly
1971	Larry Morgan	134	2	Cal Poly
1971	Lee Torres	142	3	Cal Poly
1971	Allyn Cooke	150	5	Cal Poly
1972	Larry Morgan	134	2	Cal Poly
1972	Allyn Cooke	158	3	Cal Poly
1972	Doug Stone	167	3	Humbolt
1973	Larry Morgan	134	1	Cal Poly *Most Outstanding Wrestler
1973	Allyn Cooke	158	2	Cal Poly
1972	Doug Stone	167	3	Humbolt
1974	Dick Molina	118	4	CSUB
1974	Sythell Thompson	177	3	Cal Poly
1974	Bill Van Worth	UNL	2	Humbolt
1975	Dick Molina	118	3	CSUB
1975	Mike Bull	190	4	CSUB
1976	Dick Molina	118	3	CSUB
1976	Flo Rocha	167	3	CSUB
1976	Mike Bull	190	1	CSUB
1976	Bill Van Worth	UNL	1	CSUB
1977	Franc Affentranger	134	1	CSUB * Most Outstanding Wrestler
1977	Rod Balch	150	2	CSUB
1977	Flo Rocha	167	1	CSUB
1977	Mike Anderson	177	2	CSUB
1977	Mike Bull	190	2	CSUB
1978	Fran Affentranger	134	2	CSUB
1978	Rod Balch	142	5	CSUB
1978	Tom Gongora	150	4	CSUB
1978	Mike Johnson	190	4	CSUB
1979	Joe Lopez	134	6	CSUB
1979	Tom Gongora	142	1	CSUB
1980	Jesse Reyes	134	4	CSUB
1981	Steve Nickell	142	7	CSUB
1982	Alfredo Gonzales	118	8	Sacramento
1982	Steve Nickell	142	2	CSUB
1983	Jesse Reyes	142	1	CSUB * Most Outstanding Wrestler
1984	Jesse Reyes	142	1	CSUB
1987	Tony Ramirez	118	7	Chico
1987	Mike Dallas	126	2	CSUB
1988	Tony Ramirez	126	5	Chico
1992	Ken Fontes	275	8	Portland State
2003	Pacifico Garcia	141	7	San Francisco
2005	Pacifico Garcia	149	1	San Francisco

National Association of Intercollegiate Athletics

Year	Wrestler	Weight	Place	School	Location
2002	Ivan Sanchez	125	5	Arvin	William Penn University-Iowa
2003	Isaac Pumarejo	125	7	Kingsburg	Menlo College
2004	Cleo Johnson	125	4	Firebaugh	Menlo College
2005	Jacob Hallmark	285	4	Clovis	Menlo College
2006	Jason Moreno	133	4	Firebaugh	Lindenwood University-Missouri
2006	Pablo Sanchez	133	8	Hoover	Menlo College

Bakersfield High
Left to right: Steve Varner, Don Herrera, Jack Serros, Sam Gollmyer, and Albert Valdez — all 1966 CIF Champions but Herrera, who placed 3rd

1967 Bakersfield High Wrestling Team
Back row, left to right: Jim Robesky, Dick Cook, Sam Ochoa, Richard Alvarez
Middle row, left to right: Steve Varner, Dan Sanborn, Coach Olan Polite, Karl Herrera, Paul Ronshausen, Walt Shepard
Front row, left to right: Mark Lawrance, Bones Medina, Bruce Manny, Billy Herrera

Midlands Wrestling Championships
1963-2006

Year	Weight	Wrestler	Place
1976	150	Larry Morgan	4
1977	134	Franc Affentranger	3
1979	HWT	Fred Bohna	2
1983	142	Jesse Reyes	2
1986	158	Jesse Reyes	6
1989	126	Mike Dallas	5
1994	190	Jassen Froehlich	3
1995	126	Coby Wright	6
1996	126	Coby Wright	1
1998	149	Adam Tirapelle	3
1998	165	Andy Varner	4
1999	149	Adam Tirapelle	3
1999	157	Nathan Vasquez	8
2002	157	Alex Tirapelle	5
2003	157	Alex Tirapelle	1
2004	125	Gabe Flores	7
2004	157	Alex Tirapelle	7
2005	149	Troy Tirapelle	7
2005	157	Alex Tirapelle	1
2006	184	Jake Varner	3

Troy Tirapelle
Clovis High
Three-time CIF Champion
Three-time State Champion

Alex, Adam and Troy Tirapelle
10 CIF Championships
8 State Championships

Adam Tirapelle
Buchanan High
Record: 214-7
NCAA Champion
Also placed 2nd and 3rd
University of Illinois
record: 127-21

National Wrestling Coaches All-Star Classic
East-West

Year	Wrestler
1969	Woods, John
1973	Morgan, Larry
1976	Bull, Mike
1977	Rocha, Flo
1978	Affentranger, Franc
1979	Bohna, Fred
1984	Reyes, Jesse
1997	Wright, Coby
2000	Tirapelle, Adam
2002	Pendleton, Chris
2003	Pendleton, Chris
2004	Pendleton, Chris
2005	Vasquez, Darrell
2005	Tirapelle, Alex
2006	Morgan, Nathan

Larry Morgan
Cal Poly

Nathan Morgan
Oklahoma State

Chris Pendleton
Lemoore High
Two-time NCAA
Champion
Also placed 3rd
Oklahoma State
University
Career record:
High school:
178-15
College: 115-11

Section 4
National and International Wrestling

USA Wrestling Senior National Freestyle Championships

Year	Wrestler	Weight	Place	Location
1981	Vanni, Tim	105.5	2nd	Cedar Falls, Iowa
1983	Vanni, Tim	105.5	2nd	Madison, Wisconsin
1984	Vanni, Tim	105.5	4th	Norman, Oklahoma
1985	Vanni, Tim	105.5	Champion	Lock Haven, Pennsylvania
1985	Reyes, Jessie	149.5	6th	Lock Haven, Pennsylvania
1986	Vanni, Tim	105.5	2nd.	Las Vegas, Nevada
1987	Vanni, Tim	105.5	2nd	Las Vegas, Nevada
1988	Vanni, Tim	105.5	Champion	Reno, Nevada
1988	Saenz, Pablo	114.5	6th	Reno, Nevada
1989	Vanni, Tim	105.5	Champion	Topeka, Kansas
1990	Reyes, Jesse	149.5	5th	Las Vegas, Nevada
1991	Vanni, Tim	105.5	Champion	Las Vegas, Nevada
1993	Vanni, Tim	105.5	2nd	Las Vegas, Nevada
1994	Vanni, Tim	105.5	Champion	Las Vegas, Nevada
1995	Vanni, Tim	105.5	2nd	Las Vegas, Nevada
1995	Munoz, Andy	105.5	6th	Las Vegas, Nevada
1996	Vanni, Tim	105.5	3rd	Las Vegas, Nevada
1997	Washington, Yero	127.5	4th	Las Vegas, Nevada
1998	Washington, Yero	127.5	2nd	Las Vegas, Nevada
1999	Washington, Yero	132	4th	Las Vegas, Nevada
2000	Washington, Yero	132	4th	Las Vegas, Nevada
2002	Tirapelle, Adam	145	7th	Las Vegas, Nevada
2003	Washington, Yero	132	4th	Las Vegas, Nevada
2003	Walbeck, Clint	HWT	7th	Las Vegas, Nevada
2004	Washington, Yero	132	5th	Las Vegas, Nevada

John Miller of North Bakersfield
Two-time CIF Champion 1967 and 1968
California Wrestler of the Year 1968

USA Wrestling Senior National Greco-Roman Championships

Year	Wrestler	Score	Place	Location
1986	Vanni, Tim	105.5	2nd	Las Vegas, Nevada
1987	Vanni, Tim	105.5	4th	Las Vegas, Nevada
1991	Tripp, John* ẋ	180.5	5th	Las Vegas, Nevada

*Most Falls Award

Tim Vanni

AAU National Freestyle Championships

Year	Wrestler	Weight	Place	Location
1968	Chavez, Art	114.5	Champion	Lincoln, Nebraska
1973	Morgan, Larry	149.5	2nd	Cleveland, Ohio
1974	Morgan, Larry	149.5	2nd	Long Beach, California
1975	Morgan, Larry	149.5	3rd	Bloomington, Indiana
1975	Cook, Allyn	163	6th	Bloomington, Indiana
1976	Morgan, Larry	149.5	2nd	Cleveland, Ohio
1977	Morgan, Larry	149.5	2nd	Ames, Iowa
1977	Bohna, Fred	220	3rd	Ames, Iowa
1981	Vanni, Tim	105.5	2nd	Tempe, Arizona
1981	Martinez, Rey	180.5	4th	Tempe, Arizona
1982	Vanni, Tim	105.5	4th	Lincoln, Nebraska
1982	Gutierrez, Al	114.5	4th	Lincoln, Nebraska
1982	Reyes, Jesse	149.5	6th	Lincoln, Nebraska

Tim Vanni of Monache High
Two-time Olympian

Jesse Reyes
Bakersfield High
NCAA Champion
California State
University of Bakersfield
Career record: 151-22-1

AAU National Greco-Roman Championships

Year	Wrestler	Weight	Place	Location
1967	Heath, Roy	114.5	3rd	Lincoln, Nebraska
1968	Chavez, Art	114.5	Champion	Lincoln, Nebraska
1971	Chavez, Art	136.5	3rd	San Diego, California
1974	Campbell, Guy*	149.5	Champion	Omaha, Nebraska
1975	Van Worth, Bill	HWT	2nd	Berkeley, California
1976	Morgan, Larry	149.5	Champion	Cleveland, Ohio

*Most Falls Award
*Most Outstanding Wrestler Award

Art Chavez
AAU National Champion Freestyle
AAU National Champion Greco-Roman

1995 "Doc" Buchanan Invitational
Brett Clark, Bakersfield High, First; Jarred Smith, Clovis West, Second; third unknown; Eric Rodriguez, Monache, Fourth; John Montoya, Lemoore, Fifth; sixth unknown

1962 Bakersfield High Wrestling Team
Back row, left to right: Dan McGill, John Beard, Dale Annis, Bill Harralson, Mike Munoz, Mike Roberson, Chuck Fenton
Front row, left to right: Glen Daniels, Dave Carr, Alex Blake, Rufus Morris, Dean Harthorn, (First name unknown) Wiggins

USWF National Freestyle Championships

Year	Wrestler	Weight	Place	Location
1975	Morgan, Larry	149.5	2nd	Iowa City, Iowa
1976	Morgan, Larry*	149.5	Champion	Madison, Wisconsin
1977	Morgan, Larry	149.5	Champion	Eugene, Oregon
1977	Anderson, Mike	180.5	5th	Eugene, Oregon
1977	Bohna, Fred	220	Champion	Eugene, Oregon
1981	Martinez, Rey	180.5	Champion	Cedar Falls, Iowa
1982	Vani, Tim	105.5	4th	Cedar Falls, Iowa
1982	Martinez, Rey	180.5	4th	Cedar Falls, Iowa

*Most Oustanding Wrestler Award
1977 Team Champions: Bakersfield Express

Tony Webber, left, of Bakersfield High and State Champion Joe Soto of Porterville High

1995 "Doc" Buchanan Champions

Back row, left to right: Rocky Bridges, Larry Vasquez Sr., Richard Simmons, Fred Ashley, Larry Vasquez Jr. Joe Lopeteguy, Dennis Reed. Middle row, left to right: David East, Darrell Vasquez, Andy Varner, Tony Keller, Jeremy Bridges, Kelly Miller, Steve Elisondo. Front row, left to right: Greg Canfield, Wayne Bedford, Luke Blair, Brett Clark, Nathan Vasquez

USWF National Greco-Roman Championships

Year	Wrestler	Weight	Place	Location
1970	Little, Larry	136.5	3rd	Fullerton, California
1975	Bohna, Fred	198	2nd	Iowa City, Iowa
1976	Morgan, Larry	149.5	Champion	Cleveland, Iowa

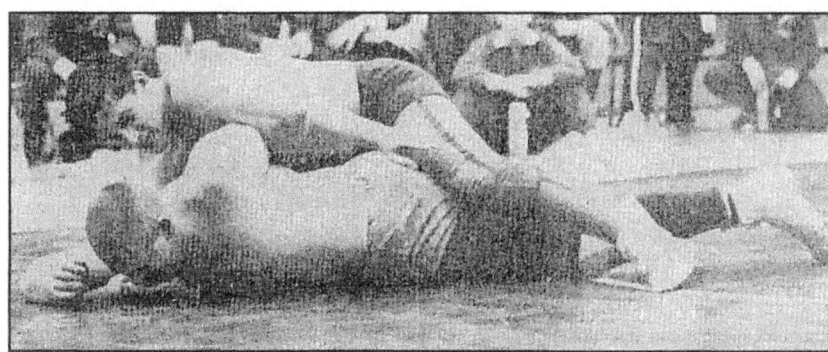

Dan McGill, bottom, of Bakersfield High and John Carter of South Bakersfield, 4th in CIF 1962

Chad Mendez
CIF Champion, Hanford High
Cal Poly All-American

Matt Boger, left, of Buchanan High and Chris Lewis of Clovis West

Larry Morgan

Matt Boger, left, 3rd in State and Ryan Flores, State Champion, Buchanan High

World Championships

Year	Wrestler	Weight	Style	Place	Location
1969	Chavez, Art	114.5	Greco	7	Mar Del Plata, Argentina
1969	Rasley, Rocky	HWT	Freestyle	5	Mar Del Plata, Argentina
1973	Morgan, Larry	136.5	Frestyle	4	Tehran, Iran
1974	Nigos, Joe	185.5	Greco	D.N.P.	Katowice, Poland
1975	Van Worth, Bill	HWT	Greco	6	Minsk, Soviet Union
1982	Vanni, Tim	105.5	Freestyle	6	Edmonton, Canada
1985	Vanni, Tim	105.5	Freestyle	10	Budapest, Hungary
1986	Vanni, Tim	105.5	Freestyle	6	Budapest, Hungary
1987	Vanni, Tim	105.5	Freestyle	5	Claremont, France
1989	Vanni, Tim	105.5	Freestyle	5	Martigny, Switzerland
1991	Vanni, Tim	105.5	Freestyle	D.N.P.	Varna, Bulgaria
1994	Vanni, Tim	105.5	Freestyle	9	Istanbul, Turkey

FILA World University Games

Year	Wrestler	Weight	Style	Place	Location
2005	Pendleton, Chris	185	Freestyle	10	Izmir, Turkey

Art Chavez
South High
Bakersfield College
Outstanding Wrestler, Far Western Conference

Tim Vanni (top)

Pan-American Games

Year	Wrestler	Weight	Style	Place	Location
1975	Van Worth, Bill	HWT	Greco	Champion	Mexico City, Mexico
1977	Bohna, Fred	220	Freestyle	Champion	
1987	Vanni, Tim	105.5	Freestyle	2	Indianapolis, Indiana
1991	Vanni, Tim	105.5	Freestyle	3	Havana, Cuba
1992	Vanni, Tim	105.5	Freestyle	2	Vancouver, Canada
1995	Vanni, Tim	105.5	Freestyle	3	Mar Del Plato, Argentina

Joe Drew of South Bakersfield versus National High School Champion from Japan 1961

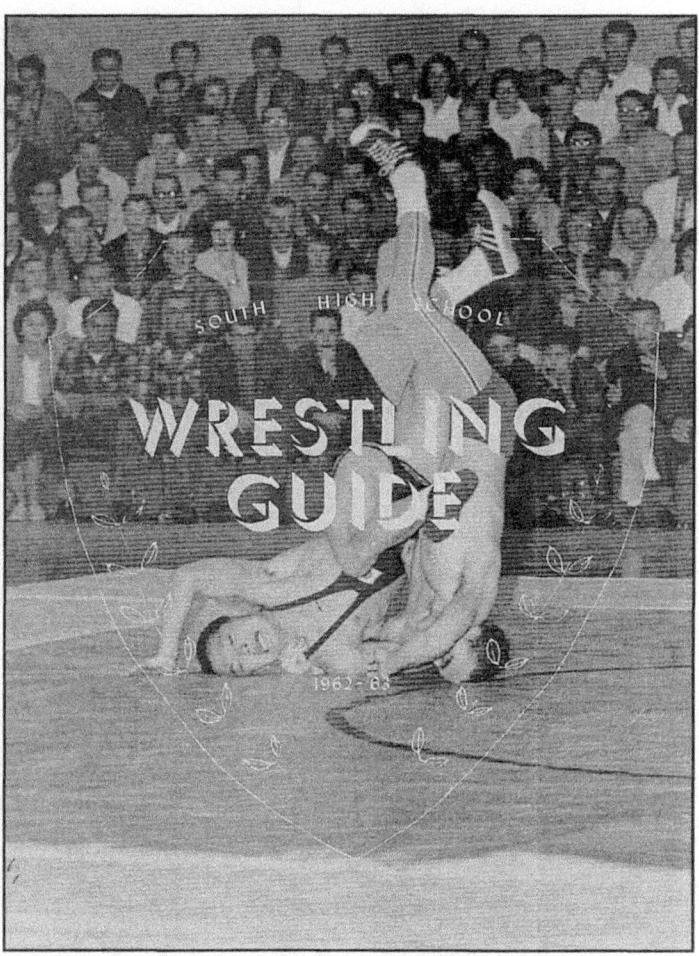

Jim Heckman of South Bakersfield versus National High School Champion Yojiro Uetake, who later went 58-0 for Oklahoma State and won three NCAA championships plus two Olympic Gold medals for Japan

Olympic Games

Year	Wrestler	Weight	Style	Location	Place
1968	Chavez, Art	114.5	Greco	Mexico City, Mexico	Medical*
1976	Morgan, Larry	149.5	Freestyle	Montreal, Canada	Alternate
1988	Vanni, Tim	105.5	Freestyle	Seoul, Korea	4
1992	Vanni, Tim	105.5	Freestyle	Barcelona, Spain	5
1996	Vanni, Tim	105.5	Freestyle	Atlanta, Georgia	Alternate

*Failed the medical exam: bleeding stomach ulcers

Tim Vanni
Olympic Games, Seoul, Korea

USA Wrestling National Championships
Freestyle – Greco-Roman

Year	Wrestler	Weight	Style	Place	Location
(Date?)	Zinkin, Harold		Freestyle	2	Bullard-Fresno State
1992	Sordi, Robbi	125.5	Freestyle	6	Madera-Fresno State
1992	Quintana, Gary	136.5	Freestyle	3	Selma-Fresno State
1996	Washington, Yero	125	Freestyle	6	Porterville-Fresno State
1997	Esquivel, Benny	127.5	Greco	6	Porterville
1998	Vasquez, Nathan	152	Greco	7	Bakersfield-CSUB
1998	Varner, Andy	167.5	Freestyle	4	Bakersfield-CSUB
1998	Nelms, Ian	167.5	Greco	8	Mt. Whitney-CSUB
2002	Pendleton, Chris	185	Freestyle	2	Lemoore-Oklahoma State
2003	Hafemeister, Sven	163	Greco	8	Lemoore-Columbia
2005	Pendleton, Chris	185	Freestyle	1	Lemoore-Oklahoma State
2006	Varner, Jake	185	Freestyle	3	Bakersfield-Iowa State
2007	Maffia, Broc	264.5	Greco	4	Tulare Western-UC Davis

Jake Varner of Bakersfield High
Two-time State Champion – 2004 and 2005
2nd in State – 2003
4th in State – 2004
Four-time CIF Champion

Renaldo Contreras, top, of Kingsburg and Roy Heath of South Bakersfield

University World
Freestyle

Year	Wrestler	Weight	Place	School	Location
2005	Pendleton, Chris	185	10th	Lemoore/Oklahoma State	Izmir, Turkey

World Cup

Year	Wrestler	Weight	Style	Place	Location
1979	Bohna, Fred	220	Freestyle	2	
1986	Vanni, Tim	105.5	Freestyle	3	Toledo, Ohio
1988	Vanni, Tim	105.5	Freestyle	3	Toledo, Ohio
1989	Vanni, Tim	105.5	Freestyle	4	Toledo, Ohio
1990	Vanni, Tim	105.5	Freestyle	2	Toledo, Ohio
1991	Vanni, Tim	105.5	Freestyle	2	Toledo, Ohio
1994	Vanni, Tim	105.5	Freestyle	3	Chattanooga, Tennessee
1999	Washington, Yero		Freestyle		

Goodwill Games

Year	Wrestler	Weight	Style	Place	Location
1994	Vanni, Tim	105.5	Freestyle	DNP	St. Petersburg, Russia

1962 South Bakersfield Wrestling Team
Back row, left to right: Gary Jackson, Ken Van Worth, Jerry Greer, Seymour Nerove, Jerry Thompson, William Andrews, Coach Bruce Pfutzenreuter
Front row, left to right: Bill Bridger, Mike Stricker, Virgil Bispo, Richard Villarreal, Arnold Villarreal, David Bracamonte

**Porterville High Wrestling Team
C.Y.L. Champions 10-0 1967**
Back row: Wall, Nelms, Keehan, Bennett
Middle row: Martinez, Storey, Wall, Rabbon, Cemo
Front row: Dames, Ensslin, Cortez, Cortez

**Roger Castaneda, CIF Champion
Porterville High**

**Everett Rabbon, CIF Champion
Porterville High**

U.S. Olympic Festival

Year	Wrestler	Weight	Style	Place	Location
1985	Vanni, Tim	105.5	Freestyle	Champion	
1987	Vanni, Tim	105.5	Freestyle	Champion	
1989	Vanni, Tim	105.5	Freestyle	Champion	

Bill Harralson of Bakersfield High
3rd in CIF

Tad Stricker of South Bakersfield
CIF Champion
2nd State

1965 CIF Finals
Roy Heath of South Bakersfield and Renaldo Contreras of Kingsburg.
Heath won 2-1
Heath: Three-time CIF Champion, career record 106-6-1
Contreras: Two-time CIF Champion, career record 96-4

ESPOIR USA Wrestling National Championships
Freestyle – Greco-Roman

Year	Wrestler	Weight	Style	Place	School
1988	Tamez, Anthony	114.5	Freestyle	5	Clovis
1988	Ravalin, Rick	198	Freestyle	5	Selma/Cal Poly
1990	Lagarreta, Eric		Greco	3	Selma
1990	Patton, Derreck	149.5	Freestyle	5	Arvin
1990	Neal, Lorenzo	286	Freestyle	Champion	Lemoore/Fresno State
1990	Neal, Lorenzo	286	Greco	Champion	Lemoore/Fresno State
1992	Aguirre, Jim	125.5	Freestyle	2	Clovis/Stanford
1992	Salven, Josh	286	Freestyle	2	Clovis West
1992	Salven, Josh	286	Greco	4	Clovis West
1993	Aguirre, Jim	136.5	Freestyle	2	Clovis/Stanford
1993	Molano, David	136.5	Freestyle	6	Golden West
1993	Mast, Chad	286	Freestyle	5	Clovis

ESPOIR FILA Juniors

Year	Wrestler	Weight	Style	Place	School
1997	Johnson, Cleo	108	Freestyle	3	Firebaugh
1997	Banuelos, Antonio	123.5	Greco	5	Clovis West
1997	Banuelos, Antonio	123.5	Freestyle	8	Clovis West
1997	Tirapelle, Adam	143	Freestyle	Champion	Buchanan, Illinois
1997	Davis, Jonte	143	Freestyle	5	Edison/Fresno State
1997	Nelms, Ian		Freestyle	8	Mt. Whitney/CSUB

Bakersfield Drillers Varsity Wrestling 1994-1995
Back row, left to right: David East, Richard Simmons, Bo Wright, Jeremy Bridges, Fred Ashley, Brett Clark, Larry Vasquez Sr., Dennis Reed
Middle row, left to right: Tony Keller, Ray Maese, Ben Sherley, unknown, Andy Varner, Luke Blair
Front row, left to right: Greg Canfield, Steve Elisondo, Larry Vasquez Jr., Nthan Vasquez, Kelly Miller, Bennett Scott

Tbilisi, U.S.S.R.

Freestyle (Known as the toughest tournament in the world)

Year	Wrestler	Weight	Place
1974	Morgan, Larry	136.5	
1980	Bohna, Fred	220	
1982	Vanni, Tim	105.5	6th
1983	Vannie, Tim	105.5	
1985	Reyes, Jessie	149.5	
1990	Vanni, Tim	105.5	Bronze

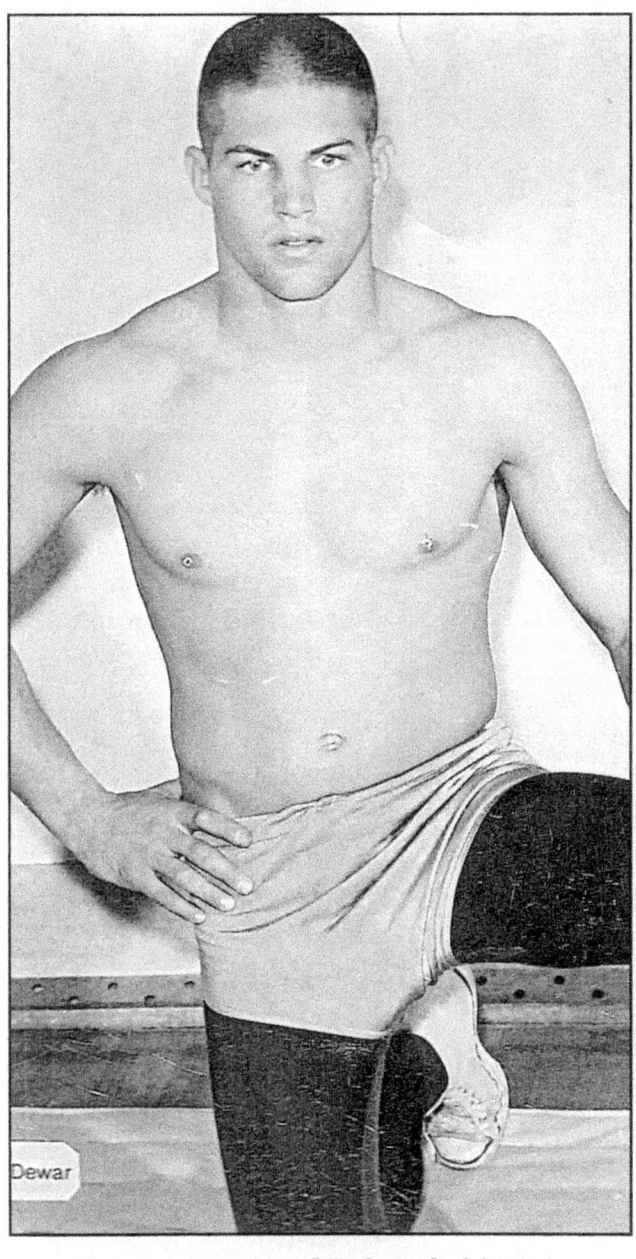

George Dewar of Bakersfield High
2nd in CIF 1961

Bakersfield High Drillers Varsity Wrestling 1992-93
Back row, left to right: Jack Serros, Paul Olejnik, David East, Brett Clark, Miles Hertkman, Jim Fenrick, Amy East
Middle row, left to right: Ray Maese, Carl Lupercio, Fred Ashley, Gabe Garcia, Phil Maicas, Eddie (last name unknown)
Front row, left to right: Andy Varner, Shon Collier, Luke Peat, Phil Schallberger, Rob McCally

Max Odom of Foothill High
National High School Free Style Champion

National YMCA Championships

Year	Wrestler	Weight	Style	Place
1972	Morgan, Larry	149.5	Freestyle	2
1972	Morgan, Larry	149.5	Greco	2

Jimmy Aguirre, Clovis, First
Parris Whitley, South Bakersfield, Second
Angel Villafana, Redwood, Third
Lou Salazar, Selma, Fourth

Detran Gant, Roosevelt, First
Roger Ramos, Merced, Second
Dave Molano, Golden West, Third
Ben Ervin, Madera, Fourth

1995 Bakersfield High
CIF Champions
Jeremy Brides (top)
Andy Varner (left)
Larry Vasquez

Alex Hernandez
Corcoran High
Two-tme CIF Champion
1968 and 1969

Larry Little
South Bakersfield
Two-time CIF Champion
1968 and 1969
4th place 1967

Section 5
Kern County Coaching Staffs
Coach/Wrestler Profiles
For the Record

Arvin High School

Year	Head Coach	Assistant Coaches
1957-58	Olan Polite	
1959	Olan Polite	
1960	Don Lukehart	
1961	Don Lukehart	
1962	John Bunton	
1963	John Bunton	
1964	John Bunton	Duane Damron
1965	John Bunton	Duane Damron
1966	John Bunton	Duane Damron, Jim Young
1967	Jim Young	Mr. Smith
1968	Jim Young	
1969	Richard Fisher	Bill Smith
1970	Richard Fischer	Gordon Shuppert
1971	Jose Gomez	Bill Satterfield
1972	Phil Bradfield	Bill Shanholtzer
1973	Phil Bradfield	Dwight Denney
1974	Phil Bradfield	A.J. Vasquez
1975	A.J. Vasquez EYL	Ruben Ramirez
1976	Ruben Ramirez	Ken Myers
1977	Ruben Ramirez	Frank Borjas
1978	Ruben Ramirez	Frank Borjas
1979	Ruben Ramirez	Frank Borjas
1980	Ruben Ramirez	
1981	Ruben Ramirez	Tom Gault, Gil Trevino
1982	Ruben Ramirez	Mike Spensko, Gil Trevino
1983	Ruben Ramirez	Gil Trevino, Eddie Morales
1984	Ruben Ramirez	Gil Trevino
		Leon Robinson
1985	Ruben Ramirez	Gil Trevino
		Leon Robinson
		Ric Cox
1986	Ruben Ramirez	George White
		Leon Robinson
		Gil Trevino
1987	Ruben Ramirez	George White
		Leon Robinson
		Gill Trevino, Mike Smithee
1988	Ruben Ramirez	George White
		Mike Smithee

Year	Head Coach	Assistant Coaches
1989	Ruben Ramirez	George White
		Jose Morales
		Mike Smithee
1990	Ruben Ramirez	George White
		Jose Morales
		Mike Smithee
1991	Ruben Ramirez	George White
		Jose Morales
		Mike Smithee
1992	Ruben Ramirez	George White
		Jose Morales
		Mike Smithee
1993	Ruben Ramirez	George White
		Jose Morales
		Steve Scarey
		Mike Leonard
1994	Ruben Ramirez	Jose Morales
1995	Jack Serros	Jose Marin
1996	Jack Serros	Jose Marin
1997	Jack Serros	Jose Marin
1998	Jack Serros	Jose Marin
1999	Jack Serros	Milo Lavario
2000	Jack Serros	Miguel Sanchez
2001	Jack Serros	Miguel Sanchez
2002	Jack Serros	Miguel Sanchez
2003	David Manriquez	Chris Carlos
		Jenard Arellano
		Anthony Adame
2004	Chris Carlos	Miguel Sanchez
		Jose Marin
2005	Miguel Sanchez	James Seiser
		Chris Alfonso
		Ivan Sanchez
		Isaias Manriquez
2006	Miguel Sanchez	Chris Alfonso
		Ivan Sanchez
		Isaias Manriquez

Bakersfield High School

Year	Head Coach	Assistant Coaches
1956-57	Paul Briggs	
1958	Paul Briggs	
1959	Paul Briggs	
1960	Olan Polite	Paul Briggs
1961	Olan Polite	
1962	Olan Polite	
1963	Olan Polite	Don Cornett
1964	Olan Polite	Don Cornett, Pat Mitchell
1965	Olan Polite	Don Cornett Nick Graham
1966	Olan Polite	Nick Graham
1967	Olan Polite	Mike Meek
1968	Olan Polite	Mike Meek
1969	Olan Polite	Joe McDonald
1970	Olan Polite	Willard Roberson
1971	Olan Polite	Willie Sandoval
1972	Olan Polite	Willie Sandoval
1973	Olan Polite	Willie Sandoval
1974	Olan Polite	Willie Sandoval
1975	Olan Polite	Steve Varner Charles Plummer
1976	Olan Polite	Steve Varner Charles Plummer
1977	Steve Varner	Charles Plummer
1978	Steve Varner	Rick Varner
1979	Steve Varner	Rick Varner
1980	Steve Varner	Tom Williams
1981	Steve Varner	Joe Smart
1982	Steve Varner	Joe Smart
1983	Jim Seay	Tony Ovalle
1984	Steve Varner	Tony Ovalle
1985	Steve Varner	Tony Ovalle
1986	Steve Varner	David East
1987	Steve Varner	David East
1988	David East	Bob Thistle Richard Simmons
1989	David East	Mike Taylor Richard Simmons
1990	David East	Paul Olejnik, Craig Oliver Richard Simmons
1991	David East	Paul Olejnik, Craig Oliver Richard Simmons
1992	David East	Paul Olejnik, Craig Oliver Richard Simmons
1993	David East	Craig Noble, Jack Serros Mel East
1994	David East	Jack Serros, Craig Noble, Joe Lopeteguy
1995	David East	Craig Noble, Joe Lopeteguy Larry Vasquez
1996	David East	Craig Noble Joe Lopeteguy Mike Battistoni Larry Vasquez
1997	David East	Kenny Wright Mike Battistoni, Mel East
1998	David East	Kenny Wright Richard Simmons Mel East, Dan Corpstein
1999	David East	Kenny Wright, Mel East Mike Battistoni Richard Simmons Larry Vasquez Joe Lopeteguy
2000	David East	Ben Sherley Larry Vasquez Mike Battistoni Larry Vasquez
2001	David East	Ben Sherley Larry Morgan Larry Vasquez Jr. Andy Varner Nathan Vasquez Larry Vasquez Steve Varner
2002	David East	Andy Varner, Nathan Vasquez, Larry Morgan, Mel East, Sean Crosswhite, Larry Vasquez, Larry Morgan, Steve Varner
2003	Andy Varner	Fidel Herrera Ray Hammond Kenny Wright, Kirk Moore Steve Varner, Larry Morgan
2004	Andy Varner	Mel East, Kenny Wright Larry Morgan Roy Hammond Steve Varner Craig Shoene Fidel Herrera
2005	Andy Varner	Larry Morgan, Mel East Ray Hammond, Kenny Wright, Danny Castaneda, Steve Varner, Fidel Herrera Craig Schoene
2006	Andy Varner	Kenny Wright, Craig Schoene, Larry Morgan Ray Hammond, Steve Varner, Fidel Herrera

Centennial High School

Year	Head Coach	Assistant Coaches
1993-94	Paul Olejnik	Claude Bradford
1995	Paul Olejnik	Claude Bradford, John Burns, Manuel Machado
1996	Paul Olejnik	Claude Bradford, John Burns, Manuel Machado, John Branch
1997	Paul Olejnik	Claude Bradford, John Burns, John Branch
1998	Paul Olejnik	Gary Chapman, Derek Scott, John Burns, John Branch
1999	Paul Olejnik	Derek Scott, Gary Chapman, Jason Froelich, John Burns
2000	Paul Olejnik	Derek Scott, Gary Chapman, Jason Froelich, John Burns
2001	Paul Olejnik	Derek Scott, Gary Chapman, Jason Froelich, John Burns
2002	Paul Olejnik	Tom Olejnik, John Archuletta, Gary Chapman
2003	Mike Hicks	Glen Smith
2004	Mike Hicks	Greg Horton, Lawrence Tatakawa, Jason Mason, Bryan Strain
2005	Mike Hicks	John Burns, Bob Thistle, Jason Mesa
2006	Mike Hicks	John Burns, Bob Thistle, Grant Newman, Juan Villalobos, Andy Sheffield, Jason Mesa

Cesar Chavez High School/Delano

Year	Head Coach	Assistant Coaches
2002-03	Jesse Ortega	
2004	Jesse Ortega	
2005	Gene Walker	Jesse Ortega
2006	Gene Walker	Ian Tablit

Delano High School

Year	Head Coach	Assistant Coaches
1957-58	Ralph Allen	
1959	Ralph Allen	
1960	Ralph Allen	
1961	Ralph Allen	
1962	Ralph Allen	
1963	Ralph Allen	Jack Mason
1964	Ralph Allen	Phillip Tincher
1965	Ralph Allen	Ted Hammock
1966	Ralph Allen	Harold Reimer
1967	James Macres	Harold Reimer
1968	James Macres	Gene Beck
1969	Terry Moreland	Gene Beck, Bob Limi
1970	Terry Moreland	Gene Beck
1971	Terry Moreland	Gene Beck
1972	Terry Moreland	Gene Beck
1973	Terry Moreland	Mike Sawyer
1974	Terry Moreland	Lon Gwyn
1975	Lon Gwyn	John Alcala
1976	Jon Talbott	John Alcala
1977	Jon Talbott	Juan Garza
1978	Jon Talbott	Juan Garza
1979	Jon Talbott	Juan Garza, Greg Reimer
1980	Robert Arballo	Juan Garza
1981	Robert Arballo	Don Noriel
1982	Robert Arballo	Joe Vega
1983	Robert Arballo	Joe Vega
1984	Robert Arballo	Tim Hartnett
1985	Ray Trask	Ernie Gonzales
1986	Ed Sibby	Ernie Gonzales, John Alcala
1987	Ed Sibby	Ernie Gonzales
1988	John Alcala	Keith Delehoy
1989	John Alcala	Ernie Gonzales, Keith Delehoy
1990	John Alcala	Ernie Gonzales, Keith Delehoy
1991	John Alcala	Jesse Ortega, John Brown
1992	Keith Delehoy	Jesse Ortega
1993	Keith Delehoy	Jesse Ortega
1994	Keith Delehoy	Jesse Ortega
1995	Keith Delehoy	Jesse Ortega, Johnny Rodriguez
1996	Jesse Ortega	
1997	Keith Delehoy	Jesse Ortega, Feliciano Romero
1998	Jesse Ortega	Ilario Prieto, Earnie Macias, David Castillo, Feliciano Romero
1999	Jesse Ortega	Ilario Prieto, Ernie Macias
2000	Jesse Ortega	Ilario Prieto, Ernie Macias
2001	Jesse Ortega	Ilario Prieto, Ernie Macias
2002	Jessie Ortega	Ilario Prieto, Ernie Macias
2003	Eric Rodriguez	Tim Bonita
2004	Eric Rodriguez	Ernie Macias
2005	Eric Rodriguez	Ernie Macias
2006	Todd Guevara	Gonzalo Quiddam, Ernie Macias

East Bakersfield High School

Year	Head Coach	Assistant Coaches
1956-57	Kay Dalton	
1958	Kay Dalton	Grover Rains
1959	Grover Rains	Bob Aston
1960	Leon Tedder	Bob Aston
1961	Leon Tedder	Bob Aston
1962	Leon Tedder	Bob Aston
1963	Leon Tedder	Bob Aston
1964	Leon Tedder	Bob Aston
1965	Leon Tedder	Bob Aston
1966	Leon Tedder	Jim Nuanez
1967	Leon Tedder	Jim Nuanez
1968	Leon Tedder	Jim Nuanez
1969	Leon Tedder	Jim Nuanez
1970	Jim Nuanez	Quinn Morgan
1971	Jim Nuanez	Quinn Morgan
1972	Jim Nuanez	Bill Pineda
1973	Leon Tedder	Bill Pineda
1974	Leon Tedder	Bill Pineda
1975	Leon Tedder	Rudy Gonzalez
1976	Rudy Gonzalez	Jim Groves
1977	Rudy Gonzalez	Jim Groves
1978	Rudy Gonzalez	Jim Groves
1979	Rudy Gonzalez	Jim Groves
1980	Rudy Gonzalez	Abe Oliveras
1981	Rudy Gonzalez	Carl Cruz
1982	Rudy Gonzalez	Leon Tedder
1983	Rudy Gonzalez	Leon Tedder
1984	Rudy Gonzalez	Steve Nickell
1985	Rudy Gonzalez	Anthony Padilla
1986	Rudy Gonzalez	Anthony Padilla
1987	Rudy Gonzalez	Anthony Padilla
		Mike Gonzalez
1988	Rudy Gonzalez	Mike Gonzalez
1989	Rudy Gonzalez	Mike Gonzalez
1990	Rudy Gonzalez	Mike Gonzalez, Joe Triggs
1991	Rudy Gonzalez	Joe Triggs
1992	Joe Triggs	Rudy Gonzalez
1993	Joe Triggs	Rudy Gonzalez
		Tony Levaro
1994	Joe Triggs	Tony Levaro
		Rudy Gonzalez
		Saul
1995	Joe Triggs	Tony Levaro
1996	Joe Triggs	Tony Levaro
1997	Joe Triggs	Brian Nava
1998	Joe Triggs	Brian Nava
1999	Joe Triggs	
2000	Joe Triggs	Cirilo Reyes
2001	Joe Triggs	David Gardner, Ken Gabin
2002	Joe Triggs	David Gardner, Ken Gabin
2003	Joe Triggs	Ken Gabin, David Gardner
2004	Joe Triggs	Ken Gabin
2005	Joe Triggs	Ken Gabin, Chris Felix
2006	Joe Triggs	Ken Gabin, Pete Gonzalez

Foothill High School

Year	Head Coach	Assistant Coaches
1962-63	Doug Collins	Harvel Pollard
1964	Doug Collins	Ray Juhl
1965	Doug Collins	Ray Juhl
1966	Grover Rains	Steve Powers
1967	Grover Rains	Dennis Tangeman
1968	Grover Rains	Dennis Tangeman
1969	Grover Rains	Lee Hammet
1970	Grover Rains	Lee Hammet
1971	Frank Sousa	Dave Edmondson
1972	Frank Sousa	Dave Olds
1973	Frank Sousa	Dave Olds
1974	Frank Sousa	Dave Edmondson
1975	Frank Sousa	Dave Edmondson
1976	Frank Sousa	Dave Edmondson
1977	Dave Edmondson	Karl Herrera
1978	David Edmondson	Karl Herrera
1979	Dave Edmondson	Karl Herrera
1980	Karl Herrera	Lloyd Dickey
1981	Karl Herrera	Lloyd Dickey, Chris Kirby
1982	Seymore Nerove	Frank Ramos
1983	Seymore Nerove	Frank Ramos
		Scott Chambers
1984	Seymore Nerove	Scott Chambers
		Richie Sinnett
1985	Seymore Nerove	Lee Noble
1986	Mark Loomis	Jeff Caputo
1987	Mark Loomis	Jeff Caputo
1988	Mark Loomis	Jeff Caputo
1989	Mark Loomis	Pat Zimmerman
1990	Mark Loomis	Pat Zimmerman
1991	Mike Dallas	Dennis Reed
1992	Alan Paradise	Matt Smith
1993	Alan Paradise	Tom Osendorf, Pat Higa

Year	Head Coach	Assistant Coaches
1994	Alan Paradise	Pat Higa
1995	Alan Paradise	Bo Steinbach
		George Anderson
1996	Alan Paradise	Bo Steinbach
		George Anderson
		Bobby Soto
1997	Alan Paradise	Bo Steinbach
		George Anderson
		Craig Noble
		Richie Sinnett
1998	Alan Paradise	Bob Steinbach
		Craig Noble
		Kirk Moore
1999	Bobby Soto	Kirk Moore
		Craig Noble
		Bo Steinbach
2000	Bo Steinbach	George Anderson
		Kirk Moore
2001	Brad Hull	Pete Hernandez
		Phillip Marquez
2002	Brad Hull	Phillip Marquez
		Steve Hernandez
		Carlos Sanches
2003	Brad Hull	Phillip Marquez
		Thomas Juarez
		Carlos Medina
2004	Brad Hull	Phillip Marquez
		Thomas Juarez
2005	Brad Hull	Thomas Juarez
		John Wren
		Robert Pfeifle
2006	Brad Hull	Thomas Juarez
		Brian Hull
		Robert Pfeifle

Correction

1982,83,84,85 Seymour Nerove

Golden Valley High School

Year	Head Coach	Assistant Coaches
2005	Aaron Wherry	Elizar Ceballos, Dan Mundanke
2006	Aaron Wherry	Elizar Ceballos, Dan Mundanke

Highland High School

Year	Head Coach	Assistant Coaches
1971-72	Joe Barton	J.R. Williams
1973	Joe Barton	Jim Kliewer
1974	Joe Barton	Jim Kliewer
1975	Joe Barton	Jim Kliewer
1976	Joe Barton	Jim Kliewer
1977	Joe Barton	Mike Spensko
1978	Joe Barton	Mike Spensko
		Jim Kliewer
1979	Jim Seay	Dick Molina
1980	Jim Seay	Chris Kirby, Dick Molina
1981	Jim Seay	Dick Molina
1982	John Gonzales	Kevin Finnel
1983	Bob Thistle	Charlie Chaney
1984	Bob Thistle	Charlie Chaney
1985	Joe Vega	Dan Richards
1986	Ted Hunter	Steve Tucker
1987	Bob Thistle	Dennis Reed
1988	Todd Owens	
1989	Jim Norsworthy	Dan Willis
1990	Dan Willis	Brian Neufeld
1991	Dan Willis	Brian Neufeld
1992	Dan Willis	Brian Neufeld
1993	Dan Willis	Brian Neufeld
1994	Dan Willis	Pete Cortez
1995	Dan Willis	Eric Williams
1996	Ernie Geronimo	Frank Ramos
1997	Ernie Geronimo	Carlos Marquez
1998	Carlos Marquez	Steve Montanio
1999	Carlos Marquez	Steve Montanio
2000	Carlos Marquez	Richard Eton
2001	Carlos Marquez	Chris Felix
2002	Carlos Marquez	
2003	Carlos Marquez	Jess Ortega
2004	Carlos Marquez	Chris Felix
2005	Ann Miller	Brian Marsh
2006	(Co-Head Coaches)	
	Anthony Gonzalez, Paul Gonzales	
		Juan Lopez

Kern Valley High School

Year	Head Coach	Assistant Coaches	Year	Head Coach	Assistant Coaches
1979-80	Denny Knight		1994	Denny Knight	
1981	Denny Knight		1995	Denny Knight	
1982	Denny Knight		1996	Denny Knight	
1983	Denny Knight		1997	Denny Knight	
1984	Denny Knight		1998	Denny Knight	
1985	Denny Knight	Marty Maciel	1999	Denny Knight	
1986	Denny Knight		2000	Denny Knight	Josh Factor
1987	Denny Knight		2001	Denny Knight	Josh Factor
1988	Denny Knight		2002	Denny Knight	Josh Factor
1989	Denny Knight	John Arcurio	2003	Denny Knight	Josh Factor, Mike Bull
1990	Denny Knight	John Arcurio	2004	Denny Knight	Josh Factor
1991	Denny Knight	John Arcurio	2005	Denny Knight	
1992	Denny Knight	Eric Allison	2006	Denny Knight	Cody Cunningham
1993	Denny Knight				Josh McCartney

Liberty High School

Year	Head Coach	Assistant Coaches
1999-2000	John Eisel	
2001	Joe Vega	Steve Elisondo
2002	Joe Vega	Coach Williams, Coach Genaro, Richard Gutierrez
2003	Jay Curtis	Ernie Lindley, Coach Williams
2004	Ernie Lindley	Rick Christensen, Doug Boothe, Sean Ponce
2005	Ernie Lindley	Ron Rogers, Dean Brown, Doug Klinchurch
2006	Ron Rogers	David East

McFarland High School

Year	Head Coach	Assistant Coaches
1968	Bob Miller	
1969	Bob Miller	David Kistler
1970	Lisle Gates	Coach Karr
1971	Lisle Gates	
1972	Lisle Gates	
1973	Lisle Gates	
1974	Lisle Gates	
1975	Lisle Gates	
1976	Lisle Gates	
1977	Lisle Gates	
1978	Lisle Gates	Jim Robesky
1979	Lisle Gates	
1980	Ed Levenson	
1981	Ed Levenson	
1982	Ed Levenson	
1983	Ed Levenson	
1984	Ed Levenson	
1985	Ed Levenson	
1986	Ed Levenson	
1987	Ed Levenson	
1988	Ed Levenson	
1989	Ed Levenson	Martin Davidson
1990	Ed Levenson	Martin Davidson
1991	Ed Levenson	Martin Davidson
1992	Ed Levenson	Jeff Nichols
		Rick Sparks
1993	Ed Levenson	Rick Sparks
1994	Ed Levenson	Rick Sparks
1995	Ed Levenson	Rick Sparks
1996	Ed Levenson	
1997	Ed Levenson	
1998	Ed Levenson	Javier Holguin
1999	Ed Levenson	Javier Holguin
2000	Ed Levenson	Javier Holguin
2001	Ed Levenson	Javier Holguin
2002	Ed Levenson	Javier Holguin
2003	Ed Levenson	Javier Holguin
2004	Ed Levenson	Coach Holguin,
		Jose Navajar
		Danny Camacho
		Coach Cardoza
2005	Ed Levenson	Javier Holguin
		Branden McFarland
		Jose Ramos
		Danny Camacho
2006	Ed Levenson	Javier Holguin
		Brandon McFarland
		George Silva
		Joey Ramos

North High School

Year	Head Coach	Assistant Coaches
1956-57	Dick Westbay	
1958	Dick Westbay	
1959	Win Bootman	
1960	Win Bootman	
1961	Win Bootman	
1962	Win Bootman	
1963	Win Bootman	Ken Kiefer
1964	Win Bootman	Gil Roberts
1965	Win Bootman	Gil Roberts
1966	Win Bootman	Roger Kelly
1967	Win Bootman	Bob Spencer
1968	Win Bootman	Bob Spencer
1969	Gary Kuster	Charles Lovell
1970	Gary Kuster	Charles Lovell
1971	Gary Kuster	Jack O'Brien
1972	Gary Kuster	Jeff Tuculett
1973	Gary Kuster	Jeff Tuculett
1974	Gary Kuster	Rick Harvick
1975	Gary Kuster	Ron Shearer
1976	Gary Kuster	Ron Shearer
1977	Gary Kuster	Ron Shearer
1978	Gary Kuster	Ron Shearer
1979	Gary Kuster	Jack O'Brien
1980	Gary Kuster	Bob Gamboa
1981	Richard Alvarez	Bob Gamboa
1982	Mark Hall	Kevin Duggan
1983	Ted Hunter	Darrin Lindsey
1984	Craig Schone	Lewis McNabb
1985	Tim Maestas	Rick Contreras
1986	Tim Maestas	Rick Contreras
1987	Rick McKinney	Armand Medina
1988	Rick McKinney	Jordan Holt
		Rocky Churchman
1989	Rick McKinney	John Branch
1990	Rick McKinney	Bill Thomas
1991	Rick McKinney	Bill Thomas
1992	Rick McKinney	Bill Thomas
		Rocky Churchman
		Lee Anderson
1993	Rick McKinney	Bill Thomas
		Rocky Churchman
		Brian Malavar
1994	Pat Huych	Bill Thomas
		Rocky Churchman
		Jeff Heberle
1995	Pat Huych	Rocky Churchman
		Jeff Heberle
		Travis Spears
1996	Rocky Churchman	Roman Aguilar
		Bobby Sherrill
		Chad Hobbs
1997	Rocky Churchman	Roman Aguilar
		Jake Shirley
1998	Rocky Churchman	Roman Aguilar
		Ted Hunter
		Tony Keller
1999	Rocky Churchman	Roman Aguilar
2000	Ty Stricker	Parris Whitley
2001	Ty Stricker	Parris Whitley
2002	Ty Stricker	Parris whitley,
		Bill Pitcher
		Jeff Tensley
2003	Ty Stricker	Bill Pitcher
		Jeff Tensley
2004	Ty Stricker	Bill Pitcher
		Jeff Tensley
		Dusi Terrell
		Mike Stricker
		Derrick Hunter
2005	Ty Stricker	Bill Pitcher
		Jeff Tensley
		Mike Stricker
2006	Ty Stricker	Bill Pitcher
		Brad Heineman
		Jeff Tensley
		Mike Stricker

Ridgeview High School

Year	Head Coach	Assistant Coaches
1993-94	Brad Case	Roman Aguilar
1995	Brad Case	Craig Oliver
1996	Brad Case	Craig Oliver
1997	Lee Ramos	Steve Montanio
1998	Lee Ramos	Steve Montanio
1999	Lee Ramos	John Paredez
2000	Lee Ramos	John Paradez, Chris Hertzog
2001	Lee Ramos	Paul Gonzales, Craig Oliver, Tony Gonzalez
2002	Lee Ramos	Craig Oliver, Paul Gonzales, Tony Gonzalez
2003	Lee Ramos	Tony Gonzalez, Sony Mord
2004	Lee Ramos	Tony Gonzalez, Bobby Sherriel, Eric Coleman
2005	Lee Ramos	Seba Wright, Anthony Gonzales, Eric Coleman, Calvin Cox
2006	Adam Setser	Seba Wright, Calvin Cox, Jarred Eades

Shafter High School

Year	Head Coach	Assistant Coaches
1965-66	Bill Hatcher	Darrell Fletcher
1967	Bill Hatcher	Darrell Fletcher
		Bill Dauphin
1968	Bill Dauphin	Darrell Fletcher
1969	Bill Dauphin	Darrell Fletcher
1970	Darrell Fletcher	Kalmon Matis
1971	Darrell Fletcher	Kalmon Matis
1972	Darrell Fletcher	Kalmon Matis
		Arlie Smith
1973	Darrell Fletcher	Kalmon Matis
		Arlie Smith
1974	Darrell Fletcher	
1975	Darrell Fletcher	Mike Spensko
1976	Darrell Fletcher	Ben Ansolabhere
		Tom Williams
1977	Darrell Fletcher	Tom Williams
1978	Darrell Fletcher	Tom Williams
1979	Don Burns	Tom Williams
1980	Lisle Gates	Dana Ellison
1981	Lisle Gates	Joe Lopez
1982	Lisle Gates	Joe Lopez
1983	Joe Lopez	Lisle Gates
1984	Joe Lopez	Roger Giovannetti
1985	Steve Nickell	
1986	Rick McKinney	Rick Sparks
1987	Gary Pederson	Rick Sparks
1988	Gary Pederson	Rick Sparks
1989	Gary Pederson	Allen Salazar
1990	Gary Pederson	Allen Salazar
1991	Gary Pederson	Rick Gabin
		Pay Hyuck
1992	Gary Pederson	Joe Lopez
		Rick Gabin
		Pat Hyuck
1993	Gary Pederson	Rick Gabin
1994	Gary Pederson	Rick Gabin
		Ken Gabin
1995	Gary Pederson	Rick Gabin
		Ken Gabin
		Julian Irigoyen
1996	Gary Pederson	Rick Gabin
		Ken Gabin
		Julian Irigoyen
1997	Gary Pederson	Julian Irigoyen
1998	Gary Pederson	John Paredez
		Joe Jolley
		Kevin Kellior
1999	Gary Pederson	Ray Organ
		Joe Jolley
		Kevin Kellior
2000	Gary Pederson	Ray Organ
		Joe Jolley
		Kevin Kellior
2001	Gary Pederson	Juan Gallardo
		Kevin Kellior
2002	Gary Pederson	Juan Gallardo
		Aaron Wherry
2003	Gary Pederson	Juan Gallardo
		Aaron Wherry
2004	Gary Pederson	Jacob Prendez
		Pat Hyuck
2005	Gary Pederson	Pat Hyuck
		Rick Cabin
		Andrew Stuebbe
2006	Gary Pederson	Rick Gabin
		Juan Gallardo
		Pat Hyuck
		Andrew Stuebbe

# South High School

Year	Head Coach	Assistant Coaches
1957-58	Bruce Pfutzenreuter	
1959	Bruce Pfutzenreuter	
1960	Bruce Pfutzenreuter	Ed Hageman
1961	Bruce Pfutzenreuter	Doug Collins
1962	Bruce Pfutzenreuter	Doug Collins
1963	Bruce Pfutzenreuter	Bob Lathrop
		Rod O'Meara
1964	Bruce Pfutzenreuter	Bob Lathrop
1965	Joe Seay	Bob Lathrop
1966	Joe Seay	Bob Lathrop
1967	Joe Seay	Bob Lathrop
1968	Joe Seay	Bob Lathrop
1969	Joe Seay	Bob Lathrop
		Bill Bruce
1970	Joe Seay	Bob Lathrop
1971	Joe Seay	Bob Lathrop
1972	Joe Seay	Bob Lathrop
1973	Art Chavez	Bob Lathrop
		Mike Stricker
1974	Art Chavez	Bob Lathrop
		Mike Stricker
1975	Bob Lathrop	Gene Walker
1976	Bob Lathrop	Gene Walker
1977	Bob Lathrop	Gene Walker
1978	Gene Walker	Art Chavez
1979	Gene Walker	Mike Stricker
1980	Gene Walker	Mike Stricker
1981	Gene Walker	Mike Stricker
1982	Gene Walker	Mike Stricker
		Jim Poteete
1983	Gene Walker	Jim Poteete
1984	Gene Walker	Mike Stricker
		Jim Poteete
1985	Gene Walker	Mike Stricker
		Jim Poteete
1986	Gene Walker	Mike Stricker
		Jim Poteete
1987	Gene Walker	Mike Stricker
		Jim Poteete
1988	Gene Walker	Mike Stricker
1989	Gene Walker	Mike Stricker
1990	Gene Walker	Mike Stricker
1991	Gene Walker	Ramon Hendrix,
		Brian Henderson
1992	Gene Walker	Brian Henderson
		Ramon Hendrix
1993	Brian Henderson	Cary Mills
1994	Brian Henderson	Cary Mills
1995	Brian Henderson	Cary Mills
1996	Brian Henderson	Cary Mills
1997	Brian Henderson	Cary Mills
1998	Brian Henderson	Cary Mills
		Andy Silvestro
1999	Brian Henderson	Cary Mills
		Ted Hunder
		Andy Silvestro
2000	Brian Henderson	Cary Mills
		Ted Hunter
		Andy Silvestro
2001	Brian Henderson	Cary Mills
		Andry Silvestro
2002	Brian Henderson	Cary Mills
		Derrick Hembree
2003	Brian Henderson	Cary Mills
2004	Brian Henderson	Cary Mills
		John Wren
		Ric Cox
2005	Brian Henderson	Cary Mills
		Tyson Jones
2006	Brian Henderson	Cary Mills

Stockdale High School

Year	Head Coach	Assistant Coaches
1991-92	Craig Schoene	
1993	Craig Schoene	Bill Graham, Tim Martin
1994	Craig Schoene	Bill Graham, Tim Martin
1995	Craig Schoene	Bill Graham, Chris McFadden
1996	Louis Chiparelli	Danny Castaneda
1997	Craig Schoene	Pat Zimmerman, Ric Cox
1998	Craig Schoene	Pat Zimmerman, Paul Garcia
1999	Craig Schoene	Pat Zimmerman, Paul Garcia
2000	Craig Schoene	Pat Zimmerman, Paul Garcia
2001	Craig Schoene	Paul Garcia
2002	Craig Schoene	Jason Mesa, Sean Ponce, Ric Cox, Joe Lopez
2003	Paul Garcia	Jason Armijo, Joe Espejo, Joe Martinez, Elizar Ceballos
2004	Paul Garcia	Jason Armijo, Elizar Ceballos, Paul Carrillo
2005	Paul Garcia	Jason Armiso, Travis Marchant, Jose Marales, Lalo Celedon
2006	Paul Garcia	Dante Borradori, Jose Morales, Joey Martinez, Lalo Celedon

Wasco High School

Year	Head Coach	Assistant Coaches
1965	Dale Dillingham	
1966	Dale Dillingham	
1967	Ted Hammack	
1968	Ted Hammack	
1969	Ted Hammack	
1970	Ted Hammack	Michael Worley
1971	Ted Hammack	Michael Worley
1972	Gerald Brandon	Ken Gladden
1973	Gerald Brandon	Keith Smith
1974	Gerald Brandon	
1975	Gerald Brandon	Larry Pearson
1976	Gerald Brandon	Larry Pearson
1977	Gerald Brandon	Larry Pearson
1978	Gerald Brandon	Larry Pearson
1979	Rod Balch	Randy Horton
1980	Jim Wooster	
1981	Jim Wooster	
1982	Lloyd Dickey	Jerry Kearns
		Al Soto
1983	Rodney Balch	Jerry Kearns
		Al Soto
1984	Jerry Kearns	Al Soto
1985	Mark Kelly	Vincent Moreno
1986	Vincent Moreno	
	George Romero	
1987	Vincent Moreno	George Romero
1988	Phil Sullivan	George Romero
1989	Dennis Reed	Cedrick Reed
		Craig Noble
1990	Rocky Bridges	
1991	Rocky Bridges	
1992	Rocky Bridges	Mark Loomis
		Brent Clark
1993	Mark Loomis	
1994	Brent Clark	
1995	Brent Clark	
1996	Brent Clark	
1997	Brent Clark	Joe Blanchard
		Juan Gallardo
1998	Brent Clark	Joe Blanchard
		Juan Gallardo
1999	Joe Blanchard	Juan Gallardo
2000	Joe Blanchard	Juan Gallardo
2001	Joe Blanchard	
2002	Stacy Hoffman	Cleo Johnson
		Jose Landin
2003	Joe Vega	Alex Gallardo
		Coach Acosta
2004	Alex Gallardo	Nacho Martinez
2005	Nacho Martinez	Orlando Landois
		Alex Gallardo
2006	Nacho Martinez	Alex Gallardo
		George Romero

West High School

Year	Head Coach	Assistant Coaches
1965-66	Ray Juhl	Floyd Thionett
1967	Ray Juhl	Gary Monji
1968	Ray Juhl	Gary Monji
1969	Ray Juhl	Ted Cano
1970	Ray Juhl	Dallas Grider
1971	Ray Juhl	Dallas Grider
1972	Ray Juhl	Dallas Grider
1973	Ray Juhl	Dallas Grider
1974	Ray Juhl	Dallas Grider
1975	Ray Juhl	Rick Varner
1976	Ray Juhl	Rick Varner
1977	Ray Juhl	Bill Kalivas
1978	Bill Kalivas	Ray Yocum
1979	Darrell Fletcher	Randy Shaw
1980	Darrell Fletcher	Mike Johnson
1981	Darrell Fletcher	Mike Johnson
1982	David East	Glen McCollough
1983	David East	Glen McCollough
1984	Don Lundgren	Darrell Fletcher
1985	Don Lundgren	Darrell Fletcher
1986	Don Lundgren	Darrell Fletcher
1987	Don Lundgren	Darrell Fletcher
1988	Joe Barton	Darrell Fletcher
		Don Lundren
		Mike Harvey
1989	Joe Barton	Darrell Fletcher
		Mike Harvey
1990	Joe Barton	Darrell Fletcher
		Ric Cox
1991	Don Lundgren	Bill Richardson
		Ric Cox

Year	Head Coach	Assistant Coaches
1992	Ric Cox	Bill Richardson
		Rich Bailey
1993	Ric Cox	Bill Richardson
		Troy Beavers
1994	Steve Lawson	Bill Richardson
		Matt Smith
1995	Ric Cox	
1996	Ric Cox	
1997	Ty Stricker	Mario Gonzales
1998	Ty Stricker	Parris Whitley
1999	Ty Stricker	Parris Whitley
2000	Terry Tabbytosavit	Trent Fussel
		Pete Hernandez
2001	Terry Tabbytosavit	Trent Fussel
2002	Ben Sherley	Scott DeGough
		Trent Fussel
		Anthony Tobin
2003	Ben Sherley	Scott DeGough
		Trent Fussel
		Anthony Tobin
2004	Ben Sherley	Scott DeGough
		Trent Fussel
2005	Ben Sherley	Scott DeGough
		Trent Fussel
2006	Ben Sherley	

Coach/Wrestler Profiles

Rodney Balch
Was CIF and State champion at Clovis High School. State Community College champion at Fresno City College. At Cal State-Bakersfield, he was a three-time CCAA Conference champion and 2nd place NCAA II champion with a 96-24-2 record. He coached at Wasco High School from 1979-1980. at Clovis High School he was assistant coach from 1980 until 1981 and head coach from 1982 to 1995. At Clovis, he led his teams to eight league championships and seven CIF championships, seven division championships. He coached six State Championship teams, 28 CIF champions and 29 state placers. He was voted California State Coach of the Year. Record at Clovis: 238-20-3. Career Record: 248-21-3. Buchanan - Assistant Coach 2001-2007

Fred Bohna
Placed 2nd and 1st in the CIF at Clovis High school. At UCLA, was NCAA champion, PAC 10 Wrestler of the Year, wrestled in the NWCA All-Star classic, was a National Champion-Freestyle. Placed 2nd in the World Cup. Pan-American Champion.

Vern Brooks
High School: Will Rogers High School, Tulsa, Oklahoma College: Northwestern State College, Oklahoma. Coaching: Springs, Wyoming, 1953 Wyoming State Wrestling Champions. Madera 1954-1965. At Madera, his teams won two Northern California Invitational Championships, five CIF Championships, and coached 27 individual CIF Central Section champions. Member of the USA Wrestling National Hall of Fame, California Chapter. Member of the California Wrestling Hall of Fame.

Mike Bull
At South High High School, he won the Sam Lynn Award for Most Outstanding Athlete in the County. Placed 3rd, 3rd and 1st in the CIF. State Champion: 44-0. National Junior Greco Roman. Placed 5th in the Olympic Champion Trials, Greco Roman, as a 17 year old. He was named California High School Wrestler of the Year in 1973. At Bakersfield College, he was State Community College Champion with a 30-2 record. At Cal State Bakersfield, he wrestled in the All-Star Classic, was a three-time All-American, second in the NCAA II championships in 1975 and first in the NCAA II championships in 1976. (Record: 85-10-1)

Bruce Burnett
At North High School, he was a two-time league champion, placing 1st, 2nd and 3rd in the CIF. At Bakersfield College, his record was 55-3. He was a two-time State Community College champion, and won the 1970 Outstanding Wrestling Award in the state meet. At Idaho State University, he was a two-time Big Sky Conference champion. He never lost a dual match in college. Coaching at Meridian High School in Idaho, he attained a 14-year record of 154-13-2, along with four state championships. He was Idaho Coach of the Year six times, and a five-time runner-up. He was assistant coach at Oklahoma State University from 1987 until 1990, and coached for USA Wrestling from 1990-2000. He served as the developmental and national freestyle coach, coaching national teams, world teams and Olympic teams. He was named Freestyle Wrestling Coach of the Year in 1995 and 1996, and named Olympic Committee Elite Coach of the Year in 1996. In 2000, he became head wrestling coach at the U.S. Naval Academy. He is a member of the Idaho State University Athletic Hall of Fame, California Wrestling Hall of Fame and Bob Elias Kern County Hall of Fame.

Art Chavez
In high school, he was a CIF champion at South High. At Bakersfield College, he placed second in the State Community College meet. At San Francisco State, he won the Far Western and was named Outstanding Wrestler. He placed 5th in the NCAA Tournament. He earned 1st place at San Jose, San Francisco State and Mare Island and third at UCLA tournaments. Internationally, he was the 7th World Greco Roman championships, and won the National AAU Freestyle and Greco Roman championships the same year. He wrestled for the San Francisco Olympic Club, winning the Olympic Trials in Freestyle in 1968. He coached two state high school champions at Gonzales High and South High and officiated the State High School Championships.

Joe Conley
Joe Conley attended high school in Chicago and Loras College in Dubuque, Iowa. He became coach at Exeter High in 1965 and coached for 30 years. His teams won more than 500 dual meets, 10 league championships and boasted seven undefeated seasons. He was a member of the Central Section Wrestling Advisory Committee for 10 years, and officiated wrestling for 10 years. He is a member of the California Wrestling Hall of Fame.

Lennis Cowell
In high school, he placed 1st, 2nd and 3rd in the Northern California championships at Pleasant Hill High School and was undefeated his senior year. At Diablo Valley College, he placed 3rd in the State Community College championships. At Cal Poly, he was a two-time CCAA champion, and placed 3rd and 4th in the NCAA II. He coached at Allan Hancock College, Cuesta College, San Luis Obispo High School and Clovis West High school. At Clovis West, his record was 97-5. He coached four league championships, three divisional championships, three CIF cham-

Coach/Wrestler Profiles

pionships and two state championships. His teams won 85 straight duals in a row. He was Southern Regional Coach of the Year in 1983 and National High School Coach of the Year in 1984. At Cal Poly, he had an 18-year record of 167-147-8. He coached 14 PAC-10 champions and eight Division 1 All-Americans. His overall record: 300-165-9. He is a member of the California Wrestling Hall of Fame.

Sam Crandall

Joining the coaching staff at Kingsburg High School, Crandall coached wrestling for more than 40 years. In 1973, he was voted Central Sequoia League Coach of the Year. His 27-year coaching record was 260-82-9. He is a member of the California Wrestling Hall of Fame.

Dennis Deliddo

He attended Bullard High School. At Fresno City College, he placed 5th in the State Community College meet, and was a two-time conference runner-up at Fresno State University. He was an assistant coach at Fresno City College before becoming coach at Clovis High School from 1971-1981. His record was 147-7-1. He led eight league championships, six divisional championships, five CIF championships and five state championships in 1974, 1975 and 1976. His teams placed 2nd in 1973 and 3rd in 1981. He was named (Valley) CIF Coach of the Year five times. At Fresno State University from 1981-2005, he coached 27 All-Americans, 58 conference champions. He was four-time WAC Coach of the Year and twice named PLAA Coach of the Year. He won seven consecutive WAC titles, nine conference titles and had 11 Top 25 finishes in the NCAA. He was a runner-up for 1993 NCAA Coach of the Year. Record at Fresno State: 314-171-4. He is a member of the Fresno County Hall of Fame and California Wrestling Hall of Fame.

Dennis Downing

At Bell Gardens High School, he placed third in the CIF. At Cerritos College, he was two-time runner-up in the State Junior College meet. At Cal Poly, he was a NCAA D-11 champion. He was assistant coach at Cal Poly for one year. He was head coach at San Luis Obispo High School one year, at Merced High School for three years, at Sierra High School for 27 years and coached one year at Heidelberg High School in Germany.

David East

At Bakersfield High School, he was CIF Champion. He attended Bakersfield College and boasted a two-year record of 75-17 at Cal State-Bakersfield. He coached at Maricopa High School for five years before coaching at West Bakersfield High School and then as assistant coach at Bakersfield High. He was head coach at Bakersfield High for 24 years. His varsity record at Bakersfield High was 204-12. He coached 14 league championship teams, two divisional championships, 3 CIF championships, one state championship team, seven state champions and 31 state place winners. He was named 2002 National High school Coaches Association Co-High School Coach of the Year.

Dick Francis

At Orange Coast College and then San Jose State University, he was undefeated in college dual meets for three years. He was the P.I.C. champion in 1953 and 1955, and 2nd in 1954. He was the Far Western AAU Champion in 1955, 1956 and 1958, and placed 3rd in 1954, 1955 and 1957 at the National AAU Championship in Freestyle. He placed 3rd in 1956 and 4th in 1957 in the National AAU Greco Roman Championship. He coached at Fresno High from 1956-1959, McLane High from 1959-1664 and Fresno State from 1964-1981. He coached two conference championship teams, and 39 individual conference champions. He is a member of the California Wrestling Hall of Fame and USA Wrestling National California Chapter Hall of Fame.

Sam Gollmyer

At Bakersfield High School, he was CIF champion. He attended Bakersfield College and Humboldt State College. He coached at Victor Valley High School from 1975-1993 with a 306-72 record, 14 league championships and one CIF championship. His teams placed 2nd two times and 3rd one time. He coached three state champions, 10 state placers and a two-time Olympian. He coached the unofficial Masters Champions/Southern Section three times and the 1987 state champions.

Al Kiddy-Madera

An outstanding three-sport star in high school, he lettered in three sports at the University of Oklahoma, where he wrestled for Port Robertson and played football for Bud Wilkerson. His coaching record is 237-15-2. He coached three Trans Valley Championship teams at Hughson High School from 1960-1964. He coached at McLane High in 1965. At Madera High, he coached six league championships, two divisional championships and two CIF championships. He was assistant coach at Fresno City College form 1976-1984.

Webber Lawson

At Cal Poly, he wrestled for the L.A. Athletic Club and was the 1948 U.S. Western Regional Olympic Trials champion. He was named Outstanding Wrestler, a thre-time Far Western Champion, was a six-time SPAAU champion, a U.S. Western Pan-Am champion and Senior Open AAU

Coach/Wrestler Profiles

champion. He coached at Inglewood High, Tulare Western and Fremont of Sunnyvale. At Fremont, his teams won 52 dual meets in a row and four Central Coast titles in a row. His teams won the Northern California Invitation in 1967 and 1968, placing 2nd in 1966. He served as president of the National High School Wrestling Association, and coached for 25 years in three different CIF sections. He is a member of the California Wrestling Hall of Fame.

Vern McCoy
At the University of Iowa, he wrestled varsity for four years and was team captain in 1948. He coached at Roosevelt High School form 1957-1966 and at McLane High School. He is a member of the USA Wrestling California Chapter National Hall of Fame.

Bill Musick
At Madera High School, Music was a CIF finalist. He was an outstanding football player in high school and in college at Bakersfield College and Fresno State. He was head football coach at Fresno City College and head wrestling coach at Fresno City for 19 years. He coached 17 league championship teams, 12 Northern California Championship teams and won four California State Community College titles. He was a four-time Community College Coach of the Year. His career record was 247-50-5. He is a member of the California Wrestling Hall of Fame and the USA Wrestling National California Chapter Hall of Fame.

Larry Morgan
At East Bakersfield High School, he was 82-2 his last two years. He was a two-time National High school Champion and Junior World Champion. In college his record at Cal Poly was 112-21-1. He placed 2nd in the NCAA II in 1971, 2nd in 1972 and was the 1973 champion He was 1973 Outstanding Wrestler in the NCAA II tournament. He placed 5th in the NCAA I tournament and wrestled in the East-West All-Star Dual in 1973. Internationally, he was 1st in the Freestyle Olympic Trials in 1973, 4th in the World Freestyle championships in 1973, 1st in the AAU Greco Roman Nationals in 1976, 1st in the U.S. Federal Nationals for Freestyle, 1st in the U.S. Federation Greco Roman Nationals and a U.S. Olympic Trials Freestyle Champion. He spent two years as a graduate assistant coach at the University of Iowa and was an assistant coach at Cal State-Bakersfield from 1979-1981. He then became an assistant at Bakersfield High . He is a member of the Cal Poly Hall of Fame, Division II Wrestling Hall of Fame, and California Wrestling Hall of Fame, and Bob Elias Kern County Hall of Wrestling Fame.

Corky Napier
Napier attended Madera High School, Fresno City College and Fresno State. He was assistant coach from 1972-1976 at Madera High, where the JV record was 55-5. He was head coach at University High School from 1976-1980, where the record was 33-3. There, he coached one State champion and three CIF champions. He was head coach at Madera High from 1980-2004, with 208 wins in the Central Section and 10 team championships. He was a six-time League Coach of the Year. He coached CIF team champions in 1990, and runners-up in 1982, 1985 and 1991. He coached six State and 28 CIF individual champions. Madera was 2nd in the state in 1984. His overall coaching record; 314-48.

Lorenzo Neal
At Lemoore High school, Neal was CIF football player of the year, a high school All-American and CAL-HI Athlete of the Year. In wrestling, he was a three-time Division and CIF champion, a runner-up for Division and CIF his freshman year and 4,2 and 1 at State. In the Junior Nationals, he placed 3rd in both styles. At Fresno State, in football, he was a two-time All Big West champion and played in the MVP Freedom Bowl. In wrestling, he was an Espoir Champion in both styles, a two-time WAC champion and placed 7th in the NCAA I. Neal has played 14 years in the NFL, with New Orleans, the New York Jets, Tampa Bay, Tennessee, Cincinnati and San Diego. He is a three-time Pro Bowl selection, a four-time Pro Bowl alternate and four-time USA Today All-Joe Team choice.

Joe Nigos
At Delano High School, Nigos was an outstanding football player and CIF champion. At Bakersfield College, his record was 52-1, and he was a two-time Community College State champion. At Cal Poly, he made the world Greco Roman team in wrestling. He was head coach at Oak Grove, an d San Jose High School, and a college wrestling referee.

Chuck Patten
Patten attended East Waterloo High School in Iowa and Northern Iowa University. He coached at Exeter High School from 1962-1963, Reedsport High School in Oregon and at Northern Iowa University for 18 years with a 217-87-8 record. He coached 10 conference championships, placed 2nd four times, coached NCAA II champions in 1975 and 1978 and placed 17 times in the Top 12. He was NCAA II Coach of the Year in 1969 and 1978, and is a member of the NCAA II Hall of Fame.

Bruce Pfutzenreuter
Pfutzenreuter coached two league championship teams at South Bakersfield High from 1957-1964. His record was 74-14-3. He coached foot-

Coach/Wrestler Profiles

ball, wrestling and was the head track coach. At Bakersfield College from 1964-1985, his coaching record was 264-81-2. He coached State Community College champions in the 1968-1969 season. His team placed 2nd three times, 3rd three times, 4th twice and 9th twice. He coached 32 tournament championship teams, 66 state placers, 16 state champions, 47 All-Americans and was named Coach of the Year in 1969. His 28-year coaching record: 338-95-5. He was named a member of the California Wrestling Hall of Fame, Bob Elias Kern County Hall of Fame and National Wrestling California Chapter Hall of Fame.

Olan Polite

At Boulder High School, Polite placed 4th in the 1949 Colorado State High School Championships at 127 lbs. He coached at Arvin High School from 1957-59 and at Bakersfield High School from 1959-1977. He coached four league championships, two divisional championships and two CIF championships. He was named California Coach of the Year, District 8 (13 states) Coach of the Year in 1979, and was nominated for National High School Wrestling Coach of the Year. His career record: 189-37-2.

Grover Rains

Rains was an NCAA champion at Oklahoma State University. He coached at Stillwater High School in Oklahoma and then at East Bakersfield and Foothill high schools in California. He is a long-time high school and college referee. He is a member of the USA Wrestling Oklahoma Chapter Hall of Fame and was awarded the Gallagher Award in 2004.

Rocky Rasley

At South Bakersfield High School, Rasley was an outstanding three-sport athlete and 2nd in the CIF. At Bakersfield College, he was again a three-sport athlete, named a Community College Football All-American and two-time Regional champion. He placed 2nd and 3rd in the State Community College championships. At Oregon State University, he wrestled and played football, placing 5th in the World Freestyle championships. He played eight years in the NFL with Detroit and San Francisco.

Jessie Reyes

At Bakersfield High School, Reyes was a two-time League champion, a Divisional champion and 3rd in the CIF. His record was 32-0 in his senior year until an injury ended his season. At Cal State-Bakersfield, he was 151-22-1, a two-time NCAA II champion, NCAA I champion and Outstanding NCAA II Wrestler (1983). In 1984 he was a member of the East-West All-Star Classic. Reyes was an assistant coach at Cal State-Bakersfield, Oklahoma State University, Arizona State University, Cal Poly and Michigan State University. He is head coach at Purdue University, were he was an all-time Victory leader with 167 wins, coaching 14 All-Americans. In 1998, he was head coach of the Junior World Freestyle Team.

Chuck Seal

At Redmond High School in Oregon, Seal was a three-time Oregon State champion. At Portland State, he was 110-14-1, placing 1st, 2nd and 1st in NCAA Division II and 3rd and 6th in Division 1. He was a member of the NCAA D-11 Wrestling Hall of Fame. He coached at Reedley High School.

Joe Seay

Attending Kansas State University, Seay was a three-time Greco Roman National champion, a two-time runner-up in Freestyle and placed second in the 1964 and 1972 Freestyle Olympic Trials. He placed third in the 1968 trials. He coached at South Bakersfield from 1964-1972 with a 117-13-2 record, coaching six league championships and four CIF championships. At Cal-State Bakersfield he coached for 12 years with a 189-56-2 record. His teams won seven NCAA II titles, 24 NCAA individual titles and placed second twice for NCAA II titles. At Oklahoma State University, he coached seven years with a 114-18-2 record. He coached five Big 8 Championships, 31 All-Americans, two NCAA I championships, five national champions and was DI Coach of the Year in 1989 and 1990. He was assistant coach at the University of Virginia and head coach at the University of Tennessee at Chattanooga, where he was named Southern Conference Coach of the Year with a 16-8-1 record. Internationally, he was head coach of the Sunkist Kids and 1971 Junior World Team. He also was head coach of the 1976 All-Star Classic World Cup (1985, 1986 and 1991) and Pan-American Games in 1995. He coached the World Team in 1993, 1995 and 2005, the Olympic Games in 1996, and was an assistant Olympics coach in 1992 and 2000. He was named Man of the Year in 1991. His record during 22 years of college coaching was 319-82-5. His record during 30 years of high school and college coaching was 436-95-7. He was named a member of the Kansas State University Hall of Fame, California Wrestling Hall of Fame, Bob Elias Kern County Hall of Fame and National Wrestling Hall of Fame.

Phil Sullivan

At Tulare Western High School, Sullivan was a two-time CIF champion. At Cal Poly, he was an NCAA II champion. He placed fifth in the National AAU Greco Roman championships. He coached at Wasco High School, and also coached numerous youth teams in the Central Section. He was named Southern Coach of the Year in 1974 and 1976.

Coach/Wrestler Profiles

Leon Tedder
Tedder was a four-year Letterman at Oklahoma State University. At East Bakersfield High School, he coached three League championships and two CIF championships. He was a long-time high school and college referee, named to the Kern County Officials Association Hall of Fame.

Tim Vanni
At Monache High School, Vanni was a three-time League champion, two-time CIF champion and two-time Divisional champion. He placed 2nd and 6th in State in 1979 and 1978, respectively, and was 70-3 his last two seasons. At Cal State-Bakersfield, he was a four-year Letterman. Internationally, he was a five-time National Freestyle champion, placing 6th in 1982, 6th in 1986, 5th in 1987, 5th in 1989 and 9th in 1994 on seven World Teams. He placed in 1982, 1983, 1984, 1986, 1989 and 1990 as a member of the U.S. Team in the Soviet Union. He placed 4th in the Olympic Team in 1988, 5th in 1992 and was an 1996 alternate. On the Pan-American Team, he placed 2nd in 1987, 2nd in 1990, 3rd in 1991 and 2nd in 1992. From 1981 until 1996, Vanni won or placed in many freestyle tournaments all over the world, including the World Cup, Canada Cup, National Sports Festival, Club Cup and World University Trials. He coached at Porterville High School for 12 years with a 68-18 record. He was assistant coach at Cal State-Bakersfield for three years and at Arizona State University for five years. Vanni is a member of the Bob Elias Kern County Sports Hall of Fame and the California Wrestling Hall of Fame.

Bill Van Worth
At South Bakersfield High School, he was an outstanding football player, a two-time league champion and two-time Division Champion, placing 1st and 2nd in the CIF. His wrestling record was 91-7 with 74 falls. He was an outstanding football player at Humboldt State, Bakersfield College and placed 2nd in the NCAA II championships at Humboldt State College. At Cal State-Bakersfield, he was a NCAA II champion with a 40-2 record. Internationally, he was a member of the Greco Roman World Team and Gold Medalist on the Pan-American Greco Roman team. At Dos Palos High School, he coached nine league champions and amassed a 126-31-1 record in 13 years.

Yero Washington
At Porterville High School, Washington was 6th in the CIF in 1990, a 1992 CIF champion and 1992 State champion. At Fresno City College, he was 2nd in the 1993 State Community College championships and a State Community College champion in 1994. At Fresno State, he placed 6th in 1996 and 3rd in 1997 at the NCAA tournament. In 1998, he was 2nd in the U.S. Open and 2nd in the World Team trials. In 1999, he was a World Cup team member, placed 4th in the U.S. Open, 4th in the World Team trials and was a Sunkist International Open Champion. Washington placed 5th in the Olympic Team trials in 2000, 4th in the U.S. Open in 2003, 5th in the U.S. Open in 2004 and placed in the Top 8 at the Olympic Team Trials. He currently coaches at Columbia University.

Hans Wiedenhoefer
At San Jose State, Wiedenhoefer was a two-time PCAA champion and Far Western champion. He coached at Fresno City College from 1959-1965, coaching five League championships, two Regional and two State Community College championships. His teams placed 2nd and twice placed third. He is a member of the California Wrestling Hall of Fame and USA Wrestling California Chapter National Hall of Fame.

Drew Williams
At Paradise High School, Williams was a three-time Northern Section CIF champion. He attended college at Yuba City College and Chico State. He coached at Los Plumas High School, Brawley High School and at Monache High school for 26 years. His career record: 386-71-4. His teams won 18 League titles, three Yosemite Division titles, one CIF championship. He coached four CIF runner-up teams, 17 CIF champions, 14 State medal winners and 60 state qualifiers. **Coaching record 401-76-4**

Floyd Winter
After wrestling all four years at Porterville High School, Winter became a 13-time Armed Forces champion for the U.S. Army. He was a 1972 World Military Greco Roman champion, a 1977 National Greco Roman champion, a three-time runner-up at the Greco Roman Nationals and four-time placer in the World Military Championships. In the U.S. Army, he was an assistant Olympic Greco Roman coach in 1984 and 1988, a World cup Greco Roman coach in 1985 and 1989, and a 1990 Olympic Festival Greco Roman coach. He was a member of the National Coaching Staff for 10 years.

John Woods
At Redwood High School in Visalia, Woods placed 1st and 2nd in the CIF with a 68-8 record. At Cal Poly, he was a three-time NCAA II All-American, an NCAA II champion in 1968, NCAA I runner-up and placed 2nd in the NCAA II. He wrestled in the East-West All-Star match. He coached at Orange Glen High School, where his four-year record was 45-9-2. At Palomar Community College, his 15-year record was 179-19-3. His teams were five-time State Community College cham-

Coach/Wrestler Profiles

pions, and he was named Community College Coach of the Year four times. He was elected to the Redwood High Hall of Fame in 1971 and named to the USA Wrestling California Chapter Hall of Fame in 1998 and California Wrestling Hall of Fame in 2000. Since 1986, Woods has been athletic director at Palomar Community College.

Howard Zink

A coach at Washington Union High School for 26 years, Zink's record was 261-97-2. He coached five Sequoia-Sierra championships, nine League championships, 96 individual League champions, 46 individual champions, nine CIF champions, 10 State medalists and one National Junior Champion.

For The Record

Fast Falls

Year	Wrestler	Weight	School	Time	Opponent
2003	Sal Magallon*		Exeter	5 seconds	vs. Redwood High
1968	Jess Winters*	138 lbs.	West Bakersfield	8 seconds	vs. R. Bann Shafter
1969	Sebastian Guerrero**	112 Lbs.	Corcoran	6 seconds	vs. R. Pallares Selma

**(Father of Eric Guerrero, three-time state champion, three-time NCAA champion and Olympian.)

Teams

Most Consecutive Dual Wins Without a Loss

Year	School	Wins	Coach
1992	Bakersfield	48	David East
1985	Clovis West	85	Lennis Cowell
1978	Monache, Porterville	39	Drew Williams (Year Ended)
1974	Delano	61	Terry Moreland
1966	South Bakersfield	39	Bruce Pfutzenreuter – Joe Seay
1963	East Bakersfield	39	Leon Tedder

Most Consecutive Wins Without a Loss

Year	Wrestler	School	Wins
2003-2005	Jake Varner	Bakersfield	88
1997-1999	Ben Martinez	Tulare	108
1964-1967	Lee Cullition	South Bakersfield	78

Most Falls in a Season

Year	Wrestler	Falls
2003-2004	Jake Varner	43 132 CAREER
1999-2000	Chris Pendleton	51

Earl Corley, South Bakersfield, Defending CIF Champion, 13-0, was declared ineligible by the CIF because he played in a church league basketball game.

In May 1960, South's Corley mixes golf with a couple of contrasting sports, football and wrestling. Shot a one under-part 71 to tie for the CIF golf title, took second after he three-putted on the second half in a sudden death playoff.

Corley went on to be named J.C. All American football player and went to wrestle 1.5 seasons as an unbeaten heavyweight and state J.C. Champion. At the semester, he transferred to the University of Arizona and placed second in the Pacific Coast Intercollegiate Championships in March 1962. After spring football, we lose track of him.

Earl Corley
South Bakersfield

Source: Cal-Hi Sports*

Matt Boger of Buchanan and Chris Lewis of Clovis West.

Matt Boger (top) of Buchanan and Nick Bardsley of Clovis West.

Matt and Josh Boger of Buchanan.

Matt Boger and Ryan Flores of Buchanan.

Matt Boger and Coach Dustin Riley.

Section 6
2007 Tournament Results

South East Yosemite League

South West Yosemite League

South Sequoia League

Sierra-Sequoia Divison

Yosemite Division

Central Section Masters

State Championships

South East Yosemite League - East High
February 10, 2007

103
Collier	Marc	EB	Fall 4:37*
Rizo	Derik	FOOT	
Delfin	Paul	B	11-4
Lenier	Jeff	LIB	
Silva	Brandon	GV	

112
Demison	Nektoe	B	9-1
Gonzalez	Peter	EB	
Bohannan	Scott	LIB	

119
Lomas	Frank	B	16-2
Tarkington	Richard	HIGH	
Miani	Keith	LIB	5-3
Berlanga	Ryan	GV	

125
Kapler	Greg	LIB	Fall 3:09
Morgan	Jacob	B	
Ramierz	Richie	HIGH	
Florez	Miguel	EB	

130
Gonzalez	Freddy	EB	12-8
Franco	Steve	HIGH	
Olmos	Juan	GV	17-2
Bryan	Jordan	LIB	
Gurlani	Andrew	B	

135
Cruz	Jonah	B	Fall 1:59
New	Mark	FOOT	
Rivera	Vince	LIB	Fall
Gutierrez	Markey	GV	
Bermudez	Jose	EB	

140
Miller	Justin	EB	8-1
Box	Anthony	B	
Rios	Robert	LIB	4-2
Matthews	Richard	GV	
Sandoval	Marcos	FOOT	19-18
Valdez	Marc	HIGH	

145
Rasmussen	Travis	B	7-4
Christensen	Colton	LIB	
Mundheneke	Aaron	GV	8-4
Gordillo	Derek	EB	
Torres	Victor	HIGH	19-8
Wren	Nathan	FOOT	

152
Rodriguez	Jamie	B	9-7
Lopez	Martin	EB	
Custer	Dylan	LIB	8-0
Marsh	Jeff	HIGH	
Hernandez	Jesus	GV	

160
Delarosa	Eric	FOOT	3-2*
Rogers	Kail	LIB	
Hernandez	Cruz	EB	5-1
Arriaga	Ruben	B	
Gutierrez	Ivan	GV	Fall 5:27
Martinez	Miguel	HIGH	

171
Carls	Brad	B	17-0
Thomas	Tim	FOOT	
Nistor	Geoff	LIB	17-8
Pena	Michael	EB	
Burnett	Josh	HIGH	Fall
Rodriguez	David	GV	

189
Travis	David	FOOT	Fall 4:34
Schoene	Brian	B	
Avena	Xzavium	LIB	Fall
Wilson	Laramie	HIGH	
Pienado	Delfino	EB	

215
Cummings	Eddie	EB	Fall 1:57
Daniel	Christen	B	
Chavez	Armando	FOOT	7-5
Goldberg	Trevor	LIB	

(Continued on next page)

South East Yosemite League - East High
February 10, 2007

285
Alvarez	Lamar	B	4-2
Cisneros	Efrain	GV	
Hernandez	Antonio	EB	Fall
Anders	Tamir	LIB	

*Outstanding wrestlers

Team results
1. Bakersfield   274
2. East Bakersfield   216
3. Liberty   194.5
4. Foothill   127
5. Golden Valley   106
6. Highland   104

South West Yosemite League - Centennial

February 10, 2007

103
Hamey	Vince	STOCK	Fall :29*
Ramierz	Jesus	RIDGE	
McKee	Nick	CEN	Fall 2:42
Cardenas	Dallas	S	

112
Tablit	Derek	CEN	Fall 2:11
Cerna	Marcus	N	
Aguilar	Chris	STOCK	

119
Hurtado	Aaron	CEN	Fall 5:26
Magno	Jon	RIDGE	
Perry	Ryan	STOCK	Dec.
Hernandez	Mike	N	
Estrada	Ruben	S	

125
Magno	Bryan	RIDGE	Fall 5:42
Staffero	Adam	CEN	
Romero	Dominic	S	Fall 4:54
DeLeon	Demetrio	N	

130
Hicks	Seth	CEN	Fall 1:56
Fuentes	Phillip	S	
Myer	Chris	STOCK	Dec.
Lozano	Jesse	RIDGE	

135
Ballard	Austin	CEN	5-0
Gonzalez	Nathan	N	
Cavazos	Kyle	RIDGE	Dec.
Pinuelas	Johnny	W	
Martinez	David	S	
Payne	Jordan	STOCK	

140
Tacket	Jack	CEN	11-9
Garcia	Rene	RIDGE	
Ryther	Nathan	STOCK	Fall 1:41
Cordova	Josh	N	
Moreno	Alex	S	

145
Endes	Dalton	CEN	10-2
Mathews	Eric	STOCK	
Arguello	Miguel	R	Fall 1:04
Jones	David	N	

152
Smith	Chris	W	14-5*
Harrison	Alex		
Beardsely	Tyler	CEN	Dec.
Navarez	Mark	RIDGE	
Nipper	Lance	S	

160
Sotelo	Nick	W	4-2
Payne	Joel	STOCK	
Velasquez	Jose	S	Forfeit
Pence	Bobby	CEN	
Farley	Dan	N	

171
Thomason	Joey	N	Fall 1:52
Sotelo	Matt	W	
Handy	Zak	CEN	11-6
Aceves	Pedro	S	

189
Ryder	Glenn	CEN	Fall 1:49
Maricich	Corban	N	
Parea	Manuel	W	Dec.
Gutierrez	Hernan	S	

215
Terrell	Lake	N	14-4
Castillo	Michael	CEN	
Mitchell	Aaron	STOCK	Fall 5:13
Davenport	Chris	S	
Hinojosa	Andrew	RIDGE	

285
Willis	Brent	N	Fall 2:18
Hinojosa	Steven	CEN	
McGill	Andrew	S	Fall 2:26
Martinez	Alex	W	

*Outstanding wrestlers

Team results
1. Centennial — 247
2. North — 180
3. Ridgeview — 119
4. Stockdale — 118.5
5. South — 109
6. West — ?

South Sequoia League - McFarland
February 9, 2007

103
Diaz	Edgar	A	Fall 2:30
Messier	Colton	TEHA	
Sanchez	Eric	WASCO	8-1
Wahl	Tommy	FRONT	

112
Steinbach	Jared	TEHA	Fall :32
Casper	Casper	FRONT	

119
Tamayo	Luis	A	Default
Martinez	Sergio	TEHA	
Blanco	Jose	WASCO	6-4
Miller	Brandon	FRONT	
Burt	Jordan	SHAFT	

125
Sanchez	Efrain	A	Fall 5:09*
Reyes	Josh	MCF	
Ramos	Ricky	WASCO	9-3
Moreno	Adam	TEHA	

130
Castillo	Frankie	A	Fall :38
Martin	Chance	FRONT	
Raya	Sal	WASCO	

135
Solorio	Phillip	WASCO	12-9
Hail	Jason	TEHA	
Campos	Ceasar	A	Fall :47
Bishop	Steven	FRONT	
Parrish	Clinton	SHAFT	

140
Varela	Abel	A	Fall 1:53
Gonzalez	Jacob	SHAFT	
Romero	Bean	WASCO	18-7
Bishop	Ryan	FRONT	
Sheahan	Ben	TEHA	

145
Rojo	Adolfo	A	15-5
Montoya	Manaury	WASCO	
Jiminez	Martin	MCF	12-1
Rocha	Austin	FRONT	
St. John	James	TEHA	

152
Molina	Guillermo	A	12-4
Mulligan	Oliver	SHAFT	
Hack	Joey	TEHA	Fall :14
Tamayo	Jose	WASCO	
Thompson	Jacob	SHAFT	

160
Ames	Joseph	SHAFT	Fall 5:58
Wehurst	Jerry	TEHA	Default
Delfino	Santino	FRONT	
Bowman	Chris	MCF	

171
Medina	Rene	SHAFT	6-4*
Hack	Tyler	TEHA	
Karr	Cody	BC	Fall 2:39
Walker	Blake	FRONT	
Alvarez	Jose	A	Default
Delfin	Tommy		

189
Abarquez	Marquez	TEHA	Fall 1:13
Doyle	Curtis	BC	
Hodges	Jeff	A	9-4
Oropeza	Diego	FRONT	

215
McBride	Evan	TEHA	Fall 2:26
Funk	James	BC	
Cantu	Felipe	WASCO	7-1
Whitesell	Nick	FRONT	
Velazquez	Senaido	A	

285
Hood	Cameron	TEHA	Fall 4:41
Rodriguez	Edgar	WASCO	
Rodriguez	Gildardo	A	Fall :29
Urrea	Jesus	MCF	
Davis	Joshua	FRONT	

*Most outstanding wrestlers

Team results

1. Arvin	208.5	5. Bakersfield Christian	63
2. Tehachapi	205	6. McFarland	50
3. Wasco	133	7. Frontier	?
4. Shafter	64		

Sierra-Sequoia Division - Tehachapi
February 16-17, 2007

103
Comacho*	Gilbert	WU		Fall 2:58
Valles	A.J.	SEL		
Martines	Chris	FIRE		12-9
Diaz	Edgar	A		
Gagnon	Jason	EX		Fall 3:02
Bacasegua	Marcos	MEN		

112
Quintana	Angelo	SEL	(28-3)	Fall 1:48
Gonzalez	Juan	KER	(25-1)	
Steinbach	Jared	TEHA		Fall 2:57
Doi	Eugene	KING		
Rico	David	WU		12-7
Casper	Torry	FRO		

119
Mendoza	Jose	SEL	(36-7)	Fall 2:26
Tomaya	Luis	AR		
Guiterrez	Emmanuel	FIRE		8-4
Martines	Sergio	TEHA		
Arroyo	Jay	DP		20-2
Huerta	Rusvel	CHO		

125
Patino	Robert	EX		O.T. Dec. 9-7
Sanchez	Efrain	AR		
Reyes	Josh	MCF		11-3
Rojas	Kevin	KER		
Felide	Joseph	COAL		10-9
Allardyce	Rafe	SIR		

130
Castillo	Frankie	AR		6-3
Areloa	Alberto	WU		
Estrada	Raul	MAD-SO		4-2
Alvardao	Nick	FOW		
Vanni	Garret	LIB-MAD		14-1
Langford	Michael	DP		

135
Hail	Jason	TEHA		7-1
Hamerslagh	Will	EX		
Solario	Phillip	WASCO		Default
Torres	Jorge	CAR		
Gomez	Kevin	MAD-SO		9-6
Alvarado	Eli	FOW		

140
Tovar	Archie	SEL	5-2	(38-7)
Varella	Abel	AR		
Doss	Nolan	LIB-MAD		Default
Ferrer	Ruben	CAR		
Hicks	Chris	KER		4-1
Jauregui	Luis	MAD-SO		

145
Cisneros	Joe	SEL	(41-3)	Fall 3:53
Rojo	Adolfo	AR		
Padraza	Lewis	MAD-SO		9-7
Pena	Manuel	FIRE		
Belew	Anthony	CAR		Default
Prieto	Raul	PAR		

152
Eskew	Bryan	KING	9-1	(25-7)
Satelo	Eric	YOSE		
Mariscal	David	FARM		Fall 2:32
Jaime	Jeff	CAR		
Mulligan	Mackenzie	SHAFT		Default
Molina	Guillermo	AR		

160
Ames*	Joseph	SHAFT		Fall 2:29
Wilson	Josh	EX		
Wehust	Jerry	TEHA		Fall 2:49
Delfino	Santino	FRO		
Guerrero	Raul	WU		Default
Dunn	Chad	YOSE		

171
Walker	Justin	SIR		9-5
Medina	Rene	SHAFT		
Hack	Tyler	TEHA		Fall 1:39
Terrones	David	WU		
Cuen	Gillero	FIRE		Fall 3:22
Cummins	Saxon	YOSE		

189
Ruiz	Abel	SEL	7-6	(38-8)
Abarquez	Marcus	TEHA		
Avila	Joey	EX		Fall 2:48
Cervantez	Johnny	FIRE		
Chase	Nath	YOSE		7-3
Doyle	Curtis	BC		

(Continued on next page)

Sierra-Sequoia Division - Tehachapi
February 16-17, 2007

215
Jiminez	Leobardo	DP	5-4
Vanderpool	Shane	LIB-MAD	
McBirde	Evan	TEHA	4-3
Renteria	Michael	WU	
Perez	Mike	SEL	Default
Madrid	Matt	COR	

285
Romero	Enrique	COR	Fall 5:29
Celodon	Jacob	SEL	
Hood	Cameron	TEHA	Fall 3:46
Rodriguez	Edgar	WASCO	
Rodriguez	Galardo	AR	Default
Tapia	David	PAR	

* Most outstanding wrestlers
( ) Record

Team results
1. Selma	217.5
2. Tehachapi	179
3. Arvin	155.5
4. Exeter	119.5
5. Firebaugh	114
6. Washington Union	106.5
7. Caruthers	74.5
8. Madera South	72.5
9. Kerman	69
10. Liberty-Madera	67.5
11. Dos Palos	64
12. Shafter	62.5
13. Kingsburg	59
14. Sierra	58
15. Yosemite	53
16. Wasco	52
17. Corcoran	47
18. Frontier	38
19. Fowler	33
20. Parlier	31
21. Famersville	26
22. McFarland	24
23. Coalinga	21
24. Mendota	20
25. Bakersfield Christian	15
26. Chowchilla	8
27. Dinuba	7
Woodlake	0
Tranquility	0

Yosemite Division – Clovis East
February 16-17, 2007

103
Done	Chris	BUC	6-4	
Collier	Marc	EB		
Zimmer	Zack	CW	13-4	
Diaz	Chris	SANG		
Ban	Jason	SUNY	5-2	
Jordan	Elmer	RED		
Gomez	Eric	MAD	5-2	
Omata	Ben	CL		

112
Demison	Nektoe	B	6-3	
Fitzgerald	Steven	CE		
Jaramillo	A.J.	LEM	2-0	
Gonzalez	Peter	EB		
Everwine	Chase	CW	Fall 1:37	
Roberts	Nathan	BUC		
Perez	Miguel	MAD	4-1	
Uribe	Victor	HW		

119
Lomas	Frank	B	5-0	
Weimer	Steve	CL		
Waters	Anthony	BUC	10-2	
Rocha	Brandon	LEM		
Tarkington	Richard	HIGH	Inj. Default	
Nam	Chantra	SUNY		
Masuta	Armajit	MAD	Default	
Magno	Jon	RIDGE		

125
Arredondo	Justin	BUC	3-1	
Ramos	Chris	BULL		
Fisher	Nick	CW	12-0	
Pered	Julian	LEM		
Chatman	Charles	ED	Fall 4:48	
Williams	Galen	TW		
Morgan	Jacob	B	8-7	
Valle	Ramiro	RED		

130
Roman-Marin	Sean	LEM	10-3	
Kelley	Cameron	CL		
Gutierrez	Isidro	BUC	Fall 3:44	
Hicks	Seth	CEN		
Gonzalez	Freddy	EB	9-3	
Franco	Steve	HIGH		
Lugan	Brian	CW	6-4	
Pavone	Ryan	PORT		

135
Rios*	John	MAD	5-4	(41-6)
Rodriguez	Alex	CD		(37-2)
Watts	David	ELD	4-2	
Cruz	Johah	B		
Pavone	Chris	PORT	10-3	
Thomas	John	CL		
Ballard	Austin	CEN	Fall :52	
Beck	Dylan	CW		

140
Larson	Tracy	CE	Fall 2:52
Rubio	Vincent	LEM	
Sakaguchi	Scott	CL	11-0
Box	Anthony	B	
Watts	Randall	ELD	4-3
Miller	Justin	EB	
Ellison	Dustin	CW	9-5
Flores	Dwight	TUL	

145
Rasmussen	Travis	B	7-2
Moralez	Mitch	TUL	
West	Stephen	BUC	Fall 2:47
Christensen	Colton	LIB-B	
Endes	Dalton	CEN	Fall 2:27
Dupras	Jake	CW	
Sierra	Nick	LEM	5-4
Vera	Hugo	CENT	

152
Balch	Andrew	BUC	1-0
Esparza	Josh	CL	
Rodriguez	Jamie	B	7-2
Moralez	Jesus	TUL	
Cook	James	CW	Fall 1:18
Smith	Christ	WB	
Jenkins	Brock	TW	Fall 4:25
Roughton	Cory	GW	

160
Montelongo	Daniel	MAD	3-0
Bracamonte	Paul	CENT	
Delarosa	Eric	FOOT	2-0
West	Craig	BUC	
Hernandez	Cruz	EB	3-0
Magna	Xavier	FRE	
Rogers	Kail	LIB-B	Fall 1:55
Pfitzer	Brent	TUL	

(Continued on next page)

Yosemite Division – Clovis East
February 16-17, 2007

171
Smith	Eric	BULL	9-3
Brant	Phil	BULL	
Allison	Dustin	MAD	4-3
Carls	Brad	B	
Villasenor	Sergio	MON	10-4
Shaver	Zack	CL	
Sanchez	Derek	HAN	Fall 5:47
Enus	Johnny	GW	

189
Garcia	Matt	LEM	3-2
Sanchez	Brett	CL	
Travis	David	FOOT	Fall 1:56
Ryder	Glen	CEN	
Medellin	Brandon	MAD	Default
Lowe	Tim	SUNY	
Gingold	Jake	BUC	Forfeit
Leavell	Jaron	HOOV	

215
Flores	Ryan	BUC	1-0
Lopez	Vince	CL	
Perez	Jose	PORT	Fall 1:01
Terrell	Lake	NB	
Gonzalez	Alex	SUNY	Forfeit
Trujillo	Robert	HAN	
Cummings	Eddie	EB	Fall 3:18
Shipman	Cameron	MCL	

285
Maxon*	Jacob	RED	1-0
Zamora	Jonathan	CL	
Garza	Austin	BUC	6-5
Baize	Lloren	LEM	
Alvarez	Lamar	B	Default
Bernard	Tyler	CENT	
Cisneros	Efren	GV	Fall 3:21
McLintock	Coby	DEL	

* Most outstanding wrestlers
( ) Record

Team results
1.	Buchanan	299.5
2.	Clovis	237.5
3.	Bakersfield	220.5
4.	Lemoore	185.5
5.	Madera	158
6.	Clovis West	132
7.	East Bakersfield	118.5
8.	Centennial	114
9.	Clovis East	107.5
10.	Tulare Union	105
11.	Bullard	90.5
12.	Sunnyside	85.5
13.	El Diamante	74.5
13.	Porterville	74.5
15.	Liberty-Bakersfield	73
16.	Redwood	72.5
17.	Central	68
18.	Foothill	66.5
19.	Monache	59
20.	Golden West	58
20.	Sanger	58
22.	Highland	52
23.	Hanford	48
24.	North Bakersfield	46
25.	Edison	43
25.	Tulare Western	43
27.	Hanford West	36.5
28.	Cesar Chavez	35.5
29.	Ridgeview	33.5
30.	Delano	31
31.	Fresno	28
32.	Stockdale	27
33.	Golden Valley	24.5
34.	McLane	24
34.	West Bakersfield	24
36.	Hoover	23
37.	Reedley	17
38.	Roosevelt	16
39.	Mt. Whitney	15
39.	South Bakersfield	15
41.	Granite Hills	3

Central Section Masters - Lemoore
February 24, 2007

103
Camacho	Gilberto	WASCO	5-0	(50-0) 38 Falls
Done	Chris	BUC		
Valles	A.J.	SEL	2-0	
Martinez	Chris	FIRE		
Diaz	Edgar	AR	8-7	
Collier	Marc	EB	(44-7)	
Zimmer	Zach	CW	3-2	
Diaz	Chris	SANG		

112
Quintana	Diego	SEL	3-2	
Gonzalez	Peter	EB		
Demison	Nektoe	BAK	12-1	(40-6)
Jaramillo	A.J.	LEM		
Fitzgerald	Steven	CE	Fall 5:17	
Roberts	Nathan	BUC		
Everwine	Chase	CW	8-4	
Gonzales	Juan	KER		

119
Lomas	Frank	BAK	4-1	(38-9)
Weimer	Steve	CLO		
Mendoza	Jose	SEL	1-0	
Rocha	Brandon	LEM		
Tarkington	Richard	HIGH	15-4	
Tomayo	Luis	AR		
Waters	Anthony	BUC	12-4	
Guiterrez	Emmanuel	FIRE		

125
Fisher*	Nick	CW	8-4
Arredondo	Justin	BUC	
Ramos	Chris	BULL	9-2
Reyes	Josh	MCF	
Sanchez	Efrain	AR	Default
Patino	Robert	EX	
Perez	Julian	LEM	7-5
Chatman	Charles	ED	

130
Roman-Marin	Sean	LEM	5-3	(48-8)
Castillo	Frankie	AR		
Kelly	Cameron	CLO	9-5	
Gutierrez	Isidro	BUC		
Hicks	Seth	CEN	8-7	
Arreola	Alberto	WASCO		
Gonzalez	Freddy	EB	12-4	
Estrada	Raul	MAS		

135
Rios	Johnny	MAD	1-0	(41-7)
Rodriguez	Alex	CE	(37-3)	
Watts	David	ELD	1-0	
Pavone	Chris	PORT		
Cruz	Johan	BAK	11-2	
Thomas	John	CLO		
Hall	Jason	THE	15-5	
Hamerslagh	Will	EX		

140
Sakaguchi	Scott	CLO	3-1
Rubio	Vincent	LEM	
Watts	Randall	ELD	3-1
Tovar	Archie	SEL	
Box	Anthony	BAK	1-0
Ellison	Dustin	CW	
Miller	Justin	EB	Fall 4:54
Hicks	Chris	KER	

145
Cisneros	Jose	SEL	6-2	(50-5)
Rasmussen	Travis	BAK	(44-5)	
West	Stephen	BUC	Default	
Moralez	Mitch	TU		
Christensen	Coltan	LIB	Default	
Dupraas	Jake	CW		
Endes	Dalton	CEN	10-3	
Rojo	Adolfo	AR		

152
Balch	Andrew	BUC	1-0
Cook	James	CW	
Rodriguez	Jamie	BAK	7-4
Esparza	Josh	CLO	
Moralez	Matt	TU	8-1
Sotelo	Eric	YOSE	
Eskew	Bryan	KING	5-2
Mariscal	David	FARM	

Central Section Masters – Lemoore
February 24, 2007

160
Montelongo*	Daniel	MAD	6-5
Dela Rosa	Eric	FOOT	
West	Craig	BUC	Default
Hernandez	Cruz	EB	
Bracamonte	Paul	CENT	10-4
Magana	Xavier	FRE	
Ames	Joseph	SHAFT	8-2
Wilson	Josh	EX	

171
Smith	Eric	BUC	10-1
Allison	Dustin	MAD	
Carls	Brad	BAK	Fall 5:03
Shaver	Zach	CLO	
Hack	Tyler	THE	6-3
Walker	Justin	SIE	
Villasenor	Sergio	MON	10-4
Terrones	David	WASCO	

189
Sanchez	Brett	CLO	7-5
Garcia	Mat	LEM	
Travis	David	FOOT	6-5
Medellin	Brandon	MAD	
Avila	Joey	EX	6-5
Abarquez	Marcus	THE	
Ruiz	Able	SEL	Fall 5:11
Cervantez	Johnny	FIRE	

215
Flores	Ryan	BUC	3-0 (56-1) 39 falls
Lopez	Vince	CLO	
Perez	Jose	POR	Fall 1:31
Jiminez	Leobardo	DP	
Terrell	Lake	NOR	2-1
McBride	Evan	THE	
Gonzalez	Alex	SUN	3-2
Vanderpool	Shane	LIB-MAD	

275
Zamora	Jonathan	CLO	6-3	(38-9)
Maxson	Jacob	RED		
Garza	Austin	BUC	11-3	
Alvarez	Lamar	BAK		
Baize	Loren	LEM	Fall 1:10	
Bernard	Tyler	CENT		
Celedon	Jacob	SEL	Fall 2:25	
Romero	Enrique	COR		

* Most outstanding wrestlers ( ) Record

Flores: 138 career falls

Team results
1. Buchanan	189.0
2. Clovis	148.0
3. Bakersfield	125.5
4. Lemoore	106.5
5. Selma	101.5
6. Madera	76.0
7. Clovis West	65.0
8. East Bakersfield	52.0
9. Arvin	47.0
10. Washington Union	35.5
11. Porterville	35.0
12. Foothill	32.0
13. Clovis East	31.0
14. Exeter	24.0
15. Tulare Union	23.0
16. Tehachapi	22.0
17. Kerman	19.0
17. Redwood	19.0
19. Dos Palos	16.0
19. Firebaugh	16.0
21. Central	14.0
22. Bullard	12.0
22. El Diamante	12.0
22. Liberty-Bakersfield	12.0
22. McFarland	12.0
26. Highland	10.0
27. Fresno	9.0
27. North	9.0
28. Sierra	7.0
29. Monache	5.0
30. Edison	3.0
30. Liberty-Madera	3.0
30. Madera South	3.0
30. West	3.0
34. Farmersville	2.0
34. Sanger	2.0
36. Kingsburg	1.0
36. Shafter	1.0
Caruthers	0
Centennial	0
Corcoran	0
Fowler	0
Fronier	0
Hanford	0
McLane	0
Sunnyside	0
Tulare Western	0
Wasco	0
Yosemite	0

2007 State Championships
Rabobank Arena, Bakersfield, California

Weight	Name	School	Place
103	Camacho, Gilberto	WU	1
	Valles, A.J.	SEL	2
	Done, Chris	BUC	4
112	Demison, Nektoe	B	3
125	Arredondo, Justin	BUC	7
	Ramos, Chris	BULL	8
130	Roman-Marin, Sean	LEM	2
	Kelly, Cameron	CL	8
135	Cruz, Jonah	B	3
	Watts, David	ELD	4
	Rios, Johny	MAD	6
140	Sakaguchi, Scott	CL	5
	Watts, Randall	ELD	8
145	Cisneros, Joe	SEL	2
	Rasmussen, Travis	B	3
152	Cook, James	CW	7
160	De La Rosa, Eric	FOOT	5
189	Sanchez, Brett	CL	7
	Medellin, Brandon	MAD	8
215	Flores, Ryan	BUC	1
	Lopez, Vince	CL	3
285	Zamora, Jonathen	CL	2

Team results

3	Buchanan	113
4	Clovis	97.5
5	Bakersfield	78
7	Selma	72
11	Lemoore	49.5

Notes/Corrections/Additions

Please e-mail to: mikestricker@valleywrestling07.com

Autographs

CAREER WRESTLING RECORDS

Flo Rocha, BHS 76-7-2
Robert Kitty, Madera 137-13
Tim Vanni, Monache 98-1
Eddie Gomez, Caruthers 141-12
David Rosario, Firebaugh/Madera 105-21
Trent Barnes, Clovis West 124-12 - 84 Falls
Harold Zinkin, Bullard, 75-8
Scott Herndon, South 79-10
Chris Olinger, South 111-35-1
Robbie Sordi, Madera 144-18
Dewayne Zinkin, Bullard 120-13
Joe Cemo, North 155-35
Terry Watts, Poway/Caruthers 177-19 – 108 Falls
Lorenzo Neal, Lemoore 147-8-1
Nick Zinkin, Clovis 198-15-3
Tad Stricker, South 116-27
Jassen Froehlich, BHS 125-16
Jimmy Aguirre, Clovis 167-21- 99 Falls
Scott Silver, Bullard 111-24 - 60 Falls
Adam Tirapelle, Hiram Johnson/Buchanan 213-7
Alfonso Tucker, Hoover 101-20-1
Lalo Moz, Hanford 126-11 - 90 Falls
Darrick Duran, Roosevelt 114-14
Ben Martinez, Tulare Union 191-15
Max Odom, Foothill 167-17 – 86 Falls
Josh Naus, Centennial 141-9 – 40 Falls
Andrew Onsurez, East 136-38
Daniel Chapman, Centennial 149-16 – TF 89
Garrett Spooner, Clovis 81-46 – 49 Falls
Chris Pendleton, Lemoore 170-25 – 106 Falls
Mike Van Worth, Dos Palos 189-32
Marcio Botellho, Lemoore 136-15 – 90 Falls
Alex Tirapelle, Clovis 190-23 – 99 Falls
Miguel Gutierrez, Foothill 203-30 – 131 Falls
Logan Ignram, Buchanan 165-24 – 88 Falls
Tony Franco, Foothill/BHS 139-33 – 79 Falls
Darrell Vasquez, BHS 191-7 – 47 Falls
Darrell Goodpaster, Buchanan 125-?
David Roberts, Bear River/Clovis West 183-13
Andrew Spradlin, BHS 191-15 – 38 Falls
Ken Van Worth, South 47-7
Tony Serros, BHS 122-9-2
Duane Williams, North 126-29
Sven Hafaemeister, Lemoore 105-12 – 61 Falls
Chad Mendes, Hanford 152-20
Gabe Flores, Madera/Clovis 170-23
Lucas Anderson, Lemoore 105-40
William Griffin, Madera 256-40

Brandon Cermello, Clovis 197-26
Anthony Torres, 159-6?
Nathan Morgan BHS 166-6
Troy Tirapelle, Clovis 198-16
Alex Herrera, BHS 154-16
Chris Martinez, Clovis West 113-25
Tyler Bernacchi, Clovis East 151-38
Bryce Thompson, Clovis 166-55
Dustin Noack, Clovis West 112-41
Keith Gibson, Mt. Whitney 136-39
Mark Anderson, Lemoore 165-53
Elijah Nacita, BHS 165-25
Alfonso Sanchez, McLane 120-19
Lucas Espericueta, Shafter 166-18
Joe Soto, Porterville 148-30
Kenneth Packard Roosevelt 131-39
Jake Varner, BHS 157-10
Josh Betancur, Buchanan 142-32
Willy Pendleton, Lemoore 181-36
Matt Boger, Coalinga/Buchanan 185-22
Ricky Alcala, Arvin 65-13
John Woods, Redwood 68-8
Richard Simmons, South 54-1
Roy Heath South, 106-6-1
Lee Culliton, South 81-3
Jack Serros, BHS 72-2
Sam King, Madera 91-11
Renaldo Contreras, Kingsburg 96-4
Herb Cosme, North 79-7
Ronnie Shearer, East 50-6
Walt Shepard, BHS 72-8
John Miller, North 112-6-1
Billy Seabourn, South 82-30-1
Eugene Walker, South 98-12-1
Larry Morgan, East 156-12 estimated
Billy Thomas, Hanford 141-?
Gary Quintana, Selma 123-7 – 43 Falls
Richard Alvarez, BHS 115-12-1
Justin Arredondo, Buchanan 131-32
Steve Nickell, East 125-21
Percy Richard, East 130-18
Jeff Heberle, North 153-40-1
Larry Little South 101-25
Tony Alvarez, BHS 94-15-1
Bill Van Worth, South 89-7
Dick Molina, South 91-18
Justin Mejia, Clovis 168-1 - 89 Falls
Vic Pierce, South 96-44

CAREER WRESTLING RECORDS

George Moreno, Firebaugh 201-25
Brad Hatch, Madera 76-1
David East, BHS 85-18-2
George Peterson, BHS 67-29
Kevin Langley, North 100-35
Kyle Griffin, Clovis East 125-24
Karl Herrera, BHS 83-13
Kirk Moore, Foothill 57-0-27 Falls
Billy Herrera, BHS 109-18
Paul Carrillo, South 114-26
Angel Olea, Farmersville 143-54
Jacob Wright, Dinuba 102-18
Gary Joint, Lemoore 180-16
Chris Delozo, Clovis North 128-26
Steve Bartlett, North 80-23
Jake Thoene, North 60-18-1
Steve Ward, North 80-45

ERRATUM AND ADDITIONS

P-15
    123 Galvez, Amador
P-31,32,33,35,326,328,330,407
    Darrel Nerove
P-111
    Wasco SSL
P-169
    photo Felez, Paul
P-175
    photo Reyes, Jessie
P-203
    Hull, Brad 5th 1993 only
P 205
    10th Roosevelt
P-215
    teams 28th Golden West 8
P-218
    Chapman, Daniel 31-3, career record 149-16 – TF 89
P-250
    119 Nishikawa, Randy - Central
P-253
    105 Magallanes, Magdaleno
P-321
    Poteete, Jim

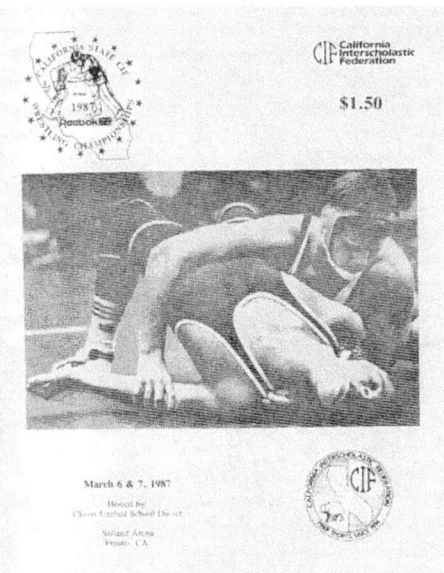

www.ingramcontent.com/pod-product-compliance
Lightning Source LLC
Chambersburg PA
CBHW060416300426
44111CB00018B/2870